CLYMER®

SCAG HYDROSTATIC

COMMERCIAL WALK-BEHIND MOWERS · 1990 & LATER

The world's finest publisher of mechanical how-to manuals

PRIMEDIA
Business Magazines & Media

P.O. Box 12901, Overland Park, Kansas 66282-2901

Copyright ©2003 PRIMEDIA Business Magazines & Media Inc.

FIRST EDITION
First Printing October, 2003

Printed in U.S.A.

CLYMER and colophon are registered trademarks of PRIMEDIA Business Magazines & Media Inc.

ISBN: 0-87288-884-3

Library of Congress: 2003112104

AUTHOR: Rodney Rom.

PRODUCTION: Clymer Staff.

COVER: Photo courtesy of Scag Power Equipment.

CONTENTS

CHAPTER FOUR
FUEL AND EXHAUST **113**

CHAPTER FIVE
KOHLER MV-18 AND MV-20 ENGINES **125**

CHAPTER SIX
KOHLER CV14 AND CV15 ENGINE **182**

QUICK REFERENCE DATA

MOWER AND ENGINE DATA

MOWER MODEL NO. _____

MOWER SERIAL NO. _____

ENGINE MODEL NO. _____

ENGINE SPEC or TYPE NO. _____

ENGINE SERIAL or CODE NO. _____

ENGINE SHORT BLOCK NO. _____

CARBURETOR NO. _____

AIR FILTER NO. _____

PRE-FILTER NO. _____

OIL FILTER NO. _____

MODEL INFORMATION

MOWER MODEL	SERIAL NO. RANGE	ENGINE MAKE[1]	MODEL	SPEC or TYPE
SWZ	xxx70001 – xxx79999	KH	CV14T, CV20S,	N.A.
		KA	FC420V, FH500V,	N.A.
		BS	303776, or 350777	N.A.
SWZ-14KA	3300001 – 3309999	KA	FC420V	HS09
SWZ-16BV	3310001 – 3319999	BS	303776	1046
SWZ-16BVE	3320001 – 3329999	BS	303777	1044
SWZ-17KA	4100001 – 4109999, 6290001 – 6299999, 7430001 – 7439999	KA	FH500V	AS09
SWZ-18BV	3330001 – 3339999	BS	350776	1046
SWZ-18KH	[2]	KH	MV18	58511
SWZ-20CVE	3340001 – 3349999	KH	CV20S	65514
SWZ-20KHE	[2]	KH	MV20S	57508
SWZ-21KAE	5210001 – 5219999, 6300001 – 6309999, 7440001 – 7449999	KA	FH641V	CS06
SWZ36-14KA	3230001 – 3239999, 4040001 – 4049999, 5120001 – 5129999	KA	FC420V	HS09
SWZ36A-14KA	6230001 – 6239999	KA	FC420V	HS09
SWZ36-14KH	3240001 – 3249999	KH	CV14T	1461
SWZ36A-15KA	7190001 – 7199999, 7370001 – 7379999	KA	FH451V	AS09
SWZ36-15KH	4050001 – 4059999, 5130001 – 5139999	KH	CV15T	41581
SWZ48-14KA	3250001 – 3259999, 4060001 – 4069999, 5140001 – 5149999	KA	FC420V	HS09
SWZ48-14KAE	3270001 – 3279999	KA	FC420V	ES17
SWZ48-14KH	3260001 – 3269999	KH	CV14T	1461
SWZ48-15KH	4070001 – 4079999, 5150001 – 5159999	KH	CV15T	41581

(continued)

MODEL INFORMATION (continued)

MOWER MODEL	SERIAL NO. RANGE	ENGINE MAKE[1]	MODEL	SPEC or TYPE
SWZ48-16BV	3280001 – 3289999	BS	303776	1046
SWZ48-17KA	4080001 – 4089999,			
	5160001 – 5169999	KA	FH500V	AS09
SWZ48A-17KA	5170001 – 5179999,			
	6260001 – 6269999,			
	7380001 – 7389999	KA	FH500V	AS09
SWZ52-17KA	5180001 – 5189999	KA	FH500V	AS09
SWZ52-17KAE	5970001 – 5979999	KA	FH500V	N.A.
SWZ52A-17KA	5190001 – 5199999,			
	6280001 – 6289999,			
	7390001 – 7399999	KA	FH500V	AS09
SWZU-21KAE	7470001 – 7479999	KA	FH641V	AS09
SWZU36-15KA	5260001 – 5269999	KA	FH451V	AS09
SWZU36A-15KA	7400001 – 7409999	KA	FH451V	AS09
SWZU36-15KH	4780001 – 4789999	KH	CV15T	41581
SWZU48-17KA	4790001 – 4799999,			
	5270001 – 5279999	KA	FH500V	AS09
SWZU48A-17KA	7410001 – 7419999	KA	FH500V	AS09
SWZU52-17KA	5280001 – 5289999	KA	FH500V	AS09
SWZU52A-17KA	7420001 – 7429999	KA	FH500V	AS09

[1]Engine Make: KH = Kohler; KA = Kawasaki; BS = Briggs & Stratton

RECOMMENDED ENGINE FUEL AND OIL*

Fuel	Unleaded gasoline with Octane rating of 87 or higher
Capacity	Approximately 5.0 U.S. gallons (18.7 liters or 4.0 Imperial gallons)
Engine oil	API service rating of SH or above
Kohler MV	
Above 32° F (0° C)	SAE 30
Between 32° F and 0° F (0° C and -18° C)	SAE 10W-30, 5W-20, or 5W-30
Below 0° F (-18° C)	SAE 5W-20 or 5W-30
Capacity	
With filter – 4 pints or 2 quarts (1.9 liters)	Without filter – 3.5 pints (1.7 liters)
Kohler CV	
Above 32° F (0° C)	SAE 10W-30
Between 32° F and 0° F (0° C and -18° C)	SAE 10W-30, 5W-20, or 5W-30
Below 0° F (-18° C)	SAE 5W-20 or 5W-30
Capacity with filter – 2.1 quarts (2.0 liters)	
Kawasaki	
Above 70° F (20° C)	SAE 40
Above 32° F (0° C)	SAE 30
Between 0° F and 95° F (-18° C and 35° C)	SAE 10W-30
Below 32° F (0° C)	SAE 5W-20

Capacity
  FC420V with filter – approximately
   3.4 pints (1.6 liters) without filter – approximately 2.7 pints (1.3 liters)
  FH451V, FH500V, and FH641V with filter – approximately 3.6 pints (1.75 liters)
  without filter – approximately 3.2 pints (1.5 liters)

(continued)

RECOMMENDED ENGINE FUEL AND OIL* (continued)

Engine oil (continued)
  Briggs & Stratton
    Above 40° F (4° C)
    Between 0° F and 40° F (-18° C and +4° C)
    Below 0° F (-18° C)
    Capacity
      With filter – 3.5 pints (1.7 liters)
      Without filter – 3.0 pints (1.42 liters)
	API service rating of SH or above
	
	SAE 30
	  SAE 10W-30
	  SAE 5W-20

* Do not use 10W-40 oil in the engine. Recommended engine oil viscosities are for petroleum-based oils. Comparable synthetic oils may be used. DO NOT MIX synthetic oil with petroleum oil.

TIRE INFLATION PRESSURE

Front caster wheel	25 psi (165 kPa)
Rear drive wheel	15 psi (100 kPa)

MAINTENANCE TORQUE SPECIFICATIONS

Blade bolt	75 Ft.-lb. (102 N·m)
Cutter deck spindle nut	150 Ft.-lb. (204 N·m)
Engine	
Fasteners	Refer to the respective Engine chapter
Spark plug(s)	See next table
Hydrostatic components	Refer to Chapter 13, Hydrostatic Drive

RECOMMENDED SPARK PLUG TYPES, GAPS, AND TORQUES[1]

ENGINE	SPARK PLUG	GAP	TORQUE
Kohler MV Kohler	Champion RV17YC[2]	.035 in. (0.9 mm)	120-180 in.-lb. (13-20 N·m)
CV14, 15	Champion RC12YC	.040 in. (1.0 mm)	335-385 in.-lb. (38-43 N·m)
CV20	Champion RC12YC	.030 in. (0.75 mm)	215-265 in.-lb. (24-30 N·m)
Kawasaki			
FC420V	Champion RN11YC, NGK BPR5ES	.028-.031 in. (0.7-0.8 mm)	
FH451V, FH500V	Champion RCJ8Y, NGK BPMR4A	.030 in. (0.75 mm)	130-135 in.-lb. (15 N·m)
FH641V	NGK BPR4ES, Champion RN14YC	.030 in. (0.75 mm)	195 in.-lb. (22 N·m)
Briggs-Stratton	Champion RC12YC, Autolite 3924	.030 in. (0.75 mm)	180 in.-lb. (20 N·m)

1. Equivalent spark plugs may be substituted. Always cross-reference accurately. Champion Premium Gold #2071 spark plug may be used in any application calling for the RC12YC plug.
2. RV17YC is for normal usage; RV15YC is recommended for continuous full-load running.

BELTS AND BLADES

MOWER SERIES and SIZE	HYDRO-DRIVE BELT	DECK-DRIVE BELT	BLADE-DRIVE BELT
SWZ 36-inch	48553	48204	N/A
SWZ 48-inch	48553	48089	48087
SWZ 52-inch	48587	48286	48285
SWZ 61-inch	48587	48088	48265
SWZ 72-inch	48587	48296	48296
SWZU 36-inch	481837	N/A	481880
SWZU 48-inch	481837	48087	481881
SWZU 52-inch	481837	48285	481922

	STANDARD BLADE	HI-LIFT BLADE	ELIMINATOR BLADE
SWZ(U) 36-inch	481707	481711	482235
SWZ(U) 48-inch	481706	481710	482241
SWZ(U) 52-inch	81707	481711	482235
SWZ 61-inch	481708	481712	482237
SWZ 72-inch	481709	N/A	482238

APPROXIMATE DIMENSIONS

DIMENSION	MOWER MODEL SWZ36	SWZ48	SWZ52	SWZ61	SWZ72
Length	74.0 in.	74.0 in.	74.0 in.	76.0 in.	76.0 in.
Width					
Overall	54.5 in.	60.0 in.	60.0 in.	70.0 in.	81.0 in
Discharge chute up	37.5 in.	53.0 in.	53.0 in.	63.0 in.	74.0 in.
Tracking	37.0 in.	42.0 in.	42.0 in.	42.0 in.	42.0 in
With grass catcher	55.0 in.	69.0 in.	69.0 in	80.0 in.	91.0 in.
Height	40.5 in.	40.5 in.	40.5 in.	40.5 in.	40.5 in.
Weight					
W/O grass catcher	515 lbs.	565 lbs.	605 lbs.	715 lbs.	755 lbs.
W/grass catcher	555 lbs.	605 lbs.	645 lbs.	755 lbs.	790 lbs.

DIMENSION	MOWER MODEL SWZU36	SWZU48	SWZU52	SWZU61
Length	77.5 in.	76.0 in.	77.0 in.	79.0 in.
Width				
Overall	46.5 in.	58.0 in.	60.0 in.	70.0 in.
Discharge chute up	37.5 in.	48.0 in.	50.0 in.	60.0 in.
Tracking	36.0 in.	38.0 in.	38.0 in.	38.0 in.
With grass catcher	55.0 in.	64.0 in.	66.0 in.	76.0 in.
Height	43.0 in.	43.0 in.	43.0 in.	43.0 in.
Weight				
W/O grass catcher	575 lbs.	640 lbs.	680 lbs.	735 lbs.
W/grass catcher	615 lbs.	680 lbs.	720 lbs.	775 lbs.

CHAPTER ONE

GENERAL INFORMATION

This Clymer shop manual covers the Scag SWZ and SWZU zero-turn walk-behind mower models. The manual gives complete information on maintenance, tune-up, repair and overhaul to keep the Scag zero-turn walk-behind operating properly. Hundreds of photos and drawings guide the reader through every step.

A shop manual is a reference tool and, as in all Clymer manuals, the chapters are thumb-tabbed for easy reference. Important items are indexed at the end of the book. All procedures, tables and figures are designed for the reader who may be working on the unit for the first time or using this manual for the first time. Frequently used specifications and capacities are summarized in the *Quick Reference Data* at the front of the manual.

MANUAL ORGANIZATION

All dimensions and capacities are expressed in both U.S. and metric standard units of measurement.

This chapter discusses equipment and tools useful for preventive maintenance, troubleshooting and repairs.

Chapter Two provides methods and suggestions for the quick and accurate diagnosis of problems. Troubleshooting procedures present typical symptoms and logical methods to pinpoint and repair the problem.

Chapter Three explains all routine maintenance necessary to keep the unit operating well. Chapter Three also includes recommended tune-up procedures, eliminating the need to constantly consult the chapters on the various assemblies.

Subsequent chapters describe specific systems such as engines, hydrostatic drive, cutter deck, electrical and brakes. Each disassembly, repair and assembly procedure is discussed in step-by-step form.

Some of the procedures in this manual specify special tools. In some cases, the tool is illustrated in use. Well-equipped mechanics may be able to substitute similar tools or fabricate a suitable replacement. However, in some cases, the specialized equipment or expertise required may make it impractical for the novice mechanic to attempt the procedure. When necessary, such operations are identified in the text with the recommendation to have a dealership or competent specialist perform the task. It may be less expensive to have a professional perform these jobs, especially when considering the cost of the equipment.

Tables 1-2 are at the end of this chapter.

Table 1 lists model information.

Table 2 lists general dimensions, including weights.

Table 3 lists conversion tables.

Tables 4-6 list general torque specification in inch sizes. **Tables 7-9** list general torque specifications for metric sizes.

Table 10 lists technical abbreviations.

WARNINGS, CAUTIONS AND NOTES

The terms WARNING, CAUTION and NOTE have specific meanings in this manual.

A WARNING emphasizes areas where injury or even death could result from negligence. Mechanical damage may also occur. WARNINGS *must be taken seriously*.

A CAUTION emphasizes areas where equipment damage could result. Disregarding a CAUTION could cause permanent mechanical damage, although personal injury is unlikely.

A NOTE provides additional information to make a step or procedure easier or clearer. Disregarding a NOTE could cause inconvenience but would probably not cause equipment damage or personal injury.

SAFETY

Professional mechanics can work for years and never sustain a serious injury or mishap. Follow these guidelines and practice common sense to safely service the vehicle.

1. Do not operate the vehicle in an enclosed area. The exhaust gasses contain carbon monoxide, an odorless, colorless, and tasteless poisonous gas. Carbon monoxide levels build quickly in enclosed areas and can cause unconsciousness and death in a short time. Make sure the work area is properly ventilated or operate the vehicle outside.

2. *Never* use gasoline or any extremely flammable liquid to clean parts. Refer to *Cleaning Parts* and *Handling Gasoline Safely* in this chapter.

3. *Never* smoke or use a torch in the vicinity of flammable liquids, such as gasoline or cleaning solvent, whether in an open or closed container.

4. If welding or brazing on the unit, remove the fuel tank and carburetor and move them to a safe distance at least 50 ft. (15 m) away.

5. Use the correct type and size of tools to avoid damaging fasteners or causing personal injury.

6. Keep tools clean and in good condition. Replace or repair worn or damaged equipment.

> *CAUTION*
> *Never hammer on any tool which has a mushroomed head (A, **Figure 1**). A hammer will likely slip off a mushroomed head, causing other damage or injury. Part B of **Figure 1** shows the correct head-shape of a hammer strike tool. Note that the striking surface is not perfectly flat but has a slight curvature, with the highest point in the center of the tool.*

7. When loosening a tight fastener, be guided by what would happen if the tool slips.

8. When replacing fasteners, make sure the new fasteners are of the same size and strength as the original ones.

9. Keep the work area clean and organized.

10. Wear eye protection (**Figure 2**) *any time* eye safety is in question. This includes procedures involving drilling, grinding, hammering, compressed air or chemicals.

11. Wear the correct clothing for the job. Tie up or cover long hair so it does not get caught in moving equipment.

12. Do not carry sharp tools in clothing pockets.

13. Always have an approved fire extinguisher available (**Figure 3**). Make sure it is rated for gasoline/flammable liquid (Class B) and electrical (Class C) fires.

14. Do not use compressed air to clean clothes, the mower or the work area. Debris may be blown into the eyes or skin. *Never* direct compressed air at yourself or someone else. Do not allow children to use or play with any compressed air equipment.

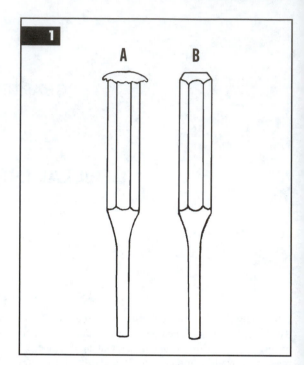

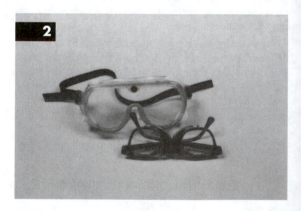

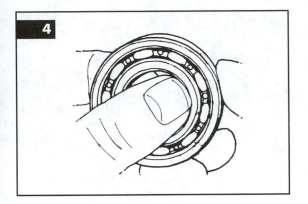

15. When using compressed air to dry bearings or other rotating parts, hold the part so it cannot rotate. Do not allow the force of the air to spin the part. The air jet is capable of rotating parts at extreme spened. The part may be damaged or disintegrate, causing serious injury. To prevent bearing damage when using compressed air, hold the inner bearing race by hand (**Figure 4**).

16. Ensure the work area is properly ventilated. Constant exposure to smoke, solvent vapors, grinding dust and welding fumes causes long-term respiratory health hazards. In addition, some types of insulating materials and gaskets may contain asbestos. Inhaling asbestos particles is hazardous. When working in restricted-ventilation areas, always use proper respirators.

17. Never work on the mower while someone is working under it.

18. When placing the unit on a stand, make sure it is secure before walking away.

Handling Gasoline Safely

Gasoline is a volatile, flammable liquid and is one of the most dangerous items in the shop.

Only use gasoline as fuel for gasoline internal combustion engines. Keep in mind when working on a vehicle that gasoline is always present in the fuel tank, fuel line and carburetor. To avoid a disastrous accident when working around the fuel system, carefully observe the following precautions:

1. *Never* use gasoline to clean parts. See *Cleaning Parts* in this chapter.

2. When working on the fuel system, work outside or in a well-ventilated area.

3. Do not add fuel to the fuel tank or service the fuel system while the vehicle is near open flames, sparks, where someone is smoking, or while the engine is running. Gasoline vapor is heavier than air; it collects in low areas and is easily ignited.

4. Allow the engine to cool completely before working on any fuel system component, unless specific instructions state otherwise.

5. When draining the carburetor, catch the fuel in a non-sparking container and then pour it into an approved gasoline storage device.

6. Do not store gasoline in glass containers. If the glass breaks, a serious explosion or fire may occur. Sunlight through glass rapidly deteriorates gasoline and may heat it to the point of explosion.

7. Immediately wipe up spilled gasoline with rags. Store the rags in an outside metal container with a lid until they can be properly disposed of, ensuring that the container itself is in a safe location.

8. Do not pour water onto a gasoline fire. Water spreads the fire and makes it more difficult to put out. Use a class B, BC or ABC fire extinguisher to extinguish a gasoline fire, as "B" is the rating which applies to flammable liquid fires.

9. Always turn off the engine before refueling. Do not spill fuel onto the engine or exhaust system. Do not overfill the fuel tank. Leave an air space at the top of the tank to allow room for the fuel to expand due to temperature fluctuations.

Cleaning Parts

Cleaning parts is one of the more tedious and difficult service jobs performed. There are many types of chemical cleaners and solvents available for shop use. Most are poisonous and extremely flammable. To prevent chemical exposure, vapor buildup, fire and serious injury, observe each product warning label and note the following:

1. Read and observe the entire product label before using any chemical. Always know what type of chemical is being used and whether it is poisonous and/or flammable.

2. Do not use more than one type of cleaning solvent at a time. If mixing chemicals is called for, measure the proper amounts according to the manufacturer's instructions and *always* mix in the specified sequence.

3. Work in a well-ventilated area.

4. Wear chemical-resistant gloves.

5. Wear safety glasses.

6. Wear a vapor respirator if the instructions call for it.

7. Wash hands and arms thoroughly after cleaning parts.

8. Keep chemical products away from children and pets.

9. Thoroughly clean all oil, grease and cleaner residue from any part that must be heated.

10. Use a brass- or nylon-bristle brush when cleaning parts. Steel-bristle brushes may cause a spark.

11. When using a parts washer, only use the solvent recommended by the manufacturer. Make sure the parts washer is equipped with a metal lid that will lower in case of fire.

Warning Labels

Most manufacturers attach informational and warning labels to the equipment. These labels contain instructions that are important to personal and bystander safety when operating, servicing, transporting and storing the equipment. Refer to the owner's manual for the description and location of labels. Order replacement labels from the manufacturer if they are missing or damaged.

BASIC SERVICE METHODS

Most of the service procedures covered in this manual are straightforward and can be performed by anyone reasonably competent with tools. However, consider personal capabilities carefully before attempting any operation involving major disassembly. Recommendations are occasionally made to refer service or maintenance to an authorized dealership or competent specialty shop. In these cases, the work will be done more quickly, economically and safely by a specialist than by a home mechanic.

Take your time and do the job right. Do not forget that a newly-rebuilt engine must be broken in the same way as a brand-new one. Keep the engine speed and load within the limits specified in the engine and equipment owner's manuals.

1. *Front*, as used in this manual, refers to the front of the mower, the section farthest away from the operator whose hands are on the handle grips, ready to operate the mower. The front of any component is the end closest to the front of the mower as it is positioned on the mower or engine. *Left-* and *right-hand* sides and *back* or *rear* refer to the position of the parts as viewed by the operator in the mowing position. For example, the speed-adjustment control is on the right-hand side. See **Figure 5**.

2. Read each procedure *completely* while looking at the actual parts before starting a job. Understand the instructions and follow the step-by-step procedure carefully.

3. Repairs are much faster and easier if the machine is clean before starting work. Degrease the unit with a commercial degreaser. Follow the directions on the container for the best results. Clean all parts with cleaning solvent as they are removed.

> *WARNING*
> ***Never*** *use gasoline as a cleaning agent. It presents an extreme fire hazard. Only use cleaning solvents in a well-ventilated area.*

> *CAUTION*
> *Do not direct high-pressure water at bearings, carburetors, hoses, linkages, or electrical components. The water will force grease out of the bearings and possibly damage the seals. Water can also be*

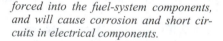
forced into the fuel-system components, and will cause corrosion and short circuits in electrical components.

4. Safely secure the mower whenever the engine or deck is being serviced or a drive train component is being removed or adjusted.

5. A compartment tray is an invaluable tool for organizing fasteners and small components (**Figure 6**). It can be made using an ordinary 12-hole muffin tin. Set it on the workbench with the three rows of four holes arranged left-to-right, and etch a number 1 next to the lower-left hole. The number 1 slot is the starting point. At the start of disassembly, begin with hole number 1 and fill the holes left-to-right, near-to-far. Each section holds the fasteners and small components for one component or system in the order of disassembly. A fine-point magic marker can be used to identify a slot's components in the case of an unfamiliar procedure. Additional trays can also be sequentially numbered, if needed. For reassembly, reverse the disassembly sequence.

A storage tray is especially helpful when working on an unfamiliar system for the first time. It also allows parts to be stored in an orderly system if the job has to wait for parts to arrive.

6. Take a photograph or make diagrams of similar-appearing parts wherever these parts are found or whenever

an unfamiliar system or component is being repaired. For instance, crankcase bolts are often not the same lengths, or left-side and right-side linkages are not always identical. Do not rely on memory alone. It is possible that carefully laid-out parts will become disturbed, making it difficult to correctly reassemble the components without a diagram or photograph.

7. Tag all similar parts for location and mark all mating parts for position. Record the number and thickness of any shims as they are removed. Larger parts can be identified by placing them in sealed and labeled plastic bags.

8. Tag disconnected wires and connectors with adhesive or masking tape and a marking pen. Again, do not rely on memory alone.

9. Protect finished surfaces from physical damage or corrosion. Keep gasoline, battery electrolyte and other chemicals off painted surfaces.

10. Use penetrating oil on frozen or tight bolts. Avoid using heat, if possible. Heat can warp, melt or affect the temper of parts. Heat also damages the finish of paint and plastics.

11. When a part is a press fit or requires a special tool for removal, the information or type of tool necessary for service is identified in the text. Otherwise, if a part is difficult to remove or install, determine the cause before proceeding.

12. Cover all openings to prevent objects or debris from falling into the engine or other undesirable locations.

13. The term *replace* means to discard a defective part and install a new part. *Overhaul* means to remove, disassemble, inspect, measure, repair and/or replace parts as required to recondition an assembly.

14. Some operations require the use of a hydraulic press. If a press is not available, have these operations performed by a shop equipped with the necessary equipment. Do not use makeshift equipment that may damage the mower or component.

15. If special tools are required, have them available before starting the procedure. When special tools are required, they will be described at the beginning of the procedure.

16. Make sure all shims and washers are reinstalled in the same location and position.

17. Wherever a rotating part contacts a stationary part, look for a shim or washer.

18. Always use new gaskets. If the manufacturer recommends sealant on a gasket, or instead of a gasket, abide by the recommendations. Do not use sealants where they are not specified.

19. If self-locking fasteners are used, replace them with new ones. Do not reuse a self-locking fastener. Also, do not install standard fasteners in place of self-locking ones.

CAUTION
*Do **not** install fasteners of a lower grade than those installed by the manufacturer. Doing so may cause component or equipment failure and personal injury. Refer to **Fasteners** in this chapter for fastener grading.*

20. Use grease to hold small parts in place if they tend to fall out during assembly. Do not apply grease to electrical or brake components, or in any location which cautions against the use of grease.

MODEL AND SERIAL NUMBERS

Identification numbers are located on the deck and the engine. Have these numbers available when ordering parts.

The mower model and serial number is located on the left-rear corner of the top of the cutter deck, just inboard of the left-rear wheel (**Figure 7**).

The engine numbers are located on a label, plate or decal on the side of the fan housing. Kohler engines use a model, spec, and serial number. Kawasaki engines use a model, type, and serial number. Briggs & Stratton engines use a model, type, and code number.

Table 1 lists mower model identification and engine usage.

FASTENERS

Proper fastener selection and installation is important to ensure that the mower operates as designed and can be serviced efficiently. Make sure that replacement fasteners meet all the same requirements as the originals.

NOTE
*When purchasing a bolt, it is important to know how to specify bolt length. The correct way to measure bolt length is to measure the length, starting from underneath the bolt head to the end of the bolt (**Figure 11**).*

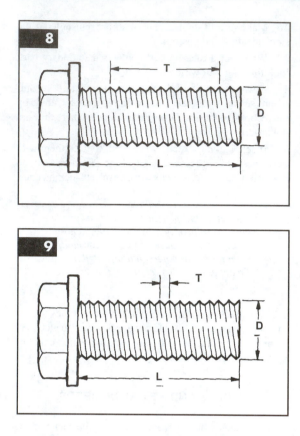

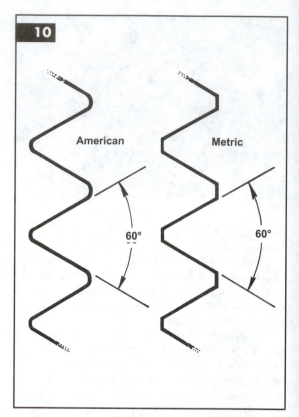

Threaded Fasteners

Threaded fasteners secure most of the components on the mower and engine. Most are tightened by turning them clockwise (right-hand threads). If the normal stress on the component would loosen the fastener, it may have left-hand threads. If a left-hand threaded fastener is used, it is noted in the text.

Three dimensions are required to match the size of the fastener – the outside diameter of the threads (D, **Figure 8** and **Figure 9**), the number of threads in a given distance (T), and the length of the fastener (L). In the case of a bolt, the head of the bolt is not figured into the length.

Two systems are currently used to specify threaded fastener dimensions, the U.S. Standard (or Society of Automotive Engineers) system (**Figure 8** and **Figure 10**) and the metric system (**Figure 9** and **Figure 10**). Pay particular attention when working with unidentified fasteners. Mismatching thread types can damage threads.

> *CAUTION*
> *To ensure that the fastener threads are not mismatched or cross-threaded, start all fasteners by hand. If a fastener is hard to start or turn, determine the cause before tightening it with a wrench.*

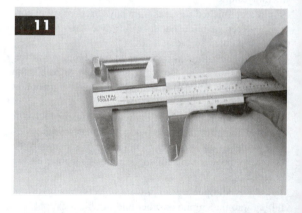

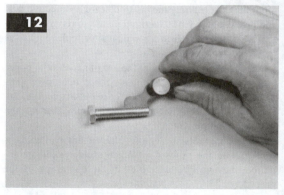

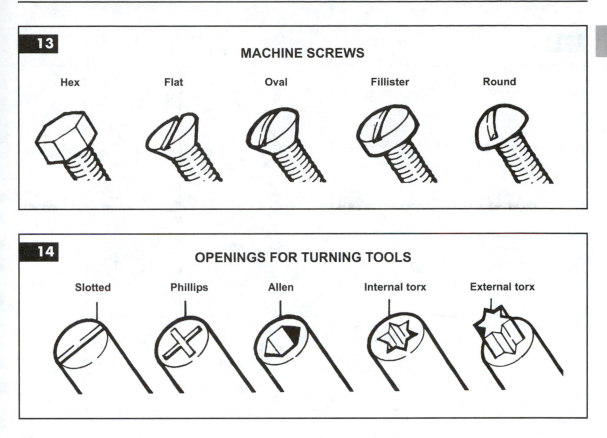

13

MACHINE SCREWS

| Hex | Flat | Oval | Fillister | Round |

14

OPENINGS FOR TURNING TOOLS

| Slotted | Phillips | Allen | Internal torx | External torx |

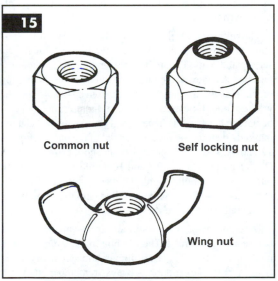

15

Common nut   Self locking nut

Wing nut

A screw-pitch gauge (**Figure 12**) is the recommended tool to use to identify any questionable thread. The gauge is made up of a number of thin plates. Each plate has a thread shape cut on one edge to match one thread pitch. When using a screw-pitch gauge to determine a thread size, try different blades onto the thread (**Figure 12**) until both threads match exactly.

Many bolts and studs are combined with nuts to secure particular components. To indicate the size of a nut, manufacturers specify the thread diameter and pitch.

The measurement across two parallel flats on a hex bolt head or nut indicates the wrench size that fits the fastener.

Figure 13 shows different head styles used on machine-thread bolts and screws. **Figure 14** shows the most popular styles of openings used to tighten and loosen bolts and screws. **Figure 15** shows some popular styles of nuts.

Inch-size fasteners

Inch-size machine-thread fasteners are classified by thread diameter (D, **Figure 8**), number of threads per inch of thread length (T), and shank length (L). A typical bolt might be identified as a 3/8-24 × 1 1/2, specifying that the bolt has a thread diameter of 3/8 inch with 24 threads per inch and a shank length of 1 1/2 inches.

The strength of inch-size bolts is normally indicated by symmetrical radial marks, or the lack thereof, on the bolt head (**Figure 16**). Grade 2 fasteners, the weakest, usually have no markings at all, although some hardware manufacturers will place an insignificant generic mark in the center of the head. Mid-strength Grade 5 bolts will be identified by three radial marks, and Grade 8, the strongest grade, has six marks. Nut strength is normally indi-

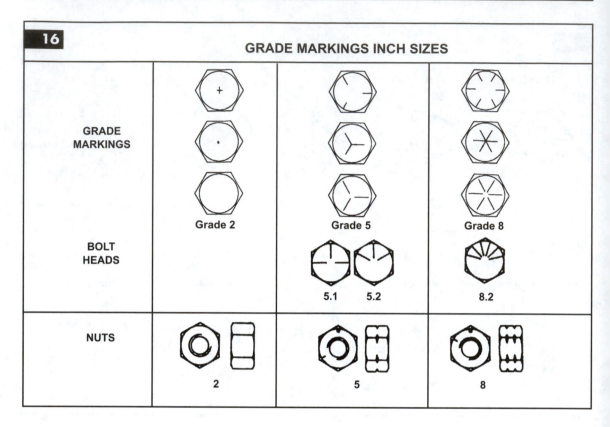

16

GRADE MARKINGS INCH SIZES

GRADE MARKINGS	Grade 2	Grade 5	Grade 8
BOLT HEADS		5.1 5.2	8.2
NUTS	2	5	8

cated by notches on the outer hex points. Grade 2 nuts have no notches, Grade 5 have one notch, and Grade 8 have two notches. Nuts should always be installed with the smooth, unmarked face *toward* the bolt head.

Inch-size fasteners are also further divided into coarse and fine threads, again determined by the number of threads per inch. The previous example, with 24 threads per inch, is the fine-thread type of 3/8-inch bolt, and would be referred to as an SAE (Society of Automotive Engineers) bolt. A coarse-thread bolt would only have 16 threads per inch and would be called a USS (United States Standard) bolt.

WARNING
Do not install fasteners with a lower-grade strength classification than what was originally installed by the manufacturer. Doing so may cause equipment failure and/or damage.

Metric fasteners

The length (L, **Figure 9**), diameter (D) and distance between thread crests (pitch) (T) classify metric screws and bolts. A typical bolt may be identified by the designation M8-1.25 × 130. This indicates the bolt has a diameter of 8 mm, the distance between thread crests is 1.25 mm and the shank length is 130 mm. Always measure bolt length

as shown in **Figure 11** to avoid purchasing replacements of the wrong length.

The numbers normally located on the head of the fastener (**Figure 17**) indicate the strength class of metric screws and bolts. The higher the number, the stronger the fastener. As shown, the numbers can be either on the top or the side of the head. Unnumbered fasteners are the weakest, and some metric bolt manufacturers do not number Grade 4.8 or 5.8 fasteners. Nut classes are also usually marked on either the face or hex flat of the nut. As **Figure 17** shows, Class 4.8 and 5.8 bolts should use at least a Class 5 nut; Class 8.8, 9.8 and 10.9 bolts need a Class 10 nut; Class 12.9 bolts should be matched with a Class 12 nut. Nuts should always be installed with the smooth, unnumbered face *toward* the bolt head.

Most metric-size fasteners are also available in both coarse and fine thread. The M8 bolt in our example has a pitch of 1.25 mm. Eight-millimeter bolts are also offered with a 1.0 mm pitch. Always remember that the coarse-thread fastener will have the higher pitch number than the fine-thread fastener of the same thread diameter.

WARNING
Do not install fasteners with a lower-grade strength classification than what was originally installed by the manufacturer. Doing so may cause equipment failure and/or damage.

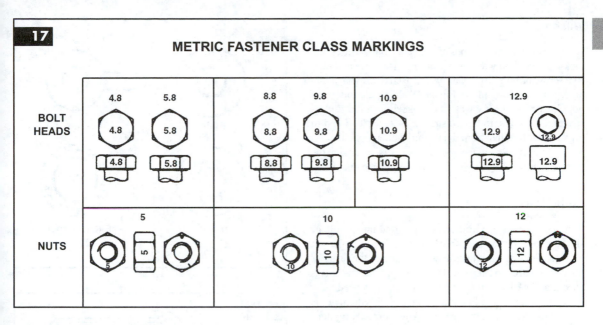

17

METRIC FASTENER CLASS MARKINGS

| BOLT HEADS | 4.8 | 5.8 | 8.8 | 9.8 | 10.9 | 12.9 |
| NUTS | 5 | | 10 | | 12 | |

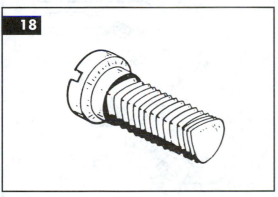

18

Torque Specifications

The materials used in the manufacture of the mower and engine may be subjected to uneven stresses if the fasteners of the various subassemblies are not installed and tightened correctly. Fasteners that are improperly installed or that work loose can cause extensive damage. Use an accurate torque wrench when tightening fasteners, and tighten each fastener to its specified torque.

Torque specifications for specific components are located in the appropriate chapters. Specifications for torque are provided in inch-pounds (in.-lb.) and/or foot-pounds (ft.-lb.) as well as Newton-meters (N·m). Refer to **Table 3** for torque conversion factors and to **Tables 4-9** for general torque values for fasteners without published specifications. **Tables 4-5** are for inch-size fasteners into steel or cast iron: **Table 4** applies to inch-size fasteners using inch-pound and Newton-meter values with dry threads; **Table 5** is for inch-size fasteners using foot-pound and Newton-meter values with dry threads. **Table 6** is for inch-size fasteners into aluminum. **Tables 7-8** are for metric fasteners into steel or cast iron: **Table 7** applies to metric fasteners using inch-pound and Newton-meter values with dry threads; **Table 8** is for metric fasteners using foot-pound and Newton-meter values with dry threads. **Table 9** is for metric fasteners into aluminum.

To use **Tables 4-9**, first determine the size of the fastener as described in *Fasteners* in this chapter. Locate that size of fastener in the appropriate table, then tighten the fastener to the indicated torque. Torque wrenches are described in the *Basic Tools* section of this chapter.

Self-Locking Fasteners

Several types of bolts, screws and nuts incorporate a system that creates interference between the two fasteners. Interference is achieved in various ways. The most common are the nylon-insert (Nylok) nut, those with a dry adhesive or Loctite-style coating on the threads of a bolt or nut, bolts with an out-of-round triangular-shaped cross-section (**Figure 18**, shown with exaggerated triangulation for emphasis), and nuts with crimped outer faces or flats.

Self-locking fasteners offer greater holding strength than standard fasteners, which improve their resistance to vibration. Most self-locking fasteners cannot be reused. The materials used to form the lock become distorted after the initial installation and removal. It is a good practice to discard and replace self-locking fasteners after their removal. Do not replace self-locking fasteners with standard fasteners.

Washers

There are two basic types of washers – flat washers and lockwashers. Flat washers are simple discs with a hole to fit a screw or bolt. Lockwashers are used to prevent a fastener from working loose. **Figure 19** shows the four most popular types of lock washers. Washers can be used as spacers and seals, to help distribute fastener load and to prevent the fastener from damaging the component.

As with fasteners, when replacing washers, make sure the replacement washers are of the same design and quality.

Cotter Pins

A cotter pin is a split metal pin inserted into a hole or slot to prevent a fastener from working loose. In certain high-load or critical-adjustment applications, the fastener must be secured in this way. For these applications, a cotter pin and castellated (slotted or castle) nut is used.

To use a cotter pin, first make sure the pin's diameter is correct for the hole in the fastener. After correctly tightening the fastener and aligning the holes, insert the cotter pin through the hole and bend the ends over the fastener (**Figure 20**). Unless specifically instructed to do so, never loosen a torqued fastener to align the holes. If the holes do not align, tighten the fastener just enough to achieve alignment.

Cotter pins are available in various diameters and lengths. Measure the length from the bottom of the head to the tip of the shortest pin.

Snap rings and E-clips

Snap rings (**Figure 21**) are circular-shaped metal retaining clips. They are required to secure parts and gears onto shafts, pins or rods. External snap rings are used to retain items on shafts. Internal snap rings secure parts within housing bores. In some applications, in addition to securing the component(s), snap rings of varying thickness also determine endplay. These are usually called selective snap rings.

Two basic types of snap rings are used – machined and stamped. Machined snap rings can be installed in either direction, since both faces have sharp edges. Stamped snap rings (**Figure 22**) are manufactured with a sharp edge and a round edge. When installing a stamped snap ring in a thrust application, install the sharp edge facing away from the part producing the thrust (**Figure 23**).

E-clips and circlips are used when it is not practical to use a snap ring or when a less-expensive retainer will suffice. Remove these clips with a flat-blade pry tool by prying between the shaft and the clip. To install an E-clip, center it over the shaft groove and push or tap it into place, or squeeze it into the slot with adjustable slip-joint pliers.

Observe the following when installing snap rings:

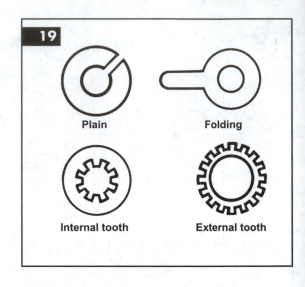

19

Plain   Folding

Internal tooth   External tooth

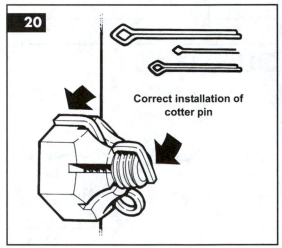

20

Correct installation of cotter pin

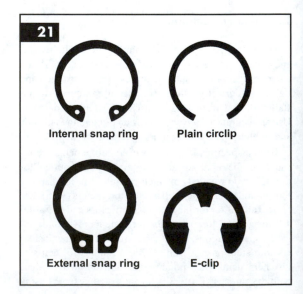

21

Internal snap ring   Plain circlip

External snap ring   E-clip

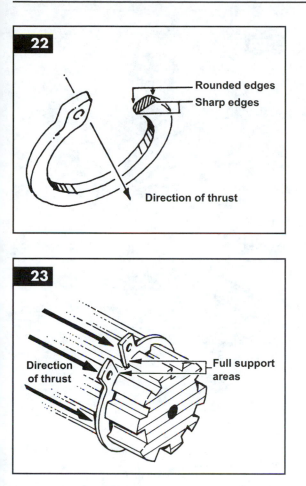

22

Rounded edges
Sharp edges
Direction of thrust

23

Direction of thrust
Full support areas

1. Wear eye protection when removing and installing snap rings.

2. Remove and install snap rings with snap ring pliers. See *Snap Ring Pliers* in this chapter.

3. Compress or expand snap rings only enough to remove or install them. If overly expanded, they lose their retaining ability.

4. In some applications, it may be necessary to replace snap rings after removing them.

5. Before installing a snap ring, make sure that the groove is clean.

6. After installing a snap ring, make sure it seats completely.

SHOP SUPPLIES

Lubricants and Fluids

Periodic lubrication helps ensure a long service life for any type of equipment. Using the correct type of lubricant is as important as performing the lubrication service. The following section describes the types of lubricants most

often required. Make sure to follow the manufacturer's recommendations for lubricant types.

Engine oils

Generally all liquid lubricants are called oil. They may be mineral-based (including petroleum bases), natural-based (vegetable and animal bases), synthetic-based, or emulsions (mixtures).

Engine oil is classified by two standards – the American Petroleum Institute (API) service classification and the Society of Automotive Engineers (SAE) viscosity rating. This information is either on the oil container label or lid. Two letters indicate the API service classification (SF, SG, CE, CF, etc.). The number or sequence of numbers and letter (10W-30 for example) is the oil's viscosity rating. The API service classification and the SAE viscosity index are not indications of oil quality.

The service classification indicates that the oil meets specific lubrication standards. Oil with a first classification letter of *S* indicates that the oil is for spark-ignited gasoline engines. Compression-ignited diesel engines require oil whose first classification letter is *C*. The second letter indicates the standard the oil satisfies. The second-letter classification started with the letter *A* and is currently at the letter *J*.

Always use oil with a classification recommended by the manufacturer. Using oil with a classification different than that recommended can cause engine damage.

Viscosity is an indication of the oil's thickness or resistance to flow. Thin oils have a low number while thicker oils have a higher number. Engine oils fall into the 5- to 50-weight range for single-grade oils. A "W" after the number indicates that the viscosity testing was done at low temperature to simulate cold-weather operation.

Most manufacturers recommend multi-grade oil. Multi-grade, or multi-viscosity, oils (for example 10W-30) are less viscous (thinner) at low temperatures and more viscous (thicker) at high temperatures. This allows the oil to perform efficiently across a wide range of engine operating conditions. The lower the number, the better the engine will start in cold climates. Higher numbers are usually recommended when operating an engine in hot weather. When selecting engine oil, follow the manufacturer's recommendation for type, classification and viscosity.

Greases

Grease is an oil to which a thickening base has been added so the end product is semi-solid. Grease is often classified by the type of thickener added, such as lithium soap. The National Lubricating Grease Institute (NLGI) grades grease. Grades range from No. 000 to No. 6, with No. 6 being the thickest. Typical multipurpose grease is

NLGI No. 2. For specific applications, manufacturers may recommend water-resistant type grease or one with an additive such as molybdenum disulfide (MoS_2).

Refer to the appropriate lubrication table for the recommended greases.

Antiseize Lubricant

Some assembly applications may specify antiseize lubricant (**Figure 24**). This compound prevents the formation of rust and corrosion, which may lock parts together, making future service and disassembly extremely difficult.

Cleaners, Degreasers and Solvents

Many chemicals are available to remove oil, grease and other residue from the mower or engine.

Before using cleaning solvents, consider how they will be used and disposed of, particularly if they are not water-soluble. EPA regulations and local ordinances may require special procedures for the disposal of various cleaning chemicals. Refer to *Safety* and *Cleaning Parts* in this chapter for more information on their use.

Use electrical contact cleaner to clean electrical connections and components without leaving any residue.

Carburetor cleaner is a powerful solvent used to remove fuel deposits and varnish from fuel system components. Use this cleaner carefully, as it may damage soft plastic components and finishes.

Generally, degreasers are strong cleaners used to remove heavy accumulations of grease from engine and frame components.

Most solvents are designed to be used in a parts-washing cabinet for individual component cleaning. For safety, use only the nonflammable or high-flash-point solvents recommended by the cabinet manufacturer.

Gasket Sealant

Sealants are used either alone or in combination with a gasket or seal. Follow the manufacturer's recommendation when using sealants. Sealants should not be used on replacement gaskets if the original gasket did not use sealant. Use extreme care when choosing a sealant different from the type originally recommended. Choose sealants based on their resistance to heat and various fluids as well as their sealing capabilities.

One of the most common sealants is RTV, or room-temperature-vulcanizing sealant. This sealant cures at room temperature over a specific time period. It allows the repositioning of components without damaging gaskets. However, some RTV manufacturers recommend against moving components while the RTV is curing in

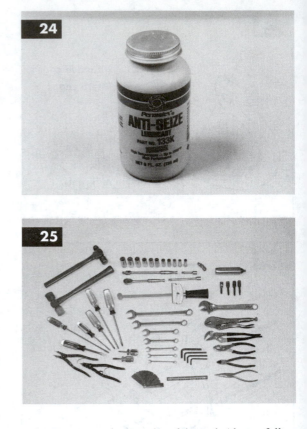

order to preserve the integrity of the seal. Always follow the RTV directions.

Moisture in the air causes the RTV sealant to cure. Always install the tube cap as soon as possible after applying RTV sealant. RTV sealant has a limited shelf life and will not cure properly if the shelf life has expired. Keep partial tubes sealed, and discard them if they have passed the expiration date.

Applying RTV sealant

Clean all old sealant residue from the mating surfaces. Remove all sealant material from blind threaded holes; it can cause inaccurate bolt torque. Spray the mating surfaces with aerosol parts cleaner, then wipe them with a lint-free cloth. The area must be clean for the sealant to adhere.

Unless otherwise instructed, apply RTV sealant in a continuous bead 2-3 mm (0.08-0.12 in.) thick. Circle all the fastener holes unless otherwise specified. Do not allow any sealant to enter these holes. Assemble and tighten the fasteners to the specified torque within the time frame recommended by the RTV sealant manufacturer.

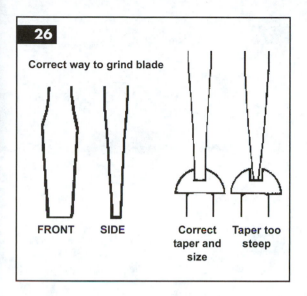

26

Correct way to grind blade

FRONT   SIDE   Correct   Taper too
                      taper and   steep
                        size

the novice mechanic. Always use the correct tools for the job at hand. Keep tools organized and clean. Store them in a tool chest with related tools organized together.

Quality tools are essential. The best tools are constructed of high-strength alloy steel. These tools are light, easy to use and resistant to wear. Their working surface is smooth, and the tool is carefully polished. They have an easy-to-clean finish and are comfortable to use. Quality tools are a good investment.

When building a new tool kit, consider purchasing a basic tool set (**Figure 25**) from a large tool supplier. These sets contain a variety of commonly-used tools, and they provide substantial savings when compared to individually purchased tools. As one becomes more experienced and tasks become more complicated, specialized tools can be added.

Gasket Remover

Aerosol gasket remover can help remove stubborn gaskets. This product can speed up the removal process and prevent damage to the mating surface that may be caused by using a scraping tool. Most of these types of products are very caustic. Follow the gasket remover manufacturer's instructions for use.

Threadlocking Compound

A threadlocking compound is a fluid applied to the threads of fasteners. After tightening the fastener, the fluid dries and becomes a solid filler between the threads. This makes it difficult for the fastener to work loose from vibration, or heat expansion and contraction. Some threadlocking compounds also provide a seal against fluid leakage.

Before applying threadlocking compound, remove any old compound from both thread areas and clean them with aerosol parts cleaner. Use the compound sparingly. Excess fluid can run into adjoining parts.

Threadlocking compounds are available in different strengths. Follow the particular manufacturer's recommendations regarding compound selection. Two popular manufacturers of threadlocking compound are Loctite and ThreeBond. They both offer a wide range of compounds for various strength, temperature and repair applications.

BASIC TOOLS

Most of the procedures in this manual can be carried out with simple hand tools and test equipment familiar to

Screwdrivers

Screwdrivers of various lengths and types are mandatory for the simplest tool kit. The two basic types are the slotted tip (flat blade) and the Phillips tip. These are available in sets that often include an assortment of tip sizes and shank lengths.

As with all tools, use a screwdriver designed for the job. Make sure the size of the tip conforms to the size and shape of the fastener. Use them only for driving screws. *Never* use a screwdriver for prying or chiseling metal. Repair or replace worn or damaged screwdrivers. A worn tip may damage the fastener, making it difficult to remove. When dressing flat-blade screwdriver tips, always be sure that the faces of the blade, when viewed from the side (**Figure 26**), are ground flat to slightly hollow-ground. Dress-grinding a flat-blade screwdriver tip with too steep a taper (bow-ground) will cause the blade tip to slip out of the screw slot when turning torque is applied, as shown by the right-side screwdriver tip in **Figure 26**.

Wrenches

Box-end, open-end and combination wrenches (**Figure 27**) are available in a variety of types and sizes. A combination wrench has one box end and one open end, usually of the same size.

The number stamped on the wrench refers to the distance between the sides of the wrench jaws. This must match the distance across two parallel flats on the bolt head or nut.

The box-end wrench is an excellent tool because it grips the fastener on all sides. This reduces the chance of the tool slipping. The box-end wrench is designed with either a 6- or 12-point opening. For stubborn or damaged fasteners, the 6-point wrench provides superior holding ability by contacting the fastener across a wider area at all six edges. For general use, the 12-point works well by allowing the wrench to be removed and reinstalled without moving the handle over a wide arc. Used carefully, a 12-point wrench can also fit square nuts and bolt heads.

An open-end wrench is fast and works best in areas with limited head access. Because it contacts the fastener at only two points, an open-end wrench is subject to slipping under heavy force or if the tool or fastener is worn. A box-end wrench is preferred in most instances, especially when applying considerable force to a fastener.

Adjustable Wrenches

An adjustable wrench or Crescent wrench (**Figure 28**) fits nearly any nut or bolt head that has clear access around its entire perimeter. An adjustable wrench is best used as a backup wrench to hold a large nut or bolt while the other end is being loosened or tightened with a box-end or socket wrench.

Adjustable wrenches contact the fastener at only two points, making them more likely to slip off the fastener. The fact that one jaw is adjustable and may loosen only aggravates this shortcoming. These wrenches are directional: Make certain the solid jaw is the one transmitting the force. In other words, if there were a right-hand threaded nut between the jaws of the wrenches in **Figure 28**, the wrenches would be positioned to tighten the nut by pulling down on the wrench handles on the right. Attempting to loosen the nut by pushing up on the handles could break the movable jaw.

Socket Wrenches, Ratchets and Handles

Sockets that attach to a ratchet handle (**Figure 29**) are available with 6-point (A) or 12-point (B) openings and different drive sizes. The drive size indicates the size of the square hole that accepts the ratchet handle. The number stamped on the socket is the size of the fastener head.

As with wrenches, a 6-point socket provides superior holding ability, while a 12-point socket needs to be moved only half as far to reposition it on the fastener.

Sockets are specified for either hand or impact use. Impact sockets are made of stronger alloys and thicker material for more durability. Compare the size and wall thickness of a 19-mm hand socket (A, **Figure 30**) and the 19-mm impact socket (B). Use impact sockets when using an impact driver or air tools. Use hand sockets with hand-driven attachments.

> *WARNING*
> *Do not use hand sockets with air or impact tools. They may shatter and cause injury. Always wear eye protection when using impact or air tools.*

Various handles are available for sockets. The speed handle is used for fast, low-torque operation. Flexible

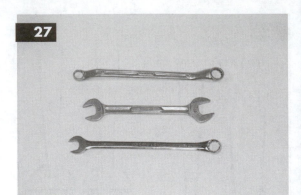

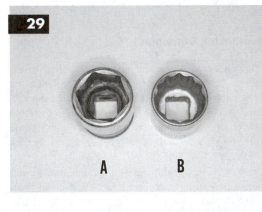

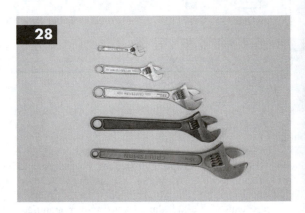

A   B

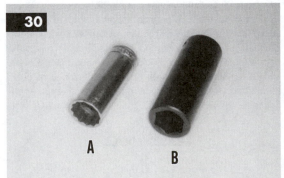

A   B

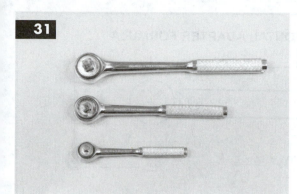

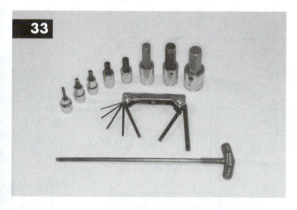

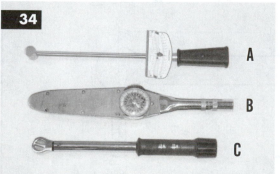

ratchet heads in varying lengths allow the socket to be turned with varying force, and at odd angles. Extension bars allow the socket to reach difficult areas. The regular ratchet (**Figure 31**) is the most versatile wrench. It allows the user to install or remove the nut without removing the socket.

Sockets combined with any number of drivers make them undoubtedly the fastest, safest and most convenient tool for fastener removal and installation.

> *WARNING*
> *Do not lengthen a socket handle with a pipe or similar item in an effort to increase loosening or tightening force. Doing so could shatter the socket or handle, causing serious injury.*

Impact Driver

An impact driver provides extra force for removing fasteners by converting the impact of a hammer into a turning motion. This makes it possible to remove stubborn fasteners without damaging them. Impact drivers and interchangeable bits (**Figure 32**) are available from most tool suppliers. When using a socket or bit with an impact driver, make sure the tool is designed for impact use. Refer to *Socket Wrenches, Ratchets and Handles* in this section.

> *WARNING*
> *Do not use hand sockets with air or impact tools. They may shatter and cause injury. Always wear eye protection when using impact or air tools.*

Allen Wrenches

Allen or setscrew wrenches (**Figure 33**) are used on fasteners with hexagonal recesses in the fastener head (**Figure 14**). These wrenches are available in L-shaped bar, socket and T-handle types. A metric set is required when working on most modern mowers. Allen bolts are sometimes called socket bolts.

Torque Wrenches

A torque wrench is used with a socket, torque adapter or similar extension to tighten a fastener to a predetermined specification. Torque wrenches come in several drive sizes (1/4, 3/8, 1/2 and 3/4) and have various methods of reading the torque value. The drive size indicates the size of the square drive that accepts the socket, adapter or extension. Common methods of reading the torque value are the deflecting beam (A, **Figure 34**), the dial indicator (B) and the audible click (C).

When choosing a torque wrench, consider the torque range, drive size and accuracy. The torque specifications

35

TORQUE WRENCH AND HORIZONTAL ADAPTER FORMULA

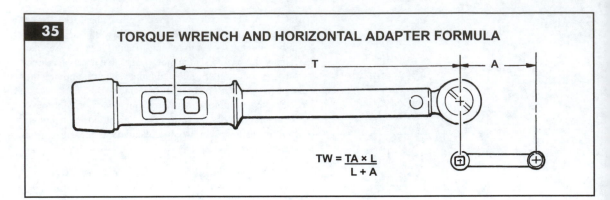

$$TW = \frac{TA \times L}{L + A}$$

36

HOW TO MEASURE TORQUE WRENCH EFFECTIVE LENGTH

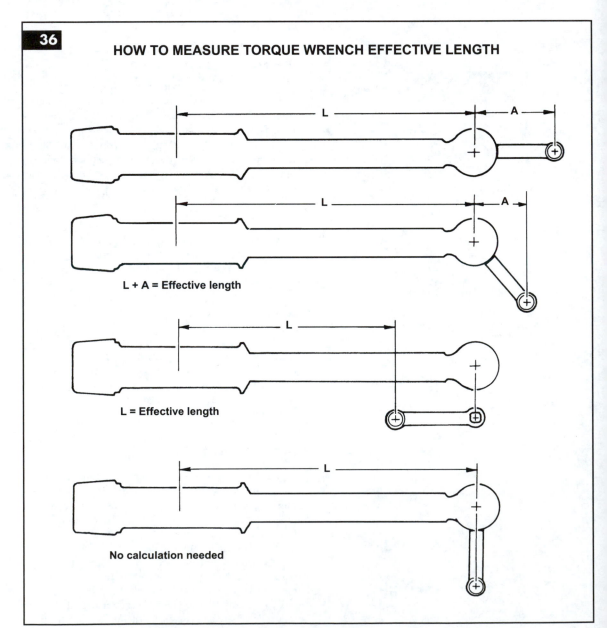

L + A = Effective length

L = Effective length

No calculation needed

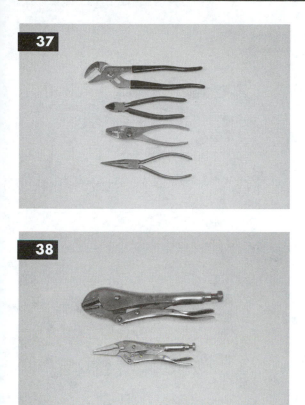

37

38

TW is the torque setting or dial reading on the wrench;

TA is the torque specification and the actual amount of torque that will be applied to the fastener;

A is the amount that the adapter increases (or in some cases reduces) the effective lever length as measured along the centerline of the torque wrench from the center of the drive to the center of adapter box end (**Figure 36**); and

L is the lever length of the wrench as measured from the center of the drive to the center of the grip.

The effective length of the torque wrench is the sum of L and A.

For example:

To apply 20 ft.-lb. of torque to a fastener using an adapter as shown in the top example in **Figure 36**:

TA = 20 ft.-lb;

A = 3 in;

L = 14 in;

$$TW = \frac{20 \times 14}{14 + 3} = \frac{280}{17} = 16.5 \text{ ft.-lb.}$$

In this example, a click-type torque wrench would be set to the recalculated torque value (TW = 16.5 ft.-lb.). When using a dial or beam-type torque wrench, tighten the fastener until the pointer aligns with 16.5 ft.-lb. In either case, although the torque wrench reads 16.5 ft.-lb., the actual torque applied to the fastener is 20 ft.-lb.

in this manual provide an indication of the range required. Torque wrenches are most accurate within the middle 50% of their range. For example, a 0-600 inch-pound torque wrench is most accurate between 150-450 in.-lb.

A torque wrench is a precision tool that must be properly cared for to remain accurate. Store torque wrenches in cases or separate padded drawers within a toolbox. Follow the manufacturer's instructions for their care and calibration.

Torque Adapters

Torque adapters extend, reduce, or make more convenient the reach of a torque wrench. The torque adapter shown in **Figure 35** is used to tighten a fastener that cannot be reached due to the size of the torque wrench head, drive, and socket. If a torque adapter changes the effective lever length (**Figure 35** and **Figure 36**) of a torque wrench, the torque reading on the wrench does not equal the actual torque applied to the fastener. It is necessary to calculate the adjusted torque reading on the wrench to compensate for the change of lever length. When a torque adapter is used at a right angle to the drive head, calibration is not required, since the effective length has not changed.

To calculate the adjusted torque reading when using a torque adapter, use the formula shown in **Figure 35**:

Pliers

Pliers come in a wide range of types and sizes. Pliers are useful for holding, cutting, bending, and crimping. Do not use them to turn fasteners. **Figure 37** shows several types of useful pliers. Each design has a specialized function. Slip-joint pliers, commonly called Channellocks, are general purpose pliers used for gripping and bending. Diagonal cutting pliers (dikes, or side cutters) cut wire and can be used to remove cotter pins. Adjustable pliers can be adjusted to hold different-sized objects. The jaws remain parallel so they grip around objects such as pipe or tubing. Needlenose pliers are used to hold or bend small objects. Locking pliers (**Figure 38**), commonly called Vise-grips, are used to hold objects very tightly. They have many uses, ranging from holding two parts together to gripping the end of a broken stud. Use caution when using locking pliers, as the sharp jaws may damage the objects they hold. If Vise-grips are used to hold more delicate components, slip pieces of fuel hose or similar material over the jaws.

Snap-Ring Pliers

Snap-ring pliers (**Figure 39**) are specialized pliers with tips that fit into the end holes of snap rings to remove and install them.

Snap-ring pliers are available with either a fixed action (either internal or external) or convertible (one tool works on both internal and external snap rings). They may have fixed tips or interchangeable ones of various sizes and angles. For general use, select a convertible pair of pliers with interchangeable tips.

WARNING
Snap rings can slip and fly off when removing and installing them. Also, the pliers' tips may break. Always wear eye protection when using snap-ring pliers.

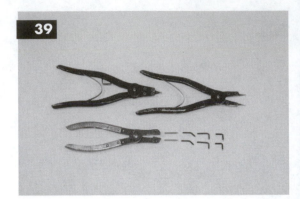

Hammers

Various types of hammers are available to fit a number of applications. A ball-peen hammer (A, **Figure 40**) is used to strike another tool, such as a punch or chisel. Soft-faced hammers (B) are required when a metal object must be struck without damaging it. *Never* use a metal-faced hammer on engine and suspension components, unless instructions require it. Damage will occur in most cases.

Always wear eye protection when using hammers. Make sure the hammer face is in good condition and the handle is not cracked. Select the correct hammer for the job and strike the object squarely. Do not use the handle or the side of the hammer to strike an object.

PRECISION MEASURING TOOLS

The ability to accurately measure components is essential to successfully rebuild an engine or precision component. Modern equipment is manufactured to close tolerances, and obtaining consistently accurate measurements is essential to determining which components require replacement or further service.

Each type of measuring instrument is designed to measure a dimension with a certain degree of accuracy and within a certain range. When selecting a measuring tool, make sure it is applicable to the task.

As with all tools, measuring tools provide the best results if cared for properly. Improper use or care can damage the tool and result in inaccurate results. If any measurement is questionable, verify the measurement using another tool. A standard gauge is usually provided with measuring tools to check accuracy and calibrate the tool.

Precision measurements can vary according to the experience of the person taking the measurement. Accurate results are possible only if the mechanic possesses a feel for using the tool. Heavy-handed use of measuring tools produces less accurate results than if the tool is handled properly. Grasp precision measuring tools gently with your fingertips so the point at which the tool contacts the object is easily felt. This feel for the equipment produces consistently accurate measurements and reduces

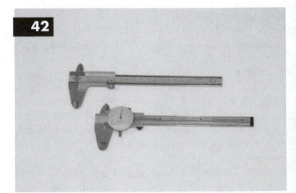

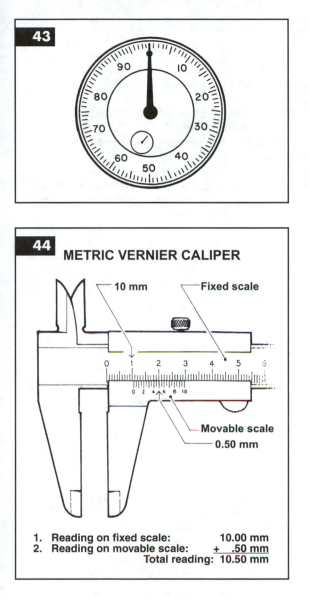

METRIC VERNIER CALIPER

10 mm

Fixed scale

Movable scale

0.50 mm

1. Reading on fixed scale:	10.00 mm
2. Reading on movable scale:	+ .50 mm
	Total reading: 10.50 mm

A common use for a feeler gauge is to measure valve clearance. Wire (round) type gauges are used to measure spark plug gaps.

Calipers

Calipers (**Figure 42**) are excellent tools for obtaining inside, outside and depth measurements. Although not as precise as a micrometer, they allow reasonable precision, typically to within 0.001 in. (0.05 mm). Most calipers have a range up to six inches (150 mm).

Calipers are available in dial, vernier or digital versions. Dial calipers have a dial readout (**Figure 43**) that provides a convenient reading. Vernier calipers have marked scales that must be compared to determine the measurement. The digital caliper uses a battery-operated LCD (liquid crystal display) to show the measurement.

Properly maintain the measuring surfaces of the caliper. There must not be any dirt or burrs between the tool and the object being measured. Never force the caliper closed around an object. Close the caliper around the highest point so it can be removed with a slight drag. Some calipers require periodic recalibration. Always refer to the manufacturer's instructions when using a new or unfamiliar caliper.

Figure 44 shows a measurement taken with a metric vernier caliper. To read the measurement, note that the fixed scale is graduated in centimeters, which is indicated by the whole numbers 1, 2, 3, etc. Each centimeter is then divided into millimeters, which are indicated by the small line between the whole numbers (1 centimeter equals 10 millimeters). The movable scale is marked in increments of 0.05 mm (five-hundredths of a millimeter). The value of a measurement equals the reading on the fixed scale plus the reading on the movable scale.

To determine the reading on the fixed scale, look for the line on the fixed scale immediately to the left of the 0-line on the movable scale. In **Figure 44**, the fixed scale reading is 1 centimeter (10 millimeters).

To determine the reading on the movable scale, note the one line on the movable scale that precisely aligns with a line on the fixed scale. Look closely; a number of lines will seem close, but only one aligns precisely with a line on the fixed scale. In **Figure 44**, the movable scale reading is 0.50 mm.

To calculate the measurement, add the fixed scale reading (10 mm) to the movable scale reading (0.50 mm) for a value of 10.50 mm.

Micrometers

A micrometer is an instrument designed for linear measurement using the decimal divisions of the inch or meter (**Figure 45**). While there are many types and styles of micrometers, most of the procedures in this manual call for

the risk of damaging the tool or component. Refer to the following sections for a description of various measuring tools.

Feeler Gauge

The feeler or thickness gauge (**Figure 41**) is used for measuring the distance between two surfaces.

A feeler gauge set consists of an assortment of strips of graduated thicknesses. Most feeler gauge strips are made of spring steel, but they can also be brass, stainless steel, or plastic. Each blade is marked with its thickness. Blades can be of various lengths and angles for different procedures.

45

DECIMAL PLACE VALUES*

0.1	Indicates 1/10 (one tenth of an inch or millimeter)
0.010	Indicates 1/100 (one one-hundreth of an inch or millimeter)
0.001	Indicates 1/1,000 (one one-thousandth of an inch or millimeter)

***This chart represents the values of figures placed to the right of the decimal point. Use it when reading decimals from one-tenth to one one-thousandth of an inch or millimeter. It is not a conversion chart (for example: 0.001 in. is not equal to 0.001 mm).**

an outside micrometer. The outside micrometer is used to measure the outside diameter of cylindrical forms and the thickness of materials.

A micrometer's size indicates the minimum and maximum size of a part that it can measure. The usual sizes (**Figure 46**) are 0-1 in. (0-25 mm), 1-2 in. (25-50 mm), 2-3 in. (50-75 mm) and 3-4 in. (75-100 mm).

Figure 47 shows the markings and parts of a standard inch micrometer. Be familiar with these terms before using a micrometer in the following sections.

Micrometers that cover a wider range of measurement are available. These use a large frame with interchangeable anvils of various lengths. This type of micrometer offers a cost savings; however, its overall size may make it less convenient.

Reading a Micrometer

When reading a micrometer, numbers are taken from different scales and added together. The following sections describe how to read the measurements of various types of outside micrometers.

For accurate results, properly maintain the measuring surfaces of the micrometer. There cannot be any dirt or burrs between the tool and the measured object. Never force the micrometer closed around an object. Close the micrometer around the highest point so it can be removed with a slight drag.

Standard inch micrometer

The standard inch micrometer is accurate to one-thousandth of an inch or 0.001. The sleeve is marked in 0.025 in. increments. Every fourth sleeve mark is numbered 1, 2, 3, 4, 5, 6, 7, 8, 9. These numbers indicate 0.100, 0.200, 0.300, and so on.

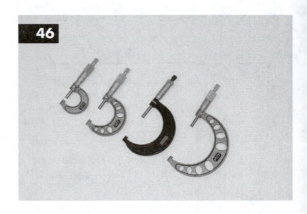

46

The tapered end of the thimble has 25 lines marked around it. Each mark equals 0.001 in. One complete turn of the thimble will align its zero mark with the first mark on the sleeve or 0.025 in.

When reading a standard inch micrometer, perform the following steps while referring to **Figure 48**.

1. Read the sleeve and find the largest number visible. Each sleeve number equals 0.100 in.

2. Count the number of lines between the numbered sleeve mark and the edge of the thimble. Each sleeve mark equals 0.025 in.

3. Read the thimble mark that aligns with the sleeve line. Each thimble mark equals 0.001 in.

NOTE
*If a thimble mark does not align exactly with the sleeve line, estimate the amount between the lines. For accurate readings in ten-thousandths of an inch (0.0001 in.), use a vernier inch micrometer (**Figure 49**).*

4. Add the readings from Steps 1-3.

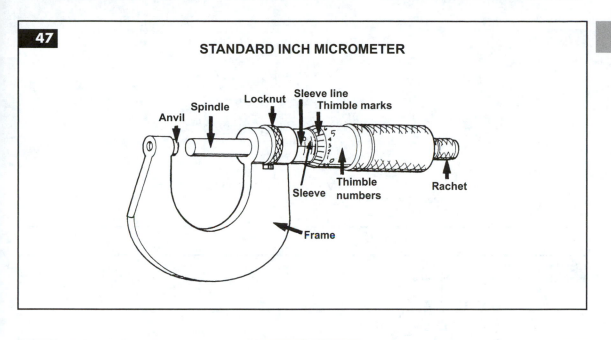

47

STANDARD INCH MICROMETER

1

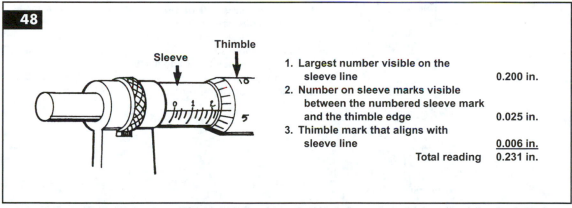

48

1. Largest number visible on the sleeve line	0.200 in.
2. Number on sleeve marks visible between the numbered sleeve mark and the thimble edge	0.025 in.
3. Thimble mark that aligns with sleeve line	0.006 in.
Total reading	0.231 in.

Vernier inch micrometer

A vernier inch micrometer is accurate to one ten-thousandth of an inch or 0.0001 in. It has the same markings as a standard inch micrometer with an additional vernier scale on the sleeve (**Figure 49** and **Figure 50**).

The vernier scale consists of 11 lines marked 1-9 with a 0 on each end. These lines run parallel to the thimble lines and represent 0.0001 in. increments.

When reading a vernier inch micrometer, perform the following steps while referring to **Figure 50**.

1. Take the initial reading in the same way as a standard micrometer.

2. If a thimble mark aligns exactly with the sleeve line, reading the vernier scale is not necessary. If they do not align, read the vernier scale in Step 3.

3. Determine which vernier scale mark aligns with one thimble mark. The vernier scale number is the amount in ten-thousandths of an inch to add to the initial reading from Step 1.

Metric micrometer

The standard metric micrometer (**Figure 51**) is accurate to one one-hundredth of a millimeter (0.01 mm). The sleeve line is graduated in millimeter and half-millimeter increments. The marks on the upper half of the sleeve line equal 1.00 mm. Every fifth mark above the sleeve line is identified with a number. The number sequence depends on the size of the micrometer. A 0-25 mm micrometer, for example, will have sleeve marks numbered 0 through 25 in 5 mm increments. This numbering sequence continues with larger micrometers. On all metric micrometers, each mark on the lower half of the sleeve equals 0.50 mm.

The tapered end of the thimble has 50 lines marked around it. Each mark equals 0.01 mm.

49

VERNIER INCH MICROMETER

Vernier scale

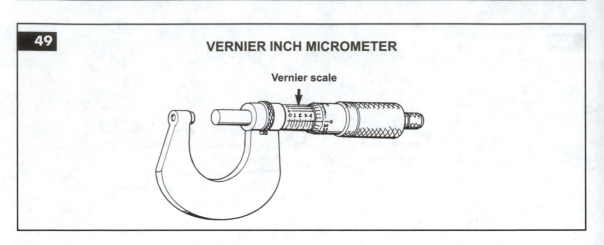

50

Vernier scale

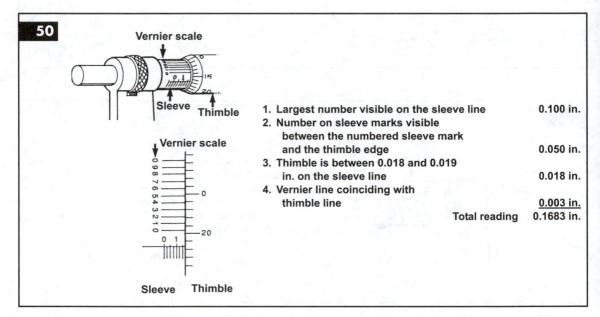

Sleeve   Thimble

Vernier scale

Sleeve   Thimble

1. Largest number visible on the sleeve line   0.100 in.
2. Number on sleeve marks visible
   between the numbered sleeve mark
   and the thimble edge   0.050 in.
3. Thimble is between 0.018 and 0.019
   in. on the sleeve line   0.018 in.
4. Vernier line coinciding with
   thimble line   0.003 in.
                                   Total reading   0.1683 in.

51

STANDARD METRIC MICROMETER

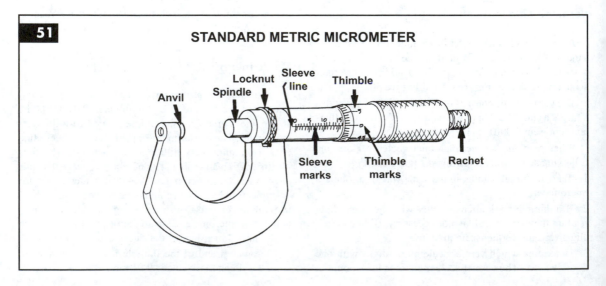

Anvil   Locknut   Sleeve   Thimble
         Spindle   line

Sleeve   Thimble   Rachet
marks   marks

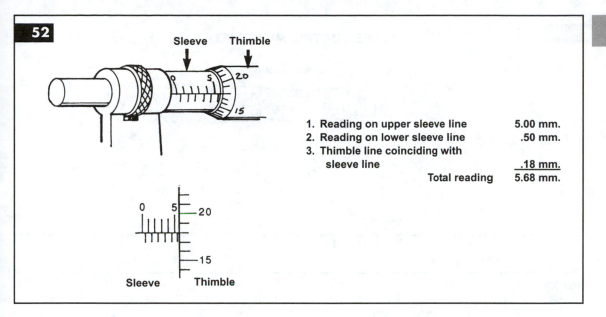

52

1. Reading on upper sleeve line	5.00 mm.
2. Reading on lower sleeve line	.50 mm.
3. Thimble line coinciding with sleeve line	.18 mm.
Total reading	5.68 mm.

One complete turn of the thimble aligns its 0 mark with the first line on the lower half of the sleeve line or 0.50 mm.

When reading a metric micrometer, add the number of millimeters and half-millimeters on the sleeve line to the hundredths of a millimeter shown on the thimble. Perform the following steps while referring to **Figure 52**.

1. Read the upper half of the sleeve line and count the number of lines visible. Each upper line equals 1 mm.

2. If the half-millimeter line is visible on the lower sleeve line, add 0.50 to the reading in Step 1.

3. Read the thimble mark that aligns with the sleeve line. Each thimble mark equals 0.01 mm.

> *NOTE*
> *If a thimble mark does not align exactly with the sleeve line, estimate the amount between the lines. For accurate readings to two-thousandths of a millimeter (0.002 mm), use a metric vernier micrometer (Figure 53).*

4. Add the readings from Steps 1-3.

Metric vernier micrometer

A metric vernier micrometer is accurate to two-thousandths of a millimeter (0.002-mm). It has the same markings as a standard metric micrometer with the addition of a vernier scale on the sleeve (**Figure 53** and **Figure 54**). The vernier scale consists of five lines marked 0, 2, 4, 6, and 8. These lines run parallel to the thimble lines and represent 0.002-mm increments.

When reading a metric vernier micrometer, perform the following steps while referring to **Figure 54**.

1. Read the micrometer in the same way as a standard metric micrometer. This is the initial reading.

2. If a thimble mark aligns exactly with the sleeve line, reading the vernier scale is not necessary. If they do not align, read the vernier scale in Step 3.

3. Determine which vernier scale mark aligns exactly with one thimble mark. The vernier scale number is the amount in two-thousandths of a millimeter to add to the initial reading from Step 1.

Micrometer Adjustment

Before using a micrometer, check its adjustment as follows.

1. Clean the anvil and spindle faces.

2A. To check a 0-1 in. or 0-25 mm micrometer:
  a. Turn the thimble until the spindle contacts the anvil. If the micrometer has a ratchet, use it to ensure that the proper amount of pressure is applied.
  b. If the adjustment is correct, the 0 mark on the thimble will align exactly with the 0 mark on the sleeve line. If the marks do not align, the micrometer is out of adjustment.
  c. Follow the manufacturer's instructions to adjust the micrometer.

2B. To check a micrometer larger than 1 in. or 25 mm, use the standard gauge supplied by the manufacturer. A standard gauge is a steel block, disc or rod that is machined to an exact size.
  a. Place the standard gauge between the spindle and anvil, and measure its outside diameter or length. If the micrometer has a ratchet, use it to ensure that the proper amount of pressure is applied.

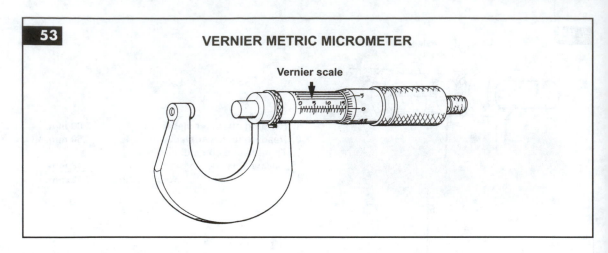

VERNIER METRIC MICROMETER

Vernier scale

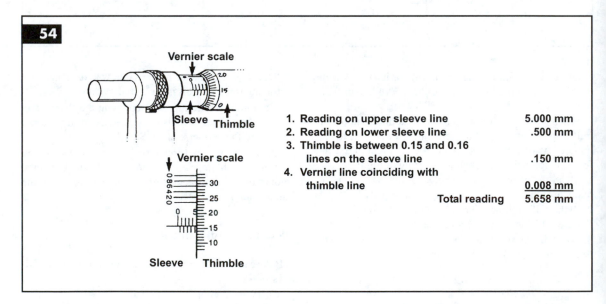

Vernier scale

Sleeve Thimble

Vernier scale

Sleeve Thimble

1. Reading on upper sleeve line	5.000 mm
2. Reading on lower sleeve line	.500 mm
3. Thimble is between 0.15 and 0.16 lines on the sleeve line	.150 mm
4. Vernier line coinciding with thimble line	0.008 mm
Total reading	5.658 mm

b. If the adjustment is correct, the 0 mark on the thimble will align exactly with the 0 mark on the sleeve line. If the marks do not align, the micrometer is out of adjustment.

c. Follow the manufacturer's instructions to adjust the micrometer.

Micrometer Care

Micrometers are precision instruments. They must be used and maintained with great care. Note the following:

1. Store micrometers in protective cases or separate padded drawers in a toolbox.

2. When in storage, make sure the spindle and anvil faces do not contact each other or another object. If they do, temperature changes and corrosion may damage the contact faces.

3. Do not clean a micrometer with compressed air. Dirt forced into the tool will cause wear and inaccurate readings.

4. Lubricate micrometers lightly with oil to prevent corrosion.

Telescoping and Small Bore Gauges

Use telescoping gauges (**Figure 55**) and small-bore gauges (**Figure 56**) to measure bores. Neither gauge has a scale for direct readings. An outside micrometer must be used to determine the reading.

To use a telescoping gauge, select the correct size gauge for the bore. Loosen the knurled handle end, then compress the movable post and carefully insert the gauge into the bore. Do not let the post faces snap into the bore walls. Carefully move the gauge in the bore to make sure it is centered at the largest diameter. Lightly tighten the knurled end of

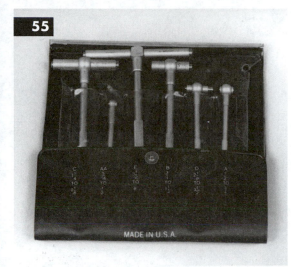

55

56

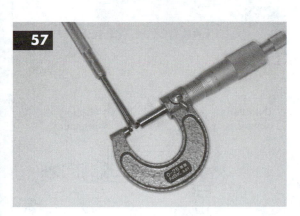

57

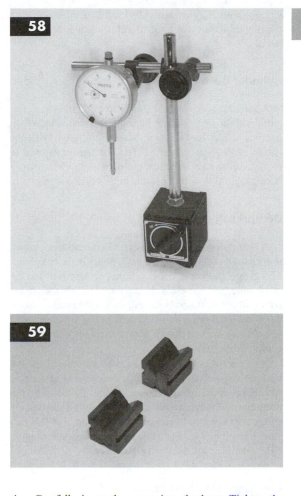

58

59

the gauge to hold the movable post in position. Remove the gauge, then measure across the posts. Telescoping gauges are typically used to measure cylinder bores.

To use a small bore gauge, select the correct size gauge for the bore. Loosen the handle knob, then compress the gauge tips. Carefully insert the gauge into the bore. Tighten the knurled end of the gauge to carefully expand the gauge fingers to the limit within the bore. Do not overtighten the gauge, as there is no built-in release. Excessive tightening can damage both the bore surface and the tool. Remove the gauge and measure the outside dimension (**Figure 57**). Small bore gauges are typically used to measure valve guides.

Dial Indicator

A dial indicator (A, **Figure 58**) is a gauge with a dial face and needle used to measure variations in dimensions and movements. Measuring shaft runout is a typical use for a dial indicator.

Dial indicators are available in various ranges and graduations and with three basic types of mounting bases: magnetic stand (B), clamp, or screw-in stud.

V-Blocks

V-blocks (**Figure 59**) are precision ground blocks used to hold a round object when checking its runout or straightness. They are normally used in conjunction with the dial indicator while the object being inspected is rotated.

Cylinder Bore Gauge

A cylinder bore gauge is similar to a dial indicator. The gauge set shown in **Figure 60** consists of a dial indicator, handle, and different length adapters (anvils) to fit the gauge to various bore sizes. The bore gauge is used to measure bore size, taper and out-of-round. When using a bore gauge, follow the manufacturer's instructions.

Compression Gauge

A compression gauge (**Figure 61**) measures combustion chamber (cylinder) pressure, usually in psi or kg/cm^2. The gauge adapter is either inserted or screwed into the spark plug hole to obtain the reading. Disable the engine so it will not start and hold both the throttle and choke in the wide-open position when performing a compression test. An engine that does not have adequate compression cannot be properly tuned.

A compression gauge will only be accurate if the engine is designed to provide full compression at starting rpm. Since most modern mower engines have some form of compression release to aid in starting, a compression gauge will not provide an accurate reading. For this reason, the best tool to use to test for compression leakage is a cylinder leakdown tester (**Figure 62**).

Cylinder Leakdown Tester

A cylinder leakdown tester (**Figure 62**) can readily determine compression leakage from either the cylinder and piston, the intake valve, or the exhaust valve. When used correctly, compression-release mechanisms have no effect on it.

Figure 62 shows a 2-gauge tester; some leakdown testers have only one gauge. Chapter 2 will discuss the use of the leakdown tester.

Multimeter

A multimeter (**Figure 63**) is an essential tool for electrical system diagnosis. The voltage function indicates the voltage applied or available to various electrical components. The ohmmeter function tests circuits for continuity and measures the resistance of a circuit.

Some manufacturers' specifications for electrical components are based on results using a specific test meter. Results may vary if using a meter other than the one recommended by the manufacturer. Such requirements are noted when applicable.

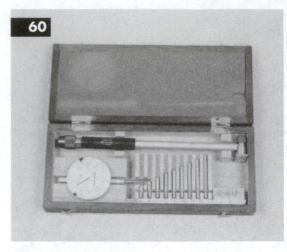

60

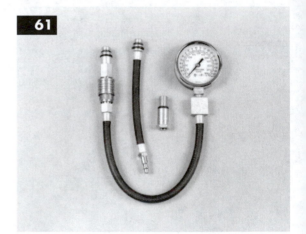

61

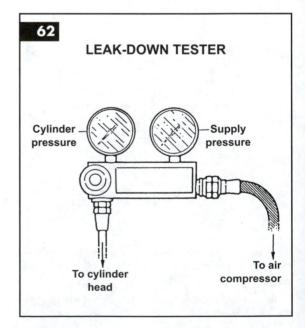

62

LEAK-DOWN TESTER

Cylinder pressure — Supply pressure

To cylinder head

To air compressor

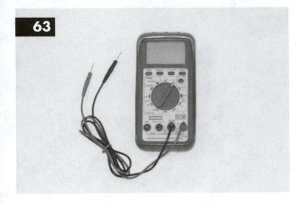

63

Ohmmeter (analog) calibration

Each time an analog ohmmeter is used or if the scale is changed, the ohmmeter must be calibrated. This process is commonly called "zeroing in" the meter. Digital ohmmeters do not require calibration. To calibrate the ohmmeter:

1. Make sure the meter battery is in good condition;
2. Make sure the meter probes are in good condition;
3. Touch the two probes together and watch the needle. It must align with the 0 mark on the scale.
4. If necessary, rotate the set-adjust knob until the needle points directly to the 0 mark.

ELECTRICAL SYSTEM FUNDAMENTALS

A thorough study of the many types of electrical systems used in today's units is beyond the scope of this manual. However, an understanding of electrical basics is necessary to perform simple diagnostic tests.

Voltage

Voltage is the electrical potential or pressure in an electrical circuit. It is expressed in volts. The more pressure (voltage) in a circuit, the more work it can perform.

Direct current (DC) voltage means the electricity flows in one direction. All circuits powered by a battery are DC circuits.

Alternating current (AC) means that the electricity constantly flows in one direction, then rapidly switches to the opposite direction. Pre-regulated alternator output is an example of AC voltage. This voltage must be changed or rectified to direct current to operate in a battery-powered system.

Resistance

Resistance is the opposition to the flow of electricity within a circuit or component. It is measured in ohms. Resistance causes a reduction in available current and voltage.

Resistance is measured in an inactive circuit with an ohmmeter. The ohmmeter sends a small amount of current into the circuit and measures how difficult it is to push the current through the circuit.

An ohmmeter, although useful, is not always a good indicator of a circuit's actual ability under operating conditions. This is due to the low voltage (1 1/2-9 volts) that the meter uses to test the circuit. The voltage in an ignition coil secondary winding can be several thousand volts. Such high voltage can cause the coil to malfunction, even though it tests acceptably during a resistance test.

Resistance generally increases with temperature. Perform all testing with the component or circuit at room temperature. Resistance tests performed at high temperatures may indicate high resistance readings and result in the unnecessary replacement of a component.

Amperage

Amperage is the unit of measure for the amount of current within a circuit. Current is the actual flow of electricity. The higher the current, the more work it can perform. However, if the current flow exceeds the circuit or component capacity, the system can be damaged.

Electrical Tests

Refer to Chapter Two for a description of various electrical tests.

SPECIAL TOOLS

Some of the procedures in this manual require special tools. These are described in the appropriate chapter and are available from either the manufacturer or a tool supplier.

In many cases, an acceptable substitute may be found in an existing tool kit. Another alternative is to make the tool or have one made.

Removing Frozen Fasteners

If a fastener cannot be removed, several methods may be used to loosen it. First, apply penetrating oil such as Liquid Wrench, Kroil or WD-40. Apply it liberally, and let it penetrate for 10-15 minutes. Rap the fastener several times with a small hammer. Do not hit it hard enough to cause damage. Reapply the penetrating oil if necessary.

For frozen screws, apply penetrating oil as described. Insert a stout screwdriver into the slot, and carefully rap the top of the screwdriver with a hammer. This loosens the rust so the screw can be removed in the normal way. If

1

the screw head is too damaged to use this method, grip the head with locking pliers and twist the screw out.

Avoid applying heat unless specifically instructed, as it may melt, warp or remove the temper from parts.

Removing Broken Fasteners

If the head breaks off a screw or bolt, several methods are available for removing the remaining portion. If a large enough portion of the fastener is still exposed, apply penetrating oil to the threads, then try gripping it with locking pliers. If the projecting portion is too small, file it to fit a wrench or cut a slot in it to fit a screwdriver (**Figure 64**).

If the head breaks off flush, use a screw extractor, commonly referred to as an EZ-out. To do this, centerpunch the exact center of the remaining portion of the screw or bolt, taking into account the part of the threads not visible in the hole. Drill a small hole in the screw and twist the extractor into the hole. Back the screw out with a wrench on the extractor (**Figure 65**).

Repairing Damaged Threads

Occasionally, threads are stripped through carelessness or impact damage. Often the threads can be repaired by running a tap (for internal threads on nuts) or die (for external threads on bolts) through the threads (**Figure 66**). If the bolt threads are damaged at the tip of the threads and a die will not start over the threads, a thread file (**Figure 67**) should be used. Begin at the good threads closest to the damaged threads and dress the threads in an unscrewing direction.

To clean or repair spark plug threads, use a spark plug tap (**Figure 68**). Be very careful to keep debris and shavings out of the cylinder. Before tapping a spark plug thread, ensure that the piston is just below TDC on the compression stroke. That way, if any debris does fall into the cylinder, compressed air and a vacuum cleaner will readily and safely remove it.

If an internal thread is damaged, it may be necessary to install a Helicoil or some other type of thread insert. Follow the manufacturer's instructions when installing their insert.

Stud Removal/Installation

A variety of stud removal tools is available from tool suppliers. These tools make the removal and installation of studs easier. If one is not available, thread two nuts onto the stud and tighten them against each other. Remove the stud by turning the lower nut. **Figure 69** shows this procedure on a right-hand threaded stud:

1. Measure the height of the stud above the surface.

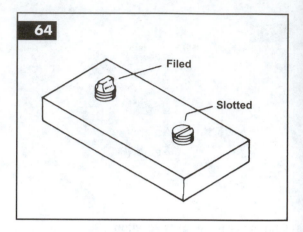

64

Filed

Slotted

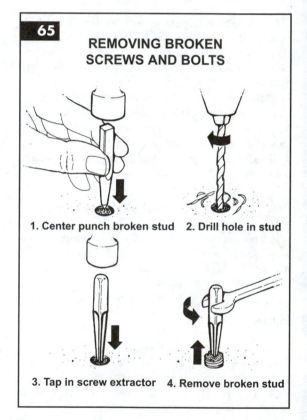

65

REMOVING BROKEN SCREWS AND BOLTS

1. Center punch broken stud

2. Drill hole in stud

3. Tap in screw extractor

4. Remove broken stud

2. Thread the stud removal tool onto the stud and tighten it, or thread two nuts onto the stud.

3. Remove the stud by turning the stud remover or the lower nut.

4. Remove any threadlocking compound from the threaded hole. Clean the threads with an aerosol parts cleaner.

5. Install the stud removal tool onto the new stud or thread two nuts onto the stud.

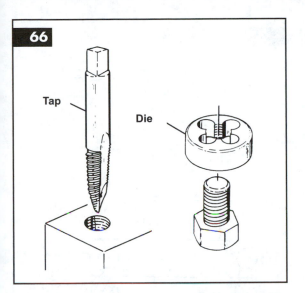

Tap

Die

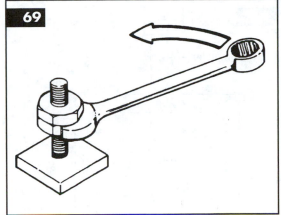

7. Install the stud and tighten with the stud removal tool or the top nut.

8. Install the stud to the height noted in Step 1 or its torque specification.

9. Remove the stud removal tool or the two nuts.

Removing Hoses

Prior to removing hoses, make sure that all fluids are drained from the part of the system attached to the hoses. Close all applicable shutoff valves.

When removing stubborn hoses, do not apply excessive force to the hose or fitting. Remove the hose clamp and carefully insert a small pick tool between the fitting and hose. Apply a spray lubricant under the hose and carefully twist the hose off the fitting. Clean the fitting of any corrosion or hose material. A wire brush can be used on metal fittings; plastic fittings will require careful use of a small knife or scraper. Replace the hose. Do not use any lubricant when installing the hose. The lubricant may allow the hose to come off the fitting, even with the clamp secure.

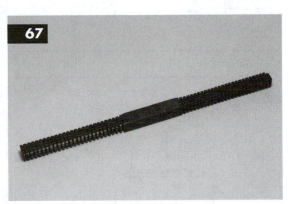

> *WARNING*
> *When working on gasoline hose fittings, always use non-sparking pick tools and wire brushes, such as brass-bristle brushes or 300-grade non-magnetic stainless steel pick tools.*

Ball and Roller Bearings

> *NOTE*
> *If there is not an unthreaded shoulder area between the bottom and top stud threads, do not use a knurled, clamp-type stud removal tool to install the stud. Top thread damage will result.*

6. Apply threadlocking compound to the threads of the stud, if necessary.

These bearings are used in the engine, cutter deck and drive train assembly to reduce power loss, heat and noise resulting from friction. Because these bearings are precision parts, they must be maintained by proper lubrication and maintenance. If a bearing is damaged, replace it immediately. When installing a new bearing, take care to prevent damaging it. Bearing replacement procedures are

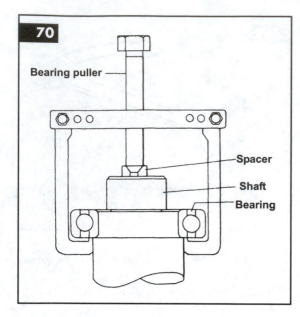

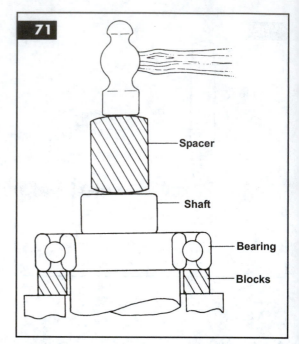

included in the individual chapters where applicable; however, use the following sections as a guideline.

NOTE
Unless otherwise specified, install bearings with the manufacturer's mark or number facing outward.

Removal

While bearings are normally removed only when damaged, there may be times when it is necessary to remove a bearing that is in good condition. However, improper bearing removal will damage the bearing and possibly the shaft or case half. Note the following when removing bearings:

1. When using a puller to remove a bearing from a shaft, take care that the shaft is not damaged. Always place a piece of metal between the end of the shaft and the puller screw. In addition, place the puller arms next to the *inner* bearing race. See **Figure 70**.

2. When using a hammer to remove a bearing from a shaft, do not strike the hammer directly against the shaft. Instead, use a brass or aluminum spacer between the hammer and shaft (**Figure 71**) and make sure to support both bearing races with wooden blocks as shown.

3. A hydraulic press is the ideal tool for bearing removal. Note the following when using a press:

   a. Always support the inner and outer bearing races with a correctly-sized wooden or aluminum ring (**Figure 72**). If only the outer race is supported, pressure applied against the balls and/or the inner race will damage them.

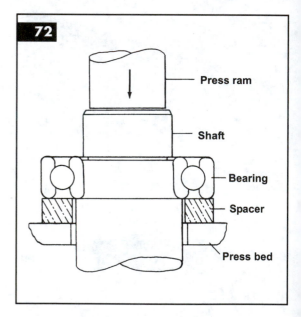

WARNING
*Always make sure the press ram (**Figure 72**) aligns with the center of the shaft and is a smaller diameter than the shaft. If the ram is not centered, it may damage the bearing and/or shaft.*

   b. The moment the shaft is free of the bearing, it will drop to the floor. Secure or hold the shaft to prevent it from falling.

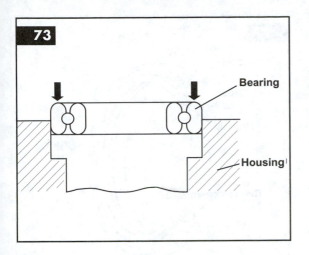

73

Bearing

Housing

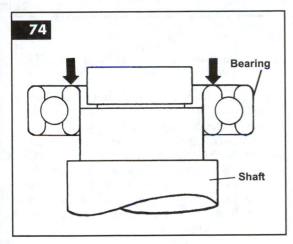

74

Bearing

Shaft

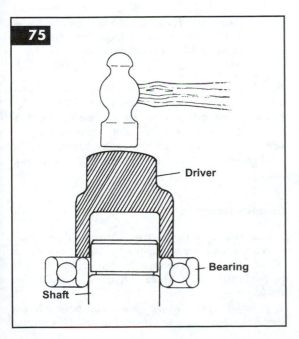

75

Driver

Bearing

Shaft

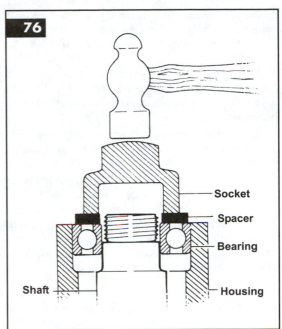

76

Socket

Spacer

Bearing

Shaft

Housing

Installation

1. When installing a bearing in a housing, apply pressure to the *outer* bearing race (**Figure 73**). When installing a bearing on a shaft, apply pressure to the *inner* bearing race (**Figure 74**).

2. When installing a bearing as described in Step 1, some type of driver is required. Never strike the bearing directly with a hammer or the bearing will be damaged. When installing a bearing, use a piece of pipe or a driver with a diameter that matches the bearing race. **Figure 75** shows the correct way to use a driver and hammer to install a bearing.

3. Step 1 describes how to install a bearing into a housing or over a shaft. However, when installing a bearing over a shaft and into a housing at the same time, a tight fit will be required for both the outer and the inner bearing races. In this situation, install a spacer underneath the driver tool so that pressure is applied evenly across both races. See **Figure 76**. If one bearing race is not supported as shown in **Figure 76**, the balls will push against the bearing races and damage the bearing.

Installing an interference fit bearing over a shaft

When a tight fit is required, the bearing inside diameter will be slightly smaller than the shaft. In this case, driving the bearing onto the shaft using normal methods may cause bearing damage. Instead, heat the bearing before installation. Note the following:

1. Secure the shaft so it is ready for bearing installation.

2. Clean all residue from the bearing surface of the shaft. Remove burrs with a file or sandpaper. Wipe a thin film of clean, light oil completely around the shaft where the bearing slides on.

3. Fill a suitable pot or container with clean mineral oil. Place a thermometer rated above 248° F (120° C) in the oil. Support the thermometer so that it does not rest on the bottom or side of the pot.

4. Remove the bearing from its wrapper and secure it with a piece of heavy wire bent to hold it in the pot. Hang the bearing so it does not touch the bottom or sides of the pot.

5. Turn the heat on and monitor the thermometer. When the oil temperature rises to approximately 248° F (120° C), remove the bearing from the pot and quickly install it. If necessary, place a driver on the inner bearing race and tap the bearing into place. As the bearing cools, it will tighten on the shaft, so installation must be done quickly. Make sure the bearing is installed completely.

> *CAUTION*
> *Do not heat the bearing with a propane or acetylene torch. Never bring a flame into contact with the bearing. The direct heat will destroy the case hardening of the bearing.*

Replacing an interference fit bearing in a housing

Bearings are generally installed into housings with a slight interference fit. Driving the bearing into the housing using normal methods may damage the housing or cause bearing damage. Instead, heat the housing before the bearing is removed or installed. Note the following:

> *CAUTION*
> *Before heating the housing, wash the housing thoroughly with detergent and water. Rinse and rewash the case as required to remove all traces of oil and other chemical deposits.*

1. Heat the housing to approximately 212° F (100° C) in an oven or on a hot plate. An easy way to check that it is at the proper temperature is to drip water onto the housing near, but not on, the bearing installation area; if it sizzles and evaporates immediately, the temperature is correct. Heat only one housing at a time.

> *CAUTION*
> *Do not heat the housing with a propane or acetylene torch. Never bring a flame into contact with the housing. The direct heat will likely warp or weaken the housing.*

2. Remove the housing from the oven or hot plate, and hold onto the housing with a kitchen potholder, heavy gloves or heavy shop cloth.

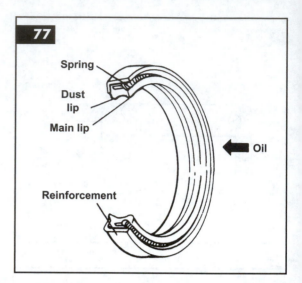

> *NOTE*
> *Remove and install the bearings with a correctly-sized driver.*

3. Hold the housing bearing-side down and tap the bearing out.

4. Repeat for all bearings in the housing.

5. Before heating the bearing housing to install a bearing, place the new bearing in a freezer, if possible. Chilling a bearing slightly reduces its outside diameter while the heated bearing housing assembly is slightly larger due to heat expansion. Prior to chilling, wipe the entire outer race area with a thin film of clean, light oil. This will make bearing installation easier.

> *NOTE*
> *Always install bearings with the manufacturer's mark or number facing outward, unless specific instructions state otherwise.*

6. While the housing is still hot, install the new bearing(s) into the housing. Install the bearing(s) by hand, if possible. If necessary, lightly tap the bearing(s) into the housing with a driver placed on the outer bearing race (**Figure 73**). Do not install bearings by driving on the inner-bearing race. Install the bearing until it seats completely.

Seal Replacement

Seals (**Figure 77**) are used to contain oil, water, grease or combustion gases in a housing or shaft. Improper removal of a seal can damage the housing or shaft. Improper installation of the seal can damage the seal. Note the following:

1. Prying is generally the easiest and most effective method of removing a seal from a housing. However, al-

ways place a rag underneath the pry tool to prevent damage to the housing.

2. Pack waterproof grease in the seal lips before the seal is installed.

3. Install seals with the manufacturer's numbers or marks facing out unless specific instructions state otherwise.

4. Install seals with a driver placed on the outside of the seal. Make sure the driver outer diameter is as near as possible to the seal outer diameter, with the seal outer diameter slightly larger. This will prevent collapsing or crushing the seal face upon installation. Drive the seal squarely into the housing. Never install a seal by hitting against the top of the seal with a hammer. If necessary, coat the outer diameter of the seal lightly with an appropriate sealant.

STORAGE

Several months of non-use can cause a general deterioration of the equipment. This is especially true in areas of extreme temperature variations. This deterioration can be minimized with careful preparation for storage. A properly-stored unit will be much easier to return to service.

Storage Area Selection

When selecting a storage area, consider the following:

1. The storage area must be dry. A heated area is best, but not necessary. It should be insulated to minimize extreme temperature variations.

2. If the building has large window areas, mask them to keep sunlight off the unit.

3. Avoid buildings in industrial areas where corrosive emissions may be present. Avoid areas close to saltwater.

4. Consider the risk of fire, theft or vandalism. Check with an insurer regarding equipment coverage while in storage.

Preparing the Unit for Storage

The amount of preparation a unit should undergo before storage depends upon the expected length of non-use, storage area conditions and personal preference. Consider the following list as minimum requirements:

1. Clean the unit thoroughly. Make sure all dirt, mud and grass debris is removed.

2. Start the engine and allow it to reach operating temperature. Drain the engine oil, regardless of the time since the last oil change. Remove the old oil filter and install a new one. Fill the engine with the recommended type of oil.

3. Start and run the engine again until normal operating temperature is reached. Stop the engine. Drain all fuel from the fuel tank, and run the engine until all the fuel is consumed from the lines and carburetor(s). To verify complete fuel consumption, disconnect the lower portion of any fuel hoses, draining any remaining fuel into an approved container. If necessary, remove, drain, and reinstall the carburetor bowl(s). Some engines have drain screws on the carburetor bowl which eliminate the necessity of removing the bowl. If bowl-drain screws are opened, make sure they are closed when the bowl is empty.

4. Remove any debris from around the spark plug(s). Remove the spark plug(s) and pour a teaspoon of engine oil into each cylinder. Place a rag over the opening(s) and slowly turn the engine over to distribute the oil. Reinstall the spark plug(s).

5. Remove and fully-charge the battery. Store the battery in a cool, dry location – the cooler, the better. A cold battery discharges more slowly than a warm battery. Do not store the battery on a dirt or concrete floor – a low shelf would be best, away from any direct sunlight. Periodically check the battery's state of charge.

6. Cover the exhaust and intake openings with a cotton or canvas material. Do not use plastic.

7. Fill the hydrostatic reservoir completely full to prevent condensation from entering the tank.

8. Disengage all belt idlers to relieve tension on the belts. If preferred, the belts can be removed to eliminate strain on the idler tension springs.

9. If the unit is to be stored for an extended period, apply a protective substance to the plastic and rubber components, including the tires. Make sure to follow the manufacturer's instructions for each type of product being used.

10. Reduce the normal tire pressure by 20 percent. Place the unit on a stand or wooden blocks so the wheels are off the ground. If this is not possible, place a piece of plywood between the tires and the ground. Inflate the tires to the recommended pressure if the vehicle cannot be elevated.

11. Cover the vehicle with canvas, old bed sheets or something similar. Do not cover it with any plastic material that will trap moisture.

Returning the Vehicle to Service

The amount of effort required when returning a vehicle to service after storage depends on the length of non-use and the storage conditions. In addition to performing the reverse of the above procedure, make sure the linkages, brakes, drives, throttle controls and engine ignition switch work properly before operating the vehicle. Refer to Chapter Three and evaluate the service intervals to determine which areas require service.

Table 1 MODEL INFORMATION AND ENGINE USAGE

MOWER MODEL	SERIAL NO. RANGE	ENGINE MAKE[1] MODEL		SPEC or TYPE
SWZ	xxx70001 – xxx79999	KH	CV14T,	[2]
			CV20S,	[2]
		KA	FC420V,	[2]
			FH500V,	[2]
		BS	303776, or	[2]
			350777	[2]
SWZ-14KA	3300001 – 3309999	KA	FC420V	HS09
SWZ-16BV	3310001 – 3319999	BS	303776	1046
SWZ-16BVE	3320001 – 3329999	BS	303777	1044
SWZ-17KA	4100001 – 4109999,			
	6290001 – 6299999,			
	7430001 – 7439999	KA	FH500V	AS09
SWZ-18BV	3330001 – 3339999	BS	350776	1046
SWZ-18KH	[2]	KH	MV18	58511
SWZ-20CVE	3340001 – 3349999	KH	CV20S	65514
SWZ-20KHE	[2]	KH	MV20S	57508
SWZ-21KAE	5210001 – 5219999,			
	6300001 – 6309999,			
	7440001 – 7449999	KA	FH641V	CS06
SWZ36-14KA	3230001 – 3239999,			
	4040001 – 4049999,			
	5120001 – 5129999	KA	FC420V	HS09
SWZ36A-14KA	6230001 – 6239999	KA	FC420V	HS09
SWZ36-14KH	3240001 – 3249999	KH	CV14T	1461
SWZ36A-15KA	7190001 – 7199999,			
	7370001 – 7379999	KA	FH451V	AS09
SWZ36-15KH	4050001 – 4059999,			
	5130001 – 5139999	KH	CV15T	41581
SWZ48-14KA	3250001 – 3259999,			
	4060001 – 4069999,			
	5140001 – 5149999	KA	FC420V	HS09
SWZ48-14KAE	3270001 – 3279999	KA	FC420V	ES17
SWZ48-14KH	3260001 – 3269999	KH	CV14T	1461
SWZ48-15KH	4070001 – 4079999,			
	5150001 – 5159999	KH	CV15T	41581
SWZ48-16BV	3280001 – 3289999	BS	303776	1046
SWZ48-17KA	4080001 – 4089999,			
	5160001 – 5169999	KA	FH500V	AS09
SWZ48A-17KA	5170001 – 5179999,			
	6260001 – 6269999,			
	7380001 – 7389999	KA	FH500V	AS09
SWZ52-17KA	5180001 – 5189999	KA	FH500V	AS09
SWZ52-17KAE	5970001 – 5979999	KA	FH500V	[2]
SWZ52A-17KA	5190001 – 5199999,			
	6280001 – 6289999,			
	7390001 – 7399999	KA	FH500V	AS09
SWZU-21KAE	7470001 – 7479999	KA	FH641V	AS09
SWZU36-15KA	5260001 – 5269999	KA	FH451V	AS09
SWZU36A-15KA	7400001 – 7409999	KA	FH451V	AS09

(continued)

Table 1 MODEL INFORMATION AND ENGINE USAGE (continued)

MOWER MODEL	SERIAL NO. RANGE	ENGINE MAKE[1] MODEL		SPEC or TYPE
SWZU36-15KH	4780001 – 4789999	KH	CV15T	41581
SWZU48-17KA	4790001 – 4799999,			
	5270001 – 5279999	KA	FH500V	AS09
SWZU48A-17KA	7410001 – 7419999	KA	FH500V	AS09
SWZU52-17KA	5280001 – 5289999	KA	FH500V	AS09
SWZU52A-17KA	7420001 – 7429999	KA	FH500V	AS09

[1]Engine Make: KH = Kohler; KA = Kawasaki; BS = Briggs & Stratton
[2]Information not available at time of publication.

Table 2   GENERAL DIMENSIONS

DIMENSION	MOWER MODEL				
	SWZ36	SWZ48	SWZ52	SWZ61	SWZ72
Length	74.0 in.	74.0 in.	74.0 in.	76.0 in.	76.0 in. Width
Overall	54.5 in.	60.0 in.	60.0 in.	70.0 in.	81.0 in
Discharge chute up	37.5 in.	53.0 in.	53.0 in.	63.0 in.	74.0 in.
Tracking	37.0 in.	42.0 in.	42.0 in.	42.0 in.	42.0 in
With grass catcher	55.0 in.	69.0 in.	69.0 in	80.0 in.	91.0 in.
Height	40.5 in.	40.5 in.	40.5 in.	40.5 in.	40.5 in.
Weight					
W/O grass catcher	515 lbs.	565 lbs.	605 lbs.	715 lbs.	755 lbs.
W/grass catcher	555 lbs.	605 lbs.	645 lbs.	755 lbs.	790 lbs.

DIMENSION	MOWER MODEL			
	SWZU36	SWZU48	SWZU52	SWZU61
Length	77.5 in.	76.0 in.	77.0 in.	79.0 in.
Width				
Overall	46.5 in.	58.0 in.	60.0 in.	70.0 in.
Discharge chute up	37.5 in.	48.0 in.	50.0 in.	60.0 in.
Tracking	36.0 in.	38.0 in.	38.0 in.	38.0 in.
With grass catcher	55.0 in.	64.0 in.	66.0 in.	76.0 in.
Height	43.0 in.	43.0 in.	43.0 in.	43.0 in.
Weight				
W/O grass catcher	575 lbs.	640 lbs.	680 lbs.	735 lbs.
W/grass catcher	615 lbs.	680 lbs.	720 lbs.	775 lbs.

Table 3 CONVERSION FORMULAS

Multiply:	By:	To get the equivalent of:
Length		
Inches	25.4	Millimeter
Inches	2.54	Centimeter
Miles	1.609	Kilometer
Feet	0.3048	Meter
Millimeter	0.03937	Inches
Centimeter	0.3937	Inches
Kilometer	0.6214	Mile
Meter	3.281	Mile
Fluid volume		
U.S. quarts	0.9463	Liters
U.S. gallons	3.785	Liters
U.S. ounces	29.573529	Milliliters
Imperial gallons	4.54609	Liters
Imperial quarts	1.1365	Liters
Liters	0.2641721	U.S. gallons
Liters	1.0566882	U.S. quarts
Liters	33.814023	U.S. ounces
Liters	0.22	Imperial gallons
Liters	0.8799	Imperial quarts
Milliliters	0.033814	U.S. ounces
Milliliters	1.0	Cubic centimeters
Milliliters	0.001	Liters
Torque		
Foot-pounds	1.3558	Newton-meters
Foot-pounds	0.138255	Meters-kilograms
Inch-pounds	0.11299	Newton-meters
Newton-meters	0.7375622	Foot-pounds
Newton-meters	8.8507	Inch-pounds
Meters-kilograms	7.2330139	Foot-pounds
Foot-pounds	12.0	Inch-pounds
Inch-pounds	0.0833	Foot-pounds
Volume		
Cubic inches	16.387064	Cubic centimeters
Cubic centimeters	0.0610237	Cubic inches
Temperature		
Fahrenheit	$(F - 32°) \times 0.556$	Centigrade
Centigrade	$(C \times 1.8) + 32$	Fahrenheit
Weight		
Ounces	28.3495	Grams
Pounds	0.4535924	Kilograms
Grams	0.035274	Ounces
Kilograms	2.2046224	Pounds
Pressure		
Pounds per square inch	0.070307	Kilograms per square centimeter
Kilograms per square centimeter	14.223343	Pounds per square inch
Kilopascals	0.1450	Pounds per square inch
Pounds per square inch	6.895	Kilopascals
Speed		
Miles per hour	1.609344	Kilometers per hour
Kilometers per hour	0.6213712	Miles per hour

1

Table 4 GENERAL TORQUE SPECIFICATIONS

INCH SIZES; INCH-POUND and N·m VALUES; DRY THREADS[1]
Bolts, Nuts, and Screws Into Steel or Cast Iron   USS = coarse thread; SAE = fine thread.
  Values first given in in.-lb.; Newton-meters (N·m) are in parentheses

Thread Size	Grade 2[2]	Grade 5	Grade 8
8-32	16-24 (1.9-2.7)	20-30 (2.3-3.3)	34-50 (3.8-5.6)
10-24 USS	26-38 (2.9-4.3)	32-48 (3.6-5.4)	– –
10-32 SAE	26-38 (2.9-4.3)	32-48 (3.6-5.4)	48-72 (5.5-8.1)
1/4-20 USS	56-84 (6.3-9.5)	98-138 (10.4-15.6)	132-198 (15.0-22.4)
1/4-28 SAE	68-102 (7.7-11.5)	112-168 (12.7-18.9)	160-240 (18.1-27.1)
5/16-18 USS	120-180 (13.6-20.4)	200-300 (22.7-34.0)	280-420 (31.7-47.5)
5/16-24 SAE	132-198 (15.0-22.4)	216-324 (24.4-36.6)	288-432 (32.6-48.8)
3/8-16 USS	208-312 (23.5-35.3)	336-504 (38.0-57.0)	480-720 (54.2-81.4)
3/8-24 SAE	240-360 (27.1-40.7)	384-576 (43.4-65.0)	– –

[1]"Dry" – Unplated or zinc-plated threads, no lubrication.
[2]For torque purposes, Grade 2 bolts between 1/4-in. and 3/4-in. in diameter with a length of six inches or less are considered Grade 1 bolts and are to be torqued to the *lowest* value specified.

Table 5 GENERAL TORQUE SPECIFICATIONS

INCH SIZES; FOOT-POUND and N·m VALUES; DRY THREADS[1]
Bolts, Nuts, and Screws Into Steel or Cast Iron   USS = coarse thread; SAE = fine thread.
  Values first given in ft.-lb.; Newton-meters (N·m) are in parentheses

Thread Size	Grade 2[2]	Grade 5	Grade 8
5/16-24 SAE	– –	– –	24-36 (32.6-48.8)
3/8-16 USS	– –	28-42 (38.0-57.0)	40-60 (54.3-81.3)
3/8-24 SAE	– –	32-48 (43.8-65.0)	48-72 (65.1-97.7)
7/16-14 USS	28-42 (38.0-57.0)	44-66 (59.7-89.5)	64-96 (86.8-130.2)
7/16-20 SAE	36-54 (49.0-73.0)	60-90 (81.4-122.0)	84-126 (113.9-170.9)
1/2-13 USS	40-60 (54.3-81.3)	64-96 (86.8-130.2)	92-138 (124.7-187.1)
1/2-20 SAE	56-84 (75.9-113.9)	84-126 (113.9-170.9)	132-198 (179.0-268.4)
9/16-12 USS	60-90 (81.4-122.0)	100-150 (135.6-203.4)	140-210 (189.8-294.8)
9/16-18 SAE	80-120 (108.5-162.7)	132-198 (179.0-268.4)	184-276 (247.9-375.9)

(continued)

Table 5 GENERAL TORQUE SPECIFICATIONS (continued)

Thread Size	Grade 2[2]	Grade 5	Grade 8
5/8-11 USS	88-132 (119.4-179.0)	144-216 (195.3-292.9)	208-312 (282.1-423.1)
5/8-18 SAE	112-168 (151.8-227.8)	184-276 (247.9-375.9)	264-396 (358.0-537.0)
3/4-10 USS	120-180 (159.4-239.2)	196-294 (265.8-398.6)	280-420 (379.6-569.6)
3/4-16 SAE	160-240 (217.0-325.4)	260-390 (352.6-528.8)	376-564 (509.8-764.7)

[1]"Dry" – Unplated or zinc-plated threads, no lubrication.
[2]For torque purposes, Grade 2 bolts of 3/4-inch or smaller diameter with a length of six inches or less are considered Grade 1 and are to be torqued to the (ital)lowest(ital) value specified.

Table 6 GENERAL TORQUE SPECIFICATIONS – INCH SIZES INTO ALUMINUM

Grade 2 or 5 fastener size	Torque value — in.-lb. (N·m)
8-32	16-24 (1.9-2.7)
10-24	26-38 (2.9-4.3)
1/4-20	56-84 (6.3-9.5)
5/16-18	120-180 (13.6-20.4)

Table 7 GENERAL TORQUE SPECIFICATIONS

METRIC SIZES; INCH-POUND and N·m VALUES; DRY THREADS*
Bolts, Nuts, and Screws Into Steel or Cast Iron
  Values first given in in.-lb.; Newton-meters (N·m) are in parentheses

Thread Size	Grade 4.8	Grade 5.8	Grade 8.8 or 9.8	Grade 10.9	Grade 12.9
M4	11-12 (1.2-1.3)	15.0-16.5 (1.7-1.9)	26-29 (2.9-3.2)	36-40 (4.1-4.5)	44-48 (5.0-5.5)
M5	22-24 (2.5-2.7)	28-31 (3.2-3.5)	51-56 (5.8-6.4)	72-79 (8.1-8.9)	86-95 (9.7-10.7)
M6	38-42 (4.3-4.7)	50-55 (5.7-6.3)	88-100 (9.9-11.0)	124-145 (14.0-16.5)	145-175 (16.5-19.0)
M8	93-105 (10.5-12.0)	120-132 (13.6-15.0)	216-240 (24.4-27.2)	300-360 (34.0-40.7)	360-420 (40.7-47.5)
M10	192-230 (21.7-26.0)	240-250 (27.1-28.3)	420-480 (47.5-54.2)	–	–
M12	324-400 (36.6-45.2)	420-445 (47.5-50.3)	–	–	–

*"Dry" – Unplated or zinc-plated threads, no lubrication.

Table 8 GENERAL TORQUE SPECIFICATIONS

METRIC SIZES; FOOT-POUND and N·m VALUES; DRY THREADS*
Bolts, Nuts, and Screws Into Steel or Cast Iron
   Values first given in ft.-Lb.; Newton-meters (N·m) are in parentheses

Thread Size	Grade 4.8	Grade 5.8	Grade 8.8 or 9.8	Grade 10.9	Grade 12.9
M10	16-19	20-21	35-40	49-60	60-70
	(21.7-25.8)	(27.1-28.5)	(47.5-54.2)	(66.4-81.3)	(81.3-95.0)
M12	27-34	35-38	61-70	86-105	103-120
	(36.6-46.0)	(47.5-52.3)	(82.7-95.0)	(117-142)	(140-163)
M14	43-52	55-60	97-110	136-165	162-190
	(58-71)	(76-81)	(132-149)	(184-224)	(220-258)
M16	90	95	175	225	300
	(122)	(129)	(237)	(305)	(407)
M18	100	125	250	350	410
	(135)	(170)	(340)	(475)	(560)
M20	150	180	350	500	580
	((205)	(245)	(475)	(675)	(800)
M22	210	250	475	675	800
	(285)	(340)	(640)	(915)	(1075)
M24	275	310	600	850	1000
	(375)	(420)	(810)	(1150)	(1350)
M27	400	450	875	1250	1500
	(540)	(610)	(1185)	(1700)	(2000)
M30	575	625	1200	1700	2000
	(775)	(850)	(1625)	(2300)	(2700)
M33	750	850	1650	2350	2750
	(1020)	(1150)	(2225)	(3150)	(3700)
M36	925	1075	2100	3000	3500
	(1250)	(1450)	(2850)	(4050)	(4750)

*"Dry" – Unplated or zinc-plated threads, no lubrication.

Table 9 GENERAL TORQUE SPECIFICATIONS – METRIC SIZES INTO ALUMINUM

Non-critical Size	In.-lb.	Ft.-lb.	N·m
M4	16-20	–	1.8-2.2
M5	32-38	–	3.6-4.4
M6	54-66	–	6.1-7.5
M8	135-165	–	15.3-18.7
M10	270-330	23-27	30.5-37.3
M12	486-594	41-49	54.9-67.1
M14	–	63-77	85.4-104.4

Table 10 TECHNICAL ABBREVIATIONS

ABDC	After bottom dead center
ATDC	After top dead center
BBDC	Before bottom dead center
BDC	Bottom dead center
BTDC	Before top dead center
C	Celsius (Centigrade)
cc	Cubic centimeters

(continued)

Table 10   TECHNICAL ABBREVIATIONS (continued)

cid	Cubic inch displacement
CDI	Capacitor discharge ignition
cu. in.	Cubic inches
F	Fahrenheit
ft.	Feet
ft.-lb.	Foot-pounds
gal.	Gallons
H/A	High altitude
hp	Horsepower
in.	Inches
in.-lb.	Inch-pounds
I.D.	Inside diameter
kg	Kilograms
kg/cm^2	Kilograms per square centimeter
kgm	Kilogram meters
km	Kilometer
kPa	Kilopascals
L	Liter
m	Meter
MAG	Magneto
ml	Milliliter
mm	Millimeter
N•m	Newton-meters
O.D.	Outside diameter
oz.	Ounces
psi	Pounds per square inch
PTO	Power take off
pt.	Pint
rpm	Revolutions per minute
qt.	Quart
TDC	Top dead center

CHAPTER TWO

TROUBLESHOOTING

Diagnosing mechanical or electrical problems is relatively simple if you use orderly procedures and keep a few basic principles in mind. The first step in any troubleshooting procedure is to define the symptoms as closely as possible, then localize the problem. Subsequent steps test and analyze those areas which could cause the symptoms. A haphazard approach may eventually solve the problem, but cost in wasted time and unnecessary parts replacement.

Proper lubrication, maintenance and periodic tune-ups as described in Chapter Three will reduce the necessity for troubleshooting. Even with the best of care, however, almost all mowers will eventually develop problems requiring troubleshooting.

Never assume anything. Do not overlook the obvious. If the engine will not start, is the spark plug wire loose? Is the fuel tank empty? If the engine dies on its own, what did it sound like? Consider this and check the easiest and most accessible problem first. A quiet death could just mean an empty fuel tank. If there is fuel in the tank, is it reaching the carburetor? Is the fuel vapor-locked? On the other hand, an engine which made screeching or knocking noises just before it quit probably indicates serious internal trouble, especially if it is now locked up.

Does the engine still run, but the drive system no longer propels the unit, or propels it in an erratic fashion? Is the grass suddenly no longer being cut, or is it cutting but leaving ridges?

If nothing obvious turns up in a quick check, look a little deeper. Learning to recognize and describe symptoms will make repairs easier for any mechanic. Gather as many symptoms as possible to aid in diagnosis. Describe problems accurately and completely.

After the symptoms are defined, analyze and test the areas which could cause the problem. Guessing may solve the problem, but usually not without frustration, wasted time, and unnecessary parts replacement.

ENGINE OPERATING FUNDAMENTALS

The engines used on these mowers are basically similar. All are technically known as internal combustion reciprocating engines.

The source of power is heat formed by the burning of a fuel and air mixture. In a reciprocating engine, this burning takes place in a closed cylinder containing a piston. Expansion resulting from the heat of combustion applies pressure on the head of the piston. The piston, mounted to a connecting rod, then turns a crankshaft.

The fuel-air mixture may be ignited by means of an electric spark (the Otto Cycle Engine) or by heat formed by compressing the air very tightly in the cylinder prior to injecting the fuel (the Diesel Cycle Engine). The complete series of events that must take place in order for the engine to run occurs in two revolutions of the crankshaft which comprise four strokes of the piston in the cylinder. This is referred to as the four-stroke cycle engine, more commonly called the four-cycle engine.

The Four-Stroke Cycle Engine

The four piston strokes of a four-cycle engine, along with the moment of ignition, are the five events necessary to produce power. This sequence is called the power cycle or the work cycle.

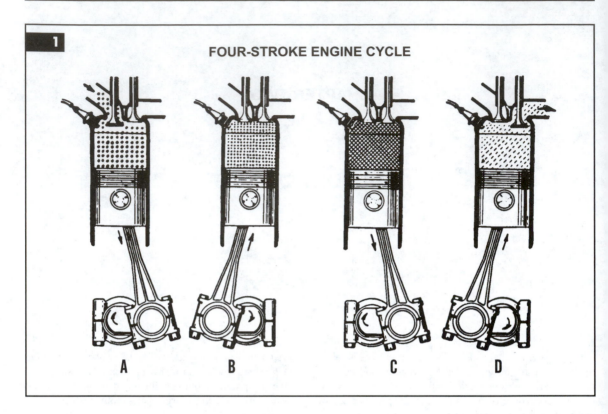

1

FOUR-STROKE ENGINE CYCLE

A   B   C   D

1. In view A, **Figure 1**, the piston is on its first downward stroke. The mechanically operated intake valve has opened the intake port and, as the piston moves down, it reduces the air pressure in the cylinder to below atmospheric pressure, creating a vacuum in the cylinder. This causes atmospheric-pressure air to be forced into the cylinder. In the Otto cycle engine, this air flows through the carburetor where it is mixed with fuel and drawn into the cylinder. In the diesel cycle engine, air alone is forced into the cylinder. Air or air-fuel mixture will continue to flow into the cylinder until the piston just passes bottom dead center (BDC), at which time the intake valve closes. This event is the Intake Stroke, the first event of the Power Cycle.

2. View B, **Figure 1** shows both valves closed, with the piston traveling back up the cylinder, compressing the air or air-fuel mixture. This is the Compression Stroke, the second event.

3. When the piston has almost reached top dead center (TDC), for ignition purposes, the cylinder air is at its point of maximum compression. At this moment, the air-fuel mixture in an Otto cycle engine is ignited by the spark plug; in the diesel cycle, the atomized fuel is injected into the cylinder and ignited by the heat of the compressed air. This is the moment of ignition, the third event.

   The difference between the total volume of the cylinder at BDC and the volume at TDC is the Compression Ratio. (Cylinder volume includes the volume of the combustion

chamber.) Otto-cycle compression ratios normally average eight-to-one, expressed as the ratio "8:1." Since the diesel-cycle air must be hot enough to ignite the injected fuel at the moment of ignition, diesel-cycle compression ratios are usually in excess of 20:1.

4. View C shows the fourth event, the Power Stroke. After the fuel-air mixture is completely ignited with the piston just past TDC, the expanding gasses drive the piston down the cylinder. Both valves are closed during this stroke.

NOTE
Do not confuse the Power Stroke with the Power Cycle. The Power Stroke is only one-fifth of the complete Power Cycle.

5. When the piston is almost at BDC, the exhaust valve opens. With the crankshaft continuing its rotation, the piston travels back up the cylinder towards TDC, pushing the burned fuel-air mix out the exhaust port. This is event No. 5, the Exhaust Stroke. When the piston is almost to TDC, the exhaust valve closes, the intake valve begins to open, and the Power Cycle is complete.

CARBURETOR FUNDAMENTALS

The function of the carburetor on a spark-ignition engine is to atomize the fuel and mix the atomized fuel in proper proportions with air flowing through the carbure-

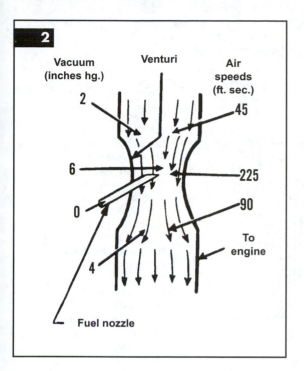

2

Vacuum (inches hg.)

Venturi

Air speeds (ft. sec.)

2

45

6

225

0

90

To engine

4

Fuel nozzle

2

a fuel stabilizer is used, follow the manufacturer's instructions precisely.

Basic Design

Carburetor design is based on the venturi principle, which simply means that a gas or liquid flowing through a narrow section (venturi) in a passage undergoes an increase in speed and a decrease in pressure as compared to its speed and pressure in the full-size sections of the passage. This principle is illustrated in **Figure 2**, which shows air passing through a carburetor throat.

The figures given for air speeds and vacuum in **Figure 2** are approximate for a typical wide-open throttle condition. Due to low pressure (high vacuum) in the venturi, fuel entering the venturi through the fuel nozzle is forced out of the nozzle into the venturi air flow by atmospheric pressure acting on the fuel. As fuel leaves the nozzle tip, it is atomized by, and mixes with, the high velocity air flow.

Float-Type Carburetor Operating Principles

Carburetors used on the engines covered in this manual are side-draft (horizontal air passage), float type carburetors. The following paragraphs describe the operating principles and design features of float-type carburetors.

A cutaway view of a typical updraft, float-type carburetor is shown in **Figure 3**. Fuel is fed into the float bowl either by gravity from a tank mounted above the carburetor or by a fuel pump if the tank is either below the level of the carburetor or some distance away. Atmospheric pressure is maintained in the fuel bowl by air entering the air horn just ahead of the choke plate and traveling through the vent passage. The fuel level is maintained just below the orifice opening in the main nozzle by the float controlling the fuel inlet valve. On some carburetors, the fuel level can be adjusted by bending the float tang.

Starting enrichment (Choking)

The ratio of fuel to air must be much richer when starting a cold engine or in cold weather than when running at warmed-up, wide-open throttle. A choke plate is the most commonly used method of obtaining a rich starting mixture.

Figure 4 shows a cutaway view of the air-fuel mixture flow. At cranking speeds, air flows through the venturi at a slow speed. Because of this, the pressure in the venturi does not usually decrease enough for atmospheric pressure to force sufficient fuel from the nozzle.

With the choke plate closed, little or no air enters the main passage. This causes atmospheric pressure acting on the fuel in the fuel bowl to force the fuel out the fuel noz-

tor into the engine. Carburetors which are used on engines operating at constant speeds and/or under even loads are of simple design because they only have to mix fuel and air in a relatively constant ratio. More complex carburetors are required for engines operating at varying speeds and loads because different fuel-air mixtures are needed to meet the wide-ranging demands of the engine.

Fuel Quality

The fuel must be fresh and of good quality.

The tetraethyl lead additive which had been used in the past as an octane booster also acted as a preservative. In the leaded-gasoline era, it was not uncommon for fuel left in an engine one autumn to start that same engine the following spring, or even three or four springs later. Since the advent of no-lead fuels, however, gasoline has a much shorter shelf-life. Most engine manufacturers do not recommend storing gasoline longer than 30 days. This is because as gasoline deteriorates, it loses its octane and thus its ability to ignite when compressed inside the cylinder and combustion chamber. In addition as it deteriorates, it forms gummy deposits. Also, many modern gasolines contain ethanol (ethyl alcohol) as an additive. Ethanol causes the fuel to absorb moisture from the atmosphere, thus further deteriorating fuel quality and performance.

Some equipment owners and shops use gasoline preservatives such as Sta-Bil or equivalent products. If such

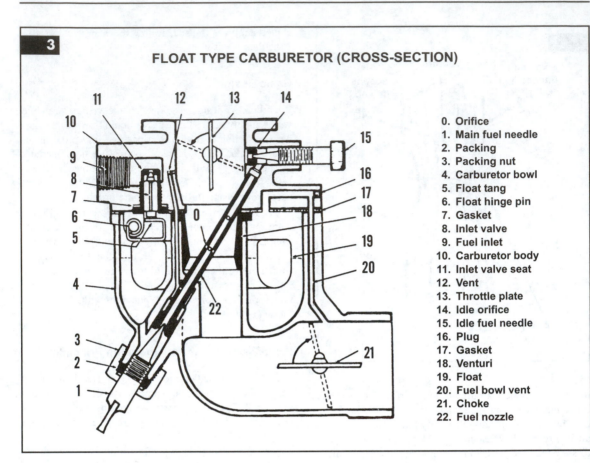

3

FLOAT TYPE CARBURETOR (CROSS-SECTION)

0. Orifice
1. Main fuel needle
2. Packing
3. Packing nut
4. Carburetor bowl
5. Float tang
6. Float hinge pin
7. Gasket
8. Inlet valve
9. Fuel inlet
10. Carburetor body
11. Inlet valve seat
12. Vent
13. Throttle plate
14. Idle orifice
15. Idle fuel needle
16. Plug
17. Gasket
18. Venturi
19. Float
20. Fuel bowl vent
21. Choke
22. Fuel nozzle

zle, thus producing a mixture rich enough to start the engine. When choke-starting an engine, the throttle plate should be in the wide-open position.

Idling

When the engine is running at slow idle speeds, the throttle plate is almost closed. This results in low air pressure downstream of the throttle plate, causing atmospheric pressure in the float bowl to force fuel through the main nozzle and out through the idle orifice where it mixes with air passing the plate (**Figure 5**).

The idle mixture is adjustable on most carburetors by turning the adjustment needle in for more air or out for more fuel as needed. The idle speed is adjustable by turning the throttle-stop screw (not shown) in for faster idle or out for slower idle, controlling the idle speed by controlling the amount of air going past the throttle plate.

Acceleration/mid-range

As the throttle plate is opened more to increase engine rpm, the speed, or velocity, of the air flow through the venturi increases, decreasing venturi pressure and draw-

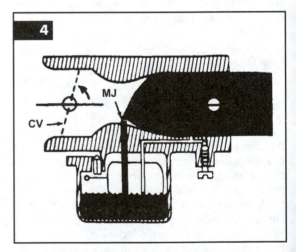

4

ing fuel from the intermediate jet (IM – **Figure 6**) instead of from the idle orifice.

High speed/wide-open throttle

When the engine is running at high speed with the throttle valve wide open **Figure 7**, almost all of the fuel required for engine operation now passes through the

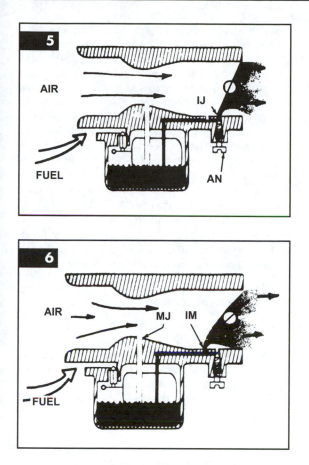

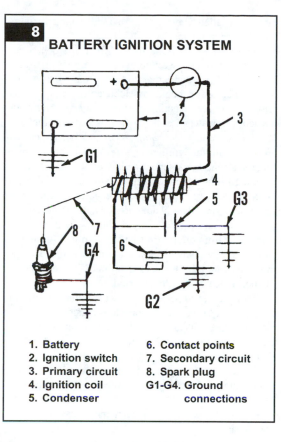

BATTERY IGNITION SYSTEM

1. **Battery**
2. **Ignition switch**
3. **Primary circuit**
4. **Ignition coil**
5. **Condenser**
6. **Contact points**
7. **Secondary circuit**
8. **Spark plug**
G1-G4. **Ground connections**

Carburetor Troubleshooting

Many operators automatically assume the carburetor is at fault when the engine does not run properly. This is not always the case. The following troubleshooting procedures will help determine the true source of what appears to be carburetor trouble.

Most carburetor-related problems fall into one of three groups – fuel starvation, flooding, or erratic engine operation due to excessively-worn carburetor components.

Fuel starvation

If fuel starvation is suspected, clean around the spark plug base and remove the spark plug. If, even after choking the engine, the plug tip is dry, fuel is not getting to the cylinder. Following are the most common causes of fuel starvation, along with the cures.

1. *Empty fuel tank*— Add clean, fresh fuel.
2. *Fuel tank shutoff valve closed*— Open the tank valve.
3. *Choke not closing completely*— Remove the air filter as necessary to inspect the choke plate function. Adjust the choke control or replace the faulty choke components.
4. *Clogged fuel lines or filters*— Carefully remove the lines to check fuel flow. Do not eliminate or bypass any

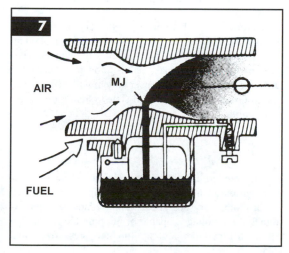

main jet orifice (**Figure 8**). This is due to the maximum air velocity and minimum air pressure in the venturi causing atmospheric pressure to push the fuel through the main jet. Some higher-pressure air in the throttle valve area will also be forced down the vent passage to mix with the fuel coming out the orifice, further atomizing the fuel for better combustion.

factory-installed filter(s). Doing so will guarantee future fuel-system problems.

5. *Debris or water in the fuel*— Water and debris normally travel to the lowest point in the carburetor, usually the main jet, lodging in that position. Remove the carburetor, if necessary, then disassemble and clean the carburetor. Before reconnecting the fuel hose, determine how the debris or water entering the fuel, and fix the problem.

6. *Malfunctioning fuel cutoff solenoid (electric-start engines)*— With the ignition switch off, place two or three fingers around the solenoid and, while both feeling and listening to the solenoid, turn the key on and off a few times. A definite "click" should be noted whenever the key is on. If the solenoid does not click, disconnect the solenoid lead and carefully repeat the test with a jumper lead direct from the positive battery terminal (ensure the battery is fully-charged). A solenoid click with the jumper indicates a fault in the chassis wiring. No click with the jumper indicates a faulty solenoid.

7. *Restricted exhaust*— Have insects built a nest in the exhaust pipe? Has a baffle come loose inside the muffler, blocking the exhaust flow? If exhaust cannot get out, fresh fuel-air mix cannot get in.

8. *Plugged fuel cap vent*— This usually causes starvation while the engine is running. Loosen the cap. If the engine immediately restarts, check and clean the cap vent or replace the cap.

9. *Low compression*— Serious internal engine component wear, or a leaking head gasket, could be preventing the engine from developing enough compression to draw the fuel through the carburetor. Perform a *Cylinder Leakdown Test* as described in this chapter.

10. *Worn carburetor components*— Although they usually just cause rough running, worn components such as a badly-worn throttle shaft and housing can sometimes suck enough air upon start-up to prevent fuel from being drawn into the cylinder. Inspect the carburetor and repair as necessary.

Flooding

If flooding is suspected, clean around the spark plug base and remove the spark plug. If the plug tip is very wet, the cylinder is flooding. Following are the most common causes of flooding, along with the cures.

1. *Plugged air filter*— Remove and inspect the filter. Replace if necessary. If a plugged air filter is found, closely inspect the carburetor throttle and choke shafts. When air cannot enter the engine where it is supposed to, it looks for any other path. That path is usually past the carburetor shafts, where abrasive, unfiltered air causes rapid shaft and housing wear.

2. *Float valve stuck*— Remove the air filter and look into the carburetor throat. Remove the dipstick and check the oil level and condition. If, aside from a wet spark plug, the carburetor throat has puddles, or the crankcase oil is

above the FULL mark and smells like fuel, the float valve (sometimes called the needle and seat), is stuck open. This floods the cylinder and carburetor, and, if allowed to run through the crankcase breather hose, the crankcase. Remove and repair the carburetor. Inspect the rest of the fuel system, as well, taking care of whatever caused the float valve to stick. Stale, gummy fuel is the usual culprit.

3. *Stale fuel*— The easiest way to identify stale fuel is by odor. Fuel which has lost its octane will not ignite *inside the combustion chamber*. Flush the fuel system in an approved manner and refill with clean, fresh fuel.

4. *Tank contains other than gasoline*—Be careful what container is used to store the gasoline. Make sure the container is unmistakably identified.

5. Spark plug not firing — If the spark plug is not firing, the fuel-air mixture will not be ignited. Refer to *Starting a Flooded Engine* and *Spark Test* in this chapter.

Worn carburetor components

As noted in the *Starvation* and *Flooding* sections, an excessively worn throttle and/or choke shaft will affect the running of the engine. Not only that, but the abrasive, unfiltered air which enters the engine past these worn shafts cases major internal damage to the intake valve, cylinder, rings, piston, and exhaust valve. The best insurance against this kind of damage is a clean, well-maintained air filter assembly.

IGNITION SYSTEM FUNDAMENTALS

The timed spark that ignites the fuel charge in the cylinders of the engines used on these mowers is supplied by a solid-state magneto ignition system. Although these engines no longer use breaker points to open and close the circuit, the point-and-condenser system will be discussed first in order to make the solid-state system more easily understood.

Theory

In the modern ignition system, a relatively weak electrical current of 6-12 volts and 2-5 amps is transformed into a momentary charge of minute amperage and extremely high voltage capable of jumping the spark plug gap in the cylinder and igniting the pressurized fuel charge.

Electricity can be thought of as a stream of electrons (negative electrical charges) flowing through a conductor (a wire). The force of the stream can be increased by restricting the volume of the electrons, or the volume can be increased by reducing the resistance of the conductor. However, the total amount of power cannot be increased except through additional outside force. The current has an inertia of motion and resists being stopped once it has

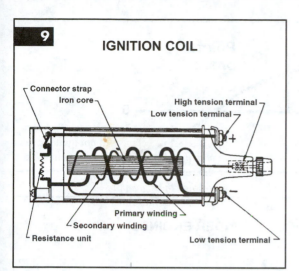

9

IGNITION COIL

Connector strap
Iron core
High tension terminal
Low tension terminal
+
−
Primary winding
Secondary winding
Resistance unit
Low tension terminal

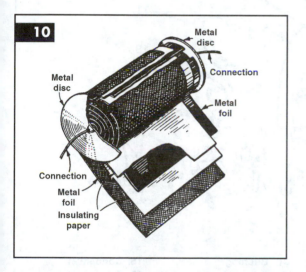

10

Metal disc
Connection
Metal disc
Metal foil
Connection
Metal foil
Insulating paper

started flowing. If the circuit is broken suddenly, the force will tend to pile up temporarily, attempting to convert the speed of flow into energy.

A brief explanation of the following electrical terms will prove useful:

1. *Ampere–* The unit of measurement which tells the quantity or amount of flow of electrical current.

2. *Ohm–* The unit of measurement designating the resistance of a conductor to current flow.

3. *Volt–* The unit of measurement telling the pressure or force of electrical current.

4. *Watt–* The unit of measurement which designates the ability of an electrical current to perform work or which measures the amount of work performed.

The preceding four terms are directly interrelated: One ampere equals the flow of current produced by one volt against a resistance of one ohm. One watt is the amount of work done by one ampere at one volt in one second.

Battery Ignition Systems

Figure 8 shows a schematic diagram of a typical battery ignition system for a 1-cylinder engine. The following subsections explain battery ignition system component function. These explanations are also the basis for understanding magneto and solid-state systems.

Ignition coil

When an electrical current is flowing through a conductor, a magnetic field exists at right angles to the current flow. If the conductor is coiled around a soft iron core, then the length of the iron core is at approximately right angles to the wire. A path is then provided for the magnetic field, and the iron core becomes a magnet whenever electrical current flows.

A second type of electrical activity happens when the magnetic field is interrupted – a pulsation of electrical energy forms at right angles to the lines of magnetic force.

In a battery ignition system, materials designed to utilize these two occurrences are assembled to form the coil (**Figure 9**). The inner and outer cores are formed of soft iron laminations which form a continuous path for a magnetic field. Wound around the inner laminated core, but insulated from it, are many coils of fine copper wire. Around this coil of fine wire, but insulated from it and the iron core, are fewer windings of heavier wire. The heavier windings are then encased in the outer laminations, followed by the protective outer case.

The heavy-wire outer winding connects to the two screw terminals on the coil case cap; this is the primary circuit. The fine-wire inner winding is grounded at one end, with the other end connected to the high-tension center post of the cap; this is the secondary circuit.

Primary circuit

The primary circuit is attached to the power source in both the battery and the magneto ignition systems. Refer to **Figure 8**.

In the battery system, the primary circuit consists of the battery, ignition switch, coil primary winding, contact points, condenser, and related wiring. **Figure 10** shows the internal construction of the typical condenser – two metal conductors separated by layers of insulating paper and rolled into a tight cylinder, with a connection to each metal conductor.

When the ignition switch and contact points are closed, the engine block and the equipment frame complete the circuit to ground (G1, G2, and G3, **Figure 8**). When the ignition switch is turned on and the points are closed, battery current flows through the primary coil winding, turning the coil core into an electromagnet, inducing a small current flow through the secondary winding. When the points open to break the circuit, the current tries to flow

2

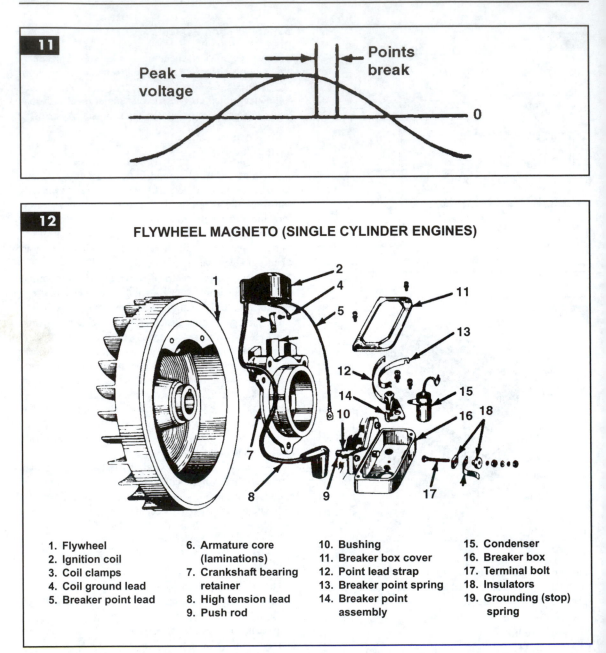

11

Peak voltage

Points break

0

12

FLYWHEEL MAGNETO (SINGLE CYLINDER ENGINES)

1. Flywheel
2. Ignition coil
3. Coil clamps
4. Coil ground lead
5. Breaker point lead
6. Armature core (laminations)
7. Crankshaft bearing retainer
8. High tension lead
9. Push rod
10. Bushing
11. Breaker box cover
12. Point lead strap
13. Breaker point spring
14. Breaker point assembly
15. Condenser
16. Breaker box
17. Terminal bolt
18. Insulators
19. Grounding (stop) spring

through the path of least resistance, the condenser, until condenser capacity is reached. At that point, the primary current stops flowing and the magnetic field starts to collapse. This collapse is hastened by the condenser, which tries to discharge its stored energy backward through the primary circuit.

Secondary circuit

The secondary circuit is comprised of the coil secondary windings (**Figure 8**), the spark plug, and related wiring.

In the preceding *Primary circuit* explanation, the magnetic field collapsed backward when the points opened. When the magnetic field collapses, extremely high voltage is induced into the coil's secondary winding. This high voltage flows through the secondary circuit to the spark plug where it arcs across the plug gap and travels to ground (G4).

Magneto Ignition Systems

In a magneto ignition system, the same principles of magnetism and electricity are involved as discussed in

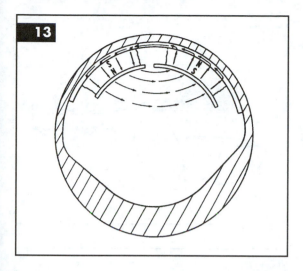

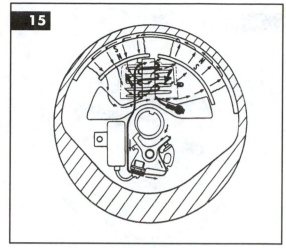

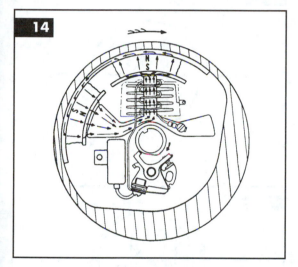

Battery Ignition Systems, but the method of application is somewhat different. Instead of the chemical energy of the battery producing 12 volts of constant direct current, the magneto's source of energy is a pulsating alternating current (AC) induced in the primary windings by permanent magnets. Because of the variations in voltage and current flow direction which characterize AC (**Figure 11**), the points must not only be correctly timed with relation to the piston near TDC, but timed also to break at or near peak voltage. The proper position of the permanent magnet in relation to this point opening is engineered into the system, and is commonly called the edge gap.

Flywheel magneto

The term "flywheel magneto" refers to the permanent magnets which activate the ignition system being a part of the engine flywheel, thereby making the flywheel the magneto rotor (**Figure 12**). Rotor, in this sense, means the rotating component which produces the electrical power by way of magnetic induction. Magnetic induction is explained under *AC Generation Theory* in this chapter.

Figure 13 shows a cross-sectional view of a typical magneto rotor – an engine flywheel used on a magneto ignition system. This particular flywheel shows the permanent magnets on the inside of the flywheel; most modern magnetos have the magnets facing the outside, with the charging system magnets on the inside.

The arrows in **Figure 13** indicate the lines of magnetic force, or flux, generated by the magnets. Since magnetic lines of force travel from the north magnetic pole to the south magnetic pole, the flux in this example travels from left to right.

Figures 14- 17 illustrate the operational cycle of a flywheel magneto.

In **Figure 14**, the flywheel magnets have moved to a position over the left and center legs of the coil core. As the magnets moved into this position, their magnetic field was attracted by the core legs and a potential voltage (electromotive force, or EMF) was induced in the coil's primary and secondary windings. However, this EMF was not sufficient to cause current to flow across the spark plug gap in the secondary circuit, and the points were open in the primary circuit.

In **Figure 15**, the flywheel magnets have advanced to where their magnetic field is being attracted by the center and right legs of the coil core while being withdrawn from the left and center legs. As indicated, lines of force are cutting *up* through the section of coil windings between the left and center core legs and are cutting *down* through the section of coil windings between the center and right legs. The resulting EMF induced in the primary circuit will cause a current to flow through the primary coil windings and breaker points, which have now been closed by action of the breaker cam.

At the instant the movement of lines of force cutting through the coil windings is at the maximum rate, the pri-

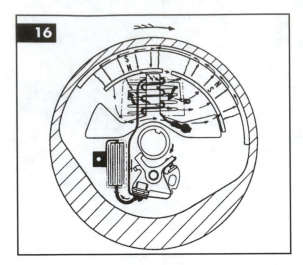

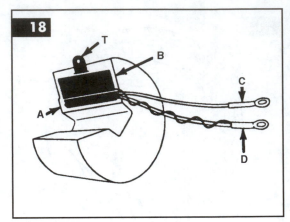

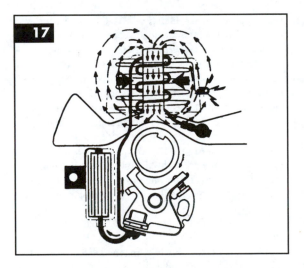

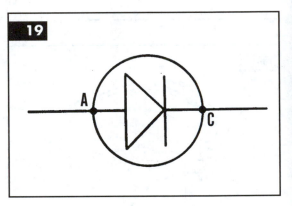

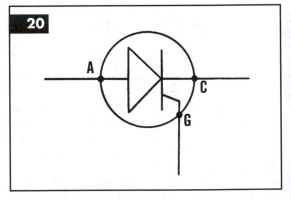

mary circuit obtains its maximum flow of current. At this time, the cam opens the breaker points, interrupting the primary circuit. For an instant, the flow of current in the primary circuit is absorbed by the condenser (**Figure 16**). An EMF is also induced in the secondary coil windings, where it allows the electromagnetic field to collapse at such a rapid rate that it induces an extremely high voltage in the coil's secondary, or high-tension, windings (**Figure 17**). This high voltage is sufficient to break down the air gap resistance between the spark plug electrodes, thereby causing a current to flow across the electrode gap in the form of an arc. This arc is the ignition spark which ignites the compressed fuel-air mixture in the combustion chamber.

Figure 18 shows a typical flywheel-magneto ignition coil. Reference A denotes the primary windings, with the secondary windings indicated by Reference B. The primary winding connection to the points and condenser is Reference C, with Reference D being the ground connection for the primary and secondary windings. Terminal T

is the secondary circuit high-tension terminal which connects to the spark plug lead. The core laminations fit through the square hole in the center of the coil.

Solid State Ignition Systems

Solid-state ignition systems normally provide trouble-free operation by eliminating required periodic maintenance.

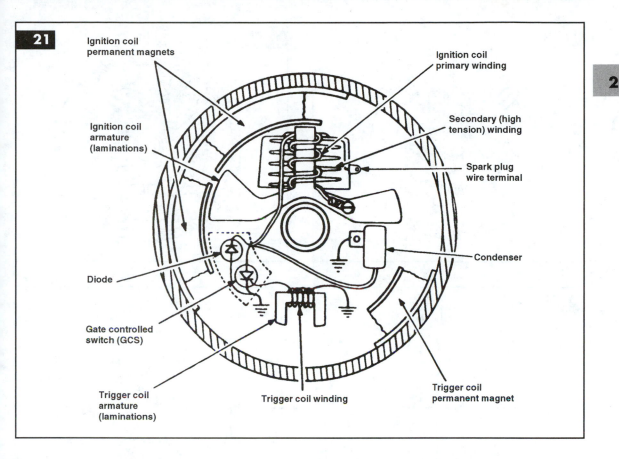

21

Ignition coil permanent magnets

Ignition coil armature (laminations)

Ignition coil primary winding

Secondary (high tension) winding

Spark plug wire terminal

Condenser

Diode

Gate controlled switch (GCS)

Trigger coil armature (laminations)

Trigger coil winding

Trigger coil permanent magnet

2

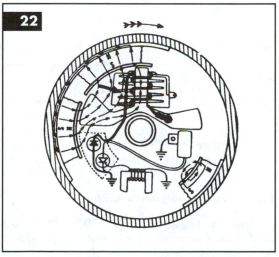

22

Solid-state ignition systems have no moving internal parts. Instead of breaker points closing and opening to control electromagnetic force, an electronic gate-controlled switch (GCS) is used. The GCS has no moving parts. Since, in a point-and-condenser system, the breaker points are closed over a longer period of crankshaft rotation than in the solid-state system, a diode is added to the circuit to provide the same characteristics as closed breaker points.

The same basic principles which explained the operation of point-and-condenser magnetos also apply to solid-state magnetos. The diode is represented in wiring diagrams by the symbol shown in **Figure 19**. It is an electronic device which will permit electrical current to flow in only one direction. In wiring diagrams and schematics, current flows from the cathode (C) to the anode (A), against the direction the arrow is pointing.

The GCS, symbolized in **Figure 20**, is a diode with a switch. Although still just a one-way path for current (C to A), it only permits current to flow when it is turned ON by a surge of positive current at the gate terminal (G). It will remain on as long as current remains positive at G, or as long as current is flowing from C to A. When there is no positive current at G, or no current flowing from C to A, the GCS is in the OFF state and will not permit current to flow.

Solid State Flywheel Magneto

The basic components for a typical solid-state flywheel magneto are shown in **Figure 21**. In **Figure 22**, the flywheel rotor is turning clockwise and the coil magnets are

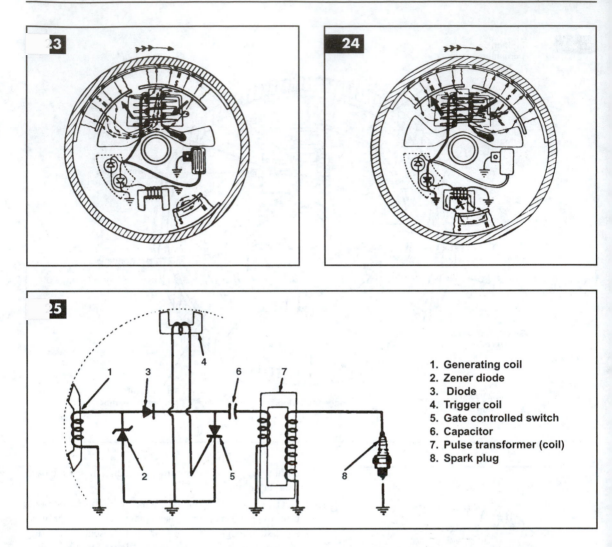

1. Generating coil
2. Zener diode
3. Diode
4. Trigger coil
5. Gate controlled switch
6. Capacitor
7. Pulse transformer (coil)
8. Spark plug

positioned so their lines of force are cutting the coil windings. This produces a surge of negative current in the primary winding. Induced current flows through the diode which, at this time, is acting like closed breaker points.

As the flywheel continues to rotate (**Figure 23**), the magnetic lines of flux are at their strongest. Now, instead of current passing through the diode, it travels to the condenser. The condenser acts as a buffer to prevent excessive voltage build-up at the GCS before it activates.

When the flywheel reaches the approximate position shown in **Figure 24**, the direction of the magnetic flux has reversed in the armature center leg, causing maximum flux density. At this time, the trigger coil magnet moves past the trigger coil armature, inducing a positive voltage on the GCS gate, triggering the GCS. The resultant surge in primary circuit current flow causes an induced secondary circuit voltage strong enough to arc across the spark plug gap electrodes, igniting the compressed fuel-air mix-

ture. While the GCS is triggered, the condenser discharges.

When the flywheel rotates the trigger magnet past the trigger armature, the GCS will cease to operate, reverting to the OFF state until it is again triggered.

Capacitive Discharge Ignition System

Capacitive discharge ignition (CDI) systems, like point-and-condenser and other solid-state systems, use a permanent magnet rotor (the flywheel), to induce current in a coil winding. In a CDI system, however, the current is stored in the capacitor, otherwise known as the condenser. At the proper timing interval, the stored current is discharged through a transformer coil to create the ignition spark.

Figure 25 shows a typical CDI system. As the flywheel magnets pass the input generating coil, half of the current produced charges a capacitor, while the other half,

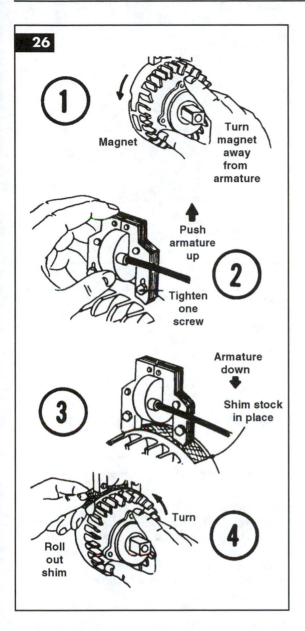

26

① Magnet / Turn magnet away from armature

② Push armature up / Tighten one screw

③ Armature down / Shim stock in place

④ Turn / Roll out shim

Armature Air Gap

To fully concentrate the magnetic field of the flywheel magnets, the magnets must pass as close as possible to the armature core without actually touching the core. The clearance between the flywheel magnets and the armature core legs is called the armature air gap.

The engines on these mowers use ignition armatures located outside the flywheel. To set the air gap, refer to **Figure 26** and follow these steps:

1. Turn the flywheel so that the magnets are not next to the ignition armature.

2. Loosen the screws holding the armature to the engine. Raise the armature to the limits allowed by the adjustment slots, then lightly tighten one screw to temporarily hold the armature away from the flywheel.

3. Rotate the flywheel to center the magnets directly under the armature legs. Place a *non-metallic* gap gauge of the correct minimum dimension (**Table 1**) between the magnets and the armature. Loosen the armature holding screw, allowing the magnets to draw the armature to the flywheel. While holding the armature snugly against the flywheel, tighten the armature screws.

> *CAUTION*
> *Do not use a steel feeler gauge to set the armature air gap. Incorrect gap settings could result. The best gap gauges to use are those supplied by the engine manufacturers.*

4. While holding one end of the gap gauge, rotate the flywheel and pull the gauge out from between the flywheel and armature. Rotate the flywheel several revolutions to be sure the flywheel does not contact the armature.

Ignition System Troubleshooting

To troubleshoot these ignition systems, refer to *Spark Test* in this chapter.

Heat

Heat is the worst enemy of a solid-state ignition armature module. It destroys internal components, rendering the entire module useless. For this reason, it is essential that the engine cooling system be constantly inspected and cleaned.

1. Keep chaff build-up removed from the flywheel intake screen.

2. If grass or leaf shavings appear to be packed between some of the cylinder fins where they are covered by the blower housing, remove the blower housing and clean the fins.

3. When mowing, always run the engine in the FAST throttle-control position to insure maximum cooling-air flow over the module and cooling fins.

blocked by the normal diode, passes through the Zener diode to complete the reverse circuit. A Zener diode is one which permits free current flow in one direction and restricted current flow in the opposite direction, after the voltage reaches a predetermined level, while limiting the maximum voltage of the forward current. As the flywheel continues to turn, the magnets pass the trigger coil where a signal current is generated. This current opens the GCS, allowing the capacitor to discharge through the primary circuit of the pulse transformer. The rapid voltage rise in the transformer primary winding induces a high voltage in the secondary winding. This secondary voltage is sent to the spark plug where it arcs across the plug gap electrodes, igniting the compressed fuel-air mixture.

Pre-ignition and detonation

Under certain conditions, the fuel-air mixture in the combustion chamber is spontaneously ignited. The names given to the two actions causing this are preignition and detonation. Although closely related and sometimes used interchangeably, they are separate and distinct.

Preignition occurs when combustion starts before the timed spark. It is usually caused by a hot spot in the combustion chamber, such as a sharp edge or a carbon deposit.

Detonation is the sudden and violent combustion of a portion of the unburned fuel ahead of the already-ignited flame front. It occurs part-way through the burning cycle when the fuel reaches its critical temperature and ignites spontaneously, causing severe heat and pressure shock. Low-octane fuel is a common cause of detonation.

Spark Plug

In any spark-ignition engine, the spark plug (**Figure 27**) provides the proper means for igniting the compressed fuel-air mixture in the combustion chamber

Thread size

The threaded portion of the spark plug shell and the mating hole in the cylinder head are manufactured to meet certain industry standards. Engines on the mowers in this manual use 14 mm threads.

Reach

The length of the threaded portion of the spark plug is also standardized throughout the engine industry. **Figure 28** shows the various reaches of the more popular plugs. On gasketed spark plugs, the reach dimension is measured from the flat gasket surface to the end of the threaded shell, not counting the gasket or ground electrode. On taper-seat spark plugs (**Figure 29**), the reach dimension is measured from the top of the taper to the end of the threaded shell, not counting the ground electrode. Taper-seat spark plugs do *not* use gaskets.

Heat range

During engine operation, part of the heat generated during the combustion process is transferred through the spark plug to the cooling medium by way of the shell, gasket (if used) and lower insulator. The operating temperature of the plug plays an important part in engine operation. If too much heat is retained by the plug, the fuel-air mixture may be ignited by contact with the plug prior to being sparked by the ignition system. This is called preignition, and causes a knocking sound in the engine. If not enough heat is retained, partially-burned com-

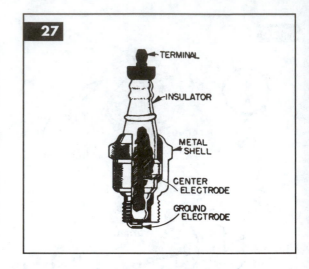

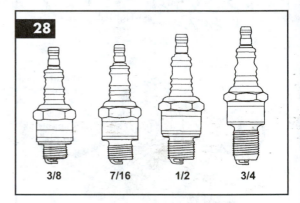

bustion products such as soot, oil, or carbon may build up on the plug tip. This results in the plug shorting out or fouling. If this happens, the secondary current from the ignition system is wasted by traveling to ground through the deposits instead of bridging the plug gap as a useful spark. In this case, the engine will misfire.

The operating temperature of the plug tip can be regulated by selecting a plug with the correct heat path length (**Figure 30**). A plug with a short insulator around the center electrode will dissipate heat faster, thereby running cooler, than a plug with a longer insulator.

Most popular-sized spark plugs are available in a number of heat ranges that are interchangeable within the group. The proper heat range is determined by engine design and the type of service. Always use caution when experimenting with a heat range other than that recommended by the manufacturer.

Heat range should not be confused with reach. Due to the externally-invisible heat range construction differences shown in **Figure 30**, there are 3/8-in. reach spark plugs which run hotter than 3/4-in. reach plugs.

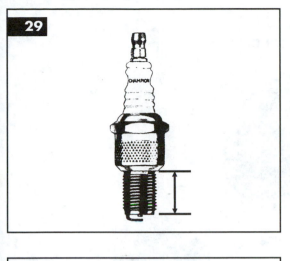

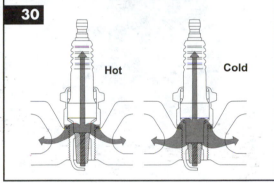

Spark Plug Troubleshooting

Valuable information can be obtained by studying a spark plug's condition. **Figure 31** shows views of seven spark plug tips after various types of service.

1. *Normal operation*— A light, even coating of tan to black deposits coupled with minimal electrode wear indicate correct heat range and proper engine operation. If not misfiring, this plug could be reused.

2. *Carbon fouling*— Dry, fluffy black carbon deposits indicate an overrich fuel mixture or faulty ignition output.

3. *Gap bridging*— Identified by deposits building up between the electrodes. The deposits reduce the gap and eventually close it entirely. Caused by oil or carbon fouling.

4. *Preignition*— If the electrodes are melted, preignition is almost certainly the cause. Caused by wrong type of fuel, incorrect ignition timing, plug heat range too hot, burned valves, or engine overheating. Find and correct the cause of preignition before returning the engine to service.

5. *Oil fouling*— Wet, oily deposits with minimal electrode wear are usually caused by worn piston rings and cylinder or intake valve guide/stem. These problems allow oil to be pumped into the combustion chamber.

6. *Worn out*— Identified by severely eroded or worn electrodes. Caused by normal wear. Install a new spark plug.

7. *Excessive overheating*— Blistered or burned insulator tips and badly worn electrodes can be caused by overheating from an obstructed cooling system or too-lean fuel mixtures, preignition, improper installation procedures, or a plug that is too hot.

> *CAUTION*
> *Do not use the abrasive-blast (sand-blast) method to clean spark plugs. When spark plugs are cleaned by this method, the abrasive grit lodges in the upper gap between the insulator and the shell. Subsequent compressed-air blowing does not remove these abrasives. This grit is only removed when the plug is reinstalled in the engine and the engine is started, heating and expanding the plug. The grit then falls into the cylinder and combustion chamber area, causing rapid internal wear and damage.*

ENGINE STARTING PROCEDURE

The starting and ignition system circuits are protected by an operator-presence switch interlock system. The positions of the control levers affect starting. The engine can only be started if the following conditions are met:

1. The neutral latches must be in the neutral lock position.

2. The speed adjustment lever must be in the neutral position.

3. The parking brake must be on.

4. The cutter blades must be disengaged.

Make sure the fuel tank has an adequate supply of clean, fresh fuel, and that the fuel shutoff valve (**Figure 32**) is in the On position.

> *WARNING*
> *Make sure ventilation is adequate if the engine is to be started in a confined area. Exhaust fumes are toxic and deadly.*

Starting a Cold Engine

1. Move the throttle control to the FAST position and pull the choke knob out (**Figure 33**).

2. On recoil-start engines, pull the rope lightly until the starter engages, then pull hard to turn the engine. Repeat as necessary if the engine does not start immediately.

3. On electric-start engines, turn the ignition switch key to the START position to activate the starter. Release the key as soon as the engine starts.

4. When the engine starts, allow it to run in the CHOKE position until it begins to lose rpm, then move the throttle

31

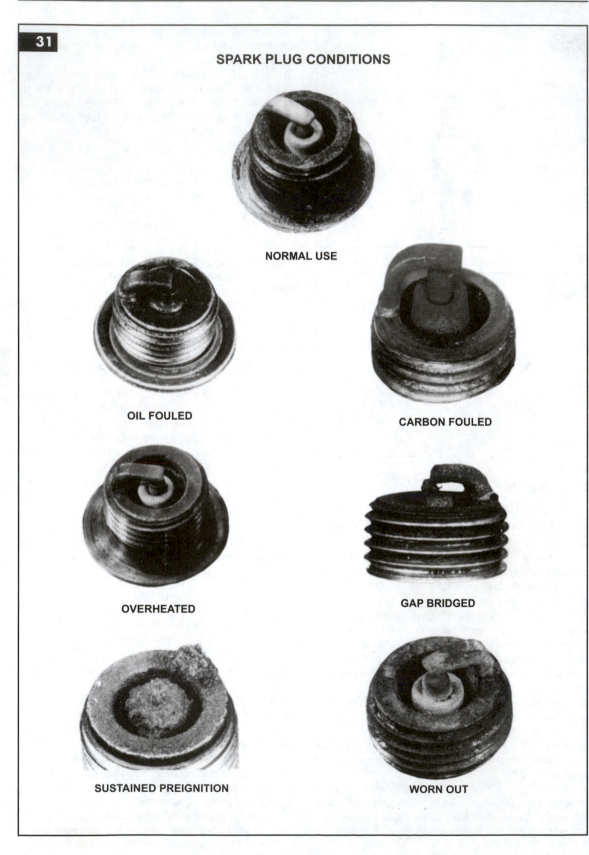

SPARK PLUG CONDITIONS

NORMAL USE

OIL FOULED

CARBON FOULED

OVERHEATED

GAP BRIDGED

SUSTAINED PREIGNITION

WORN OUT

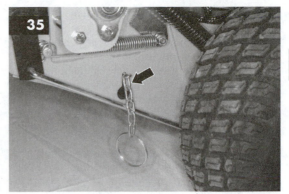

control to approximately one-half throttle, allowing the engine to warm up to operating temperature. When the engine has reached operating temperature, the throttle can be moved to FAST for mowing.

5. If a cold engine is being started in cold weather, the cold-weather start system can be activated on units so equipped. This mechanism removes the hydrostatic drive system load from the engine, and is controlled by a chain located behind the right-hand drive tire. **Figure 34** shows the chain in the normal run position. To activate the mechanism, carefully pull the chain outward to the right as far as it will go, then lift the chain up into the holding slot (**Figure 35**). Start the engine. When the engine has reached operating temperature, lightly pull out and down on the chain, then slowly return the chain back to the normal run position.

Starting a Warm or Hot Engine

1. Move the throttle control to approximately the half-throttle position. Leave the choke knob in.

2. On recoil-start engines, pull the rope lightly until the starter engages, then pull hard to turn the engine. Repeat as necessary if the engine does not start immediately.

3. On electric-start engines, turn the ignition switch key to the START position to activate the starter. Release the key as soon as the engine starts.

4. When the engine starts, allow it to run in the half-throttle position momentarily, then move the throttle to the FAST position for mowing.

Starting a Flooded Engine

1. Move the throttle control to the FAST position. Leave the choke open (choke knob in).

2. Clean the area around the spark plug base, then remove and inspect the spark plug(s). If the plug tip is wet, dry it with compressed air. Rotate the crankshaft to bring the piston near TDC on the compression stroke. Again using compressed air, carefully blow any remaining fuel

from the cylinder(s). Reinstall and retorque the spark plug(s).

3. On recoil-start engines, pull the rope lightly until the starter engages, then pull hard to turn the engine. Repeat as necessary if the engine does not start immediately.

4. On electric-start engines, turn the ignition switch key to the START position to activate the starter. Release the key as soon as the engine starts.

CAUTION
Never operate the electric starter motor more than 15 seconds at a time. Always allow at least a one minute cool-down period after each 15 second starter operation. Otherwise, the starter motor will overheat and become damaged.

If the engine does not start, remove the air filter to see if the carburetor is still flooded. If the carburetor continues to flood, refer to the appropriate engine chapter in this manual and repair the cause of the flooding.

Cylinder flooding is sometimes caused by the fuel-air mixture in the cylinder not being fired by the spark plug. This could be caused by either a faulty spark plug or a faulty ignition system.

If the spark plug is suspect, replace the plug, ensuring that the replacement plug is the correct plug for the application and that the plug is gapped correctly. Refer to **Table 2** for spark plug specifications.

If the ignition system is suspect, refer to *Spark Test* in this chapter.

ENGINE TROUBLESHOOTING

NOTE
Numbers in parentheses following the possible problem are for the chapters where solutions to the problem are found. Problems without end numbers have simple, common-sense solutions.

Engine Will Not Crank

1. Battery is weak or dead. (16)
2. Faulty ignition switch. (16)
3. Safety interlock operator-presence components faulty. (16)
4. Loose, broken, or shorted wires or connections. (16)
5. Faulty electric starter, starter drive, solenoid, or ring gear. (5-10)
6. Seized internal engine components. (5-10)

Engine Cranks But Will Not Start

1. Empty fuel tank or stale fuel. (4)
2. Fuel shutoff valve closed. (4)
3. Choke not closing completely on a cold engine. (4)

4. Dirt or water in the fuel system. (4-10)
5. Clogged fuel line. (4-10)
6. Spark plug lead(s) disconnected.
7. Faulty ignition switch. (5-10, 16)
8. Faulty ignition module(s) or kill wire(s). (5-10)
9. Faulty spark plug(s). (2, 5-10)
10. Malfunctioning carburetor solenoid. (5-10)

Engine Starts Hard

1. Cold hydrostatic fluid. (2, 3, 12)
2. Loose or faulty wires or connections. (16)
3. Dirt or water in the fuel system. (4-10)
4. Clogged fuel line. (4-10)
5. Fouled spark plug(s). (2, 5-10)
6. Faulty choke or throttle controls. (4-10)
7. Low compression. (2)
8. Stale fuel. (2, 4)
9. Faulty automatic compression release (ACR) mechanism, if equipped. (5-7)
10. Weak spark. (5-10)
11. Dirty/plugged air filter.
12. One erratic cylinder in a 2-cylinder engine. (2, 5, 7, 9, 10)

Engine Starts But Does Not Continue Running

1. Fuel tank cap vent plugged. (4)
2. Dirt or water in the fuel system. (4-10)
3. Faulty choke or throttle controls. (4-10)
4. Carburetor malfunction. (4-10)
5. Leaking cylinder head gasket. (2, 5-10)
6. Loose ignition module kill-wire connections. (5-10)
7. One erratic cylinder in a 2-cylinder engine. (2, 5, 7, 9, 10)

Engine Runs But Misses

1. Spark plug lead(s) loose.
2. Dirt or water in the fuel system. (4-10)
3. Engine overheated. See *Engine Overheats* in this chapter.
4. Dirty/plugged air filter.
5. Fouled spark plug(s). (2, 5-10)
6. Faulty ignition module. (5-10)
7. Incorrectly adjusted carburetor. (4-10)
8. Loose ignition module kill-wire connections intermittently shorting to ground. (5-10)
9. One erratic cylinder in a 2-cylinder engine. (2, 5, 7, 9, 10)

Engine Will Not Idle

1. Fuel tank cap vent restricted. (4)
2. Dirt or water in the fuel system. (4-10)

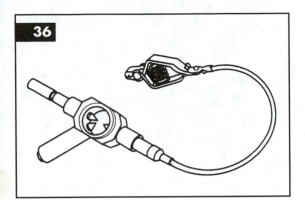

36

3. Gummy fuel deposits in the carburetor idle passages. (4-10)

4. Carburetor idle-mixture or idle-speed adjusting needles incorrectly set. (4-10)

5. Faulty spark plug(s). (2, 5-10)

6. Low compression. (2, 5-10)

7. One erratic cylinder in a 2-cylinder engine. (2, 5, 7, 9, 10)

Engine Loses Power

1. Dirty/plugged air filter.

2. Low or high crankcase oil level.

3. Contaminated fuel. (4-10)

4. Overloaded engine. (All)

5. Overheated engine. (Next section)

6. Restricted exhaust. (4-10)

7. Low compression. (2, 5-10)

8. One erratic cylinder in a 2-cylinder engine. (2, 5, 7, 9, 10)

Engine Overheats

1. Cooling fins, blower housing/shrouds, chaff screen or air intake clogged. (2)

2. Low or high crankcase oil level.

3. Overloaded engine. (All)

4. Lean fuel mixture from misadjusted or faulty carburetor or contaminated fuel. (4-10)

Engine Knocks

1. Loose engine-mount bolts.

2. Stale or improper fuel. (4)

3. Low crankcase oil level.

4. Engine overloaded. (All)

5. Excessive internal wear or damage. (5-10)

6. Malfunctioning hydraulic lifter(s). (5-7)

Engine Uses Excessive Oil

> *NOTE*
> *Factory testing has found that an engine running at full load and full governed throttle may consume up to one ounce (30 ml) of oil per hour. This amount of oil consumption is acceptable. Since running at full throttle is recommended for these units, the operator must determine oil consumption based on the load applied to the unit.*

1. Incorrect oil viscosity or type. (3)

2. Crankcase oil overfilled. (3)

3. Improperly-assembled breather. (5-10)

4. Broken piston rings; worn piston rings, cylinder bore, or valve guides or stems. (5-10)

Engine Leaking Oil

1. Clogged or inoperative crankcase breather. (5-10)

2. Broken gaskets; worn or hardened seals. (5-10)

3. Loose fasteners. (5-10)

4. Piston blowby from worn or broken piston rings or worn cylinder bore. (5-10)

5. Badly worn intake valve guide and/or stem. (5-10)

6. Exhaust restriction. (4-10)

Engine Will Not Stop

1. Ignition switch faulty. (16)

2. Loose or disconnected engine kill wire. (5-10, 16)

3. Ignition-module ground wire harness faulty. (5-10)

SPARK TEST

Perform a spark test to determine if the ignition is producing adequate spark. A spark tester (**Figure 36** and **Figure 37**) should be used as a substitute for the spark plug as it allows the spark to be more easily observed while accurately testing the ignition system.

Figure 36 shows a sealed-gap tester which can be used on any engine. This tester (Briggs & Stratton part No. 19368) is an updated version of Tester A in **Figure 37**. Tester B in **Figure 37** is an open-gap tester which should be used on capacitive discharge ignition systems for more accurate results. The Kohler CV V-twin engines use a CDI system. Tester B (Kohler part No. 24 455 02) is identified with the designation "HEI" on the tester insulator to denote its intended use on high energy CDI systems.

> *WARNING*
> *If an open-gap tester is being used (**Figure 37**), mount the spark tester away from the spark plug hole in the cylinder head so the tester cannot ignite the gasoline va-*

pors in the cylinder. *If the engine is flooded, do not perform this test without first eliminating the flooding. Fuel that is ejected through the spark plug hole can be ignited by the firing of the open-gap spark tester.*

CAUTION
Before removing the spark plugs, remove the plug leads and clean the area around each plug base with compressed air. Unscrew the plug approximately one revolution and repeat the cleaning process. Dirt that falls into the cylinder will cause rapid piston, piston ring and cylinder wear.

NOTE
Most solid-state ignition systems require a minimum of 350 rpm to produce a spark. When running a spark test, ensure that the engine rpm is sufficient, or test results will be unsatisfactory.

1. Remove the spark plug(s) from each cylinder.
2. Connect the spark plug wire to the tester and attach the tester clamp to an engine ground (**Figure 38**). Position the spark tester so the test terminals can be easily seen.
3. The starting and ignition system circuits are protected by an operator-presence switch interlock system. The positions of the control levers affect starting. The ignition system can only be properly tested if the following conditions are met:
   a. The neutral latches must be in the neutral lock position.
   b. The speed adjustment lever must be in the neutral position.
   c. The parking brake must be on.
   d. The cutter blades must be disengaged.

WARNING
Do not hold the spark plug tester, wire or connector. Serious electrical shock may result.

4. Activate the engine starter. A good spark must be evident between the tester terminals. Test both cylinders of a 2-cylinder engine simultaneously, using two testers.
5. If the spark is good at each spark plug, the ignition system is functioning properly.
6. If the spark was weak or non-existent, or if there was no spark at one of the plugs of a 2-cylinder engine, note the following:
   a. If there is no spark at one or both of the plugs, there may be a problem with the ignition grounding circuit. Access the ignition module(s) and disconnect the kill-wire terminal(s). Repeat the test. If there is now spark, the kill circuit is faulty. Refer to the appropriate engine chapter or the Electrical System chapter of this manual for kill circuit service.

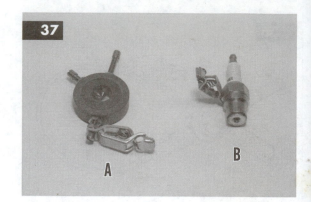

   b. If, after disconnecting the kill-wire terminal(s) and retesting, there is still no spark, check the flywheel-to-module air gap. Refer to **Table 1** for the air gap specifications.

NOTE
Do not use steel feeler gauges to set the air gap. Inaccurate gap settings could result.

   c. If the air gaps are correct, test the flywheel magnet for strength. Access the flywheel and rotate it so that the magnet is at either the 3- or 9- o'clock position. Lightly hold a medium-sized flat-bladed screwdriver so that the flat part of the tip faces the magnet and is approximately one inch from the magnet. The magnet should pull the blade tip to the flywheel. If it does not, the magnet is weak and the flywheel will need to be replaced. If the magnet is good, the ignition modules are faulty and must be replaced.

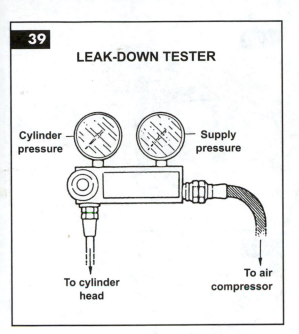

39

LEAK-DOWN TESTER

Cylinder pressure

Supply pressure

To cylinder head

To air compressor

d. On a Kohler MV opposed-twin engine, if there is no spark at only one spark tester, there is probably a fault with the spark plug wire or plug terminal, since the MV only has one module which fires both spark plugs simultaneously.

NOTE
If the engine backfires during starting attempts, the ignition timing may be incorrect. Since the flywheel key between the flywheel and the crankshaft is what sets the timing on these engines, remove the flywheel and check for a sheared flywheel key. Always torque the flywheel nut to the proper specification when installing the flywheel. Flywheel fastener torque values are listed in the appropriate engine sections. A badly sheared key could also throw the timing off to the point where the tester shows good spark but the spark is occurring at the wrong time, preventing the engine from starting or causing serious kickback.

CYLINDER LEAKDOWN TEST

An engine leakdown test locates engine problems caused by leaking valves, a blown head gasket, a worn cylinder and/or piston, or broken, worn or stuck piston rings. The leakdown test is performed by applying compressed air to a cylinder and then observing and measuring the leakage. A cylinder leakdown tester (**Figure 39**) and an air compressor are required for this test. **Figure 39** shows a 2-gauge tester; some leakdown testers only have one gauge.

Follow the manufacturer's directions along with the following information when performing a cylinder leakdown test.

2

1. If the engine will start, start and run the engine until it reaches normal operating temperature, usually three to five minutes, then turn off the engine.
2. Remove the air filter housing. Open and secure the throttle and choke so that they remain in the wide-open position.
3. If the crankcase breather tube connects directly to the air-filter side of the carburetor, remove the tube from the carburetor connection, or carefully crimp the tube, then remove the oil dipstick or fill plug. This will isolate intake valve leaks from cylinder leaks.
4. Clean around the spark plug base and remove the spark plug from the cylinder being tested.
5. Set the test-cylinder piston at TDC on its compression stroke.

CAUTION
The engine may turn over when air pressure is applied to the cylinder. To prevent this from happening, the crankshaft or flywheel must be blocked after TDC is positioned.

6. Install the leakdown tester into the spark plug hole. Connect a 75-150 psi air supply to the tester fitting.
7. Apply compressed air to the leakdown tester and perform the leakdown test, following the manufacturer's instructions. Read the rate of leakage on the gauge. Record the leakage rate for that cylinder.
8. After recording the leakage rate of the cylinder, listen for air escaping from the engine.
  a. Air escaping from the cylinder head gasket area indicates a faulty gasket, warped head, loose head bolts, or a combination of these faults.
  b. Air leaking through the exhaust pipe indicates a leaking exhaust valve or seat.
  c. Air leaking through the carburetor indicates a leaking intake valve or seat.
  d. Air leaking through the crankcase breather tube or from the oil dipstick tube or fill plug hole indicates worn piston or cylinder components.
9. Shut down the tester, disconnect the air supply, and remove the tester from the cylinder.
10. Use the tester instructions to interpret the results.
11. On a 2-cylinder engine, repeat Steps 4-8 for the second cylinder.

ELECTRICAL SYSTEM FUNDAMENTALS

The electricity used in these mowers is created either chemically, in the battery, or magnetically, by passing a magnet or magnets past a series of wire windings. For someone unfamiliar with electrical generation, the following explanation should prove helpful.

Electricity and magnetism are inseparable. Electricity cannot be produced without magnetism, and the production of electricity creates additional magnetism.

Magnetic lines of force, although invisible, can be readily observed by placing a piece of paper over the poles of a horseshoe magnet, then sprinkling iron filings onto the paper. The results are seen in **Figure 40**, as the filing positions are determined by the flux, the magnetic lines of force. Flux is more concentrated around the poles and moves outside the magnet from the North magnetic pole to the South magnetic pole (**Figure 41**). Understanding atomic structure can aid in understanding magnetism.

An atom is, by definition, the smallest particle of matter which still contains the properties of that matter; it is the most basic component of an element. An atom is made up of a center core (nucleus) which contains the neutral charges (neutrons) and the positive charges (protons) in a tight grouping. The negative charges (electrons) are constantly orbiting the nucleus.

Atoms, by nature, strive to be neutral – to have their negative charges balance their positive charges. This is the basis for the "opposite or unlike charges attract; like charges repel" principle of magnetism. It is possible to break an electron loose from its orbit around the nucleus. If this happens to an atom with an equal number of protons and electrons, then the atom is left with a positive net charge and is referred to as a positive ion. If a neutral atom receives a stray electron, it then becomes negatively charged, thereby becoming a negative ion.

The natural tendency of a positive ion is to attract an electron from a neighbor atom. The neighbor then becomes a positive ion, and a chain reaction begins in which each atom, in turn, borrows an electron from its neighbor. This electron-borrowing creates a flow of current that continues until all the atoms have achieved a state of balance. Electron transfer – the "flow" of electrons – is electricity.

Some materials such as silver and copper will readily transfer electrons from atom to atom. These materials are called conductors. Other materials such as rubber, glass, and plastic are non-conductors, more commonly known as insulators.

Electrical force – the pressure which causes electricity to "flow" – is called voltage, and refers to the potential for electrical current to flow from one point to another. For this reason, voltage is referred to as electrical potential. The unit of measurement for voltage is the volt, and the reference symbol is "V". Voltage is sometimes also referred to as electromotive force, or EMF.

Electrical volume – the amount of electricity flowing through a conductor or a system – is known as current, and is measured in amperes or, more commonly, amps.

The degree to which a conductor will not allow current to flow is called resistance and is measured in units called Ohms. The symbol for ohms is the Greek letter Omega, "Ω".

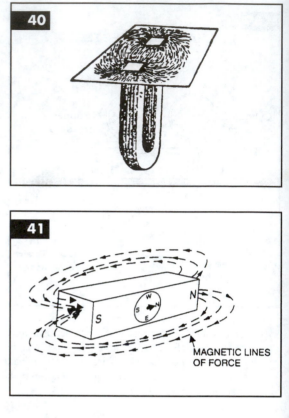

MAGNETIC LINES
OF FORCE

Electromagnetism

A magnetic field can also be created where there is none by feeding electrical current through a conductor or wire. When this is done, each end of the wire becomes a pole, and the movement of electrons inside the wire causes a magnetic field around the wire.

To determine the direction of the magnetic lines of force around the conductor, the "right-hand rule" is used.

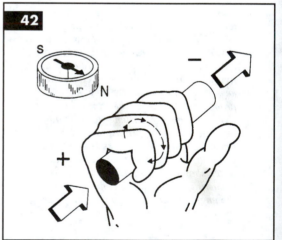

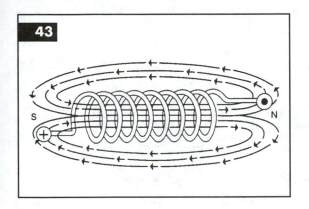

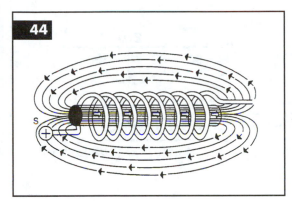

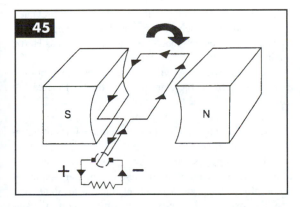

2

in the direction of current flow through the coil; the thumb then points to the coil's North pole.

To further strengthen this electromagnetic field, the coil can be wound around a core of magnetizable material, such as iron or certain steel alloys (**Figure 44**). Since air is a poor conductor of flux and since ferrous metals are good conductors, using such a core greatly increases magnetic strength.

AC Generation Theory

If the iron-filing paper were removed from the magnet in **Figure 40**, a wire conductor could be moved through the pole-to-pole magnetic field. The wire could also be held stationary while moving the magnet. If a sensitive voltmeter were connected to the wire, a voltage could be read, indicating electron flow through the conductor (**Figure 45**). This is the principle of electromagnetic induction – the movement of the conductor through the magnetic field *induces* the transfer and movement of electrons within the conductor. Stated another way: Three things are necessary to generate voltage:

    a. A magnetic field,

    b. A conductor, and

    c. Motion, either of the conductor through the magnetic field, or of the magnetic field past the conductor.

Taking the simple generator one step farther, the conductor wire could be formed into a loop and rotated inside two wider-spaced poles. By taking output from the wire ends through a rotational connection, current would flow whenever the wire was rotated. In the case of the charging systems of the engines used on these mowers, the wires are held in a fixed position and the flywheel-mounted magnets move past the wires. The result is the same — current flow.

If the magnets were rotated continuously in the same direction, one pole of the magnet would first pass one wire, then the other. This would cause current to change direction every half revolution, and is exactly what happens in the charging system alternator. The alternator is so named because it is a generator which produces *alternating current* (AC).

By connecting a meter to the conductor wire and starting out with the conductor leg mounted in the 0° or 12 o'clock position, with the north magnetic pole in the 9 o'clock position and the south magnetic pole in the 3 o'clock position (**Figure 46**), the magnet can be rotated counterclockwise to indicate the intensity and direction of current flow on the meter:

1. With the leg midway between the S and N poles (0°), both poles exert an equal force on the wire, and no electrons flow, resulting in a no-current reading on the meter.

2. As the magnet begins to rotate counterclockwise, the S pole flux begins to exert more influence on the electrons

Conventional theory states that current flows from negative to positive, so place your right hand around the conductor with the thumb pointing in the direction of current flow (**Figure 42**); the fingers will then be pointing in the direction of the flux or, in other words, to the North magnetic pole.

To strengthen this electrically-created magnetic field, the wires can be formed into a coil (**Figure 43**). With lines of magnetic force entering the coil at one end and departing the other, the coil ends form the poles, with the flux concentrated inside the coil.

To determine polarity in a coil, again use the "right-hand rule": grasp the coil with the fingers pointing

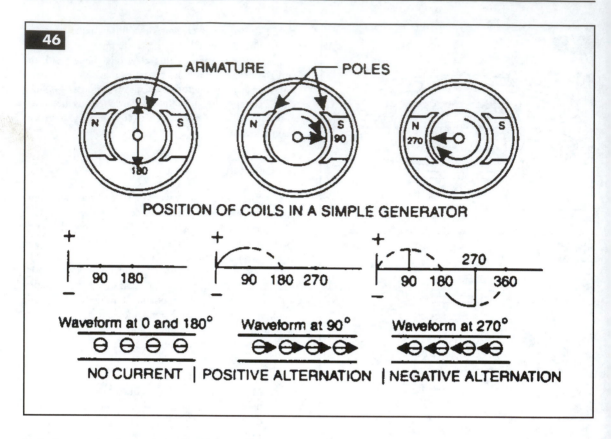

46

ARMATURE   POLES

POSITION OF COILS IN A SIMPLE GENERATOR

Waveform at 0 and 180° | Waveform at 90° | Waveform at 270°

NO CURRENT | POSITIVE ALTERNATION | NEGATIVE ALTERNATION

in the leg, causing the current to flow in the wire and the meter to begin registering (+).

3. When the magnet is rotated 90° to align the leg with the S pole, the current reaches its maximum (+) value.

4. As the magnet continues to rotate, the leg moves farther from the S pole flux concentration, causing decreasing electron and current flow and a movement of the meter needle back toward zero.

5. At the 180° (3- and 9- o'clock) positions, the leg is again equidistant from either pole, resulting in no current flow and no meter reading.

6. As the magnet continues to rotate up to the 270° (6- and 12- o'clock) positions, the leg comes under the influence of the flux from the N pole and begins moving electrons in the opposite direction, causing the meter to begin reading current flow in the (–) direction.

7. With the leg in the 270° position, the N pole exerts its strongest force on the loop, causing the meter to read maximum (–).

8. As the magnet continues to rotate back to 9- and 3- o'clock, current flow decreases and the meter needle registers decreasing (–) current flow until the leg is again at its 12:00 o'clock starting point and zero current flow.

On paper, this rotation is shown as **Figure 46**, and is referred to as the AC sine wave. It shows one "cycle" of alternating current. Rotating the magnet 60 times per second gives us an alternating current frequency of 60 cy-

cles-per-second which, until recently, was abbreviated "cps." However, electrical terminology changed somewhat, and cycles-per-second is now referred to as Hertz, abbreviated "Hz."

Since one wire loop will produce measurable, but not usable, electricity, there are three methods of increasing output:

    a. Using a stronger magnetic field.

    b. Increasing the speed used to cut the lines of force.

    c. Using more loops of wire.

The charging systems of the engines in this manual utilize all three methods for generating proper output — multiple magnets, on a flywheel rotating at 3600 rpm, passing over multi-wire windings on the stator, the stationary component mounted to the crankcase behind the flywheel.

AC Conversion to DC

Since the end-use components of the electrical systems on these mowers utilize *direct current* (DC), so the AC produced by the alternator stator must be converted. This is accomplished by using *diodes*.

A diode is a solid-state electrical device which will only allow current to pass through in one direction or, electrically speaking, will only allow one half of the AC sine wave through. The primary diode component is a sin-

2

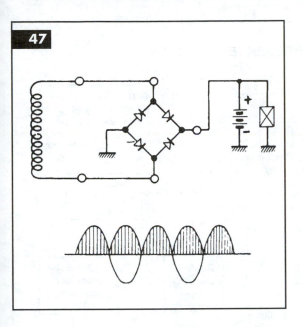

glc silicon crystal. While the diode is being manufactured, the silicon is alloyed to create two separate areas. The area at one end of the diode receives a *P-type material* having an excess of protons, thereby making it electron-deficient. The other end of the diode receives *N-type material*, giving it an excess of electrons and making it proton-deficient. Separating the P-type material from the N-type material is an area of neutral silicon called the *depletion region*.

Applying current to the diode with the negative lead connected to the N-type material and the positive lead connected to the P-type material will collapse the depletion region and allow the current to flow. This is what happens during the positive half of the AC sine wave.

Reversing the feed polarity (feeding the negative half of the AC sine wave to the diode) causes the electrons to become attracted to and bunch up around the positive lead, while the protons congregate near the negative lead. This enlarges the depletion region, preventing current from passing through it.

Current flow through the diode, then, is always positive to negative in the direction of the arrowhead on the schematic symbol. This allows DC to flow through the circuit, charging the battery and operating the accessories. To utilize as many positive sine-wave halves as possible, diodes are grouped together in what is commonly called a *rectifier bridge* or *full-wave rectifier*. This is illustrated in **Figure 47**.

ELECTRICAL SYSTEM TROUBLESHOOTING

WARNING
Always disconnect the battery before performing a resistance test. Never test an

electrically live circuit. Serious meter damage will result; personal injury may also occur.

NOTE
Resistance specifications are for an ambient temperature of 70° F (21° C) and may vary depending on the winding temperature and the test-equipment accuracy.

The electrical systems on these units consist of five main circuits:
1. Operator presence circuit,
2. Engine cranking circuit,
3. Engine ignition circuit,
4. Engine charging circuit, and
5. Cutter deck PTO clutch circuit.

Operator Presence Circuit

The operator presence circuit, sometimes referred to as the safety-interlock circuit, uses the safety-interlock switches and wiring to prevent the engine from starting or continuing to run if certain operating procedures are not followed.

The engine will not start unless:
1. The neutral latches are in the neutral lock position;
2. The speed adjustment lever is pulled back into the neutral position;
3. The parking brake is locked; and
4. The cutter blade PTO switch is in the Off position.

Once started, the operator presence levers must be held down anytime the PTO switch is activated. If the PTO switch is on and the operator presence controls are released, the engine will stop.

To troubleshoot the operator presence circuit, follow the steps in the diagram in **Figure 48**. Prior to testing the circuit:
1. Ensure that the fuses are OK;
2. Place the motion drive lever in neutral;
3. Place the PTO switch in the Off position; and
4. Start the test with the ignition switch off.

The test can be performed using either a test light or a voltmeter. Connect the positive tester lead to the positive battery terminal; connect the other tester lead to the white wire at the engine harness connector. If using a voltmeter, the meter should read battery voltage anytime a test step calls for the light to illuminate; the meter should read no voltage when a test step calls for the test light off.

Engine Cranking Circuit

The engine cranking circuit covers the wiring and components necessary to start the engine.

To troubleshoot the engine cranking circuit, follow the steps in **Figure 49**. Prior to testing the circuit:
1. Ensure that the fuses are OK;

48

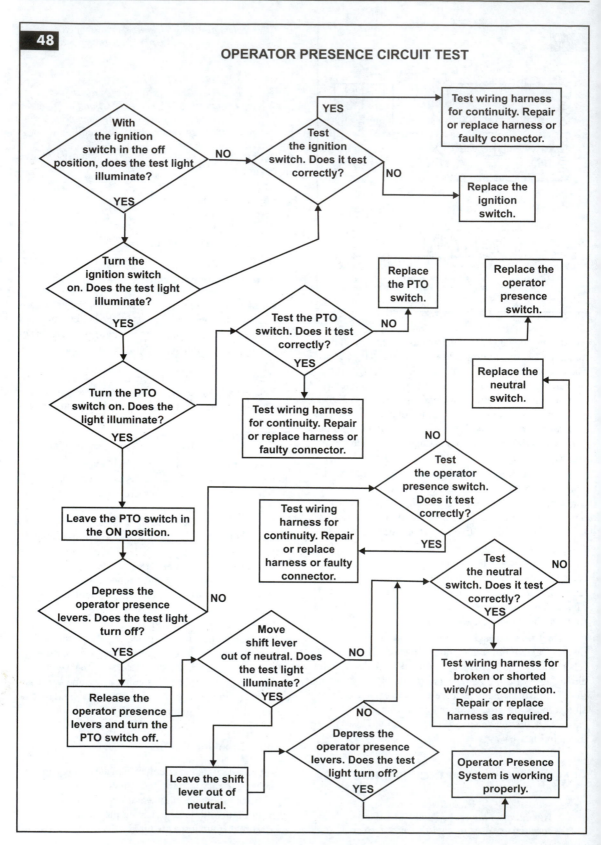

OPERATOR PRESENCE CIRCUIT TEST

2. Place the motion drive lever in neutral;

3. Place the PTO switch in the OFF position;

4. Engage the parking brake;

5. Depress and hold the operator presence lever; and

6. Test the battery.

    a. At rest, the battery should have a minimum of 12.0 volts. If not, hydrometer-test and load-test the battery. Recharge and/or replace the battery as necessary. Complete *Battery Service* is found in Chapter Three.

    b. With the ignition key turned to the START position, the battery should have a minimum of 9.0 volts. If not, perform Step 6a battery tests and service. Also test the starter motor and cables. Refer to the appropriate engine section in this manual for starter-motor service.

7. Start the test with the ignition switch on.

The test can be performed using either a voltmeter or a test light. Connect the negative tester lead to the negative battery terminal. If using a test light, the light should illuminate whenever a test step calls for voltage to be present.

Engine Ignition Circuit

Troubleshooting procedures for the engine ignition circuit are covered under *Spark Test* in this chapter, with ignition system theory covered under *Ignition System Fundamentals* in this chapter.

Engine Charging Circuit

Engine charging circuits are unique to each engine. Refer to the appropriate engine section in this manual for troubleshooting procedures for the engine charging circuit being worked on.

Charging system theory and fundamentals are discussed in the preceding *AC Generation Theory* and *AC Conversion to DC* sections in this chapter.

Cutter Deck PTO Clutch Circuit

The cutter deck PTO clutch circuit controls the engagement and disengagement of the electric clutch, which powers the blades.

> *NOTE*
> *When the PTO switch is activated and deactivated, a squealing sound may be momentarily heard under the engine. This sound is normal. It is caused by the clutch plate coming up to speed upon activation and the brake slowing the blade pulley upon deactivation. For long PTO life, do not engage or disengage the clutch under full throttle, but only between 1/2 and 3/4 throttle.*

Prior to testing the circuit, the PTO clutch windings must be checked for shorts and the airgap must be set to 0.015 inch.

Testing PTO clutch windings for shorts

Shorted windings will feed DC current into the engine crankshaft. To return to ground, the current arcs through the oil film at the main bearing surfaces, eroding and pitting the bearings and causing major engine damage. Perform the following tests with the engine off to check for shorted windings.

To perform a winding-resistance test:

1. Disconnect the main harness connector from the clutch connector.

> *NOTE*
> *Resistance specifications in Step 2 are for an ambient temperature of 70° F (21° C) and may vary depending on the winding temperature and the test-equipment accuracy. If the mower has just been used, allow the engine and clutch to cool prior to testing.*

2. Zero an ohmmeter on the R ×1 scale, then measure resistance between the two clutch-lead terminals. Resistance should read 2.4-2.9 S on the Warner Electric Model CVX clutch and 2.8-3.2 S on the Ogura Model MA-GT-EXM3X clutch.

3. Measure resistance between each clutch-lead terminal and a clean ground spot on the clutch housing. Resistance should read infinity/no-continuity at both terminal-to-ground tests.

4. Connect a 14 gauge or larger jumper wire from the positive terminal of a fully charged battery to one of the clutch-lead terminals. Touch an equal-sized jumper wire from the negative battery terminal to the engine crankshaft. Listen and watch for the clutch to engage.

5. Repeat Step 4 with the other clutch-lead terminal.

6. Reverse the battery jumper connections and repeat Steps 4-5.

7. If the clutch engaged during any of test Steps 4-6, the clutch has shorted windings and must be replaced.

A current-draw test should also be used to check for shorted windings. This test is also performed with the engine off and the main harness-to-clutch connectors disconnected. Refer to **Figure 50** and perform the following:

1. Set the test meter to the 10-amp scale.

2. Connect one ammeter lead to one terminal in the clutch-wire connector plug (A, **Figure 50**).

3. Connect the second ammeter lead to the main harness terminal, which feeds the meter-connected terminal in the clutch plug (C).

4. Connect a jumper between the remaining clutch and main harness terminals (B and D).

5. Turn the ignition switch on, but *do not start the engine.*

49

ENGINE CRANKING CIRCUIT TEST

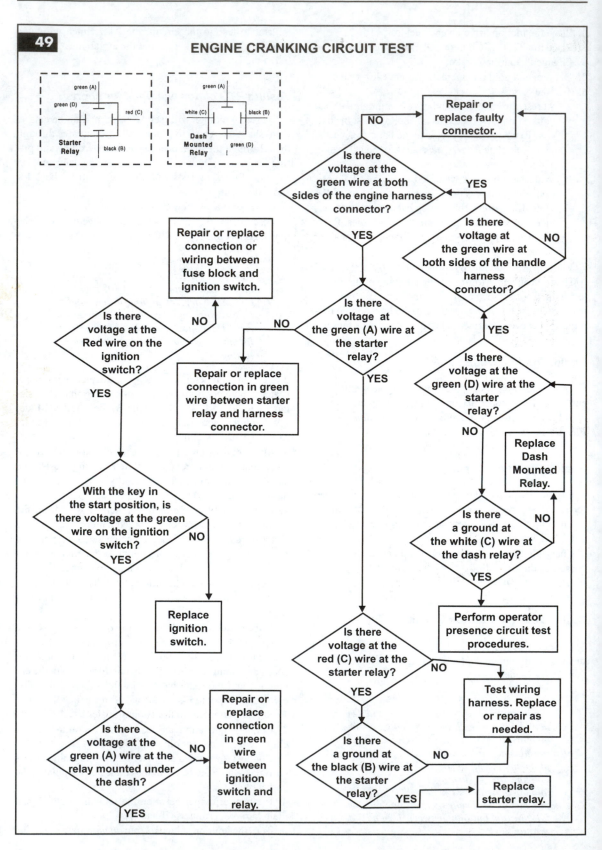

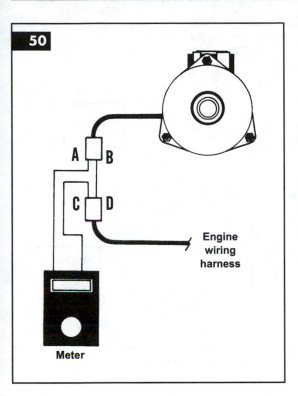

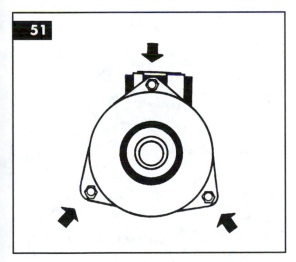

6. Activate the PTO switch. The ammeter should show a draw of approximately 4.0 amps. If the reading is significantly higher or lower than 4.0 amps, the clutch winding may be shorted or the PTO switch may be faulty. PTO switch testing will be covered in the following *Component Testing* section.

7. Turn the ignition switch off and deactivate the PTO switch.

Setting the PTO clutch airgap

To check and adjust the airgap:

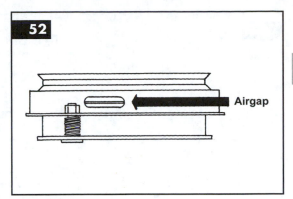

1. Access the three adjustment nuts on the bottom of the clutch (**Figure 51**).

2. Locate the airgap inspection windows on the side of the clutch housing (**Figure 52**). There is one window next to each adjusting nut.

3. Using a .015 inch feeler gauge, measure the gap between the armature and the rotor. If necessary, loosen or tighten the adjusting nut to set the airgap to specification. Do this at all three windows.

4. Repeat Step 3 two more times to ensure that the airgap did not change on one side of the clutch when the gap was adjusted on the opposite side.

5. Carefully rotate the clutch rotor pulley by hand to ensure smooth operation.

Troubleshooting the PTO circuit

To troubleshoot the PTO circuit:

1. Ensure that the battery is fully charged, the wiring integrity is good, and the operator presence circuit is functioning properly;

2. Turn the PTO switch on;

3. Turn the ignition switch to the ON position, but do not start the engine.

4. Follow the steps in the diagram in **Figure 53**.

Component Testing

Switches and other individual components may be removed and bench-tested, but for system accuracy, they should be tested in-place to ensure that the linkages which operate them are working properly. Otherwise, a switch may be thought to be at fault when the real problem is a linkage adjustment or malfunction.

Continuity (resistance) testing should be performed with an ohmmeter.

CAUTION
Never perform a resistance test on a "hot" circuit, one which is powered by the mower's battery. Serious meter damage will result; personal injury may also occur.

53

PTO CIRCUIT TEST

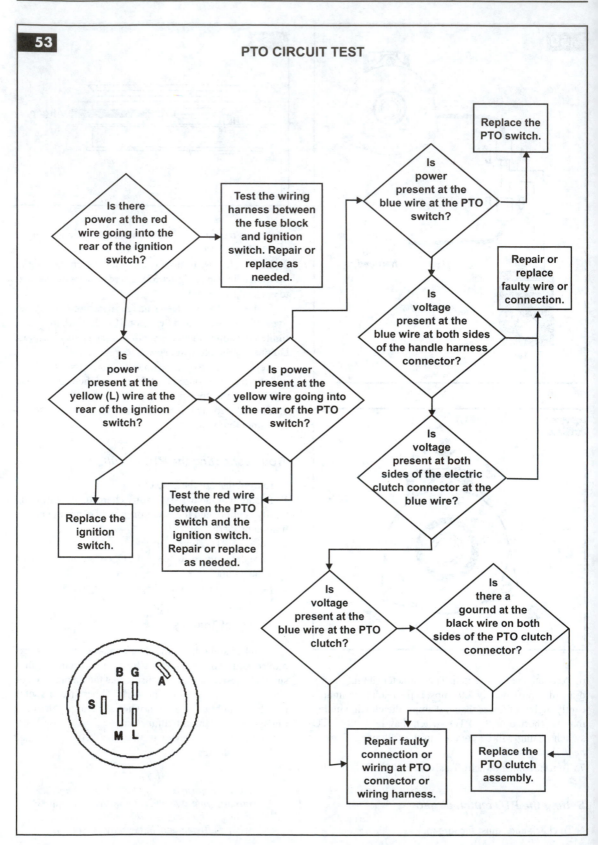

Is there power at the red wire going into the rear of the ignition switch?

Test the wiring harness between the fuse block and ignition switch. Repair or replace as needed.

Is power present at the blue wire at the PTO switch?

Replace the PTO switch.

Is power present at the yellow (L) wire at the rear of the ignition switch?

Is power present at the yellow wire going into the rear of the PTO switch?

Is voltage present at the blue wire at both sides of the handle harness connector?

Repair or replace faulty wire or connection.

Is voltage present at both sides of the electric clutch connector at the blue wire?

Replace the ignition switch.

Test the red wire between the PTO switch and the ignition switch. Repair or replace as needed.

Is voltage present at the blue wire at the PTO clutch?

Is there a gournd at the black wire on both sides of the PTO clutch connector?

Repair faulty connection or wiring at PTO connector or wiring harness.

Replace the PTO clutch assembly.

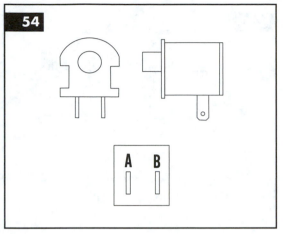

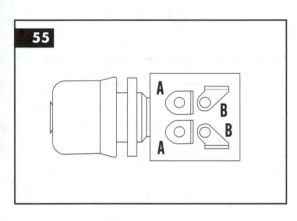

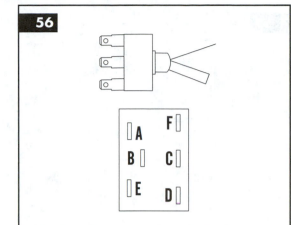

Single-pole switch

Scag single-pole switches (**Figure 54**) normally have one pair of terminals and are used in the operator presence circuit as neutral interlock switches. They are classified as normally-closed (NC) switches since, in the switch's normal position, with the spring-loaded activation plunger out, the internal contacts are closed, allowing current to pass across the two exposed terminals. To test these switches:

1. Unplug the harness connector from the switch terminals.
2. Connect the ohmmeter probes to the switch terminals.
3. The ohmmeter should read continuity between terminals A and B with the plunger out and infinity/no-continuity with the plunger in.

Double-pole switch

Scag double-pole switches (**Figure 55**) normally have two pair of terminals and are used as neutral-lever interlock switches. Only one pair of side-by-side terminals will pass current at a time, depending upon the plunger position. The switch activation plunger is spring-loaded to a normally-out position. To test these switches:

1. Unplug the harness connector(s) from the switch terminals.
2. Connect the ohmmeter probes to one pair of switch terminals at a time.
3. The ohmmeter should read continuity between the A terminals and infinity/no-continuity between the B terminals with the plunger in the out, relaxed position.
4. The ohmmeter should read continuity between the B terminals and infinity/no-continuity between the A terminals with the plunger pushed in.

PTO switches

Scag uses two styles of PTO switches – the toggle type (**Figure 56**) and the push-pull type. The push-pull type has two variations – the 5-terminal switch (**Figure 57**) and the 8-terminal switch (**Figure 58**).

Refer to the switch-terminal diagrams in **Figures 56-58** and the **Figure 59** PTO Switch Terminal Continuity Chart to test the PTO switches.

Ignition switches

Scag uses two styles of ignition switches – one for recoil-start engines (**Figure 60**) and one for electric-start engines (**Figure 61**). Abbreviations for these switches are as follows:

A = Accessories   L = Lights
B = Battery   M = Magneto
G = Ground   S = Start

To test the recoil-start switch, connect the ohmmeter leads to the two terminals, M and G. With the key off, there should be continuity between M and G. With the key in the run position, there should be no continuity between M and G.

To test the electric-start switch, connect the ohmmeter leads to the terminals noted in the following list:

1. With the key in the OFF position, there should be continuity between terminals A-M-G.

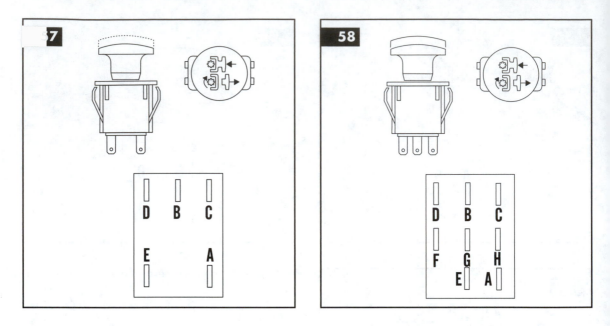

PTO Switch Terminal Continuity Chart							
SWITCH	**Toggle**		**5-Terminal Push-Pull**		**8-Terminal Push-Pull**	
POSITION	**Off**	**On**	**Off**	**On**	**Off**	**On**
CONTINUITY TERMINAL PAIRS	B-E C-D	A-B C-F	A-E C-D	B-C	C-D F-H	A-E B-C G-H
NO-CONTINUITY TERMINAL PAIRS	A-B C-F	B-E C-D	B-C	A-E C-D	A-E B-C G-H	C-D F-H

2. With the key in the RUN position, there should be continuity between terminals A-B-L.

3. With the key in the START position, there should be continuity between terminals B-L-S.

Relays

On some Scag units with electric-start Kawasaki engines, a start relay is used in the wiring harness instead of the usual solenoid mounted on or near the starter. **Figure 62** shows the relay terminal arrangement as well as the internal schematic of the relay.

Terminals B and D are connected to the internal relay winding. Terminals A and C are normally not connected, as the internal plunger is spring-loaded to keep the A-C contact strip away from the terminals. When voltage is applied to B and D, the electromagnetism created by the

winding pulls the plunger toward the winding, causing the contact strip to join A and C.

To test the relay:

1. Carefully note the relay harness positions, then disconnect the wires;

2. Connect ohmmeter leads to terminals A and C;

3. Apply 12 volts to terminals B and D (polarity is not important);

4. Note the ohmmeter reading.

If the relay is functioning properly, there will be no continuity between A and C until power is applied to B and D, at which time A and C should read continuity. Any other test results indicate a faulty relay.

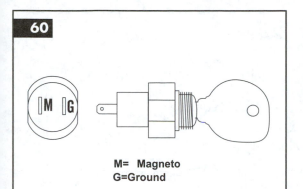

M= Magneto
G=Ground

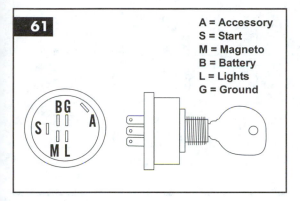

A = Accessory
S = Start
M = Magneto
B = Battery
L = Lights
G = Ground

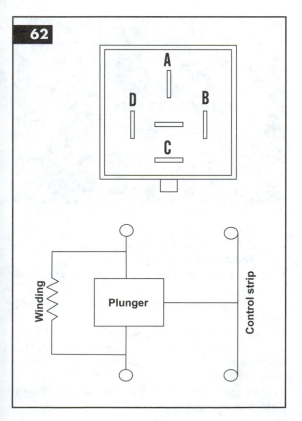

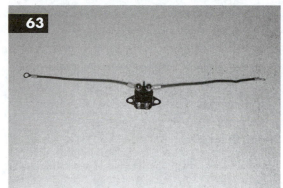

2

Solenoids

Solenoids are of two basic types – internally grounded or externally grounded. The grounding refers to the primary, low-current circuit. They can be identified by the number of terminals on the solenoid case.

All solenoids used in the starting circuits of the engines on these units have two large secondary-circuit terminals. These terminals use either 1/4 inch or 5/16 inch terminal studs, and are for the battery-to-starter cables.

Externally-grounded solenoids (**Figure 63**) have two smaller primary-circuit terminals. Internally-grounded solenoids only have one small terminal.

Troubleshooting a solenoid can usually be done quickly with the solenoid in the system.

1. To troubleshoot an internally-grounded solenoid:
   a. Remove the ignition key from the switch so the engine does not start.
   b. Ensure that the unit is in neutral and that the parking brake is set.
   c. Place the throttle control in the SLOW position.
   d. Remove the main harness wire from the small solenoid terminal.
   e. Using a short jumper wire, connect one end of the wire to the small terminal; momentarily touch the other end to the large terminal of the cable coming from the positive battery post.
   f. If the starter activates, the solenoid is good.
2. To troubleshoot an externally-grounded solenoid:
   a. Remove the ignition key from the switch so the engine does not start.
   b. Ensure that the unit is in neutral and that the parking brake is set.
   c. Place the throttle control in the SLOW position.
   d. Remove the main harness wires from the small solenoid terminals.
   e. Taking a pair of jumper wires, use one wire to connect one small solenoid terminal to the positive battery post. Connect one end of the other jumper to the other small solenoid terminal. Momentarily

touch the other end of the second jumper wire to the negative battery post.

CAUTION
Do not allow the two jumper wires to contact each other.

f. If the starter activates, the solenoid is good.

Wiring Diagrams

Engine wiring diagrams are located in each particular engine section.

Mower wiring diagrams are divided into three groups – engine deck harness, handle harness, and relay harness. These diagrams are located at the end of this book.

DRIVE SYSTEM FUNDAMENTALS

Scag SWZ(U) units use a 2-pump, 2-motor hydrostatic drive system to propel the mower. **Figure 64** shows a flow diagram of the drive circuit. The tank (reservoir) and filter are the only components shared by the system. The right-side components (pump and motor) propel only the right drive wheel; the left-side components propel only the left drive wheel.

WARNING
Hydrostatic systems operate under high pressure and uncomfortable heat. Wear appropriate protective apparel when servicing hydrostatic components. Never service a hydrostatic system with the machine running, unless specific instructions state otherwise. Always allow the engine and hydrostatic system to cool prior to servicing.

NOTE
Cleanliness is crucial to a hydrostatic system. Ensure that the external areas of the hydrostatic components are kept clean, as dirt buildup causes the pumps and motors to run hot.

NOTE
Top speed is for transport only. It should not be used when mowing.

The 2-pump, 2-motor hydrostatic system functions as follows:

1. The hydrostatic reservoir (**Figure 64**) is the tank which holds most of the oil for the system. The reservoir serves three functions.
   a. It contains the oil for the system.
   b. It cools the oil. As oil is pumped through the system to perform work, it becomes hot. Oil returning to the reservoir transfers some of this heat to the tank walls where it is dispersed into the surrounding air. This is

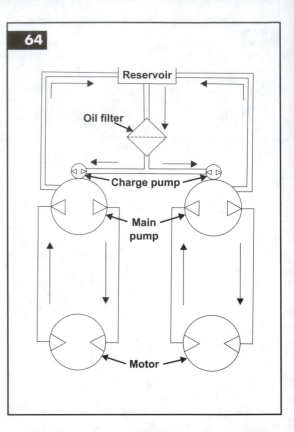

also why tanks are thin and long, as a long, thin tank has more surface area than a square-shaped tank, thus providing better cooling capacity.
   c. It allows small air bubbles in the system to break up.

2. The oil is drawn from the reservoir, through the oil filter (**Figure 64**).

3. Filtered oil then splits into two lines, one line feeding the charge pump on each main pump (**Figure 64**). The charge pump is a preliminary pump which keeps the main pump filled with oil.

4. In the main pump, the oil is pressurized and fed to the wheel motors (**Figure 64**).

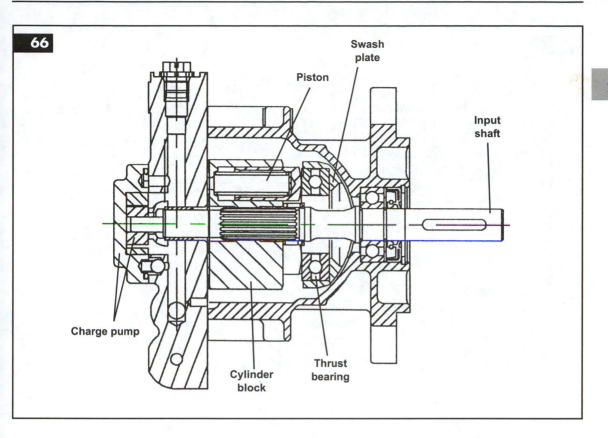

66

Swash plate

Piston

Input shaft

Charge pump

Cylinder block

Thrust bearing

2

5. After doing its work in the wheel motors, the oil returns to the main pumps where it is either sent back to the reservoir or slightly cooled and pumped back to the wheel motor.

The arrows in **Figure 64** show the direction of oil flow to propel the wheel motors forward. For reverse, the arrows between the main pumps and the wheel motors would point the opposite direction.

Figure 65 shows the hydrostatic pumps and the wheel motors as they are mounted on the mower. The pumps mount on the top of the engine deck directly behind the engine. The wheel motors mount on either side of the engine deck, with the drive wheel/tire assemblies mounted directly to the wheel motors.

Hydrostatic Pumps

Scag SWZ(U) units use Hydro-Gear® Model BDP-10L pumps to create the pressure necessary to drive the wheel motors. The BDP-10L is a variable-displacement pump with a maximum displacement of 0.61 cubic inch (10 cc) per revolution. **Figure 66** and **Figure 67** show two cutaway views of the BDP-10L. **Figure 67** is rotated 90° away from **Figure 66**.

The BDL-10L pumps use spherical-nosed pistons arranged axially around the input shaft. The pistons are spring-loaded in order to be held tightly against a thrust

bearing race. The thrust bearing rides inside a cradle-style swashplate. The swashplate uses an externally-operated lever to give direct-proportional displacement control, depending on the lever position. Reversing the direction of the swashplate angle, or tilt, reverses the flow of oil from the pump. This reverses the direction of rotation of the output shaft of the motor being powered by the pump. A fixed-displacement gerotor-style charge pump feeds a constant supply of oil from the reservoir and filter to the axial pistons.

Figure 67 is a flow chart showing the internal oil paths. Line A and Line B are the output pressure lines to the wheel motors.

The pumps are belt-driven from a pulley on the engine crankshaft, above the blade clutch (**Figure 68**, hydrostatic filter removed for clarity). A spring-loaded idler pulley keeps the belt in constant tension anytime the engine is running, except when the tension is manually released during cold-weather starts. If the chain is not in the tensioned position while mowing, the belt will slip and the traction drive will not propel the mower correctly, if at all.

Bypass valve

At times, it may be necessary to move the mower without the engine running. To do this, each pump is equipped with a bypass valve, sometimes referred to as a dump

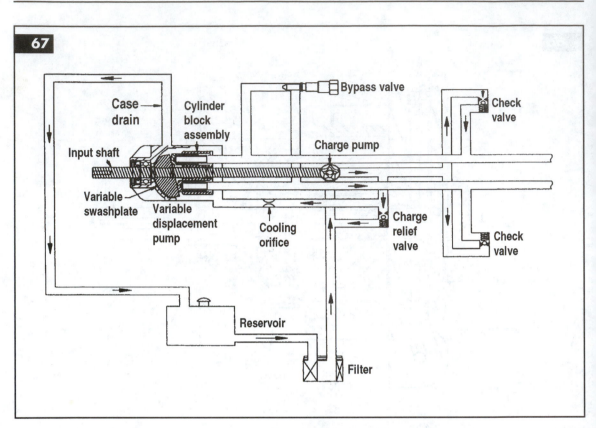

67

Case drain — Cylinder block assembly — Bypass valve — Check valve — Input shaft — Charge pump — Variable swashplate — Variable displacement pump — Cooling orifice — Charge relief valve — Check valve — Reservoir — Filter

valve. Activating the bypass valve allows oil to be internally routed directly from the inlet side of the pump through the wheel-motor circuit to the pump's outlet side.

Figure 69 shows the location of the valve on the pump. It is a screw-type bypass valve and is fully open when unscrewed two turns maximum. The left-side valve is always accessed from the rear of the mower. Depending on the model, the right-side valve can be accessed from either the rear or the front of the right-side pump.

> *WARNING*
> *Opening the bypass valve(s) will cause a loss of hydrostatic braking. Exercise extreme care when opening the bypass valves, especially on sloping ground.*

Always remember to fully close the bypass valve(s) prior to operating the mower.

Hydrostatic Wheel Motors

Scag SWZ(U) units use a pair of Ross Model MB or MF Torqmotor™ wheel motors to propel the mowers. A cutaway view of these motors is shown in **Figure 70**.

Pressurized oil from the hydrostatic pumps is fed through the system's high-pressure hoses to the wheel motors. This oil travels through the motor's internal passages (A, **Figure 70**) where it is forced against the

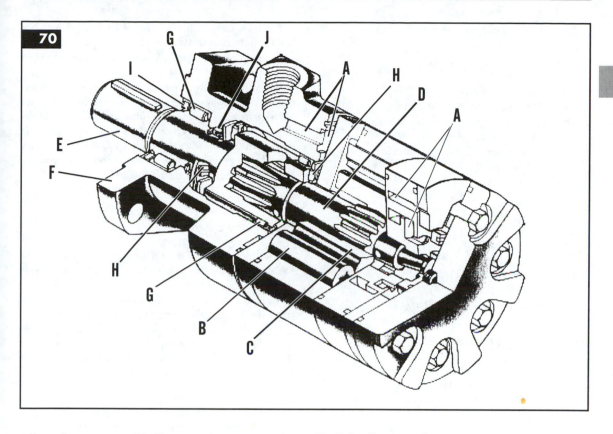

70

roller-style rotor vanes (B). The vanes, in turn, cause the vane housing (C) to rotate. Reversing the direction of the incoming oil supply reverses the direction of the vanes and vane housing, thereby reversing the motor. The vane housing is splined to the output shaft (D, **Figure 70**), and the output shaft is splined to the wheel hub shaft (E). The wheel hub shaft is held in position inside the flanged motor mount housing (F, **Figure 70**) radially by a pair of needle-style roller bearings (G) and axially by a pair of needle-style thrust bearings (H). Contaminants are prevented from entering the motor by the outer dirt-and-water seal (I, **Figure 70**) and the inner high-pressure seal (J). The flanged motor mount housing fastens directly to the mower frame, holding the wheels in alignment.

Service and parts

Only complete wheel motor assemblies are available through Scag; individual Ross wheel motor parts are not available from Scag.

DRIVE-TRAIN TROUBLESHOOTING

NOTE
Numbers in parentheses following the possible problem are for the chapters where solutions to the problem are found.

No Drive Forward Or Reverse

1. Pump bypass valves open. (2, 11, 12)
2. Hydrostatic drive belt broken or slipping. (12)
3. Control linkage not operating. (11, 12)
4. Low hydrostatic fluid level. (2, 3, 12)

No Drive At Normal Maximum Speed

1. Engine RPM not set correctly. (5-10)
2. Control linkage binding or damaged. (11, 12)
3. Bypass valves partially open. (2, 11, 12)
4. Charge check valve stuck open (problem one direction only). (12)
5. Internal component wear or leakage. (12)

Drive Jerky Or Erratic

1. Plugged filter. (3, 12)
2. Inlet air leak. (2, 12)

Drive Sluggish Under Load but Normal Without Load

1. Hydrostatic drive belt slipping. (12)
2. Low hydrostatic fluid level. (2, 3, 12)
3. Water in hydrostatic fluid. (2, 12)

4. Internal component wear or leakage. (12)

Unit Does Not Track Straight

1. Improperly inflated tire(s). (2, 3, 12)
2. Control linkage misadjusted or damaged. (11, 12)
3. One bypass valve partially open or loose. (2, 11, 12)
4. Inlet air leak. (2, 12)
5. Internal component wear or leakage. (12)
6. Incorrectly-adjusted brake. (3, 15)

Drive Runs Noisy

1. Low or contaminated oil. (2, 3, 12)
2. Excessive engine RPM. (5-10)
3. Air in hydrostatic fluid. (2, 3, 12)
4. Bypass valve loose. (2, 11, 12)
5. Pump belt drive faulty. (2, 12)
6. Damaged or blocked line or filter. (12)

Drive Components Overheating

1. Debris buildup.
2. Oil contaminated or low. (2, 3, 12)
3. Air in system or air leak. (2, 3, 12)
4. Overloaded. (2, 3)

Leaking

1. Loose connections or fasteners. (12)
2. Faulty gaskets or worn seals. (12)
3. Air trapped in oil. (2, 3, 12)
4. Hydrostatic reservoir overfilled. (2, 3, 12)

LUBRICATION

NOTE
Cleanliness is of paramount importance when working on a hydraulic system. Make sure that no dirt or debris is allowed to come into contact with any internal hydrostatic component. Also ensure that the external areas of the hydrostatic components are kept clean, as dirt buildup causes the pumps and motors to run hot.

Factory-installed lubricant is SAE 20W-50 petroleum-based oil with an API classification of SH or above. Acceptable substitutes are Mobil Super HP, Amoco Ultimate, Viscosity Oil, Shell Gemini, Aero Shell, or Helix Ultra in SAE 5W-40, SAE 10W-40, or SAE 15W-50 grades.

If synthetic oil is preferred after a complete system flush, Mobil 1 SAE 15W-50 is recommended; 5W-30 or 10W-30 are acceptable substitutes.

The reservoir is full when the oil level is one inch below the bottom of the filler neck.

To inspect the oil, use a *clean* siphon to draw a sample from the reservoir.

If the oil is bubbly or cloudy, it is usually an indication that the suction side of the system has an air leak. The suction side includes the reservoir, filter, and all hoses and fittings between the reservoir and the main pumps. Air in the system will also cause the unit drive to be jerky and/or noisy. To solve the problem, check and secure all hoses, connections, and fittings. After the air leak has been corrected, the system will need to be purged of any remaining air.

Purging the System

The amount of time needed for purging will depend on the amount of air previously drawn in. To purge the system:

1. Raise the rear of the mower so the drive wheels do not touch the floor. Safely support the mower in this position.
2. With the parking brake on, the cutter blades disengaged, the speed adjustment lever in the neutral position, and the neutral latches in the neutral lock position, start the engine and run the engine at idle speed.

WARNING
Make sure ventilation is adequate if the engine is to be run in a confined area. Exhaust fumes are toxic and deadly.

3. Release the parking brake.
4. Operate one of the wheel drive systems, going slowly from neutral to full forward, back to neutral, then into reverse and back into neutral again. Continue this process until the drive wheel operates smoothly and quietly, usually about 6-10 cycles. Check the reservoir oil level; add oil as needed. Remember that the reservoir is full when the oil level is one inch below the bottom of the filler neck.
5. Repeat Step 4 with the other side drive wheel.
6. Stop the engine and reset the parking brake.
7. Set the mower back down onto the floor.
8. Test-run the mower to ensure that all air has been purged from the system. Repeat the purging, if necessary.

Replacing the Oil

Milky oil is an indication of water in the oil. The two most likely sources of water contamination are high-pressure washing of the unit and leaving the unit out in rainy weather. Water-contaminated oil must be replaced.

Perform the following:

1. Jack up the rear of the mower so the drive wheels do not touch the floor. Safely support the mower in this position.

2. Locate the supply hose which runs from the reservoir outlet fitting to the inlet side of the oil filter base.

3. Pinch the hose just above the filter base fitting, then loosen the hose clamp and remove the hose from the base fitting.

4. Drain the reservoir oil into an approved container.

5. Loosen the two main pump return hoses from the side reservoir fittings. Direct these hose ends into a container.

6. Replace the hydrostat oil filter. Using the same new oil which the system will be refilled with, pre-fill the new filter prior to installation.

7. Using a separate flush/supply tank with the same new oil the system will be refilled with, connect the tank to the filter base inlet fitting.

8. With the parking brake on, the cutter blades disengaged, the speed adjustment lever in the neutral position, and the neutral latches in the neutral lock position, start the engine and run the engine at idle speed.

WARNING
Make sure ventilation is adequate if the engine is to be run in a confined area. Exhaust fumes are toxic and deadly.

9. Release the parking brake.

10. While carefully monitoring the oil supply in the flush tank, operate one of the wheel drive systems, going slowly from neutral to full forward, back to neutral, then into reverse and back into neutral again. Continue this process until the oil coming from the return hose is no longer milky.

11. Repeat Step 10 with the other side drive wheel.

12. Stop the engine and reset the parking brake.

13. Disconnect the flush tank.

14. Carefully clean the fitting barbs on the exposed hose fittings. Install the hoses and snugly secure all hose clamps.

15. Refill the reservoir with the proper oil to within one inch of the bottom of the filler neck.

16. Repeat Steps 8-12 to purge any remaining air from the system. Note that the tank being monitored in Step 10 is now the mower reservoir, and the oil will be returning to the reservoir. Continue to monitor the reservoir oil level while purging.

17. Stop the engine and set the mower back down onto the floor.

CUTTER-DECK TROUBLESHOOTING

NOTE
Numbers in parentheses following the possible problem are for the chapters where solutions to the problem are found. Problems without end numbers have simple, common-sense solutions.

No Deck Drive

1. Broken or slipping belt. (14)
2. Faulty PTO switch. (14, 16)
3. Wiring disconnected. (14, 16, Wiring Diagrams)
4. Faulty clutch. (14, 16)
5. Debris-jammed blade(s). (2, 13)
6. Spindle seized. (13)

Deck Drive Noisy

1. Faulty belt(s) or idler(s). (14)
2. Loose or faulty clutch. (14)
3. Worn, dry, or loose spindle bearing(s). (13)
4. Bent blade(s) or spindle shaft(s). (13)
5. Grass debris packed under deck.
6. Loose components. (13, 14)

Mowing Irregularities

The numbered items in this section are the possible causes of the problem noted in each italicized heading. Following the numbered cause, in parentheses, are the solution(s) to that problem.

NOTE
Many problems associated with poor cutting are the result of dull blades. Dull or improperly sharpened blades not only cut unsatisfactorily, they can also overheat the engine by making it work harder to cut the grass, as well as overheating the deck belt(s), pulleys and bearings by causing excessive drag.

Figure 71 shows the correct cutting-edge angle as well as the maximum amount of sharpening a blade can accept before the cutter end becomes weak and dangerous. The 30° angle is recommended for normal cutting in average soils. Decrease the angle to 20°-25° for sandy soils. Increase the angle to 35°-40° for clay or heavy soils. Original blade width is the narrowest part of the blade – in this case, from the cutting edge to the inside edge of the clearance notch between the blade center and the liftwing.

CAUTION
Never mount a blade upside-down. The cutting edge of the blade should always be at the bottom of the blade, closest to the grass. When sharpening a blade, always remove cutting-edge metal from the top of the blade, never from the bottom. A very light deburring pass is all that should be done to the bottom of the cutting edge after the top is sharpened.

When sharpening with a grinding wheel, always keep the wheel dressed. *Never* allow the blade cutting edge to

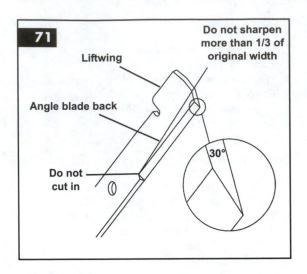

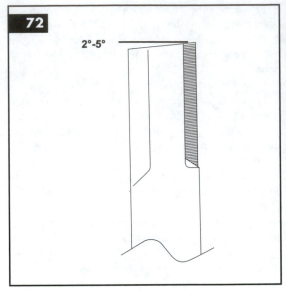

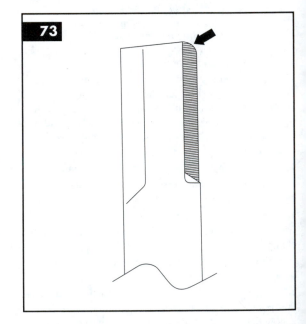

become hot enough to turn blue. This will remove the temper from the edge, thereby softening and weakening the cutting edge. Keep the cutting edge quenched while sharpening. If quenching produces steam, the cutting edge is too hot, and the metal will crystallize, further weakening the cutting edge. A quality quenching solution can be purchased from any machine-tool supply house.

Figure 72 shows the clearance angle which must be maintained on the blade ends. This prevents the end of the blade from hacking or chopping what the tip of the cutting edge may have not cut due to the traveling speed of the mower.

Figure 73 shows an unacceptable rounded cutting edge tip. This will tear the grass, giving an unsatisfactory cut. Always sharpen the blade tip as shown in **Figure 72**. Whenever a blade is sharpened, it must also be balanced. Prior to balancing, always clean all the grass debris from the blade – top, bottom, and edges. The vibration caused by out-of-balance blades is not only uncomfortable for the operator but also destructive to the mower.

NOTE
When reinstalling sharpened and balanced blades, torque the blade bolt 75 ft.-lb. (102 N•m).

Occasional stringers, or blades of uncut grass

See **Figure 74**.

1. Low engine RPM. (Run engine at full FAST setting; make sure that FAST setting is producing 3600 RPM.)

2. Ground speed too fast. (Reduce speed for conditions.)

3. Wet grass. (Allow grass to dry before cutting.)

4. Dull blades or improper sharpening. (Sharpen blades correctly.)

5. Grass debris packed under deck. (Clean underneath deck.)

6. Belt(s) slipping. (Adjust belt tension; check idler tension spring or cold-start linkage; replace belt[s] and/or pulley[s].)

Strips or streaks of uncut grass within deck swath

See **Figure 75**.

1. Dull or worn blades; improper blade sharpening. (Sharpen blades correctly.)

2. Low engine RPM. (Run engine at full FAST setting; ensure that FAST setting is producing 3600 RPM.)

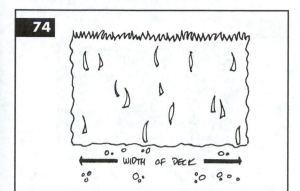

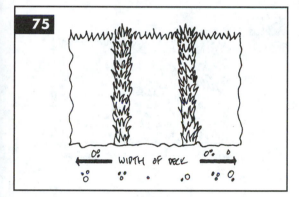

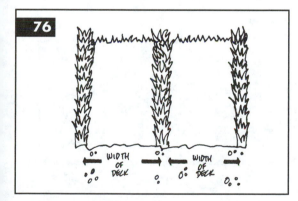

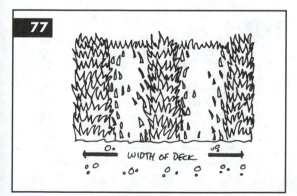

3. Belt(s) slipping. (Adjust belt tension; check idler tension spring; replace belt[s] and/or pulley[s].)

4. Grass debris packed under deck. (Clean underneath deck.)

5. Ground speed too fast. (Reduce speed for conditions.)

6. Wet grass. (Allow grass to dry before cutting.)

7. Bent blade(s) or spindle(s). (Replace blade[s] or spindle[s].)

Strips or streaks of uncut grass between deck paths

See **Figure 76**.

1. Insufficient overlap between rows. (Increase the overlap of each pass.)

Inconsistent cut on flat ground, including wavy appearance, scalloped cut, or uneven contour

See **Figure 77**.

1. Liftwing(s) worn off blade(s). (Replace blade[s].)

2. Blade(s) upside-down. (Remount blade[s] with cutting edge down, toward grass. Liftwing always mounts up, towards deck.)

3. Too much deck pitch/blade angle. (Adjust pitch and level.)

4. Deck mounted improperly. (Correctly mount the deck.)

5. Bent spindle-mount area. (Carefully straighten deck; replace deck.)

6. Dull blade(s). (Sharpen blades correctly.)

7. Grass debris packed under deck. (Clean underneath deck.)

Inconsistent cut on rough ground, including wavy appearance, scalloped cut, or uneven contour

See **Figure 78**.

1. Uneven ground. (It may help to change the direction of cut, reduce ground speed, and/or raise cutting height. Makes sure the blades are sharp and mounted correctly, and there is no grass debris packed under the deck.)

Clean but sloping cut across the width of the cutting path

See **Figure 79**.

1. Unequal tire pressures. (Check tire pressures – 25 psi [165 kPa] front/caster, 15 psi [100 kPa] rear/drive.)

2. Unequal tire diameters. (Accurately measure paired tire diameters. If a tire has just been replaced, ensure that it is identical to the original. Same-size tires from different manufacturers can be different diameters when inflated.)

3. Deck mounted incorrectly. (Correctly mount the deck.)

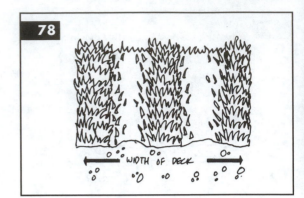

Patchy scalping; blades shaving dirt or cutting too close to the ground

See **Figure 80**.
1. Unequal or low tire pressures. (Check tire pressures – 25 psi [165 kPa] front/caster, 15 psi [100 kPa] rear/drive.)
2. Ground speed too fast. (Reduce speed for conditions.)
3. Uneven or rough ground. (It may help to change the direction of cut, reduce ground speed, and/or raise cutting height. Ensure that the blades are sharp and mounted correctly, and that there is no grass debris packed under the deck.)
4. Cutting too low for the terrain. (Raise the cutting height for ground conditions.)
5. Wet grass. (Allow the grass to dry before cutting.)

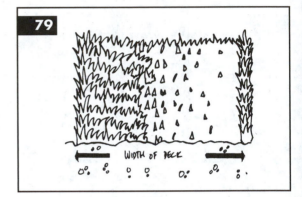

Step-cut ridge within the cutting path

See **Figure 81**.
1. Blade(s) not evenly mounted. (Correctly mount blade[s] or adjust pitch and level.)
2. Bent blade(s). (Replace blade[s].)
3. Internal spindle failure. (Repair or replace the spindle.)
4. Spindle(s) mounted improperly. (Correctly mount spindle[s].)

Each blade producing a sloped cut

See **Figure 82**.
1. Bent spindle-mount area or deck housing. (Carefully straighten deck; replace deck.)
2. Internal spindle failure(s). (Repair or replace the spindle(s).)

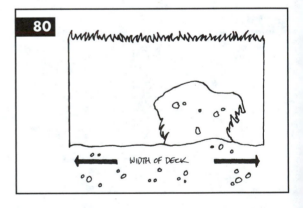

Checking for Bent Blades, Blade Bolts, or Spindles

To check the blades, spindle bolts or spindle shafts for straightness, refer to **Figure 83** and perform the following test:
1. Remove the blade drive-belt shield from the top of the deck, then:
   a. On units with spring-loaded belt idlers, carefully rotate the belt off the idler pulley;
   b. On units with fixed idlers, loosen the locknut on the J-bolt to create enough slack in the belt so the belt can be rotated off the idler pulley. This will give the spindles and blades the freedom to rotate individually.
2. Set the parking brake.
3. Raise the front of the mower to access the blades. Ensure that the mower is safely supported.

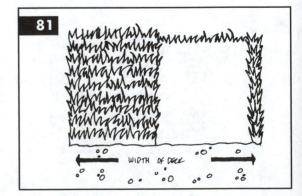

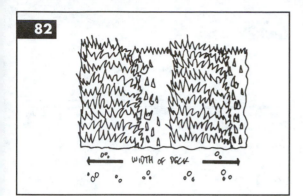

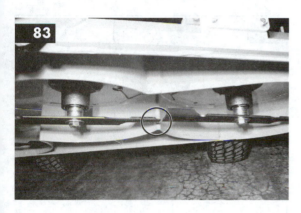

4. Using heavy gloves to guard against injury from sharp blades, rotate the left and right blades (left and center blades on 3-blade decks) so that the tips of the cutting edges align. Note the alignment.

5. While holding the left blade in position, rotate the right (center) blade 180° so that the opposite tip lines up with the stationary blade tip. Note the alignment.

6. Hold the right (center) blade in position, then rotate the left blade 180° to align the blade tips. Note the alignment.

7. On 3-blade decks, repeat Steps 4-6 with the center and right blades.

8. There should not be more than 1/16 inch misalignment between any of the tip match-ups in Steps 4-7. Any serious misalignment indicates either bent blades, bent blade bolts, bent spindle shafts, or faulty spindle bearings.

    a. If the cause of misalignment is not readily apparent, begin by rocking the spindle to check for loose bearings.

    b. If the bearings appear loose, refer to Chapter Thirteen for spindle service procedures.

    c. If the bearings are good, continue by replacing one suspect blade and blade bolt at a time.

    d. If, after replacing a pair of blades, there is still misalignment, the suspect spindle shaft is probably bent and must be replaced. Refer to Chapter Thirteen.

    e. The deck could also be bent in the area where the spindle housing mounts. Although straightening the deck is possible, it must be attempted with the utmost caution. Replacing the deck is the recommended solution.

9. Reinstall the belts onto the idler pulleys. On fixed-idler systems, refer to *Drive Belts, Fixed-Idler System* in Chapter Three for proper belt tension adjustment.

DRIVE BELTS

Belt problems have three major sources: misalignment, improper tension, and

Misalignment

Belts operate best when the pulleys are properly aligned. **Figure 84** (A) illustrates a belt running between two properly-aligned pulleys.

Tests have shown that just over 6% of belt life is lost for every degree of misalignment. **Figure 84** (B) illustrates two pulleys with plane misalignment. **Figure 84** (C) illustrates two pulleys with compound misalignment — plane misalignment plus shaft misalignment. Compound misalignment is usually caused by shaft bearing problems, especially with spring-loaded idler pulleys, as belt tension tends to pull the two pulleys together.

Some applications require a certain amount of misalignment. In these cases, the belts are designed with a deeper cross-section to reduce twisting and "rolling-over" in the pulley groove, and the pulleys have deeper, radiused flanges to "lead" the belt into the groove.

To check the alignment of pulleys, place a straightedge across the faces of the pulleys as shown in **Figure 85**. If the inner and outer edges of both pulleys contact the straightedge, the pulleys are aligned. On pulleys with different wall thicknesses, the difference between the thick and the thin wall must be compensated for along the straightedge. If misalignment is evident, locate and correct the cause.

Belt cross-section

Figure 86 shows a deep cross-section belt in a leading-groove pulley. This is an "engineered-misalignment" pulley, and the deep cross-section belt not only resists twisting in this application, but also has a large contact surface area on both sides of the belt to provide the maximum amount of grip. The more the grip, the less the slip, provided the belt is tensioned properly.

Figure 87 shows the same pulley as **Figure 86**, but with a shallow cross-section belt such as a fractional horsepower belt. In some cases, the depth of the belt is less than the top width. Even in perfect alignment situations, these belts provide unsatisfactory results in two areas: They do not have the proper gripping capacity,

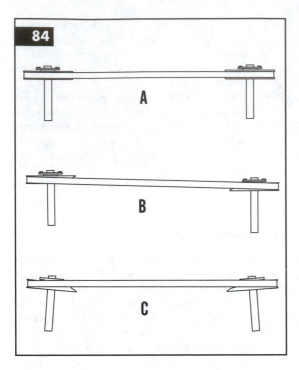

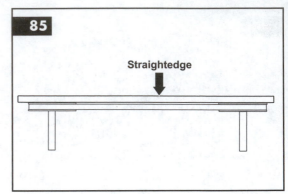

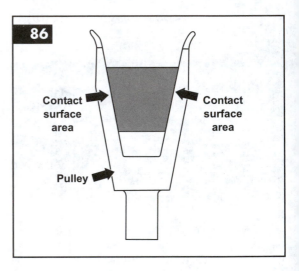

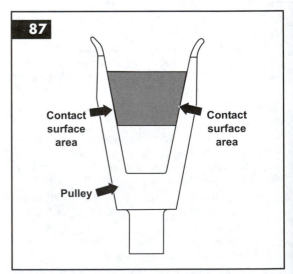

allowing slippage and overheating, especially under heavy loads, and they are more prone to twisting and rolling over due to the momentary slack created during periods of engagement and disengagement.

Figure 88 shows cross-sectional views of the two types of belt construction.

Figure 88 (A) illustrates the wrapped belt. This belt receives its name from the fact that each belt is individually manufactured, then wrapped with a rubberized fabric material covering all of the belt's internal structure. The wrap surface is not seriously affected by a slight amount of slippage, and it increases belt life by helping the belt retain its shape. This type of belt construction works well in situations where good clutching characteristics and smooth engagements are required.

Figure 88 (B) illustrates the raw edge or raw-sided belt. These belts are cut from a continuous band composed of the layers which make up the belt's internal structure. This is especially helpful when a matched set of belts is needed, as all the belts cut from the band are identical in length. The raw sides, being exposed, provide superior gripping qualities over the wrapped belt. They normally have higher strength and can handle more horsepower than wrapped belts. Because of their grip, they have limited clutch-slip ability, and are usually slightly noisier when engaged. Instead of being wrapped in rubberized fabric, these belts have laminated layers of fabric at the bottom and the top of the belt.

Although all of a belt's components are important, the component which contributes most to the strength of the belt is the layer of tensile cords which runs lengthwise inside the belt. These cords are usually either polyester or Kevlar. Polyester is most common, but it tends to stretch, requiring several adjustments over the life of the belt.

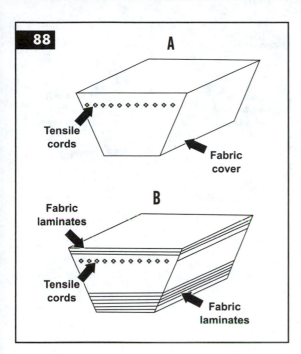

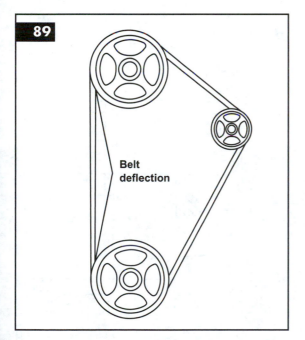

Kevlar is the strongest belt cord material and has negligible stretch, requiring minimal maintenance.

Figure 88 shows the tensile cords mounted toward the wide top of the belt. On some belts which flex both directions — forward around the drive pulleys, then backward around the "flat" idler pulleys — the layer of tensile cords is placed closer to the center of the belt to equalize flexing.

Improper Tension

Correct tension is critical toward proper belt operation and life expectancy, mainly because of heat. Testing has shown that belt life is reduced by half for every 25° F increase in belt temperature above the temperature at which the belt was designed to operate. Over-tensioning and under-tensioning both create additional heat: over-tensioning due to the excess heat of friction from the belt being too tight, and under-tensioning by slippage and the slapping of the belt against the pulley groove. Over-tensioning also overheats the pulleys, shafts and bearings due to the belt being too tight, thereby transferring additional heat to the belt.

A quality belt-tensioning tool is the best way to check belt tension. Always follow the instructions which come with the tool. Tension should be checked in the center of the longest belt span between two pulleys (**Figure 89**). The following formula can be used to calculate the amount of deflection required for proper tension. Belt span length divided by 64 equals the amount of deflection that should result when a force of 8-10 pounds is applied to the center of the belt. For example, if the span length is 32 inches, 32 divided by 64 equals 1/2. Applying 8-10 pounds of force should produce a deflection of 1/2 inch. Note that tension does not need to be checked if the idler is spring-loaded.

Heat

Belt life is reduced by 50% for every 25° F increase in belt temperature. Misalignment is one source of excess belt heat. Incorrect tension is another.

A third source of excess heat is the pulleys, themselves. A pulley running hot due to a faulty bearing will pass the heat to the belt. Grass debris buildup in the bottom of the pulley groove (**Figure 90**) reduces the normal belt-to-pulley side contact areas which is where the belt is supposed to get its traction. Debris buildup requires the load to be taken from the bottom of the belt and creates a belt rocking motion inside the pulley groove. This causes slippage, further increasing belt temperature. It also causes rapid wear on the inside diameter of the belt. Always keep the bottoms of the pulley grooves clean.

On units which operate in humid environments, especially a mower which may have been out of service for some time, check the pulley grooves for rust and corrosion. These cause additional friction between the belt and pulley grooves, producing higher belt temperatures. The roughness of the rust and corrosion also cause more rapid wear on the sides of the belt.

Load shock

A belt which seems to be in otherwise good condition but has a break area where it appears to have been pulled apart or snapped in two is a victim of load shock. When the mower is mowing, and one blade is stopped suddenly by a tree root, large rock, or other unseen solid object, the shock can be transferred to the belt. This sometimes snaps the belt in two. If this happens, also inspect the blades, blade bolts, shafts and pulleys for straightness and alignment, as the belt is the secondary recipient of the load shock, with the primary damage being done elsewhere.

Twigs

Even with the best of guards and shields, twigs, wire, hay twine and other debris can get into belt drive systems. Most of the time, they're small enough to be discharged to a harmless corner of the system. At times, though, they find their way into the belts and pulleys. When this happens, they may jam the drive, preventing it from turning; cause the belt to jump off the pulley, possibly damaging the belt; or jam against a part of the frame while rubbing against the belt or pulley, causing one or both to overheat. A large enough piece of debris rubbing against the rotating belt can even cause the belt to smoke.

Dimensioning

Some belt problems can be traced to having the wrong-sized belt, especially if the belt was recently replaced. Aside from cross-sectional differences between belts, there can also be variations in length. These differences can lead to improper tensioning and insufficient or too much idler adjustment, resulting in interference between drive components and adjoining chassis members. Always ensure that replacement belts exactly match original equipment specifications.

Pulley groove damage

A pinched groove will cause binding and momentary belt tightening every time the pulley rotates to the pinched spot.

Cast pulleys, when struck, may sometimes break off a piece of groove which may not be noticed immediately, especially if the break is on the hidden side of the pulley. The edge of the break will then scrape the belt every time the belt passes the break.

Pulley-to-shaft integrity

Pulleys should always be securely mounted to their shafts, with keys and setscrews tight.

Some of the pulleys on these mowers use a separate tapered hub which locks onto the shaft by being tightened

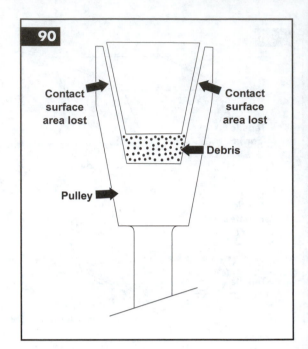

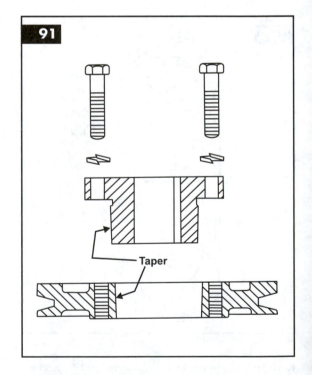

into a matching taper in the pulley (**Figure 91**). If the bolts holding the hub to the pulley should loosen, the pulley will slip on the shaft. To service these pulleys, refer to *Belt-Drive Pulleys* in Chapter Three.

TABLE 1 Flywheel-to-module air gap specifications

Briggs & Stratton	0.008-.012 in. (0.20-0.31 mm)
Kawasaki	
FC420V	0.012 in. (0.30 mm)
FH500V	0.010-.016 in. (0.25-0.40 mm)
Kohler	
CV14, CV15, MV	0.008-.012 in. (0.20-0.31 mm)
CV20	0.010-.013 in. (0.25-0.33 mm)

*Do not use a steel feeler gauge to measure air gap. A steel gap gauge will likely cause an inaccurate gap.

Table 2 RECOMMENDED SPARK PLUG TYPES, GAPS, AND TORQUES

ENGINE	SPARK PLUG	GAP	TORQUE
Kohler MV	Champion RV17YC1	0.035 in. (0.9 mm)	120-180 in.-lb. (13-20 N·m)
Kohler			
CV14, 15	Champion RC12YC	0.040 in. (1.0 mm)	335-385 in.-lb. (38-43 N·m)
CV20	Champion RC12YC2	0.030 in. (0.75 mm)	215-265 in.-lb. (24-30 N·m)
Kawasaki			
FC420V	Champion RN11YC, NGK BPR5ES	0.028-.031 in. (0.7-0.8 mm)	
FH451V, FH500V	Champion RCJ8Y, NGK BPMR4A	0.030 in. (0.75 mm)	130-135 in.-lb. (15 N·m)
FH641V	NGK BPR4ES, Champion RN14YC	0.030 in. (0.75 mm)	195 in.-lb. (22 N·m)
Briggs-Stratton	Champion RC12YC, Autolite 3924	.030 in. (0.75 mm)	180 in.-lb. (20 N·m)

1. RV17YC is for normal usage; RV15YC is recommended for *continuous full-load* running.
2. Inductive spark plug (Champion QC12YC) should be used to prevent radio frequency interference (RFI) on engines or systems with hourmeters. RFI may randomly reset hourmeters back to zero.

NOTE: Equivalent spark plugs may be substituted. Always cross-reference accurately.

CHAPTER THREE

LUBRICATION, MAINTENANCE AND TUNE-UP

This chapter covers lubrication, maintenance and tune-up procedures. To maximize the service life of these mowers while gaining the utmost in safety and performance, it is essential to perform periodic inspections and maintenance. Minor problems found during routine service can be corrected before they become serious and expensive.

Tables 1-6 list lubrication, maintenance and tune-up specifications and are at the end of this chapter.

Refer to Chapter One for the equipment and supplies necessary for performing the maintenance described in this chapter.

PRE-OPERATIONAL INSPECTION AND CHECK LIST

Perform the following checks prior to each daily use. If a component requiring service is discovered, refer to the appropriate chapter.

1. Check the engine oil level.
2. Check the fuel system for leaks, then fill the fuel tank to within one inch of the bottom of the filler neck with fresh gasoline.
3. Check the engine and hydrostatic cooling systems for debris build-up. Clean as necessary.
4. Check the hydraulic hoses and the hydrostatic components for leaks.
5. Check the air filter for security and cleanliness.
6. Check all linkages and controls for proper operation.
7. Check components and fasteners for security.

8. Check to see that all safety shields are in place and functional.
9. Check tire pressure and integrity.
10. Check the drive belts.
11. Check the battery, wiring and electrical-component integrity.
12. Ensure that the blades are sharp and straight, and that the underside of the deck is clean and free of any grass debris build-up.

Although the remaining checks are not directly mechanically related to the mower, they are essential for proper and safe equipment usage.

13. Check and remove any debris from the area to be mowed.
14. Ensure that the blade drive is disengaged, the parking brake is applied, and the wheel drive is in neutral prior to starting the engine.

MAINTENANCE SCHEDULE

Table 1 is the recommended maintenance and lubrication schedule. Strict adherence to these recommendations will ensure long service life from the mower.

For convenience when maintaining the mower, most of the services shown in **Table 1** are described in this chapter. However, some procedures which require more than minor disassembly or adjustment are covered elsewhere in the appropriate chapters.

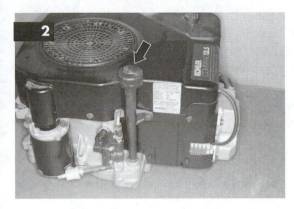

PERIODIC LUBRICATION

Perform the services listed in this section at the maintenance intervals listed in **Table 1**.

Engine Oil Level Check

Engine oil level is checked using the oil level dipstick located at the top or on the side of the engine. **Figure 1** and **Figure 2** show typical dipstick locations.

1. Ensure that the unit is sitting level.

2. Clean any dirt or debris from around the dipstick/oil fill cap area.

3. Remove the dipstick and wipe the oil from the gauge area with a clean rag.

4. Reinstall the dipstick:

   a. On B&S and Kohler Magnum (side-valve) 2-cylinder engines, reinsert the dipstick completely to obtain the correct reading;

   b. On Kohler Command (OHV) and Kawasaki engines, reinsert the dipstick into the tube and rest the oil fill cap on the tube to obtain the correct reading. Do not thread the cap onto the tube.

5. Remove the dipstick and check the oil level.

6. Add oil, if necessary. Refer to **Table 2** for the correct engine oil. Do not overfill. If the oil level is too high, care-

fully loosen the drain plug and drain off the excess oil. Recheck the oil level.

7. Inspect the O-ring seal on the oil filler cap, if applicable. Replace the O-ring if it is starting to deteriorate or harden.

8. Install the oil filler cap, and tighten it securely.

Engine Oil and Filter Change

Regular oil and filter changes contribute more to engine longevity than any other maintenance service. The recommended oil and filter change interval is listed in **Table 1**. This assumes that the mower is operated in normal, average conditions. If it is operated in severe or dusty conditions, the oil will get dirty more quickly and should be changed more frequently than recommended.

Always drain the crankcase oil with the engine warm so the oil flows freely and carries out the dirt and impurities.

Refer to **Table 2** for the recommended classification and viscosity of oil. If possible, use the same brand of oil at each oil change.

> *NOTE*
> *Never dispose of motor oil in the trash, on the ground, or down a drain. Many service stations accept used motor oil; some waste haulers provide curbside used motor oil collection. Do not combine other fluids with motor oil to be recycled. To locate a recycler, contact the American Petroleum Institute at www.recycleoil.org.*

To change the engine oil:

1. If the engine is not already hot, set the parking brake, start the engine and let it warm to normal operating temperature. Shut the engine off.

> *WARNING*
> *Make sure ventilation is adequate if the engine is to be run in a confined area. Exhaust fumes are toxic and deadly.*

2. Position the mower with the drain-plug side of the engine angled slightly downward.

3. Place a drain pan under the engine.

4. Loosen the oil filler cap. This speeds up the flow of oil.

5. Remove the oil drain plug. If the plug has a gasket, use care not to lose the gasket.

6. Allow the oil to completely drain.

7. Inspect the drain plug gasket for damage, if applicable. Replace the gasket if necessary.

8. Make sure the drain-plug threads and crankcase threads are clean, then install and tighten the drain plug.

9. Reset the mower to a level position.

10. Inspect the condition of the drained oil for contamination. After it has cooled down, check for any metal par-

ticles. If metal particles are evident, the engine may have internal damage.

11. Place the drain pan under the oil filter area. Carefully remove the oil filter.

> *CAUTION*
> *On Briggs & Stratton Model 303776, 303777 or 350777 engines with Code 92091800 or lower, do not loosen or remove the oil filter until the crankcase has been refilled with fresh oil. The oil pump design on these engines may allow an air lock, preventing proper lubrication upon start-up.*

12. Thoroughly clean the oil filter sealing surface on the crankcase. This surface must be clean to achieve a good seal with the new filter.

13. Fill the new oil filter with 2-4 ounces (60-120 ml) and rotate the filter to circulate the oil onto the entire filtering medium. Apply a light coat of clean engine oil to the rubber seal on the new filter.

14. Install the new oil filter onto the threaded fitting. Tighten the filter by hand until the rubber seal contacts the sealing surface, then tighten it an additional 1/2 to 3/4 turn.

15. If necessary, insert a funnel into the oil filler hole, then add the quantity of oil specified in **Table 2**.

16. Remove the funnel and screw in the oil filler cap securely.

17. Reset the parking brake, start the engine and let it idle.

18. Check the oil filter and drain plug for leaks. Tighten either if necessary.

19. Turn off the engine, and check the engine oil level as described in this chapter. Adjust the oil level if necessary.

> *WARNING*
> *Prolonged contact with used oil may cause skin cancer. Wash hands thoroughly with soap and water as soon as possible after handling or coming in contact with motor oil.*

General Lubrication

At the service intervals listed in **Table 1**, lubricate the cutter deck spindle bearings, caster wheel pivots and bearings, idler arm pivots, brake actuator levers, neutral cam pivots, and pump control pivots. The recommended and optional lubricants are listed in the table. Always take care to wipe any accumulated dirt off the grease fittings prior to pumping new grease into the fittings.

Control Cable Lubrication

Clean and lubricate the throttle cable and choke cable at the intervals indicated in **Table 1**. In addition, check the cables for kinks and signs of wear and damage that could cause the cables to fail or stick. Cables are expendable items that do not last forever, even under the best of conditions.

The most positive method of control cable lubrication involves the use of an aerosol lubricator with a small-diameter nozzle extension. A can of cable lube or general lubricant is required. Do *not* use chain lube as a cable lubricant.

> *NOTE*
> *Place a shop cloth at the end of the cables to catch the oil as it runs out.*

To lubricate the cables:

1. Insert the lubricant nozzle extension into the lubricator valve tip.

2. Aim the nozzle extension into the cable housing at the uppermost portion of the cable, as it is positioned on the mower (**Figure 3**).

3. Momentarily press the button on the can.

4. Repeat momentary squirts until the lubricant begins to flow out of the other end of the cable. If the cable lube will not flow through the cable at one end, try at the opposite end of the cable. It may be necessary to disconnect the lower end and raise it so the lubricant flows down the cable. Note the cable position prior to disconnection so the cable can be reinstalled in the same position. If in doubt, refer to the *Control Linkages* chapter for proper connection.

PERIODIC MAINTENANCE AND TUNE-UP

Perform the services listed in this section at the maintenance intervals listed in **Table 1**.

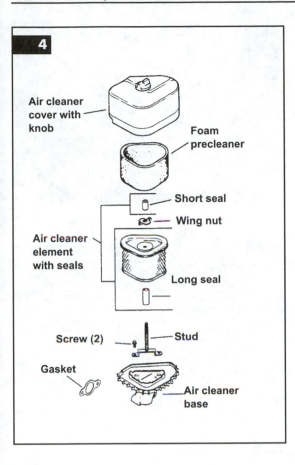

4

Air cleaner cover with knob

Foam precleaner

Short seal

Wing nut

Air cleaner element with seals

Long seal

Screw (2)

Stud

Gasket

Air cleaner base

3

Air Filter Service

Proper air filter service can ensure trouble-free service from the engine.

The air filter removes dust and abrasive particles from incoming air before it enters the carburetors and the engine. Without the air filter, very fine particles will enter the engine and cause rapid wear of the piston rings, cylinder bores and bearings. They also might clog small passages in the carburetors. Never run the mower's engine without the air filter element properly installed. The price of an air filter element is much less expensive than the cost of an engine overhaul.

Remove and clean the air filter at the interval indicated in **Table 1**. Replace the element at the specified interval or whenever it is damaged or starting to deteriorate.

NOTE
Always inspect the crankcase breather hose between the valve cover and the air filter base anytime the air filter is being serviced. If the hose is loose, cracked, or dry and brittle, replace it.

For model-specific air filter information, refer to the appropriate engine section.

For basic air filter service:

1. Thoroughly clean any dirt and debris from the area surrounding the air filter housing.

2. Remove any fasteners securing the cover to the air filter housing, and remove the cover.

NOTE
Some engines are equipped with reverse-flow air filters. On these engines, the air filter element will appear clean when the cover is removed because the air flow originates on the side of the filter which is not visible. The hidden side of the filter will be the dirty side.

3. Carefully noting the position of the air filter element within the filter housing, remove the element from the housing. **Figure 4** shows a typical dry-element air filter assembly with pre-filter.

4. Cover the air filter housing with a heavy towel to prevent the entry of objects or debris.

NOTE
If the air filter element is extremely dirty or if it has any holes, remove and clean the interior of the air filter housing prior to replacing the element. Remove any debris that may have passed through a broken element.

5. On paper-element filters:
   a. Gently tap the air filter to loosen the trapped dirt and dust. Make sure the tapping is done so the dirt falls away from the element.
   b. If low-pressure air is used, make sure that the air is blown from the clean side back through the dirty side. Using other than very low-pressure compressed air to blow through the element is not recommended, as the air pressure can damage the filter.
   c. If light tapping or blowing will not remove the dirt, replace the element. Thoroughly and carefully inspect the filter element. If it is torn or broken in any area, replace it. Do not run the engine with a damaged air filter element, as it will allow dirt to enter the engine. If the element is not damaged, it can be reused.

6. On sponge-type elements, including pre-filters, the sponge must have a light oil film in its pores in order to trap the dirt. A dry sponge is the same as not having a filter at all, as it will allow dirt to pass through. To service a sponge element:
   a. Gently wash the element in a warm water and liquid dishwash solution until the dirt and grease are removed.
   b. Rinse the element in cool water to remove all traces of dirt and soap.
   c. Pat the element dry with a soft towel or allow the element to air-dry overnight.

d. When the element is completely dry, apply a couple of tablespoons of engine oil to the element, then squeeze the element to circulate the oil. Remove any excess dripping oil.

e. Install the pre-filter over the air filter.

7. Install the air filter assembly into the housing.

8. Install the air filter cover and fasteners. Tighten the fasteners securely.

Fuel Filter Service

In order to protect the fuel system from debris-induced damage while maintaining peak performance, the fuel filter should be changed yearly.

To change the filter:

1. If possible, run the unit until it is completely out of fuel.

> *WARNING*
> *Make sure ventilation is adequate if the engine is to be run in a confined area. Exhaust fumes are toxic and deadly.*

2. If Step 1 is not practical, shut off the fuel tank valve (**Figure 5**), then run the engine until it dies. This will empty the lines and carburetor of fuel.

3. Access the fuel line at the fuel filter fitting. Loosen the hose clamp and carefully remove the hose from the filter. When removing stubborn hoses, do not apply excessive force to the hose or fitting. Remove the hose clamp and carefully insert a small pick tool between the fitting and hose. Apply a spray lubricant under the hose and carefully twist the hose off the fitting. Clean the fitting of any corrosion or hose material. A wire brush can be used on metal fittings; plastic fittings will require careful use of a small knife or scraper.

> *WARNING*
> *When working on gasoline hose fittings, always use non-sparking pick tools and wire brushes, such as brass-bristle brushes or 300-grade non-magnetic stainless steel pick tools.*

4. If the unit is being winterized at this time, direct the loosened hose into an approved container, open the tank shutoff valve and drain the fuel from the tank.

5. Install the hoses and clamps to the new fuel filter. If the new filter is a non-reversible filter, note the flow direction in relation to the fuel hoses.

> *NOTE*
> *A non-reversible filter will be marked in some fashion, usually an arrow (**Figure 6**), to denote the direction of flow. The arrow must point toward the carburetor. If the filter is installed backwards, it will not filter correctly and will clog prematurely.*

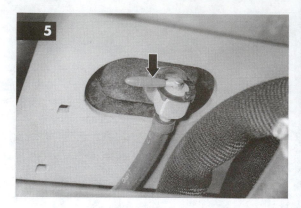

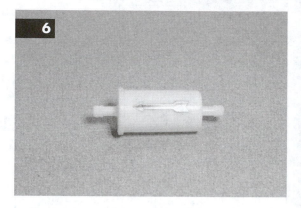

Spark Plug Service

Refer to **Table 3** for the recommended spark plugs, gaps, and plug installation torques.

> *CAUTION*
> *Before removing the spark plugs, remove the plug leads and clean the area around each plug base with compressed air. Unscrew the plug approximately one revolution and repeat the cleaning process. Dirt that falls into the cylinder will cause rapid piston, piston ring and cylinder wear.*

> *CAUTION*
> *These engines use aluminum cylinder head(s). Unless absolutely necessary, do not remove or install spark plugs while the engine is hot. The hotter the aluminum, the softer the thread, and the more easily the thread is damaged or stripped. If plugs are difficult to remove, apply penetrating oil around the base of the plug and let it soak in about 10-20 minutes. When installing the plug(s), the spark plug hole threads can be easily damaged by cross-threading of the spark plug. Make sure the plugs are correctly aligned with their holes.*

7

3

SPARK PLUG CONDITIONS

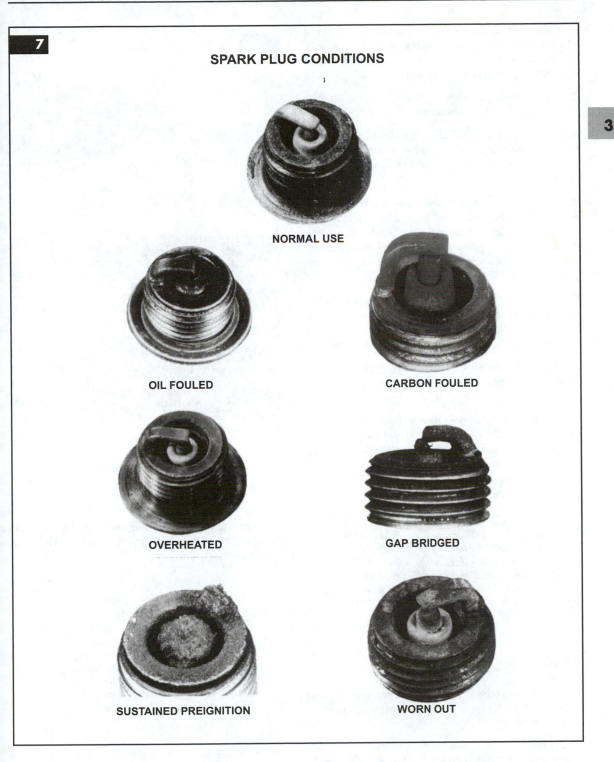

NORMAL USE

OIL FOULED

CARBON FOULED

OVERHEATED

GAP BRIDGED

SUSTAINED PREIGNITION

WORN OUT

Reading spark plugs

Valuable information regarding engine performance and a cylinder's operating condition can be obtained by studying a spark plug's condition. On 2-cylinder engines,

as each spark plug is removed, label it with its cylinder number. If anything turns up during the inspection, knowing which cylinder a plug came from will be useful.

Figure 7 shows views of seven spark plug tips after various types of service.

1. *Normal operation* — A light, even coating of tan to black deposits coupled with minimal electrode wear indicate correct heat range and proper engine operation. If not misfiring, this plug could be reused.

2. *Carbon fouling* — Dry, fluffy black carbon deposits indicate an overrich fuel mixture or faulty ignition output.

3. *Gap bridging* — Identified by deposits building up between the electrodes. The deposits reduce the gap and eventually close it entirely. Caused by oil or carbon fouling.

4. *Preignition* — If the electrodes are melted, preignition is almost certainly the cause. Caused by wrong type of fuel, incorrect ignition timing, plug heat range too hot, burned valves or engine overheating. Find and correct the cause of preignition before returning the engine to service..

5. *Oil fouling* — Wet, oily deposits with minimal electrode wear are usually caused by worn piston rings and cylinder or intake valve guide/stem. These problems allow oil to be pumped into the combustion chamber.

6. *Worn out* — Identified by severely eroded or worn electrodes. Caused by normal wear. Install a new spark plug.

7. *Excessive overheating* — Blistered or burned insulator tips and badly worn electrodes can be caused by overheating from an obstructed cooling system or too-lean fuel mixtures, preignition, improper installation procedures, or too hot a plug.

> *CAUTION*
> *Do not use the abrasive-blast (sand-blast) method to clean spark plugs. When spark plugs are cleaned by this method, the abrasive grit lodges in the upper gap between the insulator and the shell. This grit then falls into the cylinder and combustion chamber area, causing rapid internal wear and damage.*

Gapping and Installing the Plugs

Carefully gap the spark plugs to ensure a reliable, consistent spark with a special spark plug gapping tool and a wire feeler gauge.

1. Insert a wire feeler gauge between the center and side electrodes of the plug (**Figure 8**). The specified gap is listed in **Table 3**. If the gap is correct, a slight drag will be felt as the wire gauge is pulled through. If there is no drag or if the gauge will not pass through, bend the side electrode with a gapping tool (**Figure 9**) and set the gap to specification.

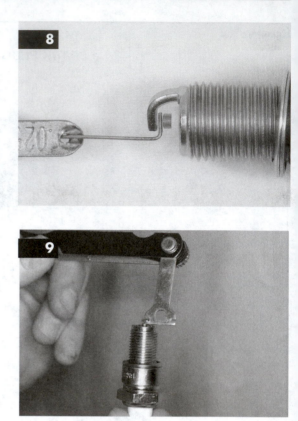

> *NOTE*
> *Do not tap the side electrode against a workbench or counter to close a wide gap. Insulator damage will result.*

3. Make sure that the spark plug threads and the plug hole threads in the cylinder head are clean and dry. Thread lubricant is not recommended.

> *NOTE*
> *To clean or repair lightly damaged spark plug threads, use a spark plug tap (**Figure 10**). Use extreme care not to get any debris or shavings in the cylinder. Before tapping a spark plug thread, ensure that the piston is just below TDC on the compression stroke. That way, if any debris does fall into the cylinder, compressed air and a vacuum cleaner will readily and safely remove it.*

If a spark plug thread is damaged, it may be necessary to install a Helicoil or some other type of thread insert. Follow the manufacturer's instructions when installing the insert.

4. Screw the spark plug in by hand until it seats. Very little effort should be required. If force is necessary, the plug

10

is cross-threaded. Unscrew it and try again. If necessary, dress the threads.

5. Tighten the plug to the torque specification listed in **Table 3**.

> *NOTE*
> *Do not overtighten the spark plug. This will only squash the gasket and destroy its sealing ability.*

> *CAUTION*
> *Do not use a plastic hammer or any type of tool to tap the plug cap assembly onto the spark plug, as the assembly will be damaged. Use fingers only.*

> *NOTE*
> *Be sure to push the plug cap all the way down to make full contact with the spark plug post. If the cap does not completely contact the plug, the engine may start to misfire and cut out at high RPM.*

Valve Adjustment

On engines which have adjustable valve tappets, the clearance should be checked and adjusted, if necessary, according to the recommendations in **Table 1**. Adjustment procedures are covered in each appropriate engine chapter.

Battery Service

On electric-start units, the battery is an important component in the electrical system. Many electrical system troubles can be traced to battery neglect. Clean and inspect the battery at periodic intervals.

Original-equipment batteries have cell caps which can be removed to check the electrolyte level and specific gravity. Some battery manufacturers offer a maintenance-free battery as a replacement. This is a sealed battery, so the electrolyte level and specific gravity cannot be checked.

On all models covered in this manual, the negative side is grounded. When removing the battery, disconnect the negative cable first, then disconnect the positive cable. This minimizes the chance of a tool shorting to ground if the positive battery cable is disconnected first.

Battery service specifications are given in this chapter for a normal room temperature of 68° F (20° C). When taking hydrometer readings, add .004 to the reading for every 10° F increase above 68° F; subtract .004 from the reading for every 10° F decrease below 68° F. Ambient temperature affects battery charging and discharging.

A cold battery will charge slower than a warm battery, but, by the same token, it will also discharge slower. For this reason, when the mower is not in use for an extended period, it is more beneficial to the battery to be stored in a cool location, provided the battery is fully-charged at the start of storage. A fully-charged battery will not freeze, even in below-zero temperatures, because the electrolyte acts as an anti-freeze. A half-charged or discharged battery will freeze more readily.

> *WARNING*
> *Battery fluid splashed into the eyes is extremely harmful. Safety glasses must always be worn while working with a battery.*

> *CAUTION*
> *Battery electrolyte is very corrosive. Avoid spilling or splashing it on skin or clothing, as it will cause burns.*

Battery removal/installation

1. Turn the ignition switch OFF.

2. Remove the insulated battery shield (3, **Figure 11**).

3. Disconnect the negative battery cable (C, **Figure 12**) from the negative battery terminal (B).

4. Move the negative cable out of the way so it will not accidentally contact the negative battery terminal.

5. Remove the protective terminal boot (F, **Figure 12**) from the positive battery terminal. Disconnect the positive battery cable (E) from the positive battery terminal (D).

6. Remove the two carriage-bolt battery holders and wingnuts (9 and 10, **Figure 11**), then remove the battery from the mower.

> *NOTE*
> *When purchasing a replacement battery, always obtain one with the terminals in the same positions as the original battery. This will prevent cable mix-up as well as allowing the cables to reach their proper battery terminals.*

3

7. To install the battery, set the battery into the battery box.

> *CAUTION*
> *Be sure the battery is positioned so the cables will connect to their proper terminals. On units with same-color cables, the ground cable is the cable with one end fastened to the mower chassis; the opposite end of this cable must be connected to the negative battery terminal. Connecting the battery backwards reverses the polarity and damages the electrical system.*

8. Install and tighten the positive battery cable (E, **Figure 12**). Fit the protective boot over the terminal.

9. Install and tighten the negative battery cable (C, **Figure 12**).

10. Coat the battery connections with dielectric grease to retard corrosion. Reinstall the protective terminal boot over the positive battery terminal.

Inspection, cleaning and testing

Battery service specifications are given in this chapter for a normal room temperature of 68° F (20° C). When taking hydrometer readings, add .004 to the reading for every 10° F increase above 68° F; subtract .004 from the reading for every 10° F decrease below 68° F. To clean and inspect the battery:

1. Remove the battery as described in this chapter. Do not clean the battery while it is mounted in the frame.

2. Inspect the battery box, holddown bolts and top shield for corrosion or damage. Clean the box and components with a baking soda and water solution, then rinse thoroughly and dry.

3. Set the battery on a stack of newspapers or cardboard to protect the workbench surface. Setting the battery on a concrete floor is not recommended.

4. Check the entire battery case (**Figure 12**) for cracks or other damage. If the battery case is warped or has a raised top, the battery has overheated from overcharging.

5. Check the battery terminals (**Figure 12**) and bolts for corrosion or damage. Clean parts thoroughly with a baking soda and water solution, then rinse and dry. Replace severely corroded bolts.

6. If corroded, clean the top, sides and bottom of the battery with a stiff bristle brush using a strong baking soda and water solution. Do *not* allow the soda solution to seep past the cell caps into the cells. Doing so will neutralize the cells' electrolyte and ruin the battery. When clean, rinse the battery case with clean water, then wipe dry.

7. Check the battery cable terminals for corrosion and damage. If corrosion is minor, clean the terminals by soaking them in a container of baking soda and water. Replace severely worn or damaged cables.

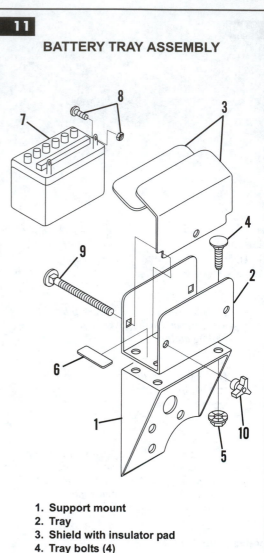

11

BATTERY TRAY ASSEMBLY

1. **Support mount**
2. **Tray**
3. **Shield with insulator pad**
4. **Tray bolts (4)**
5. **Tray nuts (4)**
6. **Rubber pad (2)**
7. **Battery**
8. **Terminal bolt assembly (2)**
9. **Holder bolt (2)**
10. **Holder wingnut (2)**

8. Connect a voltmeter across the negative and positive battery terminals (**Figure 13**). Note the following:

   a. If the battery voltage is 12.0-12.8 volts at 68° F (20° C), the battery is fully charged.

   b. If the battery voltage is below 12.0 volts at 68° F (20° C), the battery is undercharged.

9. If the battery has removable cell caps, use a hydrometer (**Figure 14**) to test the specific gravity of the electrolyte. **Table 4** shows the percent of battery charge at 68° F (20° C) based on the hydrometer float reading. When

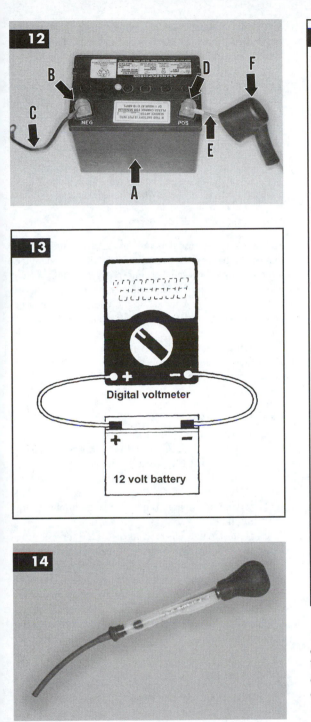

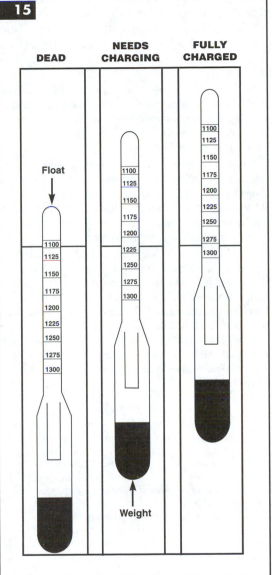

10. If either Step 8 or 9 shows the battery to be discharged, recharge it as described in this chapter. Once the battery is fully charged, reinstall the battery, then test the charging system as described in the appropriate engine chapter.

Charging

If recharging is required on a maintenance-free battery, a digital voltmeter and a charger with either an adjustable amperage output or a tapering output are required. If this equipment is not available, entrust battery charging to a shop with the proper equipment. Excessive voltage and

hydrometer testing the electrolyte (**Figure 15**), ensure that there is sufficient fluid in the tube to buoy the float and do not let the float contact the sides of the glass tube. A battery with cells below 85% is considered not fully charged.

amperage from an unregulated charger can damage the battery and shorten service life.

The battery should only self-discharge approximately one percent each day. If a battery not in use loses it charge within a week after charging, with no loads connected, the battery is defective.

If the mower is not used for long periods of time, an automatic battery charger with variable voltage and amperage outputs is recommended for optimum battery service life. Once the battery is fully-charged, an automatic trickle charger should suffice.

Ambient temperature affects battery charging and discharging. Battery service specifications are given in this chapter for a normal room temperature of 68° F (20° C). When taking hydrometer readings, add .004 to the reading for every 10° F increase above 68° F; subtract .004 from the reading for every 10° F decrease below 68° F.

A cold battery will charge slower than a warm battery, but, by the same token, it will also discharge slower. For this reason, if the mower is not in use for an extended period, it is more beneficial to the battery to be stored in a cool location, provided the battery is fully-charged at the start of storage. A fully-charged battery will not freeze, even in below-zero temperatures, because the electrolyte acts as an anti-freeze. A half-charged or discharged battery will freeze more readily. Never attempt to charge a frozen battery.

WARNING
During charging, highly-explosive hydrogen gas is released from the battery. Only charge the battery in a well-ventilated area away from open flames (including pilot lights on gas home appliances) and sparks of any kind. Do not allow anyone to smoke in the area. Never check the charge of the battery by arcing across the terminals; the resulting spark can ignite the hydrogen gas and cause a serious explosion.

CAUTION
Always disconnect the battery cables from the battery, and disconnect the ground cable first. If the cables are left connected during the charging procedure, the charger may destroy the diodes in the voltage regulator/rectifier.

1. Remove the battery from the mower as described in this chapter.

2. Set the battery on a stack of newspapers or cardboard to protect the workbench surface. Setting the battery on a concrete floor is not recommended.

3. Always follow the charger manufacturer's instructions.

4. Make sure the battery charger is turned to the OFF position prior to attaching the charger leads to the battery.

5. Connect the positive charger lead to the positive battery terminal and the negative charger lead to the negative battery terminal.

6. Set the charger to 12 volts.

7. If the amperage output of the charger is variable, select the low setting. Normally, a battery should be charged at 1/10th its given capacity. A 40-ampere-hour battery should be charged at a maximum of 4 amps.

CAUTION
Never set the battery charger to more than 5 amps. A charge of more than 5 amps can overheat and warp the cell plates, ruining the battery, as well as creating a danger of explosion.

8. The charging time depends on the discharged condition of the battery. Again, refer to the charger manufacturer's instructions concerning charging times. As a general rule, the battery state-of-charge should be checked every half-hour while the battery is on charge, unless the charger is equipped with an automatic regulator.

9. Turn the charger to the ON position.

10. After the battery has been charged for the pre-determined time, turn the charger to the OFF position and disconnect the leads. Wait 30 minutes, measure the battery voltage and test the specific gravity of the electrolyte. Refer to the following:

    a. If the battery voltage is 12.0-12.8 volts with all cells reading at least 1.260 specific gravity at 68° F (20° C), the battery is fully charged;

    b. If the battery voltage is below 12.0 volts with all cells reading below 1.260 specific gravity, the battery is undercharged and requires additional charging time.

    c. If most of the cells read at least 1.260 specific gravity after an ample charge time, with one or two cells reading significantly below 1.260, the low cells are weak and the battery is faulty.

11. If the battery remains stable for one hour, the battery is charged.

12. Install the battery into the mower as described in this chapter.

Jump-starting

If it becomes necessary to temporarily jump-start the mower, it is important to use the correct procedure not only for personal safety but also to safeguard the mower's electrical system. To jump-start:

1. Use color-coded red and black jumper cables.

2. Connect one end of the red cable to the positive terminal of the dead battery. Connect the other end to the positive terminal of the good battery (**Figure 16**).

3. Connect one end of the black cable to the negative terminal of the dead battery.

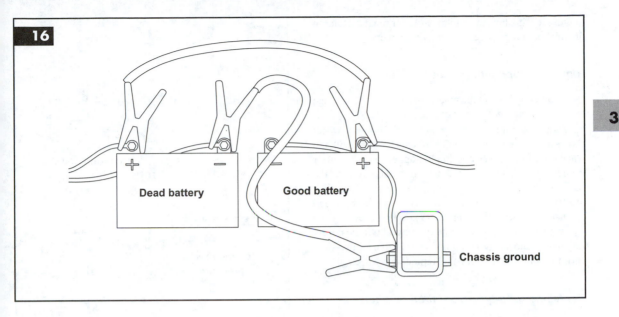

16

3

4. Connect the loose end of the black cable to a good, clean ground on the engine block or chassis of the unit with the good battery. This will prevent possible sparks from occurring near the cell caps.

5. When the machine with the dead battery starts, always disconnect the black chassis-ground connection first, followed by the black dead-battery connection. Finish by unclamping both red-cable connections.

Tires and Wheels

Tire pressure

Check and adjust tire pressure to maintain good traction and proper tracking and to prevent rim and turf damage. The recommended tire pressures for these mowers are 25 psi (165 kPa) for the front caster wheels and 15 psi (100 kPa) for the rear drive wheels.

> *NOTE*
> *After checking and adjusting the tire pressure, make sure to install the valve stem cap. The cap prevents grass debris, small pebbles and dirt from collecting in the valve stem. These could allow air leakage or result in incorrect future tire pressure readings.*

Tire pressure is critical for proper traction, driveability, tread wear and turf care.

Air pressure working against the inside of a properly-inflated tire supports the weight of the mower while maintaining a reasonably flat tread contact pattern against the ground (A, **Figure 17**). A tire with even tread wear across the tire width indicates a properly-inflated tire.

An underinflated tire (B, **Figure 17**) does not have enough air pressure to keep the tread pushing against the ground, so the weight of the mower is supported mainly by the tire sidewalls, allowing the center tread area to flex inward. This flexing at the inner corners causes the tire to run hotter than normal. It also causes rapid wear at the outer corners of the tread, with negligible center-tread wear.

Underinflation also decreases the loaded diameter of the tire. This causes the tire to travel a shorter distance for each wheel rotation than a properly-inflated tire (**Figure 18**). For this reason, a mower with two tires inflated differently will not track straight, always "pulling" toward the side with the smaller-diameter tire.

An overinflated tire (C, **Figure 17**) increases the loaded diameter of the tire by exerting too much pressure against the center of the tread area, pushing the center area away from the wheel rim while the sidewalls hold the tread edges in position. This causes accelerated tread wear in the center of the tread with negligible edge-tread wear, while giving a much harsher, rougher ride. By increasing the loaded diameter of the tire, it will travel a farther distance per wheel revolution (**Figure 18**), again causing the mower to not track straight, this time pulling toward the properly-inflated side.

Because of the additional flexing and smaller tread-load areas of the tire, underinflation and overinflation can also cause turf damage, resulting in customer complaints and dissatisfaction.

Tire inspection

Inspect the tires daily for excessive wear, bulges, cuts or abrasions. If a nail or other object is found in the tire, mark its location with chalk or a light crayon prior to removing it. This helps locate the hole for repairs. Refer to the tire changing procedures in this chapter.

Rim inspection and runout

Periodically inspect the wheel rims for cracks, warpage or dents. A damaged rim may cause an air leak.

Wheel rim runout is the amount of wobble a wheel shows as it rotates. It is possible to check runout with the wheels on the mower by simply supporting the mower frame with the wheel off the ground. Slowly turn the wheel while holding one end of a pointer solidly against the front caster leg or rear chassis with the other end against the wheel rim (**Figure 19**). When checking the rear wheels without the engine running, it will be necessary to activate the hydro pump bypass valve for that side. If rim runout seems excessive, replace the wheel.

Replacing tube-type front tires or wheels

> *WARNING*
> *Prior to doing any work on wheels or tires, always deflate the tire and remove the valve stem core. Working on a tire under pressure creates an explosion hazard.*

Refer to **Figure 20**.

1. Remove the cap and valve core from the valve stem and deflate the tire. When the tire is deflated, replace the cap lightly to prevent dirt and debris from getting inside the stem.

2. Carefully lift and support the front of the cutter deck so the tire is off the floor.

3. Remove the axle nut from the axle bolt. Slide the axle bolt out from the caster fork assembly.

4. Pull the wheel and tire assembly out of the caster fork. Do not allow the wheel bearing spacers, bearing sleeve or bearing to fall out.

5. Carefully remove and set aside the wheel bearing spacers, sleeve and bearing. Do not allow any dirt or debris to get on the bearing or in the wheel cavity.

6. Remove the four nuts holding the wheel halves onto the hub.

7. Being careful not to damage the grease fitting, remove the wheel assembly, including the tire, from the hub.

8. Carefully remove the wheel halves from the tire, taking care not to damage the inner tube valve stem.

9. Remove the inner tube from the tire.

10. Carefully inspect the tire inside and out for any punctures, cracks, splits or weak spots. Replace a faulty or questionable tire.

11. Inspect the inner tube. Inflate the tube in a pan of water and check for leaks, including the valve core. If the tube cannot be properly patched or repaired, replace it. Ensure that the replacement tube is the correct size.

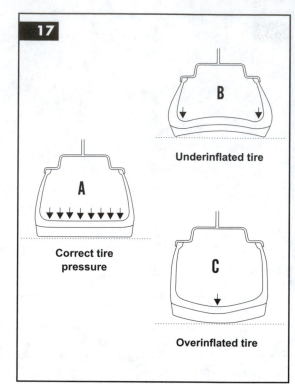

Underinflated tire

Correct tire pressure

Overinflated tire

12. Inspect the wheel halves. Check for bent or damaged rims. Ensure that the bolt holes are not elongated. Remove any rust and corrosion; refinish as necessary.

13. Carefully inspect the wheel hub for a bent flange, cracked welds, or loose studs. Ensure that the grease fitting is properly installed and that the fitting is not clogged and will pass grease.

Reassembly

Refer to **Figure 20**.

1. Install the valve core into the valve stem of the inner tube. Fit the tube into the tire. Inflate the tube just enough to almost fill the inside of the tire with the tire in the relaxed position.

2. Fit both wheel halves into the tire, taking care not to pinch or kink the valve stem. Do not pinch the inner tube between the wheel halves. Ensure that the bolt holes align.

3. Being careful not to damage the grease fitting, fit the wheel onto the hub studs. Ensure that the stud and nut threads are clean and dry, then install the four stud nuts. Torque the nuts to the value specified in **Table 5** or **Table 6**.

> *NOTE*
> *Scag uses Grade 5 wheel mount hardware.*

4. If installing a puncture sealant, deflate the inner tube, then install the sealant. Always follow the sealant manufacturer's instructions, especially concerning capacities.

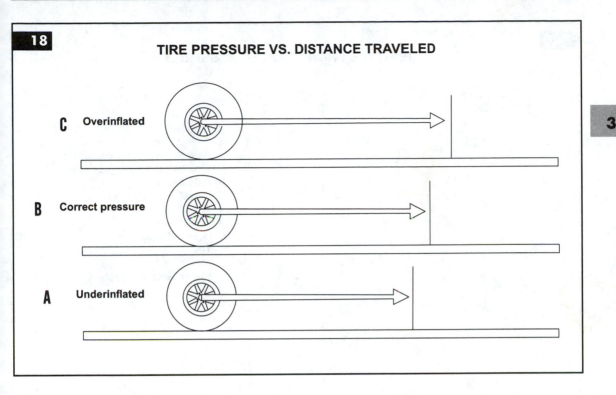

18

TIRE PRESSURE VS. DISTANCE TRAVELED

C Overinflated

B Correct pressure

A Underinflated

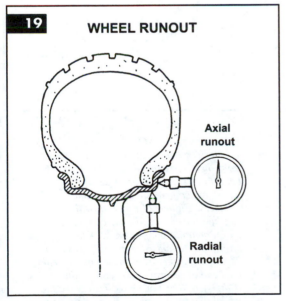

19

WHEEL RUNOUT

Axial
runout

Radial
runout

5. Inflate the tire to 25 psi (165 kPa). Install the valve stem cap.

6. Lubricate the axle bearing sleeve, bearing and the inner cavity of the hub. Insert the bearing into the hub. Insert the sleeve into the bearing, followed by the outer bearing spacers, one on each side of the bearing assembly.

7. Insert the assembled hub and wheel unit between the side plates of the caster fork, carefully aligning the inner sleeve diameter with the axle bolt holes.

8. Insert the axle bolt through the caster fork and wheel bearing spacer. Install the axle nut onto the bolt. Torque the nut to the value specified in **Table 5** or **Table 6**.

> *NOTE*
> *Scag uses Grade 5 chassis hardware.*

Replacing tubeless front tires or wheels

> *WARNING*
> *Prior to doing any work on wheels or tires, always deflate the tire and remove the valve stem core. Working on a tire under pressure creates an explosion hazard.*

> *NOTE*
> *Many owners use some form of puncture sealant inside tubeless tires to prevent minor punctures such as nails and thorns from causing equipment downtime. These sealants can create gummy residue inside the tire and may attack the finish inside the rim, causing rust and corrosion. Sealants should not be used unless an inner tube is first placed inside the tire.*

Refer to **Figure 21**.

1. Remove the cap and valve core from the valve stem and deflate the tire. When the tire is deflated, replace the

20

TUBE-TYPE FRONT CASTER ASSEMBLY

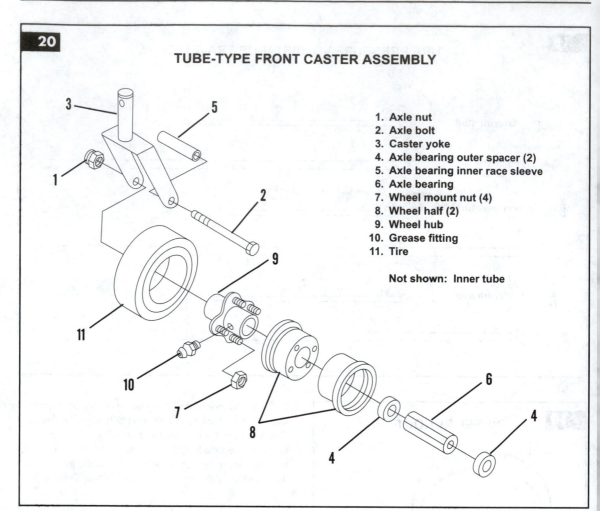

1. Axle nut
2. Axle bolt
3. Caster yoke
4. Axle bearing outer spacer (2)
5. Axle bearing inner race sleeve
6. Axle bearing
7. Wheel mount nut (4)
8. Wheel half (2)
9. Wheel hub
10. Grease fitting
11. Tire

Not shown: Inner tube

cap lightly to prevent dirt and debris from getting inside the stem.

2. Carefully lift and support the front of the cutter deck so the tire is off the floor.

3. Remove the axle nut from the axle bolt. Slide the axle bolt out from the caster fork assembly.

4. Pull the wheel and tire assembly out of the caster fork. Do not allow the wheel bearing spacers, bearing sleeve or bearings to fall out.

5. Carefully remove and set aside the wheel bearing spacers, sleeve and bearings. Do not allow any dirt or debris to get on the bearings or sleeve or inside the bearing cavity in the hub of the wheel (8).

CAUTION
*The inner rim bead areas are the sealing surfaces (**Figure 22**) on a tubeless wheel. Do not scratch the inside of the rim or damage the tire bead.*

NOTE
*Tubeless tires may be difficult to remove from their rims because of the tight tire bead-to-rim seal. **Figure 23** shows two types of commercially available bead breakers. **Figure 24** shows how the bead can be broken loose by the careful use of an automobile bumper jack. When using any of the methods shown in Figures 23 or 24, it may be necessary to attempt to break the bead at several points around the tire. If the seal does not break loose, take the wheel to a tire repair shop and have them break it loose on a tire changing machine.*

6. Press the entire bead on both sides of the tire away from the rim and into the center of the rim.

7. Lubricate both tire beads with an approved rubber lubricant. Do not use water. Water will cause rust and corrosion on the internal rim surfaces.

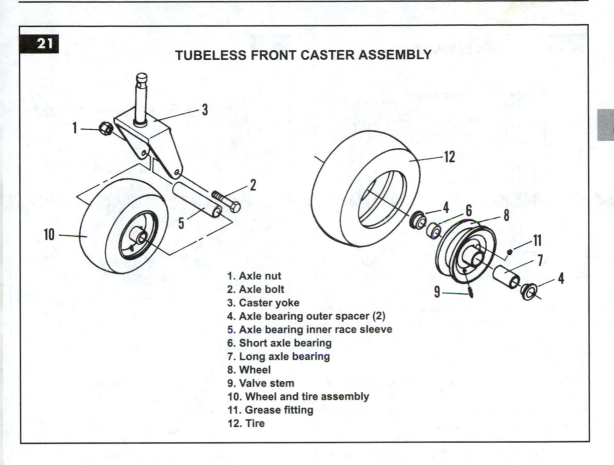

21

TUBELESS FRONT CASTER ASSEMBLY

1. Axle nut
2. Axle bolt
3. Caster yoke
4. Axle bearing outer spacer (2)
5. Axle bearing inner race sleeve
6. Short axle bearing
7. Long axle bearing
8. Wheel
9. Valve stem
10. Wheel and tire assembly
11. Grease fitting
12. Tire

3

NOTE
*To remove the tire, use only quality tire irons without sharp edges (**Figure 25**). Do not use screwdrivers or other sharp-sided tools. If necessary, file the ends of the tire irons to remove rough edges.*

8. Insert a tire iron under the top bead next to the valve stem (**Figure 26**). Force the bead on the opposite side of the tire into the center of the rim, then pry the outer bead over the rim with the tire iron.

9. Insert a second tire iron next to the first iron to hold the bead over the rim. Then work around the tire with the first tire iron, prying the bead over the rim (**Figure 27**).

10. Insert a tire iron between the second bead and the side of the rim that the first bead was pried over (**Figure 28**). From the back side of the tire, insert the second tire iron between the tire bead and the rim. Working around the rim bead area, pry the back bead off the rim (**Figure 29**).

11. Because rubber deteriorates with age, remove the old valve stem and discard it, unless it has recently been replaced.

12. Inspect the entire rim for rust, corrosion, or old tire sealer, especially the valve stem hole (**Figure 30**). If there is only minor dirt, remove the dirt and wipe the rim dry with a clean cloth. If there is any rust, corrosion or pitting, espe-

cially in the sealing area of the hole, clean, sand, prime and refinish as necessary to provide a good seal. Install a *new* valve stem and make sure it is properly seated in the rim.

13. Inspect the valve stem core rubber seal (**Figure 31**) for hardness or deterioration. Replace the valve core if necessary. **Figure 31** shows both the long and the short styles of stem cores as well as the professional core-removal tool.

14. Carefully inspect the tire inside and out for any punctures, cracks, splits or weak spots. Replace a faulty or questionable tire.

Reassembly of a tubeless front tire

1. Lubricate both beads of the tire with an approved rubber lubricant, such as RuGLYDE or equivalent. Do not use water. Water will cause rust and corrosion on the internal rim surfaces.

CAUTION
*The inner rim bead areas are the sealing surfaces (**Figure 22**) on a tubeless wheel. Do not scratch the inside of the rim or damage the tire bead.*

22

RIM INSPECTION

Rim sealing surface

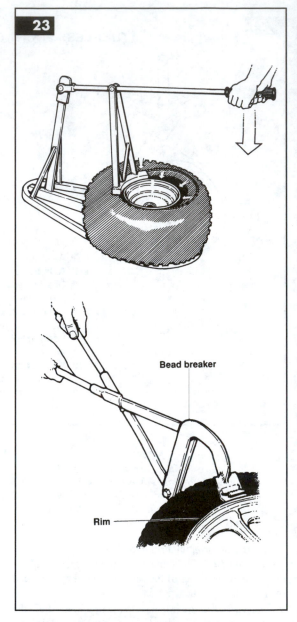

23

Bead breaker

Rim

2. Place the backside of the tire onto the rim so the lower bead sits in the center of the rim while the upper bead remains outside the rim (**Figure 29**). Work around the tire in both directions to fit the lower bead into the center of the rim.

3. Press the upper bead into the rim opposite the valve stem. Working on both sides of this initial point, pry the bead into the rim with a tire tool and work around the rim to the valve stem. If the tire wants to pull up on one side, either use another tire iron or one knee or foot to hold the tire in place. The last few inches are usually the toughest to install. If possible, continue to push the tire into the rim by hand. Relubricate the bead, if necessary. If the tire bead wants to pull out from under the rim, use both knees or feet to hold the tire in place. It may be necessary to use a tire iron for the last few inches.

4. Bounce the tire several times in different places, rotating it after each bounce. This will force the tire bead against the rim flanges.

5. Once the tire beads are in contact with the rim, place an inflatable band around the circumference of the tire. Slowly inflate the band until the tire beads are pressed against the rim. Inflate the tire enough to seat it. Deflate the band and remove it.

> *WARNING*
> *Never exceed 30 psi (215 kPa) inflation pressure as the tire could burst, causing severe injury. Never stand directly over a tire while inflating it.*

6. After inflating the tire, check to see that the beads are fully seated and that the rim lines (**Figure 32**) are the same distance from the rim all the way around the tire. If the beads will not seat, deflate the tire and relubricate the rim and beads.

7. Reinflate the tire to 25 psi (165 kPa). Install the valve stem cap.

24

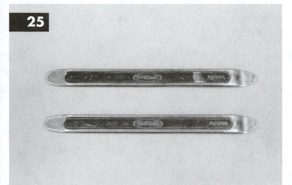

3

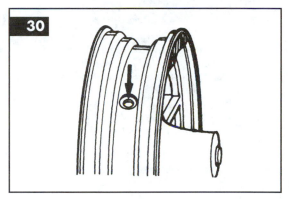

NOTE
Scag uses Grade 5 chassis hardware.

Replacing tubeless rear drive tires and wheels

WARNING
Before working on wheels or tires, always deflate the tire and remove the valve stem core. Working on a tire under pressure creates an explosion hazard.

NOTE
Many owners use some form of puncture sealant inside tubeless tires to prevent minor punctures such as nails and thorns from causing equipment downtime. These sealants can create gummy residue inside the tire and may attack the finish inside the rim, causing rust and corrosion. Sealants should not be used unless an inner tube is first placed inside the tire.

   Refer to **Figure 34**.
1. Engage the parking brake.
2. Remove the cap and valve core from the valve stem and deflate the tire. When the tire is deflated, replace the cap lightly to prevent dirt and debris from getting inside the stem.

3. Carefully lift and support the rear of the frame so the tire is off the floor.

4. Remove the four wheel-mount nuts from the studs on the drive hub.

5. Carefully slide the wheel and tire assembly off the studs. The wheel and tire assembly includes both the tire and the wheel rim. The activated parking brake will hold the brake drum onto the hub.

> *CAUTION*
> *The inner rim bead areas are the sealing surfaces (Figure 22) on a tubeless wheel. Do not scratch the inside of the rim or damage the tire bead.*

> *NOTE*
> *Removal of tubeless tires from their rims can be difficult because of the exceptionally tight tire bead-to-rim seal. Breaking the bead seal may require the use of a special tool (Figure 23 or Figure 24). If the seal does not break loose, take the wheel to a tire repair shop and have it broken down on a tire changing machine.*

6. Press the entire bead on both sides of the tire away from the rim and into the center of the rim.

7. Lubricate both tire beads with an approved rubber lubricant. Do not use water. Water will cause rust and corrosion on the internal rim surfaces.

> *NOTE*
> *To remove the tire, use only quality tire irons without sharp edges (Figure 25). Do not use screwdrivers or other sharp-sided tools. If necessary, file the ends of the tire irons to remove rough edges.*

8. Insert a tire iron under the top bead next to the valve stem (**Figure 26**). Force the bead on the opposite side of the tire into the center of the rim, then pry the outer bead over the rim with the tire iron.

9. Insert a second tire iron next to the first iron to hold the bead over the rim. Then work around the tire with the first tire iron, prying the bead over the rim (**Figure 27**).

10. Insert a tire iron between the second bead and the side of the rim that the first bead was pried over (**Figure 28**). From the back side of the tire, insert the second tire iron between the tire bead and the rim. Working around the rim bead area, pry the back bead off the rim (**Figure 29**).

11. Because rubber deteriorates with age, remove the old valve stem and discard it, unless it has recently been replaced.

12. Inspect the inside-the-tire rim area for rust, corrosion, or old tire sealer, especially the valve stem hole (**Figure 30**). If there is only minor dirt, remove the dirt and wipe the rim dry with a clean cloth. If there is any rust, corrosion or pitting, especially in the sealing area of

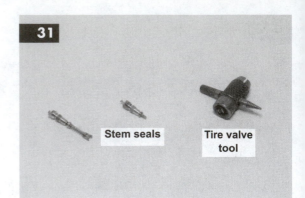

Stem seals   Tire valve tool

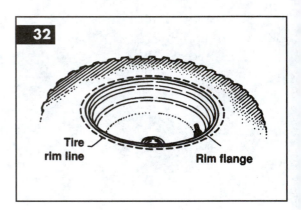

Tire rim line   Rim flange

the hole, clean, sand, prime and refinish as necessary to provide a good seal. Install a *new* valve stem and make sure it is properly seated in the rim.

13. Inspect the valve stem core rubber seal (**Figure 31**) for hardness or deterioration. Replace the valve core if necessary.

14. Carefully inspect the tire inside and out for any punctures, cracks, splits or weak spots. Replace a faulty or questionable tire.

Reassembly of a tubeless rear drive tire

1. Lubricate both beads of the tire with an approved rubber lubricant. Do not use water. Water will cause rust and corrosion on the internal rim surfaces.

> *CAUTION*
> *The inner rim bead areas are the sealing surfaces (Figure 22) on a tubeless wheel. Do not scratch the inside of the rim or damage the tire bead.*

2. Place the backside of the tire onto the rim so the lower bead sits in the center of the rim while the upper bead remains outside the rim (**Figure 29**). Work around the tire in both directions and press the lower bead, by hand, into

3

the center of the rim. Use a tire iron for the last few inches of bead (**Figure 28**).

3. Press the upper bead into the rim opposite the valve stem. Working on both sides of this initial point, pry the bead into the rim with a tire tool and work around the rim to the valve stem. If the tire wants to pull up on one side, either use another tire iron or one knee or foot to hold the tire in place. The last few inches are usually the toughest to install. If possible, continue to push the tire into the rim by hand. Relubricate the bead, if necessary. If the tire bead wants to pull out from under the rim, use both knees or feet to hold the tire in place. It may be necessary to use a tire iron for the last few inches.

4. Bounce the tire several times in different places, rotating it after each bounce. This will force the tire bead against the rim flanges.

5. Once the tire beads are in contact with the rim, place an inflatable band around the circumference of the tire. Slowly inflate the band until the tire beads are pressed against the rim. Inflate the tire enough to seat it. Deflate the band and remove it.

> *WARNING*
> *Never exceed 20 psi (135 kPa) inflation pressure, as the tire could burst, causing severe injury. Never stand directly over a tire while inflating it.*

6. After inflating the tire, check to see that the beads are fully seated and that the rim lines (**Figure 32**) are the same distance from the rim all the way around the tire. If the beads will not seat, deflate the tire and lubricate the rim and beads.

Table 1 TORQUE VALUES FOR 2-PIECE TAPER-HUB PULLEYS

Bolt Thread	Torque Value
1/4 in.	108 In.-lb. (12 N·m)
5/16 in.	180 In.-lb. (20 N·m)
3/8 in.	360 In.-lb. (40.5 N·m)

Table 2 MAINTENANCE AND LUBRICATION SCHEDULE

After 5-hour break-in period (new unit; new or overhauled engine)	Change the engine oil and the oil filter. Check all the fasteners and the linkages for security.
Every 8 hours or daily	Check the engine oil with the unit sitting level. Lubricate the two or three cutter-deck spindle bearings until grease escapes from the relief valve.[1] Lift the deck belt cover and remove any accumulated chaff or debris.

(continued)

Table 2 MAINTENANCE AND LUBRICATION SCHEDULE (continued)

Every 8 hours or daily (continued)	Check the belts for integrity and tension.
	Check the belt idler pulleys.
	Sharpen the blades, if needed.
	Check and/or clean the air filter.
	Check the tire pressure and integrity.
Every 40-50 hours or weekly	On electric-start units, check the battery electrolyte level.
	Lubricate the throttle and choke cables.
Every 100 hours or semi-monthly	Replace the air filter.
	Change the engine oil and oil filter.
	Lubricate the two caster wheel pivots.[2]
	Lubricate the two caster wheel bearings.[2]
	Lubricate the three idler arm pivots.[2]
	Lubricate the two brake actuator levers.[2]
	Clean the area around the hydrostatic oil filter and replace the filter. Replace any lost fluid.[3]
Every 200 hours or monthly	Lubricate the two neutral cam pivots.[2]
	Lubricate the two pump control pivots.[2]
Every 300 hours or semi-annually	Adjust the engine valve tappet clearances on applicable Kawasaki engines.
Every 500 hours or annually	Replace the fuel filter and fuel hoses.
	Adjust the engine valve tappet clearances on Kohler MV and Briggs & Stratton engines.
	Check all of the fasteners for proper security.
	Inspect deck, frame, and handle welds for any signs of fatigue or cracking.
	Adjust the air gap on the electric clutch.
	Drain the hydraulic system. Install fresh oil[3] and a new filter.

1. Recommended lubricant is US Lithium MP White Grease 2125. Compatible lubricants are Exxon's Ronex MP, Shell Alvania, Mobil's Mobilux #2, Conoco's Super Lub M EP #2, or Lidok EP #2.
2. Recommended lubricant is chassis grease.
3. Factory-installed lubricant is SAE 20W-50 petroleum-base oil with an API classification of SH or above. Acceptable substitutes are Mobil Super HP, Amoco Ultimate, Viscosity Oil, Shell Gemini, Aero Shell, or Helix Ultra in SAE 5W-40, SAE 10W-40, or SAE 15W-50 grades. If synthetic oil is preferred after a complete system flush, Mobil 1 SAE 15W-50 is recommended; 5W-30 or 10W-30 are acceptable substitutes.

Table 3 RECOMMENDED FUEL AND LUBRICANTS, INCLUDING CAPACITIES

Fuel capacity - approximately 5.0 U.S. gallons (18.7 liters or 4.0 Imperial gallons)	
Engine oil	API service rating of SH or above
Kohler MV	
Above 32° F (0° C)	SAE 30
Between 32° F and 0° F (0° C and -18° C)	SAE 10W-30, 5W-20, or 5W-30
Below 0° F (-18° C)	SAE 5W-20 or 5W-30
Capacity	
With filter - 4 pints or 2 quarts (1.9 liters)	Without filter - 3.5 pints (1.7 liters)
Kohler CV	
Above 32° F (0° C)	SAE 10W-30
Between 32° F and 0° F (0° C and -18° C)	SAE 10W-30, 5W-20, or 5W-30
Below 0° F (-18° C)	SAE 5W-20 or 5W-30
Capacity with filter - 2.1 quarts (2.0 liters)	

(continued)

Table 3 RECOMMENDED FUEL AND LUBRICANTS, INCLUDING CAPACITIES (continued)

Engine oil (continued)	
Kawasaki	
Above 70° F (20° C)	SAE 40
Above 32° F (0° C)	SAE 30
Between 0° F and 95° F (-18° C and 35° C)	SAE 10W-30
Below 32° F (0° C)	SAE 5W-20
Capacity	
FC420V with filter - approximately 3.4 pints (1.6 liters)	
FH500V with filter - approximately 3.6 pints (1.75 liters)	
Briggs & Stratton	
Above 40° F (4° C)	SAE 30
Between 0° F and 40° F (-18° C and +4° C)	SAE 10W-30
Below 0° F (-18° C)	SAE 5W-20
Capacity	
With filter	3.5 pints (1.7 liters)
Without filter	3.0 pints (1.42 liters)

NOTE: Do not use 10W-40 oil in the engine. Recommended engine oil viscosities are for petroleum-based oils. Comparable synthetic oils may be used. DO NOT MIX synthetic oil with petroleum oil.

Table 4 RECOMMENDED SPARK PLUG TYPES, GAPS, AND TORQUES

ENGINE	SPARK PLUG	GAP	TORQUE
Kohler MV	Champion RV17YC1	0.035 in. (0.9 mm)	120-180 in.-lb. (13-20 N·m)
Kohler			
CV14, 15	Champion RC12YC	0.040 in. (1.0 mm)	335-385 in.-lb. (38-43 N·m)
CV20	Champion RC12YC2	0.030 in. (0.75 mm)	215-265 in.-lb. (24-30 N·m)
Kawasaki			
FC420V	Champion RN11YC, NGK BPR5ES	0.028-.031 in. (0.7-0.8 mm)	[3]
FH451V, FH500V	Champion RCJ8Y, NGK BPMR4A	0.030 in. (0.75 mm)	130-135 in.-lb. (15 N·m)
FH641V	NGK BPR4ES, Champion RN14YC	0.030 in. (0.75 mm)	195 in.-lb. (22 N·m)
Briggs-Stratton	Champion RC12YC, Autolite 3924	0.030 in. (0.75 mm)	180 in.-lb. (20 N·m)

1. RV17YC is for normal usage; RV15YC is recommended for *continuous full-load* running.
2. Inductive spark plug (Champion QC12YC) should be used to prevent radio frequency interference (RFI) on engines or systems with hourmeters. RFI may randomly reset hourmeters back to zero.
3. Not specified.

NOTE: Equivalent spark plugs may be substituted. Always cross-reference accurately.

Table 5 BATTERY STATE OF CHARGE

Specific gravity reading	Percentage of charge remaining
1.120-1.140	0
1.135-1.155	10
1.150-1.170	20
1.160-1.180	30
1.175-1.195	40
1.190-1.210	50
1.205-1.255	60
1.215-1.235	70
1.230-1.250	80
1.245-1.265	90
1.260-1.280	100

Table 6 GENERAL TORQUE SPECIFICATIONS, DRY THREADS[1]

Thread Size	Grade 22	Grade 5	Grade 8
8-32	16-24 (1.9-2.7)	20-30 (2.3-3.3)	34-50 (3.8-5.6)
10-24 USS	26-38 (2.9-4.3)	32-48 (3.6-5.4)	- -
10-32 SAE	26-38 (2.9-4.3)	32-48 (3.6-5.4)	48-72 (5.5-8.1)
1/4-20 USS	56-84 (6.3-9.5)	98-138 (10.4-15.6)	132-198 (15.0-22.4)
1/4-28 SAE	68-102 (7.7-11.5)	112-168 (12.7-18.9)	160-240 (18.1-27.1)
5/16-18 USS	120-180 (13.6-20.4)	200-300 (22.7-34.0)	280-420 (31.7-47.5)
5/16-24 SAE	132-198 (15.0-22.4)	216-324 (24.4-36.6)	288-432 (32.6-48.8)
3/8-16 USS	208-312 (23.5-35.3)	336-504 (38.0-57.0)	480-720 (54.2-81.4)
3/8-24 SAE	240-360 (27.1-40.7)	384-576 (43.4-65.0)	- -

1. Unplated or zinc-plated threads, no lubrication.
2. For torque purposes, Grade 2 bolts between 1/4-in. and 3/4-in. in diameter with a length of six inches or less are considered Grade 1 bolts and are to be torqued to the (ital)lowest(ital) value specified.

Table 7 GENERAL TORQUE SPECIFICATIONS, DRY THREADS[1]

Thread Size	Grade 22	Grade 5	Grade 8
5/16-24 SAE	- -	- -	24-36 (32.6-48.8)
3/8-16 USS	- -	28-42 (38.0-57.0)	40-60 (54.3-81.3)
3/8-24 SAE	- -	32-48 (43.8-65.0)	48-72 (65.1-97.7)

(continued)

Table 7 GENERAL TORQUE SPECIFICATIONS, DRY THREADS[1] (continued)

Thread Size	Grade 22	Grade 5	Grade 8
7/16-14 USS	28-42	44-66	64-96
	(38.0-57.0)	(59.7-89.5)	(86.8-130.2)
7/16-20 SAE	36-54	60-90	84-126
	(49.0-73.0)	(81.4-122.0)	(113.9-170.9)
1/2-13 USS	40-60	64-96	92-138
	(54.3-81.3)	(86.8-130.2)	(124.7-187.1)
1/2-20 SAE	56-84	84-126	132-198
	(75.9-113.9)	(113.9-170.9)	(179.0-268.4)

1. Unplated or zinc-plated threads, no lubrication.
2. For torque purposes, Grade 2 bolts of 3/4-inch or smaller diameter with a length of six inches or less are considered Grade 1 and are to be torqued to the (ital)lowest(ital) value specified.

3

NOTES

CHAPTER FOUR

FUEL AND EXHAUST

This chapter includes service procedures for parts of the fuel, emission and exhaust systems common to all Scag SWZ(U) mowers.

The fuel system consists of the fuel tank, the fuel shut-off valve, fuel hoses and clamps, the in-line fuel filter, the carburetor, the air filter assembly and the throttle and choke control cables. An exploded view of the tank, valve, hose and filter is shown in **Figure 1**. The throttle control is mounted on the handlebar control panel; the choke control is mounted on a bracket attached to the lower left side of the fuel tank support (**Figure 2**).

The emission-control system consists of a calibrated air filter assembly, a pre-calibrated, fixed-high-speed-jet carburetor (except some Kohler MV engines), a positive crankcase ventilation (PCV) system supplied by the crankcase breather, and a solid-state ignition system for precise spark control. *Air Filter Service* is covered in Chapter Three. Service procedures for the carburetor, PCV system, crankcase breather, and solid-state ignition are covered in each appropriate engine chapter. *Carburetor Fundamentals*, *Ignition System Fundamentals* and *Ignition System Troubleshooting; Spark Test* are covered in Chapter Two.

The exhaust system consists of a short exhaust pipe and a canister-style muffler assembly. Exhaust systems are supplied by the engine manufacturers; Scag does not provide exhaust components. Some mufflers have a spark-arrestor screen mounted in the outlet pipe. **Figure 3** shows some typical mufflers for both 1- and 2-cylinder engines.

Handling Gasoline Safely

> *WARNING*
> *Gasoline is a volatile, flammable liquid and is one of the most dangerous items in the shop.*

Because gasoline is used so often, many people forget that it is hazardous. Only use gasoline as fuel for gasoline internal combustion engines. Keep in mind when working on a machine that gasoline is always present in the fuel tank, fuel line and carburetor. To avoid a disastrous accident when working around the fuel system, carefully observe the following precautions:

1. *Never* use gasoline to clean parts.

2. When working on the fuel system, work outside or in a well-ventilated area.

3. Do not add fuel to the fuel tank or service the fuel system while the vehicle is near open flames, sparks, where someone is smoking, or while the engine is running. Gasoline vapor is heavier than air; it collects in low areas and is easily ignited.

4. Allow the engine to cool completely before working on any fuel system component, unless specific instructions state otherwise.

5. When draining the carburetor, catch the fuel in a non-sparking container and then pour it into an approved gasoline storage device.

6. Do not store gasoline in glass containers. If the glass breaks, a serious explosion or fire may occur. Sunlight

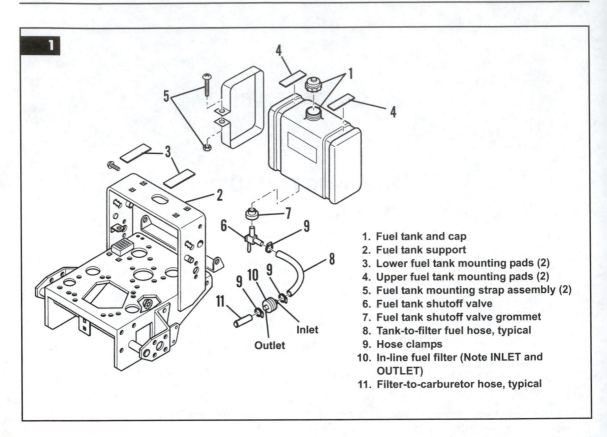

1. Fuel tank and cap
2. Fuel tank support
3. Lower fuel tank mounting pads (2)
4. Upper fuel tank mounting pads (2)
5. Fuel tank mounting strap assembly (2)
6. Fuel tank shutoff valve
7. Fuel tank shutoff valve grommet
8. Tank-to-filter fuel hose, typical
9. Hose clamps
10. In-line fuel filter (Note INLET and OUTLET)
11. Filter-to-carburetor hose, typical

through glass rapidly deteriorates gasoline as well as heating it to the point of explosion.

7. Immediately wipe up spilled gasoline with rags. Store the rags in an outside metal container with a lid until they can be properly disposed of, ensuring that the container itself is in a safe location.

8. Do not pour water onto a gasoline fire. Water spreads the fire and makes it more difficult to put out. Use a class B fire extinguisher to extinguish a gasoline fire.

9. Always turn off the engine before refueling. Do not spill fuel onto the engine or exhaust system. Do not overfill the fuel tank. Leave an air space of approximately one inch below the bottom of the filler neck to allow room for the fuel to expand due to temperature fluctuations.

FUEL TANK

The fuel tank on the Scag SWZ(U) mowers is of polymer construction and has a capacity of 5.0 U.S. gallons (18.7 liters). Fuel recommendations are as follows:

Kohler — Use only clean, fresh, *unleaded* gasoline with a pump sticker octane rating of 87 or higher. Gasohol (up to 10% ethyl alcohol, 90% unleaded gasoline by volume) is approved as a fuel for Kohler engines. Methyl Tertiary Butyl Ether (MTBE) and unleaded gasoline blends (up to a maximum of 15% MTBE by volume) are approved as a fuel for Kohler engines.

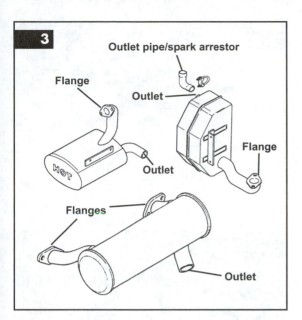

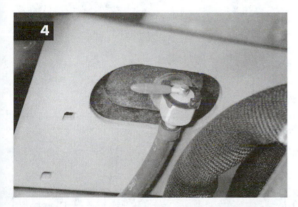

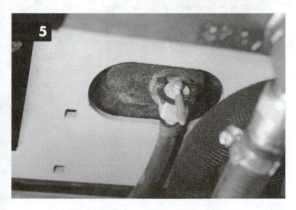

Briggs & Stratton — Use clean, fresh, regular unleaded gasoline with a minimum of 85 octane. Do not use gasoline which contains Methanol.

Kawasaki — Use only clean, fresh, unleaded regular grade gasoline with a minimum of 87 octane. Oxygenated

gasoline containing up to 10% ethanol or 15% MTBE (Methyl Tertiary Butyl Ether) or up to 5% methanol by volume may be used, as long as it also contains cosolvents and corrosion inhibitors to protect the fuel system. Gasoline containing more than 5% methanol by volume may cause starting and/or performance problems. It may also damage metal, rubber, and plastic parts of the fuel system. If knocking or pinging occurs, use a different brand of gasoline or higher octane rating.

Some equipment owners and shops use gasoline preservatives. If such a fuel stabilizer is used, follow the manufacturer's instructions precisely.

FUEL SHUT-OFF VALVE

The fuel shut-off valve is mounted directly underneath the tank. It controls the flow of fuel to the engine. **Figure 4** shows the valve in the OFF position; **Figure 5** shows the valve in the ON position. Anytime the mower is not in use, the valve should be turned off. This is especially true when the unit is being transported from one site to another. During transport, as the mower bounces in the truck or on the trailer, the carburetor float also bounces inside the carburetor. Each time the float bounces, the float valve opens. If the tank valve is open, fuel enters the carburetor, eventually flooding the engine, washing the oil from the cylinder wall and piston, and possibly diluting the crankcase oil.

Periodically check the shut-off valve for leakage. Determine whether the valve or the valve-to-tank grommet is at fault. Replace the faulty component.

If the engine is not receiving sufficient fuel, the shut-off valve may be restricted or clogged. To check for a clogged valve:

1. Turn the valve off (**Figure 4**).

2. Place a container under the fuel filter inlet fitting (10, **Figure 1**) to catch any spillage.

3. Remove the hose clamp and fuel hose (8 and 9, **Figure 1**) from the fuel filter inlet.

4. Direct the hose into the catch container.

5. Turn the valve on (**Figure 5**). If no fuel or just a dribble of fuel flows from the hose, the valve is probably clogged. Turn the valve off.

6. Siphon the fuel from the tank into an approved container.

7. Loosen the tank straps (5, **Figure 1**), then remove the tank from the mower.

8. Lay the tank on its side, noting the direction of the valve outlet fitting. work the valve from the grommet (7, **Figure 1**). Remove and discard the grommet.

9. Flush and clean the tank.

10. Remove the hose and clamp from the valve. If the valve cannot be cleaned, replace the valve.

11. Lightly oil the inner and outer grommet surfaces. First, install the grommet into the tank, then work the

shut-off valve into the grommet, ensuring that the valve outlet faces the proper direction.

12. Install the fuel hose and clamps onto the valve.

13. Remount the tank onto the mower.

14. Install a new fuel filter, then connect the tank valve hose and clamp to the filter inlet.

15. Drain and check the fuel storage container to make sure the valve-clogging debris did not come from the container.

16. Refill the tank with *fresh* fuel.

FUEL HOSES AND CLAMPS

Fuel hoses should be periodically checked for integrity. Replace any leaking, cracked or kinked hoses.

Some fuel systems use pre-formed hoses due to the tight bends required. Do not attempt to force a straight hose to bend in a location requiring a formed hose. Hose kinking and fuel starvation will result.

When removing stubborn hoses, do not apply excessive force to the hose or fitting. Remove the hose clamp and carefully insert a small pick tool between the fitting and hose. Apply a spray lubricant under the hose and carefully twist the hose off the fitting. Clean the fitting of any corrosion or hose material. A wire brush can be used on metal fittings; plastic fittings will require careful use of a small knife or scraper.

> *WARNING*
> *Never attempt to seal a loosely-fitting hose by tightening a clamp around it. Fuel leakage will eventually result. Make sure that the hose is the proper size for the fitting.*

Always match the correct hose size to the fitting. To determine the correct hose size required for a particular fitting, measure the *small diameter* of the fitting barb with a caliper (**Figure 6**). Compare the decimal reading to the nearest fractional equivalent in **Table 1**. The decimal reading will usually be slightly larger than the fractional hose size in order to ensure a snug hose fit. The reading in **Figure 6**, for example, is 0.260 inch, which is 1/4 (0.250) inch plus 0.010 inch. This fitting requires fuel hose with a 1/4 inch inside diameter. Fittings requiring 3/16 (0.187) inch hose should measure approximately 0.193-0.195 inch.

Prior to placing a hose on a fitting, always slide a clamp onto the hose just beyond where the fitting will end inside the hose. When the hose is inserted onto the fitting, slide the clamp down the hose so the clamp fits over the *large diameter* of the fitting. This will ensure maximum clamping power.

> *WARNING*
> *Never install a hose over a fuel fitting without the proper size clamp to secure it. A spring-tension style clamp is preferable*

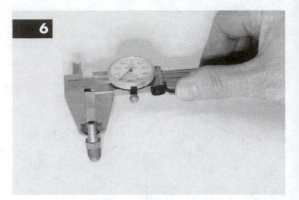

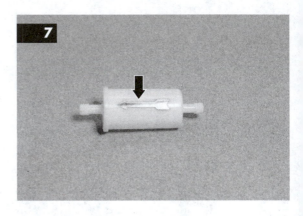

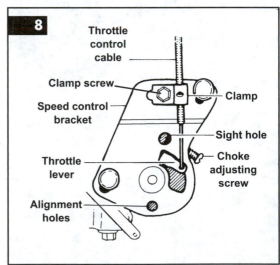

to a screw-style clamp. Reusing old clamps is not recommended.

> *NOTE*
> *Do not use any lubricant when installing fuel hose onto fittings unless a new clamp is also being installed. The lubricant may allow the hose to come off the fitting.*

9

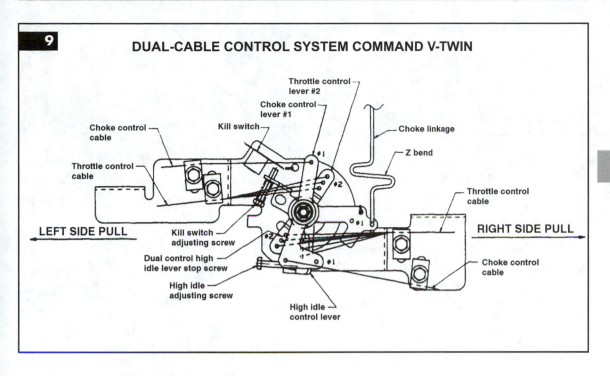

DUAL-CABLE CONTROL SYSTEM COMMAND V-TWIN

Throttle control lever #2

Choke control lever #1

Choke control cable

Kill switch

Choke linkage

Z bend

Throttle control cable

Throttle control cable

LEFT SIDE PULL

Kill switch adjusting screw

Dual control high idle lever stop screw

High idle adjusting screw

High idle control lever

RIGHT SIDE PULL

Choke control cable

4

FUEL FILTER

In order to protect the fuel system from debris-induced damage while maintaining peak performance, the fuel filter should be changed annually.

To change the filter and hoses:

1. If possible, run the unit until it is completely out of fuel.

> *WARNING*
> *Make sure ventilation is adequate if the engine is to be run in a confined area. Exhaust fumes are toxic and deadly.*

2. If Step 1 is not practical, shut off the fuel tank valve (**Figure 4**), then run the engine until it dies. This will empty the lines and carburetor of fuel.

3. Access the fuel line at the fuel filter. Loosen the hose clamps and carefully remove the hoses from the filter. When removing stubborn hoses, do not apply excessive force to the hose or fitting. Remove the hose clamp and carefully insert a small pick tool between the fitting and hose. Apply a spray lubricant under the hose and carefully twist the hose off the fitting. Clean the fitting of any corrosion or hose material. A wire brush can be used on metal fittings; plastic fittings will require careful use of a small knife or scraper.

> *WARNING*
> *When working on gasoline hose fittings, always use non-sparking pick tools and wire brushes, such as brass-bristle*

brushes or 300-grade non-magnetic stainless steel pick tools.

4. Direct the loosened hose into a drainage container, open the tank shutoff valve and drain the fuel from the tank. When the tank is completely drained, loosen the tank-fitting clamp and remove the hose from the tank fitting.

> *NOTE*
> *A non-reversible filter will be marked, usually by an arrow (**Figure 7**), to denote the direction of flow. The arrow must point toward the carburetor. If the filter is installed backwards, it will not filter correctly and will clog prematurely.*

5. Install the new hoses with new clamps to the new fuel filter. If the new filter is a non-reversible filter, note the flow direction in relation to the fuel hoses. An unmarked filter can be installed either way when new. Once installed, it should never be reversed. Reversing an unmarked filter will feed debris into the carburetor.

THROTTLE CONTROL CABLE ASSEMBLY

The throttle control cable assembly (**Figure 2**) regulates the speed of the engine. **Figure 8** shows the lower end of the cable attached to a typical 1-cylinder engine speed control. **Figure 9** shows the lower-end cable attachment for a typical 2-cylinder engine speed control.

Control Cable Lubrication

NOTE
Because of construction similarities, lubrication of both the throttle and choke cables is covered here.

Clean and lubricate the throttle cable and choke cable at the intervals indicated in **Table 2**. In addition, check the cables for kinks and signs of wear and damage that could cause the cables to fail or stick. Cables are expendable items that do not last forever, even under the best of conditions.

The most positive method of control cable lubrication involves the use of an aerosol lubricator with a small-diameter nozzle extension. A can of cable lube or general lubricant is required. Do *not* use chain lube as a cable lubricant.

NOTE
Place a shop cloth at the end of the cables to catch the oil as it runs out.

To lubricate the cables:
1. Insert the lubricant nozzle extension into the lubricator valve tip.
2. Aim the nozzle extension into the cable housing at the uppermost portion of the cable, as it is positioned on the mower (**Figure 10**).
3. Momentarily press the button on the can.
4. Repeat momentary squirts until the lubricant begins to flow out of the other end of the cable. If the cable lube will not flow through the cable at one end, try at the opposite end of the cable. It may be necessary to disconnect the lower end and raise it so the lubricant flows down the cable. Note the cable position prior to disconnection so the cable can be reinstalled in the same position.

Throttle Control Cable Adjustment

To adjust the throttle control cable, refer to **Figure 2** and the *Governor, Adjustment* section of the appropriate engine chapter, then proceed as follows:
1. Inspect the full length of the control and cable. Ensure that the cable is not rusted, kinked, or otherwise damaged, and that the Z-bends are in good condition.
2. Loosen the holddown screw holding the cable clamp to the control bracket. After loosening, the cable outer housing must be free to move under the clamp.
3. Move the throttle control to the FAST position on the control panel (**Figure 11**).
4. Perform the throttle cable adjustment by following the instructions applicable to the engine.
5. Ensure that the throttle cable is centered in the clamp channel, then tighten the clamp holddown screw. Work the throttle control between FAST and SLOW two to three times to be sure the control or cable is not binding.

6. Making sure that all safety interlocks are in their proper position, start the engine, moving the throttle control through its entire range to check control operation.

WARNING
Ensure an adequate ventilation supply if the engine is to be started in a confined area. Exhaust fumes are toxic and deadly.

Place the control in the FAST position and allow the engine to run for a minute or two to ensure that the control holds position.

7. Stop the engine.

4

CHOKE CONTROL CABLE ASSEMBLY

The choke control cable assembly (**Figure 2**) closes and opens the manual choke shutter on the engine carburetor. **Figure 12** shows a choke cable attached to a typical remote choke-control panel. Lubricate the cable as described in this chapter.

Choke Control Cable Adjustment

To adjust the choke control cable, refer to **Figure 2** and **Figure 12** and proceed as follows:

1. Remove enough of the air filter assembly so the choke shutter and choke linkage is visible (**Figure 12**).

2. Inspect the full length of the control and cable. Make sure that the cable is not rusted, kinked, or otherwise damaged, and that the Z-bends are in good condition.

3. Loosen the holddown screw holding the cable clamp to the carburetor or choke bracket. After loosening, the cable outer housing must be free to move under the clamp.

4. Push the choke knob all the way in.

5. Move the choke shutter to the wide-open position (**Figure 13**).

6. Make sure that the choke cable is centered in the clamp channel, then tighten the clamp holddown screw.

7. Pull out on the cable control until the carburetor choke shutter is completely closed (**Figure 14**). Make sure that the shutter closes completely.

8. Work the choke control out and in two or three times to make sure the control or cable is not binding.

EXHAUST SYSTEM

The exhaust system is supplied by the engine manufacturer. It is calibrated as part of the emission control system. It not only reduces exhaust noise to acceptable levels, but it also provides the proper amount of back pressure to allow the inlet and combustion components to produce rated horsepower as well as compliant emission levels.

For this reason, the exhaust system should be maintained in good repair. As the noise level increases, power decreases. Under no circumstances should the exhaust system be modified. Inspect the muffler, pipes, flanges, connections and fasteners regularly. Replace any questionable components.

Muffler Replacement

1. Allow the unit to cool.

2. Loosen all fasteners and clamps. Do *not* remove any fasteners until all of them have been loosened.

If a bolt cannot be loosened, apply penetrating oil such as Liquid Wrench, Kroil or WD-40, and let it penetrate for 10-15 minutes. Rap the fastener several times with a small hammer and punch. Do not hit it hard enough to cause damage. Reapply the penetrating oil if necessary. Use 6-sided sockets and wrenches on hex-headed bolts to reduce the chances of rounding off the hex.

For frozen screws, apply penetrating oil as described. Insert a stout screwdriver into the slot, and carefully rap the top of the screwdriver with a hammer. This loosens the rust so the screw can be removed. If the screw head is too damaged to use this method, grip the head with locking pliers and twist the screw out.

NOTE
Do not apply heat unless specifically instructed, as it may melt, warp or remove the temper from parts.

If a fastener should break off, refer to *Removing Broken Fasteners* in Chapter One.

3. Begin removing the fasteners while supporting the exhaust system. Work from the outlet pipe inward. The bolts holding the exhaust pipe flange(s) to the engine should be the last bolts removed, at which time the exhaust system can be removed and set aside.

CAUTION
Discard all used gaskets and replace with new gaskets. Also discard the old lockwashers, replacing them with new ones.

NOTE
*Remove the exhaust system carefully. Some engines have alloy steel liners inside the exhaust port(s) (**Figure 15**) for reduced cylinder head temperature. If the engine has exhaust port liners, they do not need to be removed for exhaust system replacement. If the exhaust system is being removed in order to overhaul the cylinder head(s), note the liner orientation as the liner will need to be removed for head service. Be sure that the liner is installed properly.*

4. Inspect all brackets and supports for cracks and breaks. Inspect the outlet pipe spark-arrestor screen, if equipped. Replace as necessary.

5. Carefully remove any old gasket material from the exhaust flange surfaces, and wirebrush the fastener threads.

6. With the liner(s) installed, if applicable, insert new gasket(s) onto the exhaust studs or bolts.

7. Replace all fastener lock washers and lightly coat the fastener threads with a high-temperature thread-lock compound, such as Loctite 271 or equivalent.

8. Align the exhaust system with all bracket and fastener holes, then install and hand-tighten the fasteners, beginning with the exhaust pipe flanges. Do not tighten any fasteners until all of them have been installed.

9. Beginning with the flanges, tighten all fasteners, working toward the outlet pipe.

10. Install the spark arrestor, if used.

Table 1 DECIMAL, METRIC, AND FRACTIONAL CONVERSIONS AND DRILL SIZE EQUIVALENTS

Drill/Fraction size	Decimal in.	Metric mm	Drill/Fraction size	Decimal in.	Metric mm
0.30 mm	0.0118	-	5.50 mm	0.2165	-
0.32 mm	0.0126	-	7/32 in.	0.21875	5.55625
#80	0.0135	-	5.60 mm	0.2205	-
0.35 mm	0.0138	-	#2	0.2210	-
#79	0.0145	-	5.70 mm	0.2244	-
0.38 mm	0.0150	-	#1	0.2280	-
1/64 in.	0.0156	0.39688	5.80 mm	0.2283	-
0.40 mm	0.0157	-	5.90 mm	0.2323	-
#78	0.0160	-	A	0.2340	-
0.42 mm	0.0165	-	15/64 in.	0.2344	5.95312
0.45 mm	0.0177	-	6.00 mm	0.2362	-
#77	0.0180	-	B	0.2380	-
0.48 mm	0.0189	-	6.10 mm	0.2402	-
0.50 mm	0.0197	-	C	0.2420	-
#76	0.0200	0.51	6.20 mm	0.2441	-
#75	0.0210	0.53	D	0.2460	-
			(continued)		

Table 1 DECIMAL, METRIC, AND FRACTIONAL CONVERSIONS AND DRILL SIZE EQUIVALENTS

Drill/Fraction size	Decimal in.	Metric mm	Drill/Fraction size	Decimal in.	Metric mm
0.55 mm	0.0217	-	6.30 mm	0.2480	-
#74	0.0225	-	1/4 in. and E	0.2500	6.35000
0.60 mm	0.0236	-	6.40 mm	0.2520	-
#73	0.0240	-	6.50 mm	0.2559	-
0.62 mm	0.0244	-	F	0.2570	-
#72	0.0250	0.63500	6.60 mm	0.2598	-
0.65 mm	0.0256	-	G	0.2610	-
#71	0.0260	-	6.70 mm	0.2638	-
0.70 mm	0.0276	-	17/64 in.	0.265625	6.74687
#70	0.0280	-	H	0.2660	-
#69	0.0292	-	6.80 mm	0.2677	-
0.75 mm	0.0295	-	6.90 mm	0.2717	-
#68	0.0310	-	I	0.2720	-
1/32 in.	0.03125	0.79375	7.00 mm	0.2756	-
0.80 mm	0.0315	-	J	0.2770	-
#67	0.0320	-	7.10 mm	0.2795	-
#66	0.0330	-	K	0.2810	-
0.85 mm	0.0335	-	9/32 in.	0.28125	7.14375
#65	0.0350	-	7.20 mm	0.2835	-
0.90 mm	0.0354	-	7.30 mm	0.2874	-
#64	0.0360	-	L	0.2900	-
#63	0.0370	-	7.40 mm	0.2913	-
0.95 mm	0.0374	-	M	0.2950	-
#62	0.0380	-	7.50 mm	0.2953	-
#61	0.0390	-	19/64 in.	0.296875	7.54062
1.00 mm	0.03937	-	7.60 mm	0.2992	-
#60	0.0400	-	N	0.3020	-
#59	0.0410	-	7.70 mm	0.3031	-
1.05 mm	0.0413	-	7.80 mm	0.3071	-
#58	0.0420	-	7.90 mm	0.3110	-
#57	0.0430	-	5/16 in.	0.3125	7.93750
1.10 mm	0.0433	-	8.00 mm	0.3150	-
1.15 mm	0.0453	-	O	0.3160	-
#56	0.0465	-	8.10 mm	0.3189	-
3/64 in.	0.046875	1.19062	8.20 mm	0.3228	-
1.20 mm	0.0472	-	P	0.3230	-
1.25 mm	0.0492	-	8.30 mm	0.3268	-
1.30 mm	0.0512	-	21/64 in.	0.328125	8.33437
#55	0.0520	-	8.40 mm	0.3307	-
1.35 mm	0.0531	-	Q	0.3320	-
#54	0.0550	-	8.50 mm	0.3346	-
1.40 mm	0.0551	-	8.60 mm	0.3386	-
1.45 mm	0.0571	-	R	0.3390	-
1.50 mm	0.0591	-	8.70 mm	0.3425	-
#53	0.0595	-	11/32 in.	0.34375	8.73125
1.55 mm	0.0610	-	8.80 mm	0.3465	-
1/16 in.	0.0625	1.58750	S	0.3480	-
1.60 mm	0.0630	-	8.90 mm	0.3504	-
#52	0.0635	-	9.00 mm	0.3543	-
1.65 mm	0.0650	-	T	0.3580	-
1.70 mm	0.0669	-	9.10 mm	0.3583	-
#51	0.0670	-	23/64 in.	0.359375	9.12812
1.75 mm	0.0689	-	9.20 mm	0.3622	-
#50	0.0700	-	9.30 mm	0.3661	-
1.80 mm	0.0709	-	U	0.3680	-
1.85 mm	0.0728	-	9.40 mm	0.3701	-

(continued)

4

Table 1   DECIMAL, METRIC, AND FRACTIONAL CONVERSIONS AND DRILL SIZE EQUIVALENTS

Drill/Fraction size	Decimal in.	Metric mm	Drill/Fraction size	Decimal in.	Metric mm
#49	0.0730	-	9.50 mm	0.3740	-
1.90 mm	0.0748	-	3/8 in.	0.375	9.525
#48	0.0760	-	V	0.3770	-
1.95 mm	0.0768	-	9.60 mm	0.3780	-
5/64 in.	0.078125	1.98437	9.70 mm	0.3819	-
#47	0.0785	-	9.80 mm	0.3858	-
2.00 mm	0.0787	-	W	0.3860	-
2.05 mm	0.0807	-	9.90 mm	0.3898	-
#46	0.0810	-	25/64 in.	0.390625	9.92187
#45	0.0820	-	10.00 mm	0.3937	-
2.10 mm	0.0827	-	X	0.3970	-
2.15 mm	0.0846	-	10.20 mm	0.4016	-
#44	0.0860	-	Y	0.4040	-
2.20 mm	0.0866	-	13/32 in.	0.40625	10.31875
2.25 mm	0.0866	-	Z	0.4130	-
#43	0.0890	-	10.50 mm	0.4134	-
2.30 mm	0.0906	-	27/64 in.	0.421875	10.71562
2.35 mm	0.0925	-	10.80 mm	0.4252	-
#42	0.0935	-	11.00 mm	0.4331	-
3/32 in.	0.09375	2.38125	7/16 in.	0.4375	11.11250
2.40 mm	0.0945	-	11.20 mm	0.4409	-
#41	0.0960	-	11.50 mm	0.4528	-
2.45 mm	0.0965	-	29/64 in.	0.453125	11.50937
#40	0.0980	-	11.80 mm	0.4646	-
2.50 mm	0.0984	-	15/32 in.	0.46875	11.90625
#39	0.0995	-	12.00 mm	0.4724	-
#38	0.1015	-	12.20 mm	0.4803	-
2.60 mm	0.1024	-	31/64 in.	0.484375	12.30312
#37	0.1040	-	12.50 mm	0.4921	-
2.70 mm	0.1063	-	1/2 in.	0.5000	12.7000
#36	0.1065	-	12.80 mm	0.5039	-
7/64 in.	0.109375	2.77812	13.00 mm	0.5118	-
#35	0.1100	-	33/64 in.	0.515625	13.09687
2.80 mm	0.1102	-	13.20 mm	0.5197	-
#34	0.1110	2.81	17/32 in.	0.53125	13.49375
#33	0.1130	-	13.50 mm	0.5315	-
2.90 mm	0.1142	-	13.80 mm	0.5433	-
#32	0.1160	-	35/64 in.	0.546875	13.89062
3.00 mm	0.1181	-	14.00 mm	0.5512	-
#31	0.1200	-	14.25 mm	0.5610	-
3.10 mm	0.1220	-	9/16 in.	0.5625	14.28750
1/8 in.	0.125	3.1750	14.50 mm	0.5709	-
3.20 mm	0.1260	-	37/64 in.	0.578125	14.68437
#30	0.1285	-	14.75 mm	0.5807	-
3.30 mm	0.1299	-	15.00 mm	0.5906	-
3.40 mm	0.1339	-	19/32 in.	0.59375	15.08125
#29	0.1360	-	15.25 mm	0.6004	-
3.50 mm	0.1378	-	39/64 in.	0.609375	15.47812
#28	0.1405	-	15.50 mm	0.6102	-
9/64 in.	0.140625	3.57187	15.75 mm	0.6201	-
3.60 mm	0.1417	-	5/8 in.	0.625	15.875
#27	0.1440	-	16.00 mm	0.6299	-
3.70 mm	0.1457	-	16.25 mm	0.6398	-
#26	0.1470	-	41/64 In.	0.640625	16.27187
#25	0.1495	-	16.50 mm	0.6496	-
3.80 mm	0.1496	-	21/32 in.	0.65625	16.66875

(continued)

Table 1   DECIMAL, METRIC, AND FRACTIONAL CONVERSIONS AND DRILL SIZE EQUIVALENTS

Drill/Fraction size	Decimal in.	Metric mm	Drill/Fraction size	Decimal in.	Metric mm
#24	0.1520	-	16.75 mm	0.6594	-
3.90 mm	0.1535	-	17.00 mm	0.6693	-
#23	0.1540	-	43/64 in.	0.671875	17.06562
5/32 in.	0.15625	3.96875	17.25 mm	0.6791	-
#22	0.1570	-	11/16 in.	0.6875	17.4625
4.00 mm	0.1575	-	17.50 mm	0.6890	-
#21	0.1590	-	45/64 in.	0.703125	17.85937
#20	0.1610	-	18.00 mm	0.7087	-
4.10 mm	0.1614	-	23/32 in.	0.71875	18.25625
4.20 mm	0.1654	-	18.50 mm	0.7283	-
#19	0.1660	-	47/64 in.	0.734375	18.65312
4.30 mm	0.1693	-	19.00 mm	0.7480	-
#18	0.1695	-	3/4 in.	0.75	19.05
11/64 in.	0.171875	4.36562	49/64 in.	0.765625	19.44687
#17	0.1730	-	19.50 mm	0.7677	-
4.40 mm	0.1732	-	25/32 in.	0.78125	19.84375
#16	0.1770	-	20.00 mm	0.7874	-
4.50 mm	0.1772	-	51/64 in.	0.796875	20.24062
#15	0.1800	-	20.50 mm	0.8071	-
4.60 mm	0.1811	-	13/16 in.	0.8125	20.6375
#14	0.1820	-	21.00 mm	0.8268	-
4.70 mm, #13	0.1850	-	53/64 in.	0.828125	21.03437
3/16 in.	0.1875	4.7625	27/32 in.	0.84375	21.43125
4.80 mm, #12	0.1890	-	21.50 mm	0.8465	-
#11	0.1910	-	55/64 in.	0.859375	22.82812
4.90 mm	0.1929	-	22.00 mm	0.8661	-
#10	0.1935	-	7/8 in.	0.875	22.225
#9	0.1960	-	22.50 mm	0.8858	-
5.00 mm	0.1969	-	57/64 in.	0.890625	22.62187
#8	0.1990	-	23.00 mm	0.9055	-
5.10 mm	0.2008	-	29/32 in.	0.90625	23.01875
#7	0.2010	-	59/64 in.	0.921875	23.41562
13/64 in.	0.203125	5.15937	23.50 mm	0.9252	-
#6	0.2040	-	15/16 in.	0.9375	23.8125
5.20 mm	0.2047	-	24.00 mm	0.9449	-
#5	0.2055	-	61/64 in.	0.953125	24.20937
5.30 mm	0.2087	-	24.50 mm	0.9646	-
#4	0.2090	-	31/32 in.	0.96875	24.60625
5.40 mm	0.2126	-	25.00 mm	0.9843	-
#3	0.2130	-	63/64 in.	0.984375	25.00312
			1.0 in.	1.000	25.40000

4

Table 2 MAINTENANCE AND LUBRICATION SCHEDULE

After 5-hour break-in period (new unit; new or overhauled engine)	Change the engine oil and the oil filter. Check all the fasteners and the linkages for security.
Every 8 hours or daily	Check the engine oil with the unit sitting level. Lubricate the two or three cutter-deck spindle bearings until grease escapes from the relief valve.[1] Lift the deck belt cover and remove any accumulated chaff or debris. Check the belts for integrity and tension.

(continued)

Table 2 MAINTENANCE AND LUBRICATION SCHEDULE (continued)

Every 8 hours or daily	Check the belt idler pulleys. Sharpen the blades, if needed. Check and/or clean the air filter. Check the tire pressure and integrity.
Every 40-50 hours or weekly	On electric-start units, check the battery electrolyte level. Lubricate the throttle and choke cables.
Every 100 hours or semi-monthly	Replace the air filter. Change the engine oil and oil filter. Lubricate the two caster wheel pivots.[2] Lubricate the two caster wheel bearings.[2] Lubricate the three idler arm pivots.[2] Lubricate the two brake actuator levers.[2] Clean the area around the hydrostatic oil filter and replace the filter. Replace any lost fluid.[3]
Every 200 hours or monthly	Lubricate the two neutral cam pivots.[2] Lubricate the two pump control pivots.[2]
Every 300 hours or semi-annually	Adjust the engine valve tappet clearances on applicable Kawasaki engines.
Every 500 hours or annually	Replace the fuel filter and fuel hoses. Adjust the engine valve tappet clearances on Kohler MV and Briggs & Stratton engines. Check all of the fasteners for proper security. Inspect deck, frame, and handle welds for any signs of fatigue or cracking. Adjust the air gap on the electric clutch. Drain the hydraulic system. Install fresh oil[3] and a new filter.

1. Recommended lubricant is US Lithium MP White Grease 2125. Compatible lubricants are Exxon's Ronex MP, Shell Alvania, Mobil's Mobilux #2, Conoco's Super Lub M EP #2, or Lidok EP #2.
2. Recommended lubricant is chassis grease.
3. Factory-installed lubricant is SAE 20W-50 petroleum-base oil with an API classification of SH or above. Acceptable substitutes are Mobil Super HP, Amoco Ultimate, Viscosity Oil, Shell Gemini, Aero Shell, or Helix Ultra in SAE 5W-40, SAE 10W-40, or SAE 15W-50 grades. If synthetic oil is preferred after a complete system flush, Mobil 1 SAE 15W-50 is recommended; 5W-30 or 10W-30 are acceptable substitutes.

KOHLER MV-18 AND MV-20 ENGINES

ENGINE IDENTIFICATION

The Kohler MV-18 and MV-20 engines are both four-stroke, opposed-twin-cylinder, L-head ("side valve"), vertical crankshaft air-cooled engines. They are pressure lubricated and most engines are equipped with an oil filter. Number 1 cylinder is always the cylinder closest to the flywheel. The Tables at the end of this chapter contain the engine specifications.

Engine identification and serial numbers are located on a decal (or decals) located as shown in **Figure 1**. Refer to **Figure 2** to determine engine features and date of manufacture.

The next two sections provide information on removing and reinstalling the engine as a complete, assembled unit. Subsequent sections provide disassembly, inspection, adjustment, repair/overhaul and reassembly information for the engine components.

The engine must be removed from the equipment before undertaking repairs on the internal components. In the case of external components such as the carburetor or a cylinder head, engine removal may not be necessary, as the repair job may be performed with the engine mounted on the equipment.

Kohler tools, or suitable equivalent tools, may be recommended for some procedures outlined herein. Good quality tools are also available from small-engine parts suppliers. Be careful when substituting a homemade tool for a recommended tool. Although time and money may

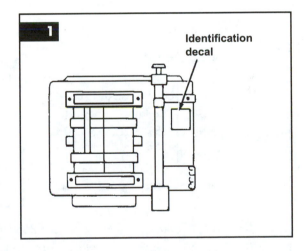

1

Identification decal

be saved if an existing or fabricated tool can be made to work, consider the possibilities if the tool does not work properly. If the substitute tool damages the engine, the cost to repair the damage, as well as the lost time, may exceed the cost of the recommended tool.

NOTE
Some procedures may require that work be performed by a professional shop. Be sure to get an estimate, then compare it with the cost of a new or rebuilt engine or shortblock (a basic engine sub-assembly).

2

ENGINE MODEL AND SERIAL NUMBER INTERPRETATION

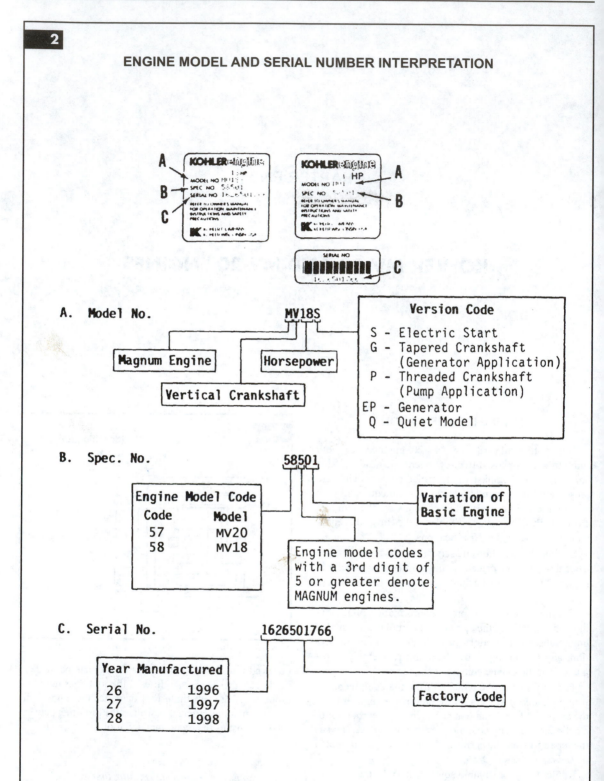

A. **Model No.** ——————————— **MV18S**

- Magnum Engine
- Vertical Crankshaft
- Horsepower

Version Code

S - Electric Start
G - Tapered Crankshaft
    (Generator Application)
P - Threaded Crankshaft
    (Pump Application)
EP - Generator
Q - Quiet Model

B. **Spec. No.** ——————————— **58501**

Engine Model Code

Code	Model
57	MV20
58	MV18

Variation of Basic Engine

Engine model codes with a 3rd digit of 5 or greater denote MAGNUM engines.

C. **Serial No.** ——————————— **1626501766**

Year Manufactured

26	1996
27	1997
28	1998

Factory Code

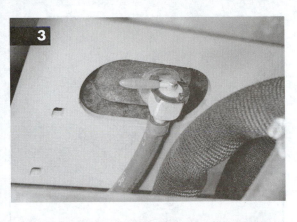

NOTE
Inch-size fasteners are used throughout these engines. Check thread compatibility before installing a fastener to prevent cross-threading.

ENGINE REMOVAL

Prior to removing the engine, drain the crankcase oil. Always drain the oil with the engine warm so the oil flows freely and carries out the dirt and impurities.

1. Be sure the engine is stopped and the ignition switch is in the OFF position. Allow the engine to cool to ambient temperature.

2. Engage the parking brake.

3. On electric-start units, disconnect the battery cables, negative terminal first, and remove the battery.

4. Close the fuel tank valve (**Figure 3**).

WARNING
Some gasoline will drain from the fuel hose during the next procedure. Wipe up any spilled gasoline immediately. Work in a well-ventilated area at least 50 feet away from any open flame, including pilot lights in gas appliances. Do not allow anyone to smoke in the area. Do not work near grinding or other source of sparks.

5. Detach the fuel hose clamp at the inlet connection to the fuel pump. Disconnect the fuel hose from the pump.

6. Disconnect the spark plug wires from both spark plugs. Ground the spark plug wires to the engine.

7. Identify and unplug the chassis wiring harness connectors and, on electric-start units, the starter motor cable.

8. Disconnect the throttle and choke control cables.

NOTE
Prior to removal, cable positions should be marked for proper reconnection during engine installation.

9. Remove the deck drive belt shield, then slacken the belt running from the engine as follows:

   a. On fixed-idler drives (**Figure 4**), apply penetrating oil to the J-bolt threads on both sides of the adjusting nut, then back the nut off to allow slack in the belt.

   b. On spring-loaded idler drives, like that in **Figure 5**, move the idler pulley bracket away from the belt. Secure the bracket to allow slack in the belt, or work the belt off the idler.

10. Chock the front wheels. Safely elevate and support the rear of the mower to gain access to the underside of the engine.

11. Unplug the PTO clutch wire connector (**Figure 5**). Support the PTO clutch while removing the clutch bolt from the crankshaft. Slide the clutch off the shaft, then remove the belt from the clutch pulley.

12. Move the hydrostatic drive idler pulley away from the drive belt so the belt slackens. Work the belt off the engine pulley, then remove the belt.

13. Remove the engine mounting bolts.

14. Carefully lift the engine off the frame.

15. Note the position of the hydrostat pulley on the crankshaft. Remove the pulley.

16. Clean the engine mounting area on the frame.

ENGINE INSTALLATION

1. Make sure that the engine mounting areas on both the frame and the bottom of the engine are clean and dry.

2. Lightly coat the crankshaft, including keyway, with anti-seize compound.

3. Install the hydrostat pulley on the crankshaft in the same position as that noted during removal.

4. Carefully set the engine in position on the frame. Ensure that the engine pan and frame fastener holes align.

5. Apply Loctite 271 or equivalent to the engine-mount fastener threads. Tighten the fasteners incrementally, alternately and securely. On fasteners with lock washers, use new lock washers.

6. Install the hydrostat belt onto the pulleys, then allow the spring-loaded idler to exert tension on the belt.

7. Apply Loctite 271 or equivalent to the electric PTO clutch mount bolt. Insert the PTO clutch belt into the clutch pulley groove. Align the clutch locator bracket, ensuring that the clutch wire is not pinched or kinked. Align the clutch key with the crankshaft keyway, then slide the clutch onto the crankshaft. While supporting the clutch, install the clutch bolt. Using the torque tables at the end of Chapter One, torque the clutch bolt.

8. Carefully remove the mower supports. Lower the unit to the floor. Make sure that the parking brake is still set, then remove the front wheel chocks.

9. Reapply tension to the deck drive belt.

   a. On fixed-idler drives, refer to the adjustment procedure under *Drive Belts* in Chapter Three to properly tension the belt.

   b. On spring-loaded idlers, reverse the belt-slacken method used during engine removal (Step 9b).

10. Install the deck drive belt shield.

11. Reconnect the throttle and choke cables using the marks noted during engine removal.

12. Reconnect the chassis wiring harness connectors to the appropriate engine plugs.

13. On electric-start units, reconnect the starter motor cable and the battery cables – negative cable last.

14. Reconnect the spark plug leads to the plugs.

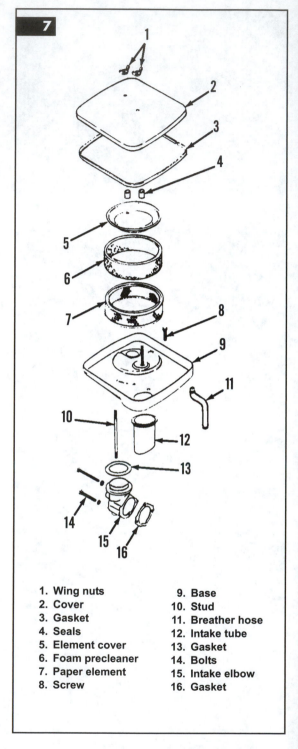

1. Wing nuts	9. Base
2. Cover	10. Stud
3. Gasket	11. Breather hose
4. Seals	12. Intake tube
5. Element cover	13. Gasket
6. Foam precleaner	14. Bolts
7. Paper element	15. Intake elbow
8. Screw	16. Gasket

15. Install a new fuel hose, including clamps, between the fuel filter and the fuel pump.

16. Refill the crankcase with the proper oil.

17. Open the fuel tank valve (**Figure 6**).

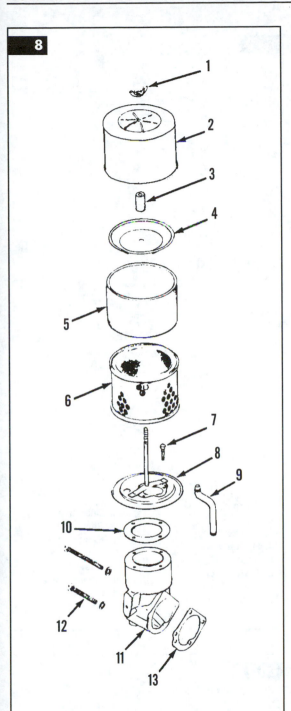

8

1. Wing nut
2. Cover
3. Seal
4. Element cover
5. Foam precleaner
6. Paper element
7. Screw
8. Base
9. Breather hose
10. Gasket
11. Intake elbow
12. Bolts
13. Gasket

5

LUBRICATION

All models are equipped with a pressure lubrication system. Refer to the *Oil Pump* section for oil pump service information.

Most engines are equipped with an oil filter. Some engines may experience oil seepage past the oil filter adapter (or block-off plate) gasket. An adapter leak kit is available from the manufacturer to correct this problem.

Periodically check the oil level, but do not overfill. To check the oil level:

1. Make sure that the mower is sitting on a level surface.
2. Clean the area around the dipstick cap to prevent dirt and debris from falling into the crankcase when the cap is removed.
3. Remove the dipstick and wipe the oil from the level indicator.
4. Reinsert the dipstick back down into the tube completely.
5. Remove the dipstick and check the oil level. The oil level should be up to, but not over, the FULL line on the dipstick.

If the engine is equipped with an oil filter, change the oil and filter after the first 5 hours of operation and every 50 hours thereafter. If the engine is not equipped with an oil filter, change oil after the first 5 hours of operation and every 25 hours thereafter. Engines used in heavy-duty operation should have the oil (and filter) changed after every 25 hours of operation.

To install a new oil filter, apply a light coating of clean engine oil to the filter gasket. Install the filter until the rubber gasket contacts the filter base, then tighten the filter an additional 1/2-3/4 turn.

Oil capacity for Models MV18 and MV20 is 3.5 pints (1.7 L) without a filter or 4 pints (1.9 L) with a filter. Refer to **Table 3** for engine oil recommendations.

NOTE
On M18 and M20 engines equipped with Oil Sentry pressure switch, an oil switch bypass kit can be installed to help eliminate engine backfiring during hot engine restart due to warm oil causing insufficient oil pressure. The bypass kit (part No. 82 755 25) is available from the engine manufacturer.

AIR FILTER

Three types of air filter assemblies are used on these engines: Square type (**Figure 7**), Dome type (**Figure 8**) and an anti-icing type (**Figure 9**).

NOTE
If a significant amount of oil is coming into the air cleaner past the crankcase breather on a Magnum vertical shaft en-

gine, serial No. 2513703355 or lower, replace the crankcase breather with the new design.

Remove and clean the air filter at the interval indicated in **Table 2**. Replace the element at the specified interval or whenever it is damaged or starting to deteriorate. To service the filter assembly, refer to *Air Filter Service* in Chapter Three as well as the following paragraphs.

NOTE
Always inspect the crankcase breather hose between the valve cover and the air filter base anytime the air filter is being serviced. If the hose is loose, cracked, or dry and brittle, replace it.

When installing the anti-icing air filter cover (2, **Figure 9**), refer to **Figure 10**. Install the cover as shown in the left view when the ambient temperature is below 45° F (10° C). Install the cover as shown in the right view when the ambient temperature is above 45° F (10° C).

FUEL FILTER

To service the fuel filter, refer to *Fuel Filter Service* in Chapter Three.

CARBURETOR

WARNING
Gasoline is a volatile, flammable liquid and is one of the most dangerous items in the shop. Wipe up any spilled gasoline immediately. Work in a well-ventilated area at least 50 feet away from any open flame, including pilot lights in gas appliances. Do not allow anyone to smoke in the area. Do not work near any grinding or any other source of sparks.

Operation and Design

Carburetor operating principles are discussed in detail under *Carburetor Fundamentals* in Chapter Two.

Models MV18 and MV20 are equipped with a Walbro float-type side-draft carburetor (**Figure 11**). Carburetors equipped with a fixed high-speed jet will not have a high-speed mixture screw.

NOTE
MV18 engines operated with a fixed high-speed jet carburetor at altitudes of 6000 feet (1830 meters) above sea level and higher should have a high-altitude jet (Kohler part No. 52 755 74) installed.

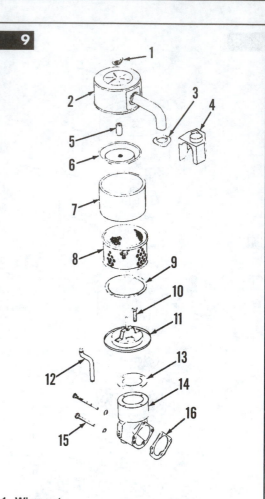

9

1. Wing nut
2. Cover
3. Heater plate
4. Heater cover
5. Seal
6. Element cover
7. Foam precleaner
8. Paper element
9. Base seal
10. Screw
11. Base
12. Breather hose
13. Gasket
14. Intake elbow
15. Bolts
16. Gasket

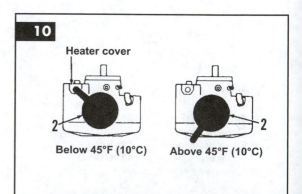

10

Heater cover

Below 45°F (10°C)   Above 45°F (10°C)

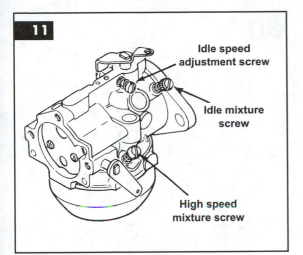

11

Idle speed
adjustment screw

Idle mixture
screw

High speed
mixture screw

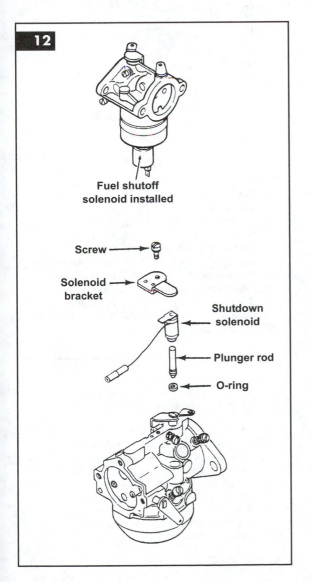

12

Fuel shutoff
solenoid installed

Screw

Solenoid
bracket

Shutdown
solenoid

Plunger rod

O-ring

On electric-start units, the carburetor may be equipped with a fuel shut-off ("anti-afterfire") solenoid. The solenoid uses a plunger to stop fuel flow through the main nozzle passage when the engine is stopped. When the ignition switch is turned ON, the plunger retracts and allows fuel to flow into the main fuel circuit. A, **Figure 12**, shows the fuel solenoid mounted on the bottom of the carburetor, in place of the bowl nut. B, **Figure 12**, shows the fuel solenoid components which mount on the top of the carburetor.

Adjustment

Initial adjustment of the idle mixture screw (**Figure 11**) should be 1 1/4 turns out from a lightly-seated position.

On models equipped with the adjustable high-speed mixture screw, the initial setting of the mixture screw is 1 1/4 turns out from a lightly-seated position on Model MV18, and one turn out on Model MV20.

Final adjustments on all models must be performed as follows:

1. With the parking brake on, the blade PTO disengaged, the speed control in neutral, and the neutral locks locked, start the engine and run it for a few minutes to reach normal operating temperature.

WARNING
Make sure ventilation is adequate if the
engine is run in a confined area. Exhaust
fumes are toxic and deadly.

2. Place the throttle control in the SLOW or IDLE position.

3. Adjust the idle speed by turning the idle speed adjustment screw to obtain 1200 rpm.

4. Run the engine at idle speed and turn the idle mixture screw counterclockwise until the engine speed decreases. Note the screw position.

5. Turn the mixture screw clockwise until the engine speed smooths out.

6. Continue turning the screw clockwise until the engine speed decreases again. Note the screw position.

7. Turn the mixture screw back counterclockwise so it is halfway between the two noted positions. If necessary, readjust the idle speed screw.

8. Accelerate the engine a few times to check the adjustment. The engine should accelerate smoothly without hesitation. If there is still slight hesitation, turn the idle mixture screw another 1/8 turn counterclockwise.

9. If necessary, repeat Step 8. If the engine still hesitates, carburetor cleaning and repair will be necessary. Refer to the *Carburetor, Repair* section.

10. If the carburetor is equipped with an adjustable high-speed mixture screw, continue to proceed as follows:

5

a. Run the engine at full speed. Turn the high-speed mixture screw counterclockwise until the engine speed decreases. Note the screw position.

b. Turn the mixture screw clockwise until the engine speed smooths out.

c. Continue turning the mixture screw clockwise until the engine speed decreases again. Note the screw position.

d. Turn the mixture screw so it is halfway between the two noted positions.

e. Operate the mower under load. If the engine appears to be running lean, turn the mixture screw an additional 1/8 turn counterclockwise. If the engine appears to be running rich, turn the mixture screw an additional 1/8 turn clockwise.

11. If the engine still does not run correctly, carburetor cleaning and repair will be necessary.

Removal

> *WARNING*
> *Some gasoline will drain from the fuel hose and/or the carburetor during this procedure. Wipe up any spilled gasoline immediately. Work in a well-ventilated area at least 50 feet away from any open flame, including pilot lights in gas appliances. Do not allow anyone to smoke in the area. Do not work near any grinding or any other source of sparks.*

1. Remove the air filter cover and the filter element assembly.

2. Carefully disconnect the crankcase breather hose from the hole in the air filter base. Inspect the hose completely. If the hose is loose, cracked, or dry and brittle, replace it.

3. Remove the screws holding the filter base to the carburetor. Remove the base.

4. Mark the position of the choke control cable, then disconnect the cable.

5. Carefully disconnect the fuel hose from the carburetor inlet fitting.

6. Unhook the throttle link from the throttle shaft and governor arm bushings.

7. If the carburetor is equipped with a fuel shutoff solenoid, disconnect the solenoid terminal.

8. Remove the nuts holding the carburetor flange to the intake manifold. Remove the carburetor.

9. Carefully remove and discard all old gaskets. Do not damage the gasket surfaces.

Disassembly

> *NOTE*
> ***Figure 13*** *shows the fixed high-speed jet carburetor. The high-speed mixture screw (**Figure 11**) is not shown. Carburetor re-*

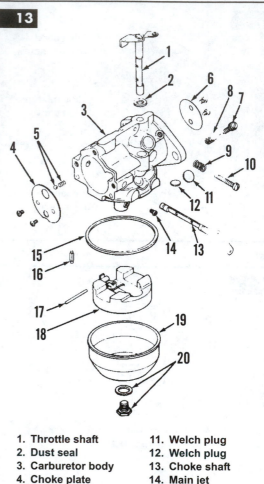

13

1. Throttle shaft
2. Dust seal
3. Carburetor body
4. Choke plate
5. Choke detent ball and spring
6. Throttle plate
7. Idle mixture needle
8. Spring
9. Spring
10. Throttle stop screw
11. Welch plug
12. Welch plug
13. Choke shaft
14. Main jet
15. Gasket
16. Fuel inlet needle
17. Float pin
18. Float
19. Float bowl
20. Plug and gasket

pair procedures are the same, except for the high-speed mixture screw.

> *CAUTION*
> *Some top-mounted fuel shutoff solenoids are wrapped with a material which is not resistant to gasoline or cleaning solvents. To prevent solenoid damage, avoid placing the solenoid in contact with gasoline or solvents and remove the solenoid before performing any cleaning operations on the carburetor.*

Refer to **Figure 13**.

1. Remove the bowl retaining plug assembly (bowl nut) or the fuel shutoff solenoid and the float bowl.

2. Remove the float pin, float assembly and fuel inlet needle. Do not attempt to remove the fuel inlet seat as it is not a serviceable item.

3. Remove the idle mixture needle, spring, throttle stop screw, spring and the main fuel jet.

4. On fully-adjustable carburetors, remove the high-speed mixture screw and spring.

5. To clean the bowl vent channel and the off-idle ports, use a small chisel-tip punch to pierce and remove the welch plugs. Use care not to damage the carburetor body during this procedure.

6. The throttle shaft and choke shaft may be removed as required. Carefully mark the orientation of the shafts and plates for proper reassembly. Use care not to lose the choke detent ball and spring while removing the choke shaft.

Cleaning, Inspection and Repair

Carburetor

1. Clean the carburetor in an approved carburetor cleaner only after all rubber and fiber washers and seals have been removed. If the carburetor is equipped with a top-mounted fuel shutoff solenoid, refer to the *Fuel Shutoff Solenoid* section immediately following this section prior to cleaning the carburetor.

2. Rinse carefully and completely according to the cleaner manufacturer's instructions.

3. Blow out all passages with compressed air.

> CAUTION
> *Do not use wire or drill bits to clean passages; calibration of the carburetor will be affected if the fuel passages are enlarged.*

4. Inspect all components. Replace any faulty or questionable items.

   a. Inspect the tip of the idle mixture needle (7, **Figure 13**) and replace the needle if the tip is bent or grooved.

   b. Inspect the fuel inlet valve (16, **Figure 13**) and replace it if the tip is grooved.

   c. Install the throttle shaft in the carburetor body and check for excessive play between the shaft and body. The body must be replaced if there is excessive play as bushings are not available.

Fuel Shutoff Solenoid

> CAUTION
> *Some top-mounted fuel shutoff solenoids are wrapped with a material which is not resistant to gasoline or cleaning solvents.*

> *To prevent solenoid damage, avoid placing the solenoid in contact with gasoline or solvents and remove the solenoid before performing any cleaning operations on the carburetor.*

On electric-start units with the fuel-shutoff solenoid mounted on the carburetor, the spring-loaded solenoid plunger should retract when the solenoid is energized (ignition switch ON), allowing fuel to flow. To test the solenoid:

1. Make sure that the battery is fully charged.

2. While listening to and/or holding the solenoid, turn the ignition switch from the OFF to the RUN position a few times.

3. An audible click should be heard and/or felt each time the key is switched.

4. If the solenoid does not click;

   a. Turn the fuel tank valve off.

   b. On bottom-mounted solenoids, place an approved non-sparking container under the carburetor to catch leaking fuel.

   c. Remove the main harness connector from the solenoid terminal.

   d. Unscrew the solenoid from the carburetor.

   e. Connect one terminal of a 9-volt dry-cell or 12-volt test battery to the solenoid case.

   f. Momentarily connect and disconnect the other battery terminal to the solenoid terminal a few times. If the solenoid still does not activate, it is faulty and must be replaced.

   g. Using a multimeter set to the 25VDC scale, place the negative meter lead on any good engine-block ground and connect the positive meter lead to the solenoid terminal in the main harness.

   h. Again turn the ignition switch on and off a few times while observing the meter dial. The meter should read mower battery voltage each time the switch is turned on. If not, the wiring is faulty. Refer to the *Wiring Diagrams* and test the wiring to determine why current is not reaching the solenoid.

Reassembly

1. Insert the choke detent spring and ball into the carburetor body bore. If the detent ball does not pass through the threaded screw hole easily, do not force it, but insert it through the choke shaft bore.

2. Using a small punch, compress the ball and spring while feeding the choke shaft through the bore. Make sure that the cutout portion of the shaft faces out.

3. Sparingly apply Loctite 609 or equivalent to the choke plate screws. Fit the choke plate to the shaft with the stamped plate numbers facing out and up. Install, but do not tighten, the screws. Operate the choke shaft to com-

5

pletely close the plate and align the plate in the bore, then torque the screws to 8-12 in.-lb. (1.0 N·m)

4. Fit the foam seal onto the throttle shaft, then insert the throttle shaft into the carburetor body bore. Make sure that the cutout portion of the shaft faces out.

5. If the idle speed adjustment screw and spring (10 and 9, **Figure 13**) have not been removed for cleaning, unscrew the adjustment screw two turns counterclockwise.

6. Sparingly apply Loctite 222 or equivalent to the throttle plate screws. Fit the throttle plate to the shaft with the stamped plate numbers facing out. Install, but do not tighten, the screws. While lightly pushing down on top of the throttle shaft, operate the shaft to completely close the plate and align the plate in the bore, then torque the screws to 8-12 in.-lb. (0.9-1.4 N·m)

7. If the idle speed adjustment screw was backed out in Step 5, screw it back in the exact same two turns. This will initially set the idle speed, presuming the idle speed was within limits prior to carburetor removal.

8. If the welch plugs were removed, reinstall them as follows:

   a. Securely position the carburetor body with the welch plug openings facing up.

   b. Make sure that the plug cavity seats are completely clean and dry.

   c. Position a new welch plug into its cavity with the convex part up (**Figure 14**).

   d. Using Kohler Tool No. KO1017 or a flat-tipped pin punch with approximately the same diameter as the welch plug, carefully *flatten* the plug, but do not cave the plug in.

   e. After installing the welch plugs, seal the plug-to-carburetor seams with a glyptal sealer or fingernail polish. Permit the sealer to dry before proceeding.

9. Install the main jet. Torque the jet to 12-16 in.-lb. (1.4-1.8 N·m).

10. Install the fuel inlet needle (float valve) onto the float tab with the needle tip pointed away from the float. Ensure that the locking clip fits on the side of the tab *opposite* the needle. Insert the float valve into the fuel passage. Position the float so the float hinge hole aligns with the carburetor body float hinge posts. Insert the float hinge pin.

11. To adjust the float level, invert the carburetor so that the float tab rests on the fuel inlet needle. The operational bottom of the float should be parallel to the bowl gasket surface (**Figure 15**). This will make the float height 0.690-0.720 inch (17.53-18.29 mm) from the carburetor body mating surface to the operational bottom of the float at the free end of the float. Carefully bend the metal fuel inlet needle tab with a small screwdriver to adjust the float height.

12. Correctly position a new fuel bowl gasket onto the carburetor, then install the bowl. Place a new gasket onto

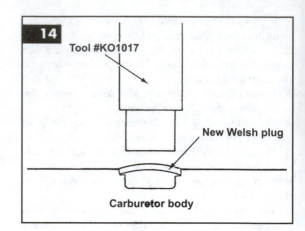

14

Tool #KO1017

New Welsh plug

Carburetor body

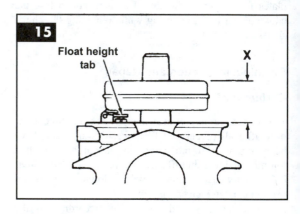

15

Float height tab

X

the bowl plug screw. Install the screw, torquing it to 45-55 in.-lb. (5-6 N·m).

13. If the idle speed adjusting screw and spring were removed for cleaning, install them now. While holding the throttle plate closed with finger pressure on the throttle shaft lever, turn the screw until the screw tip just contacts the lever. Turn the screw another 3/4 turn. This will initially set the idle speed.

14. Install the idle mixture screw and spring. Turn the screw clockwise (in) until it *lightly* bottoms, then back it out 1-1/4 turns.

15. Install the high-speed mixture screw and spring. Turn the screw clockwise (in) until it *lightly* bottoms, then back it out 1-1/4 turns for an MV18 carburetor, one turn for an MV20.

NOTE
If the muffler is covered by a sheet metal heat shield, make certain that the heat shield does not contact the carburetor bowl. Bend or indent the shield, if necessary, to prevent it from rubbing a hole in the bowl.

16

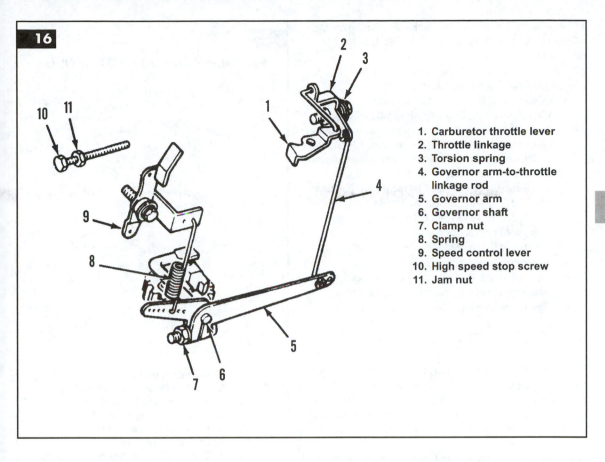

1. Carburetor throttle lever
2. Throttle linkage
3. Torsion spring
4. Governor arm-to-throttle linkage rod
5. Governor arm
6. Governor shaft
7. Clamp nut
8. Spring
9. Speed control lever
10. High speed stop screw
11. Jam nut

5

Installation

Refer to **Figure 16**.

1. Install the fuel hose, with new clamps, between the fuel pump and the carburetor location. Ensure that the hose is correctly routed *behind* the intake manifold.

2. Place a new gasket on the manifold studs, followed by the carburetor.

3. Lightly coat the manifold stud threads with Loctite 242 or equivalent, then install and tighten the stud nuts.

4. Install new link bushings in the carburetor throttle shaft and governor arm holes. Install the throttle link into the bushings. Make sure that the link is inserted into the bushings completely.

5. Perform a static governor adjustment:

    a. Make certain the governor linkage is connected to the governor arm and to the throttle lever on the intake manifold.

    b. The throttle linkage must be connected to the throttle lever on the intake manifold and the throttle lever on the carburetor as shown.

    c. Loosen the governor arm clamp bolt nut.

    d. Pull the governor arm down and away from the carburetor as far as possible to fully open the carburetor throttle plate.

    e. Turn the governor shaft clockwise as far as possible and tighten the clamp nut to 50-60 in.-lbs. (5-6 N·m).

6. Connect and clamp the fuel hose to the carburetor fitting.

7. Reconnect the choke control cable using the following procedure:

    a. Push the choke knob all the way in.

    b. Move the choke shutter to the wide-open position.

    c. Ensure that the choke cable assembly is correctly positioned under the cable clamp.

    d. Tighten the clamp holddown screw.

    e. Pull out on the cable control knob until the carburetor choke shutter closes completely.

    f. Work the choke control out and in a few times to make sure the control or cable is not binding.

8. On carburetors equipped with the anti-afterfire solenoid, connect the solenoid wire to the main harness.

9. Lightly coat the air filter elbow screws with Loctite 242 or equivalent. Using a new gasket, mount the elbow to the carburetor. Tighten the screws securely, but do not overtighten.

10. Install a new elbow-to-baseplate gasket, using Loctite 242 or equivalent on the baseplate screws.

11. Connect the breather hose to the air filter baseplate. Make sure that the hose lip completely seats in the baseplate hole.

12. Install the air filter element assembly and cover.

13. Finish adjusting the governor:

    a. Connect a tachometer to the engine.

    b. With the parking brake on, the blade PTO disengaged, the speed control in neutral, and the neutral locks locked, start the engine and run it for a few minutes in order to reach normal operating temperature.

    c. Move the throttle control to the FAST position. Note the rpm reading. The maximum no-load engine speed is 3750 rpm and is controlled by the high-speed stop screw.

14. If adjustment is required to attain 3750 rpm.

    a. Loosen the stop screw jam nut.

    b. Turn the screw (11) counterclockwise (out) to increase rpm or clockwise (in) to decrease rpm.

    c. Tighten the jam nut.

MUFFLER

The muffler is calibrated as part of the emission control system. It not only reduces exhaust noise to acceptable levels, but it also provides the proper amount of back pressure to allow the inlet and combustion components to produce rated horsepower as well as compliant emission levels.

For this reason, the exhaust system should be maintained in good repair. As the noise level increases, power decreases. Under no circumstances should the exhaust system be modified. Inspect the muffler, pipes, flanges, connections and fasteners regularly. Replace any questionable components.

Removal

1. Allow the unit to cool.

2. If the muffler is covered by a sheet metal heat shield, remove the shield fasteners, then remove the shield.

3. Loosen all fasteners and clamps. Do not *remove* any fasteners until all of them have been loosened.

If a bolt cannot be loosened, several methods of persuasion may be used. First, apply penetrating oil such as Liquid Wrench, Kroil or WD-40 and let it penetrate for 10-15 minutes. Rap the fastener several times with a small hammer and punch. Do not hit it hard enough to cause damage. Reapply the penetrating oil if necessary. Use 6-sided sockets and wrenches on hex-headed bolts to reduce the chances of rounding off the hex.

For frozen screws, apply penetrating oil as described. Insert a stout screwdriver into the slot, and carefully rap the top of the screwdriver with a hammer. This loosens the rust so the screw can be removed in the normal way. If

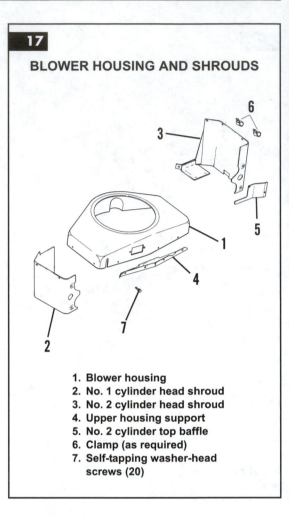

17

BLOWER HOUSING AND SHROUDS

1. Blower housing
2. No. 1 cylinder head shroud
3. No. 2 cylinder head shroud
4. Upper housing support
5. No. 2 cylinder top baffle
6. Clamp (as required)
7. Self-tapping washer-head screws (20)

the screw head is too damaged to use this method, grip the head with locking pliers and twist the screw out.

> *NOTE*
> *Avoid applying heat unless specifically instructed, as it may melt, warp or remove the temper from parts.*

If a fastener should break off, refer to *Removing Broken Fasteners* in Chapter One.

4. Begin removing the fasteners while supporting the exhaust system. Work from the outlet pipe inward. The bolts holding the exhaust pipe flange(s) to the engine should be the last bolts removed, at which time the exhaust system can be removed and set aside.

> *CAUTION*
> *Discard all used gaskets and replace with new gaskets. Also discard the old lockwashers, replacing them with new ones.*

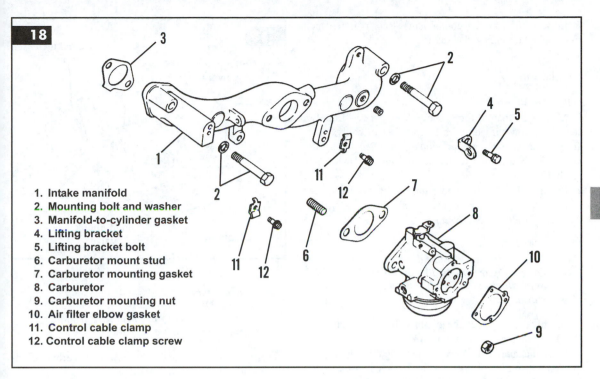

18

1. Intake manifold
2. Mounting bolt and washer
3. Manifold-to-cylinder gasket
4. Lifting bracket
5. Lifting bracket bolt
6. Carburetor mount stud
7. Carburetor mounting gasket
8. Carburetor
9. Carburetor mounting nut
10. Air filter elbow gasket
11. Control cable clamp
12. Control cable clamp screw

5

5. Inspect all brackets and supports for cracks and breaks. Inspect the outlet pipe spark-arrestor screen, if equipped. Replace as necessary.

6. Carefully remove any old gasket material from the exhaust flange surfaces, and wirebrush the fastener threads.

Installation

1. Insert new gaskets onto the exhaust studs or bolts.

2. Replace all fastener lock washers and lightly coat the fastener threads with a high-temperature thread-lock compound, such as Loctite 272 or equivalent.

3. Align the exhaust system with all bracket and fastener holes, then install and hand-tighten the fasteners, beginning with the exhaust pipe flanges. Do not tighten any fasteners until all of them have been installed.

4. Beginning with the flanges, tighten all fasteners, working toward the outlet pipe.

5. Install the heat shield and spark arrestor, if used.

NOTE
If the muffler is covered by a sheet metal heat shield, make certain that the heat shield does not contact the carburetor bowl. Bend or indent the shield, if necessary, to prevent it from rubbing a hole in the bowl.

BLOWER HOUSING, SHROUDS AND BAFFLES

Removal

Refer to **Figure 17**.

1. Unplug the spark plug wire terminals from the spark plugs, then remove the plugs. Ground the plug-wire terminals to the engine.

2. On electric-start units, unplug the rectifier-regulator connector, then unbolt the regulator from the blower housing.

3. Note the location and orientation of all brackets and clamps held in place by the blower housing fasteners.

4. Remove the self-tapping screws holding the blower housing to the engine. Two of the screws also hold the oil-fill-tube bracket to the back of the No. 1 cylinder side of the engine. Carefully lift the housing from the engine while sliding the spark plug wire grommet from its slot.

5. Remove the self-tapping screws holding the cylinder head shrouds to the engine. Remove the shrouds.

6. Remove the self-tapping screws holding the upper housing support and the No. 2 cylinder top baffle to the engine. Remove the support and baffle.

NOTE
*To gain clearance to remove the baffle, the bolt (5, **Figure 18**) holding the lift bracket to the intake manifold may need to be removed first.*

7. Inspect all removed components. Repair or replace any cracked or damaged shrouds.

Installation

Refer to **Figure 17**.

1. Make sure that all threads are clean and dry. Lightly coat the screw threads with Loctite 242 or equivalent. Torque the screws into previously threaded holes 65 in.-lb. (7.3 N·m); final-torque screws into new metal 80 in.-lb. (9.0 N·m).

2. Position the No. 2 cylinder top baffle and the upper housing support on the engine. Install and hand-tighten the screw holding them together.

> *NOTE*
> *To gain clearance to install the baffle, the bolt (5, **Figure 18**) holding the lift bracket to the intake manifold may need to be removed first.*

3. Install the cylinder head shrouds to the engine. Hand-tighten the screws at this time.

4. Slide the spark-plug wire grommet into its slot in the blower housing, then position the blower housing onto the engine. Install and hand-tighten the fasteners.

5. Make sure that all brackets and clamps have been installed in their proper positions to prevent rubbing and chafing of components.

6. Torque all fasteners to the values specified in Step 1.

7. Install the spark plugs. Torque the plugs to 120-180 in.-lb. (13-20 N·m).

FUEL PUMP

Operation

The fuel pump is operated by a lever which rides on a dedicated lobe on the camshaft (**Figure 19**). Check valves inside the pump only allow fuel to travel through the pump in one direction. The diaphragm is spring-loaded on the lever side. When the camshaft lobe pushes against the lever, the diaphragm is pulled against the spring and away from the check valves, drawing fuel into the pump body. When the camshaft lobe rotates 180°, diaphragm spring pressure pushes the diaphragm toward the check valves, expelling the fuel through the outlet.

The fuel pumps are non-serviceable items. If a fuel pump is not pumping, it must be replaced. To test the output of the pump:

> *WARNING*
> *Some gasoline will drain from the fuel hose and/or the carburetor during this procedure. Wipe up any spilled gasoline immediately. Work in a well-ventilated area at least 50 feet away from any open*

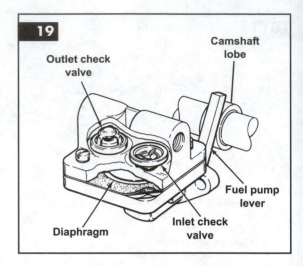

flame, including pilot lights in gas appliances. Do not allow anyone to smoke in the area. Do not work near any grinding or any other source of sparks.

1. Carefully remove the fuel hose from the carburetor inlet fitting.

2. Direct the hose into a safe catch container.

3. Disconnect the spark plug wires from both spark plugs. Ground the spark plug wires to the engine.

4. While observing the fuel hose output, use the starter to turn the engine over. Fuel should pulse from the hose on every other revolution of the flywheel. No fuel flow indicates a faulty pump.

Removal

1. Be sure the engine is stopped and the ignition switch is in the OFF position. Allow the engine to cool to ambient temperature.

2. Engage the parking brake.

3. Close the fuel tank valve (**Figure 3**).

4. On electric-start units:
   a. Disconnect the negative battery cable terminal and secure it away from the battery;
   b. Unplug the rectifier-regulator connector, then unbolt the regulator from the blower housing.

5. Unplug the spark plug wire terminals from the spark plugs, then remove the plugs. Ground the plug-wire terminals to the engine.

6. Note the location and orientation of all brackets and clamps held in place by the blower housing fasteners.

7. Remove the self-tapping screws holding the blower housing (1, **Figure 17**) to the engine. Two of the screws also hold the oil-fill-tube bracket to the back of the No. 1 cylinder side of the engine. Lift the housing from the engine.

8. Remove the self-tapping screws holding the No. 2 cylinder head shroud (3, **Figure 17**) to the engine. Remove the shroud.

9. Remove the self-tapping screws holding the upper housing support (4, **Figure 17**) and the No. 2 cylinder top baffle (5) to the engine. Remove the support and baffle.

NOTE
*To gain clearance to remove the baffle, the bolt holding the lift bracket (4, **Figure 18**) to the intake manifold may need to be removed first.*

10. Remove the air filter cover and element assembly (**Figure 8**). Carefully remove the crankcase breather hose from the baseplate, then remove the baseplate. Clean the old gasket material from the baseplate and the intake elbow.

11. Carefully remove the fuel hose from the carburetor inlet fitting.

12. Clean the area around the fuel pump mounting flange so no dirt or debris falls into the crankcase when the pump is removed.

13. Loosen the two fuel pump mounting screws and remove the pump.

14. Carefully clean all old gasket material from the crankcase mounting area. Do not allow any gasket pieces to fall into the crankcase fuel pump opening.

15. Clean and dry the pump mounting threads.

Installation

1. Always follow the instructions included with the new fuel pump.

2. Fit a new fuel hose and hose clamps onto the pump outlet fitting.

3. View the camshaft lobe through the crankcase opening. Rotate the flywheel until the low side of the lobe faces out. This will reduce the tension on the spring-loaded pump lever when performing the next step.

4. Position a new gasket onto the crankcase opening, then fit the pump lever into the crankcase opening and against the camshaft lobe.

CAUTION
Make sure that the pump lever is positioned outside of the camshaft lobe, between the lobe and the pump. Installing the pump with the lever positioned behind the camshaft will cause serious damage to both the pump and the engine.

5. Make sure that the fuel hose is routed between the crankcase and the intake manifold.

6. Install the new pump screws. Torque the screws to 40-45 in.-lb. (4.5-6.2 N·m).

7. Connect the fuel hose to the carburetor inlet fitting.

8. To install the cooling shrouds and baffles, refer to **Figure 17** and proceed as follows:

  a. Make sure that all threads are clean and dry. Lightly coat the screw threads with Loctite 242 or equivalent. Final-torque screws into previously threaded holes 65 in.-lb. (7.3 N·m); final-torque screws into new metal 80 in.-lb. (9.0 N·m).

  b. Position the No. 2 cylinder top baffle (5) and the upper housing support (4) on the engine. Install and hand-tighten the screw holding them together.

NOTE
*To gain clearance to install the baffle, the bolt holding the lift bracket (4, **Figure 18**) to the intake manifold may need to be removed first.*

  c. Install the No. 2 cylinder head shroud (3) to the engine. Hand-tighten the screws at this time.

  d. Position the blower housing (1) onto the engine. Install and hand-tighten the fasteners.

  e. Make sure that all brackets and clamps have been installed in their proper positions to prevent rubbing and chafing of components.

8. Install the spark plugs. Torque the plugs to 120-180 in.-lb. (13-20 N·m). Reconnect the spark plug wires.

9. Apply Loctite 222 or equivalent to the air filter baseplate screws. Using a new gasket, install the baseplate to the carburetor elbow. Install the air filter element assembly and cover.

10. On electric-start units:

  a. Bolt the rectifier-regulator to the blower housing, then plug in the regulator connector.

  b. Reconnect the negative battery cable terminal to the battery.

11. Open the fuel tank valve (Figure 6).

IGNITION SYSTEM

All models are equipped with an electronic magneto ignition system which consists of:

1. A magnet assembly permanently affixed to the flywheel;

2. An electronic magneto ignition module mounted on the number one cylinder.

3. A kill switch that stops the engine by grounding the primary circuit of the ignition module.

To see if the ignition module is producing spark, refer to *Spark Test* in Chapter Two.

Spark Plugs

The recommended spark plug for all models under normal usage is Champion RV17YC or equivalent; for continuous full-load running, use RV15YC. The recommended spark plug electrode gap is 0.035 inch (0.9 mm). Torque to 120-180 in.-lb. (13-20 N·m).

CAUTION
Do not use the abrasive-blast (sand-blast) method to clean spark plugs. When spark plugs are cleaned by this method, the abrasive grit lodges in the upper gap between the insulator and the shell. Subsequent compressed-air blowing does not remove these abrasives. This grit is only removed when the plug is reinstalled in the engine and the engine is started, heating and expanding the plug. The grit then falls into the cylinder and combustion chamber area, causing rapid internal wear and damage.

Module-to-Flywheel Air Gap Adjustment

The air gap between the ignition module and the flywheel should be 0.008-0.012 inch (0.21-0.31 mm). To set the air gap, refer to **Figure 20** and proceed as follows:

1. Remove the blower housing as outlined under *Blower Housing, Removal*.
2. Turn the flywheel so that the magnets are not next to the ignition module.
3. Loosen the screws holding the module to the engine.
4. Extend the module to the limits allowed by the adjustment slots, then lightly tighten one screw to temporarily hold the module away from the flywheel.
5. Rotate the flywheel to center the magnets directly under the module legs.
6. Place a *non-metallic* gap gauge of 0.008-0.012 inch (0.20-0.31 mm) between the magnets and the module.
7. Loosen the module holding screw, allowing the magnets to draw the module to the flywheel. While holding the module snugly against the flywheel, tighten the module screws.
8. Rotate the flywheel and remove the gauge.
9. Reconnect the spark plug leads.
10. Install the blower housing as described under *Blower Housing Installation*.

Module Testing

To test the ignition module:
1. Set the multimeter to read ohms.
2. Attach the ohmmeter negative test lead to the module's kill switch terminal (B, **Figure 21**).
3. Attach the positive meter lead to the coil lamination (A, **Figure 21**).
4. The ohmmeter should register 5-1000 ohms. If resistance is 0 ohms or infinite, the primary circuit is shorted or open.

5. Reverse the positions of the ohmmeter test leads to check primary resistance. The ohmmeter should register a minimum of 30,000 ohms.
6. To check secondary resistance, attach the ohmmeter test leads to the terminal ends of both spark plug cables. The ohmmeter should register 22,000-42,000 ohms.
7. If the ohmmeter readings vary considerably from the specified values in Steps 4-6, replace the ignition module.

Module Removal

1. Disconnect the spark plug wires from the spark plugs.
2. Remove the blower housing as described under *Blower Housing Removal*.
3. Remove the two hex-flange screws holding the module to the bracket on the No. 1 cylinder barrel.
4. If necessary, unbolt the module bracket from the cylinder barrel.
5. Clean all fastener threads.

Module Installation

1. Ensure that all fastener threads are clean and dry.
2. Apply Loctite 222 or equivalent to the fastener threads.
3. If the module bracket was removed from the cylinder barrel, install it now. Securely tighten the fasteners, but do not overtighten.
4. Turn the flywheel so that the magnets are not next to the ignition module.
5. Position the module on the bracket. Install the module screws finger-tight.
6. Extend the module to the limits allowed by the adjustment slots, then lightly tighten the module screw closest to the flywheel to temporarily hold the module away from the flywheel.
7. Rotate the flywheel to center the magnets directly under the module legs.
8. Place a *non-metallic* gap gauge of 0.008-0.012 inch (0.20-0.31 mm) between the magnets and the module.

21

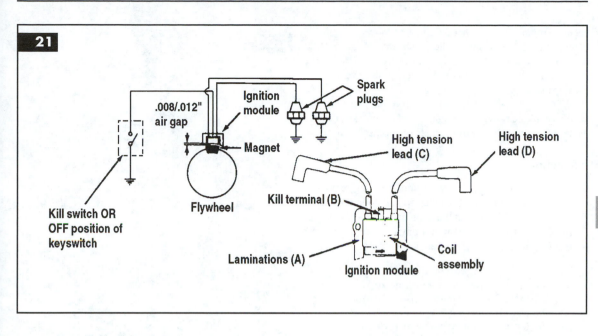

- Kill switch OR OFF position of keyswitch
- .008/.012" air gap
- Ignition module
- Magnet
- Flywheel
- Spark plugs
- High tension lead (C)
- High tension lead (D)
- Kill terminal (B)
- Laminations (A)
- Ignition module
- Coil assembly

5

22

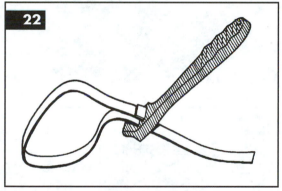

9. Loosen the module holding screw, allowing the magnets to draw the module to the flywheel. While holding the module snugly against the flywheel, tighten the module screws.

10. Rotate the flywheel and remove the gauge.

11. Reconnect the spark plug leads.

12. Install the blower housing as described under *Blower Housing, Installation*.

FLYWHEEL

Removal

CAUTION
*When loosening or tightening the flywheel or fan bolts, hold the flywheel with the recommended strap wrench No. NU-10357 (**Figure 22**). Follow the wrench manufacturer's instructions. Using a bar or wedge in the fan blades or ring gear teeth could*

cause damage. When removing the flywheel from the crankshaft, always use a proper puller. Never strike the crankshaft or flywheel, as damage could occur.

1. Disconnect the spark plug wires from the spark plugs.

2. Remove the blower housing and shroud assemblies as described under *Blower Housing, Removal*.

3. Remove the two hex-flange screws holding the module to the bracket on the No. 1 cylinder barrel.

4. Remove the grass screen from the fan. Although the flywheel can be removed with the fan installed, to prevent accidental fan blade damage, also remove the fan from the flywheel. *Do not lose* the four fan screw spacers.

5. Use the strap wrench to hold the flywheel.

6. Using the proper 6-point socket and ratchet or breaker bar, loosen the bolt assembly holding the flywheel to the crankshaft. Remove the bolt, lock washer and flat washer. On recoil-start engines, there will be two flat washers plus the starter drive cup.

7. To save time, a 1/2-inch-drive impact wrench with the proper 6-point socket can be used to remove the flywheel bolt.

CAUTION
Prior to setting the impact wrench on the bolt head, make sure that the wrench is set to turn counterclockwise, as viewing the bolt head. Accidentally applying additional tightening force to the bolt will damage the flywheel and crankshaft.

8. Using puller No. NU-3226 or equivalent, fasten the puller to the flywheel, then break the flywheel loose from the crankshaft. Always follow the puller manufacturer's instructions. **Figure 23** shows the recommended puller

set up to remove the flywheel. **Figure 24** shows an equivalent puller. When using a puller as shown in **Figure 24**, always place stout flat washers under the heads of the bolts in the flywheel so the puller jaws will have sufficient grip.

9. When the flywheel breaks loose from the crankshaft, *carefully* lift the flywheel straight up off the crankshaft so as not to damage the stator magnets under the flywheel.

Inspection

1. Carefully and thoroughly clean the flywheel, removing all dust and dirt from both the top and bottom of the flywheel, especially around the magnets.
2. Inspect the flywheel casting for cracks or damage.
3. Inspect the integrity of the magnets.

> *WARNING*
> *The magnets are not removable or serviceable. Do not attempt to reattach or tighten any loose magnet. If any magnets are loose or damaged, replace the flywheel.*

4. On electric-start units, inspect the starter ring gear. Carefully remove any debris stuck between the teeth. Light nicks or scratches may be dressed. Damaged teeth will require replacement of the flywheel assembly, as the ring gear is not available separately.
5. Inspect the tapers and keyways of both the flywheel and the crankshaft. A damaged flywheel keyway will require replacement of the flywheel. A damaged crankshaft keyway will require crankshaft replacement. The crankshaft keyway should hold the flywheel key snugly.
6. Inspect the flywheel key. Replace if questionable.

Installation

1. Make sure that the matching tapers on the crankshaft and inside the flywheel, as well as the crankshaft and bolt threads, are *clean and dry*. Make sure no debris has stuck to any of the magnets.
2. Install the flywheel key.

> *WARNING*
> *Make sure the flywheel key is installed in the (bf ital)flat area of the crankshaft keyway only (**Figure 25**). Allowing the key to slip into the curved end of the keyway will crack and damage the flywheel. If the key slides freely in the crankshaft keyway, carefully peen the edges of the keyway just enough to hold the key in position. Peen both sides of the keyway equally.*

3. Carefully lower the flywheel straight down onto the crankshaft.
4. On rewind-start engines, perform upcoming Steps 7 and 8 now, then position the starter cup onto the flywheel.

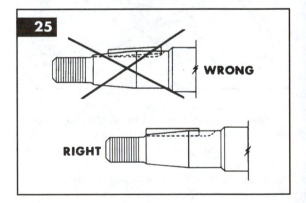

5. With the lock washer and flat washer in position on the flywheel bolt, install the bolt into the crankshaft.
6. Using the strap wrench shown in **Figure 21**, hold the flywheel in position while tightening the bolt. Torque the bolt to 40 ft.-lb. (54 N·m).
7. If the fan was removed, install it onto the flywheel, being careful to align the cutout with the magnet. Torque the fan bolts to 115 in.-lb. (13 N·m).
8. Install the grass screen onto the fan.
9. Install and gap the ignition module as described under *Module Installation* in this chapter.
10. Install the blower housing as described in this chapter.

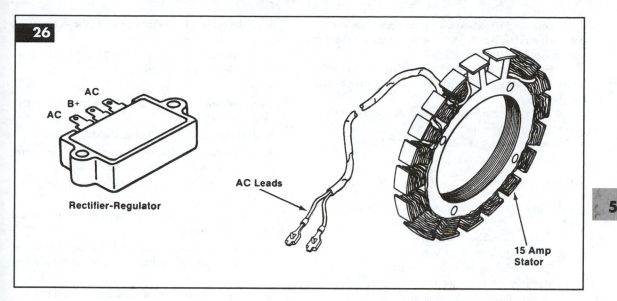

26

AC
B+
AC

Rectifier-Regulator

AC Leads

15 Amp
Stator

5

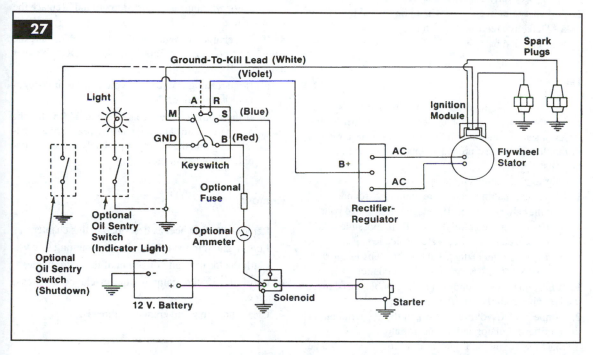

27

Spark
Plugs

Ground-To-Kill Lead (White)

(Violet)

Light

A   R
M   S   (Blue)
GND   B   (Red)

Keyswitch

Ignition
Module

Flywheel
Stator

B+   AC

AC

**Rectifier-
Regulator**

Optional
Oil Sentry
Switch
(Indicator Light)

Optional
Fuse

Optional
Ammeter

Optional
Oil Sentry
Switch
(Shutdown)

12 V. Battery

Solenoid

Starter

ALTERNATOR

Figure 26 shows the components used in these alternators. **Figure 27** shows the alternator wiring diagram.

Operation

If the alternator is functioning correctly, 12-volt DC current is being produced whenever the flywheel is rotating. The stator produces AC and the rectifier-regulator changes the AC to DC while controlling the amount of

DC based on the battery state-of-charge and the demands of the chassis electrical system. There are no adjustments required for this system.

To avoid damage to the charging system, the following precautions must be observed:

1. The negative post of the battery must be connected to the engine ground and correct battery polarity must be observed at all times.

2. The rectifier-regulator must be connected in common ground with the engine and the battery.

3. Disconnect the leads at the rectifier-regulator and the battery if electric welding is to be done on equipment in common ground with the engine.

4. Remove the battery or disconnect the battery cables when recharging the battery with an external battery charger.

5. Do not operate the engine with the battery disconnected.

6. Prevent possible grounding of the AC leads.

Troubleshooting

Defective conditions and possible causes are as follows:

1. No output. Could be caused by:
   a. Faulty windings in the stator.
   b. Defective diode(s) in the rectifier.
   c. Rectifier-regulator not properly grounded.
   d. Battery fully discharged or less than 4 volts.
2. Full charge-no regulation. Could be caused by:
   a. Defective rectifier-regulator.
   b. Defective battery.

Testing

The rectifier-regulator for the 15-amp charging system can be tested with the Kohler Tester No. 25 761 20. Instructions are included with the tester. If this tester is not available, use the test procedure that follows the precautions listed here.

Prior to performing any tests

1. Make sure that the rectifier-regulator is grounded.
2. Test the battery voltage. If voltage is less than 4 volts:
   a. Check the electrolyte level, if possible. Add deionized or distilled water as needed.
   b. Recharge the battery. Follow the steps under *Battery Service, Charging* in Chapter Three.
1. If the "no output" condition is the trouble, disconnect the B+ wire from the rectifier-regulator.
2. Connect a DC voltmeter between the B+ terminal on the rectifier-regulator and engine ground.
3. Start the engine and operate it at 3600 rpm. Voltage should be above 13.8 volts.
   a. If reading is above zero volts but less than 13.8 volts, test further for a defective rectifier-regulator.
   b. If reading is zero volts, proceed to Step 4.
   c. Stop the engine.
4. Check for a defective rectifier-regulator or a defective stator.
   a. Disconnect the AC leads from the rectifier-regulator.
   b. Connect an AC voltmeter to the two AC leads.
   c. Start the engine and operate it at 3600 rpm.
   d. Check the AC voltage output.

e. If the reading is less than 28 volts, the stator is defective.

f. If the reading is more than 28 volts, the rectifier-regulator is defective.

5. Stop the engine.

6. Using an ohmmeter, measure the resistance across the AC stator leads.
   a. If resistance is 0.1-0.2 ohm, the stator is good.
   b. If resistance is infinity/no-continuity, the stator windings are open. Replace the stator.
   c. If resistance is zero ohms, the stator windings are shorted. Replace the stator.

7. Again using an ohmmeter, measure the resistance from ground to each stator lead.
   a. If resistance is infinity/no-continuity, the stator windings are not shorted to ground and the stator is OK.
   b. If any resistance is measured during either test, the stator windings are shorted to ground. Replace the stator.

8. If "full charge-no regulation" is the trouble, start the engine and operate it at 3600 rpm. Use a DC voltmeter and check B+ to ground.
   a. If the reading is over 14.7 volts, the rectifier-regulator is defective.
   b. If the reading is between 14.0 and 14.7 volts, the alternator stator and the rectifier-regulator are satisfactory and the battery is probably defective (unable to hold a charge).

Removal

1. Remove the flywheel as described in this chapter.

2. Loosen and remove the four stator mounting screws.

3. Mark the location and direction of the stator harness.

4. Carefully lift the stator off the machined crankcase shoulder.

5. Clean the screw and crankcase threads.

Installation

1. Make sure that the screw and crankcase threads are clean and dry.

2. Lightly coat the screw threads with Loctite 222 or equivalent.

3. With the stator harness in its proper position over the base of the No. 2 cylinder, align the stator and crankcase screw holes, then carefully set the stator down onto the machined crankcase shoulder.

4. Insert the four stator screws into the crankcase threads.

5. Incrementally and alternately tighten the screws.

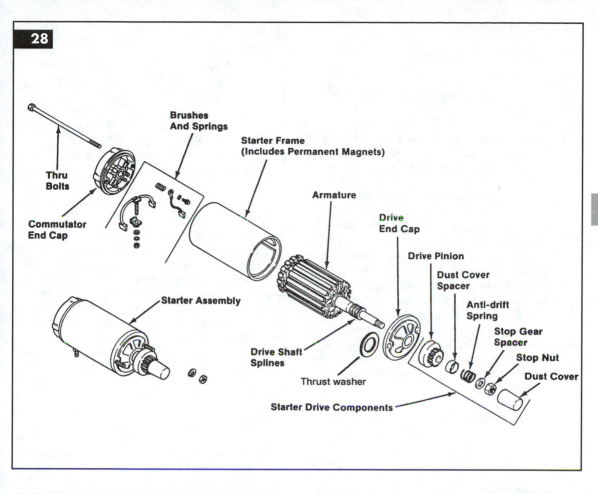

28

Thru
Bolts

Commutator
End Cap

Brushes
And Springs

Starter Frame
(Includes Permanent Magnets)

Armature

Drive
End Cap

Drive Pinion

Dust Cover
Spacer

Anti-drift
Spring

Stop Gear
Spacer

Stop Nut

Dust Cover

Starter Assembly

Drive Shaft
Splines

Thrust washer

Starter Drive Components

5

ELECTRIC STARTER MOTOR AND SOLENOID

Figure 28 shows an exploded view of the starter motor components. In this section, "starter" refers to the electric starter motor assembly.

Some later style starter motors use a retaining ring instead of a stop nut to secure the drive components to the armature. With the exception of the nut/ring removal and installation, service procedures are identical.

Starter Operation

When voltage applied to the starter through the brushes and ground, the armature rotates. As the armature spins, centrifugal force causes the drive pinion to travel up the helical splines, meshing with the flywheel ring gear teeth. When the drive pinion reaches the end of the armature shaft splines, it turns the flywheel and cranks the engine.

When the engine starts, the increased flywheel speed turns the drive pinion faster than the starter is spinning, causing the pinion to travel back down the armature shaft splines. When voltage is cut off from the starter, the armature stops and the anti-drift spring holds the pinion away from the ring gear until power is again applied to the starter.

CAUTION
Do not operate the starter continuously for more than 10 seconds. If the engine does not start, allow at least a 60-second cooling period between each 10-second operational period. Failure to allow sufficient cool-down time will burn out the starter.

If the engine false-starts by disengaging the pinion then stalling, allow the engine to come to a complete stop before attempting a restart. Engaging the starter into a rotating flywheel will damage the starter and the flywheel.

If the engine does not crank when the starter is engaged, disengage the starter immediately. Correct the engine problem prior to attempting a restart. Do not attempt to overcome the problem by jump-starting with a larger battery. Serious starter damage will result.

Do not drop the starter, strike the starter frame, or clamp the starter frame in a vise. Doing so could damage the permanent magnets inside the starter frame housing.

Starter Troubleshooting

If the starter fails to energize

1. *Battery*– Check the voltage and the specific gravity of the electrolyte. Recharge or replace the battery as necessary.
2. *Wiring*
   a. Check for corroded or loose battery or solenoid connections. Clean or tighten as necessary. Soaking the corroded terminal in a baking soda and water solution is the best cleaning method. Do not allow the solution to get into any of the cells, as it will neutralize the electrolyte. Coat the clean connections with NoCo NCP-2 or equivalent to prevent further corrosion.
   b. Replace any frayed wires or wires with disintegrated terminals.
   c. Check for corroded or rusted ground connections on the equipment chassis. Remove the rust and treat the connection with NoCo or equivalent.
3. *Solenoid*—Use a jumper cable across the two large solenoid terminals to momentarily bypass the solenoid. If the starter energizes, the fault is in either the solenoid or the wiring to the solenoid. The *Solenoid Testing* section follows the starter section.
4. *Starter components*
   a. Check the brushes. Dirty or worn brushes and/or commutator will slow a starter. Replace worn brushes or brushes with broken leads.
   b. Check the armature commutator. The commutator is an integral part of the armature. Cracked, chipped, broken, or badly-grooved commutator sections are not repairable; in these cases, the armature will need replacement. A lightly-grooved commutator may be turned on a lathe to clean up. After turning, carefully file the burrs between the commutator segments. Dirty or rough commutators should be cleaned with a suitable solvent, then lightly sanded.
   c. Check the armature shaft and bearings/bushings. A worn shaft or bearings will allow the armature laminations to rub against the frame magnets, causing drag. Replace faulty components.

Starter energizes but turns slowly

1. *Battery*– Check the voltage and the specific gravity of the electrolyte. Recharge or replace the battery as necessary.
2. *Parasitic load on the engine*– Attempting to start an engine which is connected to a hydrostatic drive system places an additional load on the starter motor, especially in cooler temperatures. If possible, disconnect the load from the engine and retry the starter. If the starter now turns the engine properly, check the hydrostatic system to find the reason for the excessive load.

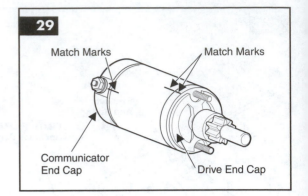

3. *Internal load on the engine*– Dirty, thick crankcase oil past its change schedule will cause slow turnover. Scored or galled internal engine components such as bearing journals, pistons and cylinders will overload the starter.
4. *Starter components*–
   a. Check the brushes. Dirty or worn brushes and/or commutator will slow a starter. Replace worn brushes or brushes with broken leads.
   b. Check the armature commutator. The commutator is an integral part of the armature. Cracked, chipped, broken, or badly-grooved commutator sections are not repairable; in these cases, the armature will need replacement. A lightly-grooved commutator may be turned on a lathe to clean up. After turning, carefully file the burrs between the commutator segments. Dirty or rough commutators should be cleaned with a suitable solvent, then lightly sanded.
   c. Check the armature shaft and bearings/bushings. A worn shaft or bearings will allow the armature laminations to rub against the frame magnets, causing drag. Replace faulty components.

Starter Removal

1. Disconnect the negative battery cable and secure the cable away from the battery.
2. Disconnect the starter cable.
3. Access the starter mount bolts by removing the blower housing.
4. Remove the nuts and lock washers holding the starter to the engine. Remove the starter.

Starter Inspection and Repair

Starter drive

1. Lightly clamp the drive pinion in a *soft-jaw* vise.

CAUTION
Overtightening the vise will distort and damage the drive pinion.

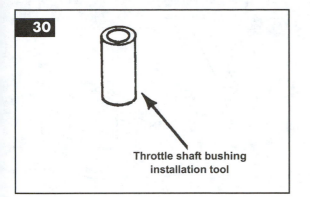

30

Throttle shaft bushing
installation tool

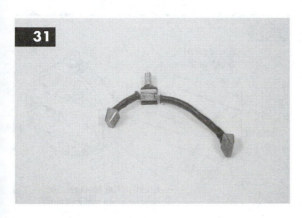

31

2. Squeeze the dust cover to remove it from the spacer groove.

3. On units with a stop nut, remove the stop nut. The armature will turn with the nut only until the pinion stops against the spacer and compressed spring. On units with a retaining ring, spread, remove and discard the ring. Remove the spacers, spring and pinion. During removal, note the orientation of the components. Replace any questionable components.

4. Carefully clean the pinion splines and armature shaft splines with a suitable solvent. Dry the splines thoroughly.

5. Lightly coat the splines and the smooth part of the shaft with Kohler Starter Drive Lubricant No. 52 357 01 or Cristolube 303. The use of other lubricants can cause sticking or binding of the pinion.

6. Lightly coat the stop nut threads with Loctite 271 or equivalent.

7. Assemble the drive components as shown in **Figure 28** — drive pinion, dust cover spacer (spring cup recess facing out), spring, flat spacer, then stop nut or retaining ring. Torque the stop nut to 240 in.-lb. (27 N·m).

8. Install the dust cover. Work the dust cover retaining ring (made into the inner base of the dust cover) into the dust cover spacer groove.

Starter motor disassembly

1. Remove the starter drive components as described as described in this chapter.
2. Rock the exposed armature shaft back and forth to check for shaft and/or bearing/bushing wear.
3. Verify that the match marks on the frame and end caps are visible for proper reassembly (**Figure 29**). Note that the match mark on the frame at the commutator end aligns with the battery cable stud. If the match marks are not clearly visible, use a scribe tool to engrave a set of match marks on both ends. Do *not* use a hammer and chisel to make match marks, as the frame magnets will be damaged.
4. Remove the through bolts.
5. Remove the commutator end cap assembly, including the brushes and springs.
6. Remove the drive end cap. Be careful not to lose the armature-to-end cap thrust washer.
7. Carefully pull the armature from the frame.
8. Clean the bolt and drive end cap threads.
9. Inspect as necessary. Replace questionable components.

Brushes and commutator end cap

1. With the brushes loose, remove the brush springs from the end cap brush holder pockets.
2. The self-tapping screws attach the negative brushes. Remove the screws, brushes and plastic brush holder.
3. Remove the nuts and washers from the positive stud terminal. Remove the stud terminal, insulator bushing and brushes from the end cap. Due to the length of the stud, the stud cannot be removed unless the insulator bushing and stud are pushed into the end cap together. If corrosion has jammed the stud insulator into the end cap, use the bushing driver from any Kohler throttle shaft kit (part No. 25 757 14 to 25 75719) (**Figure 30**) to drive the insulator into the end cap. A cotton swab with Lime-Away® or equivalent will remove any end cap corrosion. Carefully but thoroughly rinse, then dry, any corrosion-treated area.
4. Inspect the armature shaft bushing in the end cap. The bushing is not serviceable separately. If the bushing is worn beyond a reasonable limit, the end cap must be replaced.
5. Make sure that the drain hole in the commutator end cap is open and clean.
6. New brushes are approximately 1/2-inch (12 mm) in length. If the brushes are worn to 5/16-inch (8 mm) or less, replace the brushes.
7. Install the insulator bushing onto the positive brush stud. The flat part of the stud head must fit into the locator lip of the bushing, and the short brush lead must be to the left of the stud with the stud facing away from the installer (**Figure 31**). Install the brushes, bushing and stud into the

5

end cap, with the stud and bushing passing through the end cap hole. Install the outer insulator washer followed by the flat washer and shoulder nut. Tighten the nut snugly.

> *WARNING*
> *Use extreme care when assembling the positive brush stud with the insulator bushing through the end cap hole. The locator lip on the insulator bushing must be placed against the floor of the end cap, as shown in Figure 28. If, during installation, the lip breaks off or becomes damaged (Figure 32), the square stud head will twist and contact the end cap when the outer stud nut is tightened. This will cause a direct short when the starter is energized.*

8. Make sure the threads of the self-tapping screws are clean and dry. Do not use threadlocking compound on these screws, as it may prevent good ground contact. Using the self-tapping screws, install the plastic brush holder and the negative brushes into the end cap.

9. To prepare for installing the brush springs, use **Figure 33** and make a brush-holder tool.

10. Install one brush spring and brush at a time into each brush holder pocket. Make sure that the beveled-edge side of the brush faces away from the spring. Slide the tool over each brush as the brush is installed. When all four springs and brushes are installed, the tool and end cap should appear as shown, except that the positive brush stud should be 180° from the closed end of the tool, in line with the 1/2-inch armature shaft slot (**Figure 34**). This will expose both end cap through-bolt holes to permit easier starter reassembly. The end cap assembly is now ready for installation onto the starter.

Starter motor assembly

1. Carefully slide the armature into the frame housing so the magnets are at the drive end of the armature.

2. Fit the thrust washer onto the drive end of the armature.

3. Install the drive end cap over the armature, ensuring that the match marks on the cap and frame align (**Figure 29**). Note that the match mark on the frame at the commutator end aligns with the battery cable stud. Also note that when the match marks are aligned, the tabs stamped into the housing ends align with the cutout notches in the drive-end and commutator-end housings.

4. With the brush holder tool in place, fit the end cap to the frame housing and armature commutator end. Ensure that the match marks align.

5. Lightly coat the through-bolt threads with Loctite 242 or equivalent. Feed the bolts through the end cap and frame housing. Thread the bolts into the drive end cap

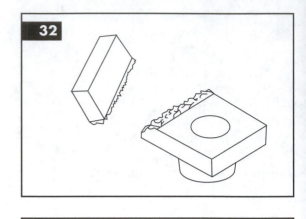

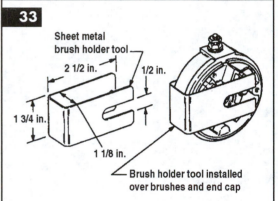

Sheet metal brush holder tool

2 1/2 in.

1/2 in.

1 3/4 in.

1 1/8 in.

Brush holder tool installed over brushes and end cap

enough to hold the starter together while still allowing a slight clearance to remove the brush holder tool.

6. Slowly slide the brush holder tool from the end cap.

7. Tighten the through bolts to 55-65 in.-lb. (6.2-7.3 N·m).

8. Install the starter drive as described in this chapter.

Starter Installation

1. Lightly coat the starter through bolt threads with Loctite 242 or equivalent.

REWIND STARTER

35

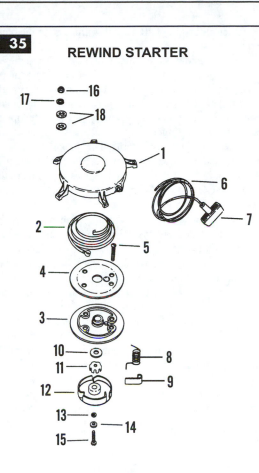

1. **Starter housing**
2. **Rewind spring**
3. **Pulley**
4. **Sheave plate**
5. **Sheave plate screw (4)**
6. **Rope**
7. **Handle grip**
8. **Pawl (3)**
9. **Pawl spring**
10. **Thrust washer**
11. **Brake**
12. **Retainer**
13. **Small diameter spacer washer**
14. **Retainer washer**
15. **Clutch screw**
16. **Hex nut 10-32 (5)**
17. **Lock washer #10 (5)**
18. **Flat washer #10 (10)**
19. **Drive cup**
20. **Flat washer 3/8" ID, 1-3/8" OD, 1/4" thick (2)**

2. Fit the starter through bolts into the starter mount holes in the crankcase, next to the No. 2 cylinder barrel.

3. Install one lock washer and nut onto each starter bolt. While holding the head of each starter bolt with a wrench, tighten the nuts.

4. Install the blower housing as described in this chapter.

5. Reconnect the starter cable, then the negative battery cable.

Solenoid Testing

Troubleshooting a solenoid can usually be done quickly with the solenoid in the system.

1. Remove the ignition key from the switch so the engine does not start.

2. Ensure that the unit is in neutral and that the parking brake is set.

3. Place the throttle control in the SLOW position.

4. Remove the main harness wire from the small solenoid winding terminal.

5. Using a short jumper wire, connect one end of the wire to the small terminal; momentarily touch the other end to the large terminal of the cable coming from the positive battery post.

6. If the starter activates, the solenoid is good.

REWIND STARTER

Refer to **Figure 35** when servicing the rewind starter.

Removal

To remove the starter, loosen and remove the five nuts, five lock washers and ten flat washers holding the starter housing to the engine blower housing.

Repair

To disassemble the starter, first release the tension of the rewind spring as follows:

1. Hold the starter assembly with the pulley facing up.

2. Pull the starter rope at least one complete pulley revolution until the notch in the pulley is aligned with the rope hole in the housing. Use thumb pressure to prevent the pulley from rotating.

3. Engage the rope in the pulley notch and pull in on the rope so the pulley can unwind freely. Slowly release thumb pressure to allow the spring to unwind until all the tension is released.

NOTE
If the rope is good, ignore Steps 6-13. If the spring is good, ignore Steps 5 and 15.

If the starter rope is worn or frayed, or if the spring is not properly rewinding, repair the starter as follows:

5

1. Remove the retainer screw assembly.

2. Remove the retainer and brake assembly. Check the pawls, pawl springs, brake, retainer and pulley for wear and replace as necessary. The brake should grip the retainer hub snugly while still allowing the retainer to rotate inside the brake. If the brake does not perform as noted, do not attempt to rebend the brake fingers as the brake is spring steel and the fingers will break off.

3. Remove the pawls and pawl springs from the pulley.

CAUTION
When removing the rope pulley, use extreme care to keep the starter spring confined in the housing.

4. With the spring tension released as previously instructed, *carefully* pull the pulley assembly off the housing center post while leaving the spring in the housing. Inspect the starter spring. Replace the spring if it is cracked, distorted, broken or rusted.

5. Note the direction of rotation of the starter spring, then carefully remove the spring.

6. Unscrew the four pulley sheave plate screws from the pulley. Remove the plate. Clean the screw threads and the threads in the pulley.

7. Carefully note the direction of rotation of the rope in the pulley track, as well as the position of the end of the rope.

8. Remove the old rope. Pull the rope through the housing hole.

9. Remove the rope from the handle grip.

10. Install a new rope into the grip.

11. Feed the rope back through the housing hole, into the starter.

12. Reinsert the rope into the pulley track.

13. Lightly coat the sheave plate screws with Loctite 222 or equivalent. Position the sheave plate onto the pulley, then install and tighten the screws.

14. Lightly coat the spring cavity in the housing and the spring side of the pulley assembly with Lubriplate® White Grease or equivalent.

15. Install the spring into the housing. The direction of rotation of the spring is shown in **Figure 35**.

16. Install the pulley onto the center post and into the housing, aligning the spring notch in the pulley hub with the hook in the end of the spring. Use a wire bent to form a hook to aid in positioning the spring hook into the hub notch.

17. Remove the wire hook and ensure that the pulley is completely seated onto the spring and into the housing.

18. Place the pawl springs into the pulley recesses with the straight ends down and the "L"-ends out. Make sure that the straight ends of the springs seat completely.

19. While pulling sideways on the "L"-end of one pawl spring, insert the pawl into its recess in the pulley. Release the "L"-end, allowing the spring to hold the pawl toward

the center of the pulley. Repeat this process for the other two pawls.

20. Make sure the friction areas on the brake and the retainer are clean and dry. Assemble the brake onto the retainer. The brake should grip the retainer hub snugly while still allowing the retainer to rotate inside the brake. If the brake does operate properly, do not attempt to rebend the brake fingers, as the brake is spring steel and the fingers will break off. Replace the brake.

21. With the thrust washer in place, place the retainer in position onto the pulley. It may be necessary to work the retainer back and forth to align the pawls into the retainer slots.

22. With the retainer and brake fully seated against the thrust washer and pulley, lightly coat the clutch screw threads with Loctite 222 or equivalent, and lightly coat the spacer washer and retainer washer with Lubriplate or equivalent. Install the spacer washer, retainer washer and clutch screw into the center post. Securely tighten the screw.

23. Align the rope notch in the pulley assembly with the rope outlet in the housing. Engage the rope in the notch and rotate the pulley to pretension the spring. The pulley should be rotated counterclockwise as the pulley is viewed inside the housing.

24. Rotate the pulley until there is no more slack in the rope. Continue rotating the pulley at least two more turns in the same direction to properly preload the starter spring.

25. Pull the rope to the fully-extended position. If the spring is properly preloaded, the rope will fully rewind when the handle grip is released. Adjust the preload, if necessary.

26. Before installing the starter on the engine, check the teeth in the drive cup for wear. Replace the cup, if necessary. When replacing the cup:

  a. Make sure that the cup is sitting squarely on the flywheel.

  b. Make sure that both flat washers are installed before installing the crankshaft bolt.

  c. Using the strap wrench shown in **Figure 21**, hold the flywheel in position while tightening the bolt. Torque the bolt to 40 ft.-lb. (54 N·m).

Installation

1. Set the starter in position on the blower housing.

2. Make sure that the starter fastener threads are clean and dry. Lightly coat the fastener threads with Loctite 222 or equivalent.

3. Install the fasteners finger tight. Refer to **Figure 35**, making certain that there are two flat washers and one lock washer under each nut.

4. Center the starter pawls inside the cup by lightly pulling out on the starter rope handle grip until all three pawls extend and contact the cup notches.

5. While the pawls are in contact with the cup, alternately tighten the starter fasteners.

6. When the fasteners are tight, release the rope grip.

OIL SENTRY

Engines equipped with the Oil Sentry oil pressure monitor will either activate a warning light or stop the engine if the oil pressure falls below approximately 3-1/2 psi.

Depending on the type of exhaust system, the Oil Sentry switch will be located either next to the oil filter, threaded into a raised boss cast into the No. 1 crankcase casting, or threaded into a special oil filter adapter base. A special 1/8 × 1/16 NPTF reducer adapter is required for the crankcase application.

Removal

Crankcase-mounted applications

1. Refer to *Muffler, Removal* in this chapter and remove as much of the exhaust system as is necessary to access the switch.

2. Disconnect the switch wire.

3. While holding the reducer with a wrench, loosen and remove the switch.

Filter base mounted applications

1. Place a pan under the oil filter to catch drippings.

2. Loosen and remove the oil filter.

3. Disconnect the switch wire.

4. Remove the screws holding the filter base to the crankcase. Remove the base. Carefully clean all old gasket material from the crankcase and base.

5. Unscrew the switch from the filter base.

Testing

The Oil Sentry switch is normally closed, and is calibrated to open and reclose when pressure is within the 2.0-5.0 psi (13.79-34.48 kPa) range. Four items will be needed to test the switch operation: A source of compressed air, a pressure regulator, a pressure gauge, and an ohmmeter.

To test the switch:

1. Connect the switch to the regulated air source.

2. Connect one ohmmeter lead to the switch case and the other lead to the switch terminal.

3. At 0 psi, the meter should read continuity.

4. As pressure is increased, the meter should change to infinity/no-continuity between 2.0 and 5.0 psi (13.8 and 34.5 kPa).

5. Gradually increase pressure to 90 psi (620 kPa). The meter should continue to read infinity. Do not apply more than 90 psi pressure to the switch.

6. Gradually decrease pressure. The meter should change back to continuity as pressure drops back between 2.0 and 5.0 psi (13.8 and 34.5 kPa). Continuity should remain all the way back to 0 psi.

7. Any results other than those specified in Steps 1-6 indicate a faulty switch. Replace the switch.

Installation

Crankcase-mounted applications

1. Make sure the switch threads and crankcase threads are clean and dry.

2. Lightly coat the switch threads with Loctite #592 Teflon sealant or equivalent. *Do not* get any sealant beyond the end of the threads, near the switch orifice.

3. Install the switch into the crankcase opening.

4. Connect the switch wire.

5. Reinstall the removed components.

Filter base-mounted applications

1. Make sure the switch threads and filter base threads are clean and dry.

2. Lightly coat the switch threads with Loctite #592 Teflon sealant or equivalent. Do *not* get any sealant beyond the end of the threads, near the switch orifice.

3. Install the switch into the filter base opening.

4. Make sure that the filter base bolt threads and crankcase threads are clean and dry. Lightly coat the bolt threads with Loctite 242 or equivalent.

5. Using a new gasket, fasten the filter base to the crankcase. Make sure the arrow stamped on the filter side of the base points toward the carburetor. Torque the base screws to 125 in.-lb. (14 N·m).

6. Connect the switch wire.

7. Install the oil filter.

INTAKE MANIFOLD

Removal

1. Remove the air filter cover and element assembly.

2. Disconnect the breather tube from the air filter base plate.

3. Remove the four screws holding the base plate to the elbow. Carefully clean all old gasket material from the base plate and elbow.

4. Note the location of the governor spring ends in the governor arm and the speed control lever. Remove the governor spring.

5. Disconnect the choke control cable from the carburetor.

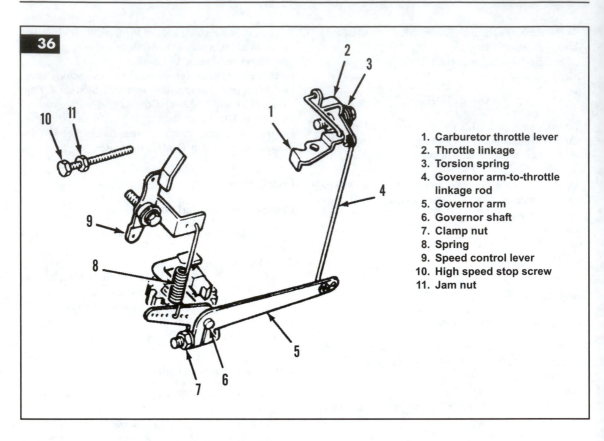

36

1. Carburetor throttle lever
2. Throttle linkage
3. Torsion spring
4. Governor arm-to-throttle linkage rod
5. Governor arm
6. Governor shaft
7. Clamp nut
8. Spring
9. Speed control lever
10. High speed stop screw
11. Jam nut

6. Refer to **Figure 36**. Unhook the governor linkage from the governor arm and the intake manifold throttle lever.

7. Unclamp the throttle control cable from the manifold. Remove the cable end from the speed control lever.

8. Undo the hose clamp and remove the fuel pump hose from the carburetor inlet fitting.

9. Refer to **Figure 18**. Loosen the four bolts holding the manifold ends to the engine. While supporting the manifold assembly, remove the bolts and washers. Remove the manifold assembly.

10. Remove all old gasket material from the manifold and cylinder mount faces.

11. If carburetor work is necessary, the carburetor can be removed from the manifold at this time. Refer to Steps 3-9 under *Carburetor, Removal*.

12. Inspect the manifold for cracks or other damage. Repair or replace as necessary.

Installation

Always use new gaskets when assembling engine components. Refer to **Figures 7-9**, **18**, **16**, and **36**.

1. Make sure the mounting bolt threads and matching cylinder threads are clean and dry.

2. Lightly coat the mounting bolt threads with Loctite 271 or equivalent.

3. Fit the four mounting bolts and washers into the manifold end holes.

4. Fit the gaskets onto the exposed ends of the bolts.

5. Position the manifold next to the engine. Screw the top two mount bolts into the engine a couple of threads, then do the same with the bottom two bolts. This will prevent the gaskets from falling off. Finish screwing the bolts in finger-tight.

6. Incrementally and alternately torque the four mount bolts to 150 in.-lb. (17 N•m).

7. If the carburetor was removed, install it now. Follow Steps 1-4 under *Carburetor, Installation*.

8. Connect the choke control cable as follows:

   a. Push the choke knob all the way in.

   b. Move the choke shutter to the wide-open position.

   c. Connect the cable Z-bend to the hole in the carburetor choke lever, and fit the cable housing into the choke clamp.

   d. Make sure that the choke cable is centered in the clamp channel, then tighten the clamp holddown screw.

   e. Pull out on the cable control until the carburetor choke shutter is completely closed. Make sure the shutter closes completely.

   f. Work the choke control out and in a couple of times to make sure the control or cable is not binding. Adjust as necessary.

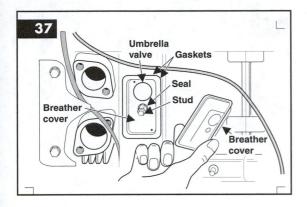

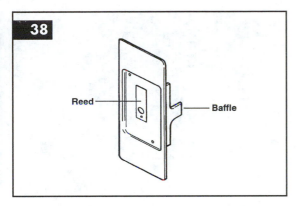

NOTE
*Early design breathers used an umbrella-style valve like that shown in **Figure 37**. Later design breathers use a reed valve-style breather (**Figure 38**). Removal, inspection and installation procedures are the same for both breathers. When removing an umbrella-style breather, replacement with a reed valve-style breather (P/N 52 035 04) is recommended.*

Removal

1. Remove the intake manifold as described in this chapter.

2. Remove the breather hose from the breather cover. Inspect the hose thoroughly. If the hose is loose, cracked, or dry and brittle, replace it.

3. Remove the hex nut and copper washer from the breather cover stud.

4. Remove the cover, seal and breather plate assembly.

5. Carefully remove all old gasket material from the cover, plate and valve chamber flange. Do not damage the gasket surfaces.

6. Inspect the breather.

   a. Make sure that the holes in the breather plate are open and clean.

   b. Check the condition of the breather valve and stud seal. Replace if either are questionable.

Installation

Always use new gaskets and a new seal when assembling breather components. Refer to **Figure 37** and **Figure 38**.

1. Place a gasket against the back side of the breather plate assembly, around the raised portion of the plate.

2. Being careful not to let the gasket slip, install the breather plate with the movable end of the reed in the UP position, toward the blower housing. This allows the baffle on the back side of the breather to fit over the crankcase hole in the valve chamber. If the breather is mounted with the reed down, oil will puddle in the valve chamber and be sucked into the air filter when the engine is operated on an angle with the No. 1 cylinder down.

3. Install the stud seal, outer gasket and breather cover. Make sure the cover hole for the breather hose is up and that the cover is aligned with the gasket and breather plate.

4. Lightly coat the stud threads with Loctite 242 or equivalent.

5. Make sure that the copper washer is in good condition. Install the copper washer and nut onto the stud. Snug the nut.

9. Connect the throttle control cable as follows:

   a. Move the throttle control to the FAST position on the control panel.

   b. Connect the cable Z-bend to the hole in the governor speed control lever, and fit the cable housing into the manifold clamp.

   c. Slide the cable housing through the clamp so the speed control lever paddle is against the high speed stop screw.

   d. Make sure that the throttle cable is centered in the clamp channel, then tighten the clamp holddown screw. Work the throttle control between fast and slow a couple of times to make sure the control or cable is not binding.

10. Complete the installation by performing Steps 5-12 under *Carburetor, Installation*. If the engine is to be run immediately, also perform Steps 13 and 14.

CRANKCASE BREATHER

NOTE
*Number 1 cylinder is always the cylinder closest to the flywheel. The breather assembly is mounted over the valve springs on the No. 1 cylinder (**Figure 37**).*

6. Install the breather hose flange into the cover hole with the other end of the hose aimed toward the air filter base.

OIL SEALS

Service With Crankshaft Installed

Oil seals at the flywheel end and the PTO end of the crankshaft prevent the oil in the engine from leaking out. Wear or damage can reduce their effectiveness and oil leakage can become a problem.

In most instances, it is possible to remove and install an oil seal without removing the crankshaft. Depending on which oil seal is leaking and the location of the engine, it may be necessary to remove the engine from the equipment.

If the oil seal at the flywheel end of the crankshaft is leaking, the flywheel must be removed (see *Flywheel, Removal*). If the oil seal at the PTO end of the crankshaft is leaking, any parts attached to the crankshaft that deny access to the oil seal must be removed.

> *NOTE*
> *Drain the engine oil if replacing the PTO oil seal.*

Removal

Before removing an oil seal, note the position of the seal in the crankcase or oil pan. Install the new seal so it is located at the same depth as the original seal.

> *CAUTION*
> *Exercise care when extracting the seal so the metal behind the seal or the crankshaft seal surface is not scratched or damaged.*

> *NOTE*
> *Special oil seal removal tools are available from small-engine tool suppliers, or and oil seal removal tool may be made by modifying a linoleum knife as shown in* **Figure 39***. Carefully grind the blade to the contour shown in the figure, then round all the blade edges so the blade will not damage the crankshaft or seal cavity.*

1. Using a small pin punch, carefully tap the seal a few times around its outer edge to break it loose from the crankcase cavity. Only tap it enough to break it loose. Do not drive it deeper into the cavity.

2. Carefully insert the tool blade under the oil seal lip and against the inside periphery of the seal, next to the crankshaft (**Figure 40**). Pry out the seal. It may be necessary to work around the seal in more than one spot before the seal will break loose.

3. Clean the seal seating area so the new seal will seat properly.

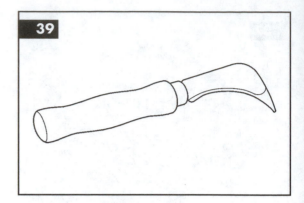

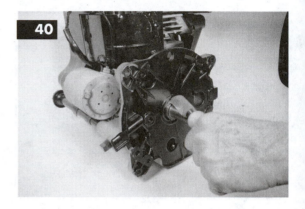

4. Check the oil seal bore in the engine and dress out any burrs created during removal. Only remove metal that is raised and will interfere with the installation of the new seal. If a deep gouge is present, clean and dry the area around the gouge, then fill the depression with a suitable epoxy so it is level with the surrounding metal.

5. Check the crankshaft seal area. Scoring, grooves, or sharp edges on the crankshaft will require that the crankshaft be replaced.

Installation

1. Apply Loctite 598 or any other oil-resistant nonhardening sealer to the edges of the oil seal prior to installation.

2. Cover keyways and threads on the crankshaft with a seal protector sleeve or thin tape so the oil seal lip will not be cut when passing the oil seal down the crankshaft.

3. Coat the lips of the seal with a light grease.

4. Position the seal so the seal lip is slanted toward the inside of the engine. Most seals are spring-loaded. The spring must be toward the engine when installing the seal.

5. Use a suitable tool with the same outside diameter as the oil seal to force the oil seal into the engine. A deep-well socket may work if the output end of the crankshaft is short. Suitable sizes of tubing or pipe may be used. Be sure the end of the tool is square and not sharp.

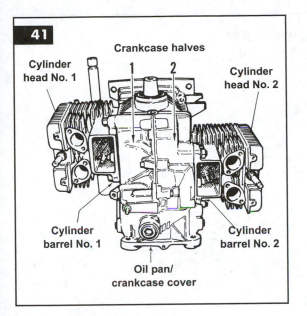

41

Cylinder head No. 1

Crankcase halves

Cylinder head No. 2

Cylinder barrel No. 1

Cylinder barrel No. 2

Oil pan/ crankcase cover

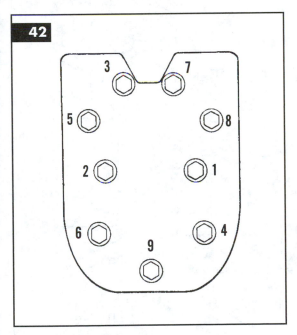

42

6. The crankshaft oil seals should be installed so they are 1/32 inch (0.79 mm) below flush with the seal bore faces.

CYLINDER HEADS

Cylinder heads should be removed at 500 hour intervals so that carbon and other deposits can be removed from the heads and combustion chambers. Clean combustion deposits using a wooden or stiff plastic scraper.

Removal

1. Remove the blower housing and the cylinder head air baffles as described under *Blower Housing, Removal* in this chapter.

2. Clean all chaff, grass clippings, or other debris from the cylinder and head cooling fins.

3. Remove the cylinder head bolts, then remove the cylinder heads and head gaskets. Note that the cylinder barrels are identified by a number 1 or number 2 stamped on the machined gasket surface near the valve spring chamber (**Figure 41**). Mark the cylinder heads with a corresponding number so they can be reinstalled in the original location.

4. Clean carbon and other combustion deposits from the cylinder heads.

5. Carefully remove all old gasket material from the heads and the cylinder barrel gasket surfaces.

6. Check the heads for distortion or other damage:

   a. Place the head, gasket face down, on a surface plate or other precision flat surface.

   b. Insert a feeler gauge between the surface plate and the head gasket area, between each pair of head bolt holes.

   c. If the head is warped more than 0.003 inch (0.076 mm), both the head and the head bolts should be replaced.

Installation

1. Lightly wire-brush the head bolt threads to remove any rust. If any bolts appear questionable, replace the entire set. Use the correct Grade 8 bolts and flat washers.

> *NOTE*
> *Lightly lubricate the cylinder head bolt threads with clean engine oil prior to assembly.*

2. Run a bottoming tap into each threaded head-bolt hole in both cylinder barrels to clean the threads for proper torquing. Do not allow tapping debris to fall into the cylinders.

3. Using new head gaskets, fit the heads onto the cylinders. Ensure that the heads are correctly matched to the cylinders. Run the head bolts in finger-tight at this time.

4. Using the sequence shown in **Figure 42**, tighten the head bolts in 50 in.-lb. or 4 ft.-lb. (5 N·m) increments to a final torque of 180-240 in.-lb. or 15-20 ft.-lbs. (20-27 N·m).

5. Reinstall the cylinder head air baffles and the blower housing using the instructions under *Blower Housing, Installation*.

43

ENGINE COMPONENTS

1. Oil seal
2. Oil pan
3. Governor assy.
4. Governor cross shaft
5. Governor stop pin
6. Governor stub shaft
7. Crankcase half
8. Cylinder barrel
9. Main bearing
10. Oil seal
11. Spacer
12. Oil pump gear
13. Oll pump shaft
14. Inner rotor
15. Outer rotor
16. Pump cover
17. Oil pressure relief valve
18. Thrust washer
19. Crankshaft
20. Screen
21. Flywheel
22. Stator

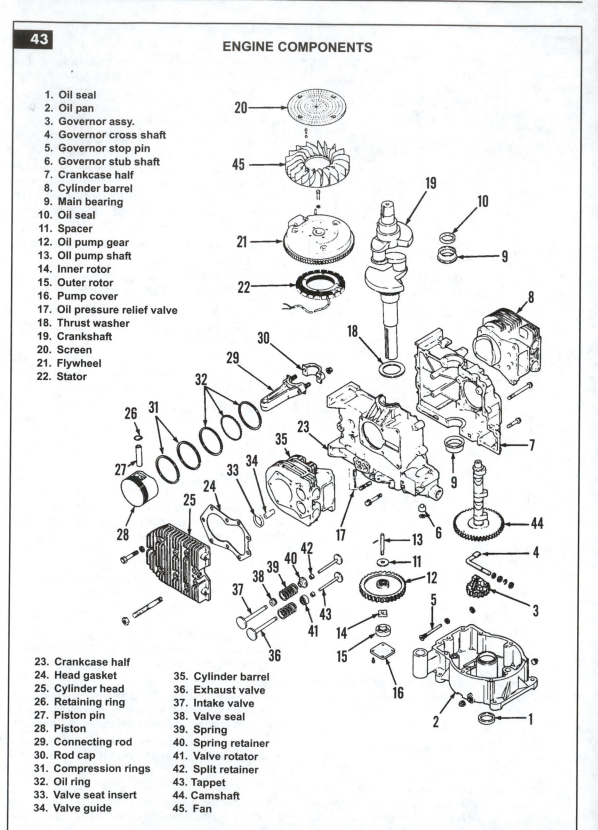

23. Crankcase half
24. Head gasket
25. Cylinder head
26. Retaining ring
27. Piston pin
28. Piston
29. Connecting rod
30. Rod cap
31. Compression rings
32. Oil ring
33. Valve seat insert
34. Valve guide
35. Cylinder barrel
36. Exhaust valve
37. Intake valve
38. Valve seal
39. Spring
40. Spring retainer
41. Valve rotator
42. Split retainer
43. Tappet
44. Camshaft
45. Fan

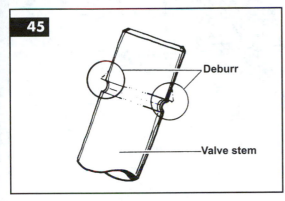

VALVES AND VALVE COMPONENTS

Valve Adjustment

NOTE
The No. 1 cylinder is the cylinder closest to the flywheel (44, Figure 43).

Valve-stem-to-tappet clearance should be checked after every 500 hours of operation. To check the clearance:

1. Remove the breather assembly from the No. 1 cylinder. **Figure 37** shows the breather assembly and cover for the No. 1 cylinder. Remove the valve cover from the No. 2 cylinder. The No. 2 cylinder only uses a cover plate and gasket. Thoroughly clean the old gasket material from the breather and covers.

2. Remove the spark plugs for visual access to the heads of the pistons and valves.

3. Rotate the flywheel so that the No. 1 piston is at top dead center on its compression stroke (both valves completely closed).

4. Use a feeler gauge to measure the clearance between the valve stem ends and the tappets.

5. Rotate the flywheel one complete turn (360°) to place the No. 2 piston at top dead center on its compression stroke.

6. Measure the valve clearance for the No. 2 cylinder.

On all models, intake valve-to-tappet clearance with the engine cold should be 0.003-0.006 inch (0.08-0.15 mm).

Recommended exhaust valve-to-tappet clearance is determined by the engine serial number as follows:
1. *Before serial number 1816500656* — 0.016-0.019 inch (0.41-0.48 mm);
2. *After serial number 1816500646 but before 1917809296* — 0.011-0.014 inch (0.30-0.35 mm);
3. *After serial number 1917809286* — 0.013-0.016 inch (0.33-0.41 mm).

If clearance is too small, remove the valves and grind the end of the valve stem to increase clearance. If clearance is too large, recut the valve seat or fit a new valve to decrease clearance.

If the valves are being adjusted as part of a major engine service, note the following:

NOTE
For accurate valve-to-tappet clearance, if the cylinder being checked has the springs removed, the valve springs of the cylinder opposite the one being checked must be off the valves. Likewise, if the valves being checked for clearance have the springs installed, the opposing cylinder must have the valve springs installed. This places an equal load on the camshaft.

Always use new gaskets when reinstalling the breather and valve covers.

Valve Removal

1. Remove the breather assembly from the No. 1 cylinder. **Figure 37** shows the breather assembly and cover for the No. 1 cylinder. Remove the valve cover from the No. 2 cylinder. The No. 2 cylinder only uses a cover plate and gasket. Thoroughly clean the old gasket material from breather and covers.

2. Follow the steps under *Cylinder Heads, Removal* in this chapter and remove the cylinder heads.

3. Using an approved spring compressor (A or B, **Figure 44**), compress the valve spring retainers and springs (49, 50 and 51, **Figure 43**) and remove the split valve spring retainer keepers (52).

4. Remove the valves from the guides. If the valves offer resistance, check the keeper groove at the base of the stem (**Figure 45**). Using a fine file, carefully deburr any flaring on the stem at the bottom end of the groove.

CAUTION
Prior to filing the keeper groove burrs, place a small rag or paper towel in the bottom of the valve chamber, below the stem end, to catch any filings. Do not let the filings fall into the engine. Before

5

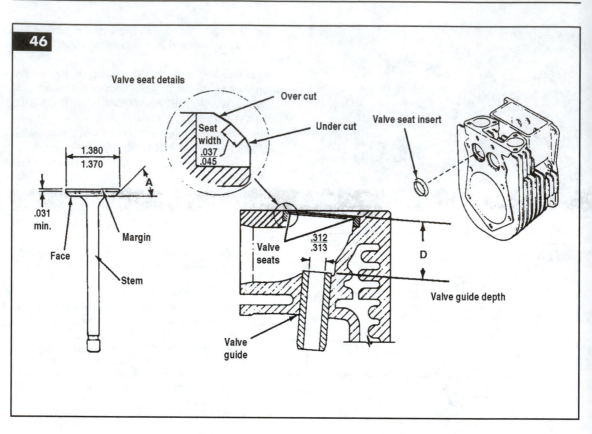

46

Valve seat details

Over cut

Under cut

Valve seat insert

Seat width
.037
.045

1.380
1.370

A

.031 min.

Margin

Face

Stem

Valve seats

.312
.313

D

Valve guide depth

Valve guide

removing the rag, remove the filings with a small magnet.

All models have replaceable hardened alloy exhaust valve seats. Intake valve face and seat angles are 45° for all models. The exhaust valve face and seat angles are 45° for early models, and 30° for later models (serial numbers 1917809296 and higher). Valve face and seat angles are 30° for all replacement exhaust valves and seats.

The standard seat width for all valves is 0.037-0.045 inch (0.94-1.14 mm) (**Figure 46**).

Valve Inspection

1. Prior to cleaning the valve, inspect it for damage and excessive wear.

   a. Gummy deposits on the intake valve (**Figure 47**) may indicate that the engine has run on gasoline that was stored for an extended period.

   b. Hard deposits on the intake valve are due to burnt oil, while hard deposits on the exhaust valve (**Figure 48**) are due to combustion byproducts and burnt oil.

   c. Moisture in the engine during storage can cause corroded or pitted valves which should be replaced.

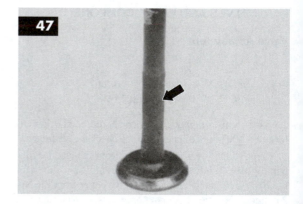

47

   d. Check the valve face (**Figure 49**) and valve seat for an irregular contact pattern. The seating ring around the face should be approximately centered on the valve face, concentric with the valve head and should be equal in dimension all around the valve. An irregular seating pattern indicates a bent valve or a poor face or seat grind.

2. Remove deposits either with a wire brush or soak the valve in parts cleaner.

3. Run a fingernail down the valve stem and check for a ledge that would indicate that the valve stem is worn. Measure the valve stem diameter. Specified minimum valve stem diameter is .3103 inch (7.882 mm) for the in-

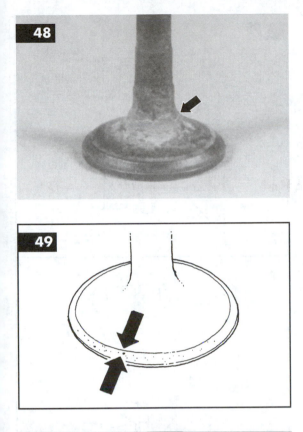

take valve and .3088 inch (7.844 mm) for the exhaust valve. Replace the valve if the valve stem is worn beyond limits. Oversize valves are not available.

4. The valve stem must be perpendicular to the valve head. To check for a bent valve, install the valve stem in the chuck of a drill press and rotate the drill by hand while measuring head runout with a dial indicator. Be sure the valve stem is centered in the drill chuck.

5. The valve rides in a replaceable valve guide. Refer to the *Valve Guide Reconditioning* in this chapter for guide service.

6. Check valve stem-to-valve guide clearance:

    a. Measure the inside diameter of the guide with a split-ball gauge. Measure at three points – top, middle and bottom of the guide. A guide with widely varying measurements should be replaced.

    b. Using an outside micrometer, measure the valve stem diameter at multiple points in the area where it travels in the guide. A valve with widely varying stem measurements should be replaced. If the dimensions are close, use the largest dimension to calculate the clearance.

    c. Stem-to-guide clearance should not exceed 0.005 inch (0.127 mm) on the intake valve or 0.007 inch (0.178 mm) on the exhaust valve.

7. Measure the valve head margin (**Figure 46**). Replace the valve if the margin is less than 0.031 inch (0.8 mm).

8. If the valve face is worn but serviceable, it can be refaced. The valve face angle (A, **Figure 46**) should be 45° on all intake valves and on original exhaust valves before Serial No. 1917809296. The exhaust valve face angle on engines beginning with Serial No. 1917809296 and on all replacement exhaust valves should be 30°.

> *NOTE*
> *Since all replacement exhaust valves have a 30° face, a valve kit must be purchased if replacing an exhaust valve in an early engine. The kit includes the 30° valve and the 30° seat. Instructions on replacing the seat are found under Valve Seat Reconditioning in this chapter.*

9. If valve face and seat machining are not necessary, the valve should be lapped against the valve seat to restore the seating surfaces. Refer to *Valve Lapping*.

10. Check the valve springs. The spring should be straight with square ends as shown in **Figure 50**. Valve spring free height should be approximately 1.69 (1-11/16) inches (42.85 mm).

Valve Lapping

1. Apply a light, even coat of lapping compound to the valve face. Lap the valve so that the sealing ring of the valve face is in the center of the face (**Figure 51**). Make

the first lap pass *very light* to check the sealing ring position.

> *NOTE*
> *For the most accurate lapping, slowly rotate the lapping tool back and forth between 1/4 and 3/8 of a turn (90°-135°). Do not spin the tool rapidly through a revolution or two, then reverse direction.*

2. If, after initial lapping, the sealing ring is too high or too low on the valve face:
    a. Recut the seat as necessary (refer to the following *Valve Seat Reconditioning* section).
    b. Reset the valve clearance.
    c. Relap the valve.
3. If the initial lap indicates the sealing ring is centered on the valve face, proceed with a full lapping.
4. Clean all lapping compound from the valve seat and valve face area.
5. After the lapping is complete, recheck the valve clearances. Adjust as necessary.

Valve Seat Reconditioning

Removal

1. Use a suitable puller (tool No. NU-11726 or NU-11913 puller, NU-11915 forcing screw, NU-11918 adapter, and a slide hammer).
2. Refer to **Figure 52** and follow the instructions included with the puller tools. View A shows the tool being installed under the seat; View B shows the seat being pulled out.

Installation

1. Thoroughly clean the seat counterbore in the cylinder barrel. Both the seat and the counterbore must be clean, dry and free of burrs or nicks.
2. Align the valve seat insert with the counterbore.
3. Press the seat insert squarely into the counterbore. Be sure the new seat is completely bottomed in the counterbore.

Cutting

1. Using a valve seat cutter (**Figure 53**), cut the new seat to match the specifications shown in **Figure 46**. Prior to each cutting, mark the face of the seat with a magic marker so the amount of seat material removed will be readily apparent.
2. Once the seat appears to be properly cut, insert the valve into the guide and adjust the valve-to-tappet clearance.
3. Remove the valve and lightly coat the seat face with Prussian Blue.

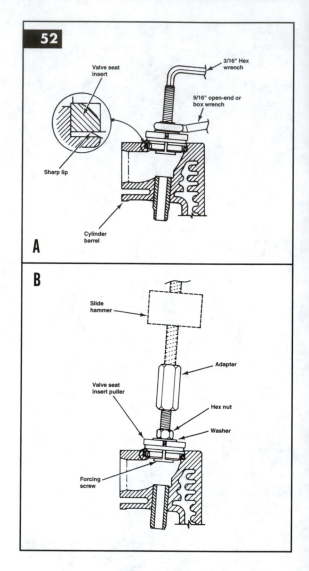

52

A — Valve seat insert / 3/16" Hex wrench / 9/16" open-end or box wrench / Sharp lip / Cylinder barrel

B — Slide hammer / Adapter / Valve seat insert puller / Hex nut / Washer / Forcing screw

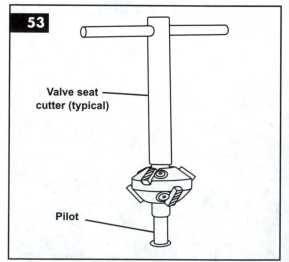

53

Valve seat cutter (typical)

Pilot

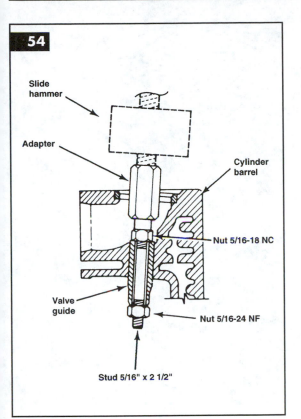

54

- Slide hammer
- Adapter
- Cylinder barrel
- Nut 5/16-18 NC
- Valve guide
- Nut 5/16-24 NF
- Stud 5/16" x 2 1/2"

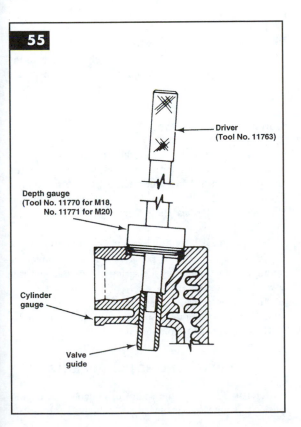

55

- Driver (Tool No. 11763)
- Depth gauge (Tool No. 11770 for M18, No. 11771 for M20)
- Cylinder gauge
- Valve guide

4. Insert the valve into the guide and lightly tap the *center* of the valve head with the ball end of a small ball-peen hammer so the Prussian Blue will leave its mark on the valve face;

5. Remove the valve. Inspect the blue dye sealing mark on the valve face.

   a. If the sealing ring is too close to the margin (too high), remove a slight amount of overcut material followed by a light seat angle cut.

   b. If the sealing ring is too close to the stem (too low), remove a slight amount of undercut material followed by a light seat angle cut.

   c. Immediately after cutting additional seat material, reset the valve-to-tappet clearance. Always ensure proper clearance prior to rechecking the sealing ring area.

6. Repeat the above steps until the valve seat and face meet specifications.

Valve Guide Reconditioning

New valve stem-to-guide clearance on all models should be 0.0025-0.0045 inch (0.064-0.114 mm) for the intake valve and 0.0045-0.0065 inch (0.114-0.165 mm) for the exhaust valve.

The standard inside diameter for intake and exhaust valve guides is 0.3125 inch (7.94 mm). If the intake valve guide inside diameter is worn 0.005 inch (0.13 mm) or more, or if the exhaust valve guide inside diameter is worn 0.007 inch (0.18 mm) or more, replace the guide(s) as follows.

1. Use a suitable puller to remove the old valve guide. **Figure 54** shows an effective puller which can be made in the shop.

2. Install the new valve guide using a suitable valve guide driver (**Figure 55**). The guide should be installed so the end surface of the guide is 1.125 inches (28.57 mm) below the top edge of the valve seat on Model MV18, or 1.390 inches (35.31 mm) on Model MV20 (D, **Figure 46**).

3. Using a split-ball gauge, measure the inside diameter of the new guide. If necessary, use a 0.3125 inch (7.94 mm) reamer and ream the inside of the guide.

Valve Installation

1. Position the valves in the cylinder barrel and check the valve clearance as described under *Valve Adjustment* in this chapter.

NOTE
For accurate valve-to-tappet clearance, if the cylinder being checked has the springs removed, the valve springs of the cylinder opposite the one being checked must be off the valves. Likewise, if the valves being

5

*checked for clearance have the springs in-
stalled, the opposing cylinder must have
the valve springs installed. This places an
equal load on the camshaft.*

2. Install new valve seals on the intake valve guides.

3. Lightly lubricate the exhaust valve stems with
Led-Plate antiseize compound or Dow Corning G-N
Metal Assembly Paste or equivalent. Lightly lubricate the
intake valve stems with engine oil. Lightly lubricate the
valve guides with engine oil.

4. Install the valve springs with the close coils facing toward the cylinder barrel and away from the spring retainers. The close-coil end is shown in **Figure 56**. Using a
valve spring compressor like the one in **Figure 57**, compress each valve spring together with its spring retainer.

5. Install the compressed springs into the valve chamber
one at a time, followed by the appropriate valve.

6. Install the split spring retainer keepers. Make sure that
the keepers (**Figure 58**) are completely seated into the
spring retainer recess (B, **Figure 59**), approximately flush
with the end of the straight diameter of the valve stem (A).

7. Using new gaskets, install the breather assembly and
valve covers.

8. Follow the steps under *Cylinder Heads, Installation* to
install the heads.

GOVERNOR

All models are equipped with a centrifugal flyweight
mechanical governor. The governor gear and flyweight
mechanism are located inside the engine crankcase and
are driven by the camshaft gear.

RPM (Static) Adjustment

Refer to **Figure 16**.

1. Make certain the governor linkage is connected to the
governor arm and to the throttle lever on the intake manifold.

2. The throttle linkage must be connected to the throttle
lever on the intake manifold and the throttle lever on the
carburetor as shown in **Figure 16**.

3. Loosen the governor arm clamp bolt nut.

4. Pull the governor arm down and away from the carburetor as far as possible to fully open the carburetor throttle
plate.

5. Turn the governor shaft clockwise as far as possible
and tighten the clamp nut to 50-60 in.-lbs. (5-6 N·m).

6. Connect a tachometer to the engine.

7. With the parking brake on, the blade PTO disengaged,
the speed control in neutral, and the neutral locks locked,
start the engine and run it for a few minutes in order to
reach normal operating temperature.

8. Move the throttle control to the FAST position. Note
the rpm reading. Maximum engine speed with no load is
3750 rpm and is controlled by a high-speed stop screw.

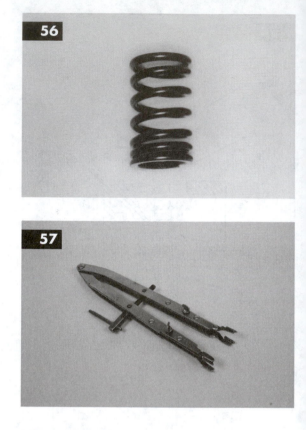

9. If adjustment is required to attain 3750 rpm:
   a. Loosen the stop screw jam nut.
   b. Turn the screw (11) counterclockwise (out) to increase rpm or clockwise (in) to decrease rpm.
   c. Tighten the jam nut.

Sensitivity Adjustment

Governor sensitivity is controlled by changing the position of the governor spring in the speed control lever or
the governor arm lever. The standard spring position is
the third hole from the cross shaft in the governor arm and
the second, or farthest, hole from the pivot point in the
speed control lever.

1. Always mark the spring location prior to removal.

2. To increase governor sensitivity, increase governor
spring tension by moving the spring in the governor arm
toward the cross shaft.

3. To decrease sensitivity and allow broader speed control, decrease spring tension by moving the spring in the
governor lever away from the cross shaft.

INTERNAL ENGINE COMPONENTS

Refer to **Table 4** at the end of this chapter for engine
Fastener Tightening Torque specifications. **Table 5** lists

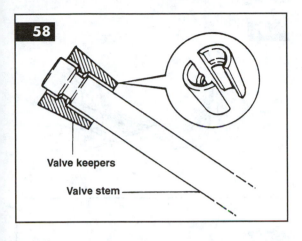

58

Valve keepers

Valve stem

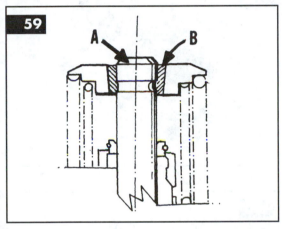

59

A B

Engine Clearances and Specifications. **Table 6** lists Recommended Silicone Sealants.

ENGINE DISASSEMBLY

Refer to the appropriate previous sections when removing the external engine components. Refer to **Figure 43**.

1. Drain the engine oil and remove the oil filter. For the most effective crankcase sludge removal, the oil should be drained hot.

2. Allow the engine to cool, then remove the muffler(s), exhaust elbows, and air cleaner.

3. Disconnect the throttle and choke control cables.

4. Carefully disconnect the fuel pump-to-carburetor fuel hose, then remove the intake manifold and carburetor as a unit. Keep the carburetor upright to prevent fuel spillage or drain the carburetor fuel into an approved container.

5. Unplug the main harness from the voltage regulator, then remove the blower housing and all cooling shrouds.

6. Mark the cylinder heads and crankcase halves as No. 1 side and No. 2 side as shown in **Figure 41**. The head and crankcase numbers should correspond to the numbers stamped into the cylinder barrels on the machined gasket surface near the valve spring chambers.

NOTE
Cylinder No. 1 is always the cylinder closest to the flywheel.

7. Remove the fuel pump, ignition module and module bracket.

8. Remove the flywheel bolt assembly, then remove the flywheel using a suitable puller.

9. Disconnect and remove the alternator and all wiring.

10. Remove the breather and valve tappet chamber covers.

11. Remove the starter motor.

12. Remove the spark plugs.

13. Remove the cylinder heads, then remove the cylinder retaining nuts and pull the cylinder barrels off the piston and connecting rod assemblies.

14. Mark the pistons as No. 1 and No. 2, then remove the piston pin retaining rings, piston pins and pistons.

15. Remove the crankcase closure plate (oil pan), oil pressure relief valve assembly and oil filter adapter.

16. Scribe a line across the camshaft bore plug and the No. 1 crankcase side. This line is used to align the plug during assembly.

17. Rotate the crankshaft so the connecting rods are at BDC, then carefully lay the crankcase assembly over, with the No. 1 side down.

18. Wrap a rubber band or tape around the valve tappet stems in the No. 2 crankcase side to prevent the tappets from falling out when the crankcase is split.

19. Remove the crankcase retaining nuts, washers and screws. With the No. 2 crankcase facing up, carefully pry the crankcase halves apart by inserting a flat-bladed pry tool into the splitting notches provided in the crankcase halves.

CAUTION
*Pry **only** between the splitting notches. Prying anywhere else between the crankcase halves will damage the sealing surfaces.*

20. Carefully rotate the crankshaft to note the crank gear and cam gear timing marks. Remove the camshaft and the camshaft bore plug from the No. 1 crankcase half.

21. Mark the tappet locations, then remove all four tappets.

NOTE
The intake valve tappet is always the tappet closest to the flywheel.

5

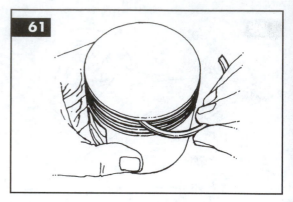

22. Remove the crankshaft, connecting rods, flywheel oil seal and crankshaft bearings as an assembly. If the crankshaft bearings are to be removed, mark them for correct reinstallation.

23. Carefully clean all old sealant from the crankcase sealing surfaces. Do not gouge the surfaces.

24. Mark the connecting rods and rod caps as No. 1 and No. 2, then remove them from the crankshaft.

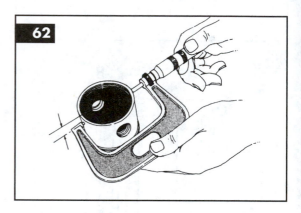

PISTON, PISTON RINGS AND PISTON (WRIST) PIN

The aluminum-alloy piston is fitted with two compression rings and one oil control ring.

To remove the pistons, follow Steps 1-14 under *Engine Disassembly.*

Disassembly

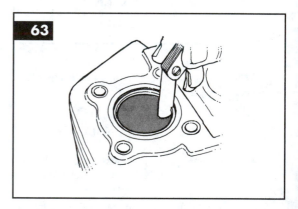

1. Remove the piston rings from the piston.

2. Carefully clean the ring grooves. Do not gouge or damage the grooves while cleaning. A professional ring groove cleaning tool is shown in **Figure 60**. A convenient substitute ring groove cleaner can be made from a broken piece of the original ring (**Figure 61**).

Inspection

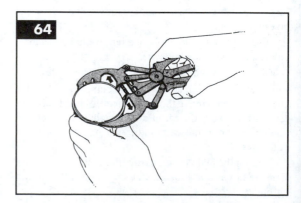

1. Check the piston for scoring, scuffing and excessive wear. To determine the piston thrust face diameter, measure the piston perpendicular to the wrist pin at a distance of 1/2-inch from the bottom of the piston (D, **Figure 63**). This measurement should be 3.1203-3.1210 inch (79.256-79.273 mm) on a new piston, with a minimum wear-limit dimension of 3.1181 inch (79.2 mm) on a used piston. Replace as necessary.

2. To measure the end gap of each piston ring (**Figure 63**):

   a. Place the ring into the top end of the cylinder.

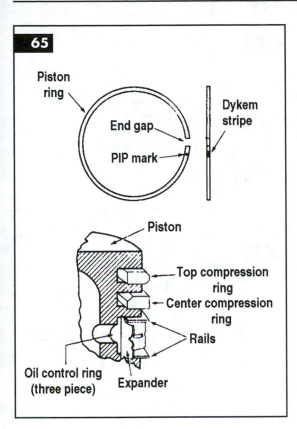

65

Piston ring

End gap

PIP mark

Dykem stripe

Piston

Top compression ring

Center compression ring

Rails

Oil control ring (three piece)

Expander

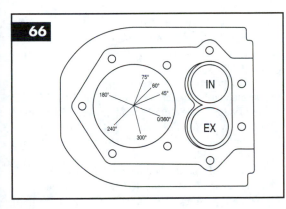

66

75° 60° 45°
180°
0/360°
240°
300°

IN

EX

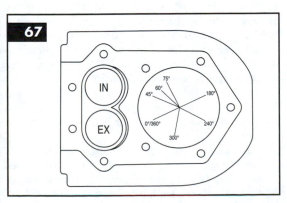

67

IN

EX

75° 60°
45° 180°
0°/360° 240°
300°

b. Use the piston to drive the ring squarely into the cylinder until the beginning of the wrist pin bore is even with the top of the cylinder.

c. Remove the piston.

d. Using a feeler gauge, measure the end gap. The piston ring end gap specification is 0.010-0.023 inch (0.254-0.584 mm) for new rings, with a 0.032 inch (0.813 mm) limit for used rings in a worn cylinder.

NOTE
Only the compression rings and the oil-control ring rails need to be gapped. The expander of a 3-piece oil-control ring is not gapped. One-piece oil-control rings in older ring sets should also be gapped.

Assembly

To avoid damaging the piston or rings, use a piston ring expander tool (**Figure 64**). To install the 3-piece oil-control ring, follow the instructions included with the replacement rings. The thin oil-control ring rails which fit over the expander are easily bent if not properly handled.

CAUTION
Do not overlap the ends of the oil-control ring expander when fitting the oil-control rails over the expander and do not use a bent oil-control ring rail.

1. Piston rings should be installed on the piston with the side of the ring marked "PIP" facing upward (**Figure 65**).

NOTE
In some replacement ring sets, the second or intermediate ring envelope showed an incorrect installation illustration: It instructs the installer to mount the ring with the "PIP" mark facing down. Always install both compression rings with the identifying "PIP" mark facing the top, or combustion area, of the piston.

2. For maximum engine power and longevity, as well as precise emission control, the ring end gaps should be spaced around the piston circumference in approximately 120° intervals as shown in **Figure 66** and **Figure 67**.

a. An imaginary line drawn from the center of the piston to the center of the exhaust valve is the 0°/360° base reference line. Degree readings will advance counterclockwise on the No. 1 cylinder, clockwise on the No. 2 cylinder.

b. The FLY mark on the piston head will be in about the 105° position.

c. The top (No. 1) compression ring should have its gap 180° from the center of the exhaust valve.

5

d. The No. 2 compression ring should have its gap at the 300° position (120° beyond the No. 1 compression ring gap).

e. The seam or gap of the oil-control ring expander should be in the 240° position (midway between the No. 1 and No. 2 compression ring gaps).

f. The top oil-control ring rail should have its gap at the 45° position.

g. The bottom oil-control ring rail should have its gap at the 75° position.

NOTE
If an older style ring set with a 1-piece oil-control ring is being installed, the ring end gap should be in the 60° position.

3. After the rings are installed on the piston, use a feeler gauge to measure the side (ring land) clearance (**Figure 68**). Ring land clearance should be a maximum of 0.006 inch (0.152 mm) with new rings. If clearance exceeds this dimension, replace the piston.

4. Measure the wrist pin (**Figure 69**). The standard piston pin diameter is 0.6247-0.6249 inch (15.867-15.872 mm) for the MV18 engine and 0.7499-0.7501 (19.047-19.053 mm) for the MV20 engine.

To install the pistons in the engine, follow Steps 15-18 in the subsequent *Engine Reassembly* section.

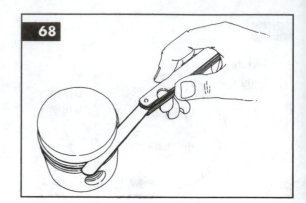

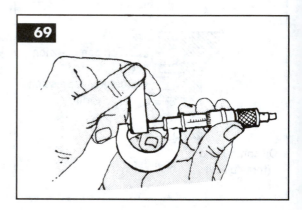

CYLINDER BARRELS

The cylinder barrels are individual cast iron alloy units with replaceable hardened alloy exhaust valve seats. The intake valve seat angle is 45° on all units. The exhaust valve seat angle is 45° on engines before serial number 1917809296 and 30° on engines beginning with serial number 1917809296. For valve seat service, refer to *Valves and Valve Components*.

Removal

The cylinders can be removed from the crankcase as separate assemblies. The No. 1 cylinder is always the cylinder closest to the flywheel; the No. 2 cylinder is the cylinder closest to the pto side of crankcase. To remove the cylinders, follow Steps 1-13 under *Engine Disassembly*.

Inspection and Reconditioning

1. Make sure all gasket and sealant material has been removed from the sealing surfaces. Sealing surfaces must be free from nicks, gouges or deep scratches.

2. Inspect the fastener holes for damaged threads or broken fasteners. Repair as necessary. If the thread holes cannot be satisfactorily repaired, replace the cylinder barrel.

3. Check for broken cooling fins. A small broken edge or corner may not affect performance. A large piece of broken-off fin will cause the cylinder to overheat. Replace any cylinder with major fin damage.

4. Check for debris packed in between the fins. Remove any heat-caked debris.

5. Check the bore for scoring.

6. The standard cylinder bore diameter is 3.1245-3.1255 inches (79.362-79.388 mm) for all models. If the bore:

a. Has worn to 3.128 inches (79.451 mm) or larger, or shows at least .003 inch (0.076 mm) wear beyond a previous rebore.

b. Is out-of-round 0.002 inch (0.05 mm) or more.

c. Is tapered 0.0015 inch (0.0381 mm) or more.

7. Rebore the cylinder to either 0.010 inch (0.254 mm), 0.020 inch (0.51 mm), or 0.030 inch (0.762 mm) oversize. If the cylinder has been previously rebored, the piston will be marked 0.010, 0.020, or 0.030 to show its oversize. A cylinder which will not clean up at 0.030 or one which has already been rebored to 0.030 and then worn beyond limits will need to be replaced.

8. Measure the cylinder bore at six points as shown in **Figure 70**. Use a telescoping bore gauge or an inside micrometer. Always follow the instructions included with the tool.

9. If new rings are being installed and the cylinder bore is within wear specifications, the bore will need to be honed so the new rings will seat properly. The crosshatch angle of the bore surface after finish-honing should be 45°-50°

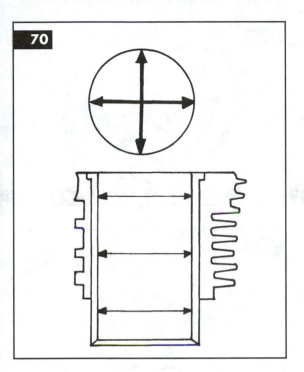

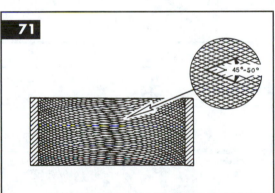

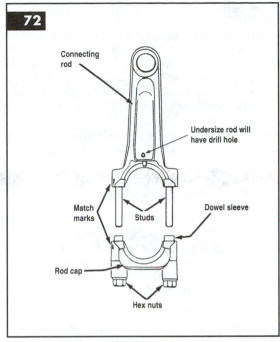

5

as shown in **Figure 71**. Too large an angle will cause high oil consumption; too small an angle will make the rings skip and wear rapidly. Follow the hone manufacturer's instructions.

10. If the cylinder is being rebored oversize, rebore to the specified original-plus-oversize dimension. Do *not* "fit" the new bore dimension to the piston. If the reboring is done to specification, the assembly clearances will be correct. Always follow the bore-machine manufacturer's instructions. The final step of a rebore should always be a finish honing. The crosshatch angle of the cylinder bore surface after finish-honing should be 45°-50° as shown in **Figure 71**.

11. After honing or reboring, thoroughly wash the cylinder barrel with plenty of soap and hot water, and rise with clean warm water. Blow-dry with compressed air. Do not use petroleum solvents (mineral spirits, kerosene, etc.) to clean the cylinder as solvents will not remove grinding dust from the cylinder bore surface.

12. Spray the bore with a moisture-displacing lubricant such as WD-40 or equivalent. Using a clean, lint-free cloth, wipe the lubricant from the bore, and the apply a light coat of engine oil to the bore to prevent rust.

CAUTION
Failure to properly clean a honed or rebored cylinder will cause rapid cylinder and piston wear and severe engine damage.

Installation

To install the cylinders in the engine, follow Steps 15-18 under *Engine Reassembly*.

CONNECTING RODS

The aluminum alloy Posi-Lock connecting rods ride directly on the crankpin journal. Posi-Lock rods can be identified by the rod cap dowel sleeves which prevent the cap from shifting on the rod studs while the engine is running (**Figure 72**).

Removal

Remove the connecting rods from the engine, as described under *Engine Disassembly*.

Inspection

Standard connecting rod-to-crankpin journal clearance is 0.0012-0.0024 inch (0.031-0.061 mm). Plastigage is the most accurate way to measure journal clearance. Plastigage comes in three sizes: 0.001-0.003 inch (.025-.076 mm); 0.002-0.006 inch (0.051-0.152 mm); and 0.004-0.009 inch (0.102-0.229 mm). To gauge the clearance:

1. Cut a strip of Plastigage slightly shorter than the width of the connecting rod (**Figure 73**). Place the Plastigage on the rod cap.
2. Position the rod on the crankshaft.
3. Tighten the rod cap to torque specifications to compress the gauge.

NOTE
When torquing the Plastigage, do not rotate the connecting rod on the crankshaft journal. Damaged Plastigage and inaccurate readings will result.

4. Remove the connecting rod.
5. Compare the flattened Plastigage width to the scale furnished with the Plastigage (**Figure 74**) to determine the clearance. If clearance exceeds 0.003 inch (0.075 mm), replace the connecting rod and/or recondition the crankshaft. A connecting rod with a 0.010 inch (0.25 mm) undersize crankshaft journal bore is available. The 0.010 inch (0.25 mm) undersize connecting rod is identified by a drilled hole in the connecting rod just above the big end bore (**Figure 72**). Standard connecting rod-to-piston pin clearance is 0.0006-0.0011 inch (0.015-0.028 mm) for all models. Standard connecting rod side play on the crankpin is 0.005-0.016 inch (0.13-0.41 mm).

Installation

To install the connecting rods into the engine, follow Steps 1-11 under *Engine Reassembly*.

CRANKSHAFT AND MAIN BEARINGS

The crankshaft is supported at each end in a sleeve type bearing (**Figure 75**).

Removal

To remove the crankshaft assembly, follow Steps 1-23 under *Engine Disassembly* section.

Inspection and Reconditioning

1. If considerable effort was required to remove the oil pan from the crankshaft, then the crankshaft is probably bent and must be discarded. If some effort was required

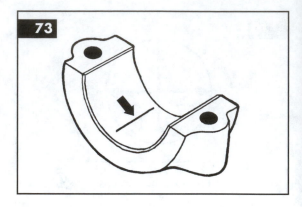

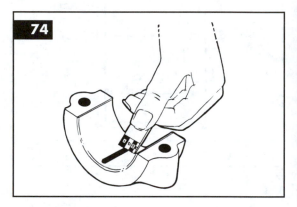

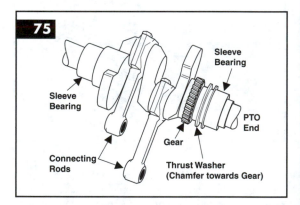

during removal, then the crankshaft should be checked for straightness by a shop with the necessary equipment. If the oil pan was easy to remove, and the bearings are within specifications, then the crankshaft is probably straight. Crankshaft runout can be used as an indicator of crankshaft straightness. Proceed to Step 2 to measure runout.

2. Measure crankshaft runout using one of the following procedures:

  a. Install the crankshaft in the engine. Be sure the main bearings are lubricated. Measure crankshaft runout at the PTO end of the crankshaft.

7. Measure the connecting rod (crankpin) journal. The crankpin journal diameter for Model MV18 should be 1.3733-1.3738 inches (34.882-34.895 mm); regrind the crankshaft if the crankpin diameter is 1.3728 inches (34.869 mm) or less. The crankshaft crankpin diameter on Model MV20 should be 1.4993-1.4998 inches (38.073-38.095 mm); regrind the crankshaft if the crankpin diameter is 1.4988 (38.069 mm) or less. On all models, if the crankpin journal is 0.0005 inch (0.013 mm) or more out-of-round, or if the journal has 0.001 inch (0.025 mm) or more taper, regrind or replace the crankshaft.

NOTE
*A connecting rod with a 0.010 inch (0.25 mm) undersize crankshaft journal bore is available. The 0.010 inch (0.25 mm) undersize connecting rod is identified by a drilled hole in the connecting rod beam just above the big end bore (**Figure 72**).*

8. Measure the main bearing journals. The standard crankshaft main bearing journal diameter is 1.7488-1.7510 in. (44.420-44.475 mm) for all models. If the journal diameter is 1.7407 in. (44.214 mm) or less, the main bearing journals should be reground undersize. Main bearings are available in .010 and .020 inch (0.254 and 0.51 mm) undersizes. A crankshaft whose main bearing journal(s) will not clean up at .020 inch (0.51 mm) undersize should be replaced.

9. Crankshaft main bearing-to-crankshaft journal clearance should be 0.0049 in. (0.1245 mm) for all models. If the clearance exceeds 0.006 in. (0.15 mm), replace the bearing and/or regrind or replace the crankshaft.

10. The inside diameter of new main bearings after installation should be 1.7439-1.7461 inches (44.295-44.351 mm) for all models.

11. If the main bearing journals are scored or galled, also inspect the main bearing cavities in the crankcase. If the crankcase cavities are scored or galled from the main bearing insert spinning in the crankcase, the crankcase will have to be replaced.

12. Some models may be equipped with a roller-style thrust bearing (**Figure 77**). Inspect the bearing rollers, roller cage, and races for pitting, gouging or overheat discoloration. Replace any questionable components.

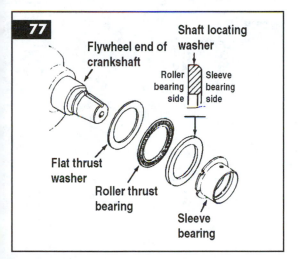

Shaft locating washer

Flywheel end of crankshaft

Roller bearing side / Sleeve bearing side

Flat thrust washer

Roller thrust bearing

Sleeve bearing

b. Support the crankshaft in V-blocks at the main bearing journals (**Figure 76**).

CAUTION
When using a dial indicator to check runout, exercise caution when the crankshaft keyway approaches the indicator anvil. Dial indicator damage could result if the keyway strikes the anvil.

c. Any measurement of more than a few thousandths of an inch would necessitate further inspection.

3. Inspect all bearing surfaces on the crankshaft for indications of scoring, scuffing or other damage. This includes the main and thrust bearing faces.

4. Check the fastener threads, such as the flywheel and PTO threads, for damage and cross-threading. Repair if possible. Install a Heli-Coil if necessary.

5. Inspect keyways and remove burrs. The keyways must be straight and unworn. The PTO extension must also be straight and unworn.

6. Check the crankshaft gear (**Figure 75**) for broken or pitted teeth. If the gear teeth are questionable, also inspect the camshaft gear teeth.

Installation

1. To begin installing the crankshaft into the crankcase, perform Steps 1-6 under *Engine Reassembly*.

2. Measure the crankshaft end play between the face of the PTO side main bearing and the crank gear thrust washer (**Figure 78**). Thrust washers are available in three thicknesses: 0.121 inch (3.07 mm), 0.130 inch (3.30 mm) and 0.139 inch (3.53 mm). The 0.130 inch thick washer is

5

considered standard. Crankshaft end play should be 0.002-0.014 inch (0.05-0.35 mm).

> *NOTE*
> *Some models may be equipped with a roller-style thrust bearing (**Figure 77**). Install the 0.039 inch (0.99 mm) thrust washer, the bearing, then the 0.156 inch (3.96 mm) shaft locating washer with the chamfered side of the washer toward the sleeve bearing.*

3. The crankshaft is now ready for additional assembly as required.

CAMSHAFT

The camshaft is supported at each end in bearings that are an integral part of the crankcase casting assembly.

Removal

To remove the camshaft, follow Steps 1-23 under *Engine Disassembly*. Be sure to identify the tappets so they can be reinstalled in their original positions if reused.

Inspection

Clearance between the camshaft journals and the bearing bores should be 0.0010-0.0025 inch (0.025-0.064 mm) for all models. To determine the clearance:

1. Remove the camshaft from the crankcase.
2. Using bolt positions 1, 3, 7, 12 and 13 from **Figure 79**, reassemble the two empty crankcase halves.
   a. Tighten all fasteners in 50 in.-lb. (5.65 N·m) increments to a final torque of 200 in.-lb. (22.6 N·m).
   b. In addition, tighten crankcase fasteners 1 and 3 in 30 in.-lb. (3.4 N·m) increments to a final torque of 260 in.-lbs. (29.4 N·m).
3. Make sure the camshaft bearing bores in the crankcase are clean and dry. Measure and note the camshaft bore dimensions at both ends of the crankcase. Add 0.0005 inch (0.0127 mm) to each dimension to compensate for the missing seam sealant.
4. Measure and note the camshaft bearing journal dimensions at both ends of the camshaft.
5. Compare the readings to the specifications.
6. Remove the crankcase bolts and separate the crankcase halves.

Camshaft end play should be 0.003-0.013 inch (0.08-0.33 mm) (**Figure 80**). Shims installed between the crankcase and the camshaft at the gear side of the camshaft control the end play.

When replacing the camshaft on engines prior to Serial No. 1917809296, a separate 30° exhaust valve kit must be installed. The valve kit includes new valves and valve

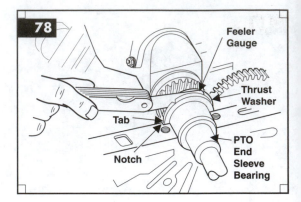

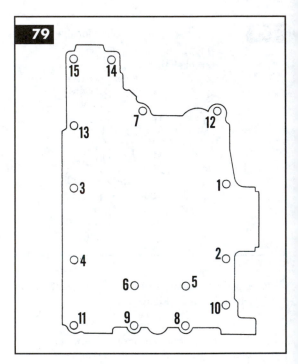

seats. Valve seat installation instructions are included with the kit.

Installation

To install the camshaft into the engine, follow Steps 7-18 under *Engine Reassembly*. When installing the camshaft, make certain that the crankshaft timing mark and the camshaft timing mark are aligned as shown in **Figure 81**.

GOVERNOR

The mechanical governor (4, **Figure 43**) is located in the crankcase and is driven by the camshaft gear.

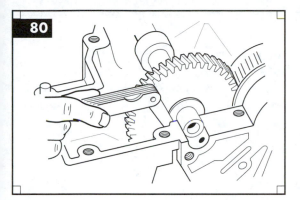

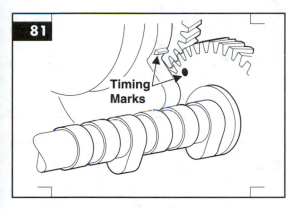

Timing Marks

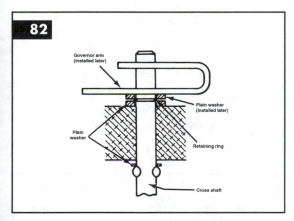

Removal

If the governor gear is damaged or broken, the crankcase halves must be split as outlined in Steps 1-19 under *Engine Disassembly* to remove the gear pieces.

After separating and emptying the crankcase halves, proceed as follows:

1. Remove the Phillips head stop pin on the outside of the No. 1 case half. Do not lose the copper washer from under the head of the stop pin.

2. Inside the case, slide the governor gear assembly off the stub shaft.

3. If necessary, remove the outer cross shaft retainer and flat washer. Remove the cross shaft and internal flat washer from inside the case.

4. If the governor gear is complete but the governor must be removed, considerable time can be saved by using the following procedure:

    a. Only remove the No.2 cylinder barrel (with piston and pin).

    b. Carefully remove the gear from the cylinder opening using the jaws of a mechanical finger.

Inspection

Engines with serial No. 1806300001 and later have a thrust washer behind the gear; do not lose this washer. Older engines prior to this serial number should be upgraded to the new style governor gear with thrust washer when replacing the original gear.

A 0.002 in. (0.05 mm) press fit holds the governor shaft (7, **Figure 43**) in position in its crankcase bore. A retainer is installed as a secondary stop. Shaft retention and fit are unaffected by normal engine operation. However, abnormal thermal expansion of the crankcase due to overheating from obstructed cooling surfaces or improper lubrication can allow the stub shaft to loosen. If failure occurs in which the crankcase is still usable but the press-fit is slightly loose, the governor shaft can be pinned to the crankcase as follows:

1. Make sure that the governor shaft bore in the crankcase is clean and dry, and use a new shaft.

2. Apply Loctite 609 to the larger outer diameter of the governor shaft as well as inside the bore in the crankcase.

3. Install the governor shaft, with the small diameter facing inward, to a dimension of 0.285 in. (7.1 mm) from the outer edge of the crankcase bore. Allow the Loctite to set.

4. Using a 3/32 or 1/8 inch cobalt or carbide-tipped drill bit, carefully drill through the curved outer boss area of the crankcase casting and about halfway into the case-hardened governor shaft. Do not allow the drill bit to walk or wander, elongating the hole.

5. Install a 3/4 to 7/8 inch long roll pin into the drilled hole. Any portion of the roll pin that is exposed may be trimmed.

6. Install a new governor shaft retainer against the shaft inside the crankcase recess.

Installation

1. If the cross shaft was removed:

    a. Install the small flat washer onto the shaft.

    b. Fit the shaft through the crankcase hole. Ensure that the paddle is positioned *away* from the governor gear stub shaft.

    c. Install one of the large outer flat washers over the shaft followed by the shaft retainer (**Figure 82**).

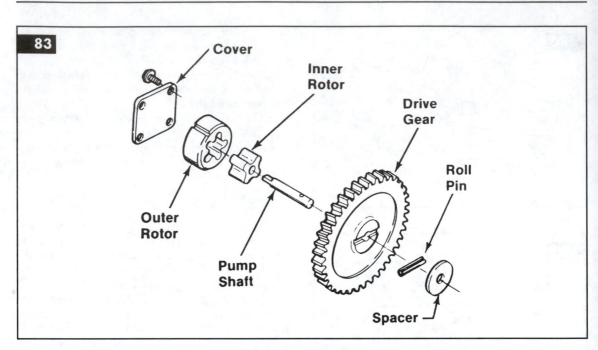

2. Lubricate the governor gear assembly, thrust washer and stub shaft with engine oil. Install the washer and gear assembly onto the shaft.

3. Make sure that the stop pin threads in the case and on the pin are clean and dry. Lightly coat the stop pin threads with Loctite 222 or equivalent.

4. Holding the gear assembly in place, install the Phillips head stop pin from outside the case. Make sure the copper washer is in place under the head of the stop pin.

5. Continue to reassemble the engine by following the necessary steps under *Engine Reassembly*. After the intake manifold and carburetor have been installed, install the second large flat washer onto the governor shaft, followed by the governor arm.

6. Connect the governor linkage, referring to **Figure 16** as necessary.

7. Adjust the governor as specified in the *Governor, External Service* section.

8. If only No. 2 cylinder was removed:
   a. Install the governor gear onto the stub shaft by using tag wire and mechanical fingers. Rock the crankshaft so the camshaft teeth will "walk" the governor gear back into place.
   b. Reassemble the engine using Steps 9 and 15-18 under *Engine Reassembly*.

OIL PUMP

All models are equipped with a rotor-type oil pump driven by the crankshaft. The oil pump assembly is located on the PTO side of the No. 1 crankcase above the oil pan. **Figure 83** shows an exploded view of the pump

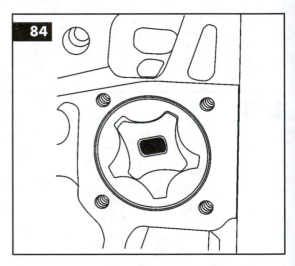

components. **Figure 84** shows the inner and outer rotors mounted in the crankcase.

The oil pump cover, rotors and pressure relief valve on all models can be serviced without splitting the crankcase. To service the oil pump drive gear and pump shaft, the crankcase must be split.

Removal

1. Drain the engine oil and remove the oil filter. For the most effective crankcase sludge removal, the oil should be drained hot.

2. Allow the engine to cool.

3. Remove the engine from the equipment.

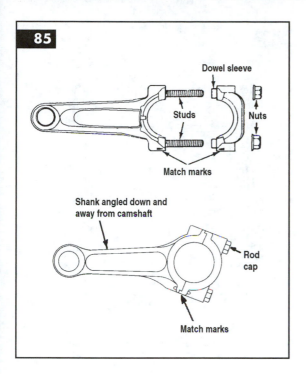

4. Set the engine up in a horizontal-crankshaft position with the PTO shaft slightly higher than the flywheel side. This will prevent the oil pressure relief valve from falling out when the oil pan is removed.

4. Remove the oil pan. Carefully clean all old silicone sealant from the sealing surfaces. Do not damage the sealing surfaces.

5. To access the oil pump rotors, remove the four pump cover screws and the cover.

6. To remove the pressure relief valve spring, ball and sleeve, use a small magnet or tilt the engine toward the PTO shaft. The components should slide out easily.

7. To split the crankcase to service the oil pump drive gear and pump shaft, follow Steps 1-19 under *Engine Disassembly* section.

Inspection

Check the rotors, crankcase rotor area and cover inner surface. Clean as necessary. Replace any scored components.

Inspect the pressure relief valve components. The free length of the oil pressure relief valve spring should be 0.992 inch (25.20 mm).

Check the clearances.

1. The oil pump shaft-to-crankcase clearance should be 0.0010-0.0025 inch (0.025-0.064 mm). To measure the clearance:
   a. Using a bore gauge or a split-ball gauge, measure the inside diameter of the pump shaft bore.

   b. Using a micrometer, measure the pump shaft where it rides in the crankcase bores.

   c. Compute the dimensional difference. This dimension is the clearance. If it is beyond specification, measure a new shaft. If the new shaft clearance dimension is within specification, replace the shaft. If the clearance is unacceptable with a new shaft, the crankcase bore is worn. Replace the crankcase.

2. The oil pump drive gear end play should be 0.010-0.029 inch (0.25-0.74 mm). The end play should be measured with a feeler gauge between the gear hub and the face of the inner pump-shaft support. If the end play is beyond specification, add a second spacer washer to reduce the end play to acceptable limits.

Installation

1. To reassemble the pump in the crankcase:
   a. Assemble the pump components, then install the pump cover. The oil pump cover outer side is marked OUT and is retained by self-tapping screws.
   b. Follow Steps 7-18 under *Engine Reassembly*.

2. When reinstalling the valve components, install the sleeve first, followed by the ball. The spring fits last, after the ball.

3. If just the oil pan was removed to service the rotors or relief valve, only perform Steps 9, 12 and 13 under *Engine Reassembly*.

ENGINE REASSEMBLY

NOTE
*These installation instructions cover the complete engine reassembly after a total teardown. For information on analyzing and setting up other major internal components such as the crankshaft, camshaft, pistons, rings, etc., refer to the appropriate individual sections. Refer to **Table 4** at the end of this chapter for Fastener Tightening Torques, **Table 5** for Engine Clearances and Specifications and **Table 6** for Recommended Silicone Sealants.*

NOTE
Always use new gaskets, O-rings and seals where applicable during reassembly.

1. Lubricate the crankshaft journals and connecting rod bores with clean engine oil.

2. The No. 1 connecting rod should be installed on the crankshaft journal closest to the flywheel end of the crankshaft, and the No. 2 connecting rod should be installed on the crankshaft journal closest to the PTO end of crankshaft. On Model MV20, install the connecting rods with the shanks angled down and away from the camshaft (**Figure 85**).

3. Make certain that the match marks on the connecting rods and the rod caps are aligned (Figures 72 and/or 86).

4. Lightly lubricate the connecting rod bolt threads with clean engine oil, then incrementally torque the rod cap nuts to 140 in.-lbs. (15.8 N·m) for new connecting rods or 100 in.-lbs. (11.3 N·m) for used connecting rods.

5. If the sleeve bearings were removed from the crankshaft upon disassembly, install them as shown in **Figure 75**. The main bearings are interchangeable, but do not switch used bearings.

6. When installing the crankshaft assembly into the No. 1 crankcase half, be sure that the locating tab of the sleeve bearing on the PTO end of the shaft is positioned in the crankcase notch. Ensure that the oil hole in the bearing on the flywheel end of the shaft is aligned with the crankcase oil passage. Position the 1-piece PTO-end thrust washer as shown in **Figure 75**, with the inner chamfer towards the crank gear. If the crankshaft is equipped with a 3-piece roller-style thrust bearing, install the bearing assembly as shown in **Figure 77**.

7. Reinstall the valve tappets into their proper locations. Wrap a rubber band or tape around the tappet stems in the No. 2 crankcase side to prevent the tappets from falling out when the crankcase is reassembled.

8. Make certain that the camshaft gear timing mark is aligned with the crankshaft timing mark (**Figure 82**).

9. Prior to joining crankcase halves or installing the oil pan or cylinders, apply a 1/16-inch bead of silicone sealant as shown in **Figures 86**, **87** and **88**. Note that in **Figure 86**, sealant must be applied to the *exterior* crankcase surface of the bolt directly below the fuel pump mounting area. Failure to apply sealant in this position will result in oil leakage. Also note in **Figure 87** that the oil passage tube protruding from the crankcase is designed to prevent sealant from entering or blocking the oil passage. *Do not remove* the tube from the crankcase.

> *NOTE*
> *Table 6 lists the recommended silicone sealants. Always follow the sealant manufacturer's instructions regarding shelf life and setting-up of the sealant.*

> *NOTE*
> *The closure plate gasket included in some gasket sets is only used on earlier horizontal-shaft twin-cylinder engines, never on the oil pan of any vertical-shaft engines.*

10. Lubricate the camshaft bore plug O-ring lightly with engine oil. Prior to assembling the two crankcase halves, position the plug in the crankcase so that the scribe mark made during disassembly is aligned with the mark on the crankcase half. While the crankcase fasteners are being tightened, maintain thumb pressure on the plug to ensure that the plug shoulder remains bottomed in the crankcase.

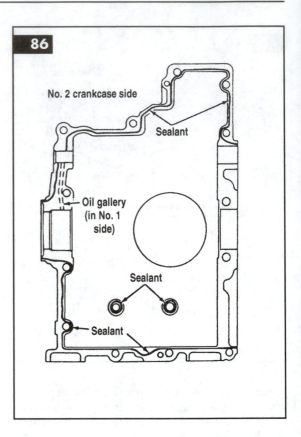

86

No. 2 crankcase side

Sealant

Oil gallery (in No. 1 side)

Sealant

Sealant

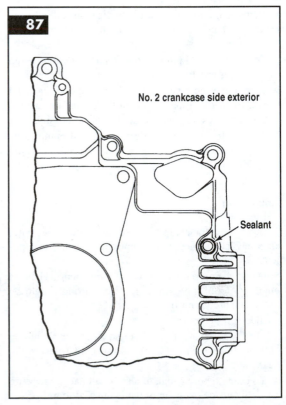

87

No. 2 crankcase side exterior

Sealant

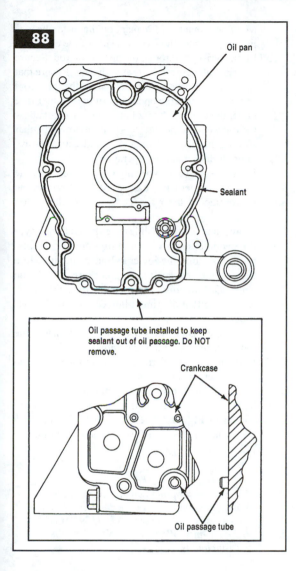

88

Oil pan

Sealant

Oil passage tube installed to keep sealant out of oil passage. Do NOT remove.

Crankcase

Oil passage tube

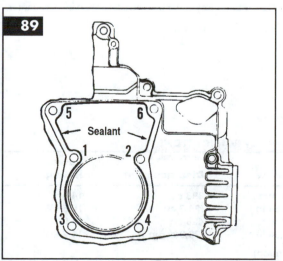

89

5   6

Sealant

1   2

3   4

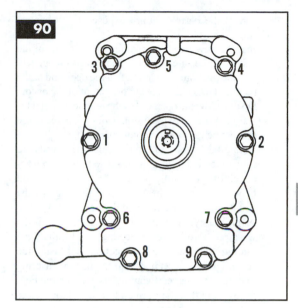

90

3   5   4

1   2

6   7

8   9

After tightening the crankcase fasteners, restake the cam plug in place using the previous stake marks.

11. Make sure that every nut has a flat washer installed between the nut and the crankcase. Tighten the crankcase fasteners in the sequence shown in **Figure 79** as follows:

   a. Tighten all fasteners in 50 in.-lb. (5.65 N·m) increments to a final torque of 200 in.-lb. (22.6 N·m).

   b. In addition, tighten crankcase fasteners 1 through 4 in 30 in.-lb. (3.4 N·m) increments to a final torque of 260 in.-lbs. (29.4 N·m).

12. Install the oil pressure relief valve sleeve, ball and spring into the crankcase.

13. Install the oil pan. Tighten the oil pan fasteners in the sequence shown in **Figure 88**. Tighten in 50 in.-lb. (5.65 N·m) increments to a final torque of 150 in.-lbs. (17 N·m).

14. Install the oil filter adapter and the crankshaft oil seals.

15. Lubricate the pistons, rings, wrist pin, wrist pin bore and cylinder bore with engine oil. Stagger the ring end gaps at 120° intervals as described under *Pistons, Wrist Pins and Rings*. There are two methods of fitting the pistons to the cylinders and the cylinders to the crankcase: Step 16 describes the first method, using a full-band type piston ring compressor (**Figure 90**); Step 17 details the second method, using a split-band type ring compressor.

16. Match the piston assembly to the cylinder barrel with the numbers marked during disassembly. Using a full-band type ring compressor (**Figure 90**), compress the piston rings, then carefully push the piston into the cylinder barrel from the cylinder-head end of the barrel. Make sure the FLY mark on the piston head is pointing toward the flywheel side of the cylinder.

   a. Push the piston through the cylinder until the wrist pin bore is completely exposed at the crankcase end of the barrel. *Do not* expose the oil control ring.

b. Install a new wrist pin retainer into one side of the piston. Make sure that the retainer seats completely into the pin bore groove and that the open end of the retainer faces either the top or bottom of the piston. Do not allow the open end of the retainer to point toward either side of the piston. Doing so could cause the retainer to loosen during operation.

c. Rotate the crankshaft so the connecting rods are fully extended from the crankcase for wrist pin accessibility. Carefully support the connecting rod being fitted so it does not strike the edge of the crankcase while performing the next step.

d. Align the cylinder and piston assembly with the wrist pin bore in the connecting rod. Fit the wrist pin into the piston and connecting rod. Install the second wrist pin retainer into the piston, ensuring that the retainer seats completely into the pin bore groove and that the open end of the retainer faces either the top or bottom of the piston.

e. Slide the cylinder barrel down over the piston and onto the crankcase studs.

f. Fit the flat washers and nuts onto the studs.

g. Tighten the cylinder barrel nuts in the sequence shown in **Figure 89**. Tighten in 50 in.-lb. (5.65 N•m) increments to a final torque of 200 in.-lbs. (22.6 N•m).

NOTE
For ease in torquing cylinder barrel nuts, Kohler offers offset extended box wrenches. Wrench No. NU-11797 fits 1/2-inch nuts. Wrench No. NU-4923 fits 9/16-inch nuts.

17. Rotate the crankshaft so the connecting rods are fully extended from the crankcase for wrist pin accessibility.

a. Using the marked numbers from the disassembly process, match the pistons to the connecting rods.

Make sure that the FLY mark on the piston head is pointing toward the flywheel side of the engine.

b. Fit the wrist pin through the piston and rod. Secure the pin with new retainers at both ends. Ensure that the retainers seat completely into the pin bore grooves and that the open ends of the retainer face either the top or bottom of the piston. Do not allow the open ends of the retainers to point toward either side of the piston. Doing so could cause the retainer to loosen during operation.

c. Using a split-band type ring compressor with the tool handle perpendicular to the wrist pin on the valve side of the cylinder, compress the piston rings.

d. Slowly and carefully slide the cylinder barrel over the piston assembly. Constantly monitor the piston rings along the lower cylinder cutouts while the cylinder pushes the ring compressor off the rings. *Do not force* the cylinder over the rings. Make sure that the rings slide easily into the cylinder.

e. When the piston rings are completely inside the cylinder, remove the ring compressor.

f. Slide the cylinder barrel down over the piston and onto the crankcase studs.

g. Fit the flat washers and nuts onto the studs.

h. Tighten the cylinder barrel nuts in the sequence shown in **Figure 89**. Tighten in 50 in.-lb. (5.65 N•m) increments to a final torque of 200 in.-lbs. (22.6 N•m).

NOTE
For ease in torquing cylinder barrel nuts, Kohler offers offset extended box wrenches. Wrench No. NU-11797 fits 1/2-inch nuts. Wrench No. NU-4923 fits 9/16-inch nuts.

18. Install the cylinder heads as described in this chapter.

Table 1 GENERAL ENGINE SPECIFICATIONS

Model	No. Cyls.	Bore	Stroke	Displacement	Power Rating
CV14	1	87 mm (3.43 in.)	67 mm (2.64 in.)	398 cc (24.3 cu. in.)	14 hp 10.5 kW
CV15	1	90 mm (3.55 in)	67 mm (2.64 in.)	426 cc (26.0 cu. in.)	15 hp 11.2 kW
			(continued)		

5

Table 2 MAINTENANCE AND LUBRICATION SCHEDULE

Except for the initial break-in period, the following recommendations are minimums. If the unit is being used in severe duty such as on dusty or sandy ground, in tall grass and weeds, or on rough terrain, maintenance should be performed more often.

After 5-hour break-in period (new unit; new or overhauled engine)	Change the engine oil and the oil filter. Check all the fasteners and the linkages for security.
Every 8 hours or daily	Check the engine oil with the unit sitting level. Do notoverfill. Check and/or clean the air filter.
Every 40-50 hours or weekly	Service the air cleaner pre-filter. On electric-start units, check the battery electrolyte level. Lubricate the throttle and choke cables.
Every 100 hours or semi-monthly	Replace the air filter and pre-filter. Change the engine oil and oil filter.
Every 500 hours or annually	Replace the fuel filter and fuel hoses. Remove cylinder heads and decarbon combustion chamber. Check all fasteners for proper security.

Table 3 ENGINE OIL

Engine oil	API service rating of SH or above
Kohler CV	
Above 32° F (0° C)	SAE 10W-30
Between 32° F and 0° F (0° C and -18° C)	SAE 10W-30, 5W-20, or 5W-30
Below 0° F (-18° C)	SAE 5W-20 or 5W-30
Capacity with filter - 2.1 quarts (2.0 liters)	

NOTE: Do not use 10W-40 oil in the engine. Recommended engine oil viscosities are for petroleum-based oils. Comparable synthetic oils may be used. DO NOT MIX synthetic oil with petroleum oil. In new or overhauled engines or short blocks, use SAE 10W-30 oil for the first 5 hours of operation, then change oil according to ambient temperature requirements. The recommended oil change interval after the 5-hour break-in period is every 100 hours of operation. The oil should be drained while the engine is warm for the most effective crankcase sludge removal.

Table 4 FASTENER TIGHTENING TORQUES

Spark plug	38-43 N·m	(335-385 in.-lb. or 28-32 ft.-lb.)
Air filter base	9.9 N·m	(88 in.-lb.)
Alternator stator	4.0 N·m	(35 in.-lb.)
Carburetor		
Fuel bowl nut	5.1-6.2 N·m	(45-55 in.-lb.)
Shutter plate screws		
(choke and throttle)	0.9-1.4 N·m	(8-12 in.-lb.)
Main fuel jet (fixed jet)	1.4-1.8 N·m	(12-16 in.-lb.)

(continued)

Table 4 FASTENER TIGHTENING TORQUES (continued)

Connecting rod (See text)		
8 mm straight-shank bolt	22.6 N·m	(200 in.-lb.)
Step-down shank bolt	14.7 N·m	(130 in.-lb.)
6 mm straight-shank bolt	11.3 N·m	(100 in.-lb.)
Crankcase cover/oil pan	24.4 N·m	(216 in.-lb.)
Cylinder head	40.7 N·m	(360 in.-lb. or 30 ft.-lb.)
Rocker arm pedestal	9.9 N·m	(88 in.-lb.)
Flywheel	66.4 N·m	(49 ft.-lb.)
Flywheel fan	9.9 N·m	(88 in.-lb.)
Fuel pump screws*	7.3/9.0 N·m	(65/80 in.-lb.)
Governor control lever	9.9 N·m	(88 in.-lb.)
Governor speed control bracket*	7.3/10.7 N·m	(65/95 in.-lb.)
Ignition module*	4.0/6.2 N·m	(35/55 in.-lb.)
Muffler	24.4 N·m	(216 in.-lb.)
Oil pump cover*	4.0/6.2 N·m	(35/55 in.-lb.)
Oil filter drain plug (1/8 in. NPT)	7.3-9.0 N·m	(65-80 in.-lb.)
Oil Sentry(tm) pressure switch	7.9 N·m	(70 in.-lb.)
Oil filter	5.7-9.0 N·m	(50-80 in.-lb.)
Starter drive pinion	15.3 N·m	(135 in.-lb.)
Valve cover*	7.3/10.7 N·m	(65/95 in.-lb.)
Fasteners not listed	Refer to Chapter One	

*When installing self-tapping fasteners into new unthreaded holes, use higher torque value; use lower torque value for installation into previously tapped holes and weld nuts.

Table 5 ENGINE CLEARANCES AND SPECIFICATIONS

Angle of Operation: Maximum angle; Full oil level; All directions		
Intermittent operation	35°	
Continuous operation	20°	
Compression		
Ratio	8.5:1	
Pressure	85+ psi	
Oil pressure		
Cold engine at start-up	Up to 60 psi	
Hot engine at idle	Down to 18 psi	
Balance shaft		
End bearing diameters		
New	19.962-19.975 mm	(0.7859-0.7864 inch)
Wear limit	19.959 mm	(0.7858 inch)
Bearing bore diameters		
New	20.000-20.025 mm	(0.7874-0.7884 inch)
Wear limit	20.038 mm	(0.7889 inch)
Running clearance	0.025-0.063 mm	(0.0009-0.0025 inch)
End play	0.0575-0.3625 mm	(0.0023-0.0143 inch)
Camshaft		
End bearing diameters		
New	19.962-19.975 mm	(0.7859-0.7864 inch)
Wear limit	19.959 mm	(0.7858 inch)
Bearing bore diameters		
New	20.000-20.025 mm	(0.7874-0.7884 inch)
Wear limit	20.038 mm	(0.7889 inch)
End play	0.076-0.127 mm	(.003-.005 inch)
Running clearance	0.025-0.063 mm	(.0010-.0025 inch)
	(continued)	

Table 5   ENGINE CLEARANCES AND SPECIFICATIONS (continued)

Lobe height (minimum lift)		
Intake	8.96 mm	(0.353 inch)
Exhaust	9.14 mm	(0.360 inch)
Carburetor		
Initial idle-mixture screw setting	One turn open	
Float level	Non-adjustable	
Connecting rod		
Crankpin clearance, new	0.030-0.055 mm	(.0012-.0022 inch)
Crankpin clearance limit	0.070 mm	(.0025 inch)
Crankpin side play	0.18-0.41 mm	(.007-.016 inch)
Wrist pin bore inside diameter		
New	19.015-19.023 mm	(0.7486-0.7489 inch)
Wear limit	19.036 mm	(0.7495 inch)
Wrist pin clearance, new	0.015-0.028 mm	(.0006-.0011 inch)
Crankshaft		
End play	0.0575-0.4925 mm	(.0023-.0194 inch)
Main bearing journal, flywheel end		
New outside diameter	44.913-44.935 mm	(1.7682-1.7691 inches)
Wear limit	44.84 mm	(1.765 inches)
Out of round	0.025 mm	(.0010 inch)
Taper	0.022 mm	(.0009 inch)
Main bearing journal, PTO end		
New outside diameter	41.915-41.935	(1.6502-1.6510 inches)
Wear limit	41.86 mm	(1.648 inches)
Out of round	0.025 mm	(.0010 inch)
Taper	0.020 mm	(.0008 inch)
Crankpin		
New outside diameter	38.958-38.970 mm	(1.5338-1.5343 inch)
Wear limit	38.94 mm	(1.5328 inch)
Out of round	0.0127 mm	(.0005 inch)
Taper	0.025 mm	(.0010 inch)
Top main or sleeve bearing		
Inside diameter, new, installed	44.965-45.003 mm	(1.7703-1.7718 inch)
Maximum wear limit	45.016 mm	(1.7723 inch)
Running clearance, new	0.03-0.09 mm	(.0012-.0035 inch)
Oil pan bearing		
Running clearance, new	0.03-0.09 mm	(.0012-.0035 inch)
Total indicated runout		
PTO end with crankshaft in engine	0.15 mm	(.0059 inch)
Crankshaft only, in V-blocks	0.10 mm	(.0039 inch)
Cylinder bore:		
New inside diameter		
CV14	87.000-87.025 mm	(3.4252-3.4262 inches)
CV15	90.000-90.025 mm	(3.5433-3.5443 inches)
Wear limit		
CV14	87.063 mm	(3.4277 inches)
CV15	90.63 mm	(3.5681 inches)
Out of round	0.12 mm	(0.0047 inch)
Taper	0.05 mm	(0.002 inch)
Cylinder head warpage, maximum	0.076 mm	(0.003 inch)
Governor		
Gear shaft diameter		
New	5.990-6.000 mm	(0.2358-0.2362 inch)
Wear limit	5.977 mm	(0.2353 inch)
Gear shaft-to-gear running clearance	0.015-0.140 mm	(0.0006-0.0055 inch)
Cross shaft diameter		
New	5.975-6.000 mm	(0.2352-0.2362 inch)
Wear limit	5.962 mm	(0.2347 inch)

(continued)

Table 5   ENGINE CLEARANCES AND SPECIFICATIONS (continued)

Cross shaft bore diameter		
New	6.025-6.050 mm	(0.2372-0.2382 inch)
Wear limit	6.063 mm	(0.2387 inch)
Cross shaft running clearance,		
Shaft-to-crankcase bore	0.025-0.075 mm	(0.0010-0.0030 inch)
Ignition		
Module to flywheel magnet air gap	0.20-0.31 mm	(0.008-0.012 inch)
Spark plug gap	1.02 mm	(0.040 inch)
Oil pump		
Pressure relief valve spring length	25.2 mm	(0.992 inch)
Piston		
Thrust face diameter (See text)		
New		
CV14	86.941-86.959 mm	(3.4229-3.4236 inches)
CV15	89.951-89.961 mm	(3.5413-3.5420 inches)
Wear limit		
CV14	86.814 mm	(3.4179 inches)
CV15	89.824 mm	(3.5363 inches)
Running clearance at thrust face(new)		
CV14	0.041-0.044 mm	(.0016-.0017 inch)
CV15	0.031-0.043 mm	(.0012-.0016 inch)
Piston rings		
End gap (compression rings)		
New		
CV14	0.3-0.5 mm	(0.012-0.020 inch)
CV15	0.27-0.5 mm	(0.010-0.020 inch)
Used limit	0.77 mm	(0.030 inch)
Ring land clearance		
Top compression ring		
CV14	0.040-0.105 mm	(0.0016-0.0041 inch)
CV15	0.060-0.105 mm	(0.0023-0.0041 inch)
Middle compression ring		
CV14	0.040-0.072 mm	(0.0016-0.0028 inch)
CV15	0.040-0.085 mm	(0.0015-0.0032 inch)
Oil-control ring		
CV14	0.551-0.675 mm	(0.0217-0.0266 inch)
CV15	0.026-0.176 mm	(0.0010-0.0069 inch)
Piston pin		
Diameter		
New	18.995-19.000 mm	(0.7478-0.7480 inch)
Wear limit	18.994 mm	(0.74779 inch)
Bore inside diameter (piston)		
New	19.006-19.012 mm	(0.7483-0.7485 inch)
Wear limit	19.025 mm	(0.7490 inch)
Selective fit, piston-to-pin	0.006-0.017 mm	(0.0002-0.0007 inch)
Rocker arms		
Inside diameter		
New	15.837-16.127 mm	(0.624-0.635 inch)
Wear limit	16.13 mm	(0.637 inch)
Rocker shaft diameter		
New	15.85-15.90 mm	(0.624-0.626 inch)
Wear limit	15.727 mm	(0.619 inch)
Valves		
Cam lobe lift, minimum		
Intake	8.96 mm	(0.353 inch)
Exhaust	9.14 mm	(0.360 inch)
Stem-to-guide running clearance (cold)		
Intake	0.038-0.076 mm	(0.0015-0.0030 inch)
Exhaust	0.050-0.088 mm	(0.0020-0.0035 inch)

(continued)

Table 5   ENGINE CLEARANCES AND SPECIFICATIONS (continued)

Guide reamer size		
Standard	7.048 mm	(0.2775 inch)
0.25 mm oversize	7.298 mm	(0.2873 inch)
Valve guide inside diameter		
Intake		
New	7.038-7.058 mm	(0.2771-0.2779 inch)
Wear limit	7.134 mm	(0.2809 inch)
Exhaust		
New	7.038-7.058 mm	(0.2771-0.2779 inch)
Wear limit	7.159 mm	(0.2819 inch)
Valve stem diameter (new, standard)		
Intake	6.982-7.000 mm	(0.2749-0.2756 inch)
Exhaust	6.970-6.988 mm	(0.2744-0.2751 inch)
Seat angle		
Intake	89°	
Exhaust	89°	

5

KOHLER CV14 AND CV15 ENGINE

ENGINE IDENTIFICATION

Both models are four-stroke, single-cylinder, over-head-valve, vertical crankshaft air-cooled engines. They are pressure lubricated and equipped with an oil filter. The tables at the end of this chapter contain the engine specifications.

Engine identification and serial numbers are located on a decal mounted on the side of the blower housing or on the cooling shroud (**Figure 1**). Refer to **Figure 2** to determine engine features and date of manufacture.

The next two sections provide information on removing and reinstalling the engine as a complete, assembled unit. Subsequent sections provide disassembly, inspection, adjustment, repair/overhaul and reassembly information for the engine components.

The engine must be removed from the equipment before undertaking repairs on the internal components. In the case of external components such as the carburetor or a cylinder head, engine removal may not be necessary, as the repair job may be performed with the engine mounted on the equipment.

Kohler tools, or suitable equivalent tools, may be recommended for some procedures outlined herein. Good quality tools are also available from small-engine parts suppliers. Be careful when substituting a "homemade" tool for a recommended tool. Although time and money may be saved if an existing or fabricated tool can be made to work, consider the possibilities if the tool does not work properly. If the substitute tool damages the engine, the cost to repair the damage, as well as the lost time, may exceed the cost of the recommended tool.

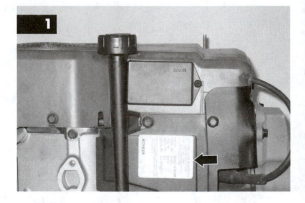

NOTE
Some procedures may require that work be performed by a professional shop. Be sure to get an estimate, then compare it with the cost of a new or rebuilt engine or shortblock (a basic engine sub-assembly).

NOTE
Metric fasteners are used throughout these engines, except for the 7/16"-20 threaded hole which holds the PTO clutch onto the bottom of the crankshaft on some engines.

ENGINE REMOVAL

Prior to removing the engine, drain the crankcase oil. Always drain the oil with the engine warm so the oil flows freely and carries out the dirt and impurities.

2

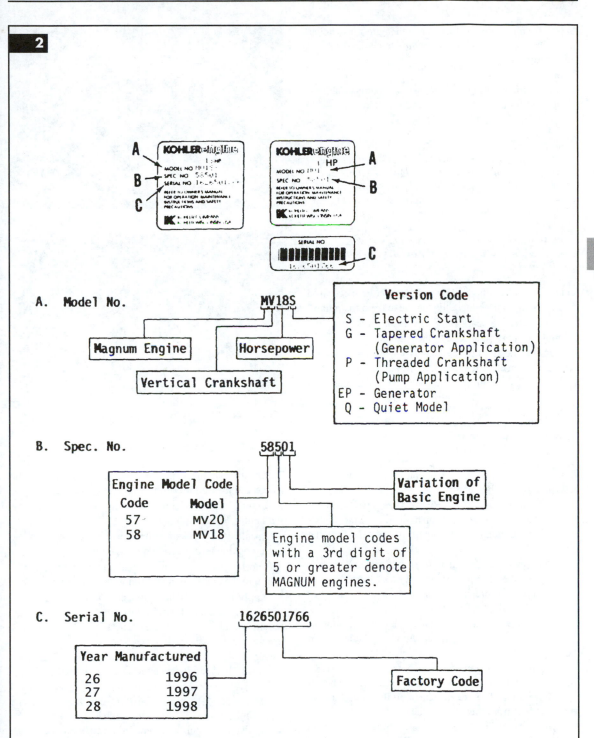

A. Model No.　　　　　　　　MV18S

Version Code
S - Electric Start
G - Tapered Crankshaft (Generator Application)
P - Threaded Crankshaft (Pump Application)
EP - Generator
Q - Quiet Model

Magnum Engine

Horsepower

Vertical Crankshaft

B. Spec. No.　　　　　　58501

Engine Model Code

Code	Model
57	MV20
58	MV18

Variation of Basic Engine

Engine model codes with a 3rd digit of 5 or greater denote MAGNUM engines.

C. Serial No.　　　　　1626501766

Year Manufactured

26	1996
27	1997
28	1998

Factory Code

6

1. Be sure the engine is stopped and the ignition switch is in the OFF position. Allow the engine to cool to ambient temperature.

2. Engage the parking brake.

3. On electric-start units, disconnect the battery cables – negative terminal first – and remove the battery.

4. Close the fuel tank valve (**Figure 3**).

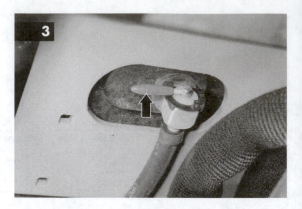

> *WARNING*
> *Some gasoline will drain from the fuel hose during the next procedure. Wipe up any spilled gasoline immediately. Work in a well-ventilated area at least 50 feet away from any open flame, including pilot lights in gas appliances. Do not allow anyone to smoke in the area. Do not work near any grinding or any other source of sparks.*

5. Detach the fuel hose clamp at the inlet connection to the fuel pump. Disconnect the fuel hose from the pump.

6. Disconnect the spark plug wire from the spark plug. Ground the spark plug wire to the engine.

7. Identify and unplug the chassis wiring harness connectors and, on electric-start units, the starter motor cable.

8. Disconnect the throttle and choke control cables.

> *NOTE*
> *Prior to removal, cable positions should be marked for proper reconnection during engine installation.*

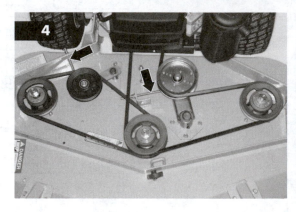

9. Remove the deck drive belt shield, then slacken the belt running from the engine:

   a. On fixed-idler drives (**Figure 4**), apply penetrating oil to the J-bolt threads on both sides of the adjusting nut, then back the nut off to allow slack in the belt.

   b. On spring-loaded idler drives, like that in **Figure 5**, move the idler pulley bracket away from the belt. Secure the bracket to allow slack in the belt, or work the belt off the idler.

10. Chock the front wheels. Safely elevate and support the rear of the mower to gain access to the underside of the engine.

11. Unplug the PTO clutch wire connector (**Figure 5**). Support the PTO clutch while removing the clutch bolt from the crankshaft. Slide the clutch off the shaft, then remove the belt from the clutch pulley.

12. Move the hydrostatic drive idler pulley away from the drive belt so the belt slackens. Work the belt off the engine pulley, then remove the belt.

13. Remove the engine mounting bolts.

14. Carefully lift the engine off the frame.

15. Note the position of the hydrostat pulley on the crankshaft. Remove the pulley.

16. Clean the engine mounting area on the frame.

ENGINE INSTALLATION

1. Ensure that the engine mounting areas on both the frame and the bottom of the engine are clean and dry.

2. Lightly coat the crankshaft, including the keyway, with anti-seize compound.

3. Install the hydrostat pulley on the crankshaft in the same position as that noted during removal.

4. Carefully set the engine in position on the frame. Ensure that the engine pan and frame fastener holes align.

5. Apply Loctite 271 or equivalent to the engine-mount fastener threads. Tighten the fasteners incrementally, alternately and securely. On fasteners with lock washers, use new lock washers.

6. Install the hydrostat belt onto the pulleys, then allow the spring-loaded idler to exert tension on the belt.

7. Apply Loctite 271 or equivalent to the electric PTO clutch mount bolt. Insert the PTO clutch belt into the clutch pulley groove. Align the clutch locator bracket, ensuring that the clutch wire is not pinched or kinked. Align the clutch key with the crankshaft keyway, then slide the clutch onto the crankshaft. While supporting the clutch, install the clutch bolt. Using the torque tables at the end of Chapter One, torque the clutch bolt.

8. Remove the mower supports. Lower the unit back down onto the floor. Ensure that the parking brake is still set, then remove the front wheel chocks.

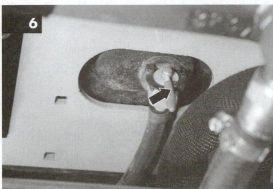

9. Reapply tension to the deck drive belt.

   a. On fixed-idler drives, refer to the adjustment procedure under *Drive Belts* in Chapter Three to properly tension the belt.

   b. On spring-loaded idlers, no adjustment is necessary.

10. Install the deck drive belt shield.

11. Reconnect the throttle and choke cables using the marks noted during engine removal.

12. Reconnect the chassis wiring harness connectors to the appropriate engine plugs.

13. On electric-start units, reconnect the starter motor cable and the battery cables – negative cable last.

14. Reconnect the spark plug leads to the plugs.

15. Install the fuel hose between the fuel filter and the fuel pump.

16. Refill the crankcase with the proper oil.

17. Open the fuel tank valve (**Figure 6**).

LUBRICATION

All models are equipped with a filtered pressure lubrication system. Refer to the *Oil Pump* section for oil pump service information.

NOTE
Fill the oil filter with oil before installation to assure adequate lubrication to components during initial engine restart. Pour the oil into the filter through the center threaded hole only. Do not fill past the bottom of the threads.

Periodically check the oil level; do not overfill. To check the oil level:

1. Make sure that the mower is sitting on a level surface.

2. Clean the area around the dipstick cap to prevent dirt and debris from falling into the crankcase when the cap is removed.

3. Remove the dipstick and wipe the oil from the level indicator.

4. Reinsert the dipstick and seat the dipstick cap on the oil fill tube. Do not screw the dipstick back down into the tube.

5. Remove the dipstick and check the oil level. The oil level should be up to, but not over, the "FULL" line on the dipstick.

It is recommended that a new oil filter be installed at each oil change. Apply a light coating of clean engine oil to the filter gasket. Install the oil filter until the rubber gasket contacts the filter adapter plate, then tighten an additional 1/2-3/4 turn.

Crankcase oil capacity is approximately 2.1 quarts (2.0 L) with oil filter. Refer to **Table 3** at the end of this chapter for oil specifications.

In new or overhauled engines or short blocks, use SAE 10W-30 oil for the first 5 hours of operation, then change oil according to ambient temperature requirements. The recommended oil change interval after the 5-hour break-in period is every 100 hours of operation. The oil should be drained while the engine is warm for the most effective crankcase sludge removal.

The engine may be equipped with a low-oil sensor. If the oil level is low, the sensor circuit will either stop the engine or trigger a warning device.

AIR FILTER

These engines are equipped with a paper-type air filter and a foam precleaner element (**Figure 7**).

Remove and clean the air filter at the interval indicated in **Table 2**. Replace the element at the specified interval or whenever it is damaged or starting to deteriorate. Service more frequently if the engine is operated in severe conditions.

To service the filter assembly, refer to *Air Filter Service* in Chapter Three.

NOTE
Always inspect the crankcase breather hose between the valve cover and the air filter base anytime the air filter is being

serviced. If the hose is loose, cracked, or dry and brittle, replace it.

NOTE
*On engines prior to serial No. 2813402183, it is recommended that a short stud seal, part No. 230046, be installed over the air filter stud above the air filter element wing nut (**Figure 7**) to prevent the wing nut from loosening during engine operation. Engines after this serial number are equipped with this seal from the factory. Make sure that the seal is in place prior to installing the air cleaner cover. (bf ital)Always ensure the long seal is in place and in good condition prior to installing the element assembly.*

FUEL FILTER

Service the fuel filter at the interval indicated in **Table 2**. Service more frequently if the engine is operated in severe conditions.

To service the fuel filter, refer to *Fuel Filter Service* in Chapter Three.

CARBURETOR

WARNING
Gasoline is a volatile, flammable liquid and is one of the most dangerous items in the shop. Wipe up any spilled gasoline immediately. Work in a well-ventilated area at least 50 feet away from any open flame, including pilot lights in gas appliances. Do not allow anyone to smoke in the area. Do not work near any grinding or any other source of sparks.

Operation and Design

Carburetor operating principles are discussed in detail under *Carburetor Fundamentals* in Chapter Two.

Figure 8 shows a view of the carburetor used on these Kohler Command single-cylinder engines. **Figure 9** shows an exploded view of the carburetor. The carburetor is equipped with a fixed, high-speed jet, with no high-speed mixture adjustment screw.

NOTE
CV14 and CV15 engines operated with a fixed high-speed jet carburetor at altitudes of 6000 feet (1830 meters) above sea level and higher should have a high-altitude jet installed (Kohler part No. 12 755 36).

On electric-start units, the carburetor may be equipped with a fuel shut-off ("anti-afterfire") solenoid. The sole-

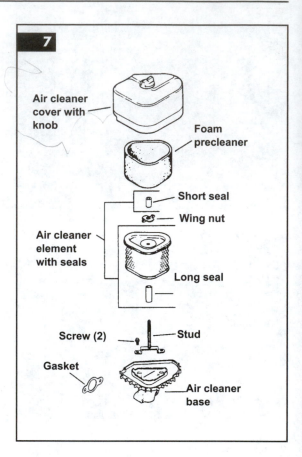

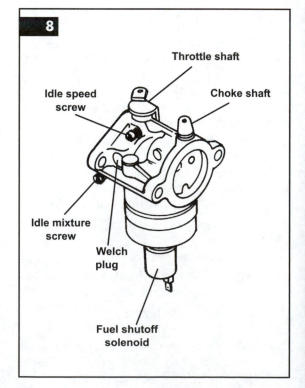

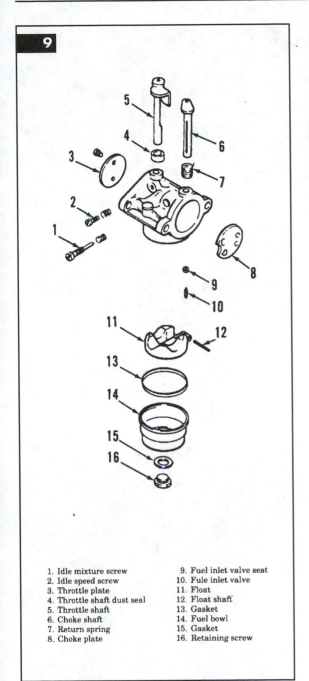

9

1. Idle mixture screw
2. Idle speed screw
3. Throttle plate
4. Throttle shaft dust seal
5. Throttle shaft
6. Choke shaft
7. Return spring
8. Choke plate
9. Fuel inlet valve seat
10. Fule inlet valve
11. Float
12. Float shaft
13. Gasket
14. Fuel bowl
15. Gasket
16. Retaining screw

10

Adjustment

The initial setting of the idle mixture screw (**Figure 8** or **Figure 10**) is one turn out on all CV models. The final adjustment of the idle mixture and idle speed screws should be made with the engine at normal operating temperature.

> *NOTE*
> *If the idle mixture screw is covered by a limiter cap (**Figure 10** and **Figure 11**), use a Walbro limiter cap removal tool (No. 500-20) or equivalent and carefully remove the cap if adjustments beyond the limit stops must be made. Follow the instructions included with the tool. Discard the original limiter cap. A new limiter cap must be reinstalled onto the mixture screw once the final adjustment has been made. After the final adjustment, install the limiter cap with the cap pointer midway between the limit stops.*

Final adjustments on all models must be performed as follows:

1. With the parking brake on, the blade PTO disengaged, the speed control in neutral, and the neutral locks locked, start the engine and run it for a few minutes to reach normal operating temperature.

> *WARNING*
> *Make sure ventilation is adequate if the engine is to be run in a confined area. Exhaust fumes are toxic and deadly.*

noid uses a plunger to stop fuel flow through the main nozzle passage when the engine is stopped. When the ignition switch is turned on and voltage is directed to the solenoid, the plunger retracts and allows fuel to flow into the main fuel circuit. **Figure 8** and **Figure 10** show the fuel solenoid mounted on the bottom of the carburetor, in place of the bowl nut. To test the solenoid prior to removing the solenoid or carburetor, refer to *Fuel Shutoff Solenoid* in this chapter.

2. Place the throttle control in the SLOW or IDLE position.

3. Adjust the idle speed screw so the engine idles at 1200 rpm.

4. Turn the idle mixture screw counterclockwise until the engine rpm begins to decrease. Note the screw position.

5. Turn the mixture screw clockwise until the engine rpm builds up, then begins to decrease again. Note the screw position.

6

6. Turn the mixture screw to the midpoint between the two noted positions.

7. Reset the idle speed screw, if necessary, to obtain the desired idle speed.

8. Accelerate the engine a few times to check the adjustment. The engine should accelerate smoothly without hesitation. If there is still slight hesitation, turn the idle mixture screw another 1/8 turn counterclockwise.

9. Repeat Step 8 one more time, if necessary. If the engine still hesitates, carburetor cleaning and repair will be necessary. Refer to the *Carburetor, Repair* section.

Removal

> *WARNING*
> *Some gasoline will drain from the fuel hose and/or the carburetor during this procedure. Wipe up any spilled gasoline immediately. Work in a well-ventilated area at least 50 feet away from any open flame, including pilot lights in gas appliances. Do not allow anyone to smoke in the area. Do not work near any grinding or any other source of sparks.*

1. Remove the air filter cover and the filter element assembly (**Figure 7**).

2. Unclamp and disconnect the valve cover breather hose from the fitting on the air filter base (**Figure 11**). Inspect the hose completely. If the hose is loose, cracked, or dry and brittle, replace it.

3. Remove the two stud nuts holding the air filter base and the carburetor to the engine. Remove the filter base.

4. If the carburetor is equipped with a fuel shutoff solenoid, disconnect the solenoid terminal and the solenoid ground wire.

5. Disconnect the fuel hose from the carburetor inlet fitting.

6. Unhook the carburetor-to-governor link from the governor arm bushing.

7. Slide the carburetor off the mount studs, taking care not to bend the linkages. When the carburetor is clear of the studs, twist the carburetor to remove the choke link.

8. Remove the plastic carburetor heat shield (**Figure 12**).

9. Remove and discard all old gaskets. Do not damage the gasket surfaces.

Disassembly

Refer to **Figure 9** and proceed as follows:

1. Remove the bowl retaining screw, gasket, bowl and bowl gasket.

2. Carefully remove the float pin, float and float valve.

3. Two types of float valve seats are used:

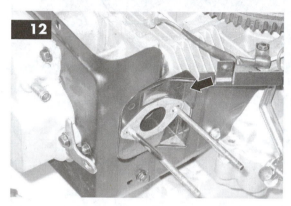

a. Engines built before Serial No. 2554000000 have a replaceable float valve seat. Using a No. 5 crochet hook or similar tool, pull the float valve seat from the carburetor. Discard the seat.

b. Engines built beginning with Serial No. 2554000000 have a non-replaceable brass seat (**Figure 13**). Do not attempt to remove this seat, as carburetor damage will result.

4. Remove the idle mixture screw and spring.

5. It is not normally necessary to remove the idle speed screw and spring. It is a good idea, however, to turn the screw counterclockwise approximately two turns so the

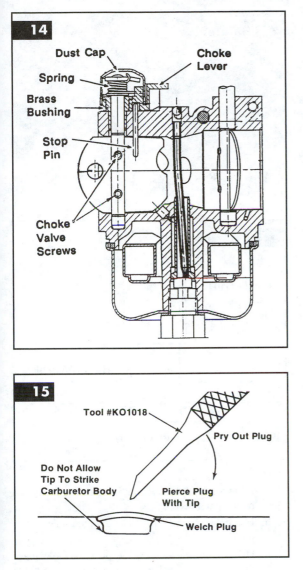

14

Dust Cap

Choke Lever

Spring

Brass Bushing

Stop Pin

Choke Valve Screws

15

Tool #KO1018

Pry Out Plug

Do Not Allow Tip To Strike Carburetor Body

Pierce Plug With Tip

Welch Plug

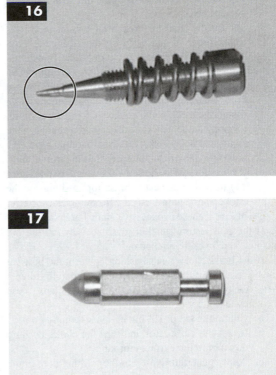

16

17

10. If necessary, carefully press the main fuel jet out of the bowl screw passageway.

Cleaning, Inspection and Repair

Carburetor

1. Clean the carburetor in an approved carburetor cleaner.

2. Rinse carefully and completely according to the cleaner manufacturer's instructions.

3. Blow out all passages with compressed air.

> *CAUTION*
> *Do not use wire or drill bits to clean passages; calibration of the carburetor will be affected if the fuel passages are enlarged.*

4. Inspect all components. Replace any faulty or questionable items.

   a. Inspect the tip of the idle mixture needle (**Figure 16**) and replace the needle if the tip is bent or grooved.

   b. Inspect the fuel inlet valve (**Figure 17**) and replace it if the tip is grooved.

   c. If the carburetor is equipped with a brass float valve seat (**Figure 13**), thoroughly inspect the seat.

throttle plate will completely seat in the bore upon reassembly.

6. The edges of the throttle and choke plates are beveled and must be installed in their original positions. Mark the choke and throttle plates before removal to ensure correct reassembly.

7. Remove the throttle shaft, then remove the shaft seal.

8A. On carburetors without the self-relieving choke, remove the choke shaft (6), then remove the return spring.

8B. On carburetors with the self-relieving choke (**Figure 14**), remove the dust cap and choke valve screws, then remove the choke shaft.

9. Use Kohler tool No. KO1018 or a small sharp chisel to carefully pierce the idle passage welch plug (**Figure 15**). Do not damage the fuel passageway under the plug. Pry the plug from the carburetor body.

6

If the seat is worn or damaged, the carburetor will
need to be replaced.

d. Inspect the float for broken tabs, holes or cracks.
Shake the float and listen for fuel inside the float,
and replace the float if any fuel is heard sloshing.

e. Inspect the float pin hinge post bores (**Figure 18**).
If a new float hinge pin indicates excessive pin
bore wear, the carburetor must be replaced.

f. Install the throttle and choke shafts in the carburetor body and check for excessive play between the
shafts and body bores. Some carburetors have a replaceable plastic top bushing for the throttle shaft.
Carburetors with the self-relieving choke (**Figure
14**) have a replaceable brass top bushing for the
choke shaft. Non-bushed carburetors must be replaced if there is excessive shaft-bore play.

5. If the plastic throttle shaft bushing is worn, the old
bushing can be easily picked out.

6. If the brass choke shaft bushing is worn, the bushing
can be removed either with a slide-hammer style puller, a
No. 3 EZ-out style screw extractor or a 12-28 tap. To use
the screw extractor or tap:

a. Clamp the tap or EZ-out in a vise, pointing up.

b. Invert the carburetor and turn the choke bushing
down onto the extractor or tap.

c. Apply penetrating oil into the bushing bore in the
carburetor body.

d. Apply a gentle twist while pulling up on the carburetor body, at the same time lightly tapping the
body casting.

Fuel Shutoff Solenoid

On electric-start units with the fuel-shutoff solenoid
mounted on the carburetor, the spring-loaded solenoid
plunger should retract when the solenoid is energized (ignition switch ON), allowing fuel to flow. To test the solenoid:

1. Make sure that the battery is fully charged.

2. While listening to and/or holding the solenoid, turn the
ignition switch from the OFF to the RUN position a few
times.

3. An audible click should be heard and/or felt each time
the key is switched.

4. If the solenoid does not click;

a. Turn the fuel tank valve off.

b. On bottom-mounted solenoids, place an approved
container under the carburetor to catch leaking
fuel.

c. Remove the main harness connector from the solenoid terminal.

d. Unscrew the solenoid from the carburetor.

e. Connect one terminal of a 9-volt dry-cell or
12-volt test battery to the solenoid case.

f. Momentarily connect and disconnect the other battery terminal to the solenoid terminal a few times.

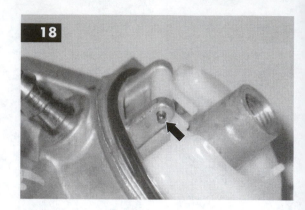

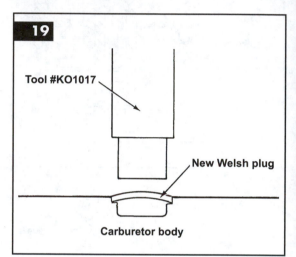

g. If the solenoid still does not activate, it is faulty and
must be replaced.

h. If Step f activates the solenoid, the solenoid is
good.

i. Using a multimeter set to the DC volts scale, place
the negative meter lead on any good engine-block
ground and connect the positive meter lead to the
solenoid terminal in the main harness.

j. Again turn the ignition switch on and off a few
times while observing the meter dial. The meter
should read mower battery voltage each time the
switch is turned on. If not, the wiring is faulty. Refer to the *Electrical Systems* section and the *Wiring
Diagrams* and test the wiring to determine why
current is not reaching the solenoid.

Reassembly

1. Press the main fuel jet into the bowl screw passageway
until it is flush with the surface.

2. If the carburetor has a replaceable plastic throttle shaft
bushing and the bushing is being replaced:

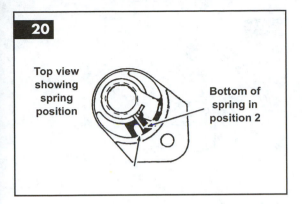

20

Top view
showing
spring
position

Bottom of
spring in
position 2

a. Use a 3/16-inch drill blank to align the bushing with the bottom shaft bushing.

b. Press the bushing completely into the body casting.

c. Fit the soft seal onto the throttle shaft, then insert the throttle shaft into the carburetor body bore. Ensure that the cutout portion of the shaft faces outwards the mounting flange.

3. If the idle speed adjustment screw and spring (2, **Figure 9**) have not been removed for cleaning and were not backed out during disassembly, unscrew the adjustment screw two turns counterclockwise.

4. Sparingly apply Loctite 609 or 222 or equivalent to the throttle plate screws. Fit the throttle plate to the shaft as noted during disassembly. Install, but do not tighten, the screws. While lightly pushing down on the top of the throttle shaft, operate the shaft to completely close the plate and align the plate in the bore, then torque the screws to 0.9-1.4 N·m (8-12 in.-lb.).

5. If the idle speed adjustment screw was backed out in Step 3 or during disassembly, screw it back in the exact same two turns. This will initially set the idle speed, presuming the idle speed was within limits prior to carburetor removal. If the idle speed adjusting screw and spring were removed for cleaning, install them now. While holding the throttle plate closed with finger pressure on the throttle shaft lever, turn the screw until the screw tip just contacts the lever. Turn the screw another 3/4 turn. This will initially set the idle speed.

6. If the carburetor does not have the self-relieving choke (**Figure 14**), proceed with Step 7 but skip Step 11. If the carburetor has the self-relieving choke, continue reassembly with Step 10. The choke will be covered in Steps 11 and 12.

NOTE
On CV engines with the self-relieving choke, the original design choke lever housing has a cavity on the underside that allows the lever to pivot around the stop pin. In dirty or dusty operation, the cavity can accumulate dirt, hindering both

movement and travel of the choke lever. Periodically remove the choke lever housing and clean the cavity, or replace the lever housing with Kohler's upgraded choke repair kit (part No. 12 757 3-S) which has an exposed cavity, preventing dirt buildup.

7. Install the choke return spring onto the choke shaft, ensuring that the hooked end of the spring fits over the choke lever.

8. Fit the choke shaft and spring into the carburetor body bore. Hook the free end of the spring onto the body, then rotate the shaft counterclockwise about 1/2 turn. This should align the shaft slot so the choke plate can be installed.

9. Fit the choke plate to the shaft as noted during disassembly. Ensure that the choke plate tabs face out and lock both sides of the choke shaft. Operate the choke shaft to completely close the plate in order to check the alignment of the plate in the bore. Adjust as necessary.

10. If the welch plug was removed, install a new plug as follows:

a. Securely position the carburetor body with the welch plug opening facing up.

b. Make sure that the plug cavity seat is completely clean and dry.

c. Position a new welch plug into its cavity with the convex part up (**Figure 19**).

d. Using Kohler tool No. KO1017 or a flat-tipped pin punch with approximately the same diameter as the welch plug, carefully *flatten* the plug, but do not cave the plug in.

e. After installing the welch plugs, seal the plug-to-carburetor seams with a glyptal sealer or fingernail polish. Permit the sealer to dry before proceeding.

11. To install the brass bushing for the self-relieving choke shaft (**Figure 14**):

a. Position the choke lever with the bottom slot over the carburetor body stop pin and with the bushing hole in the lever aligned with the bushing hole in the body casting.

b. Using a 3/16-inch drill blank to align the brass bushing with the bottom choke shaft bushing, press the bushing through the choke lever and into the body casting.

12. To assemble the self-relieving choke:

a. Fit the choke spring onto the shaft.

b. Install the choke shaft into the carburetor so the bottom arm of the spring fits in the second notch counterclockwise in the lever (**Figure 20**).

c. Sparingly apply Loctite 609 or 222 or equivalent to the choke plate screws. Fit the choke plate to the shaft as noted during disassembly. Install, but do not tighten, the screws.

6

d. While lightly pushing down on the top of the choke shaft, rotate the shaft to completely close the plate.

e. Insert a 0.010 inch (0.25 mm) feeler gauge between the top-right edge of the choke plate and the carburetor throat (**Figure 21**) to align the plate in the bore, then torque the screws to 0.9-1.4 N·m (8-12 in.-lb.).

f. Release the choke lever. The choke should spring open.

g. Rotate the choke lever to close the choke plate. The plate and lever should move together.

h. Hold the choke lever in the closed position while pushing on the long side of the choke plate. The plate should open freely, then spring closed when released.

i. Hold the choke lever to the open-choke position. The choke plate should rest against the stop pin.

j. If the choke fails to operate properly, readjust the choke using substeps d and e.

k. Snap the dust cover into place over the choke lever.

l. When the carburetor is reinstalled onto the engine, double-check the choke operation.

13. On carburetors with replaceable float valve seats, use a flat-tipped 3/16-inch (4.5 mm) pin punch or drill rod to insert the float valve seat into the carburetor so that the side with the identification ring is into the float valve passage and completely against the end of the passage. This will place the smooth side of the seat against the valve needle (**Figure 22**).

14. Install the fuel inlet needle (float valve) against the float tab with the needle tip pointed away from the float. Ensure that the locking end (**Figure 17**) fits into the float slot (**Figure 18**). Insert the float valve into the fuel passage. Position the float so the float hinge hole aligns with the carburetor body float hinge posts. Insert the float hinge pin.

15. With the carburetor inverted, the float should be parallel or nearly parallel to the bowl gasket surface. The float is not adjustable. If the float end opposite the hinge pin is much above parallel, check the float valve seat for proper installation. If necessary, replace the float or the carburetor.

16. Position a new fuel bowl gasket onto the carburetor. Make sure the gasket is seated completely around the entire float chamber shoulder (**Figure 18**). Install the bowl. Place a new gasket onto the bowl plug screw or solenoid. Install the screw or solenoid, torquing it to 45-55 in.-lb. (5-6 N·m).

17. Install the idle mixture screw and spring. Turn the screw clockwise (in) until it *lightly* bottoms, then back it out one turn.

Installation

1. Install the fuel hose, with new clamps, between the fuel filter and the carburetor location.

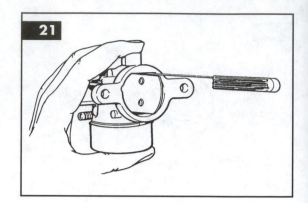

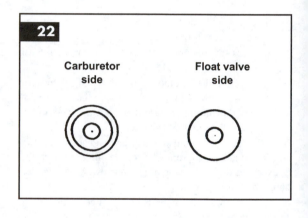

2. Install new plastic link bushings into the carburetor throttle shaft and governor lever.

3. Place a new gasket on the mount studs, followed by the plastic heat shield (**Figure 12**), then a new flange gasket.

4. While holding the carburetor just beyond the studs, tilt the carburetor so the manifold flange is up, then install the choke link into the choke lever.

5. Return the carburetor to the level position and slide it onto the mount studs. If the carburetor end of the throttle link has a Z-bend, install the link into the throttle lever bushing at this time.

6. Connect and clamp the fuel hose.

7. Slide the carburetor and manifold flange gasket all the way back against the heat shield flange.

8. If the carburetor end of the throttle link has a 90° bend, install the throttle link into the carburetor throttle shaft.

9. Install the governor end of the throttle link into the governor lever bushing. Make sure the link ends are locked securely into the bushings (**Figure 10**).

9. Lightly coat the carburetor mount stud threads with Loctite 242 or equivalent. Install a new air filter base gasket, followed by the filter base and the base nuts. Torque the nuts to 9.9 N·m (88 in.-lb.).

10. Perform a static governor adjustment using the procedure described under *Governor, Adjustment* in this chapter.

23

EXHAUST SYSTEM

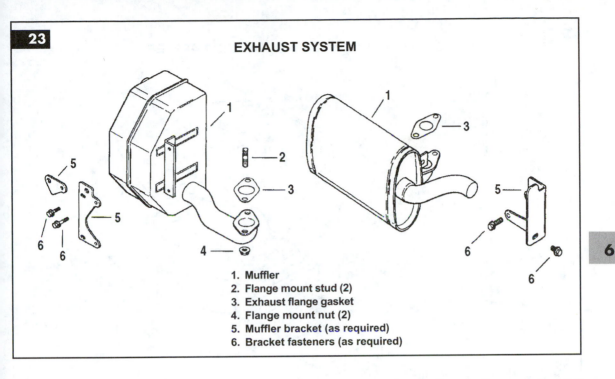

1. **Muffler**
2. **Flange mount stud (2)**
3. **Exhaust flange gasket**
4. **Flange mount nut (2)**
5. **Muffler bracket (as required)**
6. **Bracket fasteners (as required)**

6

11. Install the air filter element assembly and the filter cover.

MUFFLER

The muffler (**Figure 23**) is calibrated as part of the emission control system. It not only reduces exhaust noise to acceptable levels, but it also provides the proper amount of back pressure to allow the inlet and combustion components to produce rated horsepower as well as compliant emission levels.

For this reason, the exhaust system should be maintained in good repair. As the noise level increases, power decreases. Under no circumstances should the exhaust system be modified. Inspect the muffler, pipes, flanges, connections and fasteners regularly. Replace any questionable components.

Removal

1. Allow the unit to cool.
2. If the muffler is covered by a sheet metal heat shield, remove the shield fasteners, then remove the shield.
3. Loosen all fasteners and clamps. Do *not* remove any fasteners until all of them have been loosened.

If a bolt cannot be loosened, several methods may be used. First, apply penetrating oil such as Liquid Wrench, Kroil or WD-40. Apply it liberally, within reason, and let it penetrate for 10-15 minutes. Rap the fastener several times with a small hammer and punch. Do not hit it hard

enough to cause damage. Reapply the penetrating oil if necessary. Use 6-sided sockets and wrenches on hex-headed bolts to reduce the chances of rounding off the hex.

For frozen screws, apply penetrating oil as described. Insert a stout screwdriver into the slot, and carefully rap the top of the screwdriver with a hammer. This loosens the rust so the screw can be removed in the normal way. If the screw head is too damaged to use this method, grip the head with locking pliers and twist the screw out.

> *NOTE*
> *Do not apply heat unless specifically instructed, as it may melt, warp or remove the temper from parts.*

If a fastener should break off, refer to *Removing Broken Fasteners* in Chapter One.

4. Remove the fasteners while supporting the exhaust system. Work from the outlet pipe inward. The nuts holding the exhaust pipe flange(s) to the engine should be the last fasteners removed, at which time the exhaust system can be removed and set aside.

> *NOTE*
> *Discard the used gasket and replace it with a new gasket. Also discard any old lockwashers, replacing them with new ones.*

5. Inspect all brackets and supports for cracks and breaks. Inspect the outlet pipe spark-arrestor screen, if equipped. Replace as necessary.

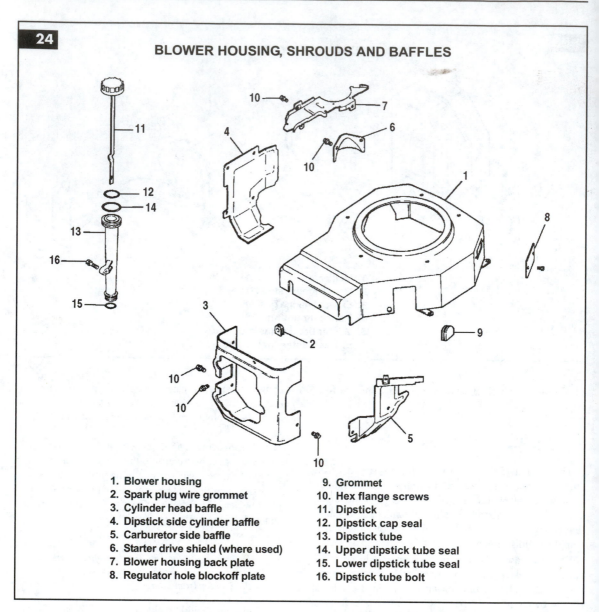

24

BLOWER HOUSING, SHROUDS AND BAFFLES

1. Blower housing
2. Spark plug wire grommet
3. Cylinder head baffle
4. Dipstick side cylinder baffle
5. Carburetor side baffle
6. Starter drive shield (where used)
7. Blower housing back plate
8. Regulator hole blockoff plate
9. Grommet
10. Hex flange screws
11. Dipstick
12. Dipstick cap seal
13. Dipstick tube
14. Upper dipstick tube seal
15. Lower dipstick tube seal
16. Dipstick tube bolt

6. Carefully remove any old gasket material from the exhaust flange surfaces, and wirebrush the fastener threads.

Installation

1. Insert a new gasket onto the exhaust studs.

2. Replace all fastener lock washers and lightly coat the fastener threads with a high-temperature thread-lock compound, such as Loctite 272 or equivalent.

3. Align the exhaust system with all bracket and fastener holes, then install and hand-tighten the fasteners, beginning with the exhaust pipe flanges. Do not tighten any fasteners until all of them have been installed.

4. Beginning with the flanges, tighten all fasteners, working toward the outlet pipe.

5. Install the heat shield and spark arrestor, if used.

BLOWER HOUSING, SHROUDS, AND BAFFLES

Removal

To remove the cooling shrouds and baffles, refer to **Figure 7** and **Figure 24** and proceed as follows:

1. Remove the air cleaner cover and disconnect the spark plug lead.

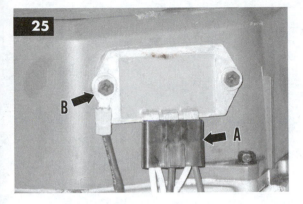

2. Clean the area around the base of the dipstick tube (13, **Figure 24**). Unscrew and remove the tube. Plug the crankcase oil-fill hole to prevent debris from contaminating the oil.

3. On recoil-start engines, the starter can be left attached to the blower housing unless it needs to be removed for service.

4. On electric-start engines, unplug the rectifier-regulator connector (A, **Figure 25**) and unscrew the regulator ground-wire terminal (B). The regulator can be left attached to the blower housing if it is not being replaced. On housings with a separate starter-drive cover, it can also be left attached to the housing.

5. Remove the exhaust system as described under *Muffler* in this chapter.

6. Remove the screws attaching the blower housing to the crankcase. Carefully lift the housing from the engine while sliding the spark plug wire grommet from its slot. A stubborn grommet may need a light application of penetrating oil for easier sliding.

7. Remove the spark plug, then remove the screws holding the cylinder head baffle to the engine. Remove the baffle. Reinstall the spark plug a few threads to prevent dirt ingestion.

8. Remove the screws which attach the dipstick side baffle to the cylinder. Remove the baffle.

9. If the engine is equipped with a carburetor-side baffle, remove its screws, then remove the baffle.

10. If necessary, remove the two screws holding the blower housing back plate to the crankcase. Remove the plate.

11. Clean and dry all fasteners and attaching threads.

12. Inspect all removed components. Repair or replace any cracked or damaged cooling shrouds. Replace any split grommets or leaking O-ring seals.

Installation

To install the cooling shrouds and baffles, refer to **Figure 7** and **Figure 24** and proceed as follows:

NOTE
Install all fasteners to finger tightness initially, then tighten to the final specification when all the baffles and shrouds are mounted.

1. If the blower housing back plate was removed, install it first.

2. If the engine uses a carburetor-side baffle (5, **Figure 24**), position the baffle onto the cylinder fins.

3. Attach the dipstick side baffle to the cylinder fins.

4. Remove the spark plug. Mount the cylinder head baffle to the head. Reinstall the spark plug, torquing the plug to 38-43 N·m (335-385 in.-lb. or 28-32 ft.-lb.).

5. Apply a few drops of penetrating oil to the groove of the spark plug wire grommet. Slide the grommet into its slot in the blower housing (1, **Figure 24**) while lowering the housing down onto the engine.

6. Install the six fasteners holding the blower housing to the engine, then tighten all of the shroud and baffle fasteners.

7. Install the exhaust system as described under *Muffler* in this chapter.

8. Reconnect the rectifier-regulator to the engine harness.

9. Make sure that the area around the dipstick tube crankcase hole is clean. With a new O-ring seal installed on the lower tube end, install the tube and tighten the fastener.

10. Install the air cleaner cover.

IGNITION SYSTEM

All models are equipped with an electronic magneto ignition system which consists of:

1. A magnet assembly permanently affixed to the flywheel.

2. An electronic magneto ignition module mounted on the No. 1 cylinder.

3. A kill switch that stops the engine by grounding the primary circuit of the ignition module.

To make sure the ignition module is producing spark, perform a *Spark Test* as described in Chapter Two.

Spark Plugs

The recommended spark plug for all models is Champion RC12YC or equivalent. The recommended spark plug electrode gap is 1.0 mm (0.040 inch). Torque the spark plug to 38-43 N·m (335-385 in.-lb. or 28-32 ft.-lb.).

CAUTION
Do no sand blast spark plugs to clean them. The grit will lodge in the upper gap between the insulator and the shell. Cleaning with compressed air does not remove all of these abrasives. This grit is only removed when the plug is reinstalled

6

in the engine and the engine is started, heating and expanding the plug. The grit then falls into the cylinder and combustion chamber area, causing rapid internal wear and damage.

Module-to-Flywheel Air Gap Adjustment

The air gap between the ignition module and the flywheel should be 0.20-0.31 mm (0.008-0.012 inch). To set the air gap, refer to **Figure 26** and proceed as follows:

1. Remove the blower housing as described under *Blower Housing* in this chapter.

2. Turn the flywheel so that the magnets are not next to the ignition module.

3. Loosen the screws holding the module to the engine.

4. Extend the module to the limits allowed by the adjustment slots, then lightly tighten one screw to temporarily hold the module away from the flywheel.

5. Rotate the flywheel to center the magnets directly under the module legs.

6. Place a *non-magnetic* gap gauge of 0.20-0.31 mm (0.008-0.012 inch) between the magnets and the module.

7. Loosen the module holding screw, allowing the magnets to draw the module to the flywheel. While holding the module snugly against the flywheel, tighten the module screws.

8. Rotate the flywheel and remove the gauge.

9. Reconnect the spark plug lead.

10. Install the blower housing as described under *Blower Housing* in this chapter.

Module Testing

> *NOTE*
> *The module cannot be tested unless it has fired a spark plug at least once. The test will not work on a new module out of the box.*

To test the ignition module:

1. Measure the resistance of the module's secondary circuit using a suitable ohmmeter. There is no test procedure for the module's primary circuit.

2. Attach one ohmmeter test lead to the spark plug boot terminal.

3. Attach the other meter lead to the coil lamination (**Figure 27**).

4. The ohmmeter should register 7900-10,850 ohms. If resistance is 0 ohms or infinite, the secondary circuit is shorted or open. If the secondary circuit registers within specification but the module still will not produce spark, the primary circuit is faulty. There is no test procedure for the primary circuit. Replace the module.

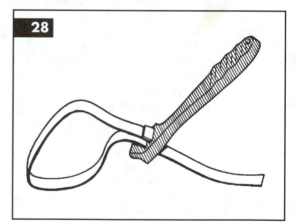

Module Removal

1. Disconnect the spark plug wire from the spark plug.

2. Remove the blower housing as described under *Blower Housing Removal* in this chapter.

3. Disconnect the ground terminal connection from the module. If there are multiple connectors, note which wire attaches to which terminal (**Figure 27**).

4. Remove the blower housing grommet from the spark plug wire.

29

30

5. Remove the two hex-flange screws holding the module to the posts on the cylinder.

6. Clean all fastener threads.

Module Installation

1. Ensure that all fastener threads are clean and dry.

2. Apply Loctite 222 or equivalent to the fastener threads.

3. Turn the flywheel so that the magnets are not next to the ignition module.

4. Position the module on the cylinder posts. Install the module screws finger-tight.

5. Extend the module to the limits allowed by the adjustment slots, then lightly tighten one module screw to temporarily hold the module away from the flywheel.

6. Rotate the flywheel to center the magnets directly under the module legs.

7. Place a *non-magnetic* gap gauge of 0.008-0.012 inch (0.20-0.31 mm) between the magnets and the module (**Figure 26**).

8. Loosen the module holding screw, allowing the magnets to draw the module to the flywheel. While holding the module snugly against the flywheel, tighten the module screws to 4.0 N·m (35 in.-lb.) for used engines or to 6.2 N·m (55 in.-lb.) on a new engine cylinder block.

9. Rotate the flywheel and remove the gauge.

10. Reconnect the spark plug lead and the module ground wire terminal(s).

11. Install the blower housing as described under *Blower Housing Installation* in this chapter.

FLYWHEEL

Removal

> *CAUTION*
> *When loosening or tightening the flywheel or fan bolts, hold the flywheel with the recommended strap wrench No. NU-10357 (**Figure 28**). Follow the wrench manufacturer's instructions. Using a bar or wedge in the fan blades or ring gear teeth could cause damage.*

> *CAUTION*
> *When removing the flywheel from the crankshaft, always use a proper puller. Never strike the crankshaft or flywheel, as damage could occur.*

1. Disconnect the spark plug wire from the spark plug.

2. Remove the blower housing described under *Blower Housing* in this chapter.

3. Remove the two hex-flange screws holding the module to the cylinder.

4. Unsnap the grass screen from the fan (**Figure 29**). On rewind-start units, perform Steps 5-8 before unsnapping the screen, as the starter cup holds the screen on. Although the flywheel can be removed with the fan installed, to prevent accidental fan blade damage, also remove the fan from the flywheel. Do not lose the four fan screw spacers.

5. Use the strap wrench to hold the flywheel.

6. Using the proper 6-point socket, loosen the bolt assembly holding the flywheel to the crankshaft. Remove the bolt, lock washer and flat washer. On recoil-start engines, also remove the starter drive cup.

7. To save time, a 1/2-inch-drive impact wrench with the proper 6-point socket can be used to remove the flywheel bolt.

> *CAUTION*
> *Prior to setting the impact wrench on the bolt head, ensure that the wrench is set to turn (bf ital)counterclockwise, viewing the bolt head. Accidentally applying additional tightening force to the bolt will damage the flywheel and crankshaft.*

8. Using puller No. NU-3226 or equivalent, fasten the puller to the flywheel, then break the flywheel loose from the crankshaft. Always follow the puller manufacturer's instructions. **Figure 30** and **Figure 31** show acceptable equivalent pullers set up to remove the flywheel. When using a puller as shown in **Figure 31**, always place stout

6

flat washers under the heads of the bolts in the flywheel so the puller jaws will have sufficient grip.

9. When the flywheel breaks loose from the crankshaft, *carefully* lift the flywheel straight up off the crankshaft so as not to damage the stator magnets under the flywheel.

Inspection

1. Thoroughly clean the flywheel, removing all dust and dirt from both the top and bottom of the flywheel, especially around the magnets.
2. Inspect the flywheel casting for cracks or damage.
3. Inspect the integrity of the magnets.

> *WARNING*
> *The magnets are not removable or serviceable. Do not attempt to reattach or tighten any loose magnet. If any magnets are loose or damaged, replace the flywheel.*

4. On electric-start units, inspect the starter ring gear. Remove any debris stuck between the teeth. Light nicks or scratches may be dressed. Damaged teeth will require replacement of the flywheel assembly, as the ring gear is not available separately.
5. Inspect the tapers and keyways of both the crankshaft (A, **Figure 32**) and the flywheel. A damaged flywheel keyway will require replacement of the flywheel. A damaged crankshaft keyway will require crankshaft replacement. The crankshaft keyway should hold the flywheel key snugly.
6. Inspect the flywheel key. Replace if questionable.

Installation

1. Make sure the matching tapers on the crankshaft and inside the flywheel, as well as the crankshaft and bolt threads, are *clean and dry*. Make sure no debris has stuck to any of the magnets.
2. Install the flywheel key.

> *WARNING*
> *Make sure the flywheel key is installed with the flat part of the key parallel to the crankshaft taper (B, **Figure 32**). If the key slides freely in the crankshaft keyway, lightly peen the edges of the keyway just enough to hold the key in position. Peen both sides of the keyway equally.*

3. Carefully lower the flywheel straight down onto the crankshaft.
4. On rewind-start units, perform Step 7 and Step 8, below, then position the starter cup over the flywheel.
5. With the lockwasher and flat washer in position on the flywheel bolt, install the bolt into the crankshaft.

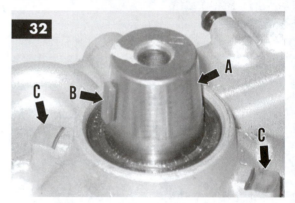

6. Using the strap wrench shown in **Figure 28**, hold the flywheel in position while tightening the bolt. Torque the bolt to 66 N·m (49 ft.-lb.).

7. If the fan was removed, install it onto the flywheel, being careful to align the cutout with the magnet. Torque the fan bolts to 9.9 N·m (88 in.-lb.).

8. Install the grass screen onto the fan.

9. Install and gap the ignition module as described under *Module Installation* in this chapter.

10. Install the blower housing as described under *Blower Housing* in this chapter.

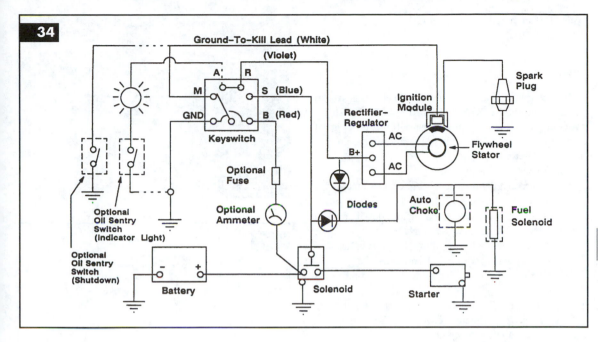

34

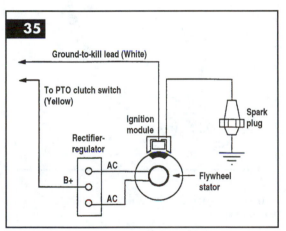

35

ALTERNATOR

Figure 33 shows the alternator stator which mounts under the flywheel. **Figure 25** shows the rectifier-regulator which mounts onto the side of the blower housing. **Figure 34** shows the alternator wiring diagram for electric-start engines. **Figure 35** shows the alternator wiring diagram for rewind-start engines.

Operation

If the alternator is functioning correctly, current is being produced whenever the flywheel is rotating. On electric-start engines, the stator produces AC and the rectifier-regulator changes the AC to DC while controlling the amount of DC based on the battery state-of-charge and the demands of the chassis electrical system. On rewind-start engines, the AC produced by the stator is converted to DC by a rectifier-regulator and fed directly through the PTO switch to the blade clutch.

To avoid damage to the charging system, the following precautions must be observed:

1. Prevent possible grounding of the AC leads.

2. The negative post of the battery must be connected to the engine ground and correct battery polarity must be observed at all times.

3. The rectifier-regulator must be connected in common ground with the engine and the battery.

4. Disconnect the leads at the rectifier-regulator and the battery if electric welding is to be done on equipment in common ground with the engine.

5. Remove the battery or disconnect the battery cables when recharging the battery with an external battery charger.

6. Do not operate the engine with the battery disconnected.

Troubleshooting

Defective conditions and possible causes are as follows:

1. No output. Could be caused by:
   a. Faulty windings in the stator.
   b. Defective diode(s) in the rectifier.
   c. Rectifier-regulator not properly grounded.
   d. Battery fully discharged or less than 4 volts.
   e. Faulty wiring.

2. Full charge-no regulation. Could be caused by:

a. Defective rectifier-regulator.

b. Defective battery.

Testing

The rectifier-regulator for the 15-amp charging system can be tested with the Kohler tester part No. 25 761 20. Instructions are included with the tester. If this tester is not available, use the test procedure that follows the precautions listed here.

Prior to performing any tests:

1. Make sure that the rectifier-regulator is grounded.

2. Test the battery voltage. If voltage is less than 4 volts:

    a. Check the electrolyte level, if possible. Add deionized or distilled water as needed.

    b. Recharge the battery. Follow the steps under *Battery Service, Charging* in Chapter Three.

On electric-start engines, if the "no output" condition is the trouble:

1. Disconnect the B+ wire from the rectifier-regulator.

2. Connect a DC voltmeter between the B+ terminal on the rectifier-regulator and engine ground.

3. Start the engine and operate it at 3600 rpm. Voltage should be above 13.8 volts.

    a. If reading is above zero volts but less than 13.8 volts, test further for a defective rectifier-regulator.

    b. If reading is zero volts, proceed to Step 4.

    c. Stop the engine.

4. Check for a defective rectifier-regulator or a defective stator.

    a. Disconnect the AC leads from the rectifier-regulator.

    b. Connect an AC voltmeter to the two AC leads.

    c. Start the engine and operate it at 3600 rpm.

    d. Check the AC voltage output.

    e. If the reading is less than 28 volts, the stator is defective.

    f. If the reading is more than 28 volts, the rectifier-regulator is defective.

5. Stop the engine.

6. Using an ohmmeter, measure the resistance across the AC stator leads

    a. If resistance is 0.1-0.2 ohm, the stator is good.

    b. If resistance is infinity/no-continuity, the stator windings are open. Replace the stator.

    c. If resistance is zero ohms, the stator windings are shorted. Replace the stator.

7. Again using an ohmmeter, measure the resistance from ground to each stator lead.

    a. If resistance is infinity/no-continuity, the stator windings are not shorted to ground and the stator is good.

    b. If any resistance is measured during either test, the stator windings are shorted to ground. Replace the stator.

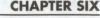

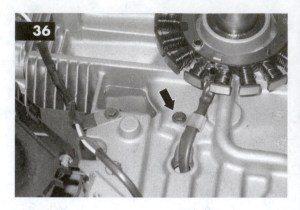

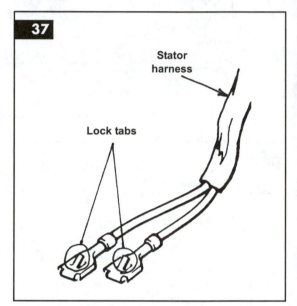

On rewind-start engines, if the "no output" condition is the trouble:

1. Check for a defective stator.

    a. Disconnect the AC lead connector from the harness.

    b. Connect an AC voltmeter to the two AC lead terminals.

    c. Start the engine and operate it at 3600 rpm.

    d. Check the AC voltage output. If the reading is less than 28 volts, the stator is defective.

2. Stop the engine.

3. Using an ohmmeter, measure the resistance across the AC stator leads

    a. If resistance is 0.1-0.2 ohm, the stator is good.

    b. If resistance is infinity/no-continuity, the stator windings are open. Replace the stator.

    c. If resistance is zero ohms, the stator windings are shorted. Replace the stator.

4. Again using an ohmmeter, measure the resistance from ground to each stator lead.

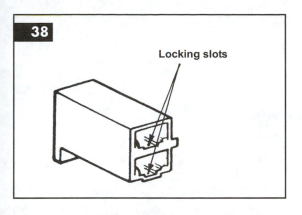

38

Locking slots

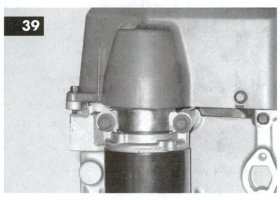

39

a. If resistance is infinity/no-continuity, the stator windings are not shorted to ground and the stator is good.

b. If any resistance is measured during either test, the stator windings are shorted to ground. Replace the stator.

If "full charge-no regulation" is the trouble:

1. Start the engine and operate it at 3600 rpm.

2. Use a DC voltmeter and check B+ to ground.

a. If the reading is over 14.7 volts, the rectifier-regulator is defective.

b. If the reading is between 14.0 and 14.7 volts, the alternator stator and the rectifier-regulator are satisfactory and the battery is probably defective (unable to hold a charge).

Removal

1. Remove the flywheel as described in this chapter.

2. Remove the stator harness clamp screw from the upper crankcase (**Figure 36**).

3. If not already done, unplug the stator harness connector from the chassis harness.

4. Using a small flat screwdriver such as those used for eyeglass repair, carefully flatten and unlock the stator terminal locking tabs (**Figure 37**) from the locking slots in the stator harness connector (**Figure 38**). The blade tip

must be inserted into the open end of the connector. Remove the terminals from the connector.

5. Loosen and remove the four stator mounting screws.

6. While guiding the stator harness through the crankcase hole, carefully lift the stator off the machined crankcase shoulder.

7. Clean the screw and crankcase threads.

Installation

1. Make sure that the screw and crankcase threads are clean and dry.

2. Lightly coat the screw threads with Loctite 222 or equivalent.

3. While guiding the stator harness through the crankcase hole, align the stator and crankcase screw holes, then carefully set the stator down onto the machined crankcase shoulder (C, **Figure 32**).

4. Insert the four stator screws into the crankcase threads.

5. Incrementally and alternately tighten the screws.

6. Install and tighten the harness clamp screw.

7. Use a very small screwdriver to carefully bend the terminal locking tabs back to the lock position as shown in **Figure 37**. Do not raise the tabs more than 2.3 mm (3/32 in.).

8. Align the terminal lock tabs with the connector slots (**Figure 38**). Insert the terminals into the connector. Terminal sequence is not important since the stator is generating AC. Make sure that the terminals are locked into the connector by lightly tugging on each stator wire. If a terminal pulls out, check the connector for obstructions, clear or replace as necessary, then reinsert the terminal.

9. Plug the harness connector into the chassis harness.

10. Replace the flywheel as described in this chapter.

ELECTRIC STARTER MOTOR AND SOLENOID

Figure 39 shows the starter motor bolted to the side of the engine, with the bendix drive shielded inside the blower housing.

Two styles of starter motors are used on these engines:

1. **Figure 40** shows an exploded view of the starter motor components on starters which use a stop nut to hold the bendix components in place. The brushes are aligned axially against the commutator in this UTE-style starter motor.

2. **Figure 41** shows an exploded view of the starter motor components on starters which use a retaining ring to hold the bendix components in place. In this Eaton-style starter motor, the brushes are aligned radially against the commutator.

In this section, "starter" refers to the electric starter motor assembly.

6

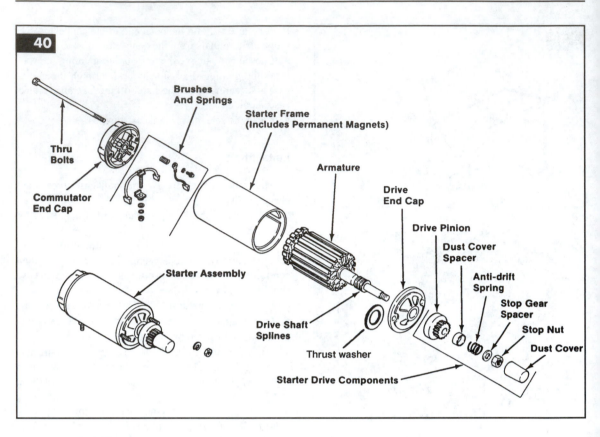

40

Thru Bolts

Brushes And Springs

Starter Frame (Includes Permanent Magnets)

Commutator End Cap

Armature

Drive End Cap

Drive Pinion

Dust Cover Spacer

Anti-drift Spring

Stop Gear Spacer

Stop Nut

Dust Cover

Starter Assembly

Drive Shaft Splines

Thrust washer

Starter Drive Components

Starter Operation

When voltage is applied to the starter through the brushes and ground, the armature rotates. As the armature spins, centrifugal force causes the drive pinion to travel up the helical splines, meshing with the flywheel ring gear teeth. When the drive pinion reaches the end of the armature shaft splines, it turns the flywheel and cranks the engine. When the engine starts, the increased flywheel speed turns the drive pinion faster than the starter is spinning, causing the pinion to travel back down the armature shaft splines. When voltage is cut off from the starter, the armature stops and the anti-drift spring holds the pinion away from the ring gear until power is again applied to the starter.

Observe the following precautions:

1. Do not operate the starter continuously for more than 10 seconds. If the engine does not start, allow at least a 60-second cooling period between each 10-second operational period. Failure to allow sufficient cool-down time will burn out the starter.

2. If the engine false-starts by disengaging the pinion then stalling, allow the engine to come to a complete stop before attempting a restart. Engaging the starter into a rotating flywheel will damage the starter and the flywheel.

3. If the engine does not crank when the starter is engaged, disengage the starter immediately. Correct the engine problem prior to attempting a restart. Do not attempt

to overcome the problem by jump-starting with a larger battery. Serious starter damage will result.

4. Do not:

   a. Drop the starter;

   b. Strike the starter frame; or

   c. Clamp the starter frame in a vise. Doing so could damage the permanent magnets inside the starter frame housing.

Starter Troubleshooting

If the starter fails to energize

Check the following:

1. Battery. Check the voltage and the specific gravity of the electrolyte. Recharge or replace the battery as necessary.

2. Wiring.

   a. Check for corroded or loose battery or solenoid connections. Clean or tighten as necessary. Soaking the corroded terminal in a baking soda and water solution is the best cleaning method. Do not allow any solution to get into any of the cells, as it will neutralize the electrolyte.

   b. Replace any frayed wires or wires with disintegrated terminals.

41

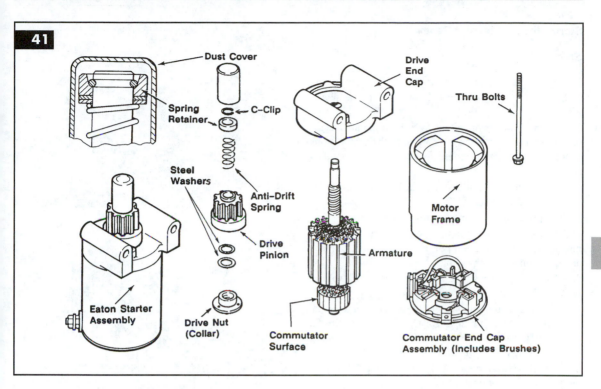

c. Check for corroded or rusted ground connections on the equipment chassis.

3. Solenoid. Use a jumper cable across the two large solenoid terminals to momentarily bypass the solenoid. If the starter energizes, the fault is in either the solenoid or the wiring to the solenoid. The *Solenoid Testing* section follows the starter section.

4. Starter components.

   a. Check the brushes. Dirty or worn brushes and/or commutator will slow a starter. Replace worn brushes or brushes with broken leads.

   b. Check the armature commutator. The commutator is an integral part of the armature. Cracked, chipped, broken, or badly-grooved commutator sections are not repairable; in these cases, the armature will need replacement. A lightly-grooved commutator may be turned on a lathe to clean up. After turning, carefully file the burrs between the commutator segments and undercut the insulator segments between the conductors, if necessary (**Figure 41**). Dirty or rough commutators should be cleaned with a suitable solvent, then lightly sanded.

   c. Check the armature shaft and bearings/bushings. A worn shaft or bearings will allow the armature laminations to rub against the frame magnets, causing drag. Replace faulty components.

If the starter energizes but turns slowly

Check the following:

1. Battery. Check the voltage and the specific gravity of the electrolyte. Recharge or replace the battery as necessary.

2. Parasitic load on the engine. Attempting to start an engine which is connected to a hydrostatic drive system places an additional load on the starter motor, especially in cooler temperatures. If possible, disconnect the load from the engine and retry the starter. If the starter now turns the engine properly, check the hydrostatic system to find the reason for the excessive load.

3. Internal load on the engine.

   a. Dirty, thick crankcase oil past its change schedule will cause slow turnover.

   b. Scored or galled internal engine components such as bearing journals, pistons and cylinders will overload the starter.

4. Starter components as listed in Step 4 under *If the starter fails to energize*, above.

Starter Removal

1. Disconnect the negative battery cable and secure the cable away from the battery.

2. Disconnect the starter cable.

3. On blower housings with removable bendix shields, unscrew and remove the shield.

4. Remove the bolts holding the starter to the engine. Remove the starter.

Starter Inspection and Repair

Starter drive

1. Lightly clamp the drive pinion in a *soft-jaw* vise.

2. Squeeze the dust cover to remove it from the spacer groove.

3. On units with a stop nut, remove the stop nut. The armature will turn with the nut only until the pinion stops against the spacer and compressed spring. On units with a retaining ring:

    a. Press the stop collar free of the retaining ring (**Figure 42**).

    b. Spread, remove and discard the ring.

   Remove the spacers, spring and pinion. During removal, note the orientation of the components. Replace any questionable components.

4. Clean the pinion splines and armature shaft splines with a suitable solvent. Dry the splines thoroughly.

5. Lightly coat the splines and the smooth part of the shaft with Kohler Starter Drive Lubricant (part No. 52 357 01) or Cristolube 303. The use of other lubricants can cause sticking or binding of the pinion.

6. On UTE-style starters, lightly coat the stop nut threads with Loctite 271 or equivalent.

7. Assemble the drive components as shown in **Figure 40** or **Figure 41**:

    a. **Figure 40** — drive pinion, dust cover spacer (spring cup recess facing out), spring, flat spacer, then stop nut. Torque the stop nut to 15.3-17.0 N·m (135-150 in.-lb.).

    b. **Figure 41** — pinion collar, two thrust washers (**Figure 43**), pinion, pinion spring washer, pinion spring, retaining ring collar, then retaining ring. Always use a new retaining ring.

8. Install the dust cover. Work the dust cover retaining ring (made into the inner base of the dust cover) into the dust cover collar groove.

Starter motor disassembly

1. Remove the starter drive components as described in Steps 1-3 of the preceding *Starter drive* section.

2. Rock the exposed armature shaft back and forth to check for shaft and/or bearing/bushing wear.

3. Make sure that the match marks on the frame and end caps are visible for proper reassembly (**Figure 44**). Note that the match mark on the frame at the commutator end aligns with the battery cable stud. If the match marks are not clearly visible, use a scribe tool to engrave a set of match marks on both ends. Do *not* use a hammer and chisel to make match marks, as the frame magnets will be damaged.

4. Remove the through bolts. Some starters have bolts which pass through the drive end cap and thread into the

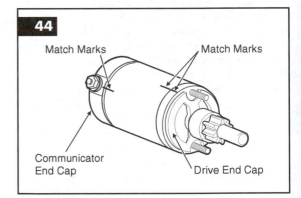

Match Marks   Match Marks

Communicator End Cap

Drive End Cap

commutator end cap; some pass through the commutator end cap and thread into the drive end cap.

5. On Eaton starters, remove the commutator end bearing plate.

6. Remove the commutator end cap/brush holder assembly, including the brushes and springs.

7. Remove the drive end cap. Be careful not to lose the armature-to-end-cap thrust washer(s).

8. Pull the armature from the frame.

9. Clean the bolt and drive end cap threads.

10. Inspect as necessary. Replace questionable components.

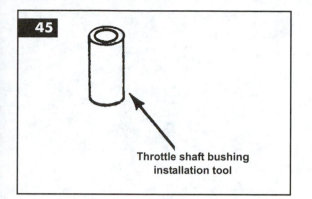

Throttle shaft bushing installation tool

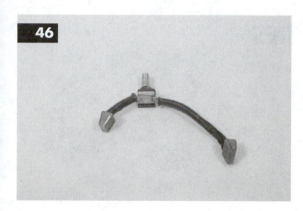

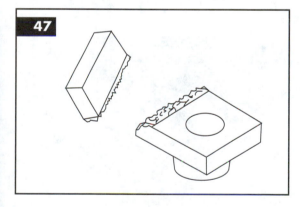

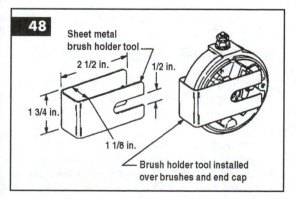

Sheet metal brush holder tool

2 1/2 in.

1/2 in.

1 3/4 in.

1 1/8 in.

Brush holder tool installed over brushes and end cap

UTE brushes and commutator end cap

1. With the brushes loose, remove the brush springs from the end cap brush holder pockets.

2. The self-tapping screws attach the negative brushes. Remove the screws, brushes and plastic brush holder.

3. Remove the nuts and washers from the positive stud terminal. Remove the stud terminal, insulator bushing and brushes from the end cap. Due to the length of the stud, the stud cannot be removed unless the insulator bushing and stud are pushed into the end cap together. If corrosion has jammed the stud insulator into the end cap, use the bushing driver from any Kohler throttle shaft kit (part Nos. 25 757 14 to 25 75719) (**Figure 45**) to carefully drive the insulator into the end cap. A cotton swab with Lime-Away or equivalent will remove any end cap corrosion. Thoroughly rinse and dry any corrosion-treated area.

4. Inspect the armature shaft bushing in the end cap. The bushing is not serviceable separately. If the bushing is worn beyond a reasonable limit, the end cap must be replaced.

5. Ensure that the drain hole in the commutator end cap is open and clean.

6. New brushes are approximately 1/2-inch (12 mm) in length. If the brushes are worn to 5/16-inch (8 mm) or less, replace the brushes.

7. Install the insulator bushing onto the positive brush stud. The flat part of the stud head must fit into the locator lip of the bushing, and the short brush lead must be to the left of the stud facing away from the installer (**Figure 46**). Install the brushes, bushing and stud into the end cap, with the stud and bushing passing through the end cap hole. Install the outer insulator washer followed by the flat washer and shoulder nut. Tighten the nut snugly.

WARNING
*Use extreme care when assembling the positive brush stud with the insulator bushing through the end cap hole. The locator lip on the insulator bushing must be placed against the floor of the end cap, as shown in **Figure 40**. If the lip breaks off or becomes damaged (**Figure 47**), the square stud head will contact the end cap when the outer stud nut is tightened. This will cause a direct short when the starter is energized.*

8. Make sure that the threads of the self-tapping screws are clean and dry. Do not use threadlocking compound on these screws, as it may prevent good ground contact. Using the self-tapping screws, install the plastic brush holder and the negative brushes into the end cap.

9. To prepare for installing the brush springs, fabricate a brush-holder tool like that shown in **Figure 48**.

10. Install one brush spring and brush at a time into each brush holder pocket. Make sure that the beveled-edge side of the brush faces away from the spring. Using the **Figure 48** tool, slide the tool over each brush

as the brush is installed. When all four springs and brushes are installed, the tool and end cap should appear as shown, except that the positive brush stud should be 180° from the closed end of the tool, in line with the 1/2-inch armature shaft slot (**Figure 49**). This will expose both end cap through-bolt holes to permit easier starter reassembly. The end cap assembly is now ready for installation onto the starter.

Eaton brushes and commutator end cap

1. With the brushes loose, remove the brush springs from the end cap brush holder pockets.

2. The through-bolt U-clips attach the negative brushes to the brush holder. Remove the clips and brushes.

3. Remove the nuts and washer(s) from the positive stud terminal. Remove the stud terminal and brushes from the brush holder.

4. Inspect the armature shaft bushing in the end cap (**Figure 50**). The bushing is not serviceable separately. If the bushing is worn beyond a reasonable limit, the end cap must be replaced.

5. Make sure that the drain holes in the end cap are open and clean.

6. Inspect the brushes. If the brushes are worn beyond a reasonable limit, replace the brushes.

7. Install the positive brushes and stud into the brush holder. The brush holder must be positioned so that the armature side of the brush holder is facing the mechanic. With the stud in the 12 o'clock position, the bare-wire short-lead brush should be in the 10:30 position, and the insulated long-lead brush should be in the 4:30 position (**Figure 51**). Install the flat washer and shoulder nut. Do not use threadlocking compound on the brush stud threads. Tighten the nut snugly.

8. Install one negative brush in the 7:30 position, with its ground clip over the 9 o'clock through-bolt hole. Install the second negative brush in the 1:30 position, placing its clip over the 3:00 through-bolt hole. Make sure the insulated positive brush lead passes *under* the 1:30 negative brush lead.

9. Make U-shaped brush holder tools as shown in **Figure 52** to hold the brushes in place so the brush holder can be easily installed over the armature commutator. A heavy paper clip can be bent as shown. The legs should be approximately 1/2 inch long to fit through the brush holder holes from the outside. **Figure 53** shows the tools in place, viewed from the armature side of the brush holder. **Figure 54** shows the tools in place from the outside. The brush holder assembly is now ready for installation onto the starter.

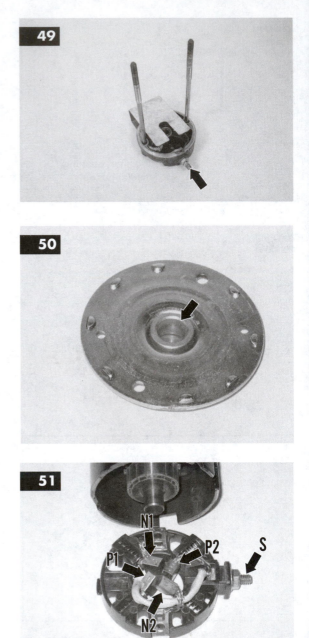

UTE Starter motor assembly

1. Slide the armature into the frame housing so the magnets are at the drive end of the armature.

2. Fit the thrust washer onto the drive end of the armature.

3. Install the drive end cap over the armature, ensuring that the match marks on the cap and frame align (**Figure 44**). Note that the match mark on the frame at the commutator end aligns with the battery cable stud.

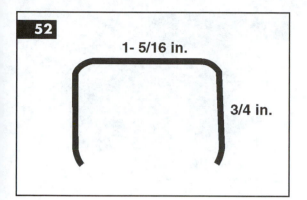

52

1- 5/16 in.

3/4 in.

Also note that when the match marks are aligned, the tabs stamped into the housing inner ends align with the cutout notches in the drive-end and commutator-end housings.

4. With the brush holder tool in place, fit the end cap to the frame housing and armature commutator end. Make sure that the match marks align.

5. Lightly coat the through-bolt threads with Loctite 242 or equivalent. Feed the bolts through the drive end cap and frame housing. Thread the bolts into the commutator end cap enough to hold the starter together while still allowing a slight clearance to remove the brush holder tool.

6. Slowly slide the brush holder tool from the end cap.

7. Tighten the through bolts to 55-65 in.-lb. (6.2-7.3 N·m).

8. Install the starter drive as described in this chapter.

53

Eaton Starter motor assembly

1. Slide the armature into the frame housing so the magnets are at the drive end of the armature.

2. Fit the thrust washer(s) onto the drive end of the armature. **Figure 55** shows the spring washer and thrust washers on an Eaton armature.

3. Install the drive end cap over the armature, ensuring that the match marks on the cap and frame align (**Figure 44**). Note that the match mark on the frame at the commutator end aligns with the battery cable stud. Also note that when the match marks are aligned, the tabs stamped into the housing inner ends align with the cutout notches in the drive-end and commutator-end housings.

54

4. With the brush holder tools in place and the housing notches aligned with the brush stud mounts and clips, slide the brush holder into the frame housing. When the brush holder is completely installed, the brush holder tools should be almost completely pushed out. Remove them now. **Figure 56** shows the brush holder installed and the brush holder tools removed. Position the bushing cap over the brush holder, ensuring that the through bolt holes align.

5. Lightly coat the through-bolt threads with Loctite 242 or equivalent. Feed the bolts through the starter. Thread the bolts into the end cap.

6. Tighten the through bolts to 55-65 in.-lb. (6.2-7.3 N·m).

7. Install the starter drive as described in this chapter.

Starter Installation

1. Lightly coat the starter mount-bolt threads with Loctite 242 or equivalent.

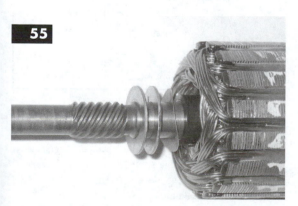

55

6

2. Fit the starter drive under the blower housing shield while aligning the mount-bolt holes with the matching threaded holes in the crankcase.

3. Install and tighten the mount bolts.

4. Reconnect the starter cable. Tighten the cable nut snugly. Do not use threadlock compound and do not overtighten the nut.

5. Reconnect the negative battery cable.

Solenoid Testing

Troubleshooting a solenoid can usually be done quickly with the solenoid in the system.

To troubleshoot the solenoid:

1. Remove the ignition key from the switch so the engine does not start.

2. Make sure that the unit is in neutral and that the parking brake is set.

3. Place the throttle control in the SLOW position.

4. Remove the main harness wire from the small solenoid winding terminal.

5. Using a short jumper wire, connect one end of the wire to the small terminal; momentarily touch the other end to the large terminal of the cable coming from the positive battery post.

6. If the starter activates, the solenoid is good.

REWIND STARTER

Refer to **Figure 57** when servicing the rewind starter. In this section, "starter" refers to the rewind starter assembly.

Removal

To remove the starter, mark the direction of the handle, then remove the five hex flange screws holding the starter to the blower housing.

To remove the starter drive cup after removing the starter:

1. Remove the blower housing as described in this chapter.

2. Use the strap wrench to hold the flywheel.

3. Using the proper 6-point socket, loosen the bolt assembly holding the flywheel to the crankshaft. Remove the bolt, lock washer and flat washer.

4. To save time, a 1/2-inch-drive impact wrench with the proper 6-point socket can be used to remove the flywheel bolt.

> *CAUTION*
> *Prior to setting the impact wrench on the bolt head, ensure that the wrench is set to*

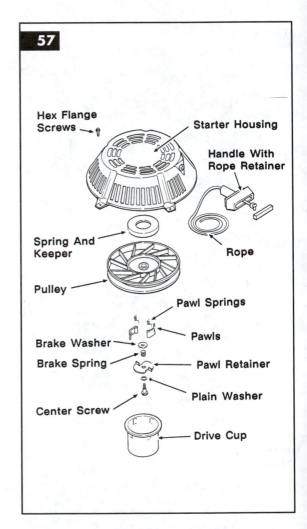

> *turn counterclockwise, viewing the bolt head. Accidentally applying additional tightening force to the bolt will damage the flywheel and crankshaft.*

5. Remove the drive cup.

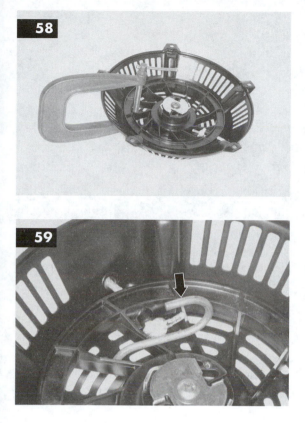

58

59

Rope Replacement

Rope unbroken

1. Pull the rope out about 12 inches (30 cm). Tie a slip knot in the rope at the housing to prevent the rope from rewinding.

2. Remove the rope retainer and handle.

3. Remove the slip knot and pull the rope all the way out. This will cause the pulley to rotate counterclockwise when viewed from inside the starter housing.

4. After performing Step 3, the spring will be almost completely tensioned, but the pulley must be held in this position to replace the rope. Three acceptable methods are:

  a. Have an assistant hold the pulley and housing to prevent the pulley from rotating.

  b. Use a C-clamp around the edge of the housing (**Figure 58**). Do *not* clamp the pulley to the housing. Place the foot of the clamp screw *between* the pulley ribs.

  c. When the rope is all the way out and the rope hole in the pulley is aligned with the rope hole in the housing, rotate the pulley one more rib counterclockwise. Place a small S-hook through one of the small-diameter slots in the housing, then allow

spring tension to lock the rib against the S-hook (**Figure 59**). The pulley and housing holes should then be nearly aligned.

5. Pull the old rope out of the starter from the inside, through the pulley hole.

6. Obtain a new No. 5 1/2 rope (4.5 mm [11/64 inch] diameter) 165 cm (65 inches) long. Burn both ends to prevent fraying. Tie a single knot at one end.

7. Feed the free end of the rope through the pulley hole, then through the housing hole. Pull the rope all the way out.

8. Feed the rope through the handle grip, then through the rope retainer.

9. Tie a single knot at the end of the rope. Slide the knot into the retainer. Fit the retainer into the handle.

10. Unlock the pulley, allowing the spring to slowly draw the rope back into the starter. The rope should draw in completely and the handle should stop against the housing hole.

11. Check starter operation.

Rope broken

1. Invert the starter and remove what remains of the rope from the pulley groove.

2. Obtain a new No. 5 1/2 rope (4.5 mm [11/64 inch] diameter) 165 cm (65 inches) long. Burn both ends to prevent fraying. Tie a single knot at one end.

3. While holding the housing stationary, rotate the pulley counterclockwise (viewed from inside the starter housing) until the spring is tight. This will require approximately six full turns of the pulley. Do *not* force the pulley once the spring is tight.

4. Rotate the pulley clockwise only until the pulley rope hole aligns with the housing rope hole. Hold the pulley in this position. Three acceptable methods of holding the pulley are:

  a. Have an assistant hold the pulley and housing to prevent the pulley from rotating.

  b. Use a C-clamp around the edge of the housing (**Figure 58**). Do *not* clamp the pulley to the housing. Place the foot of the clamp screw *between* the pulley ribs.

  c. When the rope is all the way out and the rope hole in the pulley is aligned with the rope hole in the housing, rotate the pulley one more rib counterclockwise. Place a small S-hook through one of the small-diameter slots in the housing, then allow spring tension to lock the rib against the S-hook (**Figure 59**). The pulley and housing holes should then be nearly aligned.

6

5. Feed the free end of the rope through the pulley hole, then through the housing hole. Pull the rope all the way out.

6. Feed the rope through the handle grip, then through the rope retainer.

7. Tie a single knot at the end of the rope. Slide the knot into the retainer. Fit the retainer into the handle.

8. Unlock the pulley, allowing the spring to slowly draw the rope back into the starter. The rope should draw in completely and the handle should stop against the housing hole.

9. Check starter operation.

Starter Repair

CAUTION
The rewind spring is under tension. Always wear eye protection when servicing rewind starters. Follow repair instructions accurately.

NOTE
If the rope is broken, proceed to Step 4.

1. Pull the rope out about 12 inches (30 cm). Tie a slip knot in the rope at the housing to prevent the rope from rewinding.

2. Remove the rope retainer and handle.

3. Remove the slip knot. Allow the rope to *slowly* wind back into the starter.

4. Remove the retaining screw and washer from the center of the starter.

5. Remove the pawl retainer, brake spring and washer, pawls and pawl springs. Note the position and orientation of the pawls and pawl springs.

6. Rotate the pulley *two turns clockwise* to make sure the spring tension is relieved and the spring is disengaged from the housing.

7. While holding the pulley in the housing, invert the starter, aiming the pulley away from yourself or others.

8. Carefully remove the pulley by rotating it back and forth a few degrees. The containerized spring should remain in the pulley when the pulley is removed.

NOTE
If the pulley can not be easily removed from the housing, there may still be tension on the spring or the spring could still be connected to the housing. Repeat Steps 6-8 and again try to remove the pulley.

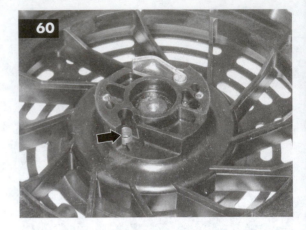

9. Note the orientation of the spring/keeper assembly inside the pulley. Carefully remove the spring and keeper as an assembly.

CAUTION
Removing the spring from the keeper could cause injury.

10. Clean and dry all parts, including the center screw and housing center post threads. Carefully inspect all components for wear or damage. Repair or replace as necessary.

NOTE
*If the pulley ribs and rope groove are distorted or folded due to ignition kickback, repair the starter, and replace the ignition module with Part No. 12 584 05. Refer to **Ignition System, Module Removal/Replacement** in this chapter. When starting the engine is in the future, pull the starter rope firmly and quickly. Pulling the starter rope slowly aggravates kickback.*

11. Lubricate the spring and the center housing shaft with grease.

12. Install the spring/keeper assembly into the pulley with the exposed spring face against the pulley and the keeper tabs in the pulley slots.

13. Install the pulley and spring assembly into the starter housing with the spring keeper against the housing.

14. Install the pawl springs into the pawl slots in the pulley (**Figure 60**). Pull the spring arms aside and insert the pawls.

15. Position the brake washer onto the center shaft, inside the pulley recess.

16. *Lightly* grease the brake spring ends. Set the spring onto the brake washer, making sure no grease gets into the center post threads.

17. Position the pawl retainer onto the pulley as shown in **Figure 61**.

18. Lightly coat the center screw threads with Loctite 271 or equivalent. Place the washer onto the screw shoulder. Install the screw, torquing it to 7.4-8.5 N·m (65-75 in.-lb.).

19. Install the rope and tension the spring as described in this chapter.

Starter Installation

1. Make sure the grass screen is in place on the flywheel fan.

2. Position the starter cup over the flywheel, into the cut-out hole in the grass screen.

3. With the lock washer and flat washer in position on the flywheel bolt, install the bolt into the crankshaft.

4. Using the strap wrench shown in **Figure 28**, hold the flywheel in position while tightening the bolt. Torque the bolt to 66 N•m (49 ft.-lb.).

5. Apply a few drops of penetrating oil to the groove of the spark plug wire grommet. Slide the grommet into its slot in the blower housing while lowering the housing down onto the engine.

6. Lightly coat the blower housing fastener threads with Loctite 242 or equivalent. Install and tighten the six fasteners holding the blower housing to the engine.

7. Position the starter onto the blower housing.

8. Lightly coat the five hex flange screw threads with Loctite 242 or equivalent. Install the screws finger-tight.

9. Center the starter pawls inside the cup by lightly pulling out on the starter rope handle grip until both pawls extend and contact the cup notches.

10. While the pawls are in contact with the cup, alternately tighten the starter fasteners.

11. When the fasteners are tight, release the rope grip.

OIL SENSOR

The engine may be equipped with an Oil Sentry oil pressure switch installed in one of the main oil galleries of the crankcase cover or oil pan, or on the oil filter adapter. The switch is designed to break contact as oil pressure increases to normal pressure and to make contact when oil pressure decreases within the range of 20.7-34.5 kpa (3-5 psi). When the switch contacts close, either the engine will stop or a "Low Oil" warning light will be activated, depending on the engine application.

Removal/Installation

1. Disconnect the wire lead from the switch.

2. Unscrew and remove the switch.

3. Before installing the switch:
   a. Make sure that the switch threads and mating engine threads are clean and dry.
   b. Apply Loctite 592 Pipe Sealant with Teflon or an equivalant sealant to the switch threads. Do not allow any sealant beyond the end thread or it could clog the switch passage.

4. Install the switch. Tighten the switch to 4.5 N·m (40 in.-lb.).

5. Connect the wire lead.

Testing

To check the sensor switch, a regulated supply of compressed air and a continuity tester are required.

1. Remove the oil pressure sensor switch as described in the previous section.

2. Connect the tester to the body of the switch and to the switch terminal.

3. The tester should indicate continuity between the switch terminal and the switch body.

4. Gradually apply air pressure to the switch oil passage.

5. As pressure increases through a range of 20.7-34.5 kpa (3-5 psi), the switch should open and the tester should indicate no continuity.

6. If the switch fails the test, install a new switch.

CRANKCASE BREATHER

The crankcase breather is a reed-type valve mounted in the upper-left corner of the cylinder head, underneath the valve cover. **Figure 62** shows the breather mounted on the head. Opposite the breather, in the upper-right corner of the head, the breather baffles can be seen. Matching baffles are a part of the inside of the rocker cover (**Figure 63**). These baffles prevent oil from being drawn through the breather hose into the air filter and carburetor. **Figure 64** shows a close-up of the reed mounted under the reed retainer. **Figure 65** shows the

6

rocker arm cover mounted on the engine, with the breather hose fitting in the upper right corner.

Removal

1. Unclamp and disconnect the breather hose from the valve cover and air filter base fittings.

2. Unbolt and remove the rocker arm cover. If the cover is stuck because of the sealant, *carefully* rap on the cover flanges at various positions with a hammer and square-edged wood block to loosen the cover. Carefully remove all sealant from the gasket surfaces. Do not gouge or damage the sealing surfaces.

3. Prior to removing the breather reed assembly, inspect the reed-to-head clearance. There should be zero-to-minimal clearance between the reed and the head surface.

4. Unbolt and remove the breather reed stop and breather reed.

Inspection

1. Check the reed for cracks or extreme wear on the reed-to-head face. Replace if questionable.

2. Inspect the head-to-crankcase breather passage for obstructions. Remove as necessary.

3. Inspect the rocker cover fitting and air filter base passages for obstructions. Clean as necessary.

4. Inspect the breather hose. Replace if dry, cracked or brittle.

5. Inspect the breather hose clamps. Replace if questionable.

Installation

1. Lightly coat the reed bolt threads with Loctite 242 or equivalent.

2. Position the reed and reed retainer onto the head. Install the bolt. Torque the bolt to 5.8 N·m (50 in.-lb.).

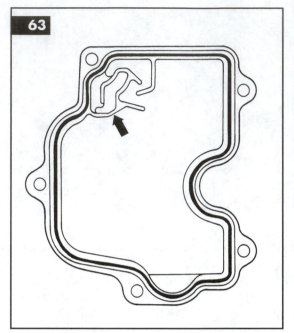

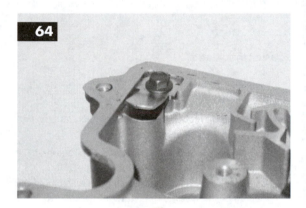

3. Apply a 1.6 mm (1/16 inch) diameter bead of sealant to the rocker cover gasket surface as shown in **Figure 63**. Applying sealant to the baffle surface is not recommended. Refer to **Table 6** at the end of this chapter for approved sealants. Always follow the sealant manufacturer's instructions regarding set time.

4. Install the rocker cover. Incrementally torque the cover bolts using the sequence shown in **Figure 66**.
   a. If the cover is being reinstalled onto a used head, lightly coat the cover bolt threads with Loctite 242 or equivalent, then torque the fasteners to 7.3 N·m (65 in.-lb.).
   b. If the cover is being installed for the first time onto a new cylinder head, do not use threadlock compound. Torque the fasteners to 10.7 N·m (95 in.-lb.).

5. Reconnect the breather hose to the rocker cover and air filter base fittings.

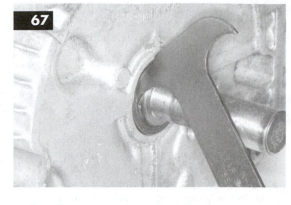

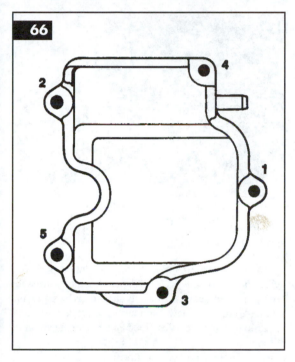

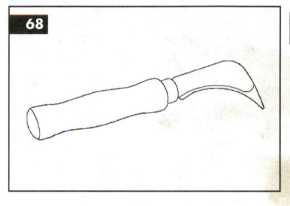

crankshaft is leaking, any parts attached to the crankshaft which deny access to the oil seal must be removed.

NOTE
Drain the engine oil if replacing the PTO oil seal.

Removal

Before removing an oil seal, note the position of the seal in the crankcase or oil pan. Install the new seal so it is located at the same depth as the original seal.

CAUTION
Exercise care when extracting the seal so the metal behind the seal or the crankshaft seal surface is not scratched or damaged.

1. Special oil seal removal tools are available from small-engine tool suppliers (**Figure 67**). An oil seal removal tool may be fabricated by modifying a linoleum knife as shown in **Figure 68**. Carefully grind the blade to the contour shown in the figure, then round all the blade edges so the blade will not damage the crankshaft or seal cavity.

2. Using a small pin punch, carefully tap the seal in a couple of places around its outer edge so as to break it

OIL SEALS

Service (With Crankshaft Installed)

Oil seals at the flywheel end and the PTO end of the crankshaft prevent the oil in the engine from leaking out. Wear or damage can reduce their effectiveness and oil leakage can become a problem, particularly if excessive amounts of oil are lost.

In most instances, it is possible to remove and install an oil seal without removing the crankshaft. Depending on which oil seal is leaking and the location of the engine, it may be necessary to remove the engine from the equipment.

If the oil seal at the flywheel end of the crankshaft is leaking, the flywheel must be removed (see *Flywheel, Removal* in this chapter). If the oil seal at the PTO end of the loose from the crankcase cavity. Only tap it enough to break it loose. Do not drive it deeper into the cavity.

3. Carefully insert the tool blade under the oil seal lip and against the inside periphery of the seal, next to the crankshaft (**Figure 69**). Pry out the seal. It may be necessary to work around the seal in more than one spot before the seal will break loose.

4. Clean and dry the seal seating area so the new seal will seat properly.

5. Check the oil seal bore in the engine and dress out any burrs created during removal. Only remove metal that is raised and will interfere with the installation of the new seal. If a deep gouge is present, carefully clean and dry the area around the gouge, then fill the depression with a suitable epoxy so it is level with the surrounding metal.

6. Check the crankshaft seal area. Scoring, grooves, or sharp edges on the crankshaft will require that the crankshaft be replaced.

Installation

1. Apply Loctite 598 or an equivalent oil-resistant non-hardening sealer to the periphery of the oil seal prior to installation.

2. Cover keyways and threads on the crankshaft with a seal protector sleeve or thin tape so the oil seal lip will not be cut when passing the oil seal down the crankshaft.

3. Coat the lips of the seal with a light grease.

4. Position the seal so the seal lip is slanted toward the inside of the engine. Most seals are spring-loaded. The spring must be toward the engine when installing the seal.

5. Use a suitable tool with the same outside diameter as the oil seal to force the oil seal into the engine. A deep-well socket may work if the output end of the crankshaft is short. Suitable sizes of tubing or pipe may be used (**Figure 70**). Be sure the end of the tool is square but not sharp.

6. The crankshaft oil seals should be installed so they are approximately 1/32 inch (0.79 mm) below flush with the seal bore faces.

ROCKER ARM COVER

Removal and installation of the valve cover is described under *Crankcase Breather* in this chapter.

Inspection of the cover will only be necessary if the cover shows evidence of leaking. If the cover is cracked or damaged in any way, especially around the breather hose fitting, it should be replaced.

ROCKER ARMS AND PUSH RODS

Three different styles of rocker arms and pivots (**Figure 71**) are used. Engines with serial No. 2617200734 and higher use the latest style, "C." If rocker arm replace-

ment is required due to valve train wear, style "B" can be upgraded to style "C" with Kohler's retrofit kit, (part No. 12 755 74-S). The self-aligning capability of the Style "C" pivot eliminates the need for the slotted push rod guide plate used with Style "B" arms. Engines with Style "A" components can only be upgraded to Style "C" by installing a complete new cylinder head. Rocker arm and push rod installation is described under *Cylinder Head* in this chapter.

Note that there are no adjustments on the rocker arms. CV14 and CV15 engines are equipped with hydraulic valve lifters that automatically maintain proper valve clearance. No periodic adjustment is required.

NOTE
New push rods are identical, interchangeable and reversible. However, if the original push rods are being reused, they must be marked to indicate whether they are for the intake or exhaust side and which end contacts the rocker arms.

CAUTION
To prevent damage to the rocker arms or other valve train components, the hydraulic valve lifters must be properly bled prior to starting a freshly reassembled engine. Refer to Cylinder Head in this chapter for the correct head and lifter

71 | **DIFFERENT STYLE ROCKER ARMS**

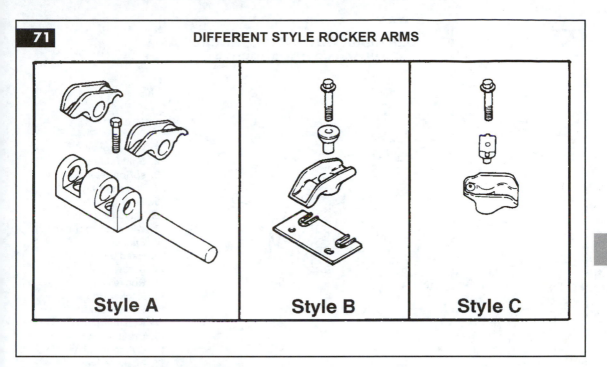

Style A | Style B | Style C

6

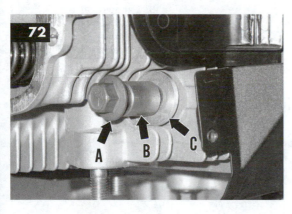

installation procedure. Refer to Hydraulic Valve Lifters in this chapter for the proper bleeding procedure.

CYLINDER HEAD

Removal

> *NOTE*
> *Refer to the appropriate sections in this chapter for specific component removal procedures noted in the following steps.*

To remove the cylinder head:

1. Remove the air cleaner assembly and base.
2. Detach the speed control cable and fuel line.
3. Remove the carburetor and muffler.

4. Remove the blower housing, cylinder head air baffles and shields.
5. Remove the rocker arm cover.
6. Remove the spark plug. Rotate the crankshaft so the piston is at top dead center on the compression stroke. Press on the rocker arms to slightly compress the valve springs, then remove the push rods. The push rods and rocker arms should be marked so they can be reinstalled in their original positions if they are being reused.
7. Unscrew and remove the five cylinder head bolts. Note the location and position of the spacer (B, **Figure 72**) and washer (C) on the bolt (A) nearest the exhaust port. Some older models do not use the washer.
8. Remove the cylinder head and gasket.

Disassembly

Style "A" Rocker Arms

> *NOTE*
> *Prior to or during disassembly, mark all components so they can be reinstalled in the same positions if they are to be reused.*

Refer to **Figure 73**.

1. Remove the spark plug.
2. Remove the breather retainer and reed.
3. Push the rocker shaft out the breather side of the rocker arm bridge, and remove the rocker arms.
4. Use a valve spring compressor tool to compress the valve springs. Remove the split retainers, release the spring tension, then remove the valve spring caps,

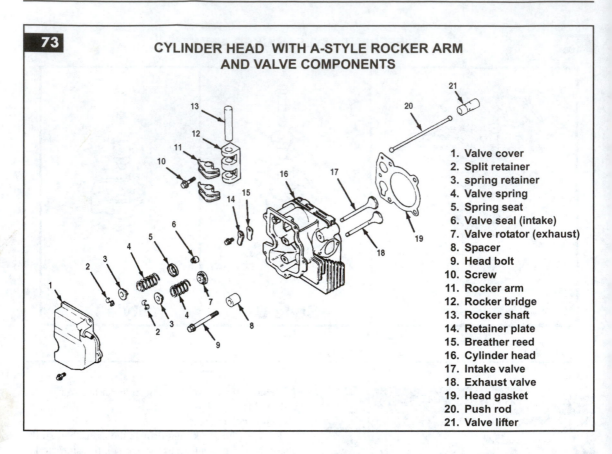

73

**CYLINDER HEAD WITH A-STYLE ROCKER ARM
AND VALVE COMPONENTS**

1. Valve cover
2. Split retainer
3. spring retainer
4. Valve spring
5. Spring seat
6. Valve seal (intake)
7. Valve rotator (exhaust)
8. Spacer
9. Head bolt
10. Screw
11. Rocker arm
12. Rocker bridge
13. Rocker shaft
14. Retainer plate
15. Breather reed
16. Cylinder head
17. Intake valve
18. Exhaust valve
19. Head gasket
20. Push rod
21. Valve lifter

springs, intake spring seat, exhaust rotator and valves from the cylinder head. If the valves offer resistance, check the keeper groove at the base of the stem (**Figure 74**). Using a fine file, carefully deburr any flaring on the stem at the bottom end of the groove. Remove and discard the valve stem seal.

5. Remove the rocker bridge bolts and bridge.

6. Clean any remaining combustion deposits from the cylinder head and components.

7. Check for cracks or other damage, especially in the combustion chamber, exhaust port and cooling fin area. Replace the cylinder head if it is cracked or damaged.

Style "B" Rocker Arms

NOTE
Prior to or during disassembly, mark all components so they can be reinstalled in the same positions if they are to be reused.

Refer to **Figure 71**.

1. Remove the spark plug, if not already removed.

2. Remove the breather retainer and reed (13 and 14, **Figure 75**).

3. Remove the rocker pivot bolts, pivot balls and rocker arms from both the intake and exhaust valves. When the

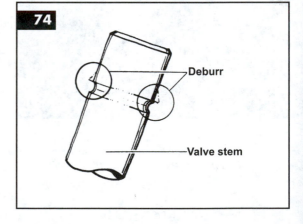

74

Deburr

Valve stem

pivot bolts are removed, the push rod guide plate can be removed.

NOTE
On engines between Serial Nos. 2421700017 and 2511700016, if the rocker pivots have part No. 24 194 02 imbedded in the upper face, there will be a spacer washer under each rocker pivot. Ensure that the washers are installed upon reassembly.

75

CYLINDER HEAD WITH B-STYLE ROCKER ARM COMPONENTS

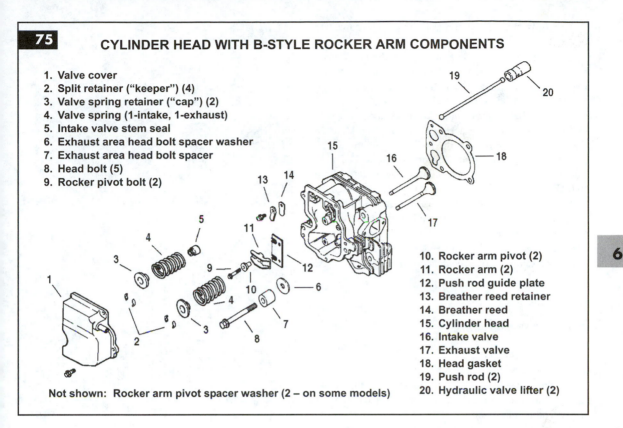

1. Valve cover
2. Split retainer ("keeper") (4)
3. Valve spring retainer ("cap") (2)
4. Valve spring (1-intake, 1-exhaust)
5. Intake valve stem seal
6. Exhaust area head bolt spacer washer
7. Exhaust area head bolt spacer
8. Head bolt (5)
9. Rocker pivot bolt (2)

10. Rocker arm pivot (2)
11. Rocker arm (2)
12. Push rod guide plate
13. Breather reed retainer
14. Breather reed
15. Cylinder head
16. Intake valve
17. Exhaust valve
18. Head gasket
19. Push rod (2)
20. Hydraulic valve lifter (2)

Not shown: Rocker arm pivot spacer washer (2 – on some models)

76

4. Remove the push rods.

5. Using a valve spring compressor, compress the valve springs and remove the split keepers.

6. Remove the valve spring caps and springs.

7. Remove and discard the intake valve stem seal.

Style "C" Rocker Arms

Cylinder head disassembly with Style "C" rocker arms is the same as the preceding Style "B" disassembly except in Step 3, there will be no guide plate to remove.

Inspection

1. Carefully remove all traces of sealant from the cylinder head and rocker cover mating surfaces. Do not gouge or damage the mating surfaces.

2. Remove all traces of gasket material from the cylinder head and cylinder block mating surfaces. Do not gouge or damage the mating surfaces.

3. Remove all carbon deposits from the valves, combustion chamber area and valve ports with a rotary wire brush. A blunt screwdriver or chisel may be used if care is taken not to damage the head, valves and spark plug threads.

4. Examine the spark plug threads in the cylinder head for damage. If damage is minor or if the threads are dirty or clogged with carbon, use a spark plug thread tap (**Figure 76**) to clean the threads. If thread damage is severe, install a Heli-Coil or equivalent replacement thread or replace the cylinder head.

5. Inspect the threads in all threaded cylinder head and crankcase holes for damage. Restore the threads with an appropriate size metric tap if necessary.

6. After the carbon is removed from the combustion chamber and the valve intake and exhaust ports, clean the entire head in cleaning solvent. Blow dry with compressed air.

7. Carefully clean all carbon from the piston crown. Do not score the crown.

8. Check for cracks or other damage to the head, especially in the combustion chamber and exhaust port. Replace the cylinder head if it is cracked or damaged, or if any cooling fins are broken off.

9. After the head has been thoroughly cleaned, place the cylinder head gasket surface on a surface plate. Measure the warpage by inserting a flat feeler gauge between the plate and the cylinder head at various locations. The maximum allowable cylinder head warpage is 0.076 mm (0.003 in.). Although resurfacing is possible, warpage beyond specification on the gasket surface indicates warpage in other head areas, as well. Replacement of the head is recommended.

10. Valve, valve guide and valve seat service is described under *Valves and Valve Components* in this chapter.

Reassembly

Style "A" Rocker Arms

Refer to **Figure 71**.

1. Make sure all threads are clean and dry.

2. Position the rocker arm bridge with the *small* counterbored hole toward the exhaust port side of the cylinder head (**Figure 77**).

3. Install the two bridge bolts. Torque the bolts to 9.9 N·m (88 in.-lb.).

4. Lightly lubricate the intake valve stem, guide and stem seal wiping lip with fresh engine oil. Always use a new stem seal. Install the intake valve, valve spring seat and valve stem seal (**Figure 78**). Install the stem seal first, pushing it over the guide until it bottoms. Rotate the valve slowly while passing through the seal to prevent damaging the seal. Push the valve all the way in until it bottoms against the seat.

5. Position the intake valve spring into the seat. Install the spring retainer. Compress the spring, then install the split retainers.

> *NOTE*
> *Apply a small amount of grease to the valve keeper groove on the valve stem before installing the split retainers ("keepers") to hold the keepers in place on the valve stem. Make sure the keepers fit snugly into the groove in the valve stem.*

6. Lightly lubricate the exhaust valve stem with Led-Plate or equivalent. Lightly lubricate the exhaust valve guide with fresh engine oil. Install the exhaust valve and rotator, if used.

7. Position the exhaust valve spring onto the valve. Install the spring retainer. Compress the spring, then install the split retainers.

8. Install the rocker arms over the valve stems, into position in the bridge. Install the rocker shaft through the bridge and arms from the breather reed side until it bottoms in the bridge. The shaft has no lock; the installed rocker cover holds it in place.

9. Install the breather reed, reed retainer and bolt. Torque the bolt to 9.9 N·m (88 in.-lb.).

10. The head is now ready for installation onto the engine.

Style "B" Rocker Arms

Refer to **Figure 71**.

1. Ensure all threads are clean and dry.

2. Lightly lubricate the intake valve stem, guide and stem seal wiping lip with fresh engine oil. Always use a new stem seal. Install the intake valve stem seal and valve. Install the stem seal first, pushing it down until it bottoms against the guide. Rotate the valve while passing through the seal to prevent damaging the seal. Push the valve all the way in until it bottoms against the seat.

3. Position the intake valve spring over the valve stem. Install the spring retainer. Compress the spring, then install the split retainers.

NOTE
Apply a small amount of grease to the valve keeper groove on the valve stem prior to installing the split retainers ("keepers") to hold the keepers in place on the valve stem. Make sure the keepers fit snugly into the groove in the valve stem.

4. Lightly lubricate the exhaust valve stem with Led-Plate or equivalent. Lightly lubricate the exhaust valve guide with fresh engine oil. Install the exhaust valve.

5. Position the exhaust valve spring onto the valve. Install the spring retainer. Compress the spring, then install the split retainers.

6. Position the push rod guide plate against the head with the raised portion of the guide slots *away from* the head.

7. Mount the rocker arms and rocker pivots. Install the pivot bolts. Torque the bolts to 14 N·m (125 in.-lb.).

8. Install the breather reed, reed retainer and bolt. Torque the bolt to 9.9 N·m (88 in.-lb.).

9. The head is now ready for installation onto the engine.

Style "C" Rocker Arms

Cylinder head reassembly with Style "C" rocker arms is the same as the preceding Style "B" reassembly except that in Step 6, there will be no guide plate to install.

While torquing the bolts, hold the arm ends in position over the valve stems so the pivots do not turn, causing misalignment.

When completely assembled and installed, the rocker arms and head will appear as shown in **Figure 79**.

Installation

CAUTION
Because these engines use hydraulic valve lifters, the specified reassembly procedure must be followed precisely to prevent damage to the valve train components.

NOTE
New cylinder head bolts should always be installed. The rust-preventive coating on the bolts affects torque retention, and most of the coating wears off the threads once the bolts are installed and tightened. Attempting to reuse old bolts results in loss of torque retention, likely causing short term head gasket failure.

1. Make sure that all cylinder block head bolt threads are clean, dry and in good repair.

2. If the hydraulic valve lifters were removed, install them now, followed by the push rods. Make sure the lower ends of the push rods are into the lifter socket holes (**Figure 80**).

3. While holding the lifters against the push rods with finger pressure, rotate the crankshaft so the piston is at TDC on the compression stroke (when neither push rod has moved for one half of a crankshaft revolution). The crankshaft PTO keyway will be in line with the piston (12 o'clock position) at this time.

4. Make sure that both cylinder head locator sleeves are in position in the cylinder block (**Figure 81**).

5. Position a new head gasket onto the block locator sleeves.

6. Fit the washer, if used, and spacer onto the exhaust port head bolt (**Figure 72**).

   a. Install the new head bolts into the head.

   b. Position the head onto the cylinder block.

6

c. Using just a deep socket, finger-tighten the bolts. If possible, align the push rods with the rocker arms prior to tightening the bolts.

7. Tighten the cylinder head bolts in increments of 14 N·m (120 in.-lb. or 10 ft.-lbs.) following the sequence shown in **Figure 82** to the final specified torque of 40.7 N·m (360 in.-lb. or 30 ft.-lbs.).

8. If it was not possible to align the push rods with the rocker arms in Step 6, do so now by pushing on each rocker arm to compress the valve spring slightly. With the spring compressed, fit each push rod into its rocker arm socket. When installed, the push rods will appear as shown in **Figure 79**.

9. Make sure that the lifters are properly bled down:

a. Attempt to rotate the flywheel clockwise by hand three full turns so the piston winds up at TDC between the exhaust and intake stroke. Again, the crankshaft PTO keyway will be in the 12 o'clock position, in line with the piston.

b. While rotating the flywheel, carefully observe the valve springs. The exhaust spring will compress first.

c. If, while rotating the flywheel, clearance between the spring coils disappears, *stop turning the flywheel* and allow the engine to rest in this position for at least 10 minutes. There should be approximately 0.25 mm (0.010 in.) clearance between the spring coils at all times.

d. After this rest, clearance should again appear between the spring coils. When it does, continue rotating the flywheel. Stop rotating the flywheel anytime the spring coils compress completely.

e. Install the spark plug, torquing it to 38-43.4 N·m (335-385 in.-lb. or 28-32 ft.-lb.).

f. If all assembly procedures have been followed correctly, the flywheel should be able to be rotated by hand with good compression being noticed and with clearance between the valve spring coils at all times.

10. Install the rocker arm cover as described in this chapter.

VALVE AND VALVE COMPONENTS

Valve Adjustment

CV14 and CV15 engines are equipped with hydraulic valve lifters that automatically maintain proper valve clearance. No periodic adjustment is required.

Valve Removal

To remove the valves, follow the steps described under *Cylinder Head, Disassembly* in this chapter.

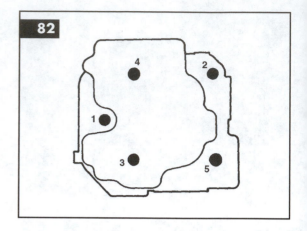

Valve Inspection

For valve, valve guide and valve seat dimensions, refer to **Figure 83** and **Table 6** at the end of this chapter.

1. Inspect the valve for damage and excessive wear prior to cleaning the valve.

a. Gummy deposits on the intake valve (**Figure 84**) may indicate that the engine has run on gasoline that was stored for an extended period.

b. Hard deposits on the intake valve are due to burnt oil during valve overlap, while hard deposits on the exhaust valve (**Figure 85**) are due to combustion byproducts and burnt oil.

c. Moisture in the engine during storage can cause corroded or pitted valves. These should be replaced.

2. Check the valve face (**Figure 86**) for an irregular seating pattern. The seating ring around the face should be centered on the face, concentric with the valve head and equal in thickness all around the valve (**Figure 87**). If the seating pattern is irregular, then the valve may be bent or the valve face or seat is damaged.

3. Remove deposits either with a wire brush or soak the valve in parts cleaner.

4. Measure the valve stem diameter. Oversize valves are available with a 0.25 mm oversize stem for installation in worn valve guides which have been reamed oversize.

5. Run a fingernail down the valve stem and check for a ledge that would indicate that the valve stem is worn. Replace the valve if the valve stem is worn.

6. The valve stem must be perpendicular to the valve head. To check for a bent valve, carefully install the valve stem in a drill chuck and rotate the drill by hand while measuring head runout with a dial indicator. Be sure the valve stem is centered in the drill chuck.

7. Measure the valve head margin. Replace the valve if the margin is less than the minimum specified dimension.

8. If the valve and valve seat are worn, but serviceable, they can be restored by machining. Take the valves and

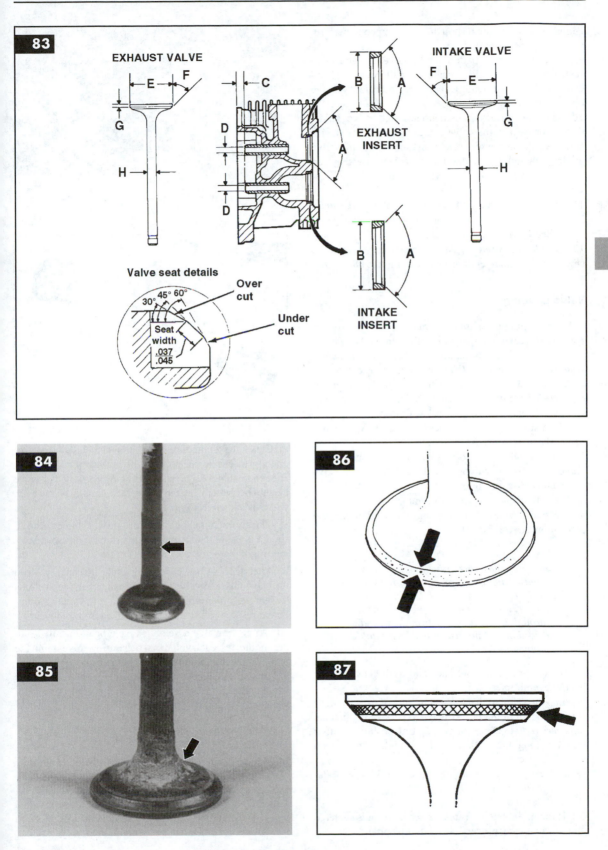

83

EXHAUST VALVE

INTAKE VALVE

EXHAUST INSERT

INTAKE INSERT

Valve seat details

30° 45° 60°

Over cut

Under cut

Seat width
.037
.045

84

85

86

87

6

engine to a professional shop that is equipped to perform valve machine work.

9. Check the contact pattern on the valve face and valve seat. The pattern should be centered on the valve face and even all the way around. Unevenness indicates warpage or a bent valve.

10. The valve rides in a nonrenewable valve guide. Check for wear in the valve guides by measuring the inside diameter at the top, middle and bottom of the valve guide. Although the guides are not replaceable, they can be reamed to accept oversize valves with 0.25 mm oversize stem.

11. If valve machining is not necessary, the valve should be lapped against the valve seat to restore the seating surfaces. See *Valve Lapping*, below.

12. Check the valve springs. The spring should be straight with square ends as shown in **Figure 88**.

Valve Lapping

Valve lapping is a simple operation which can restore the valve seal without machining if the amount of wear is not excessive. Lapping requires the use of lapping compound and a lapping tool (**Figure 89**). Lapping compound is available in either coarse or fine grade, water- or oil-mixed. Fine grade water-mixed compound is recommended. To lap a valve, proceed as follows:

1. Make sure that the valve head is smooth. Wire-brush or lightly sand, if necessary.

2. Apply a light, even coat of lapping compound to the valve face. Too much compound can fall into the valve guide and cause damage.

3. Insert the valve into the valve guide.

4. Moisten the end of the lapping tool suction cup and place it on the valve head.

> *NOTE*
> *For the most accurate lapping, slowly hand-rotate the lapping tool back and forth between 1/4 and 3/8 of a turn (90°-135°). Do not spin the tool rapidly through a revolution or two, then reverse direction. Do not use a drill to rotate the lapping tool.*

5. Rotate the lapping tool back and forth between your hands several times.

6A. Lap the valve so that the sealing ring of the valve face is in the center of the face (**Figure 87**). Make the first lap pass *very light* to check the sealing ring position. If, after initial lapping, the sealing ring is too high or too low on the valve face:

    a. Recut the seat as necessary (refer to *Valve Seat Reconditioning.*

    b. Relap the valve.

6B. If the initial lap indicates the sealing ring is centered on the valve face, proceed with a full lapping.

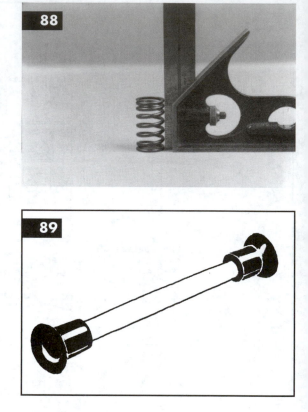

7. Clean the compound from the valve and seat frequently to check the progress of the lapping. Lap only enough to achieve a precise seating ring around the valve head. The pattern on the valve face should be an even width as shown in **Figure 87**.

8. Closely examine the valve seat in the cylinder head. It should be smooth and even with a smooth polished seating ring.

9. After lapping has been completed, thoroughly clean the valve face and valve seat areas using dampened cloths to remove all grinding compound. Any lapping compound residue left in the engine will cause rapid wear.

10. After the valve assemblies have been installed into the engine, test each valve seal by pouring solvent into the intake and exhaust ports. There should be no leakage past the seat. If fluid leaks past any of the seats, remove the valve and repeat the lapping procedure until there is no leakage.

Valve Seat Reconditioning

The cylinder heads use hardened alloy steel intake and exhaust valve seat inserts pressed into the head. The inserts are not replaceable. If the inserts are loose, cracked or seriously warped, replace the head. If the inserts are in good condition, they can be reconditioned.

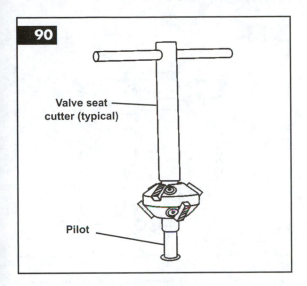

Valve seat
cutter (typical)

Pilot

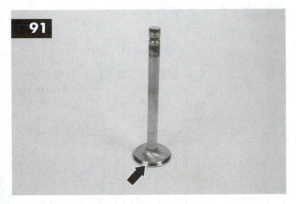

Special valve cutter tools and considerable expertise are required to recondition the valve seats in the cylinder heads.

The following procedure is provided for those who wish to attempt the job. Required tools are:

1. Valve seat cutters.

2. Vernier or dial caliper.

3. Machinist's dye or Prussian Blue.

4. Valve lapping stick.

The valve seat for both the intake and exhaust valves are machined to the same angles. The valve contact surface is cut to a 44.5° angle from center (89° total angle).

1. Carefully rotate and insert the solid pilot into the valve guide. Make sure the solid pilot is correctly seated.

2. Using the 44.5° cutter, rotate the tool one or two turns to remove roughness and clean the seat (**Figure 90**).

CAUTION
Measure the valve seat contact area in the cylinder head after each cut to make sure the contact area is correct and to prevent removing too much material. If too much

material is removed, the cylinder head must be replaced.

3. If the seat is still pitted or burned, turn the 44.5° cutter additional turns until the surface is clean. Avoid removing too much material from the cylinder head.

4. Remove the valve cutter.

5. Inspect the valve seat-to-valve face impression as follows:

    a. Spread a thin layer of Prussian Blue or machinist's dye evenly on the valve face.

    b. Moisten the suction cup tool (**Figure 89**) and attach it to the valve. Insert the valve into the guide.

    c. Using the suction cup tool, tap the valve up and down in the cylinder head. Do *not* rotate the valve or a false indication will result.

    d. Remove the valve and examine the impression left by the Prussian Blue or machinist's dye.

6. Note the impression the dye left on the valve face (**Figure 91**).

    a. If the contact area is too *low* on the valve (too close to the stem), use the 60° cutter and remove a portion of the lower area of the valve seat material. This will raise the contact area. If this narrows the seat width, use the 44.5° cutter again to bring the seat width back into specification.

    b. If the contact area is too *high* on the valve, use the 30° cutter and remove a portion of the top area of the valve seat material. This will lower the contact area. If this narrows the seat width, use the 44.5° cutter again to bring the seat width back into specification.

7. Once the contact area is properly positioned on the valve face, adjust the valve seat width:

    a. If the width is too narrow, use the 44.5° cutter to widen the seat.

    b. If the width is too wide, use the 30° and 60° cutters equally to remove material from both above and below the seat contact area. When the seat width is correct, repeat Step 5 to ensure the correct seat-to-face position.

8. After the desired valve seat position and width is obtained, use the 44.5° cutter and very lightly clean off any burrs that may have been caused by the previous cuts.

9. Check that the finish has a smooth surface. It should not be rough or show chatter marks.

10. Repeat Steps 1-9 for the remaining valve seat.

11. Lap the valves as detailed in the preceding *Valve Lapping* section.

12. Thoroughly clean the cylinder head and all valve components in solvent or detergent and hot water to remove all cutting and lapping debris.

6

Valve Guide Reconditioning

The valve guides in these heads are not replaceable. To check guide-to-stem clearance:

1. Use a split-ball gauge to measure the inside diameter of the guide. Measure in three places – the top, the middle and the bottom of the guide. Note the measurements and compare them to the specifications in **Figure 83**.

2. Use an outside micrometer to measure the valve stem along the guide wear area. Again measure at the top, middle and bottom of the wear area. Note the measurements and compare them to the specifications in **Figure 83**.

3. Subtract the smallest stem measurement from the largest guide measurement. This is the stem-to-guide clearance. Compare this dimension to the specification in **Table 5**.

4. If the guide wear is beyond specification:
   a. Use Tool No. KO-1026 to ream the guide 0.25 mm (0.010 in.) oversize. Follow the instructions included with the reamer.
   b. Install the proper oversize-stem valve.

5. If the guide is within specification but the valve stem is worn beyond limits, replace the valve with a standard valve.

Valve Installation

1. Install the valve assemblies as described under *Cylinder Head, Reassembly* in this chapter. Make sure that the keepers (B, **Figure 92**) are completely seated on the end of the valve stem (A) inside the spring retainer. After the keepers have been installed, gently tap the end of the valve stem with a soft aluminum or brass drift and hammer. This will ensure that the keepers are properly seated.

2. After the valve assemblies have been installed into the engine, test each valve seal by pouring solvent into the intake and exhaust ports. There should be no leakage past the seat. If fluid leaks past any of the seats, remove the valve and repeat the lapping procedure until there is no leakage.

3. If the cylinder head and valve components were cleaned in detergent and hot water, apply a light coat of engine oil to all bare metal surfaces to prevent any corrosion, unless the engine will be run immediately.

HYDRAULIC VALVE LIFTERS

The hydraulic valve lifters used in these engines replace the solid lifters used in other engines. The hydraulic lifter has two main advantages over solid lifters – quieter operation and the elimination of periodic valve clearance adjustments.

Figure 93 shows a cutaway view of the hydraulic lifter. The principle of operation of the lifter is as follows:

1. When the valve is closed, valve spring pressure acting through the rocker arm and push rod exerts pressure on

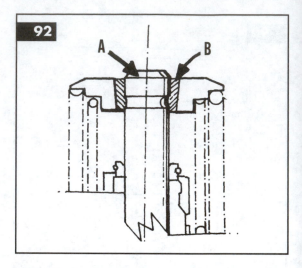

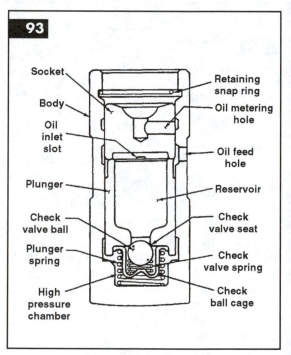

the upper socket, pushing the plunger against the plunger spring.

2. Pressurized oil from the oil pump enters the oil feed hole, opening the check valve and pressurizing the high pressure chamber.

3. The pressurized oil combines with the plunger spring to keep zero clearance in the valve train.

4. As the cam lobe raises the lifter, valve spring tension creates increased pressure in the high pressure chamber. This forces the check ball against its seat, allowing the lifter to keep zero clearance between the cam lobe, lifter, push rod, rocker arm and valve.

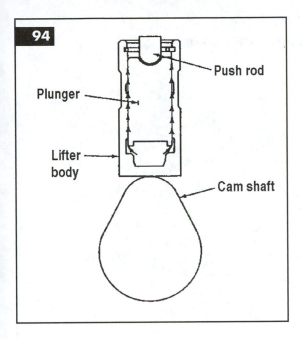

94

Push rod

Plunger

Lifter body

Cam shaft

5. Tight tolerances between the plunger and lifter body allow controlled oil leakage to compensate for system expansion, wear and bleeding of the lifter during maintenance (**Figure 94**).

If the hydraulic valve lifters are noisy after the engine has run for several minutes and reached operating temperature, it is probably an indication that either contamination is preventing the lifter check ball from seating or there is internal wear in the lifter. Individual parts are not available for the hydraulic lifters. Lifters should be replaced if faulty.

Current production engines are equipped with new style "quick-purge" lifters that reduce the lifter pump-up time and resultant noisy operation during engine start-up. The new style lifters (Kohler part No. 25 351 01) are available for service replacement on all engines.

Removal

CAUTION
Do not use magnetic pick-up tools to remove hydraulic lifters. Using magnetic tools can magnetize the small internal lifter components, trapping microscopic metal particles in the oil. This will lead to lifter malfunction and failure.

The hydraulic lifters should always be removed from the cylinder head end to prevent damage to the camshaft lobes. To remove the lifters:

1. Follow Steps 1-8 under *Cylinder Head, Removal* in this chapter.

NOTE
Some late model engines may have cylinder heads with a modified casting which will allow the lifters to be removed without removing the head. These engines can be identified by the adjustable studs which hold the rocker arms on. No adjustment procedure is available for the rocker arm studs.

2. Using Kohler Tool No. KO-1044, carefully remove the lifters one at a time.

3. Mark the lifters for reinstallation into the same bores. Switching lifters could cause rapid camshaft lobe wear. The intake valve lifter is closest to the flywheel; the exhaust valve lifter is closest to the oil pan.

Inspection

1. Visually check the crankcase lifter bores and the outside diameters of the lifters for scoring, gouging or galling.

2. Verify that the oil galleries are not obstructed.

3. Inspect the lifter components for damage. Although it is possible to disassemble and clean the lifters, it is not recommended. If in doubt, replace the lifter.

4. Use an inside micrometer or a telescoping gauge and an outside micrometer to measure the inside diameter of the lifter bore. Measure in three places – the top, the middle and the bottom of the bore. Note the measurements.

4. Use an outside micrometer to measure the lifter diameter. Again measure at the top, middle and bottom of the lifter. Note the measurements.

5. Subtract the smallest lifter measurement from the largest bore measurement. This is the running clearance. Lifter-to-crankcase bore running clearance is 0.0124-0.0501 mm (0.0005-0.0020 in.).

6. If wear is beyond specification:
   a. Measure the diameter of a new lifter.
   b. Compare the new measurement to the worn measurement.
   c. If the wear is in the lifter, replace the lifter.
   d. If the lifter is within specification but the crankcase bore is worn, the crankcase will need to be replaced.

7. Inspect the camshaft lobe rub area on the bottom of the lifter for wear.

Installation

1. If reinstalling the original lifters, note the marked positions of the lifters and install them into their proper bores.

2. If installing new lifters, lifter positions are interchangeable.

6

95

CRANKCASE/CYLINDER BLOCK ASSEMBLY

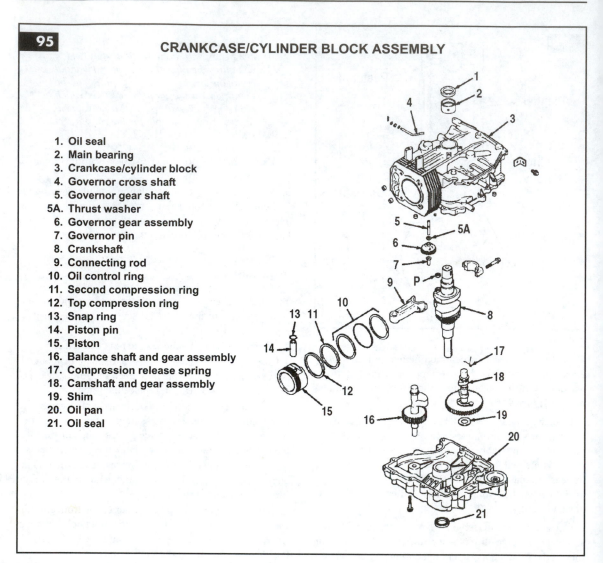

1. Oil seal
2. Main bearing
3. Crankcase/cylinder block
4. Governor cross shaft
5. Governor gear shaft
5A. Thrust washer
6. Governor gear assembly
7. Governor pin
8. Crankshaft
9. Connecting rod
10. Oil control ring
11. Second compression ring
12. Top compression ring
13. Snap ring
14. Piston pin
15. Piston
16. Balance shaft and gear assembly
17. Compression release spring
18. Camshaft and gear assembly
19. Shim
20. Oil pan
21. Oil seal

3. Continue to reassemble the engine by following the steps in the appropriate *Assembly* sections.

GOVERNOR (External Service)

A flyweight-type governor is located in the crankcase (4, 6, and 7, **Figure 95**). The governor cross-shaft extends through the crankcase to operate the external governor linkage. The governor gear is driven by the camshaft gear. Refer to the *Governor, Internal Service* section for overhaul information.

Governor Linkage Adjustment

1. Loosen the governor lever clamp nut (N, **Figure 96**).

2. Push the governor lever so the throttle is wide open.

3. While holding the throttle open, turn the governor cross shaft (S, **Figure 96**) counterclockwise as far as possible, then tighten the clamp nut.

RPM Adjustment

The maximum operating speed is 3600 rpm on the CV14 engine and 3750 rpm on the CV15 engine. Use a tachometer to check the engine speed. To adjust the high-speed setting:

1. Loosen the throttle control cable clamp screw (**Figure 97**).

2. Move the throttle control to the FAST position.

3. Align the hole in the speed-control throttle lever with the hole in the speed control bracket (**Figure 96**) by inserting a punch or drill bit through the holes.

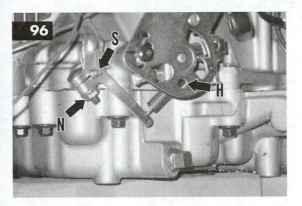

96

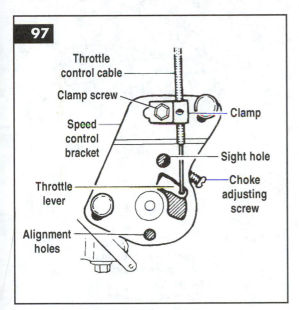

97

Throttle
control cable

Clamp screw

Clamp

Speed
control
bracket

Sight hole

Throttle
lever

Choke
adjusting
screw

Alignment
holes

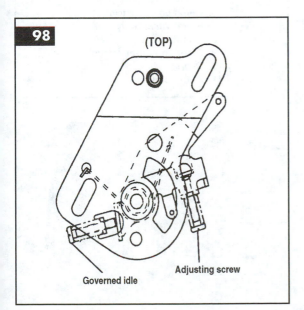

98

(TOP)

Adjusting screw

Governed idle

4. Pull up on the throttle control cable outer housing to remove slack.

5. Tighten the cable clamp screw.

6. Start the engine and allow it to reach operating temperature.

7. Repeat Step 3 to align the throttle lever and control bracket holes.

8. Loosen the speed control bracket mounting screws and move the bracket up (toward the flywheel) to decrease high speed rpm or down (toward the PTO) to increase high speed rpm.

9. When the desired speed is obtained, tighten the control bracket screws to 10.7 N·m (95 in.-lbs.) on a new short block or to 7.3 N·m (65 in.-lbs.) on all other engines.

Governor Sensitivity Adjustment

Governor sensitivity is adjusted by positioning the governor spring in different holes in the governor lever arm. On CV models, it is recommended that the spring be installed in the hole closest to governor shaft if high speed is 3600 rpm or less. If high speed is greater than 3600 rpm, use the second hole, the one farthest from the governor cross shaft.

On engines with governed idle control (**Figure 98**), proceed as follows if idle speed adjustment is necessary:

1. Manually move the governor lever so the throttle lever is tight against the idle speed stop screw (**Figure 10**).

2. Check the idle speed with a tachometer and adjust the idle speed stop screw to obtain 900-1000 rpm.

3. Release the governor lever and allow the engine to return to governed idle speed. If the idle speed is not at 1200 rpm, turn the governed idle speed adjusting screw (**Figure 98**) clockwise to increase idle speed or counterclockwise to decrease idle speed.

INTERNAL ENGINE COMPONENTS

Engine Disassembly

Refer to the appropriate previous sections when removing the external engine components. Refer to **Figure 95** for engine component references in this section.

1. Disconnect the spark plug lead and the battery cables, negative cable first.

2. Drain the engine oil and remove the oil filter and oil sentry switch. For the most effective crankcase sludge removal, the oil should be drained hot.

3. Allow the engine to cool, then remove the muffler and air cleaner.

4. Disconnect the throttle and choke control cable.

5. Carefully disconnect the carburetor fuel hose and anti-afterfire solenoid wire, then remove the carburetor, the heat shield and the external governor components. Keep the carburetor upright to prevent fuel spillage or drain the carburetor fuel into an approved container.

6

6. Unplug the main harness from the rectifier-regulator or stator connector, then remove the blower housing and all cooling shrouds. The rewind starter can be left attached to the blower housing.

7. Unbolt the starter cable. Remove the electric starter.

8. Mark and unplug the ignition module connector(s). Remove the ignition module.

9. Remove the flywheel bolt assembly and rewind starter cup, grass screen and flywheel fan. Remove the flywheel using a suitable puller.

10. Disconnect and remove the alternator stator and all wiring.

11. Remove the breather hose and rocker cover.

12. Remove the spark plug.

13. Remove the cylinder head.

14. Remove the hydraulic valve lifters.

15. Flip the engine over so the oil pan is facing up. Remove the 12 oil pan bolts. Carefully pry the oil pan from the crankcase by inserting a flat-bladed pry tool into the splitting notches provided (**Figure 99**).

CAUTION
Pry only between the splitting notches. Prying anywhere else between the crankcase and oil pan will damage the sealing surfaces.

16. Disassemble the oil pan:
   a. Remove the oil pan oil seal (**Figure 67**).
   b. Remove the oil pickup screen cover and screen (3 and 2, **Figure 100**).
   c. Remove the oil pump pressure relief valve spring, piston and body (5, 6, 7, **Figure 100**).
   d. Remove the oil pump cover and O-ring (11 and 10, **Figure 100**, early models). Later model engines have a tri-oval cover (**Figure 101**) with a standard round O-ring (**Figure 102**).
   e. Remove the inner and outer oil pump rotors (**Figure 102**).

17. Remove the camshaft end-play shim, if used. Remove the camshaft.

18. Remove the balance shaft from the crankcase.

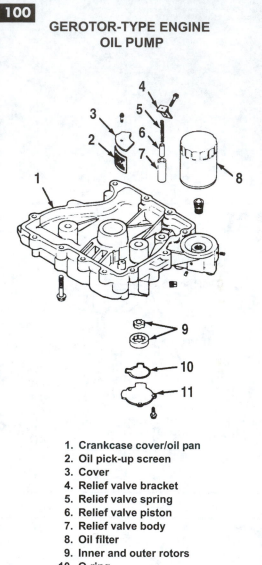

GEROTOR-TYPE ENGINE OIL PUMP

1. Crankcase cover/oil pan
2. Oil pick-up screen
3. Cover
4. Relief valve bracket
5. Relief valve spring
6. Relief valve piston
7. Relief valve body
8. Oil filter
9. Inner and outer rotors
10. O-ring
11. Pump cover

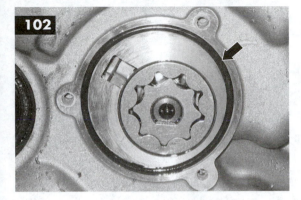

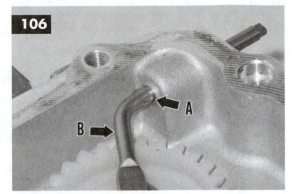

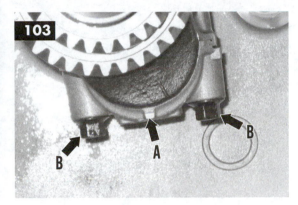

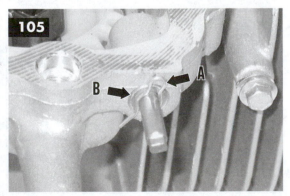

19. Prior to removing the piston and connecting rod assembly, use a ridge reamer tool to remove any ridge present at the top of the cylinder bore. Clean up any ridge shavings produced during the reaming process.

20. Rotate the crankshaft to BDC. Remove the two connecting rod cap screws (B, **Figure 103**) and cap (A). Rotate the crankshaft to TDC with the connecting rod still against the crankshaft journal, then carefully slide the connecting rod and piston assembly out of the cylinder. Do not nick the crankshaft journal while removing the rod and piston.

21. Using the cast-in pry notch (A, **Figure 104**), remove the wrist pin retainer from the piston. Remove the wrist pin (B).

22. Make sure that the flywheel key has been removed from the top of the crankshaft, then remove the crankshaft from the crankcase.

23. Remove the flywheel-side oil seal.

24. Measure the inside diameter of the top main bearing in the crankcase and compare the measurement to the specification listed in **Table 5**. If the bearing is worn beyond specification and:

    a. If the crankcase has a replaceable top main bearing, use Bearing Remover Tool No. KO-1029 and Handle No. NU-4747 to remove the bearing for replacement.

    b. If the bearing is machined into the crankcase material, replace the crankcase.

25. Remove the external hitch pin and washer (A and B, **Figure 105**) from the governor cross shaft. Remove the cross shaft (B, **Figure 106**) and internal washer (A) from the crankcase. Do not lose or confuse the washers.

26. Remove the external governor shaft seal from the crankcase (**Figure 107**).

27. If necessary for reboring or other major internal crankcase reconditioning, or if the governor gear assembly is worn or damaged, remove the governor pin spool, governor gear/flyweight assembly and thrust washer.

NOTE
The governor gear has small tabs molded internally which hold it onto the shaft. Removing the gear assembly destroys these

tabs. If the gear assembly is removed, it must be discarded and replaced with a new gear assembly.

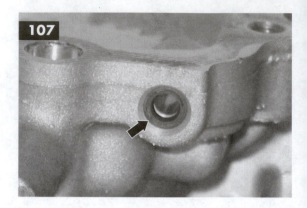

PISTON, PISTON RINGS AND PISTON (WRIST) PIN

The aluminum-alloy piston is fitted with two compression rings and one oil control ring. Piston and rings are available in standard size and oversizes of 0.25 mm and 0.50 mm (0.010 in. and 0.020 in.).

To remove the pistons, follow Steps 1-21 under *Engine Disassembly* in this chapter.

Disassembly

1. Remove and discard the piston rings. Reusing worn rings is not recommended.

2. Carefully clean the ring grooves. Do not gouge or damage the grooves while cleaning. A professional ring groove cleaning tool is shown in **Figure 108**. A convenient substitute ring groove cleaner can be made from a broken piece of the original ring (**Figure 109**).

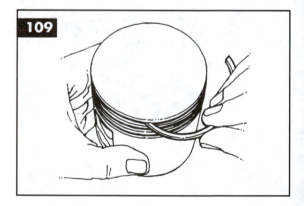

Inspection

1. Check the piston for scoring, scuffing and excessive wear. To determine the piston thrust face diameter, measure the piston perpendicular to the wrist pin at a distance of 1/2-inch from the bottom of the piston (D, **Figure 110**). Compare this dimension to the specification listed in **Table 5**. Replace if necessary.

2. Measure the wrist pin bore in the piston. Compare the measurement to the dimension listed in **Table 5**. If it is beyond specification, replace the piston.

3. Measure the wrist pin at multiple positions and compare the measurements to the dimension in **Table 5**. If it is beyond specification, replace the pin.

4. To measure the end gap of each piston ring (**Figure 111**):

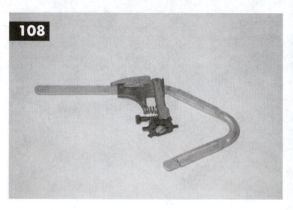

   a. Place the ring into the top end of the cylinder.

   b. Use the piston to drive the ring squarely into the cylinder until the beginning of the wrist pin bore is even with the top of the cylinder.

   c. Remove the piston.

   d. Using a feeler gauge, measure the end gap. The piston ring end gap specification is listed in **Table 5**.

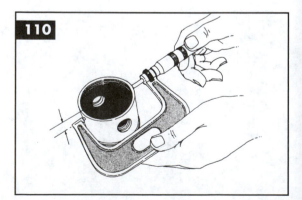

NOTE
Only the compression rings need to be gapped. The 3-piece oil-control ring is not gapped.

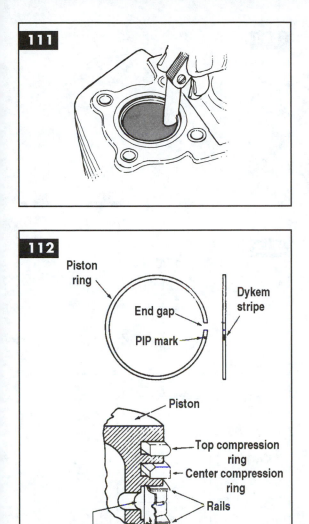

Assembly

A piston ring expander tool should be used to install the compression rings.

Prior to installing the rings, lubricate the ring grooves thoroughly with fresh engine oil.

When assembling piston rings on the piston, install the oil control ring first. To install the 3-piece oil-control ring, first install the expander, then install one end of each rail and carefully feed the rail into position with a light twisting motion. If there are instructions included with the replacement rings, precisely follow the instructions. The thin oil-control ring rails which fit over the expander are easily bent if not properly handled.

CAUTION
Do not overlap the ends of the oil-control ring expander when fitting the oil-control rails over the expander and do not use a bent oil-control ring rail.

1. Piston rings should be installed on the piston with the side of the ring marked "PIP" toward the piston crown and the colored Dykem stripe to the left of the end gap with the piston upright.(**Figure 112**).

2. For maximum engine power and longevity, as well as precise emission control, the ring end gaps should be spaced around the piston circumference in the approximate degreed intervals shown in **Figure 113**:

   a. An imaginary line drawn from the center of the piston to the 12 o'clock position is the 0°/360° base reference line. Degree readings will advance clockwise.

   b. The FLY mark on the piston head will *point to* the 0°/360° position.

   c. The top (No. 1) compression ring has a barrel-shaped face and a blue stripe. It should have its gap at the 90° position.

   d. The No. 2 compression ring (center groove) has a top bevel on the inside of the ring and a pink stripe. It should have its gap at the 270° position.

   e. The seam or gap of the oil-control ring expander should be in the 120° position.

   f. The top oil-control ring rail should have its gap at the 0°/360° position.

   g. The bottom oil-control ring rail should have its gap at the 240° position.

3. After the rings are installed on the piston, use a feeler gauge to measure the side (ring land) clearance (**Figure 114**). Ring land clearance dimensions are listed in **Table 5**. If they are beyond specification, replace the piston.

To install the piston in the engine, follow the necessary steps under *Engine Reassembly* in this chapter.

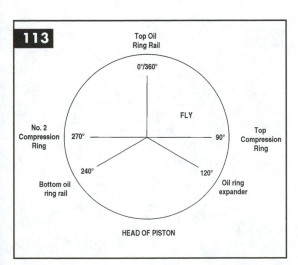

CYLINDER BLOCK/CRANKCASE

The cylinder is a cast iron alloy sleeve integrally cast into the aluminum alloy crankcase and block assembly.

To access the cylinder, follow the steps outlined in under *Engine Disassembly* in this chapter.

Pistons and ring sets are available in oversizes of 0.080 mm (0.003 in.), 0.25 mm (0.010 in.) and 0.50 mm (0.020 in.) to fit rebored cylinder bores.

Inspection and Reconditioning

1. Remove all gasket and sealant material from the sealing surfaces. Sealing surfaces must be free from nicks, gouges or deep scratches.
2. Inspect the fastener holes for damaged threads or broken fasteners.
   a. For broken fasteners, refer to *Removing Broken Fasteners* in Chapter One.
   b. For damaged threads, restore the threads with an appropriate size metric tap if necessary. If thread damage is severe, install a Heli-Coil or equivalent replacement thread. If the threaded holes cannot be satisfactorily repaired, replace the cylinder block.
3. Check for broken cooling fins. A small broken edge or corner may not affect performance. A large piece of broken-off fin will cause the cylinder to overheat. Replace the cylinder block if major fin damage is evident.
4. Check for debris packed in between the fins. Remove any heat-caked debris.
5. Check the bore for scoring.
6. Measure the bore and compare the measurements to the dimensions listed in **Table 5**.

If the cylinder has been previously rebored, the piston will be marked .080, .250 or .500 to show its oversize. A block whose cylinder will not clean up at .500 mm (0.020 in.) or one which has already been rebored to .500 mm and then worn beyond limits will need to be replaced.

> *NOTE*
> *Some oversized cylinder blocks and matching piston/ring assemblies were used in factory production. Factory-oversized engines are identified by a colored line painted along the top cooling fin, located at the side edge of the head gasket mount surface on the PTO side of the engine block. Red paint indicates a .080 mm (0.003 in.) oversize and blue paint indicates a .250 mm (0.010 in.) oversize. Factory oversizing must be taken into consideration when measuring the cylinder bore.*

When measuring a cylinder bore, six measurements must be taken to accurately determine the amount of wear in the bore (**Figure 115**). A telescoping bore gauge (**Figure 116**) or an inside micrometer can be used to precisely

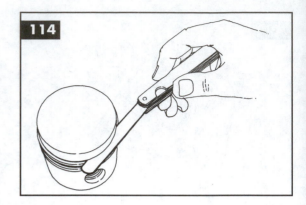

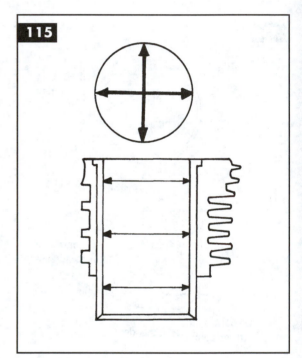

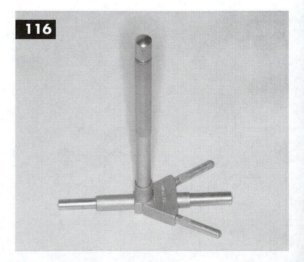

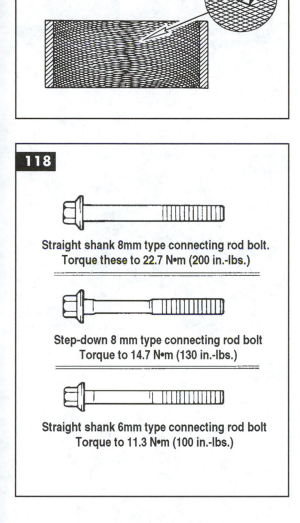

117

45°-50°

118

Straight shank 8mm type connecting rod bolt.
Torque these to 22.7 N•m (200 in.-lbs.)

Step-down 8 mm type connecting rod bolt
Torque to 14.7 N•m (130 in.-lbs.)

Straight shank 6mm type connecting rod bolt
Torque to 11.3 N•m (100 in.-lbs.)

6

honing. The crosshatch angle of the cylinder bore surface after finish-honing should be 45°-50° as shown in **Figure 117**.

After honing or reboring, wash the cylinder thoroughly in hot soapy water, then rise with clean warm water. Blow-dry with compressed air.

This will remove the microscopic grinding particles from the surface of the cylinder bore. A grease-cutting dishwash detergent is an excellent soap to use. Do not use petroleum solvents (mineral spirits, kerosene, etc.) to clean the bore. Solvents *will not remove* grinding dust from the cylinder bore surface.

After drying the cylinder, spray the bore with a moisture-displacing lubricant such as WD-40, then dry with a clean, lint-free cloth. Apply a light coat of engine oil to the bore to prevent rust.

CAUTION
Failure to properly clean a honed or rebored cylinder will cause rapid cylinder and piston wear and severe engine damage.

CONNECTING ROD

These engines use offset stepped-cap connecting rods.

NOTE
*Three different style connecting rod bolts are used. Each style bolt has a different tightening torque. Refer to **Figure 118** to identify the rod bolts and their respective torque values.*

Removal

The piston and connecting rod are removed as an assembly, then separated, as outlined under *Engine Disassembly* in this chapter.

Inspection

Connecting rod specifications are listed in **Table 5**. Replace the connecting rod if any dimensions do not meet specification.

1. The large-diameter connecting rod journal rides directly on the crankshaft crankpin (**Figure 119**). Inspect both the large and the small bearing surfaces for signs of scuffing, scoring, excessive wear or overheating. If any damage is observed, also inspect the surface of the mating crankpin or piston pin.

NOTE
If the rod bearing surface is worn due to abrasive particles (the surface texture is dull and rough), it should be replaced even if it is not worn beyond the specified

measure cylinder bores. Always follow the instructions included with the tool.

If the cylinder bore is within wear specifications, the bore will need to be honed so new rings will seat properly. The crosshatch angle of the bore surface after finish-honing should be 45°-50° as shown in **Figure 117**. Too large an angle will cause high oil consumption; too small an angle will make the rings skip and wear rapidly. Follow the hone manufacturer's instructions.

If the cylinder is being rebored oversize, rebore to the specified original-plus-oversize dimension. Do *not* "fit" the new bore dimension to the piston. If the reboring is done to specification, the assembly clearances will be correct. Follow the bore-machine manufacturer's instructions. The final step of a rebore should always be a finish *wear limit. Grit may be embedded in the aluminum, which will continue to cause wear on mating surfaces.*

2. Inspect the connecting rod for cracks, twisting and other damage.

3. Measure the connecting rod dimensions and clearances. The procedure for measuring connecting rod bearing clearance is outlined in the next section. Measure the connecting rod side clearance as follows:

    a. Install the connecting rod onto the crankshaft.

    b. Using a feeler gauge, measure the side clearance between the rod and the side of the crankpin.

Connecting Rod Bearing Clearance Measurement

Plastigage is the most popular and convenient way to measure connecting rod-to-crankshaft journal clearance. Plastigage comes in three sizes: 0.025-0.076 mm (0.001-0.003 inch); 0.051-0.152 mm (0.002-0.006 inch); and 0.102-0.229 mm (0.004-0.009 inch). To gauge the clearance:

1. Clean the crankshaft crankpin (**Figure 119**) and check for damage.

2. Position the connecting rod onto the crankshaft in the correct position on the crankpin (**Figure 120**).

3. Cut a strip of Plastigage slightly shorter than the width of the connecting rod/crankshaft journal (**Figure 120**). Place the Plastigage onto the crankpin. Make sure the Plastigage runs parallel to the crankshaft as shown in **Figure 120**. Do not place the Plastigage material over the oil hole in the crankshaft.

4. Correctly align the rod cap with the rod. Tighten the rod cap bolts to torque specification to compress the gauge.

CAUTION
When torquing the rod cap Plastigage, do not rotate the connecting rod or the crankshaft. Damaged Plastigage and inaccurate readings will result.

NOTE
*Three different style connecting rod bolts are used. Each style bolt has a different tightening torque. Refer to **Figure 119** to identify the rod bolts and their respective torque values.*

5. Loosen the cap bolts. Carefully lift the cap straight up and off the connecting rod.

6. Compare the flattened Plastigage width to the scale furnished with the Plastigage (**Figure 121**). This will tell the clearance.

    a. If clearance exceeds 0.070 mm (0.0025 in.), replace the connecting rod and recondition the crankshaft. A connecting rod with a 0.25 mm

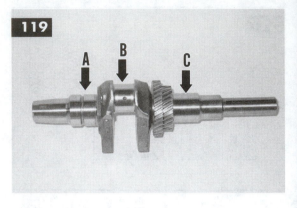

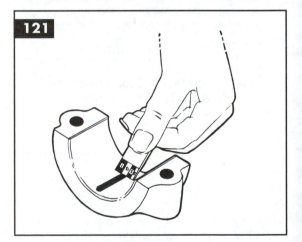

(0.010 in.) undersize crankshaft journal bore is available. The 0.25 mm (0.010 in.) undersize connecting rod is identified by a drilled hole in the connecting rod just above the big end bore (**Figure 122**).

    b. If the crankshaft must be reground to accept an undersize connecting rod, refer to the *Crankshaft* section for machining information.

7. Remove all of the Plastigage from the crankshaft and connecting rod.

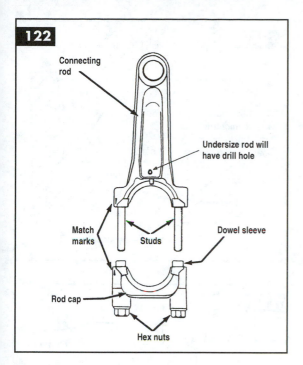

122

Connecting rod

Undersize rod will have drill hole

Match marks

Studs

Dowel sleeve

Rod cap

Hex nuts

123

Installation

To install the connecting rod into the engine, follow the necessary steps under *Engine Reassembly* in this chapter.

CRANKSHAFT AND MAIN BEARINGS

Some engines use a non-replaceable upper main bearing which is integral with and machined into the crankcase casting. Most late-model engines use a replaceable sleeve-style flywheel-side upper main bearing (2, **Figure 95**).

The lower main bearing is an integral part of the oil pan, machined into the oil pan casting (**Figure 100**).

The crankshaft is pictured in **Figure 119**.

NOTE
When replacing a crankshaft, short block, or engine, make sure that the threads on the PTO bolt which was removed from the old crankshaft are compatible with the threads in the new crankshaft. Some engines may have either metric or inch threads.

The crankshaft and main bearing specifications are listed in **Table 5**.

Removal

To remove the crankshaft, follow Steps 1-22 under *Engine Disassembly* in this chapter.

Inspection and Reconditioning

1. If considerable effort was required to remove the oil pan from the crankshaft, then the crankshaft is probably bent and must be discarded. If some effort was required during removal, then the crankshaft should be checked for straightness by a shop with the necessary equipment. If the oil pan was easy to remove, and the bearings are within specifications, then the crankshaft is probably straight. Crankshaft runout can be used as an indicator of crankshaft straightness. Proceed to Step 2 to measure runout.

2. Measure crankshaft runout using one of the following procedures:
   a. Install the crankshaft in the engine. Be sure the main bearings are lubricated. Measure crankshaft runout at the PTO end of the crankshaft.
   b. Support the crankshaft in V-blocks at the main bearing journals. **Figure 123** shows a typical crankshaft being checked for runout.

CAUTION
When using a dial indicator to check runout, exercise caution when the crankshaft keyway approaches the indicator anvil. Dial indicator damage could result if the keyway strikes the anvil.

   c. If runout exceeds the limit listed in **Table 5**, replace the crankshaft.

3. Inspect all bearing surfaces on the crankshaft for indications of scoring, scuffing or other damage. This includes the main and thrust bearing faces.

4. Check the fastener threads, such as the flywheel and PTO threads (**Figure 119**), for damage and cross-threading. Repair if possible.

5. Inspect the keyways and carefully remove any burrs. The keyways must be straight and unworn. The PTO extension must also be straight and unworn.

6

6. Check the crankshaft gears (**Figure 119**) for broken or pitted teeth. If the gear teeth are questionable, also inspect the camshaft and balance shaft gear teeth.

7. Measure the connecting rod (crankpin) journal (B, **Figure 119**). The crankpin journal diameter should be 38.958-38.970 mm (1.5338-1.5343 in.); regrind the crankshaft if the crankpin diameter is 38.94 mm (1.5328 in.) or less. If the crankpin journal is 0.0127 mm (0.0005 inch) or more out-of-round, or if the journal has 0.025 mm (0.001 inch) or more taper, regrind or replace the crankshaft.

A connecting rod with a 0.25 mm (0.010 inch) undersize crankshaft journal bore is available. The 0.25 mm (0.010 inch) undersize connecting rod is identified by a drilled hole in the connecting rod beam just above the big end bore (**Figure 122**).

> *NOTE*
> *If the crankpin is reground, the crankpin fillet should be machined as shown in **Figure 124**. If the crankpin is reground, the oil gallery plug must be removed, the gallery cleaned of all grinding debris, and a new plug installed. Refer to Steps 13 and 14.*

8. Measure the crankshaft main bearing journals:
   a. The flywheel end journal (A, **Figure 119**) should be 44.913-44.935 mm (1.7682-1.7691 in.). If the journal has worn to 44.84 mm (1.765 in.) or less, is 0.025 mm (.0010 in) out-of-round, or has at least 0.022 mm (.0009 in.) taper, replace the crankshaft.
   b. The PTO end journal (C, **Figure 119**) should be 41.915-41.935 mm (1.6502-1.6510 in.). If the journal has worn to 41.86 mm (1.648 in.) or less, is 0.025 mm (.0010 in.) out-of-round, or has at least 0.020 mm (.0008 in.) taper, replace the crankshaft.

9. The inside diameter of the upper main bearing, including a replaceable bearing measured after installation, should be 44.965-45.003 mm (1.7703-1.7718 in.).

10. If the upper main bearing journal was scored or galled and the bearing is replaceable, also inspect the main bearing bore in the crankcase. If the crankcase cavity is scored or galled from the main bearing insert spinning in the crankcase, the crankcase will have to be replaced.

11. Running clearance for both main bearings (main bearing diameter minus crankshaft journal diameter) should be 0.03-0.09 mm (0.0012-0.0035 in.).

12. To install the replaceable flywheel-end main bearing:
   a. Scribe a mark on the inside bearing bore face to show the location of the oil gallery hole (**Figure 125**).
   b. Install Handle No. NU-4747 onto Bearing Installer No. KO-1028.
   c. Install the new sleeve bearing onto KO-1028 with the bearing oil hole and the installer notch aligned.

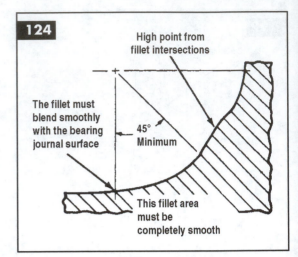

124

High point from fillet intersections

The fillet must blend smoothly with the bearing journal surface

45° Minimum

This fillet area must be completely smooth

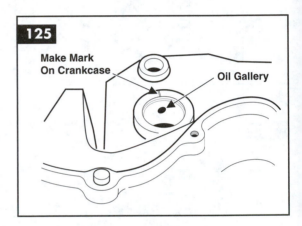

125

Make Mark On Crankcase

Oil Gallery

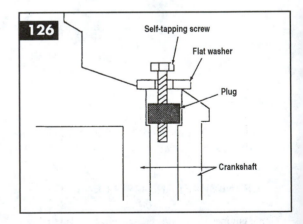

126

Self-tapping screw

Flat washer

Plug

Crankshaft

d. Position the installer with the bearing against the crankcase bore. Align the installer notch with the crankcase mark.
e. Press the bearing squarely into the crankcase until the tool bottoms against the bore face.
f. Remove the tool. Make sure the bearing oil hole is still aligned with the crankcase oil gallery.

127

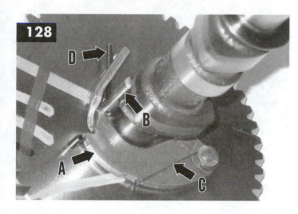

128

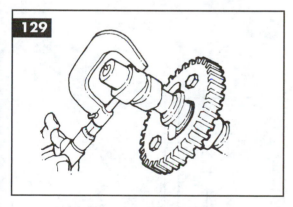

129

g. The bearing is ready for service. It does not require reaming.

13. To remove the crankshaft oil gallery plug (**Figure 126**):

a. Drill a 4.75 mm (3/16 in.) hole into the center of the plug.

b. Place a 4.75 mm (3/16 in.) flat washer over the end of the plug bore on the crankshaft.

c. Thread a 25 mm (1.0 in.) long self-tapping screw into the hole drilled into the plug.

d. Continue tightening the screw until the plug pulls out.

14. To install a new crankshaft oil gallery plug:

a. Make sure that the plug and bore are clean and dry.

b. Set the plug into the bore. Make sure that the closed end of the plug is at the bottom of the bore.

c. Using a Kohler camshaft pin (part No. 47 380 09) or a pin punch with a tip diameter just slightly smaller than the outside diameter of the plug, lightly tap the plug into the bore. Tap the plug evenly to prevent leakage and tap it until it seats completely at the bottom of the bore.

Installation

To install the crankshaft, follow the necessary steps in the *Engine Reassembly* section.

CAMSHAFT

The camshaft is shown in **Figure 127**. The camshaft bearings ride directly in bores machined into the crankcase and oil pan.

To remove the camshaft from the engine, follow the necessary steps in the *Engine Disassembly* section.

The camshaft is equipped with a compression release mechanism to aid starting (**Figure 128**). The pivoting weight mechanism (A, **Figure 128**) on the camshaft gear moves a pin (B) inside the exhaust cam lobe. During starting (RPM below 700), the pin protrudes above the bottom of the cam lobe and forces the exhaust valve to stay open longer, thereby reducing compression from the normal 8.5:1 to approximately 2:1. At running speed, centrifugal force causes the weight to pivot outward, pulling the pin arm (D, **Figure 128**) and moving the pin. This keeps the pin below the surface of the cam lobe, allowing the engine to develop full power.

Camshaft specifications are listed in **Table 5**.

1. Inspect the gear teeth for wear and cracked or broken teeth. If any teeth are damaged, the camshaft will have to be replaced.

2. Inspect the camshaft for cracks. Replace a cracked camshaft.

3. Inspect the camshaft journals and lobes for wear or scoring.

4. Measure the journals and lobes. Compare the measurements to the Table 5 dimensions.

5. Measure the lift height of the intake and exhaust lobes. Compare the measurements to the **Table 5** dimensions. To determine lift height:

a. Measure across the lift part of the lobe (**Figure 129**).

b. Measure across the narrow diameter of the lobe.

c. Subtract the measurement in substep a from the measurement in substep b.

6. Inspect the camshaft bearing surfaces in the crankcase and oil pan. The surfaces must be smooth with no signs of abrasion.

6

7. Measure the camshaft bearing bore diameters in the crankcase and oil pan. Compare the measurements to the **Table 5** dimensions.

8. Inspect the compression release mechanism. The mechanism should move freely without binding. The only replaceable component of the compression release is the spring for the pivoting weight.

9. Install the camshaft into the engine, following the necessary steps in the *Engine Reassembly* section.

COUNTERBALANCE SHAFT

Engine vibration is reduced through the use of a counterbalance shaft (**Figure 130**). The shaft gear has the same number of teeth as the crankshaft gear which drives it, thereby making it turn at the same speed as the crankshaft, only in the opposite direction. The machined-flat lower end of the shaft drives the oil pump.

To remove the balance shaft from the engine, follow the necessary steps in the *Engine Disassembly* section.

Balance shaft specifications are listed in **Table 5**.

1. Inspect the gear teeth for wear and cracked or broken teeth. If any teeth are damaged, the shaft will have to be replaced.

2. Inspect the balance shaft for cracks. Replace a cracked shaft.

3. Inspect the balance shaft journals (A, **Figure 130**) for wear or scoring.

4. Measure the journals. Compare the measurements to the **Table 5** dimensions.

5. Inspect the balance shaft bearing surfaces in the crankcase and oil pan. The surfaces must be smooth with no signs of abrasion.

6. Measure the balance shaft bearing bore diameters in the crankcase and oil pan. Compare the measurements to the **Table 5** dimensions.

To install the balance shaft into the engine, follow the necessary steps in the *Engine Reassembly* section.

GOVERNOR INTERNAL SERVICE

The engine is equipped with a flyweight mechanism mounted (A, **Figure 131**) on the governor gear (B). Gear and flyweight are available only as a unit assembly.

The governor gear assembly is mounted onto a shaft which is pressed-in to the crankcase (**Figure 132**). To remove the governor assembly from the engine, follow the necessary steps in the previous *Engine Disassembly* section.

> *NOTE*
> *The governor gear has small tabs molded internally which hold it onto the shaft. Removing the gear assembly destroys these tabs. If the gear assembly is removed, it*

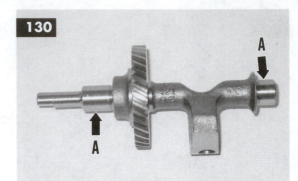

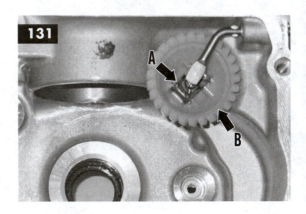

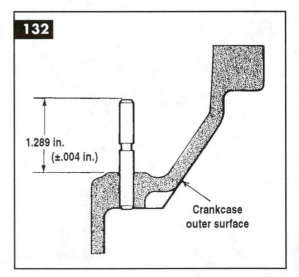

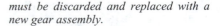

must be discarded and replaced with a new gear assembly.

Inspect the gear assembly for excess wear and damage. Governor specifications are listed in **Table 5**.

If the governor gear shaft requires replacement:

1. Locate the end of the shaft on the flywheel side of the crankcase (**Figure 132**).

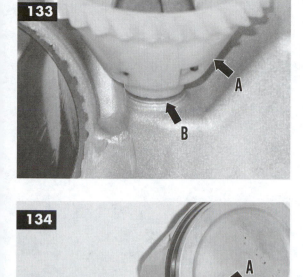

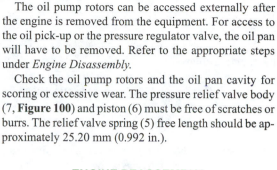

2. Using a pin punch with a smaller diameter than the shaft, carefully tap or press the shaft into the crankcase.

CAUTION
Do not remove the shaft with vise grips or pliers from inside the crankcase. Do not gouge the crankcase bore when driving the shaft into the crankcase. Do not remove the shaft by pushing the shaft to the outside of the crankcase. Damage to the crankcase will result.

3. Tap the new shaft into the bore from inside the crankcase so it protrudes 32.64-32.84 mm (1.285-1.293 in.) above crankcase face (**Figure 132**).

4. Install a new governor thrust washer (B, **Figure 133**) and gear assembly onto the shaft (A). Make sure that the internal gear locks snap into position and that the gear assembly rotates freely.

5. Installation of the remaining governor components is covered under *Engine Reassembly* in this chapter.

OIL PUMP

A gerotor-type oil pump is located in the oil pan. **Figure 102** shows a late style design with the pump rotors mounted in the pan. **Figure 100** shows the early-style

O-ring and cover. The oil pump is driven by the engine balance shaft.

The oil pump rotors can be accessed externally after the engine is removed from the equipment. For access to the oil pick-up or the pressure regulator valve, the oil pan will have to be removed. Refer to the appropriate steps under *Engine Disassembly.*

Check the oil pump rotors and the oil pan cavity for scoring or excessive wear. The pressure relief valve body (7, **Figure 100**) and piston (6) must be free of scratches or burrs. The relief valve spring (5) free length should be approximately 25.20 mm (0.992 in.).

ENGINE REASSEMBLY

1. Fit the new flywheel-side main bearing into the crankcase as noted in Step 12 under *Crankshaft and Main Bearings.*

2. Install the governor gear assembly into the crankcase as noted in the *Governor, Internal Service* section.

3. Fit the flange of the governor pin spool into the governor gear flyweights. Push the spool all the way down so the weights come together.

4. Fit a new governor cross shaft seal onto the oil seal installer tool (Kohler part No. KO-1030). Press the seal into the crankcase bore (**Figure 107**).

5. Install the small inner washer onto the governor cross shaft (**Figure 106**). Lightly lubricate the lip of the shaft seal with fresh engine oil, then insert the shaft through the oil pan bore from the inside. Carefully work the shaft back and forth as it goes through the seal to prevent damaging the seal lip. Make sure that the shaft paddle fits against the pin spool.

6. Install the large outer washer onto the exposed end of the governor shaft, followed by the hitch pin clip (**Figure 105**).

7. Lubricate the flywheel end main bearing and the flywheel end main bearing journal of the crankshaft with fresh engine oil. Install the crankshaft into the crankcase.

8. Assemble the piston rings to the piston as noted in the *Piston, Rings, and Pin* section.

9. Assemble the connecting rod to the piston.
   a. With the "FLY" mark (A, **Figure 134**) on the piston crown pointing toward the flywheel, the flat side of the connecting rod cap mating area (B) should be on the balance shaft side of the engine.
   b. Lubricate the wrist pin and the piston and rod pin bores with fresh engine oil.
   c. Insert the wrist pin through the piston and rod.
   d. Install the wrist pin retainers into the piston grooves (**Figure 104**).

CAUTION
Make sure that the retainer gap is at either the top or bottom of the piston. Installing the retainers with the gap towards the

6

sides could cause the retainers to work loose, resulting in serious engine damage.

10. Rotate the crankshaft so the connecting rod journal is at BDC.

11. Install the piston and connecting rod assembly into the engine as follows:

    a. Lubricate the cylinder bore, piston, rings, connecting rod bearing and crankshaft rod journal liberally with fresh engine oil.

    b. Make sure that the rings are still correctly staggered.

    c. Using a full-band ring compressor (**Figure 135**), compress the piston rings so the bottom oil-control ring is approximately 6 mm (1/4 inch) above the lower edge of the ring compressor.

    d. Position the connecting rod and lower part of the piston into the cylinder bore. Make sure that the FLY mark on the piston crown is pointing toward the flywheel. Rest the ring compressor on the top of the cylinder. Make sure that the compressor is seated against the cylinder around its entire perimeter.

    e. Tap the piston into the cylinder bore with the handle of a soft, rubber-grip hammer. The first tap should be quick and firm so the oil-control ring passes into the cylinder quickly without springing out of the compressor and binding.

    f. Taking care to align the crankshaft journal with the connecting rod bearing, continue pressing the piston/rod assembly into the engine until the rod bearing mates with the crankshaft journal. Do not allow the rod to nick the journal.

    g. Lubricate the connecting rod cap bearing. Align the rod cap onto the rod.

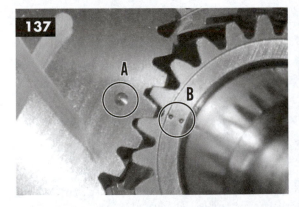

    h. Refer to **Figure 118** and determine which style of rod bolts the engine uses. Insert the rod bolts into the rod. Torque the bolts incrementally to the specification listed in **Figure 118**.

12. Rotate the crankshaft so the piston is at TDC.

13. Lubricate the upper balance shaft bearing and the matching crankcase bore with fresh oil. Insert the balance shaft into the crankcase, aligning the timing marks on the large crankshaft gear (A, **Figure 136**) and the balance shaft gear (B).

14. Lubricate the upper camshaft bearing and the matching crankcase bore with fresh oil. Insert the camshaft into the crankcase, aligning the timing marks on the small crankshaft gear (B, **Figure 137**) and the camshaft gear (A).

15. After Step 14, the crankcase should appear as in **Figure 138**.

16. Install the oil pressure relief valve components into the oil pan (4 and 7, **Figure 100**).

    a. Install the valve body first, followed by the piston and spring. The closed end of the piston fits down into the valve body.

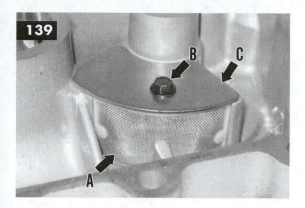

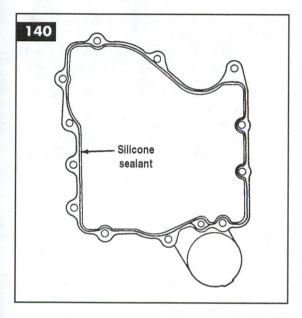

Silicone sealant

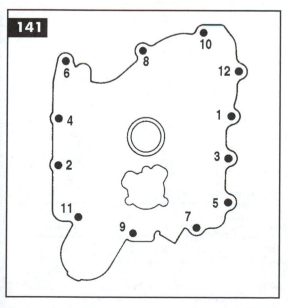

b. The bracket top should push down against the top of the valve body.

c. Make sure that the bracket screw threads and matching oil pan threads are clean and dry.

d. Lightly coat the screw threads with Loctite 242 or equivalent.

e. Secure the bracket with the hex flange screw.

17. Install the oil pick-up screen (A, **Figure 139**) and cover (C) into the oil pan.

a. Make sure that the cover screw threads (B, **Figure 139**) and the matching oil pan threads are clean and dry.

b. Lightly coat the screw threads with Loctite 242 or equivalent.

c. Install the screen, cover and cover screw. Tighten the screw.

18. If the camshaft used a spacer washer and the original crankcase, camshaft and oil pan are all being reused, place the washer onto the camshaft and prepare to install the oil pan.

19. If either the camshaft, oil pan or crankcase has been replaced, camshaft end play must be measured:

a. Install end play tool (Kohler part No. KO-1031) onto the crankcase in its proper position. Follow the instructions which come with the tool.

b. Using feeler gauges, measure camshaft end play. End play should be 0.076-0.127 mm (0.003-0.005 in.).

c. If end play is beyond specifications, determine from the measurement and the required end play specification the thickness of the necessary shim washer. Obtain the correct washer(s) from an authorized Kohler source of supply. Seven different thickness washers are available.

20. Install the oil pan:

a. Make sure that the oil pan and crankcase sealing surfaces are clean and dry.

b. No gasket is used between the crankcase and oil pan. Apply a 1.6 mm (1/16 in.) bead of silicone sealant to the *oil pan* sealing surface as shown in **Figure 140**. Approved sealants are listed in **Table 6**. Always follow the sealant manufacturer's instructions, especially regarding shelf life.

c. Make sure that the oil pan bolt threads and matching crankcase thread holes are clean and dry.

d. Lightly lubricate the crankshaft, camshaft and balance shaft bearing journals with fresh engine oil.

e. Lightly lubricate the crankshaft, camshaft and balance shaft bearing bores in the oil pan with fresh engine oil.

f. Fit the oil pan onto the crankcase.

g. Install the 12 oil pan bolts finger tight.

h. Torque the pan bolts in 6.0 N·m (50 in.-lb.) increments to a final torque of 24.4 N·m (216 in.-lb.), using the torque sequence shown in **Figure 141**.

21. Install the oil pump:

6

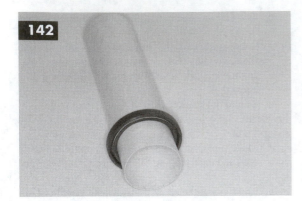

a. Lubricate the pump rotors and oil pan cavity with fresh engine oil.

b. Install the inner rotor into the cavity, onto the pump shaft. Install the outer rotor over the inner rotor.

c. Install the O-ring into the pan groove. **Figure 102** shows the late-style pump components assembled.

d. Install the pump cover with the machined side toward the rotors.

e. Make sure that the cover screw threads and the matching holes in the oil pan are clean and dry. Install and torque the three cover screws. If the screws are being reinstalled into a used pan, torque the screws to 4.0 N·m (35 in.-lb.). If the screws are being installed for the first time in a new oil pan, torque the screws to 6.2 N·m (55 in.-lb.).

22. Install the oil seals:

a. Generously lubricate the space between the oil seal lips with a light grease.

b. Slide the oil seal onto the end of the seal protector sleeve (Kohler part No. KO-1037) with the open,

spring-loaded side of the seal at the short end of the protector (**Figure 142**).

c. Slide the oil-seal end of the protector over the crankshaft until the seal contacts the engine seal bore. The closed, marked side of the seal must face out, away from the engine. The open, spring-loaded side of the seal will fit into the engine.

d. Hold the seal against the engine while sliding the seal protector off the seal and crankshaft.

e. Using Seal Driver No. KO-1027 with Handle No. KO-1036, install the seal into the seal bore until the *driver* bottoms against the crankcase or oil pan.

23. While holding the governor cross shaft (A, **Figure 143**) as far counterclockwise as it will go, install the governor lever arm (B) in the approximate position shown. Finger- tighten the nut (C, **Figure 143**) to prevent the arm from slipping off. Final tightening will be done when all of the linkage is installed.

24. Finish installing the external engine components by following the instructions in each appropriate component installation section.

Table 1 GENERAL ENGINE SPECIFICATIONS

Model	No. Cyls.	Bore	Stroke	Displacement	Power Rating
CV14	1	87 mm (3.43 in.)	67 mm (2.64 in.)	398 cc (24.3 cu. in.)	14 hp 10.5 kW
CV15	1	90 mm (3.55 in)	67 mm (2.64 in.)	426 cc (26.0 cu. in.)	15 hp 11.2 kW

Table 2 MAINTENANCE AND LUBRICATION SCHEDULE AND RECOMMENDATIONS

Except for the initial break-in period, the following recommendations are minimums. If the unit is being used in severe duty such as on dusty or sandy ground, in tall grass and weeds, or on rough terrain, maintenance should be performed more often. For engine lubricant recommendations, refer to the following Engine Lubricant table.

After 5-hour break-in period (new unit; new or overhauled engine)	Change the engine oil and the oil filter. Check all the fasteners and the linkages for security.
Every 8 hours or daily	Check the engine oil with the unit sitting level. Do not overfill. Check and/or clean the air filter.
Every 40-50 hours or weekly	Service the air cleaner pre-filter. On electric-start units, check the battery electrolyte level. Lubricate the throttle and choke cables.
Every 100 hours or semi-monthly	Replace the air filter and pre-filter. Change the engine oil and oil filter.
Every 500 hours or annually	Replace the fuel filter and fuel hoses. Remove cylinder heads and decarbon combustion chamber. Check all of the fasteners for proper security.

6

Table 3 RECOMMENDED ENGINE LUBRICANTS, INCLUDING CAPACITIES

Fuel capacity - approximately 5.0 U.S. gallons (18.7 liters or 4.0 Imperial gallons)	
Engine oil	API service rating of SH or above
Kohler CV	
Above 32° F (0° C)	SAE 10W-30
Between 32° F and 0° F (0° C and -18° C)	SAE 10W-30, 5W-20, or 5W-30
Below 0° F (-18° C)	SAE 5W-20 or 5W-30
Capacity with filter - 2.1 quarts (2.0 liters)	

NOTE: Do not use 10W-40 oil in the engine. Recommended engine oil viscosities are for petroleum-based oils. Comparable synthetic oils may be used. DO NOT MIX synthetic oil with petroleum oil. In new or overhauled engines or short blocks, use SAE 10W-30 oil for the first 5 hours of operation, then change oil according to ambient temperature requirements. The recommended oil change interval after the 5-hour break-in period is every 100 hours of operation. The oil should be drained while the engine is warm for the most effective crankcase sludge removal.

Table 4 FASTENER TIGHTENING TORQUES

Fastener	Metric	American Standard
Spark plug	38-43 N·m	(335-385 in.-lb. or 28-32 ft.-lb.)
Air filter base	9.9 N·m	(88 in.-lb.)
Alternator stator	4.0 N·m	(35 in.-lb.)
Carburetor		
Fuel bowl nut	5.1-6.2 N·m	(45-55 in.-lb.)
Shutter plate screws		
(choke and throttle)	0.9-1.4 N·m	(8-12 in.-lb.)
Main fuel jet (fixed jet)	1.4-1.8 N·m	(12-16 in.-lb.)
	(continued)	

Table 4   FASTENER TIGHTENING TORQUES (continued)

Fastener	Metric	American Standard
Connecting rod (See text)		
8 mm straight-shank bolt	22.6 N·m	(200 in.-lb.)
Step-down shank bolt	14.7 N·m	(130 in.-lb.)
6 mm straight-shank bolt	11.3 N·m	(100 in.-lb.)
Crankcase cover/oil pan	24.4 N·m	(216 in.-lb.)
Cylinder head	40.7 N·m	(360 in.-lb. or 30 ft.-lb.)
Rocker arm pedestal	9.9 N·m	(88 in.-lb.)
Flywheel	66.4 N·m	(49 ft.-lb.)
Flywheel fan	9.9 N·m	(88 in.-lb.)
Fuel pump screws*	7.3/9.0 N·m	(65/80 in.-lb.)
Governor control lever	9.9 N·m	(88 in.-lb.)
Governor speed control bracket*	7.3/10.7 N·m	(65/95 in.-lb.)
Ignition module*	4.0/6.2 N·m	(35/55 in.-lb.)
Muffler	24.4 N·m	(216 in.-lb.)
Oil pump cover*	4.0/6.2 N·m	(35/55 in.-lb.)
Oil filter drain plug (1/8 in. NPT)	7.3-9.0 N·m	(65-80 in.-lb.)
Oil Sentry(tm) pressure switch	7.9 N·m	(70 in.-lb.)
Oil filter	5.7-9.0 N·m	(50-80 in.-lb.)
Starter drive pinion	15.3 N·m	(135 in.-lb.)
Valve cover*	7.3/10.7 N·m	(65/95 in.-lb.)
Fasteners not listed	Refer to Chapter One, Tables 4-9	

*When installing self-tapping fasteners into new unthreaded holes, use higher torque value; use lower torque value for installation into previously tapped holes and weld nuts.

Table 5   ENGINE CLEARANCES AND SPECIFICATIONS

Angle of Operation: Maximum angle; Full oil level; All directions		
Intermittent operation	35°	
Continuous operation	20°	
Compression		
Ratio	8.5:1	
Pressure	85+ psi	
Oil pressure		
Cold engine at start-up	Up to 60 psi	
Hot engine at idle	Down to 18 psi	
Balance shaft		
End bearing diameters		
New	19.962-19.975 mm	(0.7859-0.7864 inch)
Wear limit	19.959 mm	(0.7858 inch)
Bearing bore diameters		
New	20.000-20.025 mm	(0.7874-0.7884 inch)
Wear limit	20.038 mm	(0.7889 inch)
Running clearance	0.025-0.063 mm	(0.0009-0.0025 inch)
End play	0.0575-0.3625 mm	(0.0023-0.0143 inch)
Camshaft		
End bearing diameters		
New	19.962-19.975 mm	(0.7859-0.7864 inch)
Wear limit	19.959 mm	(0.7858 inch)
Bearing bore diameters		
New	20.000-20.025 mm	(0.7874-0.7884 inch)
Wear limit	20.038 mm	(0.7889 inch)
End play	0.076-0.127 mm	(0.003-.005 inch)
Running clearance	0.025-0.063 mm	(0.0010-.0025 inch)
	(continued)	

Table 5   ENGINE CLEARANCES AND SPECIFICATIONS (continued)

Lobe height (minimum lift)		
Intake	8.96 mm	(0.353 inch)
Exhaust	9.14 mm	(0.360 inch)
Carburetor		
Initial idle-mixture screw setting	One turn open	
Float level	Non-adjustable	
Connecting rod		
Crankpin clearance, new	0.030-0.055 mm	(.0012-.0022 inch)
Crankpin clearance limit	0.070 mm	(.0025 inch)
Crankpin side play	0.18-0.41 mm	(.007-.016 inch)
Wrist pin bore inside diameter		
New	19.015-19.023 mm	(0.7486-0.7489 inch)
Wear limit	19.036 mm	(0.7495 inch)
Wrist pin clearance, new	0.015-0.028 mm	(.0006-.0011 inch)
Crankshaft		
End play	0.0575-0.4925 mm	(.0023-.0194 inch)
Main bearing journal, flywheel end		
New outside diameter	44.913-44.935 mm	(1.7682-1.7691 inches)
Wear limit	44.84 mm	(1.765 inches)
Out of round	0.025 mm	(.0010 inch)
Taper	0.022 mm	(.0009 inch)
Main bearing journal, PTO end		
New outside diameter	41.915-41.935	(1.6502-1.6510 inches)
Wear limit	41.86 mm	(1.648 inches)
Out of round	0.025 mm	(.0010 inch)
Taper	0.020 mm	(.0008 inch)
Crankpin		
New outside diameter	38.958-38.970 mm	(1.5338-1.5343 inch)
Wear limit	38.94 mm	(1.5328 inch)
Out of round	0.0127 mm	(.0005 inch)
Taper	0.025 mm	(.0010 inch)
Top main or sleeve bearing		
Inside diameter, new, installed	44.965-45.003 mm	(1.7703-1.7718 inch)
Maximum wear limit	45.016 mm	(1.7723 inch)
Running clearance, new	0.03-0.09 mm	(.0012-.0035 inch)
Oil pan bearing		
Running clearance, new	0.03-0.09 mm	(.0012-.0035 inch)
Total indicated runout		
PTO end with crankshaft in engine	0.15 mm	(.0059 inch)
Crankshaft only, in V-blocks	0.10 mm	(.0039 inch)
Cylinder bore:		
New inside diameter		
CV14	87.000-87.025 mm	(3.4252-3.4262 inches)
CV15	90.000-90.025 mm	(3.5433-3.5443 inches)
Wear limit		
CV14	87.063 mm	(3.4277 inches)
CV15	90.63 mm	(3.5681 inches)
Out of round	0.12 mm	(.0047 inch)
Taper	0.05 mm	(.002 inch)
Cylinder head warpage, maximum	0.076 mm	(.003 inch)
Governor		
Gear shaft diameter		
New	5.990-6.000 mm	(0.2358-0.2362 inch)
Wear limit	5.977 mm	(0.2353 inch)
Gear shaft-to-gear running clearance	0.015-0.140 mm	(0.0006-0.0055 inch)
Cross shaft diameter		
New	5.975-6.000 mm	(0.2352-0.2362 inch)
Wear limit	5.962 mm	(0.2347 inch)

(continued)

6

Table 5   ENGINE CLEARANCES AND SPECIFICATIONS (continued)

Cross shaft bore diameter		
New	6.025-6.050 mm	(0.2372-0.2382 inch)
Wear limit	6.063 mm	(0.2387 inch)
Cross shaft running clearance,		
Shaft-to-crankcase bore	0.025-0.075 mm	(0.0010-0.0030 inch)
Ignition		
Module to flywheel magnet air gap	0.20-0.31 mm	(0.008-0.012 inch)
Spark plug gap	1.02 mm	(0.040 inch)
Oil pump		
Pressure relief valve spring length	25.2 mm	(0.992 inch)
Piston		
Thrust face diameter (See text)		
New		
CV14	86.941-86.959 mm	(3.4229-3.4236 inches)
CV15	89.951-89.961 mm	(3.5413-3.5420 inches)
Wear limit		
CV14	86.814 mm	(3.4179 inches)
CV15	89.824 mm	(3.5363 inches)
Running clearance at thrust face(new)		
CV14	0.041-0.044 mm	(.0016-.0017 inch)
CV15	0.031-0.043 mm	(.0012-.0016 inch)
Piston rings		
End gap (compression rings)		
New		
CV14	0.3-0.5 mm	(0.012-0.020 inch)
CV15	0.27-0.5 mm	(0.010-0.020 inch)
Used limit	0.77 mm	(0.030 inch)
Ring land clearance		
Top compression ring		
CV14	0.040-0.105 mm	(0.0016-0.0041 inch)
CV15	0.060-0.105 mm	(0.0023-0.0041 inch)
Middle compression ring		
CV14	0.040-0.072 mm	(0.0016-0.0028 inch)
CV15	0.040-0.085 mm	(0.0015-0.0032 inch)
Oil-control ring		
CV14	0.551-0.675 mm	(0.0217-0.0266 inch)
CV15	0.026-0.176 mm	(0.0010-0.0069 inch)
Piston pin		
Diameter		
New	18.995-19.000 mm	(0.7478-0.7480 inch)
Wear limit	18.994 mm	(0.74779 inch)
Bore inside diameter (piston)		
New	19.006-19.012 mm	(0.7483-0.7485 inch)
Wear limit	19.025 mm	(0.7490 inch)
Selective fit, piston-to-pin	0.006-0.017 mm	(0.0002-0.0007 inch)
Rocker arms		
Inside diameter		
New	15.837-16.127 mm	(0.624-0.635 inch)
Wear limit	16.13 mm	(0.637 inch)
Rocker shaft diameter		
New	15.85-15.90 mm	(0.624-0.626 inch)
Wear limit	15.727 mm	(0.619 inch)
Valves		
Cam lobe lift, minimum		
Intake	8.96 mm	(0.353 inch)
Exhaust	9.14 mm	(0.360 inch)
Stem-to-guide running clearance (cold)		
Intake	0.038-0.076 mm	(0.0015-0.0030 inch)
Exhaust	0.050-0.088 mm	(0.0020-0.0035 inch)

(continued)

Table 5 ENGINE CLEARANCES AND SPECIFICATIONS (continued)

Guide reamer size		
Standard	7.048 mm	(0.2775 inch)
0.25 mm oversize	7.298 mm	(0.2873 inch)
Valve guide inside diameter		
Intake		
New	7.038-7.058 mm	(0.2771-0.2779 inch)
Wear limit	7.134 mm	(0.2809 inch)
Exhaust		
New	7.038-7.058 mm	(0.2771-0.2779 inch)
Wear limit	7.159 mm	(0.2819 inch)
Valve stem diameter (new, standard)		
Intake	6.982-7.000 mm	(0.2749-0.2756 inch)
Exhaust	6.970-6.988 mm	(0.2744-0.2751 inch)
Seat angle		
Intake	89°	
Exhaust	89°	

6

Table 6 VALVE SYSTEM DIMENSIONS

Ref.	Description	Dimension
A	Seat Angle	89
B	Insert O.D.	
	Intake	37.987-38.017 mm (1.4956-1.4967 in.)
	Exhaust	33.987-34.013 mm (1.3381-1.3391 in.)
C	Guide depth	6.5 mm (0.256 in.)
D	Guide I.D.	7.033-7.068 mm (0.2769-0.2779 in.)
E	Valve head diameter	
	Intake	35.37-35.63 mm (1.392-1.402 in.)
	Exhaust	31.37-31.63 mm (1.235-1.245 in.)
F	Valve Face Angle	45
G	Valve Margin (Min.)	1.5 mm (0.060 in.)
H	Valve Stem Diameter	
	Intake	6.982-7.000 mm (0.2749-0.2755 in.)
	Exhaust	6.97-6.988 mm (0.2745-0.2751 in.)

CHAPTER SEVEN

KOHLER CV20S ENGINE

ENGINE IDENTIFICATION

The Model CV20S is a four-stroke, twin-cylinder, overhead-valve, vertical crankshaft, air-cooled engine. The No. 1 cylinder is the cylinder closest to the flywheel. The cylinder numbers are marked on the side of the cylinders facing the flywheel. The engine is pressure lubricated and equipped with an oil filter. The Tables at the end of this chapter contain the engine specifications.

Engine identification and serial numbers are located on a decal mounted on the side of the blower housing or cylinder shroud as shown in **Figure 1**. Refer to **Figure 2** to determine engine features and date of manufacture.

The next two sections provide information on removing and installing the engine as a complete, assembled unit. Subsequent sections provide disassembly, inspection, adjustment, repair/overhaul and reassembly information for the engine components.

The engine must be removed from the equipment before undertaking repairs on the internal components. In the case of external components such as the carburetor or a cylinder head, engine removal may not be necessary, as the repair job may be performed with the engine mounted on the equipment.

Kohler tools, or suitable equivalent, may be recommended for some procedures. Good quality tools are also available from small-engine parts suppliers. Be careful when substituting a homemade tool for a recommended tool. Although time and money may be saved by substituting a tool, consider the possibilities if the tool does not work properly. If the substitute tool damages the engine,

the cost to repair the damage, as well as the lost time, may exceed the cost of the recommended tool.

NOTE
Metric fasteners are used throughout this engine, except for the 7/16"-20 threaded hole that holds the PTO clutch onto the bottom of the crankshaft on some engines. The puller holes in the flywheel might also be inch-size threads. Check thread compatibility before installing a fastener to prevent cross-threading.

ENGINE REMOVAL

Prior to removing the engine, drain the crankcase oil. Always drain the oil with the engine warm so the oil flows freely and carries out the dirt and impurities.

2

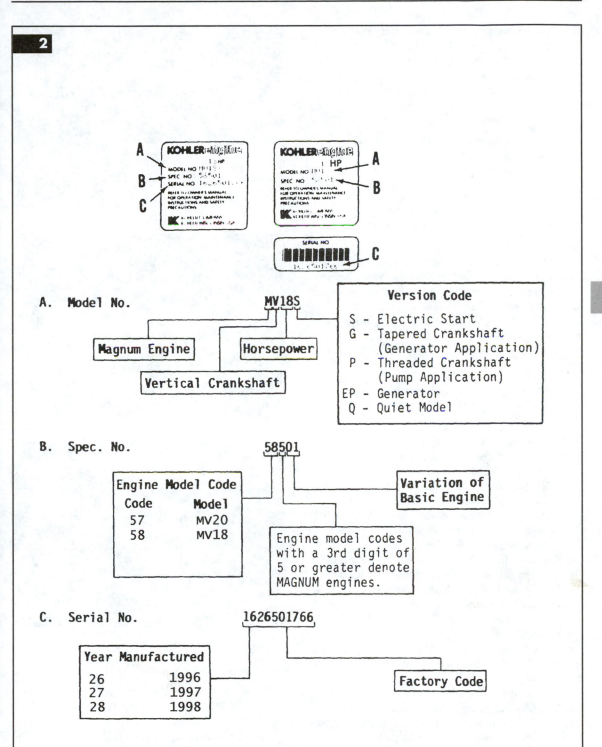

7

A. Model No. MV18S

Magnum Engine	Horsepower
Vertical Crankshaft	

Version Code

S - Electric Start
G - Tapered Crankshaft
    (Generator Application)
P - Threaded Crankshaft
    (Pump Application)
EP - Generator
Q - Quiet Model

B. Spec. No. 58501

Engine Model Code

Code	Model
57	MV20
58	MV18

Variation of
Basic Engine

Engine model codes
with a 3rd digit of
5 or greater denote
MAGNUM engines.

C. Serial No. 1626501766

Year Manufactured

26	1996
27	1997
28	1998

Factory Code

1. Allow the engine to cool to ambient temperature.

2. Engage the parking brake.

3. Disconnect the battery cables, negative terminal first, and remove the battery.

4. Close the fuel tank valve (**Figure 3**).

> *WARNING*
> *Some gasoline will drain from the fuel hose during the next procedure. Wipe up any spilled gasoline immediately. Work in a well-ventilated area at least 50 feet away from any open flame, including pilot lights in gas appliances. Do not allow anyone to smoke in the area. Do not work near grinding or any other source of sparks.*

5. Detach the fuel hose clamp at the inlet connection to the fuel pump. Disconnect the fuel hose from the pump.

6. Disconnect the spark plug wire from the spark plug. Ground the spark plug wire to the engine.

7. Identify and unplug the chassis wiring harness connectors and the starter motor cable.

8. Disconnect the throttle and choke control cables.

> *NOTE*
> *Prior to removal, cable positions should be marked for proper reconnection during engine installation.*

9. Remove the deck drive belt shield, then slacken the belt running from the engine as follows:
   a. On fixed-idler drives (**Figure 4**), back off the idler adjusting nut to allow slack in the belt.
   b. On spring-loaded idler drives, like that in **Figure 5**, move the idler pulley bracket away from the belt. Secure the bracket to allow slack in the belt, or work the belt off the idler.

10. Chock the front wheels. Raise and support the rear of the mower to gain access to the underside of the engine.

11. Unplug the PTO clutch wire connector (**Figure 5**). Remove the bolt retaining the clutch to the crankshaft. Slide the clutch off the shaft and remove the belt from the clutch pulley.

12. Move the hydrostatic drive idler pulley away from the drive belt so the belt slackens. Work the belt off the engine pulley.

13. Remove the engine mounting bolts.

14. Carefully lift the engine off the frame.

15. Note the position and orientation of the hydrostat pulley on the crankshaft. Remove the pulley.

16. Clean the engine mounting area on the frame.

ENGINE INSTALLATION

1. Make sure the engine mounting areas on both the frame and the bottom of the engine are clean and dry.

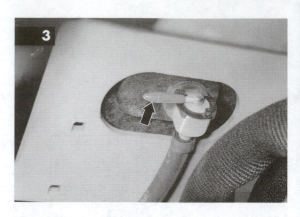

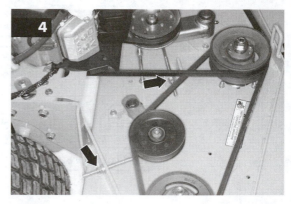

2. Lightly coat the crankshaft, including keyway, with anti-seize compound.

3. Install the hydrostat pulley on the crankshaft in the same position and orientation as that noted during removal.

4. Carefully set the engine in position on the frame. Ensure that the engine pan and frame fastener holes align.

5. Apply Loctite 271 or equivalent to the engine mount fastener threads. Tighten the fasteners securely. On fasteners with lock washers, use new lock washers.

6. Install the hydrostat belt onto the pulleys, then allow the spring-loaded idler to exert tension on the belt.

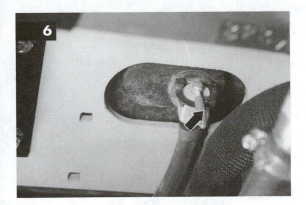

7. Insert the PTO clutch belt into the clutch pulley groove. Align the clutch locator bracket, ensuring that the clutch wire is not pinched or kinked. Align the clutch key with the crankshaft keyway, then slide the clutch onto the crankshaft. While supporting the clutch, install the clutch bolt. Using the torque tables at the end of Chapter One, tighten the clutch bolt.

8. Lower the mower onto the floor. Make sure that the parking brake is still set, then remove the front wheel chocks.

9. Reapply tension to the deck drive belt.

　a. On fixed-idler drives, refer to the adjustment procedure under *Drive Belts* in Chapter Three to properly tension the belt.

　b. On spring-loaded idlers, no adjustment is required.

10. Install the deck drive belt shield.

11. Reconnect the throttle and choke cables, using the marks noted during engine removal.

12. Reconnect the chassis wiring harness connectors to the appropriate engine plugs.

13. Connect the starter motor cable and the battery cables. Connect the negative cable last.

14. Reconnect the spark plug leads to the plugs.

15. Install a new fuel hose, including clamps, between the fuel filter and the fuel pump.

16. Refill the crankcase with the proper oil.

17. Open the fuel tank valve (**Figure 6**).

LUBRICATION

The engine is equipped with a filtered pressure lubrication system. Refer to the *Oil Pump* section for oil pump service information.

Periodically check the oil level; do not overfill. To check the oil level:

1. Make sure that the mower is sitting on a level surface.

2. Clean the area around the dipstick cap to prevent dirt and debris from falling into the crankcase when the cap is removed.

3. Remove the dipstick and wipe the oil from the level indicator.

4. Reinsert the dipstick and seat the dipstick cap on the oil fill tube. Do not screw the dipstick back down into the tube.

5. Remove the dipstick and check the oil level. The oil level should be up to, but not over, the "FULL" line on the dipstick.

NOTE
Fill a new oil filter with oil prior to installation to ensure adequate lubrication to critical components during initial engine restart. Pour the oil into the filter through the center threaded hole only. Do not fill past the bottom of the threads.

It is recommended that a new oil filter be installed at each oil change. Apply a light coating of clean engine oil to the filter gasket. Install the oil filter until the rubber gasket contacts the filter adapter plate, then tighten an additional 1/2-3/4 turn.

Crankcase oil capacity is approximately 2.1 quarts (2.0 L) with oil filter. Refer to **Table 3** for oil recommendations.

For a new or overhauled engine or short block, use SAE 10W-30 oil for the first five hours of operation, then change oil according to ambient temperature requirements. The recommended oil change interval after the five-hour break-in period is every 100 hours of operation. The oil should be drained while the engine is warm for the most effective crankcase sludge removal.

The engine may be equipped with a low-oil sensor. If the oil level is low, the sensor circuit will either stop the engine or trigger a warning device.

AIR FILTER

The engine is equipped with a paper-type air filter and a foam precleaner element (**Figure 7**).

Remove and clean the air filter at the interval indicated in **Table 2**. Replace the element at the specified interval or whenever it is damaged or starting to deteriorate. Service more frequently if the engine is operated in severe conditions.

To service the filter assembly, refer to *Air Filter Service* in Chapter Three.

NOTE
Always inspect the crankcase breather hose between the valve cover and the air filter base anytime the air filter is being serviced. If the hose is loose, cracked, or dry and brittle, replace it.

FUEL FILTER

Service the fuel filter at the interval indicated in **Table 2**. Service more frequently if the engine is operated in severe conditions.

To service the fuel filter, refer to *Fuel Filter Service* in Chapter Three.

CARBURETOR

Carburetor Design

Carburetor operating principles are discussed in detail under *Chapter Fundamentals* in Chapter Two.

Figure 8 shows a manifold-side view of the carburetor used on the Kohler CV20 engine. **Figure 9** shows an exploded view of the carburetor. The carburetor has a fixed high-speed jet, with no high-speed mixture adjustment screw.

> *NOTE*
> *Engines operated at altitudes of 6000 feet (1830 meters) above sea level and higher may need to have a high-altitude jet installed. This jet is available from Kohler.*

The carburetor may be equipped with a fuel shut-off ("anti-afterfire") solenoid. The solenoid uses a plunger to stop fuel flow through the main nozzle passage when the engine is stopped. When the ignition switch is turned on and voltage is directed to the solenoid, the plunger retracts and allows fuel to flow into the main fuel circuit. **Figure 8** shows the fuel solenoid mounted on the bottom of the carburetor, in place of the bowl nut.

Adjustment

The initial setting of the idle mixture screw (**Figure 10**) is 2 1/4 turns out from a *lightly seated* position.

> *NOTE*
> *The tapered tip of the idle mixture needle is machined to critical dimensions. If the needle is forced into its bottomed position, it will be damaged (**Figure 11**) and must be replaced. If this happens, the carburetor also may need to be replaced, as the internal mixture passage is probably similarly damaged.*

The final adjustment of the idle mixture and idle speed screws should be made with the engine at normal operating temperature.

> *NOTE*
> *If a limiter cap covers the idle mixture screw, use a Walbro Limiter Cap Removal Tool No. 500-20 or equivalent and carefully remove the cap if adjustments beyond*

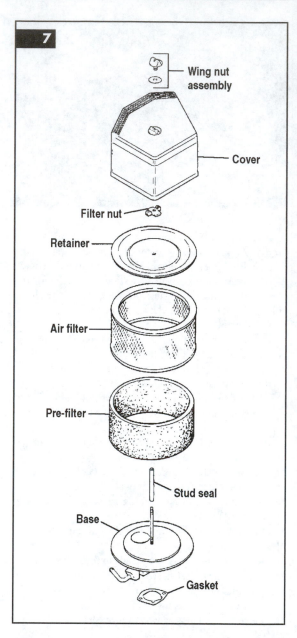

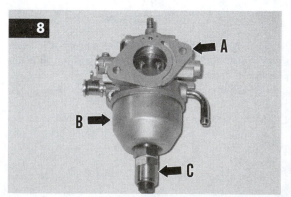

9

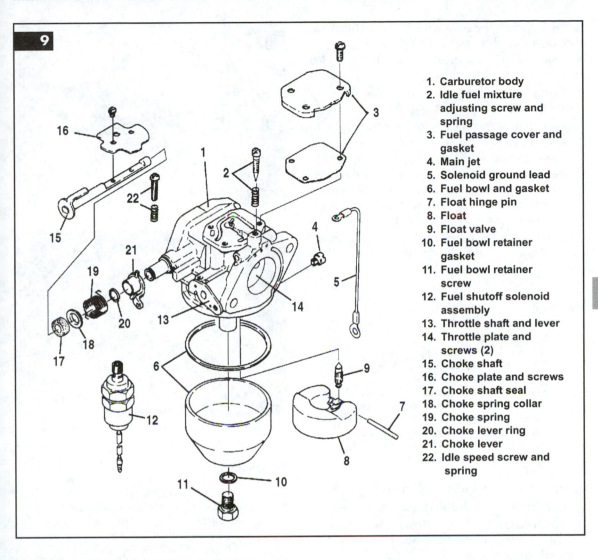

1. Carburetor body
2. Idle fuel mixture adjusting screw and spring
3. Fuel passage cover and gasket
4. Main jet
5. Solenoid ground lead
6. Fuel bowl and gasket
7. Float hinge pin
8. Float
9. Float valve
10. Fuel bowl retainer gasket
11. Fuel bowl retainer screw
12. Fuel shutoff solenoid assembly
13. Throttle shaft and lever
14. Throttle plate and screws (2)
15. Choke shaft
16. Choke plate and screws
17. Choke shaft seal
18. Choke spring collar
19. Choke spring
20. Choke lever ring
21. Choke lever
22. Idle speed screw and spring

7

10

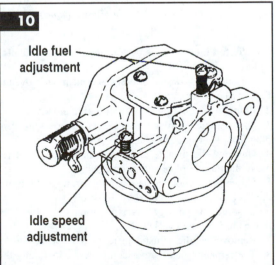

Idle fuel adjustment

Idle speed adjustment

the limit stops must be made. Follow the instructions included with the tool. Discard the original limiter cap. A new limiter cap must be installed once the final adjustment has been made. After the final adjustment, install the limiter cap with the cap pointer midway between the limit stops.

Perform the final adjustments as follows:

1. Perform the initial setting of the idle mixture screw, then connect a tachometer to the engine.

2. With the parking brake on, the blade PTO disengaged, the speed control in neutral, and the neutral locks locked, start the engine and run it for 5-10 minutes to reach normal operating temperature.

WARNING
Make sure the ventilation is adequate if the engine is operated in a confined area. Exhaust fumes are toxic and deadly.

3. Place the throttle control in the SLOW or IDLE position. Ensure the choke plate is wide open.

4. Adjust the idle speed screw so the engine idles at 1400 rpm.

5. Slowly turn the idle mixture screw clockwise until the engine rpm begins to decrease. Note the screw position.

6. Turn the mixture screw counterclockwise 3/4-1 turn.

7. Reset the idle speed screw, if necessary, to obtain the desired idle speed.

8. Accelerate the engine a few times to check the adjustment. The engine should accelerate smoothly without hesitation. If there is still slight hesitation, turn the idle mixture screw another 1/8 turn counterclockwise.

9. Repeat Step 8 one more time, if necessary. If the engine still hesitates, carburetor cleaning and repair will be necessary.

Removal

> *WARNING*
> *Some gasoline will drain from the fuel hose and/or the carburetor during this procedure. Wipe up any spilled gasoline immediately. Work in a well-ventilated area at least 50 feet away from any open flame, including pilot lights in gas appliances. Do not allow anyone to smoke in the area. Do not work near any grinding or any other source of sparks.*

1. Disconnect the negative battery lead from the battery.

2. Turn the fuel tank valve off (**Figure 3**).

3. Detach the breather hose from the air cleaner base. Inspect the hose completely. If the hose is loose, cracked, or dry and brittle, replace it.

4. Remove the air cleaner cover and elements (**Figure 7**).

5. Detach the fuel hose from the carburetor.

6. Disconnect the solenoid wire from the solenoid and unscrew the ground wire terminal from the top of the carburetor (**Figure 12**).

7. Unscrew the air cleaner base retaining nuts. Remove the air cleaner base from the carburetor.

> *NOTE*
> *The air cleaner base retaining nuts also secure the carburetor on its mounting studs.*

8. Remove the carburetor while disconnecting the throttle and choke linkage.

9. Carefully clean any gasket residue from the intake manifold, carburetor and air cleaner base. Discard all old gaskets. Do not damage the gasket surfaces.

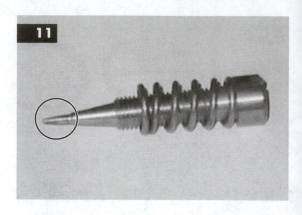

Disassembly

> *WARNING*
> *Some gasoline may drain from the carburetor during this procedure. Wipe up any spilled gasoline immediately. Work in a well-ventilated area at least 50 feet away from any open flame, including pilot lights in gas appliances. Do not allow anyone to smoke in the area.*

Refer to **Figure 9** when performing the following procedure:

1. Unscrew the bowl nut or fuel solenoid and remove the fuel bowl and gasket.

2. Remove the float pin, float and fuel inlet valve.

3. On solenoid-equipped carburetors, remove the vent plug from the center column.

4. Unscrew the throttle plate retaining screws and remove the throttle plate and throttle shaft.

5. Unscrew the choke plate retaining screws and remove the choke plate and choke shaft assembly.

6. Unscrew the passage cover retaining screws and remove the cover and gasket.

7. Remove the idle adjustment screw and spring.

8. The remaining carburetor components, including the main jet, are non-serviceable items. The carburetor is

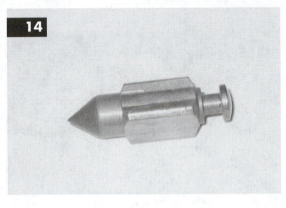

now ready for cleaning and inspection as described in the following section.

Cleaning and Inspection

Refer to **Figure 9** when performing the following procedure:

1. Clean the carburetor thoroughly using a commercial solvent such as Gumout or equivalent. Follow the solvent manufacturer's instructions, then use clean, dry compressed air to remove all traces of debris and solvent from the internal passages.

> *CAUTION*
> *Do not use wire or drill bits to clean jets.*
> *Even minor gouges in the jet can alter the*
> *flow rate and upset the air/fuel mixture.*

2. Inspect the carburetor body and components. Make sure all passages are clean (**Figure 13**).

3. Inspect the tip of the idle mixture needle. If the tip is damaged as shown in **Figure 11**, it must be replaced. If the tip is damaged, the carburetor also may need to be replaced, as the internal mixture passage is probably similarly damaged.

4. Inspect the float valve (**Figure 14**) and replace it if the tip is grooved. Inspect the valve seat in the carburetor body.

5. Install the choke and throttle shafts in the carburetor body and check for wear between the shafts and body. The carburetor must be replaced if there is excessive play, as neither a body nor bushings are available.

Fuel Shutoff Solenoid Testing

On units with the fuel-shutoff solenoid mounted on the carburetor, the spring-loaded solenoid plunger should retract when the solenoid is energized (ignition switch ON), allowing fuel to flow.

To test the solenoid:

1. Make sure that the battery is fully charged.

2. While listening to and/or holding the solenoid, turn the ignition switch from the OFF to the RUN position a few times.

3. An audible click should be heard and/or felt each time the key is switched.

4. If the solenoid does not click:

    a. Turn the fuel tank valve off.

    b. Place a container under the carburetor to catch leaking fuel.

    c. Remove the main harness connector from the solenoid terminal.

    d. Unscrew the solenoid from the carburetor.

    e. Connect the negative terminal of a 12-volt test battery to the solenoid case.

    f. Momentarily connect and disconnect the other battery terminal to the solenoid terminal a few times.

    g. If the solenoid still does not activate, it is faulty and must be replaced.

5. If substep f activates the solenoid, the solenoid is good. Check for faulty wiring as follows:

    a. Using a multimeter set to the DC volts scale, place the negative meter lead on any good engine-block ground and connect the positive meter lead to the solenoid terminal in the main harness.

    b. Again turn the ignition switch on and off a few times while observing the meter dial. The meter should read mower battery voltage each time the switch is turned on. If not, the wiring is faulty. Refer to the *Electrical Systems* section and the *Wiring Diagrams* and test the wiring to determine why current is not reaching the solenoid.

Fuel Shutoff Solenoid Cleaning

To clean the solenoid, unscrew the solenoid housing (A, **Figure 15**) from the bowl-nut fitting (B). Remove the sealing ring, plunger and plunger spring from the solenoid (**Figure 16**). All the solenoid components except the wired housing can be cleaned in the same solvent used to clean the carburetor. Do not immerse the housing in sol-

7

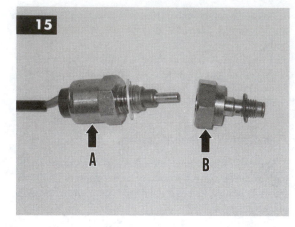

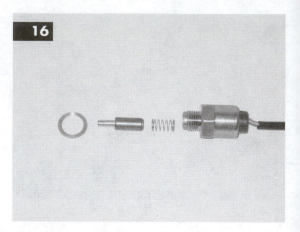

vent. If the housing plunger bore is dirty, use a cotton swab dipped in solvent. Rinse and dry.

Inspect the solenoid components. If any component appears questionable, the solenoid assembly will need to be replaced, as components are not available separately.

Reassemble the solenoid and securely tighten the fitting to the housing. Do not overtighten.

Assembly

Always use new gaskets when assembling the carburetor.

Refer to **Figure 9** when performing the following procedure:
1. Make sure that all fastener threads and threaded holes are clean and dry.
2. Install the idle mixture adjusting screw and spring. The initial setting of the idle mixture screw is 2 1/4 turns out from a *lightly seated* position.

> *NOTE*
> *The tapered tip of the idle mixture needle is machined to critical dimensions. If the needle is forced into its bottomed position, it will be damaged as shown in **Figure 11**. If this happens, the carburetor also may need to be replaced, as the internal mixture passage is probably similarly damaged.*

3. Lightly coat the passage cover screw threads with Loctite 222 or equivalent. Install the passage cover gasket, cover and screws. Tighten the screws securely, but do not overtighten.
4. Assemble the spring-loaded choke shaft. Install the choke shaft assembly into the carburetor so spring tension tries to open the choke.
5. Lightly coat the choke plate screw threads with Loctite 222 or equivalent. Install the choke plate onto the shaft as shown in **Figure 17**. Make sure that the choke shaft works freely. Realign, if necessary.

6. Assemble the throttle shaft:
   a. Lightly coat the throttle plate screw threads with Loctite 222 or equivalent.
   b. Install the throttle shaft into the carburetor body.
   c. Unscrew the idle speed screw exactly two turns so the throttle plate can be closed completely to align it with the bore.
   d. Ensuring that the beveled edges of the throttle plate match the angle of the bore, screw the plate to the shaft.
   e. Work the shaft back and forth a few times to ensure free movement. Realign, if necessary.
   f. Screw the idle speed screw in the same two turns. The throttle plate should appear as in **Figure 18**.
7. On solenoid-equipped carburetors, install the vent plug into the center column.
8. Install and measure the float height as follows:
   a. Install the float valve onto the float.
   b. With the carburetor inverted, place the valve into the seat and position the float so the float hinge pin holes align with the body holes.
   c. Install the hinge pin.
   d. Make sure that the float has freedom of movement.

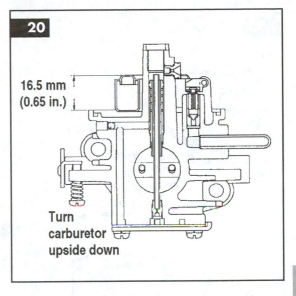

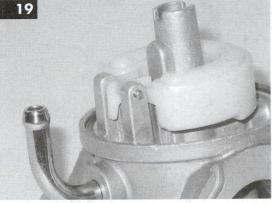

e. Allow the float arm to rest on the float valve (**Figure 19**).

f. Measure the float height as shown in **Figure 20**. The specified dimension is 16.5 mm (0.65 in.).

g. If the float height is not correct, install a new float kit. The float is not adjustable.

9. Install the fuel bowl gasket and bowl. Position the bowl nut gasket over the bowl. Tighten the screw or solenoid to 5.1-6.2 N·m (45-55 in.-lb.).

Installation

1. Position a new gasket onto the manifold studs.

2. Hook the throttle and choke links to the carburetor as shown in **Figure 21**, then slide the carburetor onto the manifold studs.

3. Install a new air-filter base gasket, then slide the filter base onto the manifold studs.

4. Install the filter base nuts. Make sure that the fuel hose support clamp is in its correct position as shown in **Figure 21**. Tighten the nuts to 9.9 N·m (88 in.-lb.).

5. Remove the passage cover screw that holds the ground wire terminal. Position the ground wire on the cover and reinstall and tighten the screw.

6. Reconnect the solenoid wire.

7. Reconnect the fuel hose between the fuel pump and carburetor.

8. Install the air filter elements and cover (**Figure 7**).

9. Reconnect and clamp the crankcase breather hose to the air filter base.

10. Turn the fuel tank valve ON and check for leaks.

11. Reconnect the negative battery lead to the battery.

12. Reset the static governor adjustment as described in the subsequent *Governor, External Adjustment* section.

13. Start the engine and adjust the carburetor as described in the previous *Adjustment* section.

MUFFLER

The muffler is calibrated as part of the emission control system. It not only reduces exhaust noise to acceptable levels, but it also provides the proper amount of back pressure to allow the inlet and combustion components to produce rated horsepower as well as compliant emission levels.

For this reason, the exhaust system should be maintained in good repair. As the noise level increases, power decreases. Under no circumstances should the exhaust system be modified. Inspect the muffler, pipes, flanges, connections and fasteners regularly. Replace any questionable components.

Removal

1. Allow the unit to cool.

2. Remove the heat shield (**Figure 22**).

21

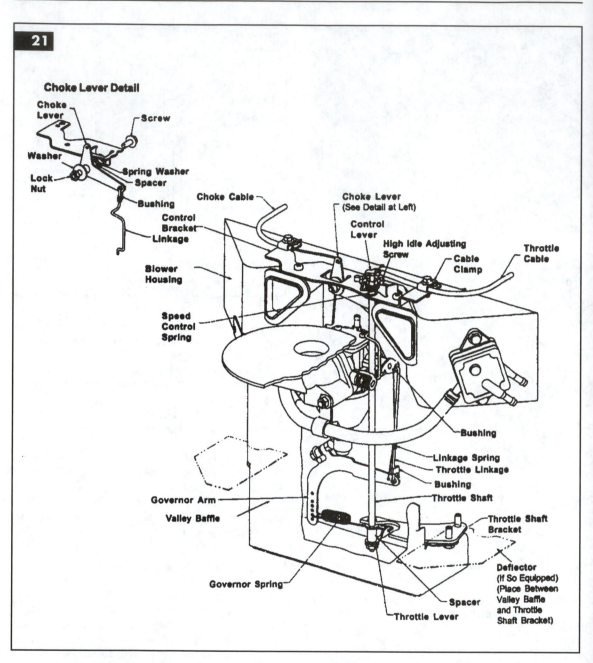

Choke Lever Detail

Choke Lever

Screw

Washer

Spring Washer

Lock Nut

Spacer

Bushing

Control Bracket Linkage

Choke Cable

Blower Housing

Speed Control Spring

Choke Lever (See Detail at Left)

Control Lever

High Idle Adjusting Screw

Cable Clamp

Throttle Cable

Bushing

Linkage Spring

Throttle Linkage

Bushing

Throttle Shaft

Governor Arm

Valley Baffle

Throttle Shaft Bracket

Deflector (If So Equipped) (Place Between Valley Baffle and Throttle Shaft Bracket)

Governor Spring

Spacer

Throttle Lever

3. Loosen all fasteners and clamps. Do not remove any fasteners until all of them have been loosened.

4. Begin removing the fasteners while supporting the exhaust system. Work from the outlet pipe inward. The nuts holding the exhaust pipe flange(s) to the engine should be the last fasteners removed, at which time the exhaust system can be removed and set aside.

5. Discard the gaskets.

6. Inspect the muffler and exhaust manifold for cracks, broken welds or indications of gas leakage. Replace the muffler if it is significantly damaged due to rust.

7. Inspect the brackets for cracks or breaks. Repair or replace as necessary.

8. Clean the mounting flange gasket surfaces and all fastener threads. Make sure the threads are clean and dry.

Installation

1. Replace all fastener lockwashers.

2. Insert new gaskets onto the exhaust studs.

3. Align the exhaust system with all bracket and fastener holes, then install and hand-tighten the fasteners, begin-

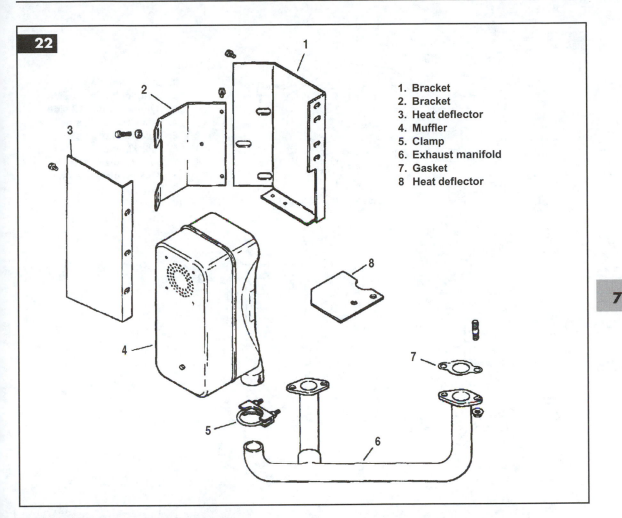

22

1. Bracket
2. Bracket
3. Heat deflector
4. Muffler
5. Clamp
6. Exhaust manifold
7. Gasket
8 Heat deflector

7

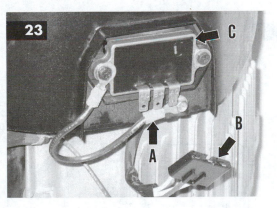

23

ning with the exhaust pipe flanges. Do not tighten any fasteners until all of them have been installed.

4. Beginning with the flanges, tighten all fasteners, working toward the outlet pipe.

5. Install the heat shield and spark arrestor, if used.

BLOWER HOUSING, SHROUDS AND BAFFLES

Removal

> *CAUTION*
> *Various length screws are used to fasten these components to the engine. Carefully note the locations of the fasteners, clamps and lift brackets as they are removed so they can be reinstalled properly.*

1. Remove the air filter assembly as described in this chapter.

2. Detach the wire connector (B, **Figure 23**) and the ground wire (A) from the regulator/rectifier (C) on the blower housing.

3. If the flywheel fan debris screen extends over the blower housing, remove the screen.

4. Remove the blower housing retaining screws and remove the blower housing (1, **Figure 24**).

5. Disconnect the spark plug leads.

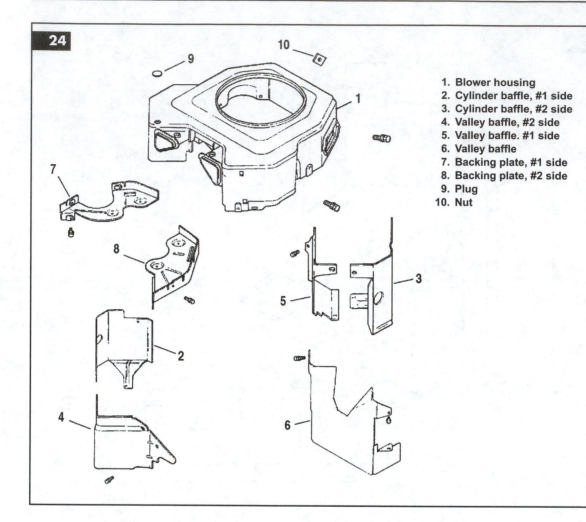

24

1. Blower housing
2. Cylinder baffle, #1 side
3. Cylinder baffle, #2 side
4. Valley baffle, #2 side
5. Valley baffle. #1 side
6. Valley baffle
7. Backing plate, #1 side
8. Backing plate, #2 side
9. Plug
10. Nut

6. Remove the outer shrouds (2, 3) and inner baffles (4, 5) from each cylinder.

7. Clean and dry all fastener threads.

8. Inspect the blower housing, shrouds and baffles for cracks or damage. Repair or replace as necessary.

Installation

Refer to **Figure 24** while performing this procedure.

1. Tighten all short screws to 4.0 N·m (35 in.-lb.). Tighten the longer screws to 6.8 N·m (60 in.-lb.).

2. Install the inner baffles. Tighten the screws finger-tight at this time.

3. Place the blower housing into position overlapping the edges of the inner baffles.

4. Install the outer shrouds. Tighten the screws finger-tight at this time. Make sure that the engine wires are routed as shown in **Figure 25** and **Figure 26**. **Figure 25** shows the starter-side wires (No. 1 cylinder); **Figure 26** shows the oil-filter side wires (No. 2 cylinder).

25

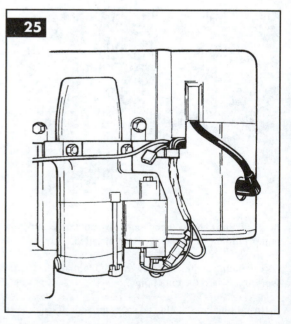

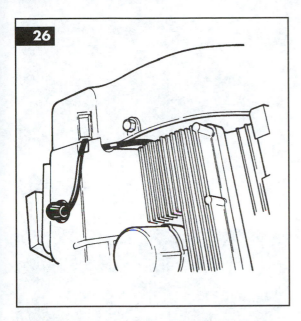

Individual parts are not available for the fuel pump. Service the fuel pump as a unit assembly.

To test the pump output:

> *WARNING*
> *Some gasoline will drain from the fuel hose and/or the carburetor during this procedure. Wipe up any spilled gasoline immediately. Work in a well-ventilated area at least 50 feet away from any open flame, including pilot lights in gas appliances. Do not allow anyone to smoke in the area. Do not work near grinding or any other source of sparks.*

1. Remove the fuel hose from the carburetor inlet fitting.
2. Direct the hose into a container.
3. Disconnect the spark plug wires from both spark plugs. Ground the spark plug wires to the engine.
4. While observing the fuel hose output, use the starter to turn the engine over. Fuel should pulse from the hose on every other revolution of the flywheel. No fuel flow indicates either a faulty pump or a plugged pulse hose or fitting.
   a. Remove the pulse hose from the crankcase fitting on the No. 2 cylinder side.
   b. Use the starter to turn the engine over while holding a fingertip over the fitting.
   c. If pressure/vacuum pulsations are felt, the fitting is clear.
   d. Remove the pulse hose from the fuel pump. Inspect the hose. If the hose is clear and not cracked or split, replace the pump.

Removal

1. Allow the engine to cool to ambient temperature.
2. Close the fuel tank valve (**Figure 3**).
3. Label the hoses at the pump (**Figure 27**):
   a. The hose coming from the crankcase fitting is the pulse hose;
   b. The hose coming from the fuel tank valve is the Inlet or supply hose; and
   c. The hose going to the carburetor is the outlet or pressure hose.
4. Loosen the hose clamps, then detach the hoses from the pump. Plug the hoses to prevent fuel leakage or contamination.
5. Remove the bolts holding the fuel pump to the blower housing and remove the fuel pump.
6. Discard the old clamps.
7. Inspect the hoses. Replace the hose(s) if they are dry, cracked, or brittle, or were in any way damaged during removal.

5. Install the blower housing screws. Tighten all fasteners to the specifications listed in Step 1.
6. Install the flywheel fan debris screen. For metal screens, tighten the screws to 9.9 N·m (88 in.-lb.).
7. Attach the wire connector and the ground wire to the regulator/rectifier on the blower housing (**Figure 23**).
8. Install the air filter assembly as outlined in this chapter.

FUEL PUMP

Operation and Testing

The engine is equipped with a diaphragm-type fuel pump (**Figure 27**) mounted on the blower housing. A pulse hose from a fitting on the engine crankcase directs crankcase pulsations to the diaphragm in the fuel pump. Diaphragm movement forces fuel through a pair of one-way valves to the fuel pump outlet, where the fuel is routed via the fuel hose to the carburetor.

7

Installation

1. Position the fuel pump against the blower housing. Install and tighten the screws to 2.3 N·m (20 in.-lb.).
2. Install new hose clamps onto the hoses.
3. Reconnect the hoses according to the identification marks made before removal.
4. Open the fuel tank valve (**Figure 6**).

IGNITION SYSTEM

All models are equipped with an electronic magneto ignition system that consists of:
1. A magnet assembly permanently affixed to the flywheel.
2. Two electronic magneto ignition modules, one mounted on each cylinder (**Figure 28**).
3. A kill switch that stops the engine by grounding the primary circuits of the ignition modules.

To see if an ignition module is producing spark, perform a *Spark Test* as described in Chapter Two.

Spark Plugs

The recommended spark plug for all models is Champion RC12YC or equivalent. The recommended spark plug electrode gap is 0.75 mm (0.030 in.). Tighten the spark plugs to 24-30 N·m (215-265 in.-lb. or 18-22 ft.-lb.).

> *CAUTION*
> *Do not use the abrasive-blast (sand-blast) method to clean spark plugs. When spark plugs are cleaned by this method, the abrasive grit lodges in the upper gap between the insulator and the shell. Subsequent cleaning with compressed air does not remove all of these abrasives. This grit is only removed when the plug is reinstalled in the engine and the engine is started, heating and expanding the plug. The grit then falls into the cylinder and combustion chamber area, causing rapid internal wear and damage.*

Module-to-Flywheel Air Gap Adjustment

The air gap between the ignition module and the flywheel should be 0.20-0.31 mm (0.008-0.012 in.). If the ignition module has been removed or its position disturbed, refer to **Figure 29** and use the following procedure to set the air gap between the ignition module and flywheel.
1. Remove the blower housing as outlined in Steps 1-5 under *Blower Housing, Removal* in this chapter.
2. Disconnect the spark plug lead and turn the flywheel so that the magnets are not next to the ignition module.

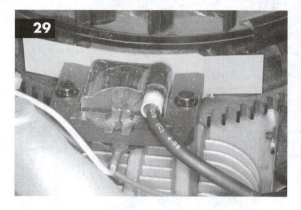

3. Loosen the screws holding the module to the engine.
4. Extend the module to the limits allowed by the adjustment slots, then lightly tighten one screw to temporarily hold the module away from the flywheel.
5. Rotate the flywheel to center the magnets directly under the module legs.
6. Place a *non-magnetic* gap gauge of 0.20-0.31 mm (.008-.012 in.) between the magnets and the module.
7. Loosen the module holding screw, allowing the magnets to draw the module to the flywheel. While holding the module snugly against the flywheel, tighten the module screws to 4.0 N·m (35 in.-lb.).
8. Rotate the flywheel and remove the gauge.
9. Measure the air gap to be sure the gap is 0.20-0.31 mm (0.008-0.012 in.).
10. If the air gap is incorrect, repeat the adjustment procedure. If the gap is not consistent after adjustment, the crankshaft and main bearings are probably worn.
11. Reconnect the spark plug lead.
12. Install the blower housing by following the applicable steps under *Blower Housing, Installation*.

Module Testing

> *NOTE*
> *The module cannot be tested unless it has fired a spark plug at least once. The test*

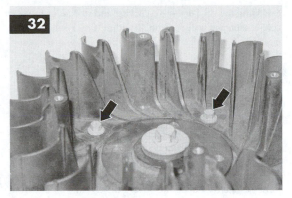

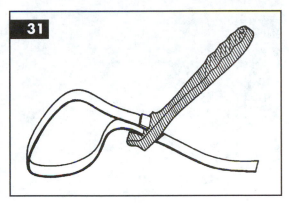

3. Turn the flywheel so that the magnets are not next to the ignition module.

4. Position the module on the cylinder posts. Install the module screws finger-tight.

5. Set the air gap between the flywheel magnets and module as described in the *Module-to-Flywheel Air Gap Adjustment* section.

6. Tighten the module screws to 4.0 N·m (35 in.-lb.) for used engines or to 6.2 N·m (55 in.-lb.) on a new engine cylinder block.

7. Reconnect the spark plug lead and the module ground wire terminal.

8. Install the blower housing by following the applicable steps under *Blower Housing, Installation*.

will not work on a new module out of the box.

Other than the *Spark Test* in Chapter Two, there is no test procedure for the ignition module. Prior to performing the spark test, disconnect the white ground wire from the module (**Figure 30**). If the module does not produce spark with the white ground wire disconnected and the flywheel air gap correctly set as outlined in the preceding section, the module is faulty.

Module Removal

1. Disconnect the spark plug wire from the spark plug.
2. Remove the blower housing as outlined in Steps 1-5 under *Blower Housing, Removal* in this chapter.
3. Disconnect the white-wire ground terminal connection from the module.
4. Remove the two hex-flange screws holding the module to the cylinder.
5. Clean all fastener threads.

Module Installation

1. Make sure that all fastener threads are clean and dry.
2. Apply Loctite 222 or equivalent to the fastener threads.

FLYWHEEL

Removal

When loosening or tightening the flywheel or fan bolts, hold the flywheel with the recommended strap wrench No. NU-10357 (**Figure 31**). Follow the wrench manufacturer's instructions. Do not use a bar or wedge in the fan blades or ring gear teeth as this could cause damage.

When removing the flywheel from the crankshaft, always use a proper puller. Never strike the crankshaft or flywheel, as damage could occur.

1. Disconnect the spark plug wire from each spark plug and properly ground the plug wires to the engine.
2. Remove the blower housing as outlined in Steps 1-5 under *Blower Housing, Removal*.
3. Disconnect the module ground wires. Remove the four hex-flange screws holding the modules to the cylinder. Remove the modules.
4. Remove the grass screen from the fan if not already removed. Although the flywheel can be removed with the fan installed, to prevent accidental fan blade damage, also remove the fan (**Figure 32**) from the flywheel. *Do not lose* the four fan screw spacers.
5. Use the strap wrench to hold the flywheel.

6. Using the proper 6-point socket and ratchet or breaker bar, loosen the bolt assembly holding the flywheel to the crankshaft. Remove the bolt and thick flat washer.

> *CAUTION*
> *If an impact wrench is used to remove the flywheel bolt, ensure that the wrench is set to turn counterclockwise, viewing the bolt head. Accidentally applying additional tightening force to the bolt will damage the flywheel and crankshaft.*

7. Using puller No. NU-3226 or equivalent, fasten the puller to the flywheel, then break the flywheel loose from the crankshaft (**Figure 33**). Always follow the puller manufacturer's instructions.

8. When the flywheel breaks loose from the crankshaft, *carefully* lift the flywheel straight up off the crankshaft so as not to damage the stator magnets under the flywheel.

Inspection

1. Thoroughly clean the flywheel, removing all dust and dirt from both the top and bottom of the flywheel, especially around the magnets.

2. Inspect the flywheel casting for cracks or damage. A cracked or damaged flywheel must be replaced.

3. Inspect the integrity of the magnets (**Figure 34**).

> *WARNING*
> *The magnets are not removable or serviceable. Do not attempt to reattach or tighten any loose magnet. If any magnets are loose or damaged, replace the flywheel.*

4. Inspect the starter ring gear. Carefully remove any debris stuck between the teeth. Light nicks or scratches may be dressed. Damaged teeth will require replacement of the flywheel assembly, as the ring gear is not available separately.

5. Inspect the tapers and keyways of both the crankshaft (A, **Figure 35**) and the flywheel. A damaged flywheel keyway will require replacement of the flywheel. A damaged crankshaft keyway will require crankshaft replacement. The crankshaft keyway should hold the flywheel key snugly.

6. Inspect the flywheel key. Replace if questionable. Use only the correct Kohler key.

Installation

1. Make sure that the matching tapers on the crankshaft and inside the flywheel, as well as the crankshaft and bolt threads, are *clean and dry*. Make sure no metal particles have stuck to any of the magnets.

37

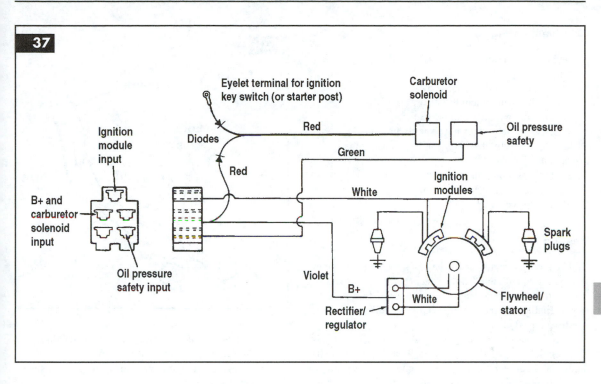

Eyelet terminal for ignition key switch (or starter post)

Carburetor solenoid

Oil pressure safety

Ignition module input

Diodes

Red

Green

Red

Ignition modules

White

B+ and carburetor solenoid input

Spark plugs

Oil pressure safety input

Violet

B+

White

Flywheel/ stator

Rectifier/ regulator

7

2. Install the flywheel key. Use only the correct Kohler key.

WARNING
Make sure the flywheel key is installed with the flat part of the key parallel to the crankshaft taper (B, Figure 35). If the key slides freely in the crankshaft keyway, lightly and carefully peen the edges of the keyway just enough to hold the key in position. Peen both sides of the keyway equally.

3. Carefully lower the flywheel straight down onto the crankshaft.

4. With the flat washer in position on the flywheel bolt, install the bolt into the crankshaft.

5. Using the strap wrench shown in **Figure 31**, hold the flywheel in position while tightening the bolt. Tighten the bolt to 66.4 N·m (49 ft.-lb.).

6. If the fan was removed, install it onto the flywheel, being careful to align the cutout with the magnet. Tighten the fan bolts to 9.9 N·m (88 in.-lb.).

7. If the grass screen fits inside the blower housing opening, install the screen onto the fan.

8. Install and gap the ignition module by following Steps 1-10 under the *Ignition System, Module-to-Flywheel Air Gap Adjustment* section of this chapter.

9. Install the blower housing by following the applicable steps under the *Blower System, Installation* section of this chapter.

ALTERNATOR/CHARGING SYSTEM

Figure 36 shows the alternator stator, which mounts under the flywheel. **Figure 23** shows the rectifier-regulator, which mounts onto the side of the blower housing. **Figure 37** shows the alternator wiring diagram.

Operation

If the alternator is functioning correctly, current is being produced whenever the flywheel is rotating. The stator produces AC and the rectifier-regulator changes the AC to DC. The rectifier-regulator also controls the amount of DC current based on the battery state-of-charge and the demands of the chassis electrical system. No adjustments are possible on this system.

To avoid damage to the charging system, the following precautions must be observed:

1. Prevent possible grounding of the AC leads.

2. The negative post of the battery must be connected to the engine ground and correct battery polarity must be observed at all times.

3. The rectifier-regulator must be connected in common ground with the engine and the battery.

4. Disconnect the leads at the rectifier-regulator and the battery if electric welding is to be done on equipment in common ground with the engine.

5. Remove the battery or disconnect the battery cables when recharging the battery with an external battery charger.

6. Do not operate the engine with the battery disconnected.

Troubleshooting

Defective conditions and possible causes are as follows:

1. No output. Could be caused by:
    a. Faulty windings in the stator.
    b. Defective diode(s) in the rectifier.
    c. Rectifier-regulator not properly grounded.
    d. Battery fully discharged or less than 4 volts.
    e. Faulty wiring.
2. Full charge-no regulation. Could be caused by:
    a. Defective rectifier-regulator.
    b. Defective battery.

Testing

The rectifier-regulator for the 15-amp charging system can be tested with the Kohler Tester (part No. 25 761 20). Instructions are included with the tester. If this tester is not available, use the test procedure that follows the precautions listed here.

Prior to performing any tests, make sure that the rectifier-regulator is properly grounded. Test the battery voltage. If voltage is less than 4 volts, check the electrolyte level, if possible. Add deionized or distilled water as needed. Recharge the battery. Follow the steps under *Charging* in Chapter Three.

No output condition

1. Disconnect the B+ wire from the rectifier-regulator.
2. Connect a DC voltmeter between the B+ terminal on the rectifier-regulator and engine ground.
3. Start the engine and operate it at 3600 rpm. Voltage should be above 13.8 volts.
    a. If reading is above zero volts but less than 13.8 volts, test further for a defective rectifier-regulator.
    b. If reading is zero volts, proceed to Step 4.
    c. Stop the engine.
4. Check for a defective rectifier-regulator or a defective stator.
    a. Disconnect the AC leads from the rectifier-regulator.
    b. Connect an AC voltmeter to the two AC leads.
    c. Start the engine and operate it at 3600 rpm.
    d. Check the AC voltage output.
    e. If the reading is less than 28 volts, the stator is defective.
    f. If the reading is more than 28 volts, the rectifier-regulator is defective.
5. Stop the engine.
6. To verify that the stator is faulty, use an ohmmeter to measure the resistance across the AC stator leads.
    a. If resistance is 0.064-0.2 ohm, the stator is good.
    b. If resistance is infinity (no-continuity), the stator windings are open. Replace the stator.

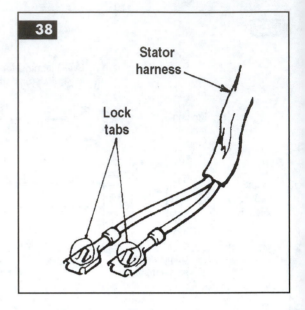

    c. If resistance is zero ohms, the stator windings are shorted. Replace the stator.
7. Again using an ohmmeter, measure the resistance from ground to each stator lead.

If any resistance is measured during either test, the stator windings are shorted to ground. Replace the stator.

Full charge-no regulation

1. Start the engine and operate it at 3600 rpm.
2. Use a DC voltmeter and check B+ to ground.
    a. If the reading is over 14.7 volts, the rectifier-regulator is defective.
    b. If the reading is between 14.0 and 14.7 volts, the alternator stator and the rectifier-regulator are satisfactory and the battery is probably defective (unable to hold a charge).

Removal

1. Remove the flywheel by following Steps 1-9 under *Flywheel, Removal* in this chapter.
2. Remove the stator harness clamp screw from the upper crankcase.
3. If not already done, unplug the stator harness connector from the chassis harness.
4. Using a small, flat screwdriver, carefully flatten and unlock the stator terminal locking tabs (**Figure 38**) from the locking slots in the stator harness connector (**Figure 39**). The blade tip must be inserted into the open end of the connector. Remove the terminals from the connector.
5. Remove the No. 2 blower housing backing plate (8, **Figure 24**). Mark the routing of the stator harness.
6. Loosen and remove the two stator mounting screws.

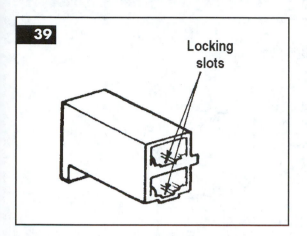

Locking slots

7. Carefully lift the stator off the machined crankcase shoulder.

8. Clean the screw and crankcase threads.

Installation

1. Ensure that the screw and crankcase threads are clean and dry.

2. Lightly coat the screw threads with Loctite 222 or equivalent.

3. Align the stator harness routing as noted during disassembly. Align the stator and crankcase screw holes, then carefully set the stator down onto the machined crankcase shoulder (**Figure 40**).

4. Tighten the two stator mount screws securely.

5. Install the No. 2 blower housing backing plate and tighten the screws.

6. Using a small, flat screwdriver, carefully bend the terminal locking tabs back to the lock position as shown in **Figure 38**. Do not raise the tabs more than 2.3 mm (3/32 in.).

7. Align the terminal lock tabs with the connector slots (**Figure 39**). Insert the terminals into the connector. Terminal sequence is not important since the stator is gener-

ating AC. Make sure that the terminals are locked into the connector by lightly tugging on each stator wire. If a terminal pulls out, check the connector for obstructions, clear or replace as necessary, and then reinsert the terminal.

8. Plug the harness connector into the chassis harness.

9. Install the flywheel by following the necessary steps under *Flywheel, Installation* in this chapter.

ELECTRIC STARTER MOTOR AND SOLENOID

In this section, "starter" refers to the electric starter motor assembly. Unless otherwise noted, starter component descriptions will refer to **Figure 41**.

Starter Operation

1. When voltage is applied to the starter through the solenoid terminal and ground, the solenoid activates, pulling the drive lever and engaging the drive pinion into the flywheel ring gear.

2. When the solenoid plunger reaches the end of its travel, its contacts close the circuit between the two large solenoid terminals, sending battery current to the starter armature through the brushes.

3. Battery current causes the armature to rotate, turning the flywheel and starting the engine.

4. When the start switch is released, current stops flowing to the starter.

    a. The internal solenoid spring retracts the plunger.

    b. The solenoid contacts and the drive pinion disengage.

    c. The armature stops turning.

Starter Troubleshooting

Starter fails to energize

Check the following:

1. Battery. Check the battery voltage and the specific gravity of the electrolyte. Recharge or replace the battery as necessary.

2. Wiring.

    a. Check for corroded or loose battery or solenoid connections. Clean or tighten as necessary. Soaking the corroded terminal in a baking soda and water solution is the best cleaning method. Do not allow any solution to get into any of the cells, as it will neutralize the electrolyte. Coat the clean connections with NoCo NCP-2 or equivalent to prevent further corrosion.

    b. Replace any frayed wires or wires with disintegrated terminals.

    c. Check for corroded or rusted ground connections on the equipment chassis. Remove the rust and treat the connection with NoCo or equivalent.

7

41

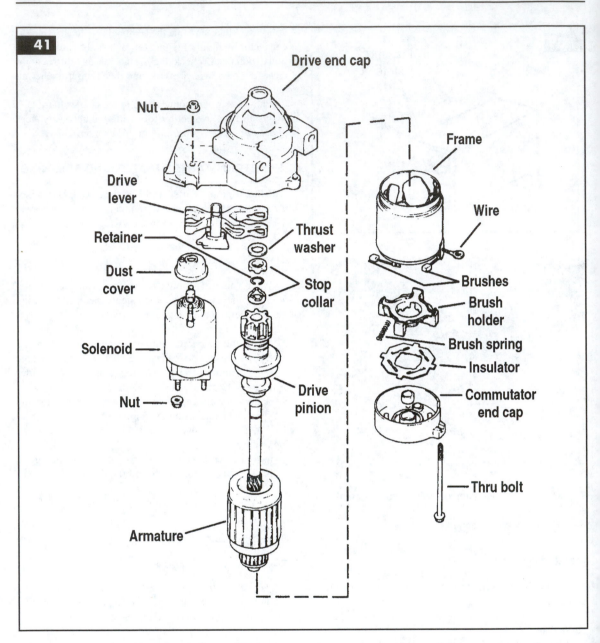

3. Solenoid. Use a jumper cable across the two large solenoid terminals to momentarily bypass the solenoid. If the starter energizes, the fault is in either the solenoid or the wiring to the solenoid. The *Solenoid Testing* section follows the starter section.

4. Starter components.

    a. Check the brushes. Dirty or worn brushes and/or commutator will slow a starter. Replace worn brushes.

    b. Check the armature commutator. The commutator is an integral part of the armature. Cracked, chipped, broken, or badly grooved commutator sections are not repairable; in these cases, the ar-

mature will need replacement. A lightly grooved commutator may be turned on a lathe to clean up.

    c. Check the armature shaft and bearings. A worn shaft or bearings will allow the armature laminations to rub against the frame magnets, causing drag. Replace faulty components.

Starter energizes but turns slowly

Check the following:

1. Battery. Check the battery voltage and the specific gravity of the electrolyte. Recharge or replace the battery as necessary.

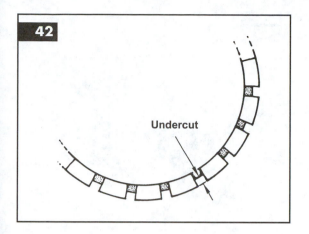

42

Undercut

43

44

b. Scored or galled internal engine components such as bearing journals, pistons and cylinders will overload the starter.

4. Starter components. Use the same checks as Step 4 in the preceding *Starter Fails to Energize* section.

Solenoid Testing

Testing a solenoid can usually be done quickly with the solenoid on the starter. To test the solenoid:

1. Remove the ignition key from the switch so the engine does not start.

2. Make sure that the unit is in neutral and that the parking brake is set.

3. Place the throttle control in the SLOW position.

4. Remove the main harness wire from the small solenoid terminal.

5. Using a short jumper wire, connect one end of the wire to the small terminal; momentarily touch the other end to the large terminal of the cable coming from the positive battery post.

6. If the starter activates, the solenoid is good.

The solenoid is not serviceable and must be replaced if faulty. To replace the solenoid, refer to the *Starter Disassembly* and *Reassembly* in this chapter.

Starter Removal

1. Disconnect the negative battery cable and secure the cable away from the battery.

2. Disconnect the starter cable.

3. Remove the bolts holding the starter to the engine. Remove the starter.

Starter Disassembly

Refer to **Figure 41** for component identification.

1. Disconnect the frame wire from the solenoid.

2. Remove the solenoid nuts from the drive end cap. Remove the solenoid (**Figure 43**). To aid in removing the slotted solenoid plunger from the drive lever, it may be necessary to pick out the dust cover once the solenoid is loose.

3. Remove the two through-bolts holding the commutator end cap and frame to the drive end cap.

4. Remove and disassemble the commutator end cap (**Figure 44**).

5. Slide the frame off the armature and drive end cap.

6. Remove the armature and drive lever assembly from the drive end cap (**Figure 45**). The flange on the drive pinion will require some careful maneuvering to work it past the dust seal inside the cap.

CAUTION
Do not lose the thrust washer.

2. Parasitic load on the engine. Attempting to start an engine that is connected to a hydrostatic drive system places an additional load on the starter motor, especially in cooler temperatures. If possible, disconnect the load from the engine and retry the starter. If the starter now turns the engine properly, check the hydrostatic system to find the reason for the excessive load.

3. Internal load on the engine.

a. Dirty, thick crankcase oil past its change schedule will cause slow turnover.

7

7. Remove the stop collar by carefully prying the two interlocking collar halves off the internal retainer ring.

    a. Early-style starters use wavy interlocking collar halves as shown in **Figure 41**.

    b. Late-style starters use recessed and shouldered collar halves as shown in the cutaway in **Figure 46**. On this style collar, the upper collar is the thrust washer.

8. Remove and discard the retainer ring.

9. Using a suitable solvent, clean the starter components.

Starter Inspection and Repair

1. Inspect all starter components. Replace any items that are cracked, broken, overheated or excessively worn.

2. Inspect the brushes. The original brushes are integral with the starter frame. To replace the brushes, use Brush Kit No. 52 221 01 and proceed as follows:

    a. Remove the grommet from the solenoid wire.

    b. Using side cutters, cut the brush lead wires where the wires meet the frame posts. *Do not* cut the solenoid wire.

    c. Carefully file any burrs from the posts.

    d. Crimp the solid portion of the replacement brushes to the posts.

    e. Solder the newly crimped ends to the posts.

    f. Reinstall the grommet back onto the solenoid wire after the solder cools.

3. Inspect the end-cap bushings. If the armature shaft rocks excessively in the bushings, the end cap(s) will need to be replaced, as the bushings are not serviceable separately. If the armature shaft bearing journals are scored, the armature will have to be replaced, as well.

4. Make sure that the drive pinion flange that contacts the drive end cap dust seal is not bent.

5. Lightly coat the splines of the armature and drive pinion and the drive-pinion area of the armature shaft with Kohler Starter Drive Lubricant (part No. 52 357 01) or Cristolube 303. The use of other lubricants can cause sticking or binding of the pinion.

6. Lubricate all contact and pivot areas of the drive lever assembly with Kohler Solenoid Starter Lubricant (part No. 52 357 02).

7. Check the armature commutator. The commutator is an integral part of the armature. Cracked, chipped, broken, or badly grooved commutator sections are not repairable; in these cases, the armature will need replacement. A lightly grooved commutator may be turned on a lathe to clean up. After turning, carefully file the burrs between the commutator segments and undercut the insulator segments between the conductors, if necessary (**Figure 42**). A dirty or rough commutator should be cleaned with a suitable solvent, then lightly sanded with ScotchBrite or equivalent.

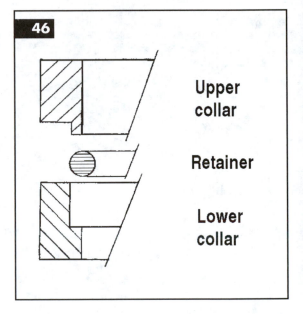

Starter Reassembly

Refer to **Figure 41** and **Figure 46** to aid in starter assembly.

1. Install the drive pinion onto the armature shaft.

2. Slide the inner collar onto the shaft, against the pinion.

3. Install and tighten a *new* retainer in the shaft groove.

4. Slide the outer collar onto the shaft, against the retainer.

5. Using two pair of pliers, evenly squeeze the two collar halves together over the retainer ring.

6. Fit the large fork of the drive lever over the drive pinion channel.

7. On early wavy-collar starters, install the thrust washer against the outer collar. Do not lose the thrust washer.

8. Install the armature and pinion lever assembly into the drive end cap. The drive lever pivot base fits into a matching recess in the end cap.

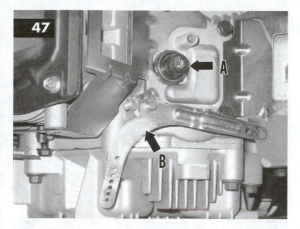

9. Set the frame on the workbench with the brushes up.
   a. Position the brush holder, open slots up, onto the end of the frame with the holder legs in between the brushes.
   b. Install one brush into each holder slot. The brush leads fit into the cutouts in the slot sides.
   c. Compress and install the brush springs into the holder slots against the back of the brushes.
   d. Snap the insulator plate into the brush holder, over the brushes and springs. The insulator is reversible.
10. Carefully install the frame assembly down onto the armature. Ensure that the drive-cap end slot aligns with the drive lever. Work the brushes against the brush springs so the frame fits down over the armature commutator and into the drive end cap.
11. Install the commutator end cap.
    a. Install the through-bolts.
    b. Tighten the bolts alternately and evenly until snug.
12. Fit the dust cover over the solenoid plunger.
13. Hold the frame solenoid wire aside and fit the solenoid into the drive end cap. Make sure the plunger slots fit into the drive lever fork fingers.
14. Install and tighten the stud nuts.
15. Install the frame wire onto the solenoid terminal. Do not use threadlocking compound on the solenoid stud or a poor connection may result.

Starter Installation

1. Lightly coat the starter mount bolt threads with Loctite 242 or equivalent.
2. Fit the starter drive under the blower housing shield while aligning the mount bolt holes with the matching threaded holes in the crankcase.
3. Install and tighten the mount bolts to 15.3 N·m (135 in.-lb.).
4. Reconnect the starter cable. Tighten the cable nut snugly. Do not overtighten the nut.
5. Reconnect the negative battery cable.

OIL SENSOR

The engine may be equipped with an Oil Sentry oil pressure switch (A, **Figure 47**) located on the crankcase breather between the cylinders. The switch is designed to break contact as oil pressure increases to normal pressure and to make contact when oil pressure decreases within the range of 20.7-34.5 kPa (3.0-5.0 psi). The switch is connected to a warning device (light) to indicate to the operator that oil pressure is low and the engine should be stopped.

Removal

1. Stop the engine and let it cool.
2. Disconnect the wire lead from the switch.
3. Unscrew and remove the switch.

Testing

To check the sensor switch, a regulated supply of compressed air and a continuity tester are required.
1. Remove the oil pressure sensor switch as described in the previous section.
2. Connect the tester probes to the body of the switch and to the switch terminal.
3. The tester should indicate continuity between the switch terminal and the switch body.
4. Gradually apply air pressure to the switch oil passage.
5. As pressure increases through a range of 20.7-34.5 kPa (3-5 psi), the switch should open and the tester should indicate no continuity.
6. If the switch fails the test, install a new switch.

Installation

1. Before installing the switch, apply Loctite 592 or equivalent pipe sealant with Teflon to the switch threads.
2. Install the switch and tighten to 4.5 N·m (40 in.-lb.).
3. Reconnect the wire lead.

INTAKE MANIFOLD

Removal

1. Remove the air cleaner assembly.
2. Remove the carburetor as described in this chapter.
3. Remove the blower housing as described in this chapter.
4. Note the location of the wire retaining straps and the orientation of the wiring, then cut the straps away from the intake manifold.
5. Remove the four intake manifold mounting bolts, then remove the intake manifold (**Figure 48**).

7

6. Discard all old gaskets. Carefully clean the manifold, cylinder head and carburetor gasket surfaces. Do not gouge or otherwise damage the gasket surfaces.

7. Clean the manifold using a suitable solvent or parts cleaner.

8. Clean and dry all fastener threads.

9. Inspect the manifold for cracks or other damage.

Installation

Prior to installation, lightly coat all fastener threads with Loctite 242 or equivalent.

1. Using new gaskets, install the intake manifold. Tighten the manifold bolts to 9.9 N·m (88 in.-lb.).

2. Noting the wiring orientation and the wire-tie strap locations marked during disassembly, fasten the wires to the manifold (**Figure 48**).

3. Install the blower housing as described in this chapter.

4. Install the carburetor as described in this chapter.

5. Install the air cleaner assembly.

CRANKCASE BREATHER

The crankcase breather system includes an oil separator canister mounted on the No. 1 cylinder rocker cover and a reed valve inside the valve lifter chamber of each cylinder. A hose connects the oil separator canister to the air cleaner base.

Removal and Installation

1. Detach the breather hose from the oil separator canister (**Figure 49**).

2. Pull the canister out of the rocker cover grommet.

3. Inspect the grommet:
   a. If the grommet color is orange, discard the grommet. The new grommet color is gray.
   b. If the grommet is dry, cracked or brittle, replace the grommet.

4. If the canister is damaged or clogged, replace it.

5. Each cylinder has a reed-style breather valve (A, **Figure 50**) mounted in the crankcase cavity below the cylinder head and between the hydraulic valve lifters (B). To access the breather, refer to *Cylinder Heads* in this chapter.

6. Inspect the reed valve. If damaged or broken, replace the valve and closely inspect the surface of the reed mounting face. If there are any small bumps or nubs protruding from the crankcase surface, use a scraping tool to remove the bump and smooth the surface. If left bumpy, the new reed valve will be similarly damaged.

7. Reinstall the cylinder heads as instructed.

8. Reassemble the grommet, canister and breather hose.

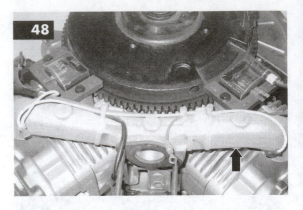

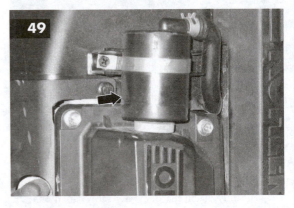

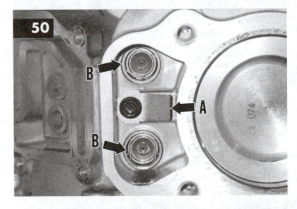

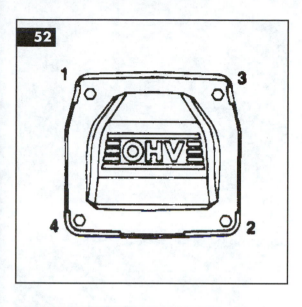

52

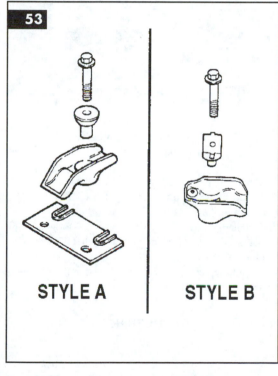

53

STYLE A | **STYLE B**

VALVE COVERS

Early models are equipped with valve covers that require a gasket and RTV sealant to seal between the cover and the cylinder head. Later models are equipped with valve covers (**Figure 51**) that use an O-ring to seal between the cover and the cylinder head. Valve cover gaskets were discontinued with the introduction of the O-ring style cover. If service requires removing early-style covers, they should be replaced with late-style covers.

Removal and Installation

1. Remove the oil separator canister from the No. 1 valve cover.

2. Unscrew the valve cover retaining screws, then remove the valve cover. Two types of valve cover screws are used: shoulder screws and straight-shank screws with spacers. Note the presence of any spacers in the cover mounting holes. Do not lose the spacers.

3. Remove and discard the O-ring, if used. Clean the mating surfaces on the cover and cylinder head.

4. Clean and dry the fastener threads.

5. Install a new O-ring seal into the cover. Do not apply any sealant to the O-ring, cover or cylinder head.

6. Install the valve cover.

    a. If used, install the spacers into the cover screw holes.

    b. Incrementally tighten the retaining screws to 7.9 N·m (70 in.-lb.) in the sequence shown in **Figure 52**.

ROCKER ARMS AND PUSH RODS

Two different styles of rocker arms and pivots (**Figure 53**) are used. Engines with serial No. 2520800017 and higher use the latest style, "B." If rocker arm replacement is required due to valve train wear, Style "A" can be upgraded to Style "B" with Kohler's retrofit kit (part No. 24 755 66). The self-aligning capability of the Style "B" pivot eliminates the need for the slotted push rod guide plate used with Style "A" arms. Rocker arm and push rod installation will be covered under *Cylinder Heads* in this chapter.

Note that there are no adjustments on the rocker arms. CV20 engines are equipped with hydraulic valve lifters that automatically maintain proper valve clearance. No periodic adjustment is required.

New push rods are identical, interchangeable and reversible. However, if the original push rods are being reused, wear patterns dictate that they be marked to denote which cylinder they fit, whether they are for the intake or exhaust side, and which end contacts the rocker arms.

Removal

1. Remove the valve cover as described in the preceding section.

2. Remove the spark plug and rotate the crankshaft so the piston is at TDC on the compression stroke. This will place both rocker arms in the full up position (**Figure 54**).

3. Mark the rocker arms so they may be reinstalled in their original positions.

4. Unscrew the rocker arm pivot screws (**Figure 55**) and remove the rocker arms and pivots.

5. Follow steps 1-4 to remove the rocker arms on the remaining cylinder head.

7

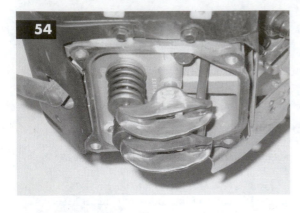

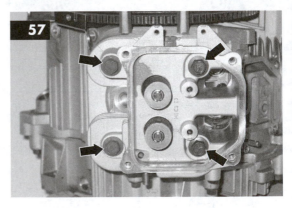

6. If necessary, remove the push rods. Mark the push rods so they may be reinstalled in their original positions and locations.

7. Clean the rocker arm pivot screw and matching cylinder head threads.

8. Inspect the rocker arms and pivots for excessive wear or damage.

Installation

1. Lubricate the ends of the push rods with engine oil. Install the push rods into their original, positions as marked during disassembly. Make sure the lower rod ball ends fit into the lifter sockets.

2. Lubricate the contact surfaces of the rocker arm and pivot with light grease such as Lubriplate or equivalent.

3. Fit each rocker arm and pivot onto its proper marked position, making sure the push rod lower end is in the lifter socket and the upper end is in the rocker arm socket.

4. Tighten the rocker arm pivot screws to 11.3 N·m (100 in.-lb.) while observing the valve springs.

    a. If the spring coils compress completely, stop tightening the bolts and allow the lifters to bleed down. There should be a minimum 0.25 mm (0.010 in.) clearance between the spring coils at all times.

    b. When proper clearance is observed between the spring coils, continue tightening the rocker pivot bolts.

5. Repeat Steps 1-4 for the other cylinder.

6. Install the spark plugs and tighten to 24.4-28.8 N·m (215-265 in.-lb.).

7. Rotate the flywheel by hand and check for good compression for both cylinders, indicating that the valves are seating properly.

8. Install the valve covers as described in the preceding section.

CYLINDER HEAD

NOTE
The cylinder heads are not identical. Each cylinder head is identified by a number embossed on the head that matches the cylinder number marked on the crankcase (Figure 56).

Removal

NOTE
Refer to the appropriate sections in this chapter for specific component removal procedures noted in the following steps.

58

CYLINDER HEAD COMPONENTS

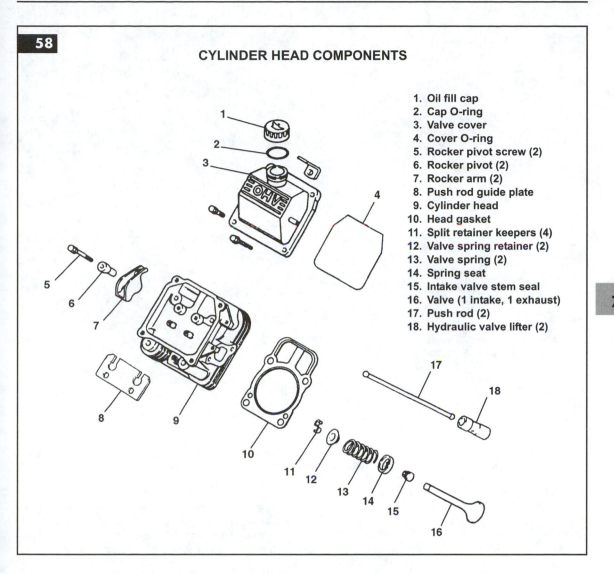

1. Oil fill cap
2. Cap O-ring
3. Valve cover
4. Cover O-ring
5. Rocker pivot screw (2)
6. Rocker pivot (2)
7. Rocker arm (2)
8. Push rod guide plate
9. Cylinder head
10. Head gasket
11. Split retainer keepers (4)
12. Valve spring retainer (2)
13. Valve spring (2)
14. Spring seat
15. Intake valve stem seal
16. Valve (1 intake, 1 exhaust)
17. Push rod (2)
18. Hydraulic valve lifter (2)

7

To remove each cylinder head:

1. Disconnect the spark plug wire from each spark plug and properly ground the spark plug wire end to the crankcase.

2. Remove the exhaust manifold and muffler.

3. Remove the intake manifold.

4. Remove any air shrouds or heat shields attached to the cylinder head.

5. Remove the spark plug. Rotate the crankshaft so the piston is at TDC on the compression stroke.

6. Unscrew the rocker arm pivot bolts (**Figure 55**) and remove the rocker arms and push rods. Mark the push rods and rocker arms as they are removed so they can be reinstalled in their original positions if reused.

7. In a crossing pattern, remove the four cylinder head bolts (**Figure 57**).

7. If necessary, loosen the cylinder head by tapping around the perimeter with a rubber or soft-faced mallet. Do not use a metal hammer.

8. Remove the cylinder head and gasket.

Disassembly

NOTE
Before or during disassembly, mark all components so they can be reinstalled in the same positions if they are to be reused.

Refer to **Figure 58**.

1. Remove the spark plug, if not already removed.

NOTE
On engines between serial Nos. 2421700017 and 2511700016, if the

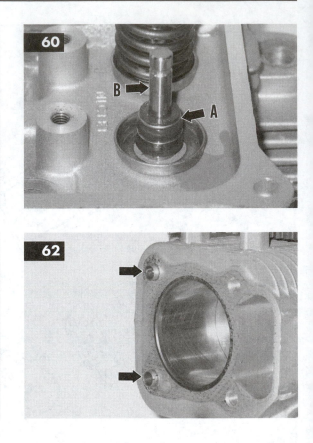

rocker pivots have Part No. 24 194 02 imbedded in the upper face, there will be a spacer washer under each rocker pivot. Ensure that the washers are installed upon reassembly.

2. Using a valve spring compressor, compress the valve springs and remove the split keepers.

3. Remove the valve spring caps, springs and valves.

4. Remove and discard the intake valve stem seal.

Inspection

1. Carefully remove all traces of sealant from the cylinder head and rocker cover mating surfaces. Do not gouge or damage the mating surfaces.

2. Remove all traces of gasket material from the cylinder head and cylinder block mating surfaces. Do not gouge or damage the mating surfaces.

3. Remove all carbon deposits from the valves, combustion chamber area and valve ports with a rotary wire brush. A blunt screwdriver or chisel may be used if care is taken not to damage the head, valves and spark plug threads.

4. Examine the spark plug threads in the cylinder head for damage. If damage is minor or if the threads are dirty or clogged with carbon, use a spark plug thread tap (**Fig-**

ure **59**) to clean the threads. Severely damaged threads can often be repaired with the installation of a Heli-Coil or equivalent replacement thread insert.

5. Inspect the threads in the cylinder head and crankcase for damage. Restore the threads with an appropriate size metric tap if necessary. If thread damage is severe, install a Heli-Coil or equivalent replacement thread insert.

6. After the carbon is removed from the combustion chamber and the intake and exhaust ports, clean the entire head in cleaning solvent. Blow dry with compressed air.

7. Check for cracks or other damage to the head, especially in the combustion chamber and exhaust port. Replace the cylinder head if it is cracked or damaged, or if any cooling fins are broken off.

8. After the head has been thoroughly cleaned, place the cylinder head gasket surface on a surface plate. Insert a flat feeler gauge between the plate and the cylinder head at various locations to check the head for distortion. The maximum allowable cylinder head warpage is 0.076 mm (0.003 in.). Resurfacing the cylinder head may be possible, however, if the head is severely warped, replacement of the head is recommended.

9. Valve, valve guide and valve seat service will be covered under *Valves and Valve Components* in this chapter.

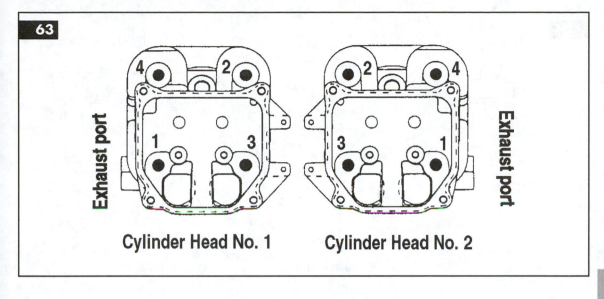

63

Exhaust port

4 **2**

1 **3**

Cylinder Head No. 1

Exhaust port

2 **4**

3 **1**

Cylinder Head No. 2

7

Reassembly

Refer to **Figure 58**.

1. Lightly lubricate the intake valve stem, guide and stem seal wiping lip with fresh engine oil. Always use a new stem seal. Install the stem seal first, pushing it down until it bottoms against the guide. Install the intake valve, rotating it while passing it through the seal to prevent damaging the seal. Push the valve all the way in until it bottoms against the seat. **Figure 60** shows the stem seal (A) in place with the valve installed (B).

3. Position the intake valve spring seat and spring over the valve stem. Install the spring retainer. Compress the spring and install the split retainers.

NOTE
Apply a small amount of grease to the valve keeper groove on the valve stem prior to installing the split keepers to hold the keepers in place on the valve stem. Make sure the keepers fit snugly into the groove in the valve stem.

4. Lightly lubricate the exhaust valve stem with Led-Plate or equivalent. Lightly lubricate the exhaust valve guide with fresh engine oil. Install the exhaust valve.

5. Position the exhaust valve spring seat and spring onto the valve. Install the spring retainer.

Compress the valve spring and install the split retainers.

NOTE
The rocker arms will be installed after the cylinder head is installed on the engine.

6. If necessary, repeat Steps 1-4 for the other cylinder head.

Installation

CAUTION
Because these engines use hydraulic valve lifters, follow the specified installation procedure precisely to prevent damage to the valve train components.

NOTE
New cylinder head bolts should always be installed. The special coating on the bolts affects torque retention, and most of the coating wears off the threads once the bolts are installed and tightened. Attempting to reuse old bolts results in loss of torque retention, likely causing head gasket failure.

Refer to **Figure 58**.

1. Make sure that all threaded holes in the cylinder block are clean, dry and in good repair.

2. If the hydraulic valve lifters (**Figure 61**) were removed, install them now.

3. Make sure that both cylinder head locator sleeves (**Figure 62**) are in position in the cylinder block.

4. Position a new head gasket onto the block locator sleeves.

NOTE
Do not apply sealer to the cylinder head gasket.

5. Install the new head bolts into the head.
   a. Position the head onto the cylinder block.
   b. Tighten the cylinder head bolts in increments of 20 N·m (15 ft.-lb.), following the sequence shown in **Figure 63**, to the final specified torque of 40.7 N·m (30 ft.-lb.).

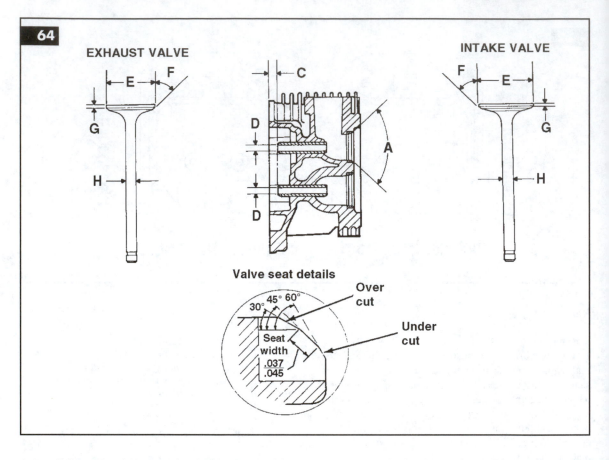

64

EXHAUST VALVE

INTAKE VALVE

Valve seat details

45° 60°
30°

Over
cut

Under
cut

Seat
width
.037
.045

6. Install the push rods. Ensure that the lower ends of the push rods are into the lifter socket holes.

7. While holding the push rods against the lifters with finger pressure, rotate the crankshaft so the piston is at TDC on the compression stroke (when neither push rod has moved for one half of a crankshaft revolution). The crankshaft PTO keyway will be in line with the cylinder at this time.

8. If equipped with Style "A" rocker arms, position the push rod guide plate against the head with the raised portion of the guide slots *toward* the head.

9. Mount the rocker arms and rocker pivots. Install the pivot bolts.

10. Carefully tighten the rocker pivot bolts to 11.3 N·m (100 in.-lb.) while observing the valve springs.

   a. If the spring coils compress completely, *stop tightening the bolts* and allow the lifters to "bleed down." There should be a minimum 0.25 mm (0.010 in.) clearance between the spring coils at all times.

   b. When suitable clearance is observed between the spring coils, continue tightening the rocker pivot bolts. Stop and allow the lifter to bleed down anytime the spring coils compress completely.

   c. Rotate the flywheel by hand three turns so the piston is at TDC between the exhaust and intake strokes. Allow the engine to rest for about 10 minutes to ensure that the lifters are properly bled down.

11. Repeat the Steps 1-10 for the other cylinder head.

12. Install the spark plugs and tighten to 24.4-28.8 N·m (215-265 in.-lb. or 18-22 ft.-lb.).

13. Rotate the flywheel by hand and check for good compression for both cylinders, indicating that the valves are seating properly.

VALVES AND VALVE COMPONENTS

Valve Adjustment

CV20 engines are equipped with hydraulic valve lifters that automatically maintain proper valve clearance. No periodic adjustment is required.

Valve Removal

To remove the valves, follow the steps outlined under *Cylinder Head, Disassembly* in this chapter.

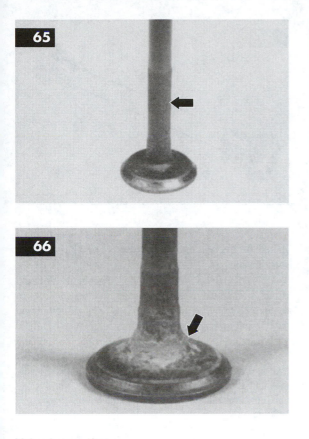

Valve Inspection

For valve, valve guide and valve seat dimensions, refer to **Figure 64** and **Table 6** at the end of this chapter.

1. Inspect the valve for damage and excessive wear prior to cleaning the valve.

    a. Gummy deposits on the intake valve (**Figure 65**) may indicate that the engine has run on gasoline that was stored for an extended period.

    b. Hard deposits on the intake valve are due to burnt oil during valve overlap, while hard deposits on the exhaust valve (**Figure 66**) are due to combustion byproducts and burnt oil.

    c. Moisture in the engine during storage can cause corroded or pitted valves. These should be replaced.

2. Check the valve face (**Figure 67**) for an irregular contact pattern with the seat. The seating ring around the face should be centered on the face, concentric with the valve head and equal in thickness all around the valve (**Figure 68**). If the seating pattern is irregular, then the valve may be bent, or the valve face or seat is damaged.

3. Remove deposits with a wire brush or soak the valve in parts cleaner.

4. Measure the valve stem diameter. Oversize valves are available with a 0.25 mm oversize stem for installation in worn valve guides that have been reamed oversize.

5. The valve stem must be perpendicular to the valve head. To check for a bent valve, carefully install the valve stem in a drill chuck and rotate the drill by hand while measuring head runout with a dial indicator. Be sure the valve stem is centered in the drill chuck.

6. Measure the valve head margin. Replace the valve if the margin is less than the minimum specified dimension.

7. If the valve and valve seat are worn, but serviceable, they can be restored by machining. Special tools are required to machine the valves and seats. If these tools are not available, take the head to a shop that is equipped to perform valve machine work.

8. The valve rides in a nonrenewable valve guide. Check for wear in the valve guides by measuring the inside diameter at the top, middle and bottom of the valve guide. Although the guides are not replaceable, they can be reamed to accept oversize valves with 0.25 mm oversize stem.

10. If valve machining is not necessary, the valve should be lapped against the valve seat to restore the seating surfaces. Refer to *Valve Lapping* in this chapter.

11. Check the valve springs. The spring should be straight with square ends as shown in **Figure 69**. The springs should also be the same length. Replace the springs if the lengths vary.

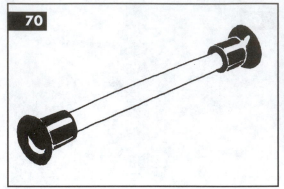

Valve Lapping

Valve lapping is a simple operation that can restore the valve seal without machining if the amount of wear is not excessive. Lapping requires the use of lapping compound and a lapping tool (**Figure 70**). Lapping compound is available in either coarse or fine grade, water- or oil-mixed. Fine-grade water-mixed compound is recommended. To lap a valve, proceed as follows:

1. Make sure that the valve head is clean and smooth.

2. Apply a light, even coat of lapping compound to the valve face. Too much compound can fall into the valve guide and cause damage.

3. Insert the valve into the valve guide.

4. Moisten the end of the lapping tool suction cup and place it on the valve head.

5. Rotate the lapping tool several times between the palms.

NOTE
For the most accurate lapping, slowly hand-rotate the lapping tool back and forth between 1/4 and 3/8 of a turn (90°-135°). Do not spin the tool rapidly through a revolution or two, then reverse direction. Do not use a drill to rotate the lapping tool.

6. The sealing ring of the valve face must be in the center of the face (Figure 68). Make the first lap pass *very light* to check the sealing ring position. If the sealing ring is too high or too low on the valve face, cut the seat as necessary (refer to the following *Valve Seat Reconditioning* section) to relocate the sealing surface. If the initial lap indicates the sealing ring is centered on the valve face, proceed with a full lapping.

7. Clean the compound from the valve and seat frequently to check the progress of the lapping. Lap only enough to achieve a precise seating ring around the valve head. The pattern on the valve face should be an even width as shown in Figure 68.

8. Closely examine the valve seat in the cylinder head. It should be smooth and even with a smoothly burnished seating ring.

9. After lapping has been completed, thoroughly clean the valve face and valve seat areas using dampened cloths to remove all grinding compound. Any lapping compound residue left in the engine will cause rapid wear.

10. After the valve assemblies have been installed into the engine, test each valve seal by pouring solvent into the intake and exhaust ports. There should be no leakage past the seat. If fluid leaks past any of the seats, remove the valve and repeat the lapping procedure until there is no leakage.

Valve Seat Reconditioning

These cylinder heads use hardened alloy steel intake and exhaust valve seat inserts pressed into the head. The inserts are not replaceable. If the inserts are loose, cracked or seriously warped, replace the head. If the inserts are in good condition, they can be reworked.

Special valve cutter tools are required to recondition the valve seats in the cylinder heads properly. If these tools are not available, remove the cylinder head and take it to a machine shop equipped to recondition valve seats.

The following procedure is provided for those who chose to perform this task.

Required tools are:

  a. Valve seat cutters.

  b. Vernier or dial caliper.

  c. Machinist's dye or Prussian Blue.

  d. Valve lapping stick.

The valve seat for both the intake and exhaust valves are machined to the same angles. The valve contact surface is cut to a 44.5° angle from center (89° total angle).

1. Carefully rotate and insert the solid pilot into the valve guide. Make sure the solid pilot is correctly seated.

2. Using the 44.5° cutter, rotate the tool one or two turns to remove roughness and clean the seat (**Figure 71**).

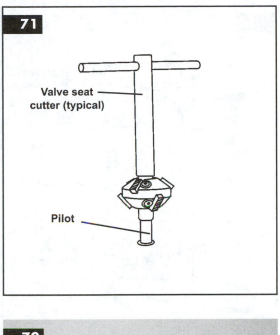

71

Valve seat cutter (typical)

Pilot

72

CAUTION
Measure the valve seat contact area in the cylinder head after each cut to make sure the contact area is correct and to prevent removing too much material. If too much material is removed, the cylinder head must be replaced.

3. If the seat is still pitted or burned, turn the 44.5° cutter additional turns until the surface is clean. Avoid removing too much material from the cylinder head.

4. Remove the valve cutter.

5. Inspect the valve seat-to-valve face impression as follows:

   a. Spread a thin layer of Prussian Blue or machinist's dye evenly on the valve face.

   b. Moisten the suction cup tool (**Figure 70**) and attach it to the valve. Insert the valve into the guide.

   c. Using the suction cup tool, tap the valve up and down in the cylinder head. Do *not* rotate the valve or a false indication will result.

6. Remove the valve and examine the impression left by the Prussian Blue or machinist's dye on the valve face (**Figure 72**).

   a. If the contact area is too low on the valve (too close to the stem), use the 60° cutter and remove a portion of the lower area of the valve seat material. This will raise the contact area.

   b. If the contact area is too high on the valve, use the 30° cutter and remove a portion of the top area of the valve seat material. This will lower the contact area.

7. Once the contact area is properly positioned on the valve face, adjust the valve seat width:

   a. If the width is too narrow, use the 44.5° cutter to widen the seat.

   b. If the width is too wide, use the 30° and 60° cutters equally to remove material from both above and below the seat contact area. When the seat width is correct, repeat Step 5 to ensure the correct seat-to-face position.

8. After the desired valve seat position and width is obtained, use the 44.5° cutter and very lightly clean off any burrs that may have been caused by the previous cuts.

9. Check that the finish has a smooth surface. It should not be rough or show chatter marks.

10. Repeat Steps 1-9 for the remaining valve seat.

11. Lap the valves as described under *Valve Lapping* in this chapter.

12. Thoroughly clean the cylinder head and all valve components in solvent or detergent and hot water to remove all cutting and lapping debris.

Valve Guide Reconditioning

The valve guides in these heads are not replaceable. To check guide-to-stem clearance:

1. Use a split-ball gauge to measure the inside diameter of the guide. Measure the top, the middle and the bottom of the guide. Note the measurements and compare them to the specifications in **Figure 64**.

2. Use an outside micrometer to measure the valve stem along the guide wear area. Again measure at the top, middle and bottom of the wear area. Note the measurements and compare them to the specifications in **Figure 64**.

3. Subtract the smallest stem measurement from the largest guide measurement. This is the stem-to-guide clearance. Compare this dimension to the specification in **Table 5**.

4. If the guide wear is beyond specification:

   a. Use Tool No. KO-1026 to ream the guide 0.25 mm (0.010 in.) oversize. Follow the instructions included with the reamer.

   b. Install the proper oversize-stem valve.

5. If the guide is within specification but the valve stem is worn beyond limits, replace the valve with a standard valve.

7

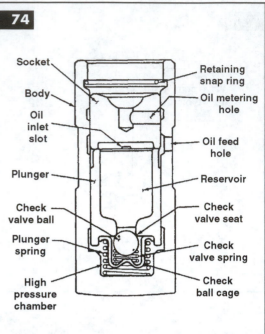

Valve Installation

1. Install the valve assemblies as described under *Cylinder Head, Reassembly* in this chapter. Make sure the keepers (B, **Figure 73**) are completely seated on the end of the valve stem (A) inside the spring retainer. After the keepers have been installed, gently tap the end of the valve stem with a soft aluminum or brass drift and hammer. This will ensure that the keepers are properly seated.

2. After the valve assemblies have been installed into the cylinder head, test each valve seal by pouring solvent into the intake and exhaust ports. There should be no leakage past the seat. If fluid leaks past any of the seats, remove the valve and repeat the lapping procedure until there is no leakage.

3. If the cylinder head and valve components were cleaned in detergent and hot water, apply a light coat of engine oil to all bare metal surfaces to prevent any corrosion, unless the engine is going to be run immediately.

HYDRAULIC VALVE LIFTERS

Hydraulic valve lifters are used in this engine. The hydraulic lifter has two main advantages over solid lifters: quieter operation and the elimination of periodic valve clearance adjustments.

Figure 74 shows a cutaway view of the hydraulic lifter. The principle of operation of the lifter is as follows:

When the valve is closed, valve spring pressure acting through the rocker arm and push rod exerts pressure on the upper socket, pushing the plunger against the plunger spring.

Pressurized oil from the oil pump enters the oil feed hole, opening the check valve and pressurizing the high-pressure chamber. The pressurized oil combines with the plunger spring to keep zero clearance in the valve train.

As the cam lobe raises the lifter, valve spring tension creates increased pressure in the high-pressure chamber.

This forces the check ball against its seat, allowing the lifter to keep zero clearance between the cam lobe, lifter, push rod, rocker arm and valve.

Tight tolerances between the plunger and lifter body allow controlled oil leakage to compensate for system expansion, wear and bleeding of the lifter during maintenance (**Figure 75**).

If the hydraulic valve lifters are noisy after the engine has run for several minutes and reached operating temperature, it is probably an indication that either contamination is preventing the lifter check ball from seating or there is internal wear in the lifter. Individual parts are not available for the hydraulic lifters. Lifters should be replaced if faulty.

Current production engines are equipped with new style "quick-purge" lifters that reduce the lifter pump-up time and resultant noisy operation during engine start-up. The new style lifters, part No. 25 351 01, are available for service replacement on all engines.

Removal

CAUTION
Do not use magnetic pick-up tools to remove hydraulic lifters. Using magnetic tools can cause the small internal lifter components to become magnetized and attract metal particles present in the oil. This will lead to lifter malfunction and failure.

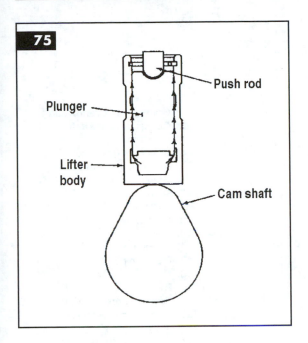

The hydraulic lifters should always be removed from the cylinder head end to prevent damage to the camshaft lobes. To remove the lifters:

1. Follow Steps 1-8 under *Cylinder Head, Removal* in this chapter.

2. Using Kohler Tool No. KO-1044, remove the lifters from their bores.

3. Mark the lifters for installation into the same bores if they are reused. Switching lifters could cause rapid camshaft lobe wear. The intake valve lifter is closest to the flywheel; the exhaust valve lifter is closest to the oil pan.

NOTE
Never reinstall used lifters if a new camshaft is being installed.

Inspection

1. Visually check the crankcase lifter bores and the outside diameters of the lifters for scoring, gouging or galling.

2. Verify that the oil galleries are not obstructed.

3. Inspect the lifter components for damage. Although it is possible to disassemble and clean the lifters, it is not recommended. If in doubt, replace the lifter.

4. Use an inside micrometer or a telescoping gauge and an outside micrometer to measure the inside diameter of the lifter bore. Measure the top, the middle and the bottom of the bore. Note the measurements.

5. Use an outside micrometer to measure the lifter diameter. Again measure at the top, middle and bottom of the lifter. Note the measurements.

6. Subtract the smallest lifter measurement from the largest bore measurement. This is the running clearance. Lifter-to-crankcase bore running clearance is 0.0124-0.0501 mm (0.0005-0.0020 in.).

7. If wear is beyond specification:
   a. Measure the diameter of a new lifter.
   b. Compare the new measurement to the worn measurement.
   c. If the wear is in the lifter, replace the lifter.
   d. If the lifter is within specification but the crankcase bore is worn, the crankcase will need to be replaced.

8. Inspect the camshaft lobe rub area on the bottom of the lifter for wear.

Installation

1. If installing the original lifters, note the marked positions of the lifters and install them into their proper bores.

2. If installing new lifters, lifter positions are interchangeable.

NOTE
If the engine will not be started immediately after assembly, apply Lubriplate or any equivalent engine camshaft break-in lubricant to the solid lifter end rather than engine oil. The camshaft break-in lubricant will adhere better to the surface and not drain away.

3. Install the cylinder head and bleed the lifters as described under *Cylinder Head, Installation* in this chapter.

GOVERNOR

External Service

A flyweight-type governor is located in the oil pan (**Figure 76**). The governor cross shaft extends through the crankcase to operate the external governor linkage (**Figure 77**). The camshaft gear drives the governor gear. Refer to the *Governor, Internal Service* section for overhaul information.

On these commercial-mower engines, the governor linkage will appear as shown in **Figure 77**. If the governor spring has been disconnected, reconnect as follows:

1. Position the spring so the open side of the spring hooks face the engine.

2. Hook the long straight end of the spring through the throttle lever.

3. Hook the short end through the appropriate hole in the governor arm.

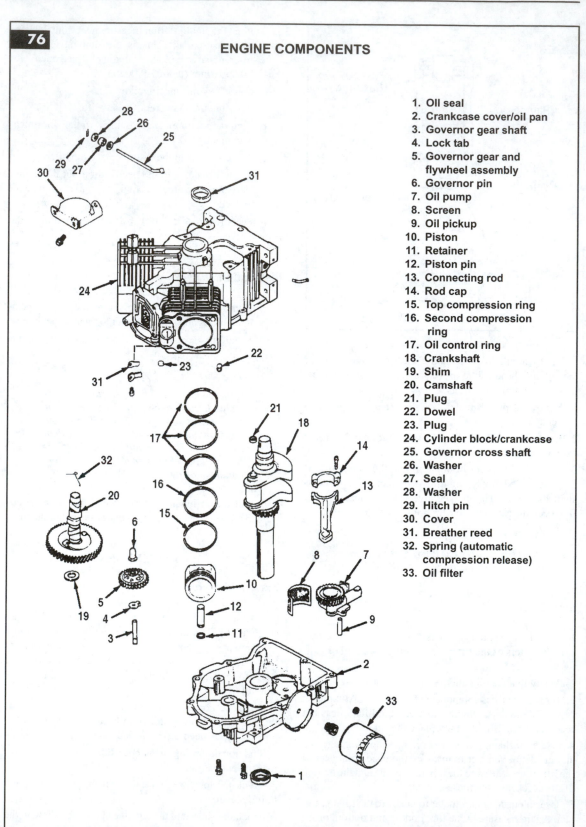

76

ENGINE COMPONENTS

1. Oil seal
2. Crankcase cover/oil pan
3. Governor gear shaft
4. Lock tab
5. Governor gear and flywheel assembly
6. Governor pin
7. Oil pump
8. Screen
9. Oil pickup
10. Piston
11. Retainer
12. Piston pin
13. Connecting rod
14. Rod cap
15. Top compression ring
16. Second compression ring
17. Oil control ring
18. Crankshaft
19. Shim
20. Camshaft
21. Plug
22. Dowel
23. Plug
24. Cylinder block/crankcase
25. Governor cross shaft
26. Washer
27. Seal
28. Washer
29. Hitch pin
30. Cover
31. Breather reed
32. Spring (automatic compression release)
33. Oil filter

77

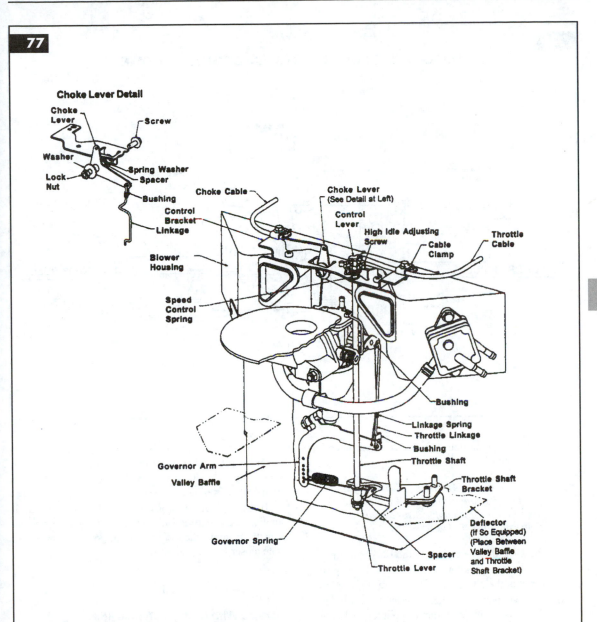

Choke Lever Detail

Choke Lever — Screw

Washer

Lock Nut

Spring Washer — Spacer

Bushing

Control Bracket — Linkage

Choke Cable

Blower Housing

Speed Control Spring

Choke Lever (See Detail at Left)

Control Lever

High Idle Adjusting Screw

Cable Clamp

Throttle Cable

Bushing

Linkage Spring

Throttle Linkage

Bushing

Throttle Shaft

Governor Arm

Valley Baffle

Throttle Shaft Bracket

Deflector (If So Equipped) (Place Between Valley Baffle and Throttle Shaft Bracket)

Governor Spring

Spacer

Throttle Lever

78

RPM Adjustment

To static-adjust the governor linkage, proceed as follows:

1. Loosen the governor lever clamp nut (A, **Figure 78**).

2. Push the governor lever so the throttle is wide open.

3. While holding the throttle open, turn the governor cross shaft (B, **Figure 78**) counterclockwise as far as possible, then torque the clamp nut 9.9 N·m (88 in.-lb.).

4. The maximum operating speed is 3600 rpm. Use a tachometer to check the engine speed. To adjust the high-speed setting:

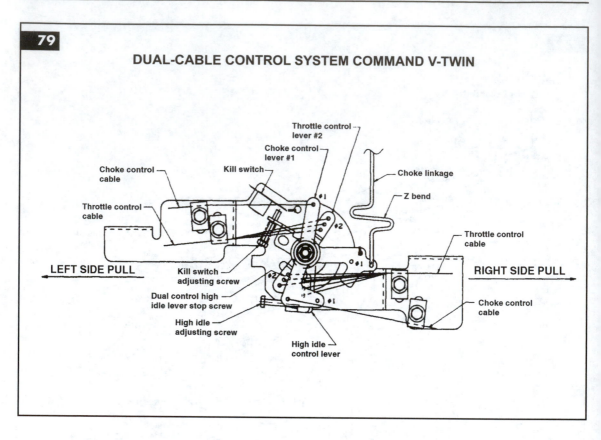

79

DUAL-CABLE CONTROL SYSTEM COMMAND V-TWIN

Throttle control lever #2
Choke control lever #1
Choke control cable
Kill switch
Choke linkage
Z bend
Throttle control cable
Throttle control cable
LEFT SIDE PULL
RIGHT SIDE PULL
Kill switch adjusting screw
Dual control high idle lever stop screw
Choke control cable
High idle adjusting screw
High idle control lever

a. Start the engine and allow it to reach operating temperature.

> *WARNING*
> *Ensure adequate ventilation if the engine is to be run in a confined area. Exhaust fumes are toxic and deadly.*

b. Move the throttle control to the FAST position.

c. Loosen the locknut on the high-idle adjusting screw of the governor control plate (**Figure 79**).

d. Observe the tachometer. Turn the high-idle screw clockwise to increase rpm or counterclockwise to decrease rpm.

e. Tighten the locknut when the correct rpm is achieved.

> *NOTE*
> *After setting the high rpm, ensure that there is at least a 0.5 mm (.020 in.) gap between the high-idle control lever and the choke control lever to allow freedom of movement.*

Sensitivity Adjustment

Governor sensitivity is adjusted by relocating the governor spring to another hole in the governor arm.

1. If the engine rpm surges when the load changes, the governor setting is too sensitive. To decrease governor sensitivity, move the short end of the governor spring to a hole farther from the cross shaft.

2. If the engine rpm drops considerably when a load is applied, the governor is not sensitive enough. To increase sensitivity, move the short end of the governor spring to a hole closer to the cross shaft.

OIL SEALS

Service With Crankshaft Installed

Oil seals at the flywheel end of the crankshaft and at the PTO end prevent the oil in the engine from leaking out. Wear or damage can reduce their effectiveness and oil leakage can become a problem, particularly if excessive amounts of oil are lost.

In some instances, it is possible to remove and install an oil seal without removing the crankshaft. Depending on the location of the engine and which oil seal is leaking, it may be necessary to remove the engine from the equipment.

If the oil seal at the flywheel end of the crankshaft is leaking, the flywheel must be removed (see the *Flywheel, Removal* section). If the oil seal at the output end of the crankshaft is leaking, any parts attached to the crankshaft

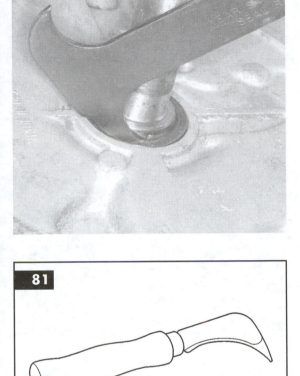

80

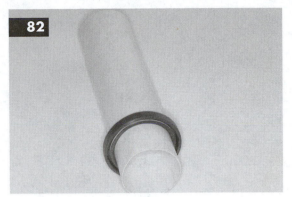

82

1. Special oil seal removal tools are available from small engine tool suppliers (**Figure 80**), or one can make an effective but inexpensive oil seal removal tool by modifying a linoleum knife as shown in **Figure 81**. Carefully grind the blade to the contour shown in the figure, then round all the blade edges so the blade will not damage the crankshaft or seal cavity.

2. Using a small pin punch, carefully tap the seal in a couple of places around its outer edge so as to break it loose from the crankcase cavity. Only tap it enough to break it loose. Do not drive it deeper into the cavity.

3. Carefully insert the tool blade under the oil seal lip and against the inside periphery of the seal, next to the crankshaft (**Figure 80**). Pry out the seal. It may be necessary to work around the seal in more than one spot before the seal will break loose.

4. Clean and dry the seal seating area so the new seal will seat properly.

5. Check the oil seal bore in the engine and dress out any burrs created during removal. Only remove metal that is raised and will interfere with the installation of the new seal. If a deep gouge is present, carefully clean and dry the area around the gouge, then fill the depression with a suitable epoxy so it is level with the surrounding metal.

6. Check the crankshaft seal area. Scoring, grooves, or sharp edges on the crankshaft will require that the crankshaft be replaced.

81

that deny access to the oil seal must be removed. Refer to the *Engine Removal* section if the engine must be removed from the mower.

NOTE
Drain the engine oil if replacing the lower crankshaft oil seal.

Removal

Before removing an oil seal, note the position of the seal in the crankcase or oil pan. Install the new seal so it is located at the same depth as the original seal.

CAUTION
Exercise care when extracting the seal so the metal in the seal bore or the crankshaft seal surface is not scratched or damaged.

Installation

1. Apply Loctite 598 or equivalent oil resistant non-hardening sealer to the periphery of the oil seal prior to installation.

2. Coat the lips of the seal with grease.

3. Cover the keyways and threads on the crankshaft with a seal protector sleeve or thin tape so the oil seal lip will not be cut when passing the oil seal down the crankshaft. **Figure 82** shows the seal installed onto a protector sleeve.

4. Position the seal so the seal lip is slanted toward the inside of the engine. Most seals are spring-loaded. The spring must be toward the engine when installing the seal.

7

5. Use a suitable tool with the same outside diameter as the oil seal to force the oil seal into the engine. A deep-well socket may work if the output end of the crankshaft is short. Suitable sizes of tubing or pipe may be used (**Figure 83**). Be sure the end of the tool is square but not sharp.

6. The crankshaft oil seals should be installed so they are approximately 0.79 mm (1/32 in.) below flush with the seal bore faces (**Figure 84**, PTO seal shown).

INTERNAL ENGINE COMPONENTS

Although some internal components can be serviced without a complete disassembly, damage to one internal engine component often affects some or all of the other parts inside the engine. Failing to inspect all of the components may result in a future repair that could have been avoided.

Refer to **Figure 76** when performing internal component procedures.

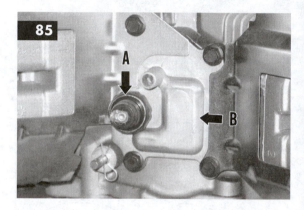

ENGINE DISASSEMBLY

Refer to the appropriate previous sections when removing the external engine components as applicable.

1. Disconnect the battery, negative cable first.
2. Turn the fuel tank valve off (Figure 3).
3. Disconnect and ground the spark plug leads.
4. Drain the engine oil and remove the engine from the equipment. Remove the oil filter.
5. Remove the muffler and exhaust system.
6. Remove the air filter assembly.
7. Remove the external governor controls.
8. Remove the blower housing, shrouds and baffles.
9. Remove the intake manifold and carburetor.
10. Remove the ignition modules.
11. Remove the flywheel and alternator stator.
12. Remove the blower housing baseplates.
13. Remove the electric starter motor.
14. Remove the crankcase breather chamber cover plate (B, **Figure 85**) and Oil Sentry switch (A).

15. Remove the spark plugs, then remove the cylinder heads.

16. Mark and remove the push rods.

17. Remove the hydraulic lifters and identify them so they can be reinstalled in their original location.

> *CAUTION*
> *Do not use magnetic pick-up tools to remove hydraulic lifters. Using magnetic tools can cause the small internal lifter*

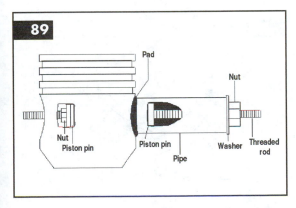

components to become magnetized and attract metal particles present in the oil.
This will lead to lifter malfunction and
failure.

18. Turn the crankshaft so the pistons are below TDC.
Run a fingernail over the top portion of the cylinder and
determine if a ridge exists. If so, use a ridge reamer and
remove the ridge at the top of the cylinder.

19. If not previously removed, remove any parts attached
to the crankshaft.

20. Remove any rust or burrs from the crankshaft. This
will prevent damage to the main bearings. A strip of em-

ery cloth can be used to remove rust. Use a fine file to
remove any burrs found adjacent to the keyways.

21. Unscrew the 10 oil pan retaining screws (**Figure 86**;
not all screws shown).

22. To break the oil pan loose from the crankcase, position the square drive end of a 1/2-inch breaker bar between the tabs on the oil pan and the bosses on the
crankcase (**Figure 87**). Rotating the breaker bar will separate the oil pan from the crankcase.

23. Remove the oil pan. If binding occurs when removing the oil pan, determine if an obstruction on the crankshaft, such as a burr, is causing the binding. If no
obstruction is present, then the crankshaft might be bent.

NOTE
*Do not lose the thrust washer shim on the
end of the camshaft.*

24. Remove the camshaft.

25. Unscrew the connecting rod cap bolts and remove the
rod cap from the No. 2 cylinder connecting rod (nearer the
oil pan).

NOTE
*Be careful not to damage the bearing sur-
face of the crankshaft, connecting rod and
rod cap.*

26. Push the No. 2 cylinder connecting rod and piston out
the top of the engine.

27. Repeat steps 25 and 26 for the No. 1 cylinder.

28. Remove the crankshaft.

The major components of the engine should now be removed from the engine crankcase. Refer to the following
sections for further disassembly and inspection.

PISTONS, PISTON RINGS AND PISTON (WRIST) PINS

The aluminum-alloy pistons are each fitted with two
compression rings and one oil control ring. Pistons and
rings are available in standard size and 0.25 mm and 0.50
mm (0.010 in. and 0.020 in.) oversize. Refer to the *Cylinders* section if a 0.08 mm (0.003 in.) oversize piston is en-
countered upon engine disassembly.

To remove the pistons, follow Steps 1-27 in the *Engine
Disassembly* section.

Disassembly

1. Extract the piston pin retaining clips (**Figure 88**).
2. Push or tap out the piston pin.

NOTE
*If the piston pin is stuck in the piston, a
puller tool like that shown in **Figure 89**
can be fabricated to extract the pin.*

3. Separate the piston from the connecting rod.

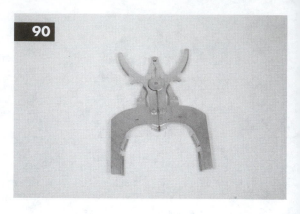

> *NOTE*
> *A suitable piston ring expander tool (**Figure 90**) should be used to remove or install the piston rings. Although the rings can be removed or installed by hand, there is less chance of piston ring breakage or gouging the piston ring grooves when the ring expander tool is used.*

4. Remove the piston rings while noting the following:
   a. Remove the top compression ring (closest to the piston crown) first.
   b. Remove the No. 2 compression ring second.
   c. Remove the oil control ring last.

5. Move the rings toward the piston crown for removal. Discard the piston rings. Reusing worn rings is not recommended.

6. Thoroughly clean the ring grooves. Do not gouge or damage the grooves while cleaning. A professional ring groove cleaning tool is shown in **Figure 91**. A convenient substitute ring groove cleaner can be made from a broken piece of the original ring (**Figure 92**).

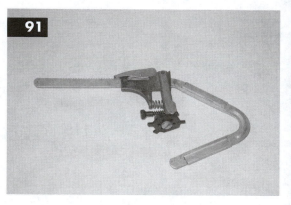

Inspection

1. Inspect the piston for damage. Replace the piston if it is cracked, scored, scuffed or scratched. Be sure to inspect the underside of the piston around the piston pin bosses for cracks, as well as the piston ring grooves. The piston crown must be smooth except for machining or casting marks.

2. Check the piston for excessive wear. To determine the piston thrust face diameter, measure the piston perpendicular to the wrist pin at a distance of 6.0 mm (1/4 in.) from the bottom of the piston (**Figure 93**). Standard piston diameter is 76.967-76.985 mm (3.0302-3.0309 in.). Replace the piston if the diameter is less than 76.840 mm (3.0252 in.).

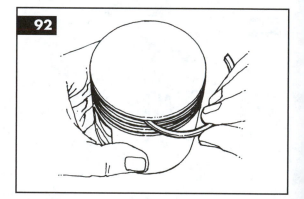

> *NOTE*
> *A factory replacement piston assembly includes the piston, rings, wrist pin and pin retainers. Neither the piston nor the wrist pin is available separately.*

3. Measure the wrist pin bore in the piston. A new bore diameter is 17.006-17.012 mm (0.6695-0.6698 in.). The wear limit is 17.025 mm (0.6703 in.). If beyond specification, replace the piston assembly.

4. Measure the wrist pin at multiple positions. A new pin diameter is 16.995-17.000 mm (0.6691- 0.6693 in.). The wear limit is 16.994 mm (0.6691 in.). If beyond specification, replace the piston assembly.

5. Install new compression rings onto the piston, then use a feeler gauge to measure the side (ring land) clearance

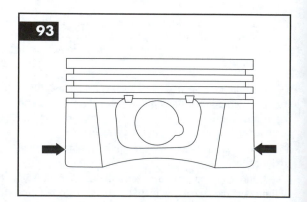

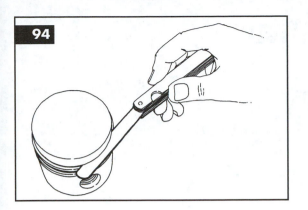

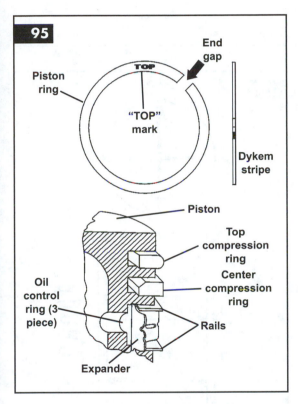

NOTE
Only the compression rings need to be gapped. The 3-piece oil control ring is not gapped.

Assembly

A piston ring expander tool (**Figure 90**) should be used to install the compression rings. Before installing the rings, lubricate the ring grooves thoroughly with fresh engine oil.

1. When assembling piston rings on the piston, install the oil control ring first. To install the 3-piece oil control ring, first install the expander, then install one end of each rail and carefully feed the rail into position with a light twisting motion. If there are instructions included with the replacement rings, follow the instructions. The thin oil control ring rails that fit over the expander are easily bent if not properly handled.

CAUTION
Do not overlap the ends of the oil control ring expander when fitting the oil control rails over the expander and do not use a bent oil control ring rail.

2. The two compression rings should be installed on the piston with the side of the ring marked TOP toward the piston crown and the colored Dykem stripe to the left of the end gap with the piston upright.(**Figure 95**).

   a. The top (No. 1) compression ring has a barrel-shaped face.

   b. The No. 2 compression ring (center groove) has a top bevel on the inside of the ring.

3. The ring end gaps should be spaced around the piston circumference in the approximate intervals as shown in **Figure 96** and **Figure 97**. **Figure 96** is the gap spacing recommendation for the No. 1 piston; **Figure 97** is for the No. 2 piston.

4. After the rings are installed on the piston, use a feeler gauge to measure the side (ring land) clearance (**Figure 94**). Replace the piston if a new top or second piston ring has a side clearance of 0.040-0.080 mm (0.0016-0.0031 in.) or greater.

To install the pistons into the engine, follow the necessary steps in the *Engine Reassembly* section.

CYLINDERS/CYLINDER BLOCK/CRANKCASE

The cylinders are cast-iron alloy sleeves integrally cast into the aluminum alloy crankcase and block assembly.

To access the cylinders, follow the steps outlined in the previous *Engine Disassembly* section.

Pistons and ring sets are available in oversizes of 0.25 mm (0.010 in.) and 0.50 mm (0.020 in.) to fit rebored cylinder bores.

(**Figure 94**). Ring land clearance dimensions are listed in **Table 5**. If beyond specification, replace the piston.

6. To measure the end gap of each piston ring:

   a. Place the ring into the top end of the cylinder.

   b. Use the piston to drive the ring squarely into the cylinder until the beginning of the wrist pin bore is even with the top of the cylinder.

   c. Remove the piston.

   d. Using a feeler gauge, measure the end gap. The end gap of new rings in a new or rebored cylinder bore should be 0.25-0.45 mm (0.0098-0.0177 in.). The maximum allowable gap of new rings in a worn cylinder is 0.77 mm (0.030 in.).

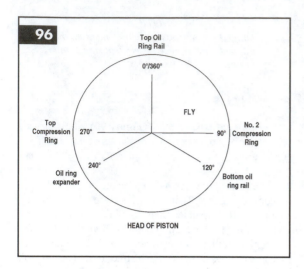

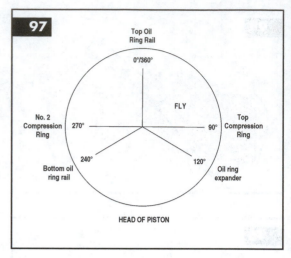

Inspection and Reconditioning

1. Make sure all gasket and sealant material has been carefully and completely removed from the sealing surfaces. Sealing surfaces must be free from nicks, gouges or deep scratches.

2. Inspect the fastener holes for damaged threads or broken fasteners.

   a. For broken fasteners, refer to *Special Tools, Removing Broken Fasteners* in Chapter One.

   b. For damaged threads, restore the threads with an appropriate size metric tap if necessary. If thread damage is severe, a Heli-Coil or equivalent replacement thread can be installed. If the threaded holes cannot be satisfactorily repaired, replace the cylinder block.

3. Check for broken cooling fins. A small broken edge or corner may not affect performance. A large piece of broken-off fin will cause the cylinder to overheat. Replace the cylinder block if major fin damage is evident.

4. Check for debris packed in between the fins. Carefully and completely remove any heat-caked debris.

5. Check the bore for scoring.

6. If the cylinder has been previously rebored, the piston will be marked .080, .250 or .500 to show its oversize. A block whose cylinder will not clean up at .500 mm (0.020 in.) or one that has already been rebored to .500 mm and then worn beyond limits must be replaced.

> *NOTE*
> *Some oversized cylinder blocks and matching piston/ring assemblies were used in factory production. Factory-oversized engines are identified by a colored line painted along the top cooling fin on the PTO side of the engine block. Red paint indicates a .080 mm (0.003 in.) oversize and blue paint indicates a .250 mm*

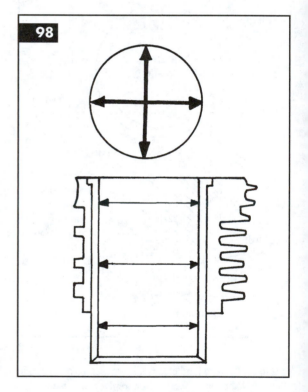

(0.010 in.) oversize. Factory oversizing must be taken into consideration when measuring the cylinder bore.

7. Measure the cylinder bore parallel with the crankshaft and at right angles to the crankshaft at the top, center and bottom of ring travel (**Figure 98**). Compare the measurements to the dimensions listed in **Table 5**.

8. If the cylinder bore is within the specified wear limit, the bore will need to be honed so new rings will seat properly. The crosshatch angle of the bore surface after finish

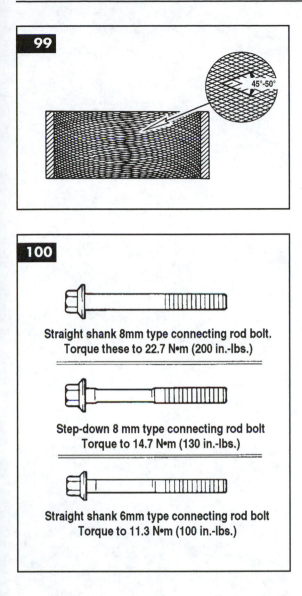

99

45°-50°

100

Straight shank 8mm type connecting rod bolt.
Torque these to 22.7 N•m (200 in.-lbs.)

Step-down 8 mm type connecting rod bolt
Torque to 14.7 N•m (130 in.-lbs.)

Straight shank 6mm type connecting rod bolt
Torque to 11.3 N•m (100 in.-lbs.)

NOTE
Do not use petroleum solvents (mineral spirits, kerosene, etc.) to clean the bore. Solvents will not remove grinding dust from the cylinder bore surface.

  b. Rinse with clean warm water.

  c. Blow-dry with compressed air.

12. After drying the cylinder, spray the bore with a moisture-displacing lubricant such as WD-40 or equivalent.

  a. Use a clean, lint-free cloth to wipe the lubricant from the bore. If gray residue shows up on the wiping cloth, the cylinder is not clean. Repeat Step 11 until no gray residue appears;

  b. Apply a light coat of engine oil to the bore to prevent rust.

CAUTION
Failure to properly clean a honed or rebored cylinder will cause rapid cylinder and piston wear and severe engine damage.

CONNECTING RODS

Removal

The piston and connecting rod are removed from the engine as an assembly, then separated, as outlined in the previous *Engine Disassembly* section.

NOTE
*Three different style connecting rod bolts are used. Each style bolt has a different tightening torque. Refer to **Figure 100** to identify the rod bolts and their respective torque values.*

Inspection

1. The connecting rod journal rides directly on the crankshaft crankpin. Inspect both the crankpin and the wrist pin bearing surfaces for signs of scuffing, scoring, excessive wear or overheating. If any damage is observed, also inspect the surface of the mating crankpin or piston pin.

NOTE
If the rod bearing surface is worn due to abrasive particles (the surface texture is dull and rough), it should be replaced even if it is not worn beyond the specified wear limit. Grit may be embedded in the aluminum, which will continue to cause wear on mating surfaces.

2. Inspect the connecting rod for cracks, twisting and other damage.

honing should be 45°-50° as shown in **Figure 99**. Too large an angle will cause high oil consumption; too small an angle will make the rings skip and wear rapidly. Always follow the hone manufacturer's instructions.

9. If the cylinder is being rebored oversize, rebore to the specified original-plus-oversize dimension. Follow the bore machine manufacturer's instructions. The final step of a rebore should always be a finish honing.

11. After honing the cylinder:

  a. Thoroughly wash the cylinder with plenty of soap and hot water. This will remove the microscopic grinding particles from the surface of the cylinder bore. A grease-cutting dishwashing detergent is an excellent soap to use.

7

3. Measure the connecting rod dimensions and clearances. Replace the connecting rod if any dimensions do not meet the specifications listed in **Table 5**.

4. The procedure for measuring connecting rod-to-crankshaft bearing clearance is outlined in the next section. To measure side play:

   a. Install the connecting rods onto the crankshaft.

   b. Using a feeler gauge, measure the side clearance between the rods or between either rod and the side of the crankpin shoulder.

5. Measure the small end diameter of the connecting rod and the diameter of the wrist pin. The difference between the two dimensions is the wrist pin clearance.

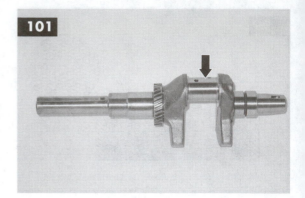

Connecting Rod-to-Crankshaft Bearing Clearance Measurement

Plastigage is the most popular and convenient way to measure connecting rod-to-crankshaft journal clearance. Plastigage comes in three sizes: 0.025-0.076 mm (0.001-0.003 inch); 0.051-0.152 mm (0.002-0.006 inch); and 0.102-0.229 mm (0.004-0.009 inch). To gauge the clearance:

1. Clean the crankshaft crankpin (**Figure 101**) and check for damage.

2. Position the connecting rod onto the crankshaft in the correct position on the crankpin. The No. 1 rod fits at the flywheel end of the journal.

3. Cut a strip of Plastigage slightly shorter than the width of the connecting rod/crankshaft journal (**Figure 102**). Place the Plastigage onto the crankpin. Make sure the Plastigage runs parallel to the crankshaft, as shown in **Figure 102**. Do not place the Plastigage material over the oil hole in the crankshaft.

4. Correctly align the rod cap with the rod (**Figure 103**). Tighten the rod cap bolts to the specified torque.

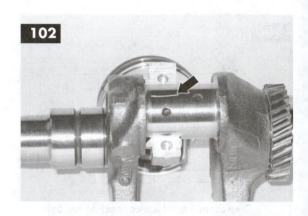

> *CAUTION*
> *When tightening the rod cap bolts, do not rotate the connecting rod or the crankshaft. Damaged Plastigage and inaccurate readings will result.*

> *NOTE*
> *Three different style connecting rod bolts are used. Each style bolt has a different tightening torque. Refer to **Figure 100** to identify the rod bolts and their respective torque values.*

5. Loosen the rod cap bolts. Carefully lift the cap straight up and off the connecting rod.

6. Compare the flattened Plastigage width to the scale furnished with the Plastigage (**Figure 104**). This will tell the clearance.

   a. If clearance exceeds 0.070 mm (0.0025 in.), replace the connecting rod and recondition the

crankshaft. A connecting rod with a 0.25 mm (0.010 in.) undersize crankshaft journal bore is available. The 0.25 mm (0.010 in.) undersize connecting rod is identified by a drilled hole in the connecting rod just above the big end bore (**Figure 105**).

   b. If the crankshaft must be reground to accept an undersize connecting rod, refer to the *Crankshaft* section for machining information.

7. Remove all of the Plastigage from the crankshaft and connecting rod.

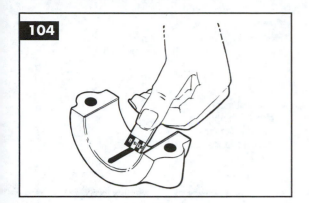

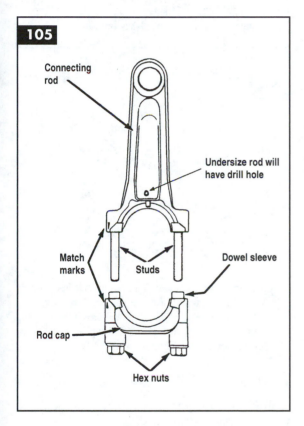

Installation

To install the connecting rod into the engine, follow the necessary steps under *Engine Reassembly* in this chapter.

CRANKSHAFT AND MAIN BEARINGS

These engines use a non-replaceable upper main bearing that is machined into the crankcase casting. The lower main bearing is an integral part of the oil pan, machined into the oil pan casting.

NOTE
When replacing a crankshaft, short block, or engine, make sure the threads on the PTO bolt that was removed from the old crankshaft are compatible with the threads in the new crankshaft. An engine may have either metric or inch threads.

The crankshaft and main bearing specifications are listed in **Table 5**.

Removal

To remove the crankshaft, follow Steps 1-28 under *Engine Disassembly* in this chapter.

Inspection and Reconditioning

Inspect the crankshaft as follows:
1. If considerable effort was required to remove the oil pan from the crankshaft, then the crankshaft is probably bent and must be discarded. Crankshaft runout can be used as an indicator of crankshaft straightness. Proceed to Step 2 to measure runout.
2. Measure crankshaft runout using one of the following procedures:
   a. Install the crankshaft in the engine. Be sure the main bearings are lubricated. Using a dial indicator fastened to the oil pan, measure crankshaft runout at the PTO end of the crankshaft.
   b. On the workbench, support the crankshaft in V-blocks at the main bearing journals. Use a dial indicator to measure runout at the PTO end of the crankshaft.

CAUTION
When using a dial indicator to check run-out, exercise caution when the crankshaft keyway approaches the indicator anvil. Dial indicator damage could result if the keyway strikes the anvil.

   c. Replace the crankshaft if runout exceeds the limits specified in **Table 5**.
3. Inspect all bearing surfaces on the crankshaft for indications of scoring, scuffing or other damage. This includes the main and thrust bearing faces.
4. Check the fastener threads, such as the flywheel and PTO threads, for damage and cross-threading. Repair if possible, using a Heli-Coil or other thread replacement insert.
5. Inspect the keyways and carefully remove any burrs. The keyways must be straight and unworn. The PTO extension must also be straight and unworn.
6. Check the crankshaft gears for broken or pitted teeth. If the gear teeth are questionable, also inspect the camshaft and balance shaft gear teeth.

7

7. Measure the connecting rod (crankpin) journal. Regrind or replace the crankshaft if the crankpin diameter is 35.94 mm (1.4150 in.) or less. If the crankpin journal is 0.025 mm (0.001 in.) or more out-of-round, or if the journal has 0.018 mm (0.0007 in.) or more taper, regrind or replace the crankshaft.

8. A connecting rod with a 0.25 mm (0.010 in.) undersize crankshaft journal bore is available. The 0.25 mm (0.010 in.) undersize connecting rod is identified by a drilled hole in the connecting rod beam just above the big end bore (**Figure 105**).

> *NOTE*
> *If the crankpin is reground, the crankpin fillet should be machined as shown in **Figure 106**.*

9. Measure the crankshaft main bearing journals:
   a. If the flywheel journal has worn to 40.84 mm (1.608 in.) or less, is 0.025 mm (.0010 in) out-of-round, or has at least 0.022 mm (.0009 in.) taper, replace the crankshaft.
   b. If the PTO journal has worn to 40.84 mm (1.608 in.) or less, is 0.025 mm (.0010 in.) out-of-round, or has at least 0.020 mm (.0008 in.) taper, replace the crankshaft.

10. Measure the main bearing bores:
   a. If the upper main bearing has worn to 41.016 mm (1.6148 in.) or more, replace the crankcase.
   b. If the lower main (oil pan) bearing has worn to 41.025 mm (1.6152 in.) or more, replace the crankcase.

11. Main bearing-to-crankshaft running clearance should be 0.03-0.09 mm (0.0012-0.0035 in.) for the upper bearing and 0.039-0.074 mm (0.0015-0.0029 in.) for the lower bearing.

> *NOTE*
> *If the crankpin is reground, the oil gallery plug must be removed, the gallery cleaned of all grinding debris, and a new plug installed. Refer to Step 12 and Step 13.*

12. To remove the crankshaft oil gallery plug (**Figure 107**):
   a. Drill a 4.75 mm (3/16 in.) hole into the center of the plug.
   b. Place a large-diameter 4.75 mm (3/16 in.) flat washer over the end of the plug bore on the crankshaft.
   c. Thread a 25 mm (1.0 in.) long self-tapping screw into the hole drilled into the plug.
   d. Continue tightening the screw until the plug pulls out.

13. To install a new crankshaft oil gallery plug:
   a. Make sure that the plug and bore are clean and dry.
   b. Set the plug into the bore. Make sure that the closed end of the plug is at the bottom of the bore.

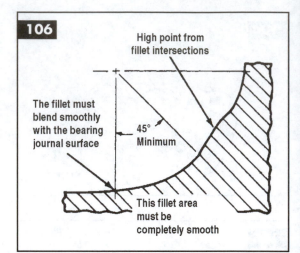

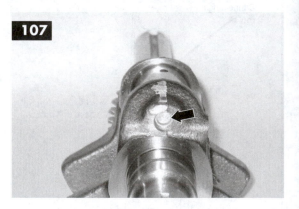

   c. Using a pin punch with a tip diameter just slightly smaller than the outside diameter of the plug, lightly tap the plug into the bore. Tap the plug evenly to prevent leakage and tap it until it seats completely at the bottom of the bore.

Installation

To install the crankshaft, follow the necessary steps under *Engine Reassembly* in this chapter.

CAMSHAFT

The camshaft (**Figure 108**) rides directly in bores machined into the aluminum of the crankcase and oil pan.

To remove the camshaft from the engine, follow the necessary steps under *Engine Reassembly* in this chapter.

The camshaft is equipped with a compression release mechanism to aid starting. The sliding weight mechanism on the camshaft gear and inside the camshaft moves pins inside the exhaust cam lobes. During starting (RPM below 700), the pins protrude above the bottom of the cam lobes and force the exhaust valves to stay open longer,

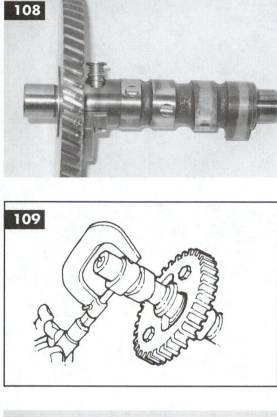

108

109

110

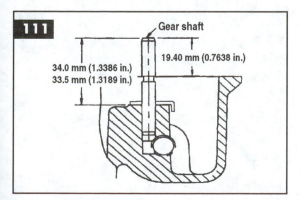

111

Gear shaft

19.40 mm (0.7638 in.)

34.0 mm (1.3386 in.)
33.5 mm (1.3189 in.)

thereby reducing compression from the normal 8.5:1 to approximately 2:1. At running speed, centrifugal force causes the weight to pivot outward, pulling the internal arm and moving the pins. This keeps the pins below the surface of the cam lobes, allowing the engine to develop full power.

Camshaft specifications are listed in **Table 5**.

1. Inspect the gear teeth for wear and cracked or broken teeth. If any teeth are damaged, the camshaft will have to be replaced.

2. Inspect the camshaft journals and lobes for wear or scoring.

3. Measure the end bearing journals. Compare the measurements to the specifications in **Table 5**.

4. Measure the lift height of the intake and exhaust lobes. To determine the minimum lift height:

   a. Measure across the lift part of the lobe (**Figure 109**).

   b. Measure across the narrow diameter of the lobe.

   c. Subtract the measurement in substep b from the measurement in substep a. The minimum lift height should be 8.07 mm (0.3177 inch) for all lobes.

5. Inspect the camshaft bearing surfaces in the crankcase and oil pan. The surfaces must be smooth with no signs of abrasion.

6. Measure the camshaft bearing bore diameters in the crankcase and oil pan. Compare the measurements to the dimensions in **Table 5**.

7. Determine the camshaft bearing running clearances by subtracting the Step 4 dimensions from the Step 7 dimensions. Running clearance should be 0.025-0.063 mm (.0010-.0025 in.).

8. Inspect the compression release mechanism. It should move freely without binding. The mechanism has no replaceable components. If the compression release mechanism is faulty, replace the camshaft.

To install the camshaft into the engine, follow the necessary steps under *Engine Reassembly* section.

GOVERNOR

Internal Service

The engine is equipped with a flyweight mechanism mounted on the governor gear (**Figure 110**). The gear and flyweight are available only as a unit assembly.

The governor gear assembly is mounted on a shaft that is pressed into the crankcase (**Figure 111**). To access the governor assembly inside the engine, follow the necessary steps in the previous *Engine Disassembly* section.

NOTE
The governor gear has small tabs molded internally that hold it onto the shaft. Removing the gear assembly destroys these

7

tabs. If the gear assembly is removed, it must be discarded and replaced with a new gear assembly.

Inspect the gear assembly for excess wear and damage. Governor specifications are listed in **Table 5**.

1. If the governor gear shaft requires replacement:
   a. Carefully pull the old shaft from the oil pan.

CAUTION
Failure to pull straight when removing the shaft will damage the crankcase.

   b. Tap the new shaft into the bore in the oil pan so it protrudes as shown in **Figure 111**.
   c. Install a new governor locator washer and gear assembly onto the shaft (**Figure 110**). Make sure that the internal gear locks snap into position and that the gear assembly rotates freely.

2. If the governor cross shaft (**Figure 112**) requires replacement:
   a. Remove the cross shaft retaining clip (B, **Figure 113**) and flat washer (C) from outside the crankcase.
   b. Slide the shaft into the crankcase (**Figure 114**). Take care not to lose the small flat washer.
   c. Install a new shaft seal in the crankcase bore (**Figure 115**) with the flat seal face toward the outside. Drive the new seal into the bore so the outer face is just below the small diameter of the countersink.
   d. Lightly lubricate the seal lip with fresh engine oil.
   e. Carefully install the shaft through the crankcase bore. Do not damage the seal. Make sure that the small flat washer is positioned on the inner shaft tabs (**Figure 114**).
   f. Install the flat washer and retaining clip onto the shaft (**Figure 113**).

Installation of the remaining governor components is described under *Engine Reassembly* in this chapter.

OIL PUMP

The rotor-type oil pump is located in the oil pan (**Figure 116**). The crankshaft gear drives the oil pump gear. Individual components are not available.

1. To access the oil pump assembly inside the engine, follow the necessary steps under *Engine Disassembly*.
2. Remove the retaining screws, then remove the oil pump (**Figure 117**).
3. Remove, clean and inspect the pick-up screen (**Figure 118**). If questionable, replace it.
4. Inspect the oil pump. If the pump is excessively worn or damaged, replace the pump as a unit assembly.
5. Inspect the oil pump surface in the oil pan (**Figure 118**). If the surface is worn or scored, replace the oil pan.
6. When installing the oil pump, alternately tighten the oil pump mounting screws in 2.2 N·m (20 in.-lb.) increments

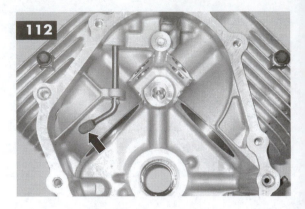

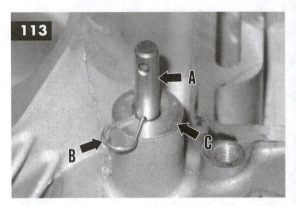

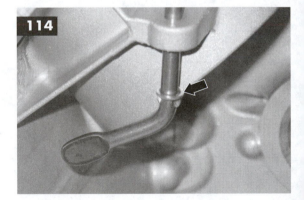

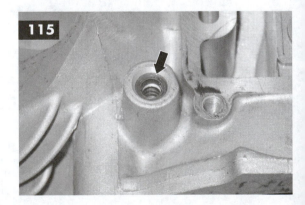

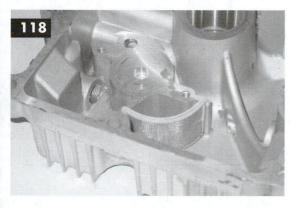

to 6.7 N•m (60 in.-lb.). Check the pump operation by rotating the drive gear. If the pump binds, loosen the screws, relocate the pump and recheck the pump operation.

ENGINE REASSEMBLY

Refer to the appropriate sections when installing the external engine components. Refer to **Figure 76** for internal engine component identification.

Before assembling the engine, be sure all components are clean. Any residue or debris left in the engine will cause rapid wear and/or major damage when the engine runs.

NOTE
Lubricate all internal component contact/wear surfaces with fresh engine oil immediately prior to assembly.

NOTE
Lightly coat all fastener threads, except the cylinder head bolts, with Loctite 242 or equivalent immediately prior to assembly. Do not use threadlock compound on the head bolts.

1. Rotate the governor cross shaft so the paddle is toward the outside (**Figure 112**).

2. Install the crankshaft into the crankcase. If the flywheel-side oil seal has already been installed, use a seal protector sleeve or adhesive tape to prevent the crankshaft from damaging the seal.

3. Assemble the pistons to the connecting rods:

   a. Install one of the piston pin clips in each piston pin bore.

CAUTION
Make sure that the gap of the clip is at either the top or bottom of the piston. Installing the clips with the gap towards the sides could cause the clips to work loose during engine operation, resulting in serious engine damage.

   b. Assemble the piston and connecting rod for No. 1 cylinder so the long side of the rod is on the same side as the FLY mark on the piston crown (**Figure 119**).

   c. Assemble the piston and connecting rod for No. 2 cylinder so the long side of the rod is on the opposite side of the FLY mark on the piston crown (**Figure 119**).

   d. Insert the piston pins.

   e. Install the remaining piston pin retaining clips. Be sure the piston pin retaining clips are securely positioned in the piston grooves.

4. Install the piston/connecting rod assemblies into the engine:

   a. Rotate the crankshaft so the connecting rod journal is at BDC on the No. 1 cylinder.

   b. Using a ring compressor, compress the piston rings. Make sure that the oil ring is approximately 6 mm (1/4 in.) above the bottom edge of the compressor.

   c. With the rod cap removed, install the piston and rod assembly in the cylinder so the FLY mark stamped on the piston crown points toward the flywheel side of the engine.

   d. Use the grip end of a hammer with a hard steady pressure, to push the piston into the cylinder.

7

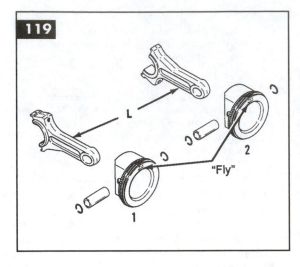

CAUTION
Do not use excessive force when installing the piston and rod. If binding occurs, remove the piston and rod and try again. Excessive force can damage or break the piston rings, piston ring lands, connecting rod or crankshaft.

e. When the piston clears the ring compressor, stop pushing and set the compressor aside.

f. Continue pushing the piston into the cylinder by hand until the rod journal bearing is completely into the crankcase area.

g. Rotate the crankshaft and carefully guide the connection rod onto the crankshaft journal. Do not allow the end of the rod to scratch the crankshaft.

h. Install the cap onto the rod, matching the chamfer of the cap to the chamfer of the rod (**Figure 103**). Note in **Figure 100** which style rod bolt is used, then install and tighten the rod cap bolts.

i. Repeat substeps a-h for the No. 2 cylinder.

5. Rotate the crankshaft to check for freedom of movement of the pistons and rods. Stop the crankshaft with the camshaft timing mark pointing toward the camshaft location. Install the camshaft, meshing the gears and aligning the match marks with the crankshaft (**Figure 120**).

6. Measure camshaft end play:

a. Install the thrust washer shim that was removed during disassembly onto the camshaft.

b. Fasten Kohler End Play Tool (part No. KO-1031) onto the crankcase above the camshaft. Follow the directions included with the tool.

c. Using feeler gauges, measure the camshaft end play. End play should be 0.076-0.127 mm (0.003-0.005 in.).

d. If end play is beyond specifications, determine from the measurement and the required end play specification the thickness of the necessary shim

washer. Seven different thickness washers are available.

e. Remove the end play tool.

7. Install the oil pan:

a. Make sure that the oil pan and crankcase sealing surfaces are clean and dry.

b. Make sure that the pan-to-block oil gallery O-ring is properly installed in the pan bore (**Figure 121**).

c. Make sure that the two oil pan locator sleeves are properly installed in the crankcase. **Figure 122** shows the sleeve just below the No. 2 cylinder.

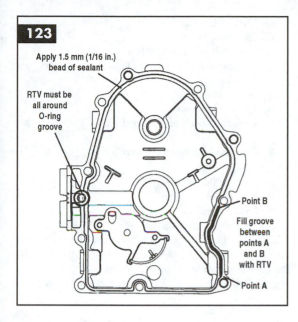

123

Apply 1.5 mm (1/16 in.)
bead of sealant

RTV must be
all around
O-ring
groove

Point B

Fill groove
between
points A
and B
with RTV

Point A

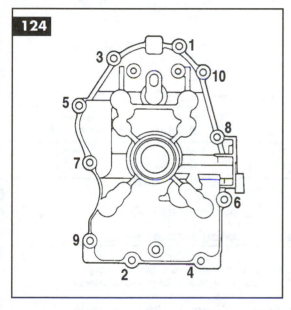

124

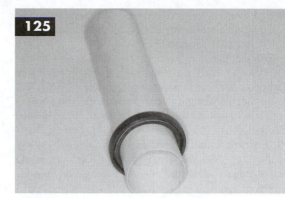

125

NOTE
*Approved sealants are listed in **Table 6**. Always follow the sealant manufacturer's instructions, especially regarding shelf life.*

e. Make sure that the oil pan bolt threads and matching crankcase thread holes are clean and dry.

f. If the oil seal has already been installed into the pan, use a seal protector sleeve or adhesive tape to prevent the crankshaft from damaging the seal.

g. Make sure that the governor cross shaft is still toward the outside of the crankcase (**Figure 112**).

h. Fit the oil pan onto the crankcase, taking care to properly mesh the oil pump gear with the crankshaft gear.

NOTE
Do not force the oil pan onto the crankcase. If binding occurs, remove the oil pan and determine the cause.

i. Install the 10 oil pan bolts finger-tight.

j. Tighten the pan bolts in 6.0 N·m (50 in.-lb.) increments to a final torque of 24.4 N·m (216 in.-lb.) using the torque sequence shown in **Figure 124**.

8. Install the oil seals if they have not already been installed:

a. Generously lubricate the space between the oil seal lips with light grease.

b. Slide the oil seal onto the end of an appropriate seal protector sleeve with the open, spring-loaded side of the seal at the short end of the protector (**Figure 125**).

c. Slide the seal protector over the crankshaft until the seal contacts the engine seal bore. The closed, marked side of the seal must face out, away from the engine. The open, spring-loaded side of the seal will fit into the engine.

d. Hold the seal against the engine while sliding the seal protector off the seal and crankshaft.

d. No gasket is used between the crankcase and oil pan. Apply a 1.6 mm (1/16 in.) bead of silicone sealant to the *oil pan* sealing surface as shown in **Figure 123**. Make sure that when the groove between Points A and B is filled with RTV, the RTV is 1.6 mm (1/16 in.) above the sealing surface.

NOTE
*Some early models may not have a groove between Points A and B as shown in **Figure 123**. If there is no groove, apply a consistent 1.6 mm (1/16 in.) bead all the way around the pan.*

e. Using an appropriate seal driver, install the seal into the seal bore until the driver bottoms against the crankcase or oil pan.

9. While holding the governor cross shaft as far counterclockwise as it will go, install the governor lever arm in the approximate position shown in **Figure 47**. Snug, but do not tighten, the nut to prevent the arm from slipping off. Final tightening will be done when all of the linkage is installed.

10. Fill the oil filter with oil prior to installing it. Lightly oil the filter gasket with fresh engine oil. The filter should be tightened 1/2-3/4 turn after the filter gasket contacts the flange.

11. Finish installing the external engine components by following the instructions in each appropriate component installation section. The recommended sequence is as follows:

    a. Blower housing backing plates.
    b. Alternator stator.
    c. Flywheel, fan and screen.
    d. Hydraulic lifters.
    e. Push rods and cylinder heads.
    f. Breather chamber cover, Oil Sentry and inner cylinder baffles.
    g. Intake manifold.
    h. Ignition modules.
    i. Blower housing and outer shields.
    j. Carburetor.
    k. Governor and throttle controls.
    l. Valve covers.
    m. Electric starter motor.
    n. Fuel pump.
    o. Exhaust system.
    p. Air cleaner assembly.

12. During final installation, make sure that the crankcase is filled with the correct type and amount of oil, and the governor is static-adjusted. Do not attempt to run the engine until the governor has been properly adjusted.

Table 1   GENERAL ENGINE SPECIFICATIONS

Model	No. Cyls.	Bore	Stroke	Displacement	Power Rating
CV20	2	77 mm (3.03 in.)	67 mm (2.64 in.)	624 cc (38.1 cu. in.)	20 hp 14.9 kW

Table 2   MAINTENANCE AND LUBRICATION SCHEDULE

After 5-hour break-in period (new or overhauled engine)	Change the engine oil and the oil filter. Check all the fasteners for proper tightness.
Every 8 hours or daily	Check the engine oil with the unit sitting level. Do not overfill. Check and/or clean the air filter.
Every 40-50 hours or weekly	Service the air cleaner pre-filter. Check the battery electrolyte level. Lubricate the throttle and choke cables.
Every 100 hours or semi-monthly	Replace the air filter and pre-filter. Change the engine oil and oil filter.
Every 500 hours or annually	Replace the fuel filter and fuel hoses. Remove cylinder heads Clean the combustion chamber. Check all of the fasteners for proper tightness.

Table 3 RECOMMENDED ENGINE FUEL AND LUBRICANTS

Fuel	Unleaded gasoline with octane rating of 87 or higher
Capacity	5.0 U.S. gallons (18.7 liters or 4.0 Imperial gallons)
Engine oil	API service rating of SH or above
Above 32° F (0° C)	SAE 10W-30
Between 32° F and 0° F (0° C and -18° C)	SAE 10W-30, 5W-20, or 5W-30
Capacity with filter	2.1 quarts (2.0 liters)

NOTE: Do not use 10W-40 oil in the engine. Recommended engine oil viscosities are for petroleum-based oils. Comparable synthetic oils may be used. DO NOT MIX synthetic oil with petroleum oil.

Table 4 FASTENER TORQUE VALUES

Spark plug	24.4-29.8 N·m	(215-265 in.-lb. or 18-22 ft.-lb.)
Air filter base	9.9 N·m	(88 in.-lb.)
Alternator stator	4.0 N·m	(35 in.-lb.)
Alternator rectifier (to blower housing)	4.0 N·m	(35 in.-lb.)
Blower housing		
M5 fasteners	4.0 N·m	(35 in.-lb.)
M6 fasteners	6.8 N·m	(60 in.-lb.)
Breather cover	7.3 N·m	(65 in.-lb.)
Carburetor		
Mounting fasteners	9.9 N·m	(88 in.-lb.)
Fuel bowl nut	5.1-6.2 N·m	(45-55 in.-lb.)
Shutter plate screws		
(choke and throttle)	0.9-1.4 N·m	(8-12 in.-lb.)
Main fuel jet (fixed jet)	1.4-1.8 N·m	(12-16 in.-lb.)
Connecting rod (See text)		
8 mm straight-shank bolt	22.6 N·m	(200 in.-lb.)
Step-down shank bolt	14.7 N·m	(130 in.-lb.)
6 mm straight-shank bolt	11.3 N·m	(100 in.-lb.)
Crankcase cover/oil pan	24.4 N·m	(216 in.-lb.)
Cylinder head	40.7 N·m	(360 in.-lb. or 30 ft.-lb.)
Rocker arm pivot	11.3 N·m	(100 in.-lb.)
Electric starter mount	15.3 N·m	(135 in.-lb.)
Electric starter drive pinion	15.3 N·m	(135 in.-lb.)
Flywheel	66.4 N·m	(49 ft.-lb.)
Flywheel fan	9.9 N·m	(88 in.-lb.)
Fuel pump screws	2.3 N·m	(20 in.-lb.)
Governor control lever	9.9 N·m	(88 in.-lb.)
Governor speed control bracket*	7.3 N·m	(65 in.-lb.)
New unthreaded hole	10.7 N.m	(95 in.-lb.)
Ignition module*	4.0 N·m	(35 in.-lb.)
New unthreaded hole	6.2 N.m	(55 in.-lb.)
Intake manifold	9.9 N·m	(88 in.-lb.)
Muffler	24.4 N·m	(216 in.-lb.)
Oil filter mount nipple	54.2 N·m	(480 in.-lb. or 40 ft.-lb.)
Oil diverter drain, plastic	40.7 N·m	(360 in.-lb. or 30 ft.-lb.)
Oil drain plug	13.6 N·m	(120 in.-lb.)
Oil Sentry pressure switch	7.9 N·m	(70 in.-lb.)
Oil filter (See text)	5.7-9.0 N·m	(50-80 in.-lb.)
Valve cover*	7.3 N·m	(65 in.-lb.)
New unthreaded hole	10.7 N.m	95 in.-lb.)
Fasteners not listed	Refer to Chapter One, Tables 4-13:	

*When installing self-tapping fasteners into new unthreaded holes, use higher torque value. Use the lower torque value for installation into previously tapped holes and weld nuts.

Table 5 ENGINE CLEARANCES AND SPECIFICATIONS

Angle of Operation:		
Maximum angle; Full oil level;		
All directions	25°	
Compression		
Ratio	8.5:1	
Pressure	85+ psi	
Oil pressure		
Cold engine at start-up	Up to 60 psi	
Hot engine at idle	Down to 18 psi	
Camshaft		
End bearing diameters		
New	19.962-19.975 mm	(0.7859-0.7864 in.)
Wear limit	19.959 mm	(0.7858 in.)
Bearing bore diameters		
New	20.000-20.025 mm	(0.7874-0.7884 in.)
Wear limit	20.038 mm	(0.7889 in.)
End play (shimmed)	0.076-0.127 mm	(.003-.005 in.)
Running clearance	0.025-0.063 mm	(.0010-.0025 in.)
Lobe height (minimum lift)		
Intake	8.07 mm	(0.3177 in.)
Exhaust	8.07 mm	(0.3177 in.)
Carburetor		
Initial idle-mixture screw setting	2¼ turns open	
Float level	Non-adjustable	
Connecting rod		
Crankpin clearance, new	0.030-0.055 mm	(.0012-.0022 in.)
Crankpin clearance limit	0.070 mm	(.0028 in.)
Crankpin side play	0.26-0.63 mm	(.0102-.0248 in.)
Piston pin bore inside diameter		
New	17.015-17.023 mm	(0.6699-0.6702 in.)
Wear limit	17.036 mm	(0.6707 in.)
Piston pin clearance, new	0.015-0.028 mm	(.0006-.0011 in.)
Crankshaft		
End play	0.070-0.480 mm	(.0028-.0189 in.)
Main bearing journal, flywheel end		
New outside diameter	40.913-40.935 mm	(1.6107-1.6116 in.)
Wear limit	40.84 mm	(1.608 in.)
Out of round	0.025 mm	(.0010 in.)
Taper	0.022 mm	(.0009 in.)
Main bearing journal, PTO end		
New outside diameter	40.913-40.935	(1.6107-1.6116 in.)
Wear limit	40.84 mm	(1.608 in.)
Out of round	0.025 mm	(.0010 in.)
Taper	0.020 mm	(.0008 in.)
Crankpin		
New outside diameter	35.955-35.973 mm	(1.4156-1.4163 in.)
Wear limit	35.94 mm	(1.4150 in.)
Out of round	0.025 mm	(.0010 in.)
Taper	0.018 mm	(.0007 in.)
Top main bearing		
Inside diameter, new	40.965-41.003 mm	(1.6128-1.6143 in.)
Maximum wear limit	40.016 mm	(1.6148 in.)
Running clearance, new	0.03-0.09 mm	(.0012-.0035 in.)
Oil pan bearing		
Inside diameter, new	40.974-40.987 mm	(1.6131-1.6137 in.)
Maximum wear limit	41.025 mm	(1.6152 in.)
Running clearance, new	0.039-0.074 mm	(.0015-.0029 in.)
	(continued)	

Table 5 ENGINE CLEARANCES AND SPECIFICATIONS (continued)

Total indicated runout		
PTO end with crankshaft in engine	0.15 mm	(.0059 in.)
Crankshaft only, in V-blocks	0.10 mm	(.0039 in.)
Cylinder bore:		
New inside diameter	77.000-77.025 mm	(3.0315-3.0325 in.)
Wear limit	77.063 mm	(3.0340 in.)
Out of round	0.12 mm	(.0047 in.)
Taper	0.05 mm	(.002 in.)
Cylinder head warpage, maximum	0.076 mm	(.003 in.)
Governor		
Gear shaft diameter		
New	5.990-6.000 mm	(0.2358-0.2362 in.)
Wear limit	5.977 mm	(0.2353 in.)
Gear shaft-to-gear running clearance	0.015-0.140 mm	(0.0006-0.0055 in.)
Cross shaft diameter		
Early-style 6 mm:		
New	5.975-6.012 mm	(0.2352-0.2367 in.)
Wear limit	5.962 mm	(0.2347 in.)
Late-style 8 mm:		
New	7.975-8.012 mm	(0.3140-0.3154 in.)
Wear limit	7.962 mm	(0.3135 in.)
Cross shaft bore diameter		
Early-style 6 mm:		
New	6.025-6.050 mm	(0.2372-0.2382 in.)
Wear limit	6.063 mm	(0.2387 in.)
Late-style 8 mm:		
New	8.025-8.050 mm	(0.3160-0.3169 in.)
Wear limit	8.063 mm	(0.3174 in.)
Cross shaft running clearance,		
Shaft-to-crankcase bore	0.013-0.075 mm	(0.0005-0.0030 in.)
Ignition		
Module to flywheel magnet air gap	0.20-0.31 mm	(0.008-0.012 in.)
Spark plug gap	1.02 mm	(0.040 in.)
Oil pump		
Pressure relief valve spring length	25.2 mm	(0.992 in.)
Oil seal		
Distance of outer face below		
crankcase surface	2.0 mm	(0.0787 in.)
Piston		
Thrust face diameter (See text)		
New	76.967-76.985 mm	(3.0302-3.0309 in.)
Wear limit	76.840 mm	(3.0252 in.)
Running clearance		
At thrust face(new)	0.035-0.078 mm	(.0014-.0031 in.)
Piston rings		
End gap (compression rings)		
New	0.25-0.45 mm	(0.0098-0.0177 in.)
Used limit	0.77 mm	(0.030 in.)
Ring land clearance		
Top compression ring	0.040-0.080 mm	(0.0016-0.0031 in.)
Middle compression ring	0.040-0.080 mm	(0.0016-0.0031 in.)
Oil-control ring	0.060-0.202 mm	(0.0024-0.0080 in.)
Piston pin		
Diameter		
New	16.995-17.000 mm	(0.6691-0.6693 in.)
Wear limit	16.994 mm	(0.6691 in.)
Bore inside diameter (piston)		
New	17.006-17.012 mm	(0.6695-0.6698 in.)
Wear limit	17.025 mm	(0.6703 in.)

(continued)

7

Table 5 ENGINE CLEARANCES AND SPECIFICATIONS (continued)

Selective fit, piston-to-pin	0.006-0.017 mm	(0.0002-0.0007 in.)
Valves		
Cam lobe lift, minimum		
Intake	8.96 mm	(0.353 in.)
Exhaust	9.14 mm	(0.360 in.)
Stem-to-guide running clearance (cold)		
Intake	0.038-0.076 mm	(0.0015-0.0030 in.)
Exhaust	0.050-0.088 mm	(0.0020-0.0035 in.)
Guide reamer size		
Standard	7.048 mm	(0.2775 in.)
0.25 mm oversize	7.298 mm	(0.2873 in.)
Valve guide inside diameter		
Intake		
New	7.038-7.058 mm	(0.2771-0.2779 in.)
Wear limit	7.134 mm	(0.2809 in.)
Exhaust		
New	7.038-7.058 mm	(0.2771-0.2779 in.)
Wear limit	7.159 mm	(0.2819 in.)
Valve stem diameter (new, standard)		
Intake	6.982-7.000 mm	(0.2749-0.2756 in.)
Exhaust	6.970-6.988 mm	(0.2744-0.2751 in.)
Seat angle		
Intake	89°	
Exhaust	89°	

Table 6 VALVE SYSTEM DIMENSIONS

Ref.	Description	Dimension
A	Seat Angle	89
B	Insert O.D.	
	Intake	37.987-38.017 mm (1.4956-1.4967 in.)
	Exhaust	33.987-34.013 mm (1.3381-1.3391 in.)
C	Guide depth	6.5 mm (0.256 in.)
D	Guide I.D.	7.033-7.068 mm (0.2769-0.2779 in.)
E	Valve head diameter	
	Intake	35.37-35.63 mm (1.392-1.402 in.)
	Exhaust	31.37-31.63 mm (1.235-1.245 in.)
F	Valve Face Angle	45
G	Valve Margin (Min.)	1.5 mm (0.060 in.)
H	Valve Stem Diameter	
	Intake	6.982-7.000 mm (0.2749-0.2755 in.)
	Exhaust	6.97-6.988 mm (0.2745-0.2751 in.)

KAWASAKI FC420V ENGINE

This section provides engine service information for the Kawasaki FC420V engine. This engine is an air-cooled, four-stroke, vertical-crankshaft 1-cylinder engine equipped with overhead valves. It is pressure lubricated and equipped with an oil filter.

This chapter provides information on removing and reinstalling the engine as a complete, assembled unit. Subsequent sections provide disassembly, inspection, adjustment, repair/overhaul and reassembly information for the engine components. The engine must be removed from the equipment before undertaking repairs on the internal components. In the case of external components such as the carburetor or a cylinder head, engine removal may not be necessary, as the repair job may be performed with the engine mounted on the equipment.

Kawasaki tools, or suitable equivalents, may be recommended for some procedures. The tools are available from Kawasaki dealers and service centers. Good quality tools are also available from small engine parts suppliers. Be careful when substituting a homemade tool for a recommended tool. Although time and money may be saved if an existing or fabricated tool can be made to work, consider the possibilities if the tool does not work properly. If the substitute tool damages the engine, the cost to repair the damage, as well as lost time, may exceed the cost of the recommended tool.

> *NOTE*
> *Metric fasteners are used throughout the engine. Check the thread compatibility before installing a fastener.*

ENGINE IDENTIFICATION

Engine identification is provided by information found on the decal affixed to the crankcase (**Figure 1**). The decal lists the engine model number and serial number ("E/NO"). Both numbers are required when ordering parts and for using applicable service procedures.

ENGINE REMOVAL

Prior to removing the engine, drain the crankcase oil. Always drain the oil with the engine warm so the oil flows freely and carries out the dirt and impurities.

1. Allow the engine to cool to ambient temperature.
2. Engage the parking brake.
3. On electric-start units, disconnect the battery cables – negative terminal first – and remove the battery.

4. Close the fuel tank valve (**Figure 2**).

WARNING
Some gasoline will drain from the fuel hose during the next procedure. Wipe up any spilled gasoline immediately. Work in a well-ventilated area at least 50 feet away from any open flame, including pilot lights in gas appliances. Do not allow anyone to smoke in the area. Do not work near any grinding or any other source of sparks.

5. Detach the fuel hose clamp at the inlet connection to the fuel pump. Disconnect the fuel hose from the pump.

6. Disconnect the spark plug wire from the spark plug. Ground the spark plug wire to the engine.

7. Identify and unplug the chassis wiring harness connectors and, on electric-start units, the starter motor cable.

8. Access and disconnect the throttle and choke control cables.

NOTE
Prior to removal, cable positions should be marked for proper reconnection during engine installation.

9. Remove the deck drive belt shield, then slacken the belt running from the engine:
   a. On fixed-idler drives (**Figure 3**), back the belt idler adjuster nut off to allow slack in the belt.
   b. On spring-loaded idler drives, like that in **Figure 4**, move the idler pulley bracket away from the belt. Secure the bracket to allow slack in the belt, or work the belt off the idler.

10. Chock the front wheels. Safely raise and support the rear of the mower to gain access to the underside of the engine.

11. Unplug the PTO clutch wire connector (**Figure 4**). Support the PTO clutch while removing the clutch bolt from the crankshaft. Slide the clutch off the shaft, then remove the belt from the clutch pulley.

12. Move the hydrostatic drive idler pulley away from the drive belt so the belt slackens. Work the belt off the engine pulley, then remove the belt.

13. Remove the engine mounting bolts.

14. Carefully lift the engine off the frame.

15. Note the position and orientation of the hydrostat pulley on the crankshaft. Remove the pulley.

16. Clean the engine mounting area on the frame.

ENGINE INSTALLATION

1. Ensure that the engine mounting areas on both the frame and the bottom of the engine are clean and dry.

2. Lightly coat the crankshaft, including keyway, with antiseize compound.

3. Install the hydrostat pulley on the crankshaft in the same position and orientation as that noted during removal.

4. Set the engine in position on the frame. Ensure that the engine pan and frame fastener holes align.

5. Apply Loctite 271 or equivalent to the engine mount fastener threads. Tighten the fasteners incrementally, alternately and securely. On fasteners with lockwashers, use new lockwashers.

6. Install the hydrostat belt onto the pulleys, then allow the spring-loaded idler to exert tension on the belt.

7. Apply Loctite 271 or equivalent to the electric PTO clutch mount bolt. Insert the PTO clutch belt into the

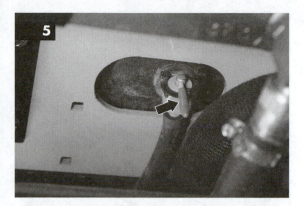

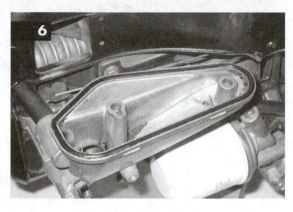

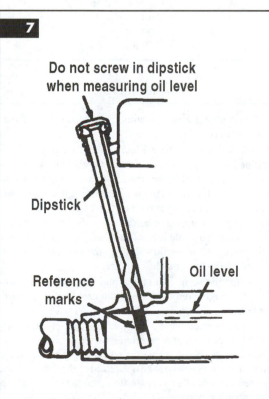

clutch pulley groove. Align the clutch locator bracket, ensuring that the clutch wire is not pinched or kinked. Align the clutch key with the crankshaft keyway, then slide the clutch onto the crankshaft. While supporting the clutch, install the clutch bolt and tighten it securely. Refer to the applicable torque chart at the end of Chapter One for the standard torque value.

8. Remove the mower supports. Lower the unit onto the floor. Ensure that the parking brake is still set, then remove the front wheel chocks.

9. Reapply tension to the deck drive belt.

    a. On fixed-idler drives, refer to the adjustment procedure under *Drive Belts* in Chapter Three to properly tension the belt.

    b. On spring-loaded idlers, no adjustment is necessary.

10. Install the deck drive belt shield.

11. Reconnect the throttle and choke cables using the marks noted during engine removal.

12. Reconnect the chassis wiring harness connectors to the appropriate engine plugs.

13. On electric-start units, reconnect the starter motor cable and the battery cables, negative cable last.

14. Reconnect the spark plug leads to the plugs.

15. Install a new fuel hose, including clamps, between the fuel filter and the fuel pump.

16. Refill the crankcase with the proper oil.

17. Open the fuel tank valve (**Figure 5**).

LUBRICATION

All models are equipped with a filtered pressure lubrication system. Refer to the *OIL PUMP* section for oil pump service information.

                NOTE
*Fill the oil filter (**Figure 6**) with oil before installation to assure adequate lubrication to critical components during initial engine restart. Pour the oil into the filter through the center threaded hole only. Do not fill past the bottom of the threads.*

Periodically check the oil level; do not overfill. To check the oil level:

1. Ensure that the mower is sitting on a level surface.

2. Clean the area around the dipstick cap to prevent dirt and debris from falling into the crankcase when the cap is removed.

3. Remove the dipstick and wipe the oil from the level indicator.

4. Reinsert the dipstick and seat the dipstick cap on the oil fill tube. Do not screw the dipstick back down into the tube (**Figure 7**).

5. Remove the dipstick and check the oil level. The oil level should be up to, but not over, the FULL line on the dipstick.

It is recommended that a new oil filter be installed at each oil change. Apply a light coating of clean engine oil to the filter gasket. Install the oil filter until the rubber gasket contacts the filter adapter plate, then tighten an additional ½-3/4 turn.

Crankcase oil capacity is approximately 3.4 pints (1.6 L) with oil filter or 2.7 pints (1.3 L) without the filter, although changing the oil without changing the filter is not recommended.

Refer to **Table 3** for oil recommendations.

> *NOTE*
> *DO NOT use SAE 10W-40 oil. Do not mix synthetic oil with petroleum-base oil.*

In new or overhauled engines or short blocks, use SAE 30 oil for the first five hours of operation, then change oil according to ambient temperature requirements. Do not run break-in oil for more than five hours or serious short-term engine damage could result. The recommended *minimum* oil change interval after the five-hour break-in period is every 100 hours of operation. The oil should be drained while the engine is warm for the most effective crankcase sludge removal.

AIR FILTER

These engines are equipped with a paper-type air filter and a foam pre-cleaner element (**Figure 8**). The air filter assembly mounts to the carburetor, just above the oil filter (**Figure 9**).

Remove and clean the air filter at the interval indicated in **Table 2**. Replace the element at the specified interval or whenever it is damaged or starting to deteriorate. Service more frequently if the engine is operated in severe conditions.

To service the filter assembly, refer to *Periodic Maintenance, Air Filter Service* in Chapter Three. Install a new housing O-ring (7, **Figure 8** and A, **Figure 10**) at each filter change.

> *NOTE*
> *Always inspect the crankcase breather hose between the breather and the air filter base (B, **Figure 10**) anytime the air filter is being serviced. If the hose is loose, cracked, or dry and brittle, replace it.*

FUEL FILTER

Service the fuel filter at the interval indicated in **Table 2**. To service the fuel filter, refer to *Periodic Maintenance, Fuel Filter Service* in Chapter Three.

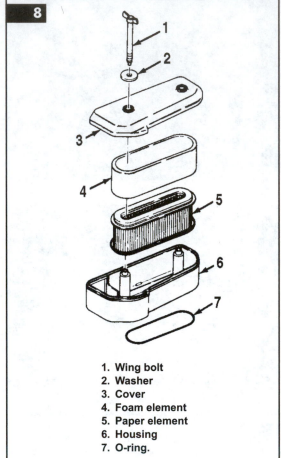

1. Wing bolt
2. Washer
3. Cover
4. Foam element
5. Paper element
6. Housing
7. O-ring.

CARBURETOR

This engine is equipped with a float-type side draft carburetor (**Figure 11**).

The carburetor operates according to the principles outlined in Chapter Two. A float in the fuel bowl controls the amount of fuel in the bowl. When the engine is running, fuel is drawn into the nozzle through the removable main jet. Fuel in the nozzle then exits into the carburetor bore through a discharge hole. Fuel is also drawn into the idle circuit to the idle fuel jet and then to the idle mixture adjustment screw. Airflow through the carburetor is controlled by throttle and choke plates.

Air for the main fuel circuit and idle circuit is introduced through a removable air jet located in the carburetor bore.

The carburetor may be equipped with a fuel shutoff solenoid. The solenoid is controlled by the equipment electrical system. A rod inside the solenoid projects into the main fuel jet. When voltage is directed to the solenoid, the rod retracts and allows fuel to flow into the main fuel circuit of the carburetor.

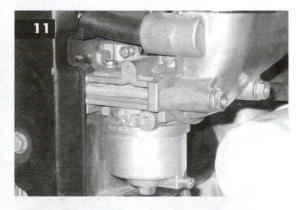

Adjustments

The high-speed fuel mixture is not adjustable on this engine. A fixed main jet controls the high-speed fuel mixture. Different size main jets are available for various higher-altitude operations.

Idle speed adjustment

1. Connect an accurate tachometer to the engine.
2. With the parking brake on, the blade PTO disengaged, the speed control in neutral, and the neutral locks locked, start the engine and run it for a few minutes to reach normal operating temperature.

> *WARNING*
> *Make sure ventilation is adequate if the engine is run in a confined area. Exhaust fumes are toxic and deadly.*

3. Place the remote throttle control in the SLOW position.
4. Turn the idle speed screw (A, **Figure 12**) clockwise to increase idle speed or counterclockwise to decrease idle speed. The recommended engine idle speed is 1450-1650 rpm.

Idle mixture adjustment

1. With the parking brake on, the blade PTO disengaged, the speed control in neutral, and the neutral locks locked, start the engine and run it for a few minutes to reach normal operating temperature.

> *WARNING*
> *Make sure ventilation is adequate if the engine is to be run in a confined area. Exhaust fumes are toxic and deadly.*

2. Adjust the idle speed screw (A, **Figure 12**) so the engine idles at the recommended 1450-1650 rpm.
3. Adjust the mixture screw to obtain maximum engine idle speed, then turn the mixture screw out (counterclockwise) 1/4 turn. If the limit stop will not allow this much adjustment:
   a. Carefully remove and discard the original plastic limiter cap (B, **Figure 12** and **Figure 13**).
   b. Turn the mixture screw (underneath the limiter cap) in (clockwise) until it is *lightly seated*. Do not force.
   c. Turn the pilot screw out (counterclockwise) 1 1/2 turns.
   d. Repeat the Step 3 adjustment.
   e. Install a new limiter cap in the mid-range adjustment position.
4. If necessary, readjust the idle speed screw (A, **Figure 12**) so the engine idles at the recommended 1450-1650 rpm.

8

Removal

WARNING
Some gasoline will drain from the fuel hose and/or the carburetor during this procedure. Wipe up any spilled gasoline immediately. Work in a well-ventilated area at least 50 feet away from any open flame, including pilot lights in gas appliances. Do not allow anyone to smoke in the area. Do not work near any grinding or other source of sparks.

1. Turn the fuel tank valve off (**Figure 2**).
2. Remove the air filter assembly.
3. Unclamp and remove the fuel inlet hose.
4. Unscrew the bowl drain screw (A, **Figure 14**) and drain the fuel from the carburetor into a container.
5. If equipped with a fuel shutoff solenoid, disconnect the solenoid terminal and the ground wire.
6. Remove the air filter base mounting nuts (B, **Figure 14**). Remove the base and discard the gasket. Note that the base nuts also hold the carburetor onto the engine.
7. Slide the carburetor off the mounting studs while working the choke and throttle linkages off the carburetor. Discard the carburetor mounting gasket.

Disassembly

1. Refer to **Figure 15** for component identification.
2. Disassemble the carburetor completely. The float valve seat (**Figure 16**) is not replaceable.
3. Mark the positions of the throttle plate and choke plate for reassembly.

Cleaning, Inspection and Repair

1. Clean carburetor parts (except plastic components) using a carburetor cleaner. Follow the cleaner manufacturer's instructions.
2. Do not clean jets or passages with drill bits or wire, as enlargement of passages will affect calibration of the carburetor.
3. Rinse parts in warm water to neutralize the corrosive action of the carburetor cleaner.
4. Dry the carburetor with compressed air.

Reassembly

1. Use new gaskets and seals when reassembling the carburetor.
2. Lightly coat the throttle and choke plate screws with Loctite 222 or equivalent prior to installation.
3. The float should be parallel with the carburetor body when the carburetor is inverted as shown in B, **Figure 17**.

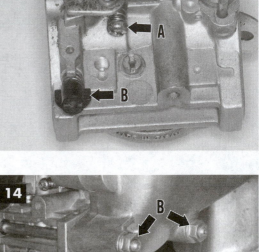

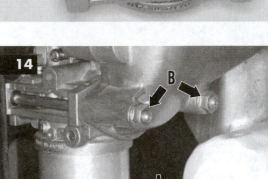

a. On floats with metal arms, bend the float valve tab to set the float height.
b. If equipped with a white plastic float, the float height is not adjustable; replace any components that are damaged or excessively worn and adversely affect the float position.

4. Make sure that the throttle and choke plates are reinstalled as marked during disassembly.
   a. The throttle plate center dimple must fit into the shaft, with the numbers to the left (**Figure 18**).
   b. The choke plate cutout will be to the bottom, with the plate hole and number both on the right side (**Figure 19**). The throttle and choke must operate freely once assembled.
5. Refer to *Adjustments* in this chapter for the proper screw settings.

Installation

1. Reverse the removal process to install the carburetor.
2. Always use new gaskets when installing the carburetor.
3. When the carburetor is in position on the studs, ensure the linkages work correctly without binding.
4. Lightly coat the stud end threads with Loctite 242 or equivalent prior to installing the air filter base and nuts.

15

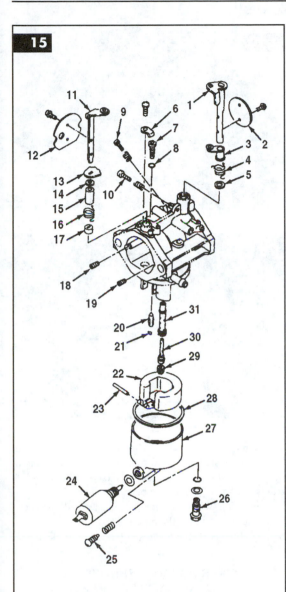

16

17

18

19

1. Throttle shaft	17. Ring
2. Throttle plate	18. Pilot air jet
3. Ring	19. Main air jet
4. spring	20. Fuel inlet needle
5. Seal	21. Clip
6. Retainer plate	22. Float
7. Pilot jet	23. Pin
8. O-ring	24. Fuel shut-off
9. Pilot screw	solenoid
10. Idle speed screw	25. Drain screw
11. Choke shaft	26. Special bolt
12. Choke plate	27. Float bowl
13. Plate	28. Gasket
14. Seal	29. Main jet
15. Ring	30. Bleed pipe
16. Spring	31. Main nozzle

8

MUFFLER

The muffler is calibrated as part of the emission control system. It not only reduces exhaust noise to acceptable levels, but it also provides the proper amount of back pressure to allow the inlet and combustion components to produce rated horsepower as well as compliant emission levels.

For this reason, the exhaust system should be maintained in good repair. As the noise level increases, power decreases. Under no circumstances should the exhaust system be modified. Inspect the muffler, pipe, flanges, connections and fasteners regularly. Replace any questionable components.

Removal

1. Allow the unit to cool.
2. If the muffler is covered by a sheet metal heat shield, remove the shield.
3. Loosen all fasteners and clamps. Do not remove any fasteners until all of them have been loosened.
4. If a bolt cannot be loosened, liberally apply penetrating oil such as Liquid Wrench, Kroil or WD-40, and let it penetrate for 10-15 minutes. Rap the fastener several times with a small hammer and punch. Do not hit it hard enough to cause damage. Reapply the penetrating oil if necessary. Use 6-sided sockets and wrenches on hex-headed bolts to reduce the chances of rounding off the hex.

If a fastener should break off, refer to *Removing Broken Fasteners* in Chapter One.

5. Begin removing the fasteners while supporting the exhaust system. Work from the outlet pipe inward. The nuts holding the exhaust pipe flange(s) to the engine should be the last fasteners removed, at which time the exhaust system can be removed and set aside.

> *CAUTION*
> *Discard the used gasket and replace it with a new gasket. Also discard any old lockwashers, replacing them with new ones.*

6. Inspect all brackets and supports for cracks and breaks. Inspect the outlet pipe spark arrestor screen, if equipped. Replace as necessary.
7. Carefully remove any old gasket material from the exhaust flange surfaces.

Installation

1. Insert a new gasket onto the exhaust studs.
2. Replace all fastener lock washers and lightly coat the fastener threads with a high-temperature thread-lock compound, such as Loctite 272 or equivalent.

3. Align the exhaust system with all bracket and fastener holes, then install and hand-tighten the fasteners, beginning with the exhaust pipe flanges. Do not tighten any fasteners until all of them have been installed.
4. Beginning with the flanges, tighten all fasteners, working toward the outlet pipe.
5. Install the heat shield and spark arrestor, if used.

BLOWER HOUSING, SHROUDS AND BAFFLES

Removal/Installation

1. If equipped with a rewind starter, proceed as follows:
   a. Remove the rewind starter as described in this chapter.
   b. Remove the blower housing retaining screws, then remove the blower housing (A, **Figure 20**), cylinder head shield (A, **Figure 21**) and cylinder side shields.
2. If not equipped with a rewind starter, proceed as follows:
   a. Remove the debris screen (B, **Figure 20**).
   c. Remove the blower housing retaining screws, then remove the blower housing (A, **Figure 20**), cylinder head shield (A, **Figure 21**) and cylinder side shields.

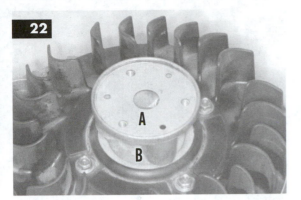

22

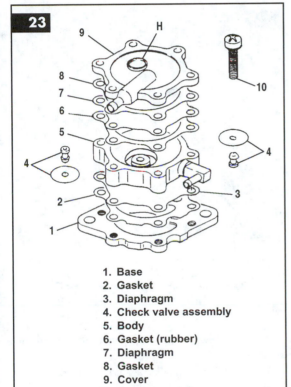

23

1. Base
2. Gasket
3. Diaphragm
4. Check valve assembly
5. Body
6. Gasket (rubber)
7. Diaphragm
8. Gasket
9. Cover
10. Screws
H. Vent hole and screen

FUEL PUMP

The engine is equipped with a diaphragm-type fuel pump (**Figure 23**) mounted on the blower housing. A pulse hose from the engine directs crankcase pulsations to the diaphragm in the fuel pump. Diaphragm movement forces fuel through a pair of one-way valves to the fuel pump outlet, where the fuel is routed via the fuel hose to the carburetor.

Testing

WARNING
Wipe up any spilled gasoline immediately. Work in a well-ventilated area at least 50 feet away from any open flame, including pilot lights in gas appliances. Do not allow anyone to smoke in the area. Do not work near any grinding or other source of sparks.

1. Disconnect the outlet fuel hose from the fuel pump.
2. Connect a hose from the fuel pump outlet into a suitable container.
3. Connect an auxiliary fuel supply to the carburetor.
4. Run the engine.
5. If the fuel pump does not pump fuel into the container, remove and inspect the pump. Be sure the vent hole (H, **Figure 23**) is open.
6. If the pump does not function, remove, disassemble, clean, inspect and repair as necessary.

Removal

1. Label the hoses at the pump.
2. Loosen the hose clamps, then detach the hoses from the pump. Plug the hoses to prevent fuel leakage or contamination.
3. Remove the bolts holding the fuel pump to the mounting bracket. Remove the fuel pump.

Disassembly

Refer to **Figure 23**.

1. Mark the pump base, body and cover prior to disassembly so these components can be properly aligned during reassembly.
2. Follow the instructions included with the pump repair kit.
3. Lightly coat the pump screws with Loctite 242 or equivalent prior to reassembly.
4. Tighten the pump screws alternately and incrementally. Use the torque value listed in **Table 4**.

8

3. Install the blower housing and shields by reversing the removal steps.

   a. Lightly coat the blower housing fasteners with Loctite 242 or equivalent prior to installation.

   b. On models without a rewind starter, measure the clearance between the debris screen knife edges (C, **Figure 20**) and the blower housing. The clearance should be 1.5 mm (0.060 in.). If necessary, remove or install shims (A, **Figure 22**) between the screen support (B) and the screen to obtain the recommended clearance.

Installation

1. Replace the hoses and hose clamps as necessary.

2. Installation is the reverse of the preceding steps. Re-connect the hoses according to the identification marks made before removal.

IGNITION SYSTEM

The engine is equipped with a two-piece solid-state ignition system that uses an ignition coil located under the blower housing adjacent to the flywheel (A, **Figure 24**) and a separate ignition control unit. The ignition switch grounds the module to stop the engine. There is no periodic maintenance or adjustment required for the ignition system, other than setting the air gap for the coil, ensuring that the coil and control unit are properly grounded to the engine and keeping the cooling system free of chaff and debris.

Spark Plug

The recommended spark plug is NGK BPR5ES or Champion RN11YC. Remove, clean and gap the spark plug after every 100 hours of operation. The specified spark plug gap is 0.7-0.8 mm (0.028-0.031 in.).

> *CAUTION*
> *Do not use the abrasive-blast (sand-blast) method to clean spark plugs. When spark plugs are cleaned by this method, the abrasive grit lodges in the upper gap between the insulator and the shell. Cleaning with compressed air does not remove all of these abrasives. This grit is only removed when the plug is reinstalled in the engine and the engine is started, heating and expanding the plug. The grit then falls into the cylinder and combustion chamber area, causing rapid internal wear and damage.*

Coil Air Gap Adjustment

If the ignition coil has been removed or its position disturbed, set the air gap between the coil and flywheel as follows:

1. Rotate the flywheel so the flywheel magnet is away from the ignition coil.

2. Loosen the coil retaining bolts (B, **Figure 24**), move the coil as far away from the coil as the adjusting slots will allow and tighten one bolt to hold the coil in position.

3. Rotate the flywheel so the flywheel magnet is aligned with the coil legs.

4. Place a 0.30 mm (0.012 in.) plastic or brass flat feeler gauge between the flywheel and the ignition module armature legs (**Figure 25**).

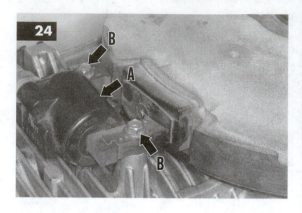

> *CAUTION*
> *Do not use a steel feeler gauge to set the air gap. An erroneous air gap setting could result.*

5. Allow the flywheel magnet to pull the ignition module toward the flywheel.

6. While holding the module against the magnet, tighten the module fasteners to the value specified in **Table 4**.

7. Measure the air gap to be sure the gap is still 0.30 mm (0.012 in.).

8. If the air gap is incorrect, repeat the adjustment procedure.

Testing

Ignition coil

1. Remove the blower housing and disconnect the spark plug lead (**Figure 26**).

2. Connect ohmmeter test leads between the coil core (ground) and the high tension (spark plug) terminal. Secondary coil resistance should be 10.9k-16.3k ohms.

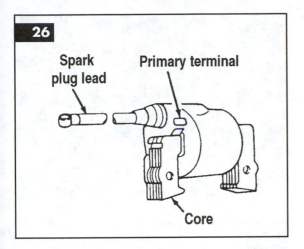

26

Spark plug lead

Primary terminal

Core

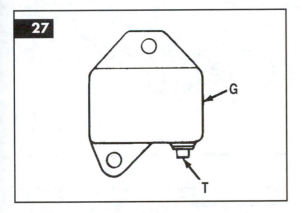

27

G

T

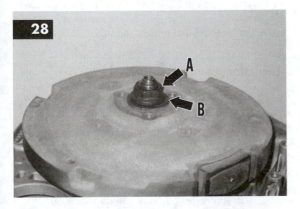

28

A

B

3. Remove the test lead connected to the high tension terminal and connect the lead to the coil primary terminal. Primary coil resistance should be 0.48-0.72 ohms.

4. If readings vary significantly from specifications, replace the ignition coil.

Control unit

1. Refer to **Figure 27** and disconnect all electrical leads.

2. Connect a positive ohmmeter lead to terminal and a negative ohmmeter lead to the ground lead or control unit case according to the engine being serviced.

3. The ohmmeter reading should be 400-600 ohms.

4. Reverse the ohmmeter leads.

5. The ohmmeter reading should be 60-100 ohms.

6. If the ohmmeter readings are not as specified, the control unit is faulty.

FLYWHEEL

Removal

The flywheel is secured to the crankshaft by a flanged nut (A, **Figure 28**) and a flat washer (B). To remove the flywheel, proceed as follows:

1. Remove the blower housing as previously detailed.

2. Remove the ignition coil as described in the preceding section.

3. If equipped with an electric starter, remove the debris screen support (B, **Figure 22**).

4. Hold the flywheel using a strap wrench, then remove the flywheel retaining nut (A, **Figure 28**) and washer (B).

5. If equipped with a rewind starter, remove the starter cup.

6. Remove the cooling fan.

7. Install a suitable flywheel puller. **Figure 29** shows the recommended puller setup using the threaded holes adjacent to the crankshaft. If the flywheel is not equipped with threaded holes, use a jaw-type puller.

WARNING
Do not strike the flywheel or crankshaft. Doing so will cause damage.

8. Rotate the puller screw until the flywheel pops free.

9. Remove the flywheel by carefully pulling straight up so as not to damage the alternator stator or magnets under the flywheel.

10. Remove the flywheel key, if necessary (A, **Figure 30**).

Inspection

1. Thoroughly clean the flywheel, removing all dust and dirt from both the top and bottom of the flywheel, especially around the magnets.

2. Inspect the flywheel casting for cracks or damage. A cracked or damaged flywheel must be replaced.

3. Inspect the integrity of the inner ring of stator magnets and the outer ignition module magnet (B, **Figure 31**).

WARNING
The magnets are not removable or serviceable. Do not attempt to reattach or tighten any loose magnet. If any magnets are loose or damaged, replace the flywheel.

8

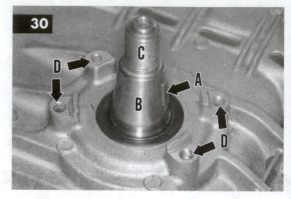

4. Inspect the starter ring gear. Carefully remove any debris stuck between the teeth. Light nicks or scratches may be dressed. Damaged teeth will require replacement of the ring gear.

5. Inspect the flywheel and the crankshaft tapers. The tapered portion of the crankshaft (B, **Figure 30**) and flywheel must be clean and smooth with no damage due to movement between the flywheel and crankshaft.

6. Check the fit of the flywheel on the crankshaft. There should be no looseness or wobbling.

7. Be sure the keyways in the crankshaft and flywheel are not damaged or worn.

8. Inspect the flywheel key (A, **Figure 30**). If the key is partially sheared or in any other way damaged, replace it.

9. Check the crankshaft threads (C, **Figure 30**) for damage. Repair the threads if necessary.

Installation

Reverse the removal procedure to install the flywheel. Note the following:

1. Tighten the fasteners to the torque values listed in **Table 4**.

2. Install the cooling fan so the extended pegs on the fan blades fit around the flywheel magnet.

3. If so equipped, install the starter cup so the holes fit in their proper positions.

4. Tighten the flywheel retaining nut to 137 N·m (101 ft.-lb.).

ALTERNATOR/CHARGING SYSTEM

Stator Testing

1. Disconnect the stator connector (**Figure 31**) from the main harness.

2. Connect a tachometer to the engine and an AC voltmeter to Terminals A and B, shown in **Figure 31**.

3. With the parking brake on, the blade PTO disengaged, the speed control in neutral, and the neutral locks locked,

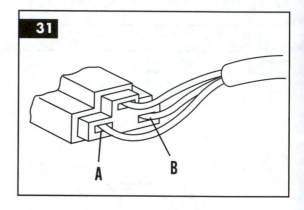

start the engine and run it for a few minutes to reach normal operating temperature.

4. Run the engine at 3350 rpm. Note the voltage reading. If the reading is less than 30 VAC, the stator is faulty. Remove the flywheel and replace the stator.

Regulator Testing

1. Disconnect all the harness plugs from the regulator. The rear of the regulator should appear as in **Figure 32**.

2. Test each pair of terminals as shown in the **Figure 32** chart specifications.

NOTE
Different meters may show slightly different test results. Testing should show consistent and proportional results.

3. If any pair of terminals tests notably and inconsistently different from the specifications, the regulator is faulty.

ELECTRIC STARTER MOTOR AND SOLENOID

In this section, "starter" refers to the electric starter motor assembly. Unless otherwise noted, starter component descriptions will refer to **Figure 33**.

32

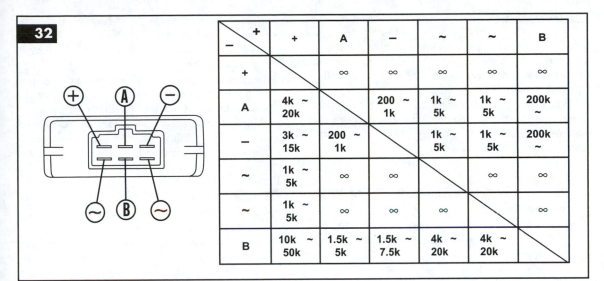

−	+	+	A	−	~	~	B
+			∞	∞	∞	∞	∞
A	4k ~ 20k			200 ~ 1k	1k ~ 5k	1k ~ 5k	200k ~
−	3k ~ 15k	200 ~ 1k			1k ~ 5k	1k ~ 5k	200k ~
~	1k ~ 5k	∞	∞			∞	∞
~	1k ~ 5k	∞	∞	∞			∞
B	10k ~ 50k	1.5k ~ 5k	1.5k ~ 7.5k	4k ~ 20k	4k ~ 20k		

33

8

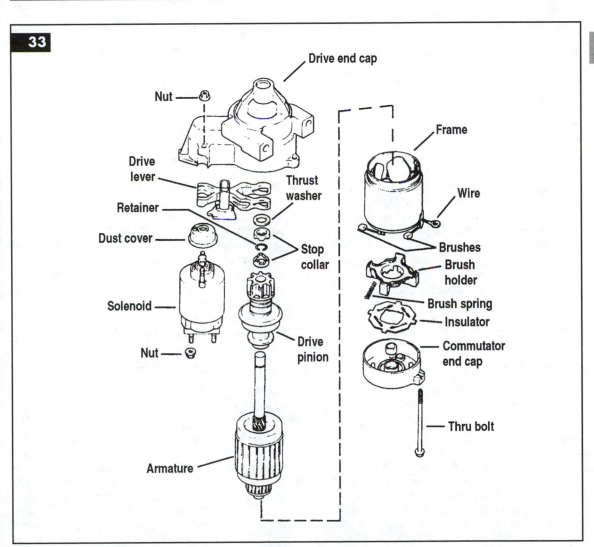

Starter Operation

1. When voltage is applied to the starter through the solenoid terminal and ground, the solenoid activates, pulling the drive lever and engaging the drive pinion into the flywheel ring gear.

2. When the solenoid plunger reaches the end of its travel, its contacts close the circuit between the two large solenoid terminals, sending battery current to the starter armature through the brushes.

3. Battery current causes the armature to rotate, turning the flywheel and starting the engine.

4. When the start switch is released, current stops flowing to the starter.

    a. The internal solenoid spring retracts the plunger.

    b. The drive pinion disengages from the flywheel ring gear.

    c. The armature stops turning.

Starter Precautions

1. Do not operate the starter continuously for more than 10 seconds. If the engine does not start, allow at least a 60-second cooling period between each 10-second operational period. Failure to allow sufficient cool-down time will burn out the starter.

2. Do not activate the starter while the engine is already turning. Engaging the starter into a rotating flywheel will damage the starter and the flywheel.

3. If the engine does not crank when the starter is engaged and the pinion contacts the ring gear, disengage the starter immediately. Correct the engine problem prior to attempting a restart. Do not attempt to overcome the problem by jump-starting with a larger battery. Serious starter damage will result.

4. Do not strike the starter frame or clamp it in a vise. Take care not to drop the starter. Doing so could damage the permanent magnets inside the starter frame housing.

Starter Troubleshooting

Starter fails to energize

Check the following:

1. Battery. Check the voltage and the specific gravity of the electrolyte. Recharge or replace the battery as necessary.

2. Wiring.

    a. Check for corroded or loose battery or solenoid connections. Clean or tighten as necessary. Soaking the corroded terminal in a baking soda and water solution is the best cleaning method. Do not allow any solution to get into any of the cells, as it will neutralize the electrolyte. Coat the clean connections with NoCo NCP-2 or equivalent to prevent further corrosion.

    b. Replace any frayed wires or wires with disintegrated terminals.

    c. Check for corroded or rusted ground connections on the equipment chassis. Remove the rust and treat the connection with NoCo or equivalent.

3. Solenoid. Use a jumper cable across the two large solenoid terminals to momentarily bypass the solenoid. If the starter energizes, the fault is in either the solenoid or the wiring to the solenoid. The *Solenoid Testing* section follows the starter section.

4. Starter components.

    a. Check the brushes. Dirty or worn brushes and/or commutator will slow a starter.

    b. Check the armature commutator. The commutator is an integral part of the armature. Cracked, chipped, broken, or badly grooved commutator sections are not repairable. In these cases, the armature will need replacement. A lightly grooved commutator may be turned on a lathe to clean up.

    c. Check the armature shaft and bearings. A worn shaft or bearings will allow the armature laminations to rub against the frame magnets, causing drag. Replace faulty components.

Starter energizes but turns slowly

Check the following:

1. Battery. Check the voltage and the specific gravity of the electrolyte. Recharge or replace the battery as necessary.

2. Parasitic load on the engine. Attempting to start an engine that is connected to a hydrostatic drive system places an additional load on the starter motor, especially in cooler temperatures. If possible, disconnect the load from the engine and retry the starter. If the starter now turns the engine properly, check the hydrostatic system to find the reason for the excessive load.

3. Internal load on the engine.

    a. Dirty, thick crankcase oil past its change schedule will cause slow turnover.

    b. Scored or galled internal engine components such as bearing journals, pistons and cylinders will overload the starter.

4. Starter components. (Same checks as Step 4 in the preceding *If the starter fails to energize* section.)

    a. Check the brushes. Dirty or worn brushes and/or commutator will slow a starter.

    b. Check the armature commutator. The commutator is an integral part of the armature. Cracked, chipped, broken, or badly grooved commutator sections are not repairable. In these cases, the armature will need replacement. A lightly grooved commutator may be turned on a lathe to clean up.

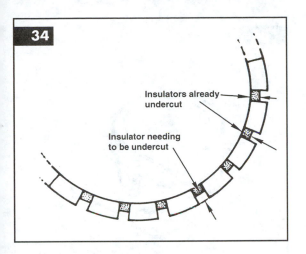

34

Insulators already undercut

Insulator needing to be undercut

c. Check the armature shaft and bearings. A worn shaft or bearings will allow the armature laminations to rub against the frame magnets, causing drag. Replace faulty components.

Solenoid Testing

Testing a solenoid can usually be done quickly with the solenoid on the starter. To test the solenoid:
1. Remove the ignition key from the switch so the engine does not start.
2. Ensure that the unit is in neutral and that the parking brake is set.
3. Place the throttle control in the SLOW position.
4. Remove the main harness wire from the small terminal on the solenoid.
5. Using a short jumper wire, connect one end of the wire to the small terminal. Momentarily touch the other end to the large terminal of the cable coming from the positive battery post.
6. If the starter activates, the solenoid is good.

The solenoid is not serviceable and must be replaced if faulty. To replace the solenoid, refer to *Starter Disassembly* and *Reassembly* in this chapter.

Starter Removal
1. Disconnect the negative battery cable and secure the cable away from the battery.
2. Disconnect the starter cable.
3. Remove the bolts holding the starter to the engine. Remove the starter.

Starter Disassembly

Refer to **Figure 33** for component identification.
1. Place alignment marks on the pinion housing, frame and end cover before disassembly so they can be reinstalled in their original position.
2. Disconnect the frame wire from the solenoid.

3. Remove the solenoid nuts from the drive end cap. Remove the solenoid. To aid in removing the slotted solenoid plunger from the drive lever, it may be necessary to pick out the dust cover once the solenoid is loose.

4. Remove the two through-bolts holding the commutator end cap and frame to the drive end cap.

5. Remove and disassemble the commutator end cap.

6. Slide the frame off the armature and drive end cap.

7. Remove the armature and drive lever assembly from the drive end cap. The flange on the drive pinion will require some careful maneuvering to work it past the dust seal inside the cap.

CAUTION
Do not lose the thrust washer.

8. Remove the stop collar by carefully prying the two wavy interlocking collar halves off the internal retainer ring. Remove and discard the retainer ring.

9. Using a suitable solvent, clean and dry the starter components.

Starter Inspection and Repair

1. Inspect all starter components. Replace any items that appear to be cracked, broken, overheated or excessively worn.

2. Inspect the brushes. Replace the brushes if their length is less than 6.0 mm (0.24 in.). The original brushes are semi-permanently attached to the starter. Carefully follow the instructions included with the replacement brushes.

3. Inspect the end cap bushings. If the armature shaft rocks excessively in the bushings, the end cap(s) will need to be replaced, as the bushings are not serviceable separately. If the armature shaft bearing journals are scored, the armature will have to be replaced as well.

4. Make sure that the drive pinion flange that contacts the drive end cap dust seal is not bent.

5. Lightly coat the splines of the armature and drive pinion and the drive pinion area of the armature shaft with Cristolube 303 or equivalent high-temperature multipurpose grease.

6. Check the armature commutator. The commutator is an integral part of the armature. Cracked, chipped, broken, or badly grooved commutator sections are not repairable; in these cases, the armature will need replacement. A lightly grooved commutator may be turned on a lathe to clean up. After turning, carefully file the burrs between the commutator segments and undercut the insulator segments between the conductors, if necessary (**Figure 34**). A dirty or rough commutator should be cleaned with a suitable solvent, then lightly sanded.

8

Starter Reassembly

Refer to **Figure 33** to aid in starter assembly.

1. Install the drive pinion onto the armature shaft.
2. Slide the inner collar onto the shaft, against the pinion.
3. Install and tighten a *new* retainer in the shaft groove.
4. Slide the outer collar onto the shaft, against the retainer.
5. Using two pair of pliers, evenly squeeze the two collar halves together over the retainer ring.
6. Fit the large fork of the drive lever over the drive pinion channel.
7. Install the thrust washer against the outer collar. Do not lose the thrust washer.
8. Install the armature/pinion/lever assembly into the drive end cap. The drive lever pivot base fits into a matching recess in the end cap.
9. Set the frame on the workbench with the brushes up.
   a. Position the brush holder, open slots up, onto the end of the frame with the holder legs in between the brushes.
   b. Install one brush into each holder slot. The brush leads fit into the cutouts in the slot sides.
   c. Compress and install the brush springs into the holder slots against the back of the brushes.
   d. Snap the insulator plate into the brush holder, over the brushes and springs. The insulator is reversible.
10. Carefully install the frame assembly down onto the armature. Ensure that the drive-cap end slot aligns with the drive lever. Work the brushes against the brush springs so the frame fits down over the armature commutator and into the drive end cap.
11. Install the commutator end cap.
   a. Install the through-bolts.
   b. Tighten the bolts alternately and evenly until snug.
12. Fit the dust cover over the solenoid plunger.
13. Hold the frame solenoid wire aside and fit the solenoid into the drive end cap. Make sure the plunger slots fit into the drive lever fork fingers.
14. Install and tighten the solenoid stud nuts.
15. Install the frame wire onto the solenoid terminal. Do not use threadlocking compound on the solenoid stud, or a poor connection may result.

Starter Installation

1. Lightly coat the starter mount bolt threads with Loctite 242 or equivalent.
2. Fit the starter drive under the blower housing shield while aligning the starter bolt holes with the matching threaded holes in the crankcase.
3. Install and tighten the mount bolts to 16 N·m (140 in.-lb.).

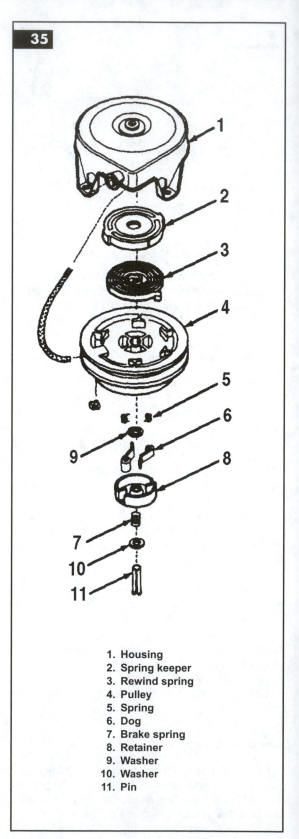

35

1. Housing
2. Spring keeper
3. Rewind spring
4. Pulley
5. Spring
6. Dog
7. Brake spring
8. Retainer
9. Washer
10. Washer
11. Pin

4. Reconnect the starter cable. Tighten the cable nut snugly. Do not use threadlock compound and do not overtighten the nut.

5. Reconnect the negative battery cable.

REWIND STARTER

The rewind starter is a pawl type starter. When the rope is pulled, two pawls extend outward to engage notches in the starter cup attached to the flywheel.

In this section, "starter" refers to the rewind starter assembly.

Refer to **Figure 35** for typical component identification. The starters on this engine use a shoulder bolt in place of the press pin.

> *WARNING*
> *Use extreme caution when servicing the starter. The rewind spring is under considerable tension and must be handled with the utmost care.*

Removal/Installation

1. To remove the rewind starter, remove the starter housing retaining nuts and remove the rewind starter.

2. To install the starter, perform the following:
   a. Position the starter onto the blower housing. Ensure that the handle is oriented in the proper direction.
   b. Lightly coat the fastener threads with Loctite 242 or equivalent. Install the fasteners finger tight.
   c. Center the starter pawls inside the cup by lightly pulling out on the starter rope handle grip until both pawls extend and engage the cup notches.
   d. While the pawls are in contact with the cup, alternately tighten the starter fasteners.
   e. When the fasteners are tight, release the rope grip.

Unbroken Starter Rope Replacement

> *NOTE*
> *Do not discard the rope before measuring its length and diameter. The same length and diameter of rope must be installed, which is either determined by measuring the old rope or consulting a parts manual.*

To replace an unbroken rope, remove the rewind starter as previously described, then proceed as follows:

1. Pull out the rope to its fully extended length so the rope end in the pulley is towards the housing rope outlet, then hold the pulley by installing a restraining device so the spring cannot rewind.

2. Pull out the rope knot in the pulley, untie or cut off the knot, then pull the rope out of the pulley.

3. Detach the rope from the rope handle.

4. Measure the rope and obtain a replacement rope of the same length and diameter. If the new rope is made of nylon, melt each rope end with a match to prevent fraying. Wipe the melted ends with a clean rag so the rope will fit through the pulley and housing holes.

5. Tie a knot in one end of the rope.

6. Thread the rope through the pulley rope hole and out the rope outlet in the housing.

7. Attach the rope handle to the rope.

8. Release the restraining device on the rope pulley and slowly allow the rope to wind onto the pulley.

9. Check starter operation.

Broken Starter Rope Replacement

> *NOTE*
> *Do not discard the rope before measuring its total length. The same length of rope must be installed, which is either determined by measuring the old rope or consulting a parts manual.*

To replace a broken rope, remove the starter as previously outlined, then proceed as follows:

1. Pull the rope out of the hole in the rope pulley. If the rope pulley must be removed for access to the rope, remove the rope pulley as outlined in the following procedure for rewind spring removal.

2. Detach the rope from the rope handle.

3. Measure the rope and obtain a replacement rope of the same length and diameter. If the new rope is made of nylon, melt each rope end with a match to prevent fraying. Wipe the melted ends with a clean rag so the rope will fit through the pulley and housing holes.

4. Rotate the rope pulley counterclockwise as far as possible, then allow the pulley to turn clockwise so the rope hole in the pulley and the rope outlet in the housing are aligned. Hold the pulley by installing a restraining device so the spring cannot rewind.

5. Tie a knot in one end of the rope.

6. Thread the rope through the pulley rope hole and out the rope outlet in the housing.

7. Attach the rope handle to the rope.

8. Hold the pulley, release the restraining device on the rope pulley and slowly allow the rope to wind onto the pulley.

9. Check starter operation.

Disassembly/Reassembly

Refer to **Figure 35** for typical component identification. The starters on this engine use a shoulder bolt in place of the press pin.

1. Remove the rope handle and allow the rewind spring to wind the rope into the starter.

2. Remove the shoulder bolt, washer and spring.

8

3. Remove the pawl retainer, pawls and pawl springs.

4. Remove the pulley, spring and keeper as an assembly.

5. Carefully remove the spring and keeper from the pulley.

6. Clean and inspect all components. Replace any questionable items.

7. Reverse the disassembly process to reassemble the starter, noting the following:

   a. Lightly coat all rotating parts with multipurpose grease.

   b. Make sure the spring end hooks mate properly with the catches on the pulley and housing.

   c. Make sure the pawl spring ends are toward the outside of the pawls, holding the pawls into the center of the pulley.

   d. Lightly coat the shoulder bolt threads with Loctite 222 or equivalent prior to installation.

8. Install the rope as instructed in the preceding rope replacement sections.

OIL SENSOR

Model FC420V may be equipped with an oil pressure sensor located on the oil filter adapter, if equipped with an oil filter, or on the oil passage cover if not equipped with an oil filter. The switch should be closed at zero pressure and open at 29.4 kPa (4.3 psi). The switch is connected to a warning device.

Removal/Installation

1. Stop the engine and let it cool.

2. Disconnect the wire lead from the switch.

3. Unscrew and remove the switch.

Testing

To check the sensor switch, a regulated supply of compressed air and a continuity tester are required.

1. Remove the oil pressure sensor switch as described in the previous section.

2. Connect the tester probes to the body of the switch and to the switch terminal.

3. The tester should indicate continuity between the switch terminal and the switch body.

4. Gradually apply air pressure to the switch oil passage.

5. As pressure increases to 29.4 kPa (4.3 psi), the switch should open and the tester should indicate no continuity.

6. If the switch fails the test, install a new switch.

Installation

1. Before installing the switch, apply Loctite 592 or equivalent pipe sealant with Teflon to the switch threads.

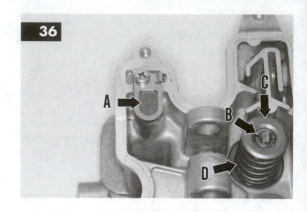

2. Install the switch. Tighten the switch to 4.5 N·m (40 in.-lb.).

3. Reconnect the wire lead.

CRANKCASE BREATHER

Crankcase pressure is vented to the cylinder head. A reed valve is located under the valve cover in the rocker arm chamber (**Figure 36**). Renew the reed valve (**Figure 37**) if the tip of the reed stands up more than 2.0 mm (0.080 in.), or if the reed is damaged or worn excessively.

Inspect the breather hose (B, **Figure 10**) anytime the air filter is serviced. If the hose is loose, cracked, or dry and brittle, replace it.

CYLINDER HEAD COVER (VALVE COVER)

The valve cover is fastened to the cylinder head with four screws (B, **Figure 21**). Remove the cover to access the crankcase breather reed valve, rocker arm assembly, valve springs and cylinder head bolts.

Once the cover is removed, thoroughly clean all gasket material from the cover and head mating surfaces. Do not damage the mating surfaces. Discard the old gasket.

When reinstalling the cover, install a new gasket. Tighten the screws in a staggered pattern to the torque value shown in **Table 4**.

38 **CYLINDER HEAD COMPONENTS**

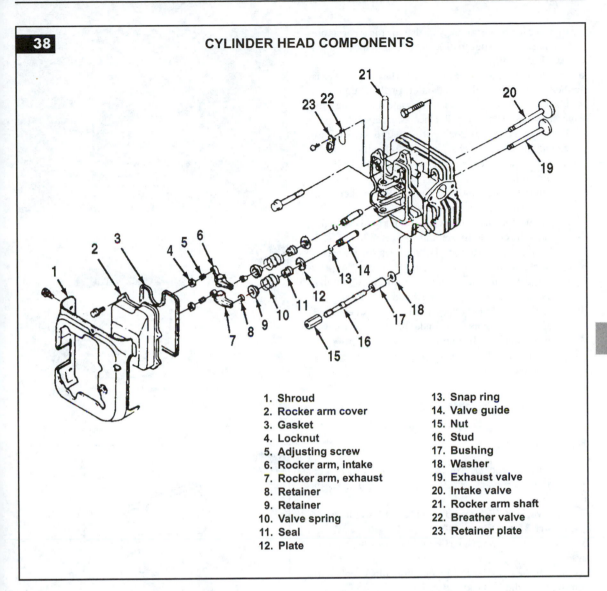

1. Shroud
2. Rocker arm cover
3. Gasket
4. Locknut
5. Adjusting screw
6. Rocker arm, intake
7. Rocker arm, exhaust
8. Retainer
9. Retainer
10. Valve spring
11. Seal
12. Plate
13. Snap ring
14. Valve guide
15. Nut
16. Stud
17. Bushing
18. Washer
19. Exhaust valve
20. Intake valve
21. Rocker arm shaft
22. Breather valve
23. Retainer plate

8

ROCKER ARMS AND PUSH RODS

Automatic Compression Release (ACR) Test

1. Remove the spark plug to relieve compression.

2. Ensure the valve clearance is set at 0.15 mm (0.006 in.) on both valves.

3. Mount a dial indicator to the engine to measure movement of the exhaust valve rocker arm at the valve stem.

4. Rotate the flywheel slowly clockwise while observing the movement of the rocker arms.

5. Immediately after the intake valve closes, the exhaust valve should open briefly at least 0.6 mm (0.024 in.).

6. Failure of the exhaust rocker arm/valve stem to move this amount indicates a faulty ACR mechanism on the camshaft. Refer to the subsequent *Camshaft* section.

Removal/Installation

Refer to **Figure 38** when performing the following procedure, unless otherwise noted:

1. Remove the cylinder head cover as described in the preceding section.

2. Remove the spark plug.

3. Rotate the crankshaft to position the piston at TDC between the compression and power strokes. At this point, there should be clearance between both valve stem ends and both rocker arms.

4. The rocker shaft is held in place by a shoulder on the bottom shaft support (A, **Figure 39**) and by the valve cover at the top (B, **Figure 39**). Carefully pull the rocker shaft up and out of the supports.

5. Remove the rocker arms. Note that the rocker arms are not interchangeable due to different offsets at the push rod end (C, **Figure 39**).

6. If necessary, remove the push rods. Mark the push rods so they may be reinstalled in their original positions.

7. Inspect the push rods, rocker arms and rocker shaft for excessive wear or damage. Replace as necessary.

8. Install the push rods, rocker arms and rocker shaft by reversing the removal steps. Note the following:

   a. Lubricate the ends of the push rods with fresh engine oil.

   b. Lubricate the contact surfaces of the rocker arms and shaft with fresh engine oil.

   c. Be sure the push rod ends are properly seated in the valve lifters and rocker arm sockets.

   d. Position the piston at TDC between the compression and power strokes.

   e. Correctly align the rocker arm offsets (C, **Figure 39**) with the appropriate push rods.

   f. When installing the rocker shaft, make sure the top of the shaft clears the cylinder head-to-valve cover gasket surface (B, **Figure 39**).

   g. Adjust the valve clearance as described in this chapter.

CYLINDER HEAD

Removal

1. Remove the rocker arm cover, rocker arms, rocker shaft and push rods as described under *Rocker Arms* in this chapter.

2. Remove the cylinder head shroud and blower housing (A, **Figure 21** and **Figure 20**).

3. Remove the carburetor (**Figure 11**) and the exhaust system.

4. Loosen the cylinder head mounting bolts evenly and remove the cylinder head and gasket.

> *NOTE*
> *Mark the positions of the head bolts, spacers and washers. They must be reassembled in the same positions.*

Disassembly

1. Compress one valve spring with a valve compressor tool (**Figure 40**). Remove the valve keepers (B, **Figure 36**). Release and remove the valve compressor tool.

2. Remove the valve spring retainer (C, **Figure 36**) and the valve spring (D).

3. Prior to removing the valve, remove any burrs from the valve stem (**Figure 41**). Otherwise, the valve guide will be damaged.

4. Remove the valve.

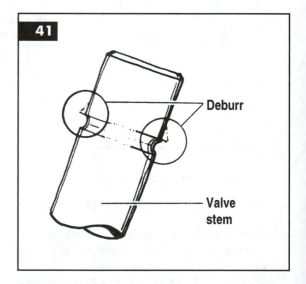

5. Remove the stem seal from the valve guide (**Figure 42**). Discard the old seal.

6. Repeat Steps 1-5 for the remaining valve.

7. Mark all parts as they are disassembled so that they can be installed in their original locations. The exhaust valve is adjacent to the exhaust port and the intake valve is located next to the intake port.

42

43

44

Inspection

1. Carefully remove all traces of gasket material from the cylinder head and valve cover mating surfaces. Do not gouge or damage the mating surfaces.

2. Carefully remove all traces of gasket material from the cylinder head and cylinder block mating surfaces. Do not gouge or damage the mating surfaces.

3. Remove all carbon deposits from the valves, combustion chamber area and valve ports with a rotary wire brush. A blunt screwdriver or chisel may be used if care is taken not to damage the head, valves and spark plug threads.

4. Examine the spark plug threads in the cylinder head for damage. If damage is minor or if the threads are dirty or clogged with carbon, use a spark plug thread tap (**Figure 43**) to clean the threads. If thread damage is severe, it may be possible to install a Heli-Coil or equivalent replacement thread to restore the damaged threads.

5. Inspect the threads in all threaded cylinder head and crankcase holes for damage. If damage is slight, dress the threads with an appropriate size metric tap if necessary. If thread damage is severe, installation of a Heli-Coil or equivalent replacement thread may be required.

6. After the carbon is removed from the combustion chamber and the valve intake and exhaust ports, clean the entire head in cleaning solvent. Blow dry with compressed air.

7. Carefully clean all carbon from the piston crown. Do not score the crown.

8. Check for cracks or other damage to the head, especially in the combustion chamber and exhaust port. Replace the cylinder head if it is cracked or damaged, or if any cooling fins are broken off.

9. After the head has been thoroughly cleaned, place the cylinder head gasket surface on a surface plate. Insert a flat feeler gauge between the plate and cylinder head at various locations to check the head for distortion. Replace the cylinder head if warpage exceeds 0.05 mm (0.002 in.). Machining or grinding the cylinder head surface to remove warpage is not recommended.

10. Valve, valve guide and valve seat service are described under *Valves and Valve Components* in this chapter.

Reassembly

1. Install new stem seals on the valve guides.

2. Lubricate the *intake* valve stem and guide bore with fresh engine oil. To avoid damage to the valve stem seal, turn the valve slowly while inserting the valve into the cylinder head. Push the valve all the way in until it seats.

3. Install the valve spring.

4. Position the valve spring retainer on top of the valve spring.

5. Compress the valve spring with a compressor tool (**Figure 40**).

6. Apply a small amount of grease to the valve keeper groove on the valve stem, then install both keepers. The grease will hold the keepers in place on the valve stem. Make sure the keepers fit snugly in the groove in the valve stem.

7. Slowly remove the compressor tool, allowing the keepers to slide into the spring retainer taper.

8. After the spring has been installed, gently tap the end of the valve stem with a soft aluminum or brass drift and hammer. This will ensure that the keepers are properly seated (**Figure 44**).

9. Repeat for the *exhaust* valve assembly. When performing Step 2, lightly lubricate the stem with Led-Plate

8

or equivalent, and lubricate the guide with fresh engine oil.

Installation

1. To install the cylinder head, reverse the removal procedure. Make sure that:
   a. The piston is at TDC between the compression and power strokes.
   b. Both locator sleeves are in position in the cylinder block (**Figure 45**).
   c. Prior to installing the rocker arms, the exhaust valve rotator cap (**Figure 44**) is installed on the end of the valve stem, inside the spring retainer cavity.
2. The cylinder head gasket surfaces are coated with a sealant and do not require additional sealant.
3. Push rods should be installed in their original positions.
4. If the head bolts are not all equal, install them into the positions shown in **Figure 46** as follows:
   a. Regular bolt in Positions 1, 3 and 4.
   b. Long nut and spacer in Position 2.
   c. Long nut and washer in Position 5.
5. Tighten the cylinder head bolts in the sequence shown in **Figure 46**. Tighten the bolts in 7.0 N·m (60 in.-lb.) increments to a final torque of 52 N·m (455 in.-lb. or 38 ft.-lb.).
6. Adjust the valve clearance as described in this chapter.

VALVES AND VALVE COMPONENTS

Valve Adjustment

Check and adjust the clearance between the valve stem ends and rocker arms after every 300 hours of operation. The engine must be cold for valve adjustment.
1. Remove the cylinder head cover as described under *Valve Cover* in this chapter.
2. Remove the spark plug.
3. Rotate the crankshaft to position the piston at TDC between the compression and power strokes. At this point, there should be clearance between both valve stem ends and both rocker arms.
4. Measure the valve clearance gap (A, **Figure 47**). Clearance should be 0.15 mm (0.006 in.) for both valves.
5. Loosen the locknut (B, **Figure 47**) and turn the setscrew to obtain the desired clearance.
6. Tighten the locknut (B, **Figure 47**) to 20 N·m (175 in.-lb.) and recheck the adjustment. Readjust, if necessary.

Valve Service

General practice among those who do their own service is to remove the cylinder head and take it to a ma-

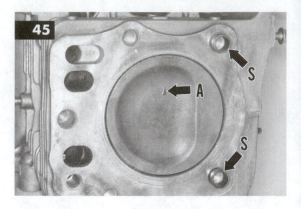

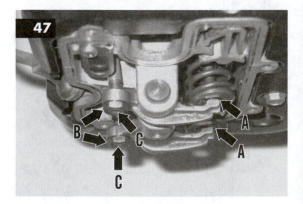

chine shop equipped to service cylinder heads and valves. Since the cost is relative to the required effort and equipment, this is the best approach even for experienced mechanics.

This procedure is included for those who chose to do their own valve service. Refer to **Figure 38** when performing this procedure.

Valve Removal

To remove the valves, follow the steps described under *Cylinder Head, Disassembly* in this chapter.

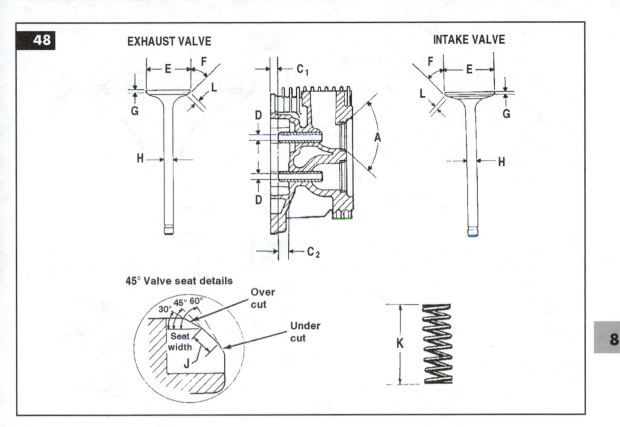

48

EXHAUST VALVE

INTAKE VALVE

45° Valve seat details

Over cut

Under cut

Seat width

8

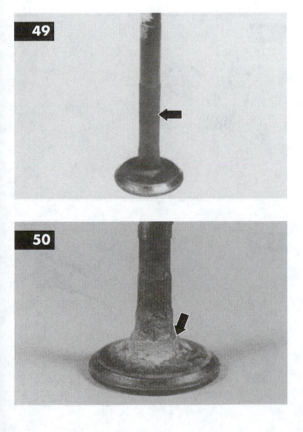

49

50

Valve Inspection

Refer to **Table 6** at the end of this chapter and **Figure 48** for valve service dimensions.

1. Inspect the valve for damage and excessive wear. Inspect the valve before cleaning. Gummy deposits on the intake valve (**Figure 49**) may indicate that the engine has run on gasoline that was stored for an extended period. Hard deposits on the intake valve are due to burnt oil, while hard deposits on the exhaust valve (**Figure 50**) are due to combustion byproducts and burnt oil. Moisture in the engine during storage can cause corroded or pitted valves, which should be replaced.

2. Check the valve face and seat for an irregular contact pattern. The seating ring around the valve face should be centered on the face, concentric with the valve head and equal in thickness all around the valve (**Figure 51**). If the seating pattern is irregular, then the valve may be bent or the valve face or seat is damaged.

3. Remove deposits with a wire brush or soak the valve in parts cleaner.

4. Measure the valve stem diameter in multiple locations where the valve rides in the guide. Replace the valve if the stem is worn.

5. The valve stem must be perpendicular to the valve head. To check for a bent valve, carefully install the valve stem in a drill chuck and rotate the drill. Be sure the valve

stem is centered in the drill chuck. If the stem or head wobbles, replace the valve.

6. Measure the valve head margin (**Figure 48**). Replace the valve if the margin is less than specified.

7. The valves and seats can be machined to restore their seating surfaces if they are worn but still serviceable. Use the specifications in **Figure 48**.

8. If valve machining is not necessary, the valve should be lapped against the valve seat to restore the seating surfaces. Refer to *Valve Lapping* in this chapter.

9. The valves ride in nonrenewable valve guides. Check for wear in the valve guides by measuring the inside diameter of the valve guide. Replace the cylinder head if the valve guide is excessively worn.

10. Check the valve springs:

   a. The spring should be straight and square as shown in **Figure 52**. Check multiple locations around the spring circumference.

   b. Measure the spring free length (**Figure 53**). Replace the valve spring if the free length is less than specification.

Valve Lapping

Valve lapping is a simple operation that can restore the valve seal without machining if the amount of wear or distortion is not excessive. Lapping requires the use of lapping compound and a lapping tool (**Figure 54**). Lapping compound is available in either coarse- or fine-grade, water- or oil-mixed. Fine-grade water-mixed compound is recommended. To lap a valve, proceed as follows:

1. Make sure that the valve head is smooth. Wire brush or lightly sand the head, if necessary.

2. Apply a light, even coat of lapping compound to the valve face. Too much compound can fall into the valve guide and cause damage.

3. Insert the valve into the valve guide.

4. Moisten the end of the lapping tool suction cup and place it on the valve head.

5. Rotate the lapping tool back and forth by hand several times.

> *NOTE*
> *For the most accurate lapping, slowly hand-rotate the lapping tool back and forth between 1/4 and 3/8 of a turn (90°-135°). Do not spin the tool rapidly and do not use a drill to rotate the lapping tool.*

Lap the valve so that the sealing ring of the valve face is in the center of the face (**Figure 55**). Make the first lap pass very light to check the sealing ring position. If, after initial lapping, the sealing ring is too high or too low on the valve face:

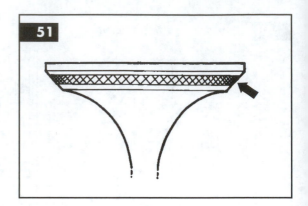

51

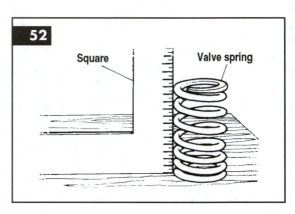

52

Square   Valve spring

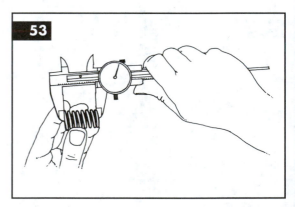

53

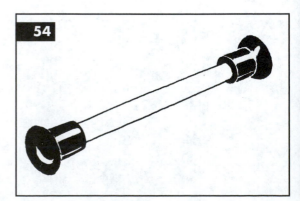

54

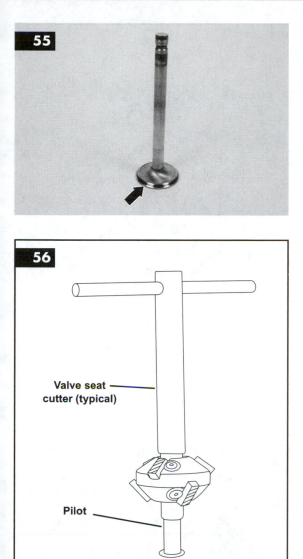

55

56

Valve seat
cutter (typical)

Pilot

10. After the valve assemblies have been installed into the engine, test each valve seal by pouring solvent into the intake and exhaust ports. There should be no leakage past the seat. If fluid leaks past any of the seats, remove the valve and repeat the lapping procedure until there is no leakage.

Valve Seat Reconditioning

These cylinder heads use hardened alloy steel intake and exhaust valve seat inserts pressed into the head. The inserts are not replaceable. If the inserts are loose, cracked or seriously warped, replace the head. If the inserts are in good condition, they can be reworked.

Special valve cutter tools and the proper expertise are required to recondition the valve seats in the cylinder heads properly. If the required tools are not available, take the cylinder head to a machine shop for service.

The following procedure is provided for those who choose to perform this task.

The following tools are needed for this procedure: Valve seat cutters, Vernier or dial caliper, machinist's dye or Prussian Blue and a valve lapping stick.

The valve seats for both the intake and exhaust valves are machined to the same angles. The valve contact surface is cut to a 45° angle from center (90° total angle).

1. Carefully rotate and insert the solid pilot into the valve guide. Make sure the solid pilot is correctly seated.

2. Using the 45° cutter, rotate the tool (**Figure 56**) one or two turns to remove roughness and clean the seat.

CAUTION
Measure the valve seat contact area in the cylinder head after each cut to make sure the contact area is correct and to prevent removing too much material. If too much material is removed, the cylinder head must be replaced.

3. If the seat is still pitted or burned, continue turning the 45° cutter until the surface is clean. Avoid removing too much material from the cylinder head.

4. Remove the valve cutter.

5. Inspect the valve seat-to-valve face impression as follows:

    a. Spread a thin layer of Prussian Blue or machinist's dye evenly on the valve face.

    b. Moisten the suction cup tool (**Figure 54**) and attach it to the valve. Insert the valve into the guide.

    c. Using the suction cup tool, tap the valve up and down in the cylinder head. Do *not* rotate the valve or a false indication will result.

    d. Remove the valve and examine the impression left by the Prussian Blue or machinist's dye.

6. Note the impression the dye left on the valve face (**Figure 55**).

    a. Recut the seat as necessary. Refer to *Valve Seat Reconditioning* in this chapter.

    b. Relap the valve.

6. If the initial lap indicates the sealing ring is centered on the valve face, proceed with a full lapping.

7. Clean the compound from the valve and seat frequently to check the progress of the lapping. Lap only enough to achieve a precise seating ring around the valve head. The pattern on the valve face should be an even width as shown in **Figure 51**.

8. Closely examine the valve seat in the cylinder head. It should be smooth and even with a burnished seating ring.

9. After lapping has been completed, thoroughly clean the valve face and valve seat areas, using dampened cloths to remove all grinding compound. Any lapping compound residue left in the engine will cause rapid wear.

8

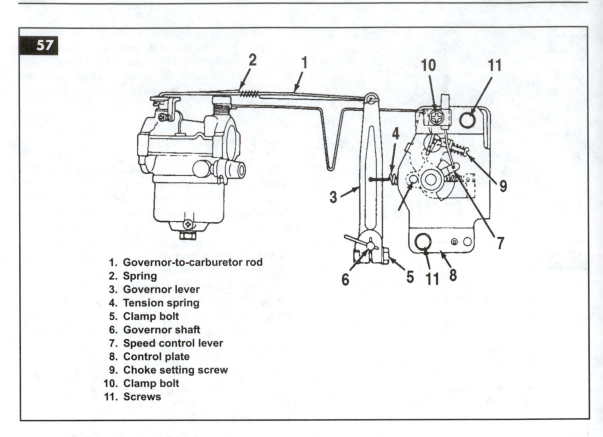

57

1. Governor-to-carburetor rod
2. Spring
3. Governor lever
4. Tension spring
5. Clamp bolt
6. Governor shaft
7. Speed control lever
8. Control plate
9. Choke setting screw
10. Clamp bolt
11. Screws

a. If the contact area is too *low* on the valve (too close to the stem), use the 60° cutter and remove a portion of the lower area of the valve seat material. This will raise the contact area. If this narrows the seat width, use the 45° cutter again to bring the seat width back into specification.

b. If the contact area is too *high* on the valve, use the 30° cutter and remove a portion of the top area of the valve seat material. This will lower the contact area. If this narrows the seat width, use the 45° cutter again to bring the seat width back into specification.

7. Once the contact area is properly positioned on the valve face, adjust the valve seat width:

a. If the width is too narrow, use the 45° cutter to widen the seat.

b. If the width is too wide, use the 30° and 60° cutters equally to remove material from both above and below the seat contact area. When the seat width is correct, repeat Step 5 to ensure the correct seat-to-face position.

8. After the desired valve seat position and width is obtained, use the 45° cutter and very lightly clean off any burrs that may have been caused by the previous cuts.

9. Check that the finish has a smooth surface. It should not be rough or show chatter marks.

10. Repeat Steps 1-9 for the remaining valve seat.

11. Lap the valves as described under *Valve Lapping* in this chapter.

12. Thoroughly clean the cylinder head and all valve components in solvent or detergent and hot water to remove all cutting and lapping debris.

13. Install the valve assemblies into the cylinder head as described in this chapter. Fill the ports with solvent to check for leaks. If any leaks are present, the valve seats must be inspected for foreign matter or burrs that may be preventing a proper seal.

14. If the cylinder head and valve components were cleaned in detergent and hot water, apply a light coat of engine oil to all bare metal surfaces to prevent any corrosion formation.

Valve Guide Reconditioning

Check for wear in the valve guides by measuring the inside diameter of the guides. Compare the measurements to the **Figure 48** specifications in **Table 6**.

Valve guides (14, **Figure 38**) can be replaced using a suitable valve guide driver.

1. Press out the old guide from the combustion chamber side by supporting the head on a 5° angle. The spark plug side of the head must be angled up.

2. Press the guides into cylinder head until the snap ring just contacts the cylinder head.

a. Press from the rocker arm side of the head.
b. Support the head on a 5° angle. The spark plug side of the head must be angled down.
3. Ream new guides to specification with a 7.0 mm valve guide reamer.

Valve Installation

To install the valves, follow the steps under *Cylinder Head, Reassembly* in this chapter.

GOVERNOR

External Service

Throttle control adjustment (engine stopped)

1. Place the remote throttle control in the FAST position.
2. Align the hole in the control plate with the hole in the throttle lever (H, **Figure 57**).
3. Insert a 15/64-inch drill bit through the hole to keep the lever and plate aligned.
4. Loosen the throttle cable housing clamp screw, pull the cable housing tight and retighten the screw.
5. Rotate the choke lever screw on back side of bracket counterclockwise so there is a gap between the screw and the choke control lever, then turn the screw back in until it *just touches* the lever.
6. Remove the drill bit.
7. With the throttle control lever in the CHOKE position, the carburetor choke plate should be closed. If not, repeat the procedure.

Static Adjustment (engine stopped)

Before adjusting the governor linkage, make certain all linkages and springs are in good condition and that the tension spring (4, **Figure 57**) is not stretched.
1. Place the engine throttle control in the FAST position. The spring around the governor-to-carburetor rod must pull the governor lever and throttle lever toward each other.
2. Loosen the governor lever clamp nut.
3. Turn the governor shaft clockwise as far as possible.
4. Tighten the clamp nut.

High RPM Adjustment

The maximum no-load engine speed should be 3550-3600 rpm. Adjust the maximum no-load speed as follows:
1. Connect an accurate tachometer to the engine.
2. With the parking brake on, the blade PTO disengaged, the speed control in neutral, and the neutral locks locked, start the engine and run it for a few minutes to reach normal operating temperature.

WARNING
Make sure ventilation is adequate if the engine is to be run in a confined area. Exhaust fumes are toxic and deadly.

3. Stop the engine.
4. Align the holes in the speed control lever (7, **Figure 57**) and bracket (8) and insert a 15/64-inch drill bit through the hole (H).
5. Restart and run the engine under no load and note engine speed.
6. If engine speed is not 3550-3600 rpm:
a. Loosen the bracket retaining screws.
b. Reposition the bracket to obtain the desired engine speed.
c. Retighten the bracket screws and recheck the engine speed.
d. Check for proper choke operation as described under *Throttle Control Adjustment* in this chapter. Readjust, if necessary.

OIL SEALS

Service With Crankshaft Installed

Oil seals at the flywheel end of the crankshaft and at the PTO end prevent the oil in the engine from leaking out. Wear or damage can reduce their effectiveness and oil leakage can become a problem, particularly if excessive amounts of oil are lost.

In some instances, it is possible to remove and install an oil seal without removing the crankshaft. Depending on the location of the engine and which oil seal is leaking, it may be necessary to remove the engine from the equipment.

If the oil seal at the flywheel end of the crankshaft is leaking, the flywheel must be removed as described in this chapter. If the oil seal at the output end of the crankshaft is leaking, any parts attached to the crankshaft that deny access to the oil seal must be removed. Refer to *ENGINE REMOVAL* in this chapter if the engine must be removed from the mower.

NOTE
Drain the engine oil if replacing the lower crankshaft oil seal.

Removal

CAUTION
Exercise care when extracting the seal so the metal in the seal bore or the crankshaft seal surface is not scratched or damaged.

1. Special oil seal removal tools (**Figure 58**) are available from small-engine tool suppliers, or one can make an effective but inexpensive oil seal removal tool by modify-

58

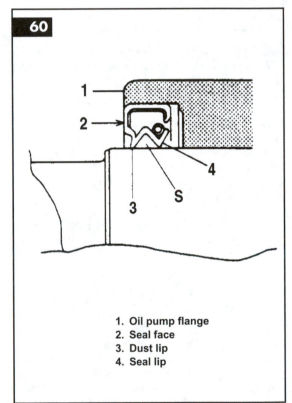

59

60

1. Oil pump flange
2. Seal face
3. Dust lip
4. Seal lip

ing a linoleum knife as shown in **Figure 59**. Carefully grind the blade to the contour shown in the figure, then round all the blade edges so the blade will not damage the crankshaft or seal cavity.

2. Using a small pin punch, carefully tap the seal in a couple of places around its outer edge so as to break it loose from the crankcase cavity. Only tap it enough to break it loose. Do not drive it deeper into the cavity.

3. Carefully insert the tool blade under the oil seal lip and against the inside periphery of the seal, next to the crankshaft (**Figure 58**). Pry out the seal. It may be necessary to work around the seal in more than one spot before the seal will break loose.

4. Clean and dry the seal seating area so the new seal will seat properly.

5. Check the oil seal bore in the engine and remove any burrs. Only remove metal that is raised and will interfere with the installation of the new seal. If a deep gouge is present, carefully clean and dry the area around the gouge, then fill the depression with a suitable epoxy so it is level with the surrounding metal.

6. Check the crankshaft seal area. Scoring, grooves, or sharp edges on the crankshaft will require that the crankshaft be replaced.

Installation

1. Apply Loctite 598, or equivalent oil resistant non-hardening sealer, to the periphery of the oil seal prior to installation.

2. Coat the lip of the seal with all-temperature grease. On double-lip seals (**Figure 60**), pack the cavity between the lips with the grease.

3. Cover keyways and threads on the crankshaft with a proper size seal protector sleeve or adhesive tape so the oil seal lip will not be cut when passing the oil seal down

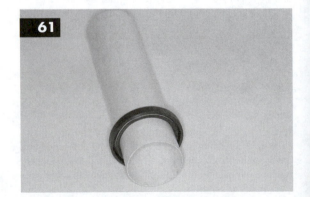

61

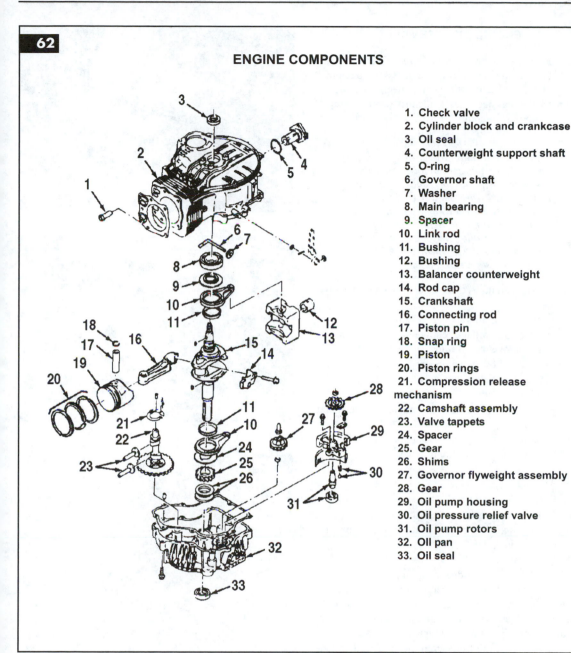

62

ENGINE COMPONENTS

1. Check valve
2. Cylinder block and crankcase
3. Oil seal
4. Counterweight support shaft
5. O-ring
6. Governor shaft
7. Washer
8. Main bearing
9. Spacer
10. Link rod
11. Bushing
12. Bushing
13. Balancer counterweight
14. Rod cap
15. Crankshaft
16. Connecting rod
17. Piston pin
18. Snap ring
19. Piston
20. Piston rings
21. Compression release mechanism
22. Camshaft assembly
23. Valve tappets
24. Spacer
25. Gear
26. Shims
27. Governor flyweight assembly
28. Gear
29. Oil pump housing
30. Oil pressure relief valve
31. Oil pump rotors
32. Oil pan
33. Oil seal

8

the crankshaft. **Figure 61** shows the seal installed onto a protector sleeve.

4. Position the seal so the seal lip is slanted toward the inside of the engine. Most seals are spring-loaded. The spring must be toward the engine when installing the seal.

5. Use a suitable tool with the same outside diameter as the oil seal to drive the oil seal into the engine. Suitable sizes of tubing or pipe may be used. Be sure the seal-driving end of the tool is square but not sharp. The outer face of both seals should be flush with the face of each seal bore.

INTERNAL ENGINE COMPONENTS

Although some internal components can be serviced without a complete disassembly, damage to one internal engine component often affects some or all of the other parts inside the engine. Failing to inspect all of the components may result in a future repair that could have been avoided.

Refer to **Figure 62** when performing internal component procedures.

ENGINE DISASSEMBLY

Use the following procedure to disassemble the engine, referring to previous sections where necessary to remove the external components. If the components are to be re-used, mark them as necessary to identify them for proper placement upon reassembly.

> *WARNING*
> *Some gasoline may drain from the fuel pump and/or the carburetor during this procedure. Wipe up any spilled gasoline immediately. Work in a well-ventilated area at least 50 feet away from any open flame, including pilot lights in gas appliances. Do not allow anyone to smoke in the area. Do not work near any grinding or any other source of sparks.*

1. On electric-start units, disconnect the battery, negative cable first.
2. Turn the fuel shutoff valve off (**Figure 2**).
3. Drain the engine oil and remove the engine from the equipment. Remove the oil filter.
4. Remove the following components:
   a. PTO clutch, pulley and keys.
   b. Muffler and exhaust system.
   c. Fuel pump, blower housing, cooling shrouds and baffles.
   d. Air filter assembly and carburetor.
   e. Ignition coil and control module.
   f. Flywheel.
   g. Alternator stator.
   h. External governor controls.
   i. Electric starter motor, if used.
   j. Spark plug, valve cover, rocker arm assembly and cylinder head.
   k. Push rods.
5. Remove the carbon ridge at the top of the cylinder bore. Run a fingernail over the top portion of the cylinder to determine if a wear ridge exists. Use a ridge reamer to remove the ridge at the top of the cylinder. Remove any shavings or grit from the ridge removal process.
6. Remove any rust or burrs from the crankshaft extensions. This will prevent damage to the main bearings. A strip of emery cloth can be used to remove rust. Burrs may be found adjacent to the keyways. It may be necessary to file down the end of the crankshaft to the original crankshaft diameter.
7. Unscrew the oil pan retaining screws and remove the oil pan. Carefully tap the pan side flanges with a soft-faced mallet, if necessary. Do not pry between the mating surfaces. Do not use excessive force against the oil pan. Applying excessive force may damage the main bearing or oil pan. If binding occurs, determine if an obstruction on the crankshaft, such as a burr, is causing the binding. If no obstruction is present, then the crankshaft

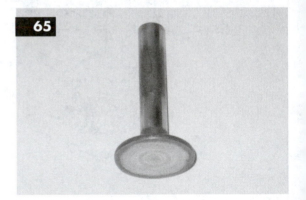

may be bent. If the crankshaft is bent, then a replacement short block should be considered, depending on the condition of the other internal engine components.

> *WARNING*
> *When a crankshaft becomes bent, stresses are introduced that weaken the crankshaft. Attempting to straighten a bent crankshaft is not recommended. A bent crankshaft must be replaced.*

8. Remove the crankshaft thrust washer (**Figure 63**).

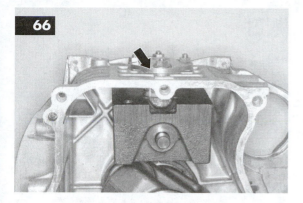

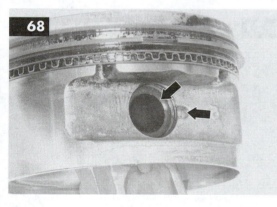

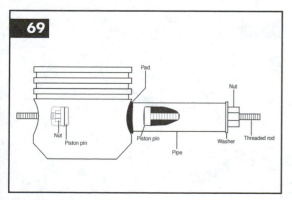

9. Position the engine so the cylinder points down. This will move the tappets away from the camshaft lobes so the lobes and tappets are not damaged when removing the camshaft.

10. Rotate the crankshaft so the timing marks on the crankshaft gear and camshaft gear are aligned (**Figure 64**).

11. Remove the camshaft.

12. Mark, then remove, the tappets (**Figure 65**). The tappets must be marked so they can be reinstalled in their original positions.

13. Unscrew the connecting rod cap retaining screws and remove the rod cap.

NOTE
Care must be exercised not to damage the bearing surface of the crankshaft, connecting rod and rod cap.

14. Push the connecting rod and piston assembly out the top of the engine.

15. Remove the counterbalance support shaft from the outside of the crankcase (**Figure 66**).

16. Remove the crankshaft and counterbalance assembly as a unit (**Figure 67**).

17. Removal of the oil pump and governor shaft assemblies will be covered in subsequent sections.

The major components of the engine should now be removed from the engine crankcase. Refer to the following sections for further disassembly and inspection of major components.

PISTON, PISTON RINGS AND PISTON PIN (WRIST PIN)

Disassembly

Use the following procedure to separate the piston from the connecting rod.

1. Insert a small pry tool in the wrist pin notch and extract the pin retaining clips (A, **Figure 68**).

2. Push or tap out the piston pin (B, **Figure 68**).

NOTE
*If the piston pin is stuck in the piston, a puller tool like that shown in **Figure 69** can be fabricated to extract the pin. Make sure the inside diameter of the tubing is larger than the outside diameter of the pin.*

3. Separate the piston from the connecting rod.

NOTE
*A suitable piston ring expander tool (**Figure 70**) should be used to remove or install the piston compression rings. Although the rings can be removed or installed by hand, there is less chance of piston ring*

breakage or gouging the piston ring grooves when the ring expander tool is used.

4. Remove the piston rings and note the following:
   a. Remove the top compression ring (closest to the piston crown) first.
   b. Remove the No. 2 compression ring second.
   c. Remove the oil control ring last.

Move the rings toward the piston crown for removal. Use care not to gouge the ring lands. Due to the flexibility of the oil control ring rails, carefully twist them out of the groove rather than use the expander tool. Discard the piston rings. Reusing worn rings is not recommended.

5. Clean the piston ring grooves. One method for cleaning piston ring grooves is to pull the end of a broken piston ring through the groove, as shown in **Figure 71**. Use care not to gouge or otherwise damage the groove. Professional piston ring groove cleaning tools are also available (**Figure 72**).

Inspection

> *NOTE*
> *Pistons and rings are available in standard size as well as 0.25 mm (0.010 in.), 0.50 mm (0.020 in.) and 0.75 mm (0.030 in.) oversize. The cylinder must be bored to the proper oversize dimension prior to installing oversize piston or rings.*

1. Clean the top of the piston using a soft wire brush. Soak the piston in carburetor cleaner to remove hard deposits.

2. Inspect the piston for damage. Replace the piston if it is cracked, scored, scuffed or scratched. Inspect the underside of the piston around the piston pin bosses, as well as the piston ring grooves, for cracks. The piston crown must be smooth except for machining or casting marks.

3. Place a new piston ring in the clean top piston ring groove and measure the side (ring land) clearance using a feeler gauge, as shown in **Figure 73**. Repeat for the second ring. Replace the piston if the side clearance exceeds 0.17 mm (0.007 in.) for the top ring or 0.15 mm (0.006 in.) for the second ring.

4. Inspect the piston pin and the piston pin bores in the piston for scoring and other damage. The piston pin is only available in the standard size; replace the piston and pin if wear exceeds specification. The maximum inside diameter of the pin bore in the piston is 22.037 mm (0.8676 in.). The piston pin outside diameter wear limit is 21.977 mm (0.8652 in.). The maximum piston-to-pin clearance is 0.06 mm (0.0024 in.).

5. Measure the piston pin diameter at several points to determine if the piston pin is worn or out-of-round. Replace the pin if any measurement is smaller than 21.977 mm (0.8652 in.).

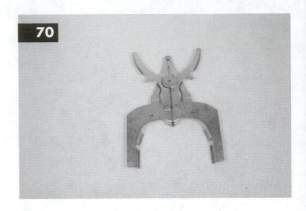

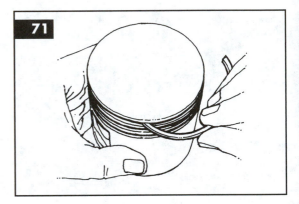

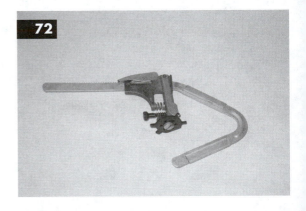

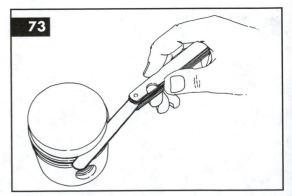

74

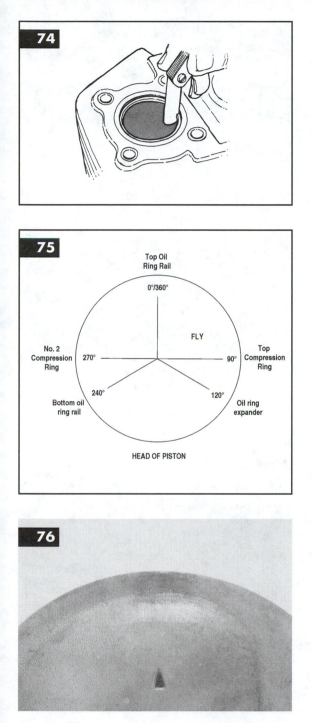

75

Top Oil Ring Rail

0°/360°

FLY

No. 2 Compression Ring — 270°

90° — Top Compression Ring

240°

120°

Bottom oil ring rail

Oil ring expander

HEAD OF PISTON

76

6. Measure the end gap of each piston ring. Place the piston ring in the cylinder bore, then push the piston ring down into the bore with the piston so the ring is square in the bore. Position the piston ring 25 mm (1.0 in.) down in the bore from the top of the cylinder and measure the piston ring end gap as shown in **Figure 74**. The maximum allowable end gap is 0.90 mm (0.035 in.) for the

77

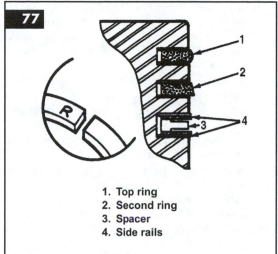

1. **Top ring**
2. **Second ring**
3. **Spacer**
4. **Side rails**

compression rings and 1.30 mm (0.051 in.) for the oil control ring. If the piston ring gap is greater than specified, check the cylinder bore for wear.

Reassembly

Lubricate the piston ring grooves, rings, wrist pin and pin bores with fresh engine oil prior to assembly.

1. Use a suitable piston ring expander tool (**Figure 70**) to install the piston rings. Although the rings can be removed or installed by hand, there is less chance of piston ring breakage or gouging the piston ring grooves when the ring expander tool is used.

2. For maximum engine power and longevity, as well as precise emission control, the ring end gaps should be spaced around the piston circumference in the approximate degreed intervals, as shown in **Figure 75**.

    a. The arrow on the piston head (**Figure 45** and **Figure 76**) will indicate the 0°/360° position.

    b. Refer to **Figure 77** for a top and cross-sectional view of the rings.

    c. The top (No. 1) compression ring should have its gap at the 90° position.

    d. The No. 2 compression ring (center groove) should have its gap at the 270° position.

    e. The seam or gap of the oil control ring expander should be in the 120° position.

    f. The top oil control ring rail should have its gap at the 0°/360° position.

    g. The bottom oil control ring rail should have its gap at the 240° position.

3. Install the oil control ring first using the following procedure:

    a. Install the ring expander in the ring groove. The expander ring ends must abut, not overlap (**Figure 78**).

8

b. Twist one of the rails in a spiral and work it into the top piston ring groove (**Figure 79**), then into the center groove, and finally into the oil ring groove, placing the first rail against the bottom of the expander ring.

c. Install the second rail using the same procedure so it fits above the expander and the end gap is properly positioned. The installed oil control ring should appear as shown in **Figure 78**. The oil control ring assembly must rotate without binding in the piston ring groove.

4. Install the center compression ring, then the top compression ring. Note that the top side of each compression ring (toward the piston crown) has an identifying R, N or NPR mark to indicate the top. Refer to the instructions included with the replacement rings.

NOTE
Install new piston pin clips. Do not reuse removed clips.

5. Assemble the piston and connecting rod for the No. 1 cylinder so the arrow on the piston crown (**Figure 45** and **Figure 76**) is toward the MADE IN JAPAN side of the connecting rod (**Figure 80**).

a. Lubricate the piston pin bores and pin.

b. Install one of the piston pin clips in its piston pin bore groove.

c. Insert the piston pin.

d. Install the remaining piston pin retaining clip.

e. Be sure the piston pin retaining clips are securely positioned in the piston grooves.

CAUTION
Make sure that the gap of the clip is at either the top or bottom of the piston and not aligned with the clip removal cutout (A, Figure 68). Installing the clips with the gap towards the sides could cause the clips to work loose during engine operation, resulting in serious engine damage.

CONNECTING ROD

The connecting rod rides directly on the crankshaft crankpin. If the rod and crankpin are worn beyond specification, the crankpin can be reground and a 0.50 mm (0.020 in.) undersize connecting rod installed. Refer to *Crankshaft* in this chapter for regrinding specifications.

Disassembly

The piston and connecting rod are removed from the engine as an assembly, then separated, as outlined in the preceding section.

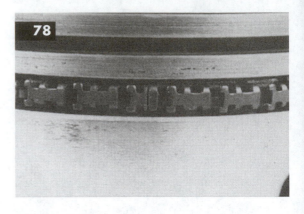

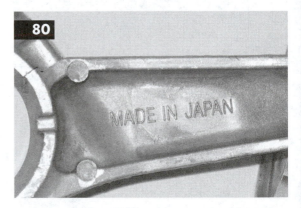

Inspection

1. Inspect the bearing surfaces for signs of scuffing and scoring. If any damage is observed, also inspect the surface of the crankpin or piston pin.

NOTE
If the rod bearing surface is worn due to abrasive particles (the surface texture is dull and rough), it should be replaced even if it is not worn beyond the specified wear limit. Grit may be embedded in the aluminum that will continue to cause wear on mating surfaces.

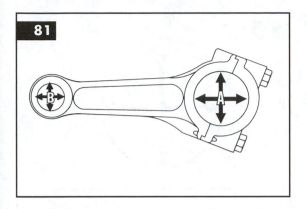

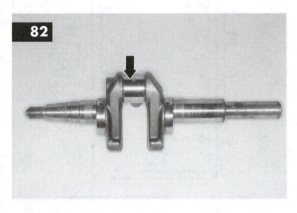

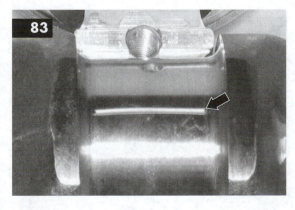

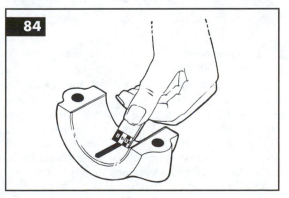

2. Inspect the connecting rods for cracks, twisting and other damage. Inspect the alignment of each connecting rod. If there is evidence of abnormal piston or cylinder wear, have the connecting rod inspected at a machine shop. Specialized equipment is required to accurately determine if a rod is bent or twisted.

3. Assemble the connecting rod.

    a. Apply a small amount of oil to the connecting rod bolt threads.

    b. Tighten the rod bolts to 20 N·m (180 in.-lb.).

4. Measure the big end diameter of the connecting rod (A, **Figure 81**). The maximum allowable inside diameter for the connecting rod big end bearing surface is 41.068 mm (1.6169 in.). Maximum connecting rod-to-crankpin clearance is 0.14 mm (0.006 in.).

5. Measure the small end diameter of the connecting rod (B, **Figure 81**). The maximum inside diameter of the connecting rod small end is 22.059 mm (0.8685 in.). Maximum allowable connecting rod-to-piston pin clearance is 0.08 mm (0.003 in.).

6. Replace the connecting rod if any Step 4 or 5 measurements do not meet specification.

Connecting Rod Bearing Clearance Measurement

Plastigage is the most popular and convenient way to measure connecting rod-to-crankshaft journal clearance. Plastigage comes in three sizes: 0.025-0.076 mm (0.001-0.003 inch); 0.051-0.152 mm (0.002-0.006 inch); and 0.102-0.229 mm (0.004-0.009 inch). To gauge the clearance:

1. Clean the crankshaft crankpin (**Figure 82**).

2. Position the connecting rod onto the crankshaft in the correct position on the crankpin.

3. Cut a strip of Plastigage slightly shorter than the width of the connecting rod/crankshaft journal (**Figure 83**). Place the Plastigage onto the crankpin. Make sure the Plastigage runs parallel to the crankshaft as shown in **Figure 83**. Do not place the Plastigage material over the oil hole in the crankshaft.

4. Correctly align the rod cap with the rod. Tighten the rod cap bolts to the torque specification of 20 N·m (180 in.-lb.) to compress the gauge.

CAUTION
When tightening the rod cap bolts, do not rotate the connecting rod or the crankshaft. Damaged Plastigage and inaccurate readings will result.

5. Loosen the cap bolts. Carefully lift the cap straight up and off the connecting rod.

6. Compare the flattened Plastigage width to the scale furnished with the Plastigage (**Figure 84**). This will tell the clearance.

8

a. If clearance exceeds 0.14 mm (0.006 in.), replace the connecting rod and recondition the crankshaft. A connecting rod with a 0.50 mm (0.020 in.) undersize crankshaft journal bore is available.

b. If the crankshaft must be reground to accept an undersize connecting rod, refer to the *Crankshaft* section for machining information.

7. Remove the Plastigage from the crankshaft and connecting rod.

CYLINDER, CYLINDER BLOCK AND CRANKCASE

The cylinder is a cast iron alloy sleeve integrally cast into the aluminum alloy crankcase and block assembly.

To access the cylinder, follow the steps under *Engine Disassembly* in this chapter.

The piston and ring set is available in the standard size as well as 0.25 mm (0.010 in.), 0.50 mm (0.020 in.) and 0.75 mm (0.030 in.) oversize.

Inspection and Reconditioning

Thoroughly inspect the cylinder block:

1. Make sure all gasket and sealant material has been completely removed from the head, oil pan and breather sealing surfaces. Sealing surfaces must be free from nicks, gouges or deep scratches.

2. Inspect the fastener holes for damaged threads or broken fasteners.

a. For broken fasteners, refer to *Removing Broken Fasteners* in Chapter One.

b. For damaged threads, restore the threads with an appropriate size metric tap if necessary. If thread damage is severe, install a Heli-Coil or equivalent replacement thread to restore the damaged threads. If the threaded holes cannot be satisfactorily repaired, replace the cylinder block.

3. Check for broken cooling fins. A small broken edge or corner may not affect performance. A large piece of broken-off fin will cause the cylinder to overheat. Replace the cylinder block if major fin damage is evident.

4. Check for debris packed in between the fins. Carefully and completely remove any heat-caked debris.

5. Check the bores for scoring or other damage.

6. Measure the cylinder bore parallel with the crankshaft and at right angles to the crankshaft at the top, center and bottom of ring travel (**Figure 85**). A telescoping bore gauge (**Figure 86**) or an inside micrometer can be used to precisely measure cylinder bores. Always follow the instructions included with the tool. Compare the measurements to the following:

a. The standard cylinder bore diameter is 88.90-89.00 mm (3.500-3.504 in.).

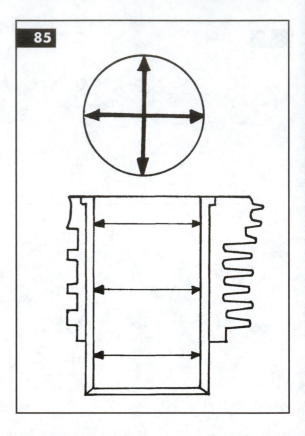

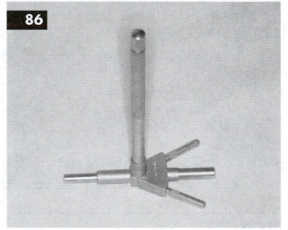

b. The standard cylinder bore wear limit is 89.076 mm (3.5069 in.).

c. Maximum out-of-round is 0.063 mm (0.0025 in.).

7. If the cylinder has been previously rebored, the piston crown will be marked 0.25, 0.5, or 0.75 to show its oversize. A block whose cylinder will not clean up at 0.75 mm oversize or one which has already been rebored to 0.75 mm oversize and then worn beyond limits will need to be replaced. The maximum wear limit for an oversized cylinder is 89.816 mm (3.510 in.).

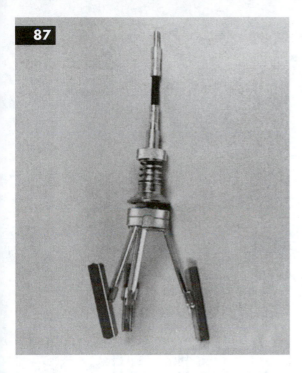

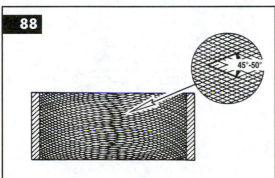

CAUTION
If one cylinder is worn beyond specification, both cylinders must be rebored and fitted with oversize pistons to preserve engine balance integrity.

8. If the cylinder bore is within the specified wear limits, the bore will need to be honed so new rings will seat properly. A hone such as that pictured in **Figure 87** works well. Always follow the hone manufacturer's instructions.

9. The crosshatch angle of the bore surface after finish honing should be 45°-50° as shown in **Figure 88**. Too large an angle will cause high oil consumption; too small an angle will make the rings skip and wear rapidly. The crosshatch pattern retains oil in the microscopic grooves, thus allowing the piston rings to seat properly.

10. If the cylinder is being bored oversize, bore to the specified original-plus-oversize dimension.
   a. Oversize cylinder dimension at 0.25 mm is 89.210-89.230 mm (3.5122-3.5130 in.).
   b. Oversize cylinder dimension at 0.50 mm is 89.460-89.480 mm (3.5220-3.5228 in.).
   c. Oversize cylinder dimension at 0.75 mm is 89.710-89.730 mm (3.5329-3.5327 in.).

Always follow the boring machine manufacturer's instructions. The final step of a rebore should always be a finish honing. The crosshatch angle of the cylinder bore surface after finish honing should be 45°-50° as shown in **Figure 88**.

11. After honing, thoroughly wash the cylinder with plenty of soap and hot water and rise in clean warm water. Blow-dry with compressed air. This will remove the microscopic grinding particles from the surface of the cylinder bore. A grease-cutting dishwashing detergent is an excellent soap to use. Do not use petroleum solvents (mineral spirits, kerosene, etc.) to clean the bore. Solvents *will not remove* embedded grinding dust from the cylinder bore surface.

12. After drying the cylinder, spray the bore with a moisture displacing lubricant such as WD-40 or equivalent. Use a clean, lint-free cloth to wipe the lubricant from the bore. If gray residue shows up on the wiping cloth, the cylinder is not clean. Repeat Step 11 until no gray residue appears.

13. Apply a light coat of engine oil to the bore to prevent rust.

CAUTION
Failure to properly clean a honed or rebored cylinder will cause rapid cylinder and piston wear and severe engine damage.

CRANKSHAFT, COUNTERBALANCE AND MAIN BEARINGS

The crankshaft (**Figure 82**) is supported on the flywheel side by a ball-type main bearing (A, **Figure 89**) and on the PTO side by a plain bearing machined into the oil pan casting (A, **Figure 90**).

A reciprocating balancer rides on separate crankshaft journals (**Figure 67** and **Figure 91**).

> *NOTE*
> *When replacing a crankshaft, short block, or engine, ensure that the threads on the PTO bolt that was removed from the old crankshaft are compatible with the threads in the new crankshaft.*

The crankshaft and main bearing specifications are listed in **Table 5**.

Removal

To remove the crankshaft, follow the steps under *Engine Disassembly* in this chapter.

The bearing on the flywheel side should be a press fit on the crankshaft and in the bearing bore of the crankcase.

Disassembly

> *NOTE*
> *Prior to disassembling the crankshaft and counterbalance unit, mark all components so they can be reassembled properly.*

Refer to **Figure 62**.
1. Remove the flywheel-side ball bearing.
2. Remove the crankshaft gear.
3. Remove the thrust spacer from the flywheel side of the crankshaft.
4. Remove the thrust washer from the PTO side of the crankshaft.
5. Turn the crankshaft/counterbalance assembly so both components are lying on the workbench.
6. Being careful not to damage the crankshaft connecting rod journal, slide both counterbalance links off the crankshaft and counterweight journals.
7. Thoroughly clean all components.

Inspection and Reconditioning

Inspect the crankshaft as follows:
1. If considerable effort was required to remove the oil pan from the crankshaft, then the crankshaft is probably bent and must be discarded. If some effort was required during removal, then the crankshaft should be checked for straightness by a shop with the necessary equipment. If the oil pan was easy to remove, and the bearings are within specifications, then the crankshaft is probably straight. Crankshaft runout can be used as an indicator of crankshaft straightness. Proceed to Step 2 to measure runout. Maximum allowable crankshaft runout is 0.05 mm (0.002 in.).

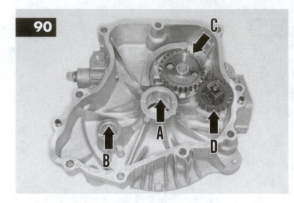

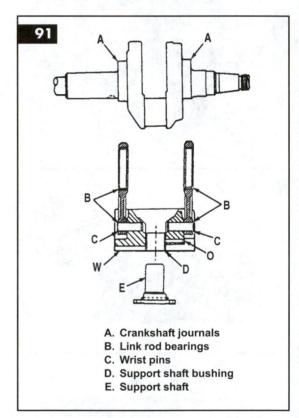

A. Crankshaft journals
B. Link rod bearings
C. Wrist pins
D. Support shaft bushing
E. Support shaft

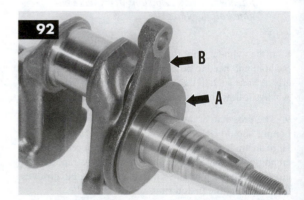

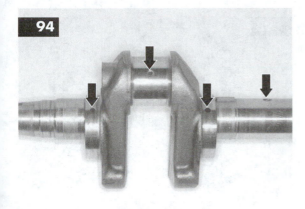

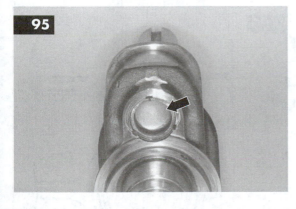

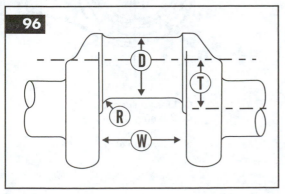

WARNING
When a crankshaft becomes bent, stresses are introduced that weaken the crankshaft. Attempting to straighten a bent crankshaft is not recommended. A bent crankshaft must be replaced.

2. Measure crankshaft runout using one of the following procedures:

    a. Install the crankshaft in the engine. Be sure the main bearings are lubricated. Measure crankshaft runout at the PTO end of the crankshaft.

    b. Support the crankshaft in V-blocks at the main bearing journals. **Figure 93** shows a typical crankshaft being checked for runout.

CAUTION
When using a dial indicator to check runout, exercise caution when the crankshaft keyway approaches the indicator anvil. Dial indicator damage could result if the keyway strikes the anvil.

3. Inspect all mating surfaces on the crankshaft for indications of scoring, scuffing and other damage.

4. Check the flywheel threads and the PTO threads for damage and cross threading. Dress or repair if possible.

5. Inspect the keyways and remove any burrs. The keyway must be straight and unworn.

6. The crankshaft gear is removable. Check the crankshaft gear for broken or pitted teeth.

7. Be sure all oil passages (**Figure 94**) are clean and unobstructed.

8. Be sure the connecting rod crankpin plug (**Figure 95**) is tight.

CAUTION
*Removing and/or replacing the crankshaft oil gallery plug (**Figure 95**) is not recommended. If the connecting rod journal must be reground undersize, thoroughly flush the galleries to remove all traces of grinding grit. Failure to properly flush the oil gallery behind the plug will cause rapid crankshaft, main bearing and connecting rod wear and severe internal engine damage.*

9. Measure the crankpin journal. The crankpin journal minimum diameter is 40.928 mm (1.6113 in.). If the crankpin is worn beyond standard specification, the crankpin can be reground and a 0.50 mm (0.020 in.) undersize connecting rod installed. Refer to **Figure 96** for regrinding dimensions.

10. Measure the main bearing journals (**Figure 82**). Main bearing journals cannot be machined undersize.

    a. The minimum flywheel-side journal dimension is 34.945 mm (1.3757 in.).

8

b. The minimum PTO-side journal dimension is 34.919 mm (1.3747 in.).

11. Measure the crankshaft counterbalance link journals. The minimum dimension is 53.950 mm (2.1240 in.). The counterbalance link journals cannot be machined under-size.

12. Measure the PTO inside bearing diameter in the oil pan (A, **Figure 90**). The maximum inside diameter for the integral bore in the oil pan is 35.069 mm (1.3807 in.).

13. Measure the counterbalance link bearings (**Figure 97**):

a. The maximum big end dimension is 54.121 mm (2.1307 in.). Big end bushings are replaceable.

b. The maximum small end dimension is 12.60 mm (0.4748 in.). Replace the link if the small-end bore exceeds this dimension.

14. Measure the counterweight shaft bushing inside diameter (A, **Figure 98**). The maximum bushing diameter is 26.097 mm (1.0274 in.).

a. The support shaft bushing is replaceable. When installing a new support shaft bushing, make sure that the oil hole in the bushing is aligned with the oil passage in the counterweight.

b. Replace the counterweight if the link pins are worn or damaged.

Counterbalance Link Bushing Replacement

1. Carefully support the link while driving out the old bushing (B, large end, **Figure 91**).

2. Position the seam (S, **Figure 99**) of the bushing 90° from the centerline of the link rod.

3. Press the bushing into the link rod from the side opposite oil grooves.

4. Install the bushing so the depth below the machined surface of the link rod is 1.0 mm (0.040 in.).

Assembly

To assemble the crankshaft and counterbalance:

1. Install the balance weight (W, **Figure 91**) with the oil hole (O) toward the flywheel side of the crankshaft.

2. Install the link rods (B, **Figure 91**) with the oil grooves (G, **Figure 99**) facing away from the crankshaft.

3. Install the spacer with the chamfered face toward the link rod.

4. Install the spacer so the conical face is out.

Installation

To install the crankshaft, follow the necessary steps under *Engine Reassembly* in this chapter.

When installing the crankshaft/counterbalance assembly into the crankcase:

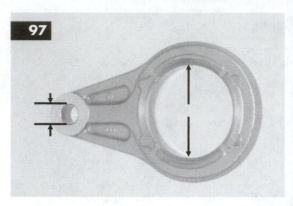

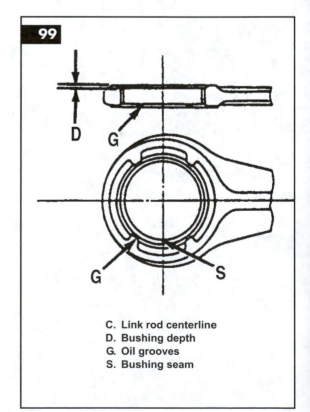

C. Link rod centerline
D. Bushing depth
G. Oil grooves
S. Bushing seam

To remove the camshaft from the engine, follow the necessary steps under *Engine Disassembly* in this chapter.

The camshaft is equipped with a compression release mechanism to aid starting. The pivoting weight mechanism on the camshaft gear moves an arm that fits next to the exhaust cam lobe. During starting, the arm protrudes above the bottom of the cam lobe and forces the exhaust valve to stay open longer, thereby reducing compression. At running speed, centrifugal force causes the weight to pivot outward, pulling the arm away from the lobe. This allows the engine to develop full power.

Camshaft specifications are listed in **Table 5**.

1. Inspect the gear teeth for wear and cracked or broken teeth. If any teeth are damaged, the camshaft will have to be replaced.

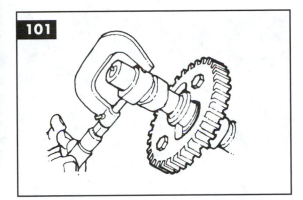

NOTE
If the camshaft is replaced, the crankshaft gear will also need replacing. Also replace the lifters.

2. Inspect the camshaft for cracks. Replace a cracked camshaft.

3. Inspect the camshaft journals and lobes for wear or scoring.

4. Measure the journals and lobes. Compare the measurements to the **Table 5** dimensions.

5. Measure the lift height of the intake and exhaust lobes. Compare the measurements to the **Table 5** dimensions. To determine lift height:

   a. Measure across the lift part of the lobe (**Figure 101**).

   b. Measure across the narrow diameter of the lobe.

   c. Subtract the measurement in substep b from the measurement in substep a.

6. Inspect the camshaft bearing surfaces in the crankcase and oil pan. The surfaces must be smooth with no signs of abrasion.

7. Measure the camshaft bearing bore diameters in the crankcase and oil pan. Compare the measurements to the **Table 5** dimensions.

8. Inspect the compression release mechanism. The mechanism should move freely without binding. The only replaceable component of the compression release is the spring for the pivoting weight.

To install the camshaft into the engine, follow the necessary steps under *Engine Reassembly* in this chapter.

1. Align the balancer weight bushing with the hole in the crankcase.

2. Insert the support shaft (4, **Figure 62**, and **Figure 66**).

   a. Use a new O-ring (5, **Figure 62**).

   b. Lightly coat the shaft fastener threads with Loctite 242 or equivalent prior to tightening.

CAMSHAFT

The camshaft is shown in **Figure 100**. The camshaft bearing journals ride directly in bores machined into the crankcase and oil pan.

GOVERNOR (Internal Service)

The internal centrifugal flyweight governor is mounted in the oil pan (A, **Figure 102**). The governor is driven by the camshaft gear and, in turn, drives the oil pump gear (B, **Figure 102**).

To remove the governor assembly from the oil pan, use two flat-bladed pry tools, one under either side of the gear, to snap the governor gear and flyweight assembly off the governor stub shaft. The governor gear has internal lock tabs and will be damaged when removed. Discard the original governor gear.

To install a new governor:

1. Clean any debris from the locking groove of the pan-mounted governor shaft.

2. Install the thrust washer (A, **Figure 103**) onto the shaft.

3. Install the flange of the sleeve (B, **Figure 103**) between the flyweight fingers (C).

CAUTION
The sleeve (bf ital)must be installed into the weights prior to installing the gear onto the shaft.

4. Lubricate the shaft and gear with engine oil.

5. Push the gear onto the shaft until the internal lock tabs snap into the shaft groove.

Governor Shaft Oil Seal Replacement

Refer to **Figure 104**.

1. Remove the shaft retainer clip (A, **Figure 105**).

2. Push the shaft (B, **Figure 105**) into the crankcase. Do not lose the inner shaft washer (**Figure 106**).

3. Carefully pry out the seal.

4. Install the new seal, lip facing in, so the outer face is just below flush with the face of the seal bore (**Figure 104**).

5. Lubricate the shaft bore and seal lip with engine oil.

6. Reinstall the shaft and retainer clip.

   a. Make sure that the inner washer is correctly mounted on the shaft (**Figure 106**).

   b. Position the shaft and clip *exactly* as pictured in **Figure 105**, or the governor will not operate properly.

OIL PUMP

The trochoid-type oil pump (**Figure 107**) is mounted in the oil pan (**Figure 108**). To service the oil pump:

1. Remove the pump drive gear (B, **Figure 102**).

2. Remove the two bolts (B, **Figure 108**) retaining the pump housing and remove the housing, outer rotor and inner rotor/shaft (**Figure 107**) together from the oil pan.

3. Remove the inlet screen (**Figure 109**).

4. Unbolt the relief valve retainer plate (C, **Figure 108**). Remove the relief valve ball and spring (5, **Figure 110**).

5. Inspect the seating of the relief valve ball.

6. Measure the relief valve spring free length. Replace the spring if the free length is less than 19.00 mm (0.748 in.).

7. Measure the diameter of the rotor shaft (6, **Figure 110**); the wear limit is 12.63 mm (0.497 in.).

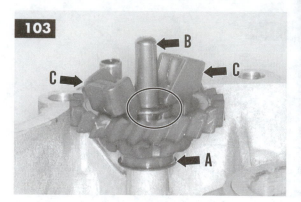

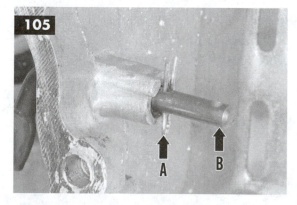

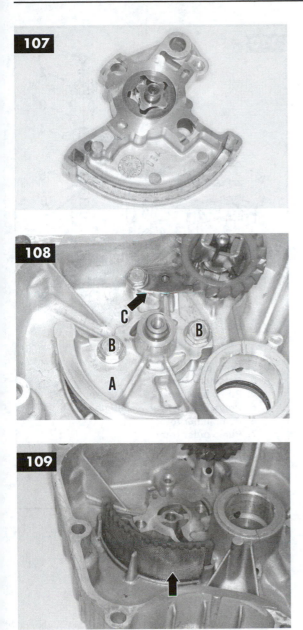

8. Measure the inside diameter of the rotor shaft bearing surface in the pump housing; the wear limit is 12.76 mm (0.502 in.).

9. To reinstall the pump:
   a. Lubricate the parts with fresh engine oil.
   b. Reverse the removal procedure.

ENGINE REASSEMBLY

Refer to the appropriate previous sections when assembling the internal engine components and installing the external engine components as applicable. Refer to **Figure 62** for internal engine component identification.

Before assembling the engine, be sure all components are clean. Any residue or debris left in the engine will cause rapid wear and/or major damage when the engine runs.

NOTE
Thoroughly lubricate all internal component contact/wear surfaces with fresh engine oil immediately prior to assembly.

Lightly coat all fastener threads, except the cylinder head bolts and the connecting rod bolts, with Loctite 242 or equivalent immediately prior to assembly. Do not use threadlock compound on the head or rod bolts.

During final installation, make sure that new gaskets are installed and the correct torque sequences and values are strictly followed. Torque values are listed in **Table 4**.

The following components should be already assembled before proceeding:
   a. Pistons, piston rings and connecting rods.
   b. Oil pump assembly.
   c. Flyweight governor.
   d. Governor shaft.
   e. Crankshaft and counterbalance.

Use the following procedure to assemble the internal engine components:

1. Lubricate the flywheel-side main crankshaft bearing with engine oil.

2. Insert the crankshaft/balancer assembly into the crankcase.
   a. Align the balancer weight bushing with the hole in the crankcase.
   b. Using a new O-ring (5, **Figure 62**), insert the support shaft (4, **Figure 62**, and **Figure 66**).
   c. Lightly coat the shaft fastener threads with Loctite 242 or equivalent prior to tightening.

3. Proceed as follows and install the piston/connecting rod assembly:
   a. Lubricate the piston, piston pin and piston rings with engine oil.
   b. Position the piston ring end gaps as specified under *Pistons, Reassembly* in this chapter.
   c. Use a ring compressor (**Figure 111**) to compress the piston rings. Ensure that the top and bottom edges of the snugged compressor band are not misaligned. The projections on the compressor band must be toward the piston skirt and the oil ring must be at least 6 mm (1/4 in.) above the bottom edge of the compressor.
   d. Install the piston and rod assembly in the cylinder so the arrow cast into the piston crown (**Figure 45** and **Figure 76**) points toward the flywheel side of the engine.
   e. Lubricate the cylinder bore with Lubriplate White Grease or fresh engine oil.
   f. Insert the connecting rod and piston through the top of the engine so the piston ring compressor rests against the engine.

8

g. Liberally lubricate the connecting rod bearing and the crankshaft crankpin with engine oil.

h. Push the piston into the cylinder bore while guiding the connecting rod onto the crankshaft crankpin.

CAUTION
Do not use excessive force when installing the piston and rod. If binding occurs, remove the piston and rod and try again. Excessive force can damage or break the piston rings, piston ring lands, connecting rod or crankshaft.

i. Mate the connecting rod with the crankshaft crankpin, then rotate the crankshaft so the cap can be installed.

j. Install the rod cap. Apply oil to the connecting rod bolts before installation. Tighten the rod bolts to 20 N·m (180 in.-lb.).

k. Rotate the crankshaft to position the piston at TDC.

4. Lubricate the shafts and ends of the valve lifters and install them into their correct positions in the crankcase.

NOTE
If a new camshaft is being installed, also install new lifters.

5. Lubricate the camshaft and camshaft bearing in the crankcase with engine oil.

6. Install the camshaft. Align the timing marks (**Figure 64**) on the crankshaft and camshaft gears.

7. Install the thrust washer onto the end of the crankshaft (**Figure 63**).

8. Be sure the oil pan locating sleeves are installed in the appropriate crankcase holes.

9. Install the crankcase gasket.

10. Lubricate the crankshaft main bearing and camshaft bearing in the oil pan.

11. Install the oil pan. Rotate the crankshaft to help engage the governor gear.

NOTE
Do not force the oil pan onto the crankcase. If binding occurs, remove the oil pan, then determine and correct the cause.

a. Install the oil pan with the original thrust washer shim(s) (**Figure 63**).

b. Use a dial indicator to measure the crankshaft end play.

c. Add or remove shims as necessary to obtain the specified end play of 0.09-0.22 mm (0.004-0.009 in.).

12. Install the oil pan bolts. Tighten the oil pan bolts in 5.0 N·m (45 in.-lb.) increments in the sequence shown in **Figure 112**. Tighten the screws to a final torque of 26 N·m (230 in.-lb.).

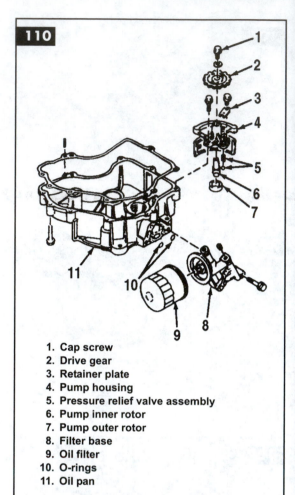

110

1. Cap screw
2. Drive gear
3. Retainer plate
4. Pump housing
5. Pressure relief valve assembly
6. Pump inner rotor
7. Pump outer rotor
8. Filter base
9. Oil filter
10. O-rings
11. Oil pan

111

13. Install the oil seals. Follow the steps in the *OIL SEAL* section.

14. Install the PTO shaft keys, pulley and clutch. The assembled engine block can now be installed onto the mower, if desired, for installation of the external components.

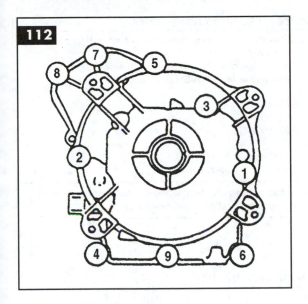

15. Paying close attention to the location and orientation marks made during disassembly, install the external components.

  a. Crankcase breather.
  b. Push rods.
  c. Cylinder head.
  d. Rocker arm assembly.
  e. Valve cover.
  f. Spark plug.
  g. Electric starter motor, if used.
  h. External governor components.
  i. Alternator stator.
  j. Flywheel.
  k. Ignition coil and control module.
  l. Carburetor and air filter assembly.
  m. Blower housing (including rewind starter, if used), cooling shrouds and baffles.
  n. Fuel pump.
  o. Exhaust system and muffler.
  p. Oil filter. Fill the oil filter with oil prior to installation. Fill the crankcase with the correct type and amount of oil.

16. Static-adjust the governor.

> *CAUTION*
> *Prior to starting the engine, the governor linkage must have the static adjustment performed or serious engine overspeed damage could result. Once the engine is started, the governor must be adjusted for high speed as described in this chapter.*

8

Table 1   GENERAL ENGINE SPECIFICATIONS

Model	No. Cyls.	Bore	Stroke	Displacement	Power Rating
FC420V	1	89 mm (3.50 in.)	68 mm (2.68 in.)	423 cc (25.8 cu. in.)	14 hp 10.5 kW

Table 2   MAINTENANCE AND LUBRICATION SCHEDULE

After 5-hour break-in period (new unit; new or overhauled engine)	Change the engine oil and the oil filter. Check all the fasteners and the linkages for security.
Every 8 hours or daily	Check the engine oil with the unit sitting level. Do not overfill. Check and/or clean the air filter. Clean the cooling system grass screen.
Every 40-50 hours or weekly	Service the air cleaner pre-filter. Clean the paper air filter. On electric-start units, check the battery electrolyte level. Lubricate the throttle and choke cables.
Every 100 hours or semi-monthly	Change the engine oil and oil filter. Clean the cooling system.
Every 300 hours or semi-annually	Replace the air filter and pre-filter. Adjust the valve clearance.
Every 500 hours or annually	Replace the fuel filter and fuel hoses. Remove and clean the cylinder heads. Clean and lap the valves. Check all of the fasteners for proper tightness.

Table 3 RECOMMENDED ENGINE FUEL AND LUBRICANTS

Fuel	Unleaded pump gasoline with Octane rating of 87 or higher
Capacity	5.0 U.S. gallons (18.7 liters or 4.0 Imperial gallons)
Engine oil	API service rating of SH or above
Viscosity	
Above 70° F (20° C)	SAE 40
Above 32° F (0° C)	SAE 30
Between 0° F and 95° F (-18° C and 35° C)	SAE 10W-30
Capacity	
With filter	3.4 pints (1.6 liters)
Without filter	2.7 pints (1.3 liters)

NOTE: Do not use 10W-40 oil in the engine. Recommended engine oil viscosities are for petroleum-based oils. Comparable synthetic oils may be used. Do not mix synthetic oil with petroleum oil.

Table 4 FASTENER TORQUE VALUES

Connecting rod	20 N·m	(177 in.-lb.)
Crankshaft (PTO end)	38 N·m	(28 ft.-lb.)
Cylinder head	52 N·m	(38 ft.-lb.)
Electric starter mount	16 N·m	(140 in.-lb.)
Engine mount flange to frame	20 N·m	(180 in.-lb.)
Flywheel	137 N·m	(101 ft.-lb.)
Oil drain plug	23 N·m	(204 in.-lb.)
Oil pan	26 N·m	(19 ft.-lb.)
Rocker arm adjusting nut	20 N·m	(180 in.-lb.)
Bolts not listed		
M5	3.5 N·m	(30 in.-lb.)
M6	6.0 N·m	(50 in.-lb.)
M8	15 N·m	(130 in.-lb.)

Table 5 ENGINE SERVICE SPECIFICATIONS

Compression pressure	483 kPa	(71 psi)
Camshaft		
Lobe height (minimum)		
Intake and exhaust	36.75 mm	(1.446 in.).
Bearing journal OD (minimum)		
PTO end	20.912 mm	(0.8233 in.)
Flywheel end	19.912 mm	(0.7839 in.)
Bearing bore ID (maximum)		
Oil pan bearing	21.076 mm	(0.8298 in.)
Crankcase bearing.	20.076 mm	(0.790 in.)
Connecting rod		
Small end ID, maximum	22.059 mm	(0.8685 in.)
Large end ID, maximum	41.068 mm	(1.6169 in.)
Counterbalance		
Link rod journal OD	53.950 mm	(2.1240 in.)
Link rod big end ID	54.121 mm	(2.1307 in.)
Link rod small end ID	12.06 mm	(0.475 in.)
Support shaft bushing ID	26.097 mm	(1.0274 in.)
Support shaft OD	25.927 mm	(1.0208 in.)
Crankcase breather		
Reed valve gap	1.0-2.0 mm	(0.04-0.08 in.)
(continued)		

Table 5 ENGINE SERVICE SPECIFICATIONS (continued)

Crankshaft		
Balancer link rod journal		
Minimum OD	53.950 mm	(2.1240 in.)
Connecting rod journal		
Minimum OD	40.928 mm	(1.6113 in.)
Main journal		
Minimum OD		
PTO end	34.919 mm	(1.3747 in.)
Flywheel end	34.945 mm	(1.3758 in.)
Main bearing		
Maximum ID		
PTO end	35.069 mm	(1.3807 in.)
End play	0.09-0.22 mm	(0.0035-0.0087 in.)
Runout, maximum	0.05 mm	(0.002 in.)
Cylinder		
Bore ID		
Standard, maximum	89.076 mm	(3.5069 in.)
Rebore	See text	
Out-of-round	0.063 mm	(0.0025 in.)
Cylinder head		
Warpage (Maximum)	0.05 mm	(0.002 in.)
Electric starter motor		
Brush length (Minimum)	6.0 mm	(0.24 in.)
Cummutator		
Undercut depth	0.5-0.8 mm	(0.020-0.030 in.)
Runout	0.40 mm	(0.016 in.)
Ignition system		
Spark plug		
Type	RN11YC Champion or BPR5ES NGK	
Gap	0.7-0.8 mm	(0.028-0.031 in.)
Coil-to-flywheel air gap	0.3 mm	(0.012 in.)
Piston		
Ring groove clearance (maximum)		
Upper compression ring	0.17 mm	(0.0067 in.)
Second compression ring	0.15 mm	(0.0059 in.)
Oil control ring	0.20 mm	(0.0079 in.)
Compression ring end gap		
Maximum; both rings	0.9 mm	(0.035 in.)
Wrist pin bore (maximum)	22.037 mm	(0.8676 in.)
Wrist pin diameter (minimum)	21.977 mm	(0.8652 in.)
Push rod runout	0.3 mm	
(0.012 in.)		
Rocker arm shaft OD		
Wear limit	12.94 mm	(0.509 in.)
Rocker arm ID		
Wear limit	13.07 mm	(0.515 in.)
Valve clearance		
Intake and exhaust	0.15 mm	(0.006 in.)

Table 6 VALVE SYSTEM DIMENSIONS

Ref.	Description	Dimension
A	Seat Angle	45° from guide centerline; 90° total included
B	Insert Diameter (OD)	Not serviceable
C_1	Guide Depth	See text
C_2	Guide Protrusion	See text
	(continued)	

Table 6   VALVE SYSTEM DIMENSIONS (continued)

Ref.	Description	Dimension
D	Guide Diameter (ID)	
	Wear limit:	7.065 mm (0.2781 in.)
	Reamed replacement:	7.000-7.015 mm (0.2756-0.2762 in.)
E	Valve Head Diameter	Not specified
F	Valve Face Angle	45° from stem centerline
G	Valve Margin (Minimum)	0.60 mm (0.020)
H	Valve Stem Diameter	
	Wear limit:	
	Intake	6.930 mm (0.2728 in.)
	Exhaust	6.915 mm (0.2722 in.)
	Stem runout (Maximum)	0.03 mm (0.001 in.)
J	Valve Seat Width	1.10-1.46 mm (0.039-0.057 in.)
K	Valve Spring Free Length	Minimum 37.5 mm (1.47 in.)
L	Valve Face Width	Completely concentric

CHAPTER NINE

KAWASAKI FH451V, FH500V AND FH641V ENGINES

This section provides engine service information for the Kawasaki FH451V, FH500V and FH641V engines. These engines are air-cooled, four-stroke, vertical-crankshaft engines equipped with overhead valves. The two cylinders are arranged at 90° to each other, with both connecting rods sharing one crankpin. They are pressure lubricated and equipped with an oil filter.

The tables at the end of this chapter contain the engine specifications.

The next two sections in this chapter provide information on removing and reinstalling the engine as a complete, assembled unit. Subsequent sections provide disassembly, inspection, adjustment, repair/overhaul and reassembly information for the engine components.

The engine must be removed from the equipment before undertaking repairs on the internal components. In the case of external components such as the carburetor or a cylinder head, engine removal may not be necessary, as the repair job may be performed with the engine mounted on the equipment.

Kawasaki tools, or suitable equivalents, may be recommended for some procedures. The tools are available from Kawasaki dealers and service centers. Good quality tools are also available from small engine parts suppliers. Be careful when substituting a homemade tool for a recommended tool. Although time and money may be saved by using an existing or fabricated tool, consider the possibilities if the tool does not work properly. If the substitute tool damages the engine, the cost to repair the damage, as

well as lost time, may exceed the cost of the recommended tool.

NOTE
Metric fasteners are used throughout the engine. Check for thread compatibility before installing a fastener.

ENGINE IDENTIFICATION

Engine identification information is found on the decal affixed to the crankcase (**Figure 1**). The decal lists the engine model number and serial number ("E/NO"). Both numbers are required when ordering parts and for using applicable service procedures.

CYLINDER IDENTIFICATION

The top cylinder (closest to the flywheel) is the number 1 cylinder. Refer to **Figure 2**. Each cylinder number is also cast into its matching cylinder head (**Figure 3**).

ENGINE REMOVAL

Before removing the engine, drain the crankcase oil. Always drain the oil with the engine warm so the oil flows freely and carries out the dirt and impurities.

1. Be sure the ignition switch is in the OFF position. Allow the engine to cool to ambient temperature.
2. Engage the parking brake.
3. On electric-start units, disconnect the battery cables (negative terminal first) and remove the battery.
4. Close the fuel tank valve (**Figure 4**).

WARNING
Some gasoline will drain from the fuel hose during the next procedure. Wipe up any spilled gasoline immediately. Work in a well-ventilated area at least 50 feet from open flame, including pilot lights in gas appliances. Do not allow anyone to smoke in the area. Do not work near any grinding or other source of sparks.

5. Detach the fuel hose clamp at the inlet connection to the fuel pump. Disconnect the fuel hose from the pump.
6. Disconnect the spark plug wires from the spark plugs. Ground the spark plug wires to the engine.
7. Identify and unplug the chassis wiring harness connectors and the starter motor cable on electric start units.
8. Disconnect the throttle and choke control cables.

NOTE
Prior to removal, mark the cable positions for proper reconnection during engine installation.

9. Remove the deck drive belt shield, then slacken the belt running from the engine:
   a. On fixed-idler drives (**Figure 5**), loosen the belt tension adjuster nut to allow slack in the belt.
   b. On spring-loaded idler drives (**Figure 6**), move the idler pulley bracket away from the belt. Secure the bracket to allow slack in the belt, or work the belt off the idler.
10. Securely block the front wheels. Safely raise and support the rear of the mower to gain access to the underside of the engine.
11. Unplug the PTO clutch wire connector (**Figure 6**). Support the PTO clutch while removing the clutch bolt from the crankshaft. Slide the clutch off the shaft, and then remove the belt from the clutch pulley.

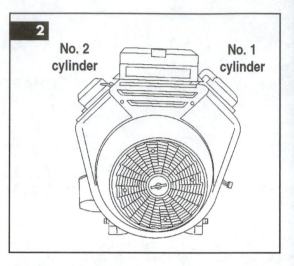

No. 2 cylinder / No. 1 cylinder

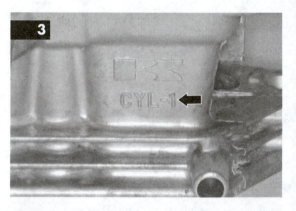

12. Move the hydrostatic drive idler pulley away from the drive belt so the belt slackens. Work the belt off the engine pulley and remove the belt.
13. Remove the engine mounting bolts.
14. Carefully lift the engine off the frame.
15. Note the position and orientation of the hydrostat pulley on the crankshaft. Remove the pulley.
16. Clean the engine mounting area on the frame.

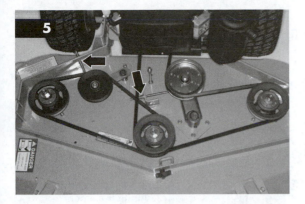

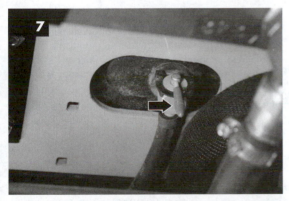

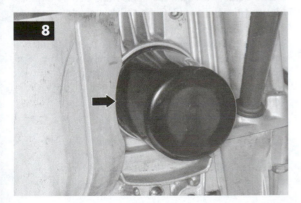

ENGINE INSTALLATION

1. Ensure that the engine mounting areas on both the frame and the bottom of the engine are clean and dry.

2. Lightly coat the crankshaft, including keyway, with anti-seize compound.

3. Install the hydrostat pulley on the crankshaft in the same position and orientation as that noted during removal.

4. Carefully set the engine in position on the frame. Make sure that the engine pan and frame fastener holes align.

5. Apply Loctite 271 or equivalent to the engine mount fastener threads. Tighten the fasteners incrementally, alternately and securely. On fasteners with lock washers, use new lock washers.

6. Install the hydrostat belt onto the pulleys and allow the spring-loaded idler to exert tension on the belt.

7. Apply Loctite 271 or equivalent to the electric PTO clutch mount bolt. Insert the PTO clutch belt into the clutch pulley groove. Align the clutch locator bracket, ensuring that the clutch wire is not pinched or kinked. Align the clutch key with the crankshaft keyway, then slide the clutch onto the crankshaft. While supporting the clutch, install the clutch bolt and tighten it securely. Refer to the applicable torque table at the end of Chapter One for the standard torque value.

8. Remove the mower supports. Lower the unit onto the floor.

9. Reapply tension to the deck drive belt.

   a. On fixed-idler drives, refer to the adjustment procedure under *Drive Belts* in Chapter Three to properly tension the belt.

   b. On spring-loaded idlers, no adjustment is necessary.

10. Install the deck drive belt shield.

11. Reconnect the throttle and choke cables using the marks noted during engine removal.

12. Reconnect the chassis wiring harness connectors to the appropriate engine plugs.

13. On electric-start units, reconnect the starter motor cable and the battery cables – negative cable last.

14. Reconnect the spark plug leads to the plugs.

15. Install a new fuel hose, including clamps, between the fuel filter and the fuel pump.

16. Refill the crankcase with the proper oil.

17. Open the fuel tank valve (**Figure 7**).

LUBRICATION

All models are equipped with a filtered pressure lubrication system. Refer to the *Oil Pump* section for oil pump service information.

NOTE
*Fill the oil filter (**Figure 8**) with oil before installation to assure adequate lubrication to critical components during initial*

9

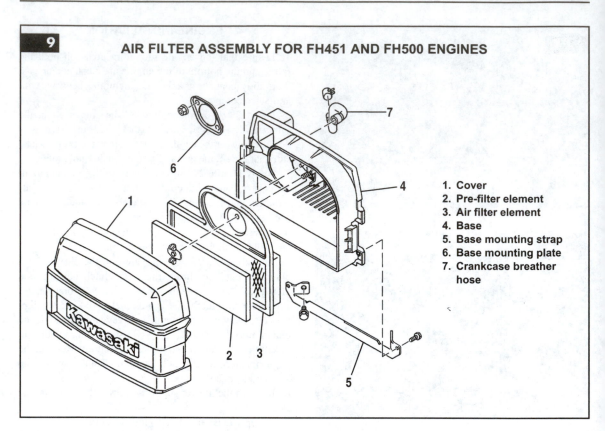

9

AIR FILTER ASSEMBLY FOR FH451 AND FH500 ENGINES

1. Cover
2. Pre-filter element
3. Air filter element
4. Base
5. Base mounting strap
6. Base mounting plate
7. Crankcase breather hose

engine restart. Pour the oil into the filter through the center threaded hole only. Do not fill past the bottom of the threads.

Periodically check the oil level; do not overfill. To check the oil level:

1. Make sure that the mower is sitting on a level surface.
2. Clean the area around the dipstick cap to prevent dirt and debris from falling into the crankcase when the cap is removed.
3. Remove the dipstick and wipe the oil from the level indicator.
4. Reinsert the dipstick and seat the dipstick cap on the oil fill tube. Do not screw the dipstick back down into the tube.
5. Remove the dipstick and check the oil level. The oil level should be up to, but not over, the "FULL" line on the dipstick.

Install a new oil filter at each oil change. Apply a light coating of clean engine oil to the filter gasket. Install the oil filter until the rubber gasket contacts the filter adapter plate, then tighten an additional 1/2-3/4 turn.

Crankcase oil capacity is approximately 3.6 pints (1.75 L) with oil filter or 3.2 pints (1.5 L) without the filter, although changing the oil without changing the filter is not recommended.

Refer to **Table 3** at the end of this chapter for oil recommendations.

In new or overhauled engines or short blocks, use SAE 30 oil for the first five hours of operation, then change oil according to ambient temperature requirements. The recommended minimum oil change interval after the five-hour break-in period is every 100 hours of operation. The oil should be drained while the engine is warm for the most effective crankcase sludge removal.

AIR FILTER

These engines are equipped with a paper-type air filter and a foam pre-cleaner element. **Figure 9** shows the air filter assembly used on the FH451 and FH500 engines. **Figure 10** shows the FH641 air filter assembly.

Remove and clean the air filter at the interval indicated in **Table 2**. Replace the element at the specified interval or whenever it is damaged or starting to deteriorate. Service more frequently if the engine is operated in severe conditions. To service the filter assembly, refer to *Periodic Maintenance, Air Filter Service* in Chapter Three.

NOTE
Always inspect the crankcase breather hose between the breather and the air filter base any time the air filter is serviced. If the hose is loose, cracked, or dry and brittle, replace it.

10

AIR FILTER ASSEMBLY FOR FH641 ENGINES

1. Cover
2. Pre-filter element
3. Air filter element
4. Base
5. Crankcase breather hose
6. Breather hose baffle

FUEL FILTER

Service the fuel filter at the interval indicated in **Table 2**. To service the fuel filter, refer to *Periodic Maintenance, Fuel Filter Service* in Chapter Three.

CARBURETOR
FH451V AND FH500V

Operation

The carburetor operates according to the principles outlined in Chapter Two. A float in the fuel bowl controls the amount of fuel in the bowl. When the engine is running, fuel is drawn into the nozzle through the removable main jet. Fuel in the nozzle then exits into the carburetor bore through a discharge hole. Fuel is also drawn into the idle circuit to the idle fuel jet and then to the idle mixture adjustment screw. Airflow through the carburetor is controlled by throttle and choke plates.

Air for the main fuel circuit and idle circuit is introduced through a removable air jet located in the carburetor bore.

If the engine does not perform well at high altitude, high-altitude main jets are available. See **Table 4**.

The carburetor may be equipped with a fuel shut-off solenoid. The solenoid is controlled by the equipment electrical system. A rod inside the solenoid projects into the main fuel jet. When 12 volts is directed to the solenoid, the rod retracts and allows fuel to flow into the main fuel circuit of the carburetor.

Adjustments

Idle Speed Adjustment

The idle speed is governed. With an accurate tachometer connected to the engine, use the following procedure to adjust the idle speed.

1. Remove the air cleaner for access to the carburetor adjustment.
2. Run the engine and hold the carburetor throttle lever against the idle speed screw on the carburetor (9, **Figure 11**).
3. Adjust the carburetor idle speed screw so the engine idles at 1450 rpm.
4. Release the carburetor throttle lever.
5. Adjust the governed idle speed by rotating the governed idle speed screw (S, **Figure 12**) so the engine idles at 1550 rpm.
6. Stop the engine and install the air cleaner.

Idle Mixture Adjustment

To comply with emissions requirements, the idle mixture screw is equipped with a limiter cap (6, **Figure 11**).

9

11 ONE-BARREL CARBURETOR AND INTAKE MANIFOLD

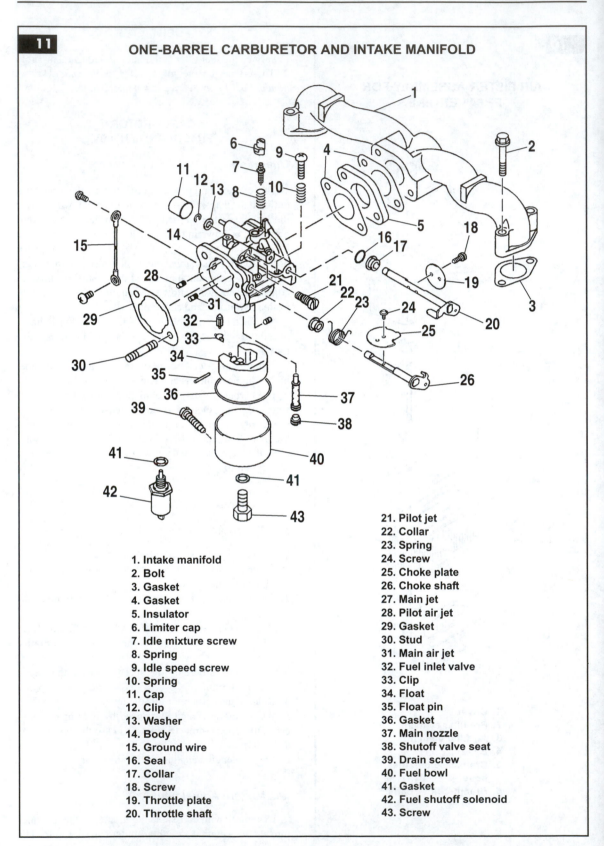

1. Intake manifold
2. Bolt
3. Gasket
4. Gasket
5. Insulator
6. Limiter cap
7. Idle mixture screw
8. Spring
9. Idle speed screw
10. Spring
11. Cap
12. Clip
13. Washer
14. Body
15. Ground wire
16. Seal
17. Collar
18. Screw
19. Throttle plate
20. Throttle shaft
21. Pilot jet
22. Collar
23. Spring
24. Screw
25. Choke plate
26. Choke shaft
27. Main jet
28. Pilot air jet
29. Gasket
30. Stud
31. Main air jet
32. Fuel inlet valve
33. Clip
34. Float
35. Float pin
36. Gasket
37. Main nozzle
38. Shutoff valve seat
39. Drain screw
40. Fuel bowl
41. Gasket
42. Fuel shutoff solenoid
43. Screw

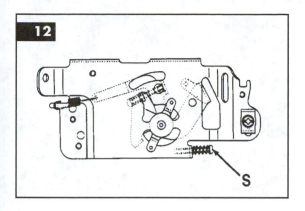

12

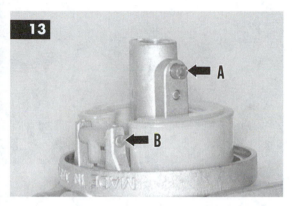

13

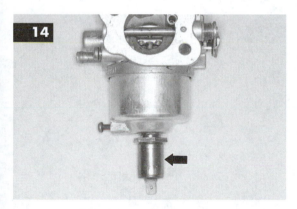

14

The position of the idle mixture screw (7) is established at the factory to obtain best performance while complying with emissions requirements. The limiter cap prevents movement of the idle mixture screw to positions that will adversely affect engine operation.

NOTE
Be sure the choke is wide open and the engine is at normal operating temperature when performing this adjustment procedure.

1. Adjust the idle mixture by turning the limiter cap so the engine idles at the highest speed with the engine at

normal operating temperature. If the engine does not idle properly due to improper idle mixture, the carburetor may require cleaning or repair, or the limiter cap may be incorrectly installed.

NOTE
After adjusting the idle mixture, adjust the engine idle speed as described in this chapter.

2. Remove and discard the original limiter cap. Never reinstall a used limiter cap.
3. Turn IN the idle mixture screw until it is lightly seated.
4. Turn OUT the idle mixture screw 2 1/4 turns.
5. Install a new limiter cap on the idle mixture screw so the cap is at the midpoint of its travel.
6. Adjust the idle mixture with the engine running as described in Step 1.

High speed mixture adjustment

The main fuel jet (A, **Figure 13**) located inside the carburetor controls the high-speed mixture. No external high-speed mixture adjustments can be made to this carburetor. The main fuel jet may be removed and replaced with a jet having a different orifice size to alter the high-speed fuel mixture. For near sea level operation, the standard main jet size is #125. Additional main jets are available for high altitude operation as listed in **Table 4**.

Removal

WARNING
Some gasoline will drain from the fuel hose during this procedure. Wipe up any spilled gasoline immediately. Work in a well-ventilated area at least 50 feet away from any open flame, including pilot lights in gas appliances. Do not allow anyone to smoke in the area. Do not work near any grinding or any other source of sparks.

1. Disconnect the negative battery cable from the battery. Secure the cable so it cannot contact the battery.
2. Remove the air filter cover and elements (**Figure 9**).
3. On FH500 engines:
   a. Disconnect the electrical wire from the fuel shutoff solenoid (**Figure 14**).
   b. Disconnect the ground wire (**Figure 15**) from the carburetor.

NOTE
*The air cleaner base plate (**Figure 9**) retaining nuts also secure the carburetor onto its mounting studs.*

4. Unscrew the air cleaner base retaining nuts. While working the filter base off the carburetor, unclamp and re-

9

move the crankcase breather hose from the back of the base. Discard the filter base gasket.

5. Unclamp and detach the fuel hose from the carburetor.

6. Remove the carburetor while disconnecting the throttle and choke linkages.

7. Clean any gasket residue from the insulator, carburetor and air cleaner base.

> *NOTE*
> *If the insulator detaches from the intake manifold, install a new gasket between the insulator and intake manifold after carefully cleaning the old gasket material from the insulator and manifold.*

Disassembly

> *WARNING*
> *Some gasoline may drain from the carburetor during this procedure. Wipe up any spilled gasoline immediately. Work in a well-ventilated area at least 50 feet away from any open flame, including pilot lights in gas appliances. Do not allow anyone to smoke in the area. Do not work near any grinding or any other source of sparks.*

Refer to **Figure 11** when performing the following procedure.

> *NOTE*
> *Do not attempt to remove any passage balls.*

1. Remove the fuel bowl:
   a. On FH451 engines, unscrew the fuel bowl retaining screw and remove the fuel bowl and gasket.
   b. On FH500 engines, unscrew the fuel solenoid (**Figure 14**) and remove the fuel bowl and gasket.

2. Remove the main jet (A, **Figure 13**).

3. Remove the float pin (B, **Figure 13**), float and fuel inlet valve.

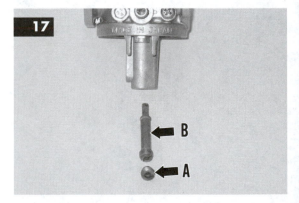

> *NOTE*
> *The float pin has a head on one end. Carefully remove the float pin by pushing or pulling the pin toward the head end.*

4. Remove the shutoff valve seat (A, **Figure** 16 and **Figure** 17) and nozzle (B, **Figure 17**) in the carburetor column.

> *NOTE*
> *The fuel valve seat in the carburetor body (B, **Figure 16**) is not removable.*

5. Remove the throttle shaft cap (A, **Figure 18**), clip and washer (12 and 13, **Figure 11**).

6. Unscrew the throttle plate retaining screws and remove the throttle plate (B, **Figure 18**) and throttle shaft.

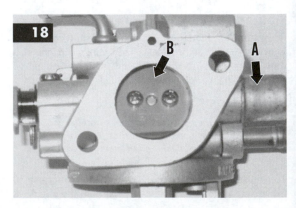

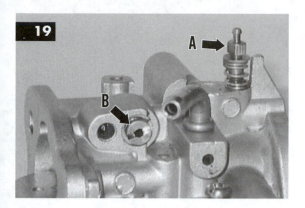

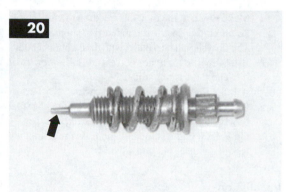

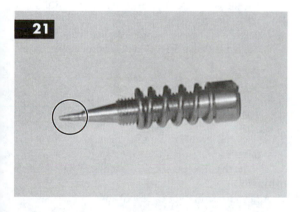

7. Unscrew the choke plate retaining screws and remove the choke plate and choke shaft assembly (25 and 26, **Figure 11**).

8. Mark the position of the idle mixture limiter cap. When removing the idle mixture screw limiter cap, do not change the setting of the idle mixture screw (A, **Figure 19**).

9. Remove the cap. While counting the number of turns, screw IN the idle mixture screw until it lightly seats. Write down the number of turns so the idle mixture screw can be reinstalled in its original position.

10. Remove the pilot jet (B, **Figure 19**).

11. The carburetor should now be ready for cleaning and inspection as described in the following section.

Cleaning and Inspection

1. Inspect the carburetor and components.

> *CAUTION*
> *Do not use wire or drill bits to clean jets. Even minor gouges in the jet can alter the fuel flow rate and upset the air/fuel mixture.*

2. Inspect the tip of the idle mixture needle (**Figure 20**) and replace if the tip is bent or grooved. If the tapered tip of the needle is damaged as in **Figure 21**, the carburetor may require replacement, as a seriously damaged needle usually has corresponding damage to the passage.

3. Inspect the fuel inlet valve (**Figure 22**) and replace if the tip is grooved.

4. Inspect the fuel valve seat (B, **Figure 16**). The valve seat is not removable. Replace the carburetor body if the valve seat is worn or damaged.

5. Install the throttle shaft in the carburetor body and check for excessive play between the shaft and body. The body must be replaced if there is excessive play as bushings are not available.

6. Clean the carburetor components in an approved solvent. Do not attempt to clean rubber or plastic components in solvents. Discard all old gaskets, seals and O-rings.

7. To test the fuel-shutoff solenoid on the FH500V engines, proceed as follows:

   a. Connect the negative terminal of a 12-volt test battery to the solenoid case.

   b. Momentarily connect and disconnect the positive battery terminal to the solenoid terminal a few times.

> *NOTE*
> *It may be necessary to slightly push the solenoid plunger to trigger retraction with the solenoid removed from the carburetor.*

   c. If the solenoid does not operate, it is faulty and must be replaced.

9

Assembly

Always use new gaskets when reassembling the carburetor. Refer to **Figure 11**.

1. Make sure that all fastener threads and threaded holes are clean and dry.

2. Install the pilot jet (B, **Figure 19**).

3. Install the idle mixture needle screw and spring (A, **Figure 19**). Turn the screw in until it lightly seats in the carburetor. *Do not force.* After bottoming, unscrew the needle the same number of turns noted in Step 9 of *Disassembly.* If the number of turns was not recorded, unscrew the needle 2 1/4 turns.

NOTE
*The tapered tip of the idle mixture adjusting needle is machined to critical dimensions. If the needle is forced into its bottomed position, it will be damaged as shown in **Figure 21**. If this happens, the carburetor may need to be replaced, as the internal mixture passage is probably similarly damaged.*

4. Install a new limiter cap on the idle mixture screw so the cap is at the midpoint of its travel.

5. Install the throttle shaft assembly:
   a. Install the throttle shaft spacer so the large diameter contacts the O-ring.
   b. Lightly coat the throttle plate screw threads with Loctite 222 or equivalent.
   c. Install the throttle plate so the numbers on the plate are down and toward the outside of the carburetor (B, **Figure 18**).
   d. Install the washer, clip and cap.

6. Assemble the spring-loaded choke shaft:
   a. Install the spring and spring bushing onto the shaft.
   b. Install the choke shaft assembly into the carburetor.
   c. Lightly coat the choke plate screw threads with Loctite 222 or equivalent.
   d. Install the choke plate so it fits properly in the carburetor and so spring tension tries to open the choke (**Figure 23**).
   e. Make sure that the choke shaft works freely. Realign, if necessary.

7. Install the nozzle (B, **Figure 17**) and shutoff valve seat (A, **Figure 16** and **Figure 17**) into the carburetor column.

8. Install the main jet (A, **Figure 13**).

9. Install and measure the float:
   a. Install the float valve onto the float. Make sure that the float tab fits between the float valve clip and the base of the valve.
   b. With the carburetor inverted, place the valve into the seat and position the float so the float hinge pin holes align with the body holes.
   c. Install the float pin so the head end (B, **Figure 13**) is positioned as shown.

   d. Make sure that the float has freedom of movement.
   e. To check the float level, invert the carburetor body. The float should be parallel with the carburetor body.
   f. If the float level is not correct, install a new float kit. The float is not adjustable.

10. Install the fuel bowl gasket and bowl:
   a. On FH451 engines, install and tighten the fuel bowl retaining screw and seal (43 and 41).
   b. On FH500 engines, install and tighten the fuel solenoid and seal (42 and 41).

Installation

Install the carburetor by reversing the removal steps. Note the following:

1. Install one new gasket between the carburetor and insulator, and one between the carburetor and air cleaner base.

NOTE
The insulator between the carburetor and intake manifold has an indexing pin that must fit into the recess in the intake manifold.

2. Be sure the throttle rod spring is attached to the carburetor throttle arm (B, **Figure 15**).

3. Tighten the air cleaner base retaining nuts to 6.9 N•m (61 in.-lb.).

4. Adjust the carburetor as described in this chapter.

CARBURETOR (FH641V)

Operation

The model FH641V is equipped with a float type carburetor that is equipped with two throttle bores, each of which controls the air-fuel mixture for one cylinder. A single choke plate enriches the mixture for both cylinders during starting.

The carburetor operates according to the principles outlined in Chapter 2. A float in the fuel bowl controls the amount of fuel in the bowl. When the engine is running, fuel is drawn into the fuel circuit through removable main jets,

24

TWO-BARREL CARBURETOR AND INTAKE MANIFOLD

1. Intake manifold
2. Stud
3. Bolt
4. Gasket
5. Gasket
6. Insulator
7. Gasket
8. Plug
9. Idle mixture screw
10. Hose
11. Body
12. Idle speed screw
13. Spring
14. Seal
15. Collar
16. Throttle plate
17. Screw

18. Throttle shaft
19. Collar
20. Choke plate
21. Screw
22. Choke shaft
23. Float pin
24. Fuel inlet valve
25. Float
26. Gasket
27. Pilot jet
28. Main jet
29. Gasket
30. Plug
31. Drain screw
32. Spring
33. Bracket
34. Screw

35. Fuel bowl
36. Screw
37. Gasket
38. Fuel shutoff solenoid

39. Gasket
40. Air cleaner base
41. Bolt
42. Nut
43. Washer
44. Breather hose

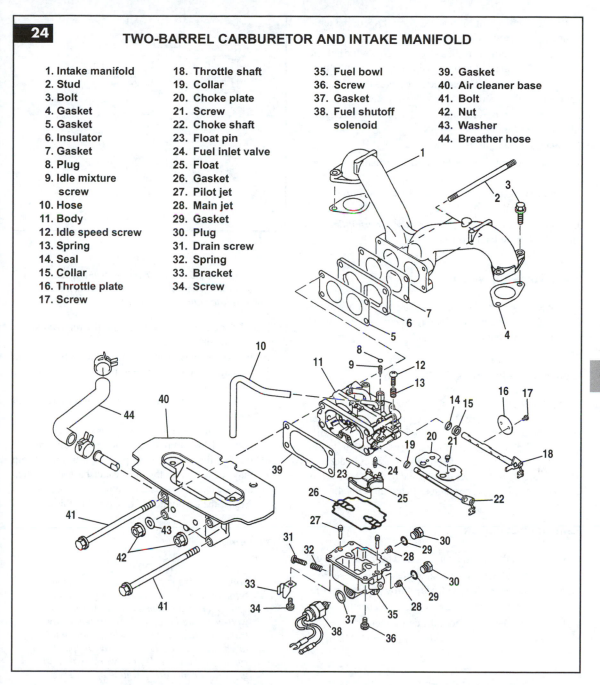

9

one for each cylinder. Fuel in the fuel circuit then exits into the carburetor bore through a discharge hole. Fuel is also drawn into the idle circuit to the removable idle fuel jets and then to the idle mixture adjustment screws. Airflow through the carburetor is controlled by throttle and choke plates.

If the engine does not perform well at high altitude, high-altitude main jets are available. Refer to **Table 5**.

The carburetor may be equipped with a fuel shut-off solenoid. The solenoid is controlled by the equipment electrical system. A rod inside the solenoid projects into the carburetor. When 12 volts is directed to the solenoid, the rod retracts and allows fuel to flow into the main fuel circuit of the carburetor.

Idle Speed Adjustment

The idle speed is governed. Use the following procedure to adjust the idle speed. Refer to **Figure 24**.

1. Run the engine until it reaches normal operating temperature, then stop the engine.

2. Insert a long No. 2 Phillips screwdriver into the hole in the blower housing to the right of the horsepower number.

3. Run the engine and hold the carburetor throttle lever against the idle speed screw on the carburetor.

4. Adjust the carburetor idle speed screw so the engine idles at 1450 rpm.

5. Release the carburetor throttle lever.

6. Adjust the governed idle speed by rotating the idle speed screw.

7. Adjust the governed idle speed screw (S, **Figure 12**) so the engine idles at 1550 rpm.

8. Stop the engine. Refer to *Governor, External Service* for the high-speed adjustment.

Idle Mixture Adjustment

Pilot screws control the idle mixture. It is pre-set at the factory. Do not adjust the pilot screws unless the carburetor requires overhaul.

High Speed Mixture Adjustment

A main fuel jet inside the carburetor controls the high-speed fuel mixture for each cylinder. The main fuel jet may be removed and replaced with a jet having a different orifice size to alter the high-speed fuel mixture. Standard main jet size is #136 for the left cylinder and #140 for the right cylinder. Additional main jets are available for high altitude operation as listed in **Table 4**.

Removal/Installation

1. Disconnect the negative battery lead from the battery.

2. Unclamp and detach the crankcase breather hose from the air cleaner base. Do not lose the baffle (6, **Figure 10**).

3. Remove the air cleaner cover and elements.

4. Detach the fuel hose from the carburetor.

5. Disconnect the electrical wire from the fuel shutoff solenoid.

> *NOTE*
> *The air cleaner base retaining bolts and nuts also secure the carburetor to the intake manifold.*

6. Unscrew the air cleaner base retaining bolts and nuts. Remove the air cleaner base from the carburetor.

7. Remove the carburetor while disconnecting the throttle and choke linkage.

8. Clean any gasket residue from the insulator, carburetor and air cleaner base.

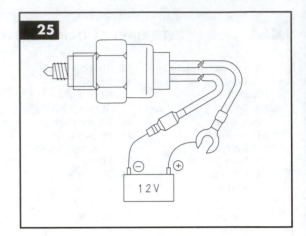

> *NOTE*
> *If the insulator detaches from the intake manifold, install a new gasket between the insulator and intake manifold.*

9. Install the carburetor by reversing the removal steps. Note the following:

   a. Install one new gasket between the carburetor and insulator, and one between the carburetor and air cleaner base.

   b. Tighten the air cleaner base retaining nuts to 6.9 N•m (61 in.-lb.).

   c. Be sure the fuel hose clamp ends (at the carburetor end of the hose) point in a horizontal direction. If the fuel hose clamp ends point upward, the clamp may loosen when the air cleaner base is installed and the base contacts the clamp.

   d. Adjust the carburetor as described in this chapter.

Disassembly

> *WARNING*
> *Some gasoline may drain from the carburetor during this procedure. Wipe up any spilled gasoline immediately. Work in a well-ventilated area at least 50 feet away from any open flame, including pilot lights in gas appliances. Do not allow anyone to smoke in the area. Do not work near any grinding or any other source of sparks.*

Refer to **Figure 24** when performing the following procedure.

> *NOTE*
> *Do not attempt to remove any passage balls.*

1. Remove the fuel solenoid (38) and gasket (37).

2. Remove the main jet plugs (30) and gaskets (29).

3. Remove the main jets (28).

4. Remove the fuel bowl (35) and gasket.

> *NOTE*
> *The float pin is flattened on one end. Remove the float pin by pushing or pulling the float pin toward the flattened end.*

5. Remove the float pin (23), float (25) and fuel inlet valve (24).

6. Remove the pilot jets (27) in the fuel bowl.

7. Mark the throttle plates and choke plate so they can be reinstalled in their original positions.

8. Unscrew the throttle plate retaining screws and remove the throttle plates (16) and throttle shaft (18).

9. Unscrew the choke plate retaining screws and remove the choke plate (20) and choke shaft assembly (22).

10. The pilot screws (9) are sealed by plugs (8) to prevent routine adjustment. The pilot screws do not require adjustment unless the carburetors are overhauled, the pilot screws are incorrectly adjusted, or if the pilot screws require replacement. The following procedure describes how to remove and install the pilot screws.

   a. Using an awl or other suitable tool, pierce the Welch plug and pry it out.

   b. While counting the number of turns, turn the pilot screw IN until it *lightly seats*. During reassembly, reinstall the pilot screw to the same position.

   c. Remove the pilot screw assembly from the carburetor body.

   d. Repeat for the other pilot screw.

   e. Inspect the O-ring and the end of the pilot screw. Replace the screw and/or O-ring if damaged or worn (grooved).

> *NOTE*
> *If the pilot screw was incorrectly adjusted, refer to the specifications in Tables 5 and 8.*

   f. Install the pilot screw in the same position as noted during removal or to the specification listed in **Table 5**.

   g. Install a new plug by tapping it into place with a punch. Apply a small amount of glyptol sealant or fingernail polish to the plug seam after installation.

Cleaning and Inspection

1. Inspect the carburetor and components.

> *CAUTION*
> *Do **not** use wire or drill bits to clean jets. Even minor gouges in the jet can alter the fuel flow rate and upset the air/fuel mixture.*

2. Inspect the tip of the idle mixture needle and replace if the tip is bent or grooved.

3. Inspect the fuel inlet valve and replace if the tip is grooved.

4. Inspect the fuel valve seat. The valve seat is not removable. Replace the carburetor body if the valve seat is worn or damaged.

5. Install the throttle shaft in the carburetor body and check for excessive play between the shaft and body. The body must be replaced if there is excessive play as bushings are not available.

6. To test the fuel-shutoff solenoid, proceed as follows:

   a. Connect a 12-volt test battery to the solenoid as shown in **Figure 25**.

   b. Momentarily connect and disconnect the battery to the solenoid connectors a few times.

> *NOTE*
> *It may be necessary to slightly push the solenoid plunger to trigger retraction with the solenoid removed from the carburetor.*

   c. If the solenoid does not operate, it is faulty and must be replaced.

Reassembly

Assemble the carburetor by reversing the disassembly procedure while noting the following:

1. Install the throttle and choke plates using marks made during disassembly so they are reinstalled in their original positions. Apply a small amount of Loctite 222 or equivalent to the retaining screws.

2. Install the float pin so the flattened end is toward the throttle lever side of the carburetor.

3. To check the float level, invert the carburetor body, allowing the float to rest on the valve and seat. Do not push on the float. The float should be parallel with the carburetor body gasket surface. If the float level is not correct, install a new float kit. The float is not adjustable.

EXHAUST SYSTEM

Muffler

1. Unscrew the muffler inlet pipe clamp screw (A, **Figure 26**).

2. Remove the muffler bracket screw (B, **Figure 26**).

3. Remove the muffler.

4. Inspect the muffler for indications of gas leakage. Replace the muffler if it is significantly rusted or otherwise damaged.

5. Install the muffler by reversing the removal steps.

Exhaust Manifold

1. Remove the muffler as previously described.

9

2. Unscrew the exhaust manifold retaining nuts. Clean the fastener threads.

3. Remove the exhaust manifold. Discard the used gaskets.

4. Inspect the exhaust manifold for indications of gas leakage. Replace the exhaust manifold if it is significantly rusted or otherwise damaged.

5. Install the exhaust manifold by reversing the removal steps. Always use new gaskets. Tighten the exhaust manifold retaining nuts to 15.0 N•m (133 in.-lb.).

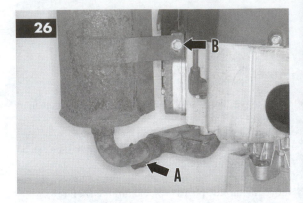

FUEL PUMP

The engine is equipped with a diaphragm-type fuel pump (**Figure 27**) mounted on the blower housing. A pulse hose from the engine directs crankcase pulsations to the diaphragm in the fuel pump. Diaphragm movement forces fuel through a pair of one-way valves to the fuel pump outlet, where the fuel is routed via the fuel hose to the carburetor.

Individual parts are not available for the fuel pump. Service the fuel pump as a unit.

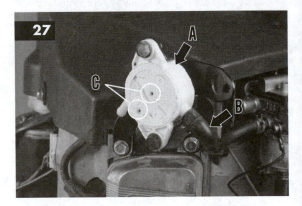

Testing

> *WARNING*
> *Exercise care when performing the following procedure. Wipe up any spilled gasoline immediately. Work in a well-ventilated area at least 50 feet away from any open flame, including pilot lights in gas appliances. Do not allow anyone to smoke in the area. Do not work near any grinding or any other source of sparks.*

1. Disconnect the outlet fuel hose (B, **Figure 27**) from the fuel pump.

2. Connect a hose from the fuel pump outlet into a suitable container.

3. Connect an auxiliary fuel supply to the carburetor.

4. Run the engine.

5. If the fuel pump does not pump fuel into the container, remove and inspect the pump. Be sure the vent holes (C, **Figure 27**) are open.

> *NOTE*
> *Be sure to inspect the vent hole on the back of the pump.*

6. Unplug the vent holes with vacuum. Do not blow into the holes or the diaphragm will be damaged. After cleaning the vents, retest the pump.

7. If the fuel pump does not pump fuel, replace it.

Removal/Installation

> *WARNING*
> *Gasoline may drain from the fuel pump and hoses during this procedure. Wipe up any spilled gasoline immediately. Work in a well-ventilated area at least 50 feet from any open flame, including pilot lights in gas appliances. Do not allow anyone to smoke in the area. Do not work near any grinding or any other source of sparks.*

1. Label the hoses at the pump.

2. Loosen the hose clamps, then detach the hoses from the pump. Plug the hoses to prevent fuel leakage or contamination.

3. Remove the bolts holding the fuel pump to the mounting bracket. Remove the fuel pump.

4. Replace the hoses and hose clamps as necessary.

5. Installation is the reverse of the preceding steps. Reconnect the hoses according to the identification marks made before removal.

REWIND STARTER

The rewind starter is a pawl type starter. When the rope is pulled, two pawls extend outward to engage notches in the starter cup attached to the flywheel.

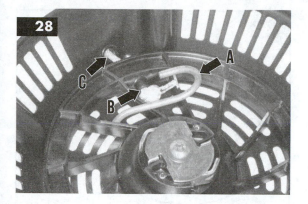

To remove the rewind starter, remove the starter housing retaining nuts, then remove the rewind starter.

To install the starter:

1. Position the starter onto the blower housing. Ensure that the handle is oriented in the proper direction.

2. Install the fasteners finger-tight.

3. Center the starter pawls inside the cup by lightly pulling out on the starter rope handle grip until both pawls extend and engage the cup notches.

4. While the pawls are in contact with the cup, alternately tighten the starter fasteners.

5. When the fasteners are tight, release the rope grip.

Replace an Unbroken Starter Rope

NOTE
Do not discard the rope before measuring its length and diameter. The same length and diameter of rope must be installed, which is either determined by measuring the old rope or consulting a parts manual.

To replace an unbroken rope, remove the rewind starter as previously described, then proceed as follows:

1. Pull out the rope to its fully extended length so the rope end in the pulley is towards the housing rope outlet, then hold the pulley by installing a restraining device so the spring cannot rewind. An S-hook (A, **Figure 28**) or a

C-clamp (**Figure 29**) may be used to prevent pulley rotation.

2. Pull out the rope knot in the pulley, untie or cut off the knot, then pull the rope out of the pulley.

3. Detach the rope from the rope handle.

4. Measure the rope and obtain a replacement rope of the same length and diameter. If the new rope is made of nylon, melt each rope end with a match to prevent fraying. Wipe the melted ends with a clean rag so the rope will fit through the pulley and housing holes.

5. Tie a knot in one end of the rope.

6. Thread the rope through the pulley rope hole (B, **Figure 28**) and out the rope outlet (C) in the housing.

7. Attach the rope handle to the rope.

8. Hold the pulley, release the restraining device on the rope pulley and slowly allow the rope to wind onto the pulley.

9. Check starter operation.

Replace a Broken Starter Rope

NOTE
Do not discard the rope before measuring its total length. The same length of rope must be installed, which is either determined by measuring the old rope or consulting a parts manual.

To replace a broken rope, remove the starter as previously outlined, then proceed as follows:

1. Pull the rope out of the hole in the rope pulley. If the rope pulley must be removed for access to the rope, remove the rope pulley as outlined in the following procedure for rewind spring removal.

2. Detach the rope from the rope handle.

3. Measure the rope and obtain a replacement rope of the same length and diameter. If the new rope is made of nylon, melt each rope end with a match to prevent fraying. Wipe the melted ends with a clean rag so the rope will fit through the pulley and housing holes.

4. Rotate the rope pulley counterclockwise as far as possible, then allow the pulley to turn clockwise so the rope hole in the pulley and the rope outlet in the housing are aligned. Hold the pulley by installing a restraining device so the spring cannot rewind. An S-hook (A, **Figure 28**) or C-clamp (**Figure 29**) may be used to prevent pulley rotation.

5. Tie a knot in one end of the rope.

6. Thread the rope through the pulley rope hole (B, **Figure 28**) and out the rope outlet (C) in the housing.

7. Attach the rope handle to the rope.

8. Hold the pulley, release the restraining device on the rope pulley and slowly allow the rope to wind onto the pulley.

9. Check starter operation.

9

Disassembly/Reassembly

Refer to **Figure 30** when performing this procedure.
1. Remove the rope handle and allow the pulley to totally unwind.
2. Remove the pulley retaining screw (A, **Figure 31**), washer (B) and retainer (C).
3. Remove the brake spring (A, **Figure 32**).
4. Remove the washer (A, **Figure 33**) and pawls (B).
5. Remove the pawl springs (**Figure 34**).

> *CAUTION*
> *Wear appropriate safety eyewear and gloves before disengaging the pulley from the starter as the spring may uncoil violently.*

6. Lift the pulley out of the housing; the spring and cup should remain in the pulley. Do not attempt to separate the spring from the cup as they are a unit assembly.
7. Inspect the components for damage and excessive wear.
8. Reverse the disassembly procedure to install the components while noting the following:
   a. Install the spring and cup into the pulley (**Figure 35**). Due to the asymmetrical location of the lugs, the cup only fits properly in the pulley one way.

> *NOTE*
> *The spring cup will fall out of the pulley if the pulley is inverted.*

   b. With the housing positioned so the open side is down, install the pulley into the housing. Rotate the pulley counterclockwise so the inner spring end engages the spring anchor in the housing (**Figure 36**).
   c. Be sure to install the pawl spring and pawl so the angled end of the spring (B, **Figure 32**) forces the pawl inward.
   d. Tighten the center screw (A, **Figure 31**) to 8.0 N•m (70 in.-lb.).
   e. Install the rope as previously described.

ELECTRIC STARTER MOTOR

> *CAUTION*
> *The starter motor field magnets are made of ceramic material. Do not clamp the starter housing in a vise or hit the housing as the field magnets may be damaged.*

Starter Removal/Installation

1. Disconnect the negative battery cable from the battery.
2. Disconnect the solenoid cable from the starter terminal.

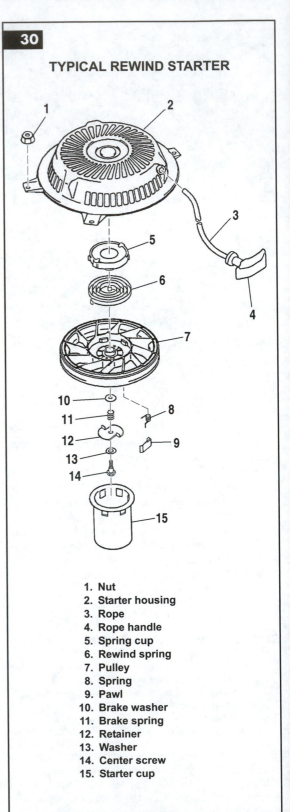

30

TYPICAL REWIND STARTER

1. Nut
2. Starter housing
3. Rope
4. Rope handle
5. Spring cup
6. Rewind spring
7. Pulley
8. Spring
9. Pawl
10. Brake washer
11. Brake spring
12. Retainer
13. Washer
14. Center screw
15. Starter cup

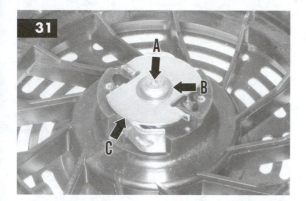

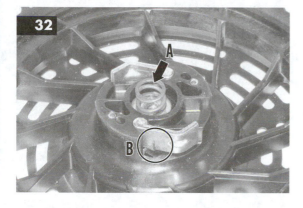

9

3. Remove the starter motor mounting bolts and remove the starter motor from the engine.

4. Installation is the reverse of removal. Tighten the mounting bolts to 15 N•m (133 in.-lb.).

Starter Disassembly

Refer to **Figure 37**.

1. Remove the cap (**Figure 38**).

2. Push down the collar (A, **Figure 39**) and remove the retainer ring on the armature shaft.

3. Remove the spring (B, **Figure 39**), drive pinion (C) and washer.

4. Unscrew and remove the bolts (A, **Figure 40**) securing the commutator end cap and starter frame to the drive end cap.

5. Remove the commutator end cap (B, **Figure 40**), then withdraw the armature from the frame.

Starter Inspection

1. Inspect the armature for damage or wear. Replace if necessary.

2. Inspect the commutator (**Figure 41**). Minimum commutator diameter is 31.1 mm (1.225 in.). The mica in a good commutator is below the surface of the copper bars.

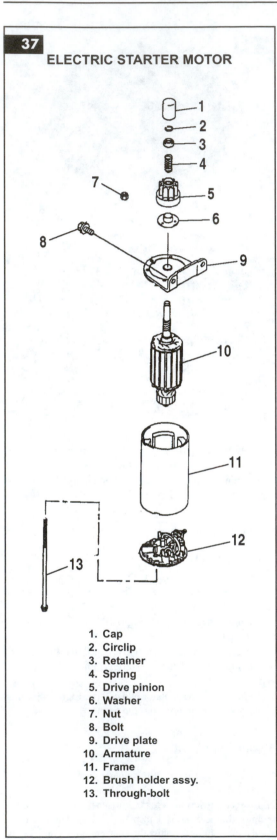

37

ELECTRIC STARTER MOTOR

1. Cap
2. Circlip
3. Retainer
4. Spring
5. Drive pinion
6. Washer
7. Nut
8. Bolt
9. Drive plate
10. Armature
11. Frame
12. Brush holder assy.
13. Through-bolt

38

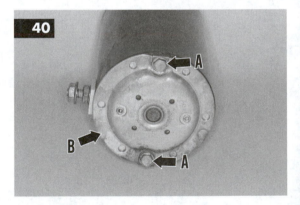

39

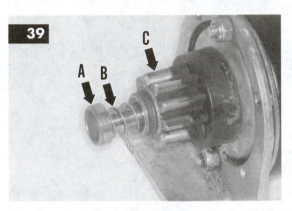

40

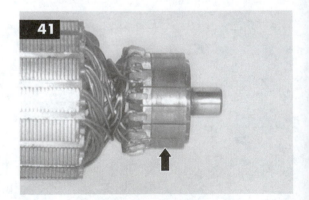

41

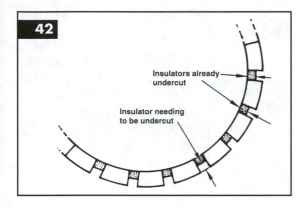

42

Insulators already
undercut

Insulator needing
to be undercut

46

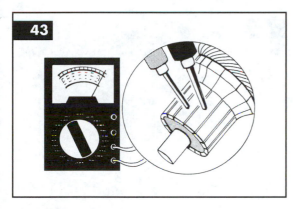

43

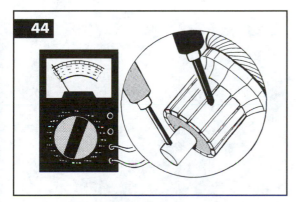

44

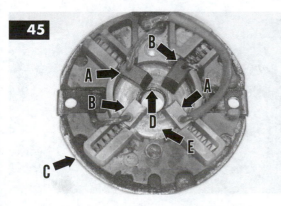

45

On a worn commutator, the mica and copper bars may be worn to the same level (**Figure 42**).

3. Inspect the commutator copper bars for discoloration. If a pair of bars is discolored, grounded armature coils are indicated. Replace the armature.

4. Use an ohmmeter to perform the following:

   a. Check for continuity between the commutator bars (**Figure 43**); there should be continuity (indicated resistance) between pairs of bars.

   b. Check for continuity between the commutator bars and the shaft (**Figure 44**); there should be no continuity (infinite resistance).

   c. If the armature fails either of these tests, replace the armature.

5. Use an ohmmeter to perform the following:

   a. Check for continuity between the positive brushes (A, **Figure 45**) and the brush holder (C); there should be no continuity (infinite resistance). If the ohmmeter indicates continuity, replace the brush holder assembly.

   b. Check for continuity between the negative brushes (B, **Figure 45**) and the brush holder (C); there should be continuity (indicated resistance). If the ohmmeter does not indicate continuity, replace the brush holder assembly.

6. Inspect the commutator end cap and bushing (D, **Figure 45**) for wear or damage. The bushing is not available as a replacement part. If either is damaged, replace the end cap assembly.

7. Inspect the bushing in the drive bracket (**Figure 46**) for wear, damage or deterioration. If damaged, replace the drive bracket.

8. Inspect the brushes and brush holder. Minimum brush length is 6.4 mm (0.25 in.). If worn beyond limits, replace the brushes.

9. Check the strength of the brush springs. The spring must force the brush against the commutator with sufficient pressure to ensure good contact.

10. Inspect the frame assembly for wear or damage. Make sure the field coils are bonded securely in place.

9

11. Clean and inspect the drive assembly components. Replace broken, cracked or excessively worn parts. The pinion gear should rotate clockwise freely, but not turn counterclockwise.

Starter Reassembly

Refer to **Figure 37**.

1. Insert the armature into the drive bracket.
2. Install the washer and drive pinion onto the armature shaft.
3. Install the spring and stop collar onto the armature shaft.
4. Install a new retainer clip into the groove in the armature shaft.
5. Force the stop collar over the retainer clip.
6. Install the frame onto the armature while meshing the tab on the drive bracket with the notch in the frame (A, **Figure 47**).
7. Install the washer into the brush holder (E, **Figure 45**) so the cupped side is down.
8. Push the brushes back into their receptacles while pulling up on the cup washer so it prevents the brushes from coming out as shown in **Figure 48**. Continue to pull the washer (A, **Figure 48**) up so it is flush with the brush holder walls (B). When installing the end cap, the end of the commutator will push the washer below the brushes, thereby releasing the brushes against the commutator.
9. Install the end cap while meshing the tab on the end cap with the notch in the frame (B, **Figure 47**).
10. Install and tighten the through-bolts.

STARTER MOTOR SOLENOID

Electric current for the electric starter motor is routed from the battery through a solenoid mounted on the power unit. Refer to Chapter Two for troubleshooting information.

BLOWER HOUSING

Removal/Installation

1. If equipped with a rewind starter, proceed as follows:
   a. Remove the rewind starter as described in this chapter.
   b. Remove the blower housing retaining screws, then remove the blower housing.
2. If not equipped with a rewind starter, proceed as follows:
   a. Remove the debris screen (**Figure 49**).
   b. Remove the blower housing retaining screws, then remove the blower housing.
3. Install the blower housing by reversing the removal steps.

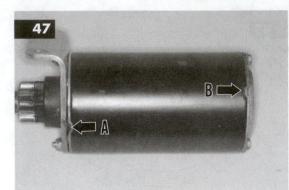

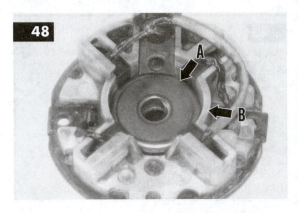

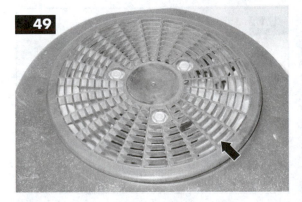

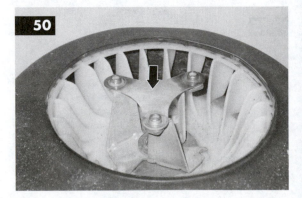

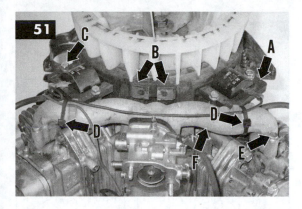
51

52

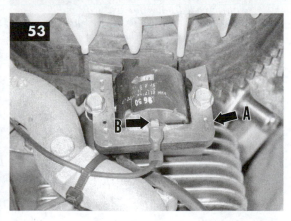
53

4. On models without a rewind starter, measure the clearance between the debris screen (**Figure 49**) and the blower housing. The clearance must be 1.0-3.0 mm (0.040-0.120 in.). If necessary, install a spacer plate (**Figure 50**) onto the support plate to obtain the specified clearance.

IGNITION MODULES

The engine is equipped with a solid-state ignition system that uses two ignition modules, one for each cylinder. The ignition modules are located under the blower housing adjacent to the flywheel, and are fastened to each corresponding cylinder (A, **Figure 51**). The ignition switch grounds the modules to stop the engine. There is no periodic maintenance or adjustment required for the ignition system other than setting the air gap for each module.

Air Gap Adjustment

If the ignition module has been removed or its position disturbed, set the air gap between the ignition module and flywheel as follows:
1. Rotate the flywheel so the flywheel magnet is away from the ignition module being adjusted (B, **Figure 51**).
2. Loosen the module retaining bolts (C, **Figure 51**).

> *NOTE*
> *A retaining stud nut may be used instead of a flanged retaining bolt.*

3. Place a 0.30 mm (0.012 in.) plastic or brass flat feeler gauge between the flywheel and the ignition module armature legs (**Figure 52**).

> *NOTE*
> *Do not use a steel feeler gauge to set the air gap. An incorrect air gap setting could result.*

4. Allow the flywheel magnet to pull the ignition module toward the flywheel.
5. While holding the module against the magnet, tighten the module fasteners:
    a. Tighten the flange bolts to 5.9 N·m (52 in.-lb.)
    b. Tighten the stud nuts to 7.8 N·m (69 in.-lb.).
6. Measure the air gap to be sure the gap is 0.20-0.40 mm (0.008-0.016 in.).
7. If the air gap is incorrect, repeat the adjustment procedure.

Testing

To test the ignition module, proceed as follows:
1. Disconnect the spark plug cable and the stop switch wire (B, **Figure 53**).
2. Using an ohmmeter, connect the test leads to the following test points:
    a. Coil leg.
    b. Stop switch terminal.
    c. Spark plug cap.

> *NOTE*
> *Figure 53 shows the flywheel magnets adjacent to the ignition module. For accu-*

9

*rate test results, rotate the flywheel so the magnets are away from the module (**Figure 51**).*

3. Refer to the chart in **Figure 54** and check the resistance readings at the test points specified.

4. If the readings vary significantly from the specifications noted in the table, replace the ignition module.

Removal/Installation

1. Disconnect the spark plug wire from the spark plug.

2. Remove the blower housing as described in this chapter.

3. Disconnect the kill wire from the ignition module (B, **Figure 53**).

4. Rotate the flywheel so the magnet is away from the ignition module (B, **Figure 51**).

5. Remove the module retaining bolts (C, **Figure 51**).

> *NOTE*
> *Retaining stud nuts may be used instead of flanged retaining bolts.*

6. Remove the module.

7. Install the ignition modules by reversing the removal procedure while noting the following:

   a. Install the ignition module so the wire terminal (B, **Figure 53**) is up.

   b. Position the ignition module so it is at the farthest distance from the flywheel, then temporarily hold the module in place by hand-tightening the retaining bolts.

   c. Adjust the air gap as described in this chapter.

FLYWHEEL

Removal/Installation

The flywheel is secured to the crankshaft by a retaining bolt. To remove the flywheel, proceed as follows:

1. Remove the blower housing as described in this chapter.

2. Remove the ignition modules as described in this chapter.

3. Remove the debris screen support plate (**Figure 50**).

4. Hold the flywheel using a strap wrench and unscrew the flywheel retaining bolt (A, **Figure 55**) and washer (B).

4. If equipped with a rewind starter, remove the starter cup.

5. If so equipped, remove the debris screen bracket (C, **Figure 55**).

6. Remove the cooling fan.

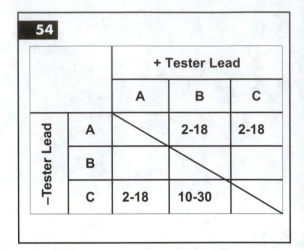

		+ Tester Lead		
		A	**B**	**C**
−Tester Lead	**A**		2-18	2-18
	B			
	C	2-18	10-30	

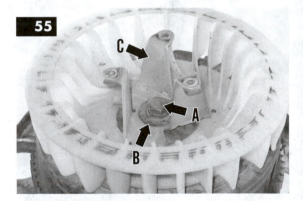

> *NOTE*
> *The flywheel may or may not be equipped with threaded holes for use with puller bolts. If not, a jaw-type puller must be used to remove the flywheel.*

7. Install a suitable flywheel puller. **Figure 56** shows a typical puller setup using threaded holes adjacent to the crankshaft.

> *WARNING*
> *Do not strike the flywheel or crankshaft. Doing so will cause damage.*

8. Rotate the puller screw until the flywheel pops free.

9. Remove the flywheel by carefully pulling straight up so as not to damage the alternator stator or magnets under the flywheel.

10. Remove the flywheel key, if necessary (A, **Figure 57**).

56

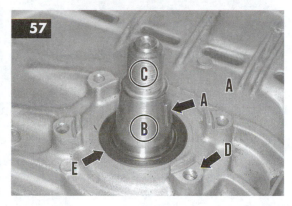

57

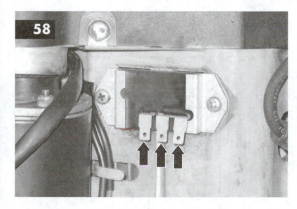

58

Inspection

1. Thoroughly clean the flywheel, removing all dust and dirt from both the top and bottom of the flywheel, especially around the magnets.

2. Inspect the flywheel casting for cracks or damage. A cracked or damaged flywheel must be replaced.

3. Inspect the integrity of the inner ring of stator magnets and the outer ignition module magnet (B, **Figure 51**).

WARNING
The magnets are not removable or serviceable. Do not attempt to reattach or

tighten any loose magnet. If any magnets are loose or damaged, replace the flywheel.

4. Inspect the starter ring gear. Carefully remove any debris stuck between the teeth. Light nicks or scratches may be dressed. Damaged teeth will require replacement of the ring gear, if the ring gear is either plastic composite or aluminum alloy. Ring gear replacement is covered in this chapter.

5. Inspect the flywheel and the crankshaft tapers. The tapered portion of the crankshaft (**Figure 57**) and flywheel must be clean and smooth with no damage due to movement between the flywheel and crankshaft.

6. Check the fit of the flywheel on the crankshaft. There should be no looseness or wobbling.

7. Be sure the keyways in the crankshaft and flywheel are not damaged or worn.

8. Inspect the flywheel key (A, **Figure 57**). If the key is partially sheared or in any other way damaged, replace it.

Installation

To install the flywheel, reverse the removal procedure and note the following:

1. Install the cooling fan so the extended pegs on the fan blades fit around the flywheel magnet.

2. Install the cooling fan plate so the notch indexes into the slot in the flywheel.

3. If so equipped, install the starter cup so the holes fit around the tabs on the cooling fan plate.

4. Tighten the flywheel retaining nut to 56 N•m (41 ft.-lb.).

ALTERNATOR

Two alternator designs are used on these engines. Engines equipped with an electric starter use a two-wire alternator stator that connects to a regulator/rectifier. Engines not equipped with an electric starter may be equipped with a single-wire alternator stator that provides current for the electric PTO clutch.

Testing

Electric start models

The following tests may be used to determine the condition of the alternator stator. Refer also to Chapter Two for charging system troubleshooting information.

1. Disconnect the alternator stator connector from the regulator/rectifier (**Figure 58**).

2. Connect an AC voltmeter to the stator connector terminals.

3. Start the engine and let it reach normal operating temperature, then shut off the engine.

9

4. Connect a portable tachometer to the engine, following the manufacturer's instructions.

5. Start the engine and run it at 3000 rpm.

6. The voltmeter should read at least 26 volts. If the charging voltage is less than 26 volts, stop the engine and check the stator coil resistance as described in the following steps.

7. Connect an ohmmeter to the alternator connector terminals.

8. Stator coil resistance should be 0.01-0.1 ohms.

> *NOTE*
> *If the stator coil resistance is as specified,*
> *but the voltage test is less than specified,*
> *the flywheel magnets may be weak.*

9. Using an ohmmeter or continuity tester, check for continuity between the connector terminals and engine ground. There should be no continuity (infinite resistance).

10. Replace the alternator stator if it fails the preceding tests.

Models Without Electric Starter

The following test may be used to determine the condition of the alternator stator. Refer also to Chapter Two for charging system troubleshooting information.

1. Start the engine and let it reach normal operating temperature, then shut off the engine.

2. Disconnect the alternator stator connector from the main chassis harness.

3. Connect an AC voltmeter to the connector terminal and engine ground.

4. Connect a portable tachometer to the engine following the manufacturer's instructions.

5. Start the engine and run it at 3000 rpm.

6. The voltmeter should read at least 26 volts. If the charging voltage is less than 26 volts, stop the engine and check the stator coil resistance as described in the following steps.

7. Connect an ohmmeter to the alternator connector and engine ground.

8. Stator coil resistance should be 4.5-15.0 ohms.

> *NOTE*
> *If the stator coil resistance is as specified,*
> *but the voltage test is less than specified,*
> *the flywheel magnets may be weak.*

9. Replace the alternator stator if it fails the preceding tests.

Removal/Installation

1. Remove the flywheel as described in this chapter.

2. Disconnect the alternator stator wires.

59

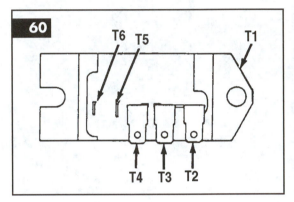

60

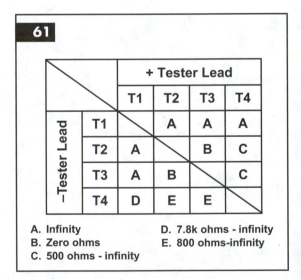

61

	+ Tester Lead			
		T1	T2	T3	T4
−Tester Lead	T1		A	A	A
	T2	A		B	C
	T3	A	B		C
	T4	D	E	E	

A. Infinity   D. 7.8k ohms - infinity
B. Zero ohms   E. 800 ohms-infinity
C. 500 ohms - infinity

3. Remove the alternator stator retaining screws, then remove the stator (**Figure 59**).

4. Reverse the removal steps to install the alternator stator while noting the following:

   a. Be sure the wires are positioned on the underside of the stator.

   b. Tighten the stator retaining bolts to 3·4 N·m (30 in.-lb.).

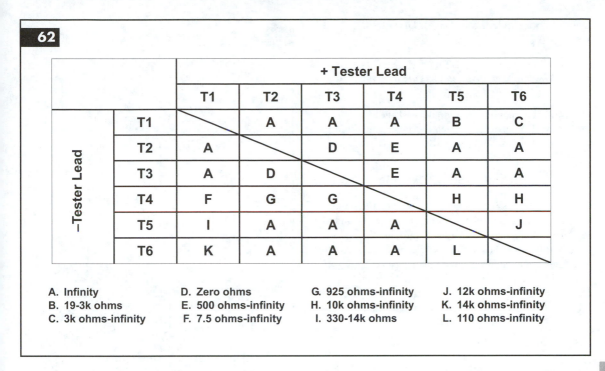

62

		\+ Tester Lead					
		T1	**T2**	**T3**	**T4**	**T5**	**T6**
−Tester Lead	**T1**		A	A	A	B	C
	T2	A		D	E	A	A
	T3	A	D		E	A	A
	T4	F	G	G		H	H
	T5	I	A	A	A		J
	T6	K	A	A	A	L	

A. Infinity
B. 19-3k ohms
C. 3k ohms-infinity

D. Zero ohms
E. 500 ohms-infinity
F. 7.5 ohms-infinity

G. 925 ohms-infinity
H. 10k ohms-infinity
I. 330-14k ohms

J. 12k ohms-infinity
K. 14k ohms-infinity
L. 110 ohms-infinity

9

REGULATOR/RECTIFIER

Engines equipped with an electric starter are also equipped with a regulator/rectifier that provides regulated DC current to charge the battery. Engines not equipped with an electric starter are equipped with a diode in the alternator wire that rectifies the alternating current to direct current to operate the electric PTO clutch.

Testing

Models Without Electric Starter

CAUTION
The mower blades will be engaged during this test. Use all necessary precautions to prevent injury.

1. Connect an ammeter in series with the alternator lead.

CAUTION
Make sure the ammeter test leads cannot touch ground.

2. Run the engine and engage the PTO switch.
3. The ammeter should indicate current. The amount of current will vary according to engine speed.
4. If no current is indicated, stop the engine and test the alternator as described in this chapter.
5. If the alternator tests good, replace the alternator lead containing the diode.

Models With Electric Starter

1. Detach the wire connectors from the regulator/rectifier (**Figure 58**).

NOTE
*The engine may be equipped with a three- or five-terminal rectifier/regulator. The configurations are similar, except terminals T6 and T5 shown in **Figure 60** are not used on the three-terminal regulator.*

2. Connect an ohmmeter to the rectifier/regulator terminals shown in **Figure 60** using the specifications in the Figures 61 and 62 charts. **Figure 61** is for the 3-terminal regulator; **Figure 62** is for the 5-terminal regulator.
3. Replace the rectifier/regulator if the test specifications in **Figure 61** or **Figure 62** are not obtained.

INTAKE MANIFOLD

Removal/Installation

1. Remove the blower housing as described in this chapter.
2. Remove the carburetor as previously described.
3. Note the location of the wire retaining straps (D, **Figure 51**), then cut them away from the intake manifold.
4. Remove the intake manifold retaining bolts (E, **Figure 51**) and remove the intake manifold (F).
5. Inspect the manifold for cracks and other damage. Clean the manifold using a suitable solvent or parts cleaner. Carefully remove any gasket material on the

manifold or cylinder head flanges. Discard the old gaskets.

> *NOTE*
> *The intake manifold gaskets are asymmetrical. Be sure they fit properly.*

6. Install the intake manifold and gaskets by reversing the removal procedure. Tighten the intake manifold retaining bolts to 6.9 N•m (61 in.-lb.).

CRANKCASE BREATHER

The engine is equipped with a closed breather system. Crankcase pressure is vented through a separator and filter on the crankcase, then routed through the cylinder head and breather hose to the air cleaner. The separator and filter are located behind a cover located on the flywheel side of the crankcase between the cylinders. A filter element catches solid particles, but does not require periodic maintenance other than replacement when plugged.

Removal/Installation

1. Remove the intake manifold as described in this chapter.
2. Remove the flywheel as described in this chapter.
3. Remove the crankcase breather cover (2, **Figure 63**).
4. Remove and discard the breather element (4, **Figure 63**).
5. Be sure the plate (5, **Figure 63**) is in place in the breather cavity.
6. On FH641 engines, a reed-type valve is mounted in the crankcase cavity (**Figure 64**). Replace the reed valve if damaged. Exercise care when installing the mounting screw to prevent cross threading.
7. Clean and dry the cover and crankcase mating surfaces.
8. Install a new breather element.
9. Apply RTV sealant to the crankcase mating surface, then install the cover and gasket. Tighten the cover retaining screws to 5.9 N•m (52 in.-lb.).

> *NOTE*
> *Refer to the cylinder head section in this chapter for service information on the breather valve in each cylinder head.*

CYLINDER HEAD COVERS (VALVE COVERS)

Removal/Installation

1. Unscrew the head cover retaining screws, then remove the head cover.
2. Remove the gasket and clean the mating surfaces on the cover and cylinder head.

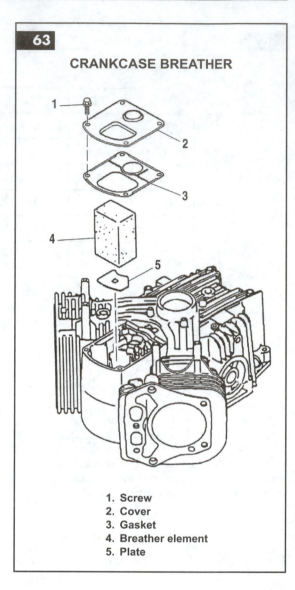

63

CRANKCASE BREATHER

1. Screw
2. Cover
3. Gasket
4. Breather element
5. Plate

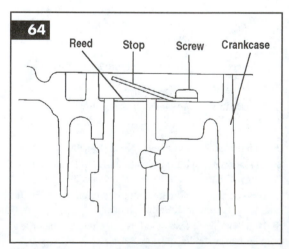

64

Reed   Stop   Screw   Crankcase

65

CYLINDER HEAD

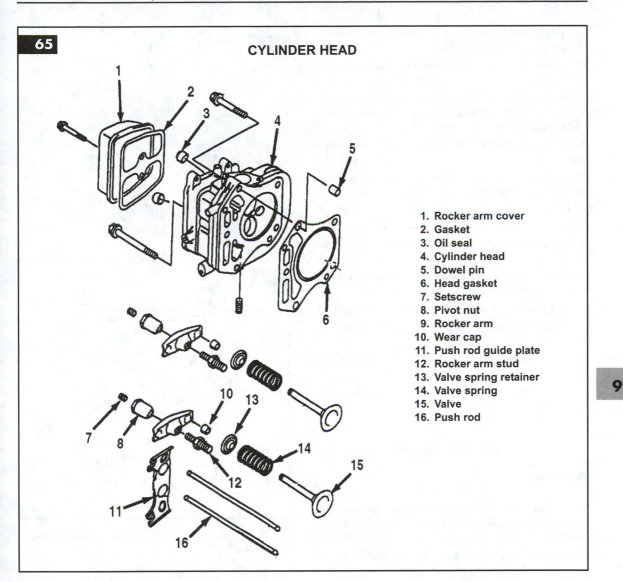

1. Rocker arm cover
2. Gasket
3. Oil seal
4. Cylinder head
5. Dowel pin
6. Head gasket
7. Setscrew
8. Pivot nut
9. Rocker arm
10. Wear cap
11. Push rod guide plate
12. Rocker arm stud
13. Valve spring retainer
14. Valve spring
15. Valve
16. Push rod

9

66

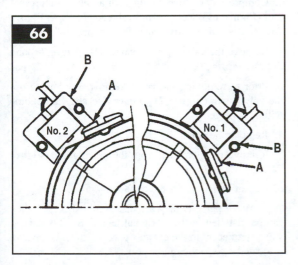

3. Install the gasket and cylinder head cover. Tighten the retaining screws to 5.9 N•m (52 in.-lb.).

ROCKER ARMS AND PUSH RODS

Removal/Installation

Refer to **Figure 65**.

1. Remove the cylinder head cover as described in the preceding section.

2. Remove the blower housing as described in this chapter.

3. Rotate the flywheel clockwise so the leading edge of the second outer flywheel magnet pole (A, **Figure 66**) aligns with the leading edge of the ignition coil leg of the cylinder being serviced. Be sure both valves are closed. If

not, rotate the flywheel one revolution clockwise and re-align the magnet and coil leg.

4. Loosen the setscrew (B, **Figure 67**) and remove the pivot nut.

5. Remove the rocker arm. Mark the pivot nut and rocker arm so they may be reinstalled in their original positions and not mixed with other parts.

6. Repeat Steps 4 and 5 to remove the remaining rocker arm.

7. If necessary, remove the push rods. Mark the push rods so they may be reinstalled in their original positions.

8. Follow steps 1-5 to remove the rocker arms and push rods on the remaining cylinder head.

9. Replace the rocker arms and pivots if worn or damaged.

10. Install the push rods and rocker arm assemblies by reversing the removal steps. Note the following:

    a. Lubricate the ends of the push rods with engine oil.

    b. Lubricate the contact surfaces of the rocker arm and pivot with grease.

    c. Be sure the push rod ends are properly seated in the valve lifters and rocker arm sockets.

    d. Adjust the valve clearance as described in this chapter.

CYLINDER HEADS

Removal

1. Disconnect the spark plug wire from each spark plug and properly ground the spark plug wire ends to the engine.

2. Remove the exhaust manifold and muffler as described in this chapter.

3. Remove the intake manifold as previously described.

4. Remove any air shrouds or heat shields attached to the cylinder heads.

5. Remove the rocker arm assemblies and push rods as described in this chapter.

6. Remove the cylinder head bolts in 1/4-turn steps in the sequence shown in **Figure 68**.

7. Loosen the cylinder head by tapping around the perimeter with a rubber or soft-faced mallet. Do not use a metal hammer.

8. Remove the cylinder head and gasket. Discard the gasket. Never reinstall a used head gasket.

NOTE
The cylinder heads are not identical. Each cylinder head is identified by the cylinder number cast into the head (Figure 3).

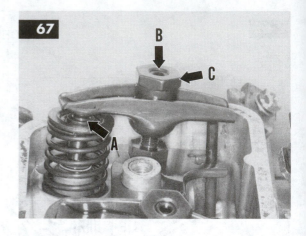

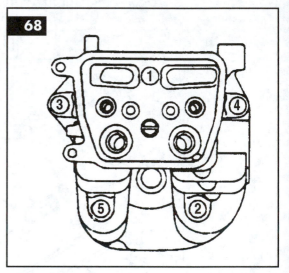

Disassembly

1. Compress one valve spring with a valve compressor tool (**Figure 69**). Remove the valve keepers (A, **Figure 70**). Release and remove the valve compressor tool.

2. Remove the valve spring retainer (B, **Figure 70**) and the valve spring (C).

3. Prior to removing the valve, remove any burrs from the valve stem (**Figure 71**). Otherwise, the valve guide will be damaged.

4. Remove the valve.

5. Remove the stem seal from the valve guide (**Figure 72**).

6. Repeat Steps 1-5 for the remaining valve.

7. Mark all parts as they are disassembled so that they can be installed in their original locations. The exhaust valve is adjacent to the exhaust port and the intake valve is located next to the intake port.

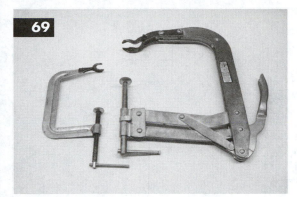

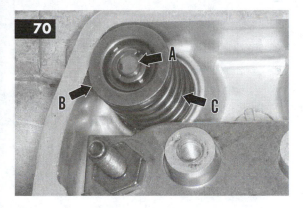

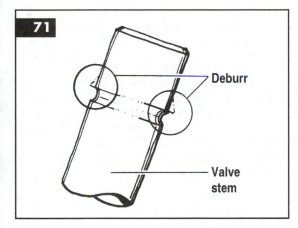

Deburr

Valve
stem

Inspection

1. Carefully remove all traces of gasket material from the cylinder head and valve cover mating surfaces. Do not gouge or damage the mating surfaces.

2. Carefully remove all traces of gasket material from the cylinder head and cylinder block mating surfaces. Do not gouge or damage the mating surfaces.

3. Remove all carbon deposits from the valves, combustion chamber area and valve ports with a rotary wire brush. A blunt screwdriver or chisel may be used if care is

taken not to damage the head, valves and spark plug threads.

4. Examine the spark plug threads in the cylinder head for damage. If damage is minor or if the threads are dirty or clogged with carbon, use a spark plug thread tap to clean the threads. If thread damage is severe, it may be possible to install a Heli-Coil or equivalent replacement thread to restore the damaged threads.

5. Inspect the threads in all threaded cylinder head and crankcase holes for damage. If damage is slight, repair the threads with an appropriate size metric tap if necessary. If thread damage is severe, installation of a Heli-Coil or equivalent replacement thread may be required.

6. After the carbon is removed from the combustion chamber and the valve intake and exhaust ports, clean the entire head in cleaning solvent. Blow dry with compressed air.

7. Carefully clean all carbon from the piston crown. Do not score the crown.

8. Check for cracks or other damage to the head, especially in the combustion chamber and exhaust port. Replace the cylinder head if it is cracked or damaged, or if any cooling fins are broken off.

9. After the head has been thoroughly cleaned, place the cylinder head gasket surface on a surface plate. Insert a flat feeler gauge between the plate and the cylinder head at various locations to check the head for distortion. Replace the cylinder head if warpage exceeds 0.05 mm (0.002 in.). Machining or grinding the cylinder head surface to remove warpage is not recommended.

10. Valve, valve guide and valve seat service will be covered in the following *Valves and Valve Components* section.

Reassembly

1. Install new stem seals on the valve guides.

2. Lubricate the intake valve stem and guide bore with fresh engine oil. To avoid damage to the valve stem seal, turn the valve slowly while inserting the valve into the cylinder head. Push the valve all the way in until it seats.

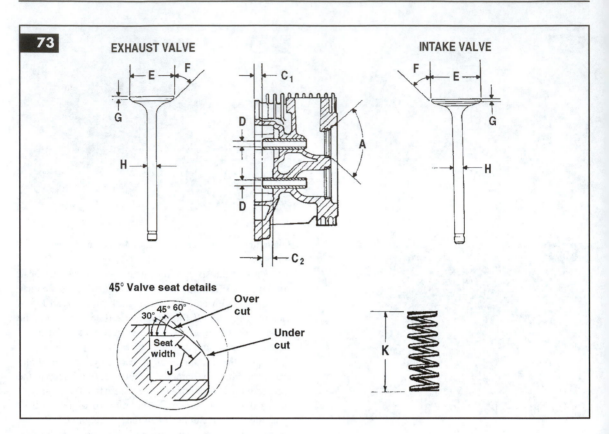

EXHAUST VALVE

INTAKE VALVE

45° Valve seat details

Over cut

Under cut

Seat width

---

3. Install the valve spring.

4. Position the valve spring retainer on top of the valve spring.

5. Compress the valve spring with a compressor tool (**Figure 69**).

6. Apply a small amount of grease to the valve keeper groove on the valve stem, then install both keepers. The grease will hold the keepers in place on the valve stem. Make sure the keepers fit snugly in the groove in the valve stem.

7. Slowly remove the compressor tool, allowing the keepers to slide into the spring retainer taper.

8. After the spring has been installed, gently tap the end of the valve stem with a soft aluminum or brass drift and hammer. This will ensure that the keepers are properly seated (**Figure 70**).

9. Repeat for the exhaust valve assembly. When performing Step 2, lightly lubricate the stem with Led-Plate or equivalent, and lubricate the guide with fresh engine oil.

Installation

1. If removed, install the cylinder head locating sleeves into the cylinder block. There should be two sleeves in the block to correspond to head bolt Positions 3 and 4 in **Figure 68**.

NOTE
Do not apply sealer to the cylinder head gasket.

2. Position the head gasket onto the sleeves.

3. Install the cylinder head onto the cylinder.

4. Install the cylinder head bolts.

5. Tighten the cylinder head bolts in 5.0 N•m (45 in.-lb.) increments in the sequence shown in **Figure 68**. Tighten to a final torque of 25 N•m (225-230 in.-lb.).

6. Install the remaining components by reversing the removal steps as outlined in this chapter.

VALVES AND VALVE COMPONENTS

Valve Adjustment

Check and adjust the clearance between the valve stem ends and rocker arms after every 300 hours of operation. The engine must be cold for valve adjustment.

1. Remove the cylinder head cover.

2. Remove the blower housing as described in this chapter.

3. Rotate the flywheel clockwise so the leading edge of the second outer flywheel magnet pole (A, **Figure 66**) aligns with the leading edge of the ignition coil leg (B) of the cylinder being serviced. Be sure both valves are

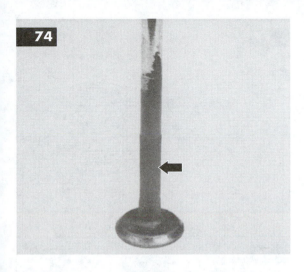

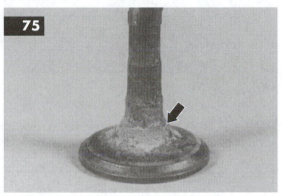

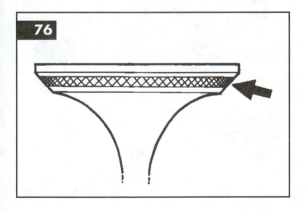

closed. If not, rotate the flywheel one revolution clockwise and realign the magnet and coil leg.

4. Measure the valve clearance gap (A, **Figure 67**) for both valves, which should be 0.075-0.125 mm (0.003-0.005 in.).

5. Loosen the setscrew (B, **Figure 67**) and turn the pivot nut (C) to obtain the desired clearance.

6. Tighten the setscrew (B, **Figure 67**) and recheck the adjustment.

Valve Service

General practice among those who do their own service is to remove the cylinder head and take it to a machine shop equipped to service cylinder heads and valves. Since the cost is relative to the required effort and equipment, this is the best approach even for experienced mechanics.

This procedure is included for those who chose to do their own valve service. Refer to **Figure 65** when performing this procedure, unless other figures are noted.

Valve Removal

To remove the valves, follow the steps outlined under *Cylinder Head, Disassembly* in this chapter.

Valve Inspection

Refer to **Table 9** at the end of this chapter and **Figure 73** for valve service dimensions.

1. Inspect the valve for damage and excessive wear. Note the condition of the valve prior to cleaning. Gummy deposits on the intake valve (**Figure 74**) may indicate that the engine has run on gasoline that was stored for an extended period. Hard deposits on the intake valve are due to burnt oil, while hard deposits on the exhaust valve (**Figure 75**) are due to combustion byproducts and burnt oil. Moisture in the engine during storage can cause corroded or pitted valves, which should be replaced.

2. Check the valve face and seat for an irregular contact pattern. The seating ring around the valve face should be centered on the face, concentric with the valve head and equal in thickness all around the valve (**Figure 76**). If the seating pattern is irregular, then the valve may be bent or the valve face or seat is damaged.

3. Remove deposits either with a wire brush or soak the valve in parts cleaner.

4. Using a micrometer, measure the valve stem diameter in multiple locations where the valve rides in the guide. Replace the valve if the stem is worn.

5. The valve stem must be perpendicular to the valve head. To check for a bent valve, carefully install the valve stem in a drill chuck and rotate the drill. Be sure the valve stem is centered in the drill chuck. If the stem or head wobbles, replace the valve.

6. Measure the valve head margin (**Figure 73**). Replace the valve if the margin is less than specified.

7. The valves and seats can be machined to restore their seating surfaces if they are worn but still serviceable.

8. If valve machining is not necessary, the valve should be lapped against the valve seat to restore the seating surfaces. Refer to *Valve Lapping* in this chapter.

9. The valves ride in nonrenewable valve guides. Check for wear in the valve guides by measuring the inside di-

9

ameter of the valve guide. Replace the cylinder head if the valve guide is excessively worn.

10. Check the valve springs:
   a. The spring should be straight and square as shown in **Figure 77**. Check multiple locations around the spring circumference.
   b. Measure the spring free length (**Figure 78**). Replace the valve spring if the free length is less than specification.

Valve Lapping

Valve lapping is a simple operation that can restore the valve seal without machining if the amount of wear or distortion is not excessive. Lapping requires the use of lapping compound and a lapping tool (**Figure 79**). Lapping compound is available in either coarse- or fine-grade, water- or oil-mixed. Fine-grade water-mixed compound is recommended. To lap a valve, proceed as follows:

1. Make sure that the valve head is smooth. Wire brush or lightly sand the head, if necessary.

2. Apply a light, even coat of lapping compound to the valve face. Too much compound can fall into the valve guide and cause damage.

3. Insert the valve into the valve guide.

4. Moisten the end of the lapping tool suction cup and place it on the valve head.

5. Rotate the lapping tool back and forth between your hands several times.

> *NOTE*
> *For the most accurate lapping, slowly hand-rotate the lapping tool back and forth between 1/4 and 3/8 of a turn (90°-135°). Do not spin the tool rapidly or use a drill to rotate the lapping tool.*

6. Lap the valve so that the sealing ring of the valve face is in the center of the face (**Figure 80**). Make the first lap pass *very light* to check the sealing ring position. If, after initial lapping, the sealing ring is too high or too low on the valve face:
   a. In necessary, recut the valve seat as described in this chapter.
   b. Relap the valve.

7. If the initial lap indicates the sealing ring is centered on the valve face, proceed with a full lapping.

8. Clean the compound from the valve and seat frequently to check the progress of the lapping. Lap only enough to achieve a precise seating ring around the valve head. The pattern on the valve face should be an even width as shown in **Figure 76**.

9. Closely examine the valve seat in the cylinder head. It should be smooth and even with a smooth burnished seating ring.

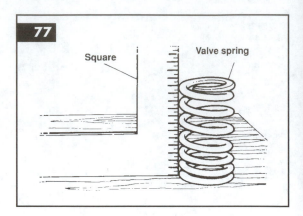

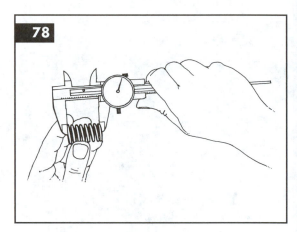

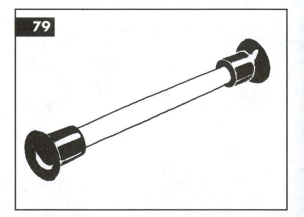

10. After lapping has been completed, thoroughly. Any lapping compound residue left in the engine will cause rapid wear.

11. After the valve assemblies have been installed into the engine, test each valve seal by pouring solvent into the intake and exhaust ports. There should be no leakage past the seat. If fluid leaks past any of the seats, remove the valve and repeat the lapping procedure until there is no leakage.

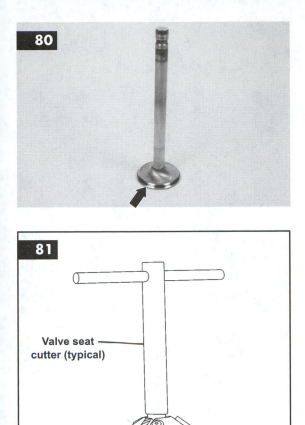

Valve seat cutter (typical)

Pilot

1. Carefully rotate and insert the solid pilot into the valve guide. Make sure the solid pilot is correctly seated.
2. Using the 45° cutter, rotate the tool (**Figure 81**) one or two turns to remove roughness and clean the seat.

> *CAUTION*
> *Measure the valve seat contact area in the cylinder head after each cut to make sure the contact area is correct and to avoid removing too much material. If too much material is removed, the cylinder head must be replaced.*

3. If the seat is still pitted or burned, continued turning the 45° cutter until the surface is clean. Avoid removing too much material from the cylinder head.
4. Remove the valve cutter.
5. Inspect the valve seat-to-valve face impression as follows:
   a. Spread a thin layer of Prussian Blue or machinist's dye evenly on the valve face.
   b. Moisten the suction cup tool (**Figure 79**) and attach it to the valve. Insert the valve into the guide.
   c. Using the suction cup tool, tap the valve up and down in the cylinder head. Do *not* rotate the valve or a false imprint will result.
   d. Remove the valve and examine the impression left by the Prussian Blue or machinist's dye.
6. Note the impression the dye left on the valve face (**Figure 80**).
   a. If the contact area is too *low* on the valve (too close to the stem), use the 60° cutter and remove a portion of the lower area of the valve seat material. This will raise the contact area. If this narrows the seat width, use the 45° cutter again to bring the seat width back into specification.
   b. If the contact area is too *high* on the valve, use the 30° cutter and remove a portion of the top area of the valve seat material. This will lower the contact area. If this narrows the seat width, use the 45° cutter again to bring the seat width back into specification.
7. Once the contact area is properly positioned on the valve face, adjust the valve seat width.
   a. If the width is too narrow, use the 45° cutter to widen the seat.
   b. If the width is too wide, use the 30° and 60° cutters equally to remove material from both above and below the seat contact area. When the seat width is correct, repeat Step 5 to ensure the correct seat-to-face position.
8. After the desired valve seat position and width is obtained, use the 45° cutter and very lightly clean off any burrs that may have been caused by the previous cuts.
9. Check that the finish has a smooth surface. It should not be rough or show chatter marks.
10. Repeat Steps 1-9 for the remaining valve seat.

Valve Seat Reconditioning

These cylinder heads use hardened alloy steel intake and exhaust valve seat inserts pressed into the head. The inserts are not replaceable. If the inserts are loose, cracked or seriously warped, replace the head. If the inserts are in good condition, they can be reworked.

Special valve cutter tools and the proper expertise are required to recondition the valve seats in the cylinder heads properly. If the required tools are not available, take the cylinder head to a machine shop equipped to service the cylinder head.

The following procedure is provided if you choose to perform this task yourself.

Required tools are: valve seat cutters, Vernier or dial caliper, machinist's dye or Prussian Blue and a valve lapping stick.

The valve seats for both the intake and exhaust valves are machined to the same angles. The valve contact surface is cut to a 45° angle from center (90° total angle).

9

11. Lap the valves as detailed in the preceding *Valve Lapping* section.

12. Thoroughly clean the cylinder head and all valve components in solvent or detergent and hot water to remove all cutting and lapping debris.

13. Install the valve assemblies into the cylinder head as described in this chapter and fill the ports with solvent to check for leaks. If any leaks are present, the valve seats must be inspected for foreign matter or burrs that may be preventing a proper seal.

14. If the cylinder head and valve components were cleaned in detergent and hot water, apply a light coat of engine oil to all bare metal surfaces to prevent any corrosion formation.

Valve Guide Reconditioning

The valves ride in nonrenewable valve guides. Check for wear in the valve guides by measuring the inside diameter of the valve guide. Compare the measurements to the **Figure 73** specifications. Replace the cylinder head if the valve guide is excessively worn.

Valve Installation

To install the valves, follow the steps outlined under *Cylinder Head, Reassembly* in this chapter.

GOVERNOR CONTROL PANEL

The governor control panel (**Figure 82**) includes levers and linkage that coordinate the operator controls with the governor, throttle and choke controls so the engine runs at the desired speed.

Static Adjustment

The static governor adjustment must be made any time the governor arm (A, **Figure 83**) is loosened or removed from the governor shaft (B), or the carburetor mounting fasteners are loosened.

To static-adjust the governor:

1. On FH451 and FH500 engines, remove the air filter assembly and mount strap (**Figure 9**).

2. Remove the governor control panel assembly bolts (B, **Figure 82**). Noting the position of the governor spring and choke link, remove the panel (A).

3. Inspect all the linkages and springs. Replace any worn or broken components.

4. Loosen the clamp nut (E, **Figure 83**) on the governor lever (A).

5. Push up on the right end of the lever to position the throttle wide open.

6. Rotate the governor shaft (B, **Figure 83**) counterclockwise as far as it will go. Do not force the shaft.

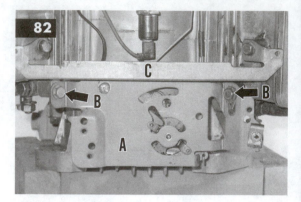

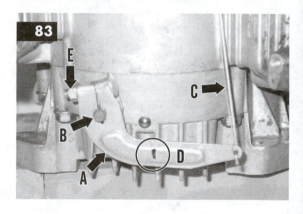

7. Ensure that the governor shaft protrudes 6.5-7.5 mm (0.25-0.30 in.) beyond the governor lever clamping area.

8. Tighten the clamp nut to 7.8 N•m (70 in.-lb.).

9. Reinstall the removed components.

Governed High Speed Adjustment

NOTE
The air cleaner must be installed while running the engine.

1. Run the engine until it reaches normal operating temperature, then stop the engine.

2. Connect a tachometer to the engine.

3. Loosen the governor control panel retaining screws (B, **Figure 82**).

4. Start the engine and set the throttle control to full throttle. The engine must be operating with no load.

5. Move the right side of the control panel up or down as needed so the engine runs at 3500-3600 rpm. If the panel is at the end of the adjustment slot and the specified rpm is unattainable, replace the governor spring and readjust the panel.

6. Tighten the panel retaining screws.

7. Recheck the full-throttle engine operating speed. Readjust, if necessary.

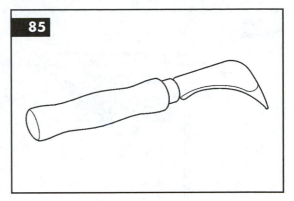

Removal/Installation

1. On FH451 and FH500 engines, remove the air filter assembly and mount strap (**Figure 9**).

2. On electric-start models, disconnect the ground wire.

3. Remove the control panel retaining screws (B, **Figure 82**).

5. Remove the control panel while disengaging the governor spring and choke rod.

6. Inspect the control panel components. Be sure all parts move freely without binding.

7. Reinstall the governor control panel by reversing the removal procedure while noting the following:

   a. Adjust the high-speed governed speed as described in the preceding section.

   b. Adjust the idle governed speed as described under *Carburetor, Idle Speed Adjustment* in this chapter.

OIL SEALS

Service With Crankshaft Installed

Oil seals at the flywheel end of the crankshaft and at the PTO end prevent the oil in the engine from leaking out. Wear or damage can reduce their effectiveness and oil leakage can become a problem, particularly if excessive amounts of oil are lost.

In some instances, it is possible to remove and install an oil seal without removing the crankshaft. Depending on the location of the engine and which oil seal is leaking, it may be necessary to remove the engine from the equipment.

If the oil seal at the flywheel end of the crankshaft is leaking, the flywheel must be removed (see *Flywheel, Removal* in this chapter). If the oil seal at the output end of the crankshaft is leaking, any parts attached to the crankshaft that deny access to the oil seal must be removed. Re-

fer to the previous *Engine Removal* section if the engine must be removed from the mower.

> *NOTE*
> *Drain the engine oil if replacing the lower crankshaft oil seal.*

Removal

Before removing an oil seal, note the position of the seal in the crankcase or oil pan. Install the new seal so it is located at the same depth as the original seal.

> *CAUTION*
> *Exercise care when extracting the seal so the metal in the seal bore or the crankshaft seal surface is not scratched or damaged.*

1. Special oil seal removal tools are available from small-engine tool suppliers (**Figure 84**), or one can make an effective but inexpensive oil seal removal tool by modifying a linoleum knife as shown in **Figure 85**. Carefully grind the blade to the contour shown in the figure, then round all the blade edges so the blade will not damage the crankshaft or seal cavity.

2. Using a small pin punch, carefully tap the seal in a couple of places around its outer edge so as to break it loose from the crankcase cavity. Only tap it enough to break it loose. Do not drive it deeper into the cavity.

3. Carefully insert the tool blade under the oil seal lip and against the inside periphery of the seal, next to the crankshaft (**Figure 84**). Pry out the seal. It may be necessary to work around the seal in more than one spot before the seal will break loose.

4. Clean and dry the seal seating area so the new seal will seat properly.

5. Check the oil seal bore in the engine and dress out any burrs created during removal. Only remove metal that is raised and will interfere with the installation of the new seal. If a deep gouge is present, carefully clean and dry the area around the gouge, then fill the depression with a suitable epoxy so it is level with the surrounding metal.

9

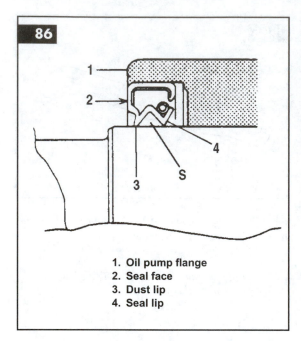

1. Oil pump flange
2. Seal face
3. Dust lip
4. Seal lip

6. Check the crankshaft seal area. Scoring, grooves, or sharp edges on the crankshaft will require that the crankshaft be replaced.

Installation

1. Apply Loctite 598 or equivalent oil resistant non-hardening sealer to the periphery of the oil seal prior to installation.

2. Coat the lip of the seal with all-temperature grease. On double-lip seals (**Figure 86**), pack the cavity between the lips (S) with the grease.

3. Cover keyways and threads on the crankshaft with a proper-sized seal protector sleeve or adhesive tape so the oil seal lip will not be cut when passing the oil seal down the crankshaft. **Figure 87** shows the seal installed onto a protector sleeve.

4. Position the seal so the seal lip is slanted toward the inside of the engine. Most seals are spring-loaded. The spring must be toward the engine when installing the seal.

5. Use a suitable tool with the same outside diameter as the oil seal to drive the oil seal into the engine. Suitable sizes of tubing or pipe may be used (**Figure 88**). Be sure the seal-driving end of the tool is square but not sharp. The outer face of both seals should be flush with the face of each seal bore.

INTERNAL ENGINE COMPONENTS

Although some internal components can be serviced without a complete disassembly, damage to one internal engine component often affects some or all of the other

parts inside the engine. Failing to inspect all of the components may result in a future repair which could have been avoided.

ENGINE DISASSEMBLY

Use the following procedure to disassemble the engine, referring to previous sections where necessary to remove the external components. If the components are to be re-used, mark them as necessary to identify them for proper placement upon reassembly.

Refer to **Figure 89**.

1. On electric-start units, disconnect the battery, negative cable first.

2. Turn the fuel tank shutoff valve off.

3. Drain the engine oil and remove the engine from the equipment. Remove the oil filter.

4. Remove the following components:
    a. PTO clutch, pulley and key(s).
    b. Muffler and exhaust system.
    c. Fuel pump, blower housing, cooling shrouds and baffles.
    d. Air filter assembly, carburetor and intake manifold.
    e. Ignition modules.
    f. Flywheel.
    g. Alternator stator.

89

ENGINE EXPLODED VIEW

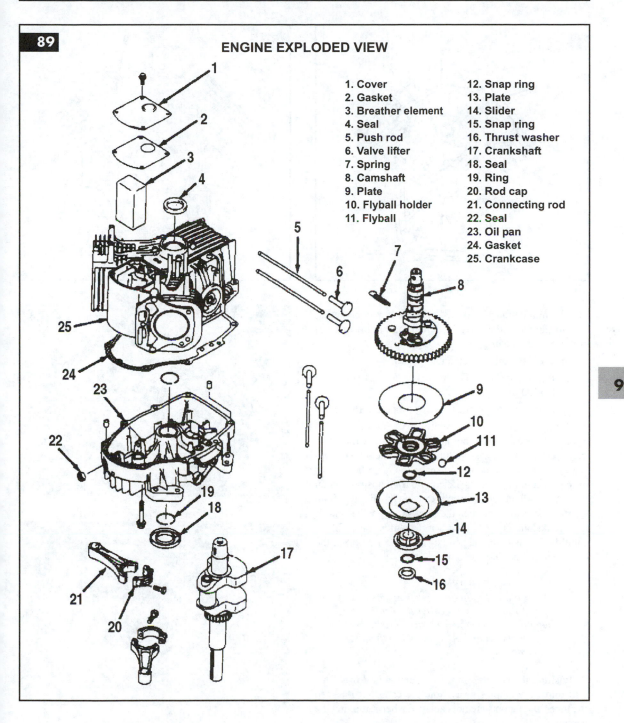

1. Cover	12. Snap ring
2. Gasket	13. Plate
3. Breather element	14. Slider
4. Seal	15. Snap ring
5. Push rod	16. Thrust washer
6. Valve lifter	17. Crankshaft
7. Spring	18. Seal
8. Camshaft	19. Ring
9. Plate	20. Rod cap
10. Flyball holder	21. Connecting rod
11. Flyball	22. Seal
	23. Oil pan
	24. Gasket
	25. Crankcase

9

h. External governor controls.

i. Blower shroud base plate.

j. Electric starter motor, if used.

k. Spark plugs, valve covers, rocker arm assemblies and cylinder heads.

l. Push rods.

m. Crankcase breather.

5. Remove the carbon ridge at the top of the cylinder bore. Run a fingernail over the top portion of the cylinder to determine if a wear ridge exists. Use a ridge reamer to remove the ridge at the top of the cylinder. Remove any shavings or grit from the ridge removal process.

6. Remove any rust or burrs from the crankshaft extensions. This will prevent damage to the main bearings. A strip of emery cloth can be used to remove rust. Burrs

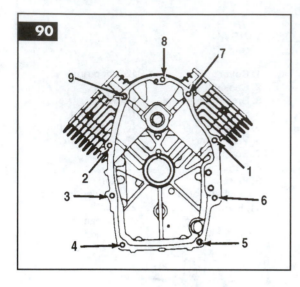

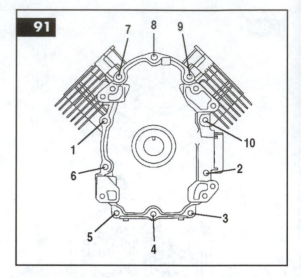

may be found adjacent to the keyways. It may be necessary to file down the end of the crankshaft to the original crankshaft diameter.

7. Unscrew the oil pan retaining screws:

    a. **Figure 90** shows the nine screws on the FH451 and FH500 pans.

    b. **Figure 91** shows the ten screws on the FH641 pan.

8. Remove the oil pan. Carefully tap with a soft-faced mallet, if necessary. Do not pry between the mating surfaces. Do not use excessive force against the oil pan. Applying excessive force may damage the main bearing or oil pan. If binding occurs, determine if an obstruction on the crankshaft, such as a burr, is causing the binding. If no obstruction is present, then the crankshaft may be bent. If the crankshaft is bent, then a replacement short block should be considered, depending on the condition of the other internal engine components.

> *WARNING*
> *When a crankshaft becomes bent, stresses are introduced that weaken the shaft. Attempting to straighten a bent crankshaft is not recommended. A bent crankshaft must be replaced.*

9. Position the engine so the cylinders point down. This will move the tappets away from the camshaft lobes so the lobes and tappets are not damaged when removing the camshaft.

10. Rotate the crankshaft so the timing marks on the crankshaft gear and camshaft gear are aligned (**Figure 92**).

11. Remove the camshaft.

12. Mark, then remove, the tappets. The tappets must be marked so they can be reinstalled in their original positions.

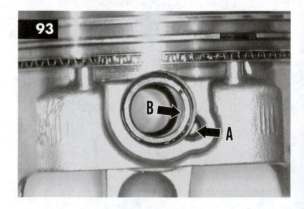

13. Unscrew the connecting rod cap retaining screws and remove the rod cap on the No. 2 cylinder connecting rod (nearer the crankshaft PTO end).

> *NOTE*
> *Care must be exercised not to damage the bearing surface of the crankshaft, connecting rod and rod cap.*

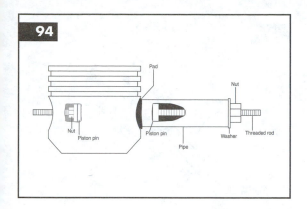

94

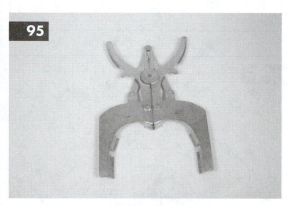

95

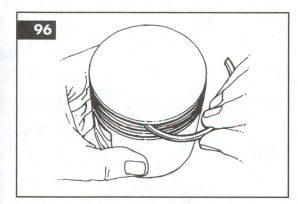

96

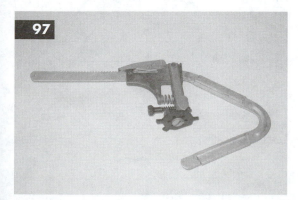

97

14. Push the connecting rod and piston in the No. 2 cylinder out the top of the engine.

15. Repeat steps 13 and 14 for the No. 1 cylinder.

16. Remove the crankshaft.

17. Removal of the oil pump and governor shaft assemblies from the oil pan will be covered in subsequent sections.

PISTON, PISTON RINGS AND PISTON PIN (WRIST PIN)

Disassembly

Use the following procedure to separate the piston from the connecting rod.

1. Insert a small pry tool in the wrist pin notch and extract the pin retaining clips (A, **Figure 93**).

2. Push or tap out the piston pin (B, **Figure 93**).

NOTE
*If the piston pin is stuck in the piston, a puller tool like that shown in **Figure 94** can be fabricated to extract the pin. Make sure the inside diameter of the tubing (2) is larger than the outside diameter of the pin.*

3. Separate the piston from the connecting rod.

NOTE
*A suitable piston ring expander tool (**Figure 95**) should be used to remove or install the piston compression rings. Although the rings can be removed or installed by hand, there is less chance of piston ring breakage or gouging the piston ring grooves when the ring expander tool is used.*

4. Move the rings toward the piston crown for removal. Use care not to gouge the ring lands. Due to the flexibility of the oil control ring rails, carefully twist them out of the groove rather than use the expander tool. Discard the piston rings. Reusing worn rings is not recommended.

Remove the piston rings as follows:

   a. Remove the top compression ring (closest to the piston crown) first.

   b. Remove the No. 2 compression ring second.

   c. Remove the oil control ring last.

5. Clean the piston ring grooves. One method for cleaning piston ring grooves is to pull the end of a broken piston ring through the groove as shown in **Figure 96**. Use care not to gouge or otherwise damage the groove. Professional piston ring groove cleaning tools are also available (**Figure 97**).

9

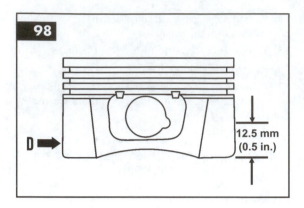

12.5 mm
(0.5 in.)

D ➡

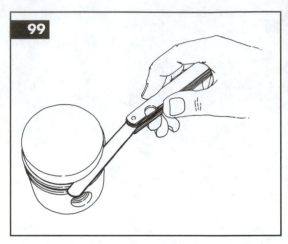

Inspection

1. Measure the cylinder bore as described under *Cylinder* in this chapter. If a cylinder overbore is required, then piston inspection is unnecessary. If the cylinder bore is within specification, proceed with Step 2.

> *CAUTION*
> *If one cylinder is worn beyond specification, both cylinders must be rebored and fitted with oversize pistons to preserve engine balance integrity.*

> *NOTE*
> *Pistons and rings are available in standard size as well as 0.50 mm (0.020 in.) oversize.*

2. Clean the top of the piston using a soft wire brush. Soak the piston in carburetor solvent to remove hard deposits.

3. Inspect the piston for damage. Replace the piston if it is cracked, scored, scuffed or scratched. Be sure to inspect the underside of the piston around the piston pin bosses for cracks, as well as the piston ring grooves. The piston crown must be smooth except for machining or casting marks.

4. Measure the piston diameter at a point 12.5 mm (1/2 in.) from the bottom of the skirt and perpendicular to the piston pin bore (D, **Figure 98**).

   a. On Models FH451V or FH500V, replace the piston if the diameter is less than 67.79 mm (2.669 in.).

   b. On Model FH641V, replace the piston if the diameter is less than 74.99 mm (2.952 in.).

5. Place a new piston ring in the clean top piston ring groove and measure the side (ring land) clearance using a feeler gauge as shown in **Figure 99**. Repeat for the second ring. Replace the piston if a new top or second piston ring has a side clearance exceeding the specification listed in **Table 8**. Oil ring clearance is not specified.

6. Inspect the piston pin and the piston pin bores in the piston for scoring and other damage. The piston pin is

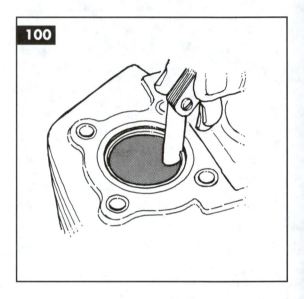

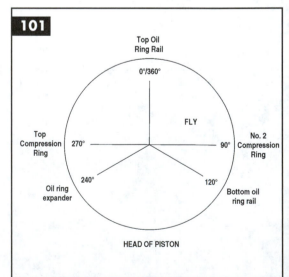

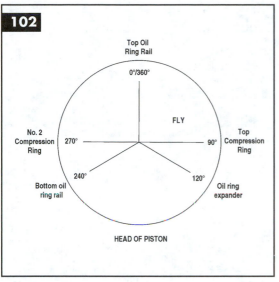

102

Top Oil
Ring Rail

0°/360°

FLY

No. 2
Compression   270°   90°   Top
Ring   Compression
                                            Ring

240°   120°

Bottom oil   Oil ring
ring rail   expander

HEAD OF PISTON

103

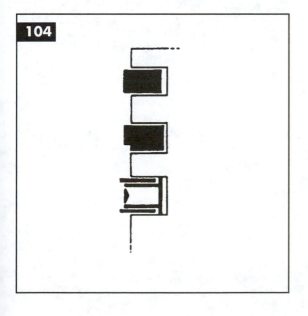

104

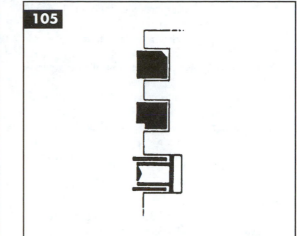

105

only available in the standard size; replace the piston and pin if wear exceeds specification.

7. Measure the piston pin diameter at several points to determine if the piston pin is worn or out-of-round. Replace the pin if the measurements exceed the specifications listed in **Table 8**.

8. Measure the piston pin bore in the piston at several points to determine if the bore is worn or out-of-round. Replace the piston if the measurements exceed the specifications listed in **Table 8**.

9. Measure the end gap of each piston ring. Place the piston ring in the cylinder bore, then push the piston ring down into the bore with the piston so the ring is square in the bore. Position the piston ring 25 mm (1.0 inch) down in the bore from the top of the cylinder and measure the piston ring end gap as shown in **Figure 100**. Reject sizes for the piston ring end gaps are listed in **Table 8**.

Assembly

1. Use a suitable piston ring expander tool (**Figure 95**) to install the piston rings. Although the rings can be removed or installed by hand, there is less chance of piston ring breakage or gouging the piston ring grooves when the ring expander tool is used.

2. For maximum engine power and longevity, as well as precise emission control, the ring end gaps should be spaced around the piston circumference in the approximate degreed intervals as shown in Figures 101 and 102. **Figure 101** is the gap spacing recommendation for the No. 1 piston; **Figure 102** is for No. 2 piston.

    a. The arrow on the piston head (**Figure 103**) will indicate the 0°/360° position.

    b. Refer to Figures 104 and 105 for cross-sectional views of the rings. **Figure 104** shows the rings for the FH451 and FH500 engines; **Figure 105** shows the FH641 rings.

9

c. The top (No. 1) compression ring should have its gap at the 90° position.

d. The No. 2 compression ring (center groove) should have its gap at the 270° position.

e. The seam or gap of the oil control ring expander should be in the 120° position.

f. The top oil control ring rail should have its gap at the 0°/360° position.

g. The bottom oil control ring rail should have its gap at the 240° position.

3. Lubricate the rings and ring grooves in the piston prior to assembly.

4. Install the oil control ring first using the following procedure:

a. Install the ring expander in the ring groove. The expander ring ends must abut, not overlap.

b. Twist one of the rails in a spiral and work it into the top piston ring groove (**Figure 106**), then into the center groove, and finally into the oil ring groove, placing the first rail against the bottom of the expander ring.

c. Install the second rail using the same procedure so it fits above the expander and the end gap is properly positioned. The installed oil control ring should appear as shown in **Figure 107**. The oil control ring assembly must rotate without binding in the piston ring groove.

5. Install the center compression ring, then the top compression ring. Note that the top side of each compression ring (toward the piston crown) may have an identifying mark to indicate top. Refer to the instructions included with the replacement rings.

NOTE
Install new piston pin clips. Do not reuse removed clips.

6. Assemble the piston and connecting rod for the No. 1 cylinder so the arrow on the piston crown (**Figure 103**) and the K on the side of the rod (**Figure 108**) are on opposite sides (B, **Figure 109**).

a. Lubricate the piston pin bores and pin.

b. Install one of the piston pin clips in its piston pin bore groove.

c. Insert the piston pin.

d. Install the remaining piston pin retaining clip.

e. Be sure the piston pin retaining clips are securely positioned in the piston grooves.

CAUTION
Make sure that the gap of the clip is at either the top or bottom of the piston and not aligned with the clip removal cutout (A, Figure 93). Installing the clips with the gap towards the sides could cause the clips to work loose during engine operation, resulting in serious engine damage.

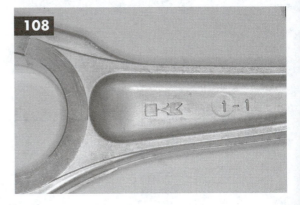

7. Assemble the piston and connecting rod for the No. 2 cylinder so the arrow on the piston (**Figure 103**) and the K on the side of the rod (**Figure 108**) are on the same side (C, **Figure 109**).

CONNECTING ROD

The connecting rod rides directly on the crankshaft crankpin. If the rod and crankpin are worn beyond specification, the crankpin can be reground and a 0.50 mm (0.020 in.) undersize connecting rod installed. Refer to *Crankshaft* in this chapter for regrinding specifications.

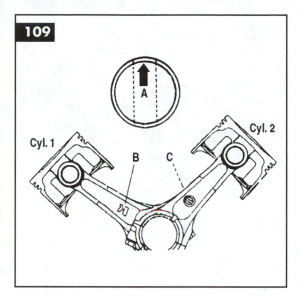

109

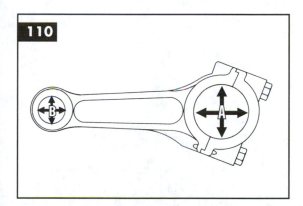

110

Disassembly

The piston and connecting rod are removed from the engine as an assembly, then separated as outlined in the preceding section.

Inspection

1. Inspect the bearing surfaces for signs of scuffing and scoring. If any damage is observed, also inspect the surface of the crankpin or piston pin.

> *NOTE*
> *If the rod bearing surface is worn due to abrasive particles (the surface texture is dull and rough), it should be replaced even if it is not worn beyond the specified wear limit. Grit may be embedded in the aluminum, which will continue to cause wear on mating surfaces.*

2. Inspect the connecting rods for cracks, twisting and other damage. Inspect the alignment of each connecting rod. If there is evidence of abnormal piston or cylinder wear, have the connecting rod inspected at a machine shop. Specialized equipment is required to accurately determine if a rod is bent or twisted.

3. Assemble the No. 1 connecting rod.
   a. Apply a small amount of oil to the connecting rod bolt threads.
   b. On Models FH451V and FH500V, tighten the rod bolts to 5.9 N•m (52 in.-lb.).
   c. On Model FH641V, tighten the rod bolts to 21 N•m (186 in.-lb.).

4. Measure the big end diameter of the connecting rod (A, **Figure 110**).
   a. On Models FH451V and FH500V, maximum inside diameter of the connecting rod big end is 39.50 mm (1.555 in.).
   b. On Model FH641V, maximum inside diameter of the connecting rod big end is 43.10 mm (1.697 in.).

5. Measure the small end diameter of the connecting rod (B, **Figure 110**). Maximum inside diameter of the connecting rod small end is 16.05 mm (0.632 in.).

6. Measure the big end width of the connecting rod.
   a. On Models FH451V and FH500V, minimum width of the connecting rod big end is 18.80 mm (0.740 in.).
   b. On Model FH641V, minimum width of the connecting rod big end is 19.90 mm (0.783 in.).

7. Repeat Steps 3-6 for the No. 2 connecting rod.

8. Replace the connecting rod if any Step 4-6 measurements do not meet specification.

CYLINDERS, CYLINDER BLOCK, AND CRANKCASE

The cylinders are cast-iron alloy sleeves integrally cast into the aluminum alloy crankcase and block assembly.

To access the cylinders, follow the steps described under *Engine Disassembly* in this chapter.

Pistons and ring sets are available in standard size as well as an oversize of 0.50 mm (0.020 in.).

Inspection and Reconditioning

1. Make sure all gasket and sealant material has been carefully and completely removed from the head, oil pan and breather sealing surfaces. Sealing surfaces must be free from nicks, gouges or deep scratches.

2. Inspect the fastener holes for damaged threads or broken fasteners.
   a. For broken fasteners, refer to *Removing Broken Fasteners* in Chapter One.
   b. For damaged threads, restore the threads with an appropriate size metric tap if necessary. If thread

9

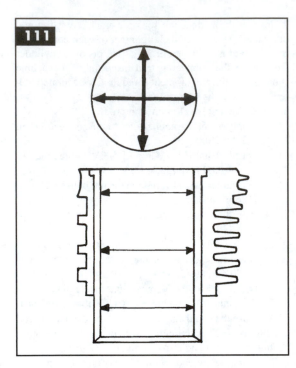

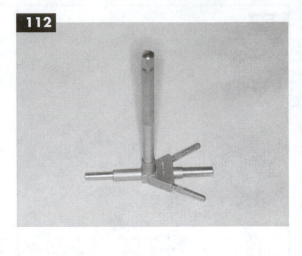

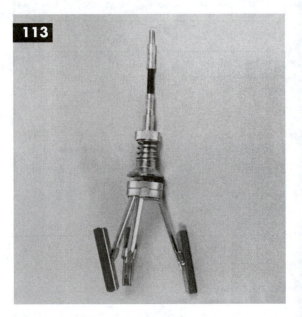

damage is severe, a satisfactory repair can sometimes be made by the installation of a Heli-Coil or equivalent replacement thread. If the threaded holes cannot be satisfactorily repaired, replace the cylinder block.

3. Check for broken cooling fins. A small broken edge or corner may not affect performance. A large piece of broken-off fin will cause the cylinder to overheat. Replace the cylinder block if major fin damage is evident.

4. Check for debris packed in between the fins. Carefully and completely remove any heat-caked debris.

5. Check the bores for scoring or other damage.

6. Measure the cylinder bore parallel with the crankshaft and at right angles to the crankshaft at the top, center and bottom of ring travel (**Figure 111**). A telescoping bore gauge (**Figure 112**) or an inside micrometer can be used to precisely measure cylinder bores. Always follow the instructions included with the tool. Compare the measurements to the dimensions listed in **Table 8**.

    a. On Models FH451V and FH500V, rebore the cylinder if the diameter exceeds 68.10 mm (2.681 in.).

    b. On Model FH641V, rebore the cylinder if the diameter exceeds 75.28 mm (2.964 in.).

    c. Maximum out-of-round for all models is 0.056 mm (0.0022 in.).

7. If the cylinder has been previously rebored, the piston will be marked "0.5" to show it is oversize. A block whose cylinder will not clean up at 0.5 mm oversize or one which has already been rebored to 0.5 mm oversize and then worn beyond limits will need to be replaced. Wear limits for overbored cylinders are:

    a. For Models FH451 and FH500: 68.60 mm (2.701 in.).

    b. For Model FH641: 75.78 mm (2.983 in.).

CAUTION
If one cylinder is worn beyond specification, both cylinders must be rebored and fitted with oversize pistons to preserve engine balance integrity.

8. If the cylinder bore is within the wear limit, the bore will need to be honed so new rings will seat properly. A hone such as that pictured in **Figure 113** works well. Always follow the hone manufacturer's instructions. The crosshatch angle of the bore surface after finish honing should be 45°-50° as shown in **Figure 114**. Too great an angle will cause high oil consumption; too small an angle

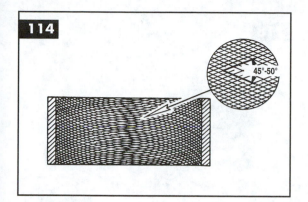

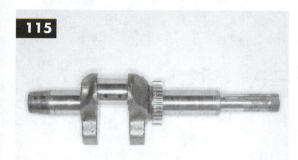

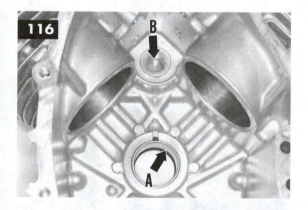

will make the rings skip and wear rapidly. The crosshatch pattern retains oil in the microscopic grooves, thus allowing the piston rings to seat properly.

9. If the cylinder is being bored oversize, bore to the specified original-plus-oversize dimension.

    a. On Models FH451 and FH500, oversize cylinder dimension is 68.48-68.50 mm (2.696-2.697 in.).

    b. On Model FH64, oversize cylinder dimension is 75.68-75.70 mm (2.979-2.980 in.).

10. The final step of a rebore should always be a finish honing. The crosshatch angle of the cylinder bore surface after finish honing should be 45°-50° as shown in **Figure 114**.

11. After honing, thoroughly wash the cylinder with plenty of soap and hot water and rinse with clean warm water. Blow-dry with compressed air. This will remove the microscopic grinding particles from the surface of the cylinder bore. A grease-cutting dishwashing detergent is an excellent cleanser. Do not use petroleum solvents (mineral spirits, kerosene, etc.) to clean the bore. Solvents *will not remove* embedded grinding dust from the cylinder bore surface.

12. After drying the cylinder, spray the bore with a moisture displacing lubricant such as WD-40 or equivalent. Use a clean, lint-free cloth to wipe the lubricant from the bore. If gray residue shows up on the wiping cloth, the cylinder is not clean. Repeat Step 11 until no gray residue appears.

13. Apply a light coat of engine oil to the bore to prevent rust.

> *CAUTION*
> *Failure to properly clean the cylinder after honing will cause rapid cylinder and piston wear and severe engine damage.*

CRANKSHAFT AND MAIN BEARINGS

The crankshaft is pictured in **Figure 115**.

These engines use non-replaceable sleeve-style main bearings. The upper (flywheel-side) main bearing is A, **Figure 116**. The lower (oil pan) main bearing is shown in **Figure 117**.

> *NOTE*
> *When replacing a crankshaft, short block, or engine, ensure that the threads on the PTO bolt that was removed from the old crankshaft are compatible with the threads in the new crankshaft.*

The crankshaft and main bearing specifications are listed in **Table 8**.

9

Removal

To remove the crankshaft, follow the steps under *Engine Disassembly* in this chapter.

Inspection and Reconditioning

Inspect the crankshaft as follows:

1. If considerable effort was required to remove the oil pan from the crankshaft, then the crankshaft is probably bent and must be discarded. If some effort was required during removal, then the crankshaft should be checked for straightness by a shop with the necessary equipment. If the oil pan was easy to remove, and the bearings are within specifications, then the crankshaft is probably straight. Crankshaft runout can be used as an indicator of crankshaft straightness. Maximum allowable crankshaft runout is 0.05 mm (0.002 in.).

2. Measure crankshaft runout using one of the following procedures:

    a. Install the crankshaft in the engine. Be sure the main bearings are lubricated. Measure crankshaft runout at the PTO end of the crankshaft.

    b. Support the crankshaft in V-blocks at the main bearing journals. **Figure 118** shows a typical crankshaft being checked for runout.

> *CAUTION*
> *When using a dial indicator to check runout, exercise caution when the crankshaft keyway approaches the indicator anvil. Dial indicator damage could result if the keyway strikes the anvil.*

3. Inspect all mating surfaces on the crankshaft for scoring, scuffing and other damage.

4. Check the flywheel threads and the PTO threads for damage and cross threading. Dress or repair if possible.

5. Inspect the keyways and remove any burrs. The keyway must be straight and unworn.

6. Check the crankshaft gear (A, **Figure 119**) for broken or pitted teeth.

7. Be sure all oil passages (B, **Figure 119**) are clean and unobstructed.

8. Be sure the crankpin plug (**Figure 120**) is tight.

> *CAUTION*
> *The crankshaft oil gallery plug (**Figure 120**) is not replaceable. If the connecting rod journal must be reground undersize, thoroughly flush the galleries to remove all traces of grinding grit. Failure to properly flush the oil gallery will cause rapid crankshaft, main bearing and connecting rod wear and severe internal engine damage.*

9. Measure the crankpin journal:

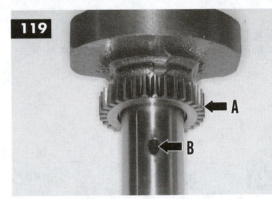

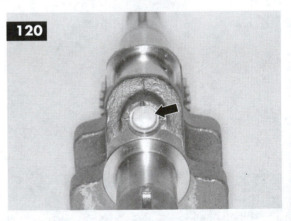

    a. Crankpin journal minimum diameter on Models FH451V and FH500V is 34.94 mm (1.376 in.).

    b. Crankpin journal minimum diameter on Model FH641V is 37.94 mm (1.494 in.).

    c. If the crankpin is worn beyond standard specification and must be reground, refer to **Figure 121** for regrinding dimensions.

10. Measure the crankpin width (W, **Figure 121**).

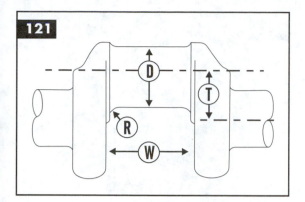

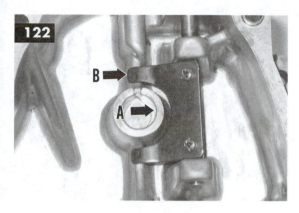

a. Maximum allowable crankpin width on Models FH451V and FH500V is 39.50 mm (1.555 in.).

b. Maximum allowable crankpin width on Model FH641V is 43.10 mm (1.697 in.).

11. Measure the main bearing journals (**Figure 115**). Refer to **Table 8** for specified wear limits. Main bearing journals cannot be machined undersize.

12. Measure the inside bearing diameter in the crankcase (**Figure 116**) and oil pan (**Figure 117**).

a. Maximum allowable bearing diameter on Models FH451V and FH500V is 35.15 mm (1.384 in.).

b. Maximum allowable bearing diameter on Model FH641V is 40.15 mm (1.581 in.).

c. The main bearing bushings are not replaceable.

Installation

To install the crankshaft, follow the necessary steps under *Engine Reassembly* in this chapter.

CAMSHAFT, VALVE LIFTERS AND COMPRESSION RELEASE

The camshaft rides directly in the machined aluminum bores of the crankcase (B, **Figure 116**) and oil pan (A, **Figure 122**).

The camshaft is equipped with a compression reduction device to aid starting (**Figure 123**). With the engine stopped or at cranking speed, the spring (A, **Figure 124**) holds the actuator cam weight (B) inward against the actuator rod (C). The actuator rod forces the compression release balls (**Figure 123**) in the exhaust lobes to protrude, which in turn holds the exhaust valves open slightly during the compression stroke. This compression release greatly reduces the power needed for cranking.

The camshaft also houses the governor flyball assembly (**Figure 123**). Refer to the following *Governor* section for service information.

1. Inspect the camshaft and gear for wear on the journals, cam lobes and gear teeth.

2. Measure the diameter of the camshaft bearing journals. Minimum allowable camshaft journal diameter is 15.985 mm (0.6293 in.).

3. Measure the height of the intake and exhaust lobes.

a. Minimum cam lobe height for intake and exhaust valves on Models FH451V and FH500V is 29.131 mm (1.147 in.).

b. Minimum cam lobe height for intake and exhaust valves on Model FH641V is 29.621 mm (1.166 in.).

4. Inspect the camshaft bearing surfaces in the crankcase (B, **Figure 116**) and oil pan (A, **Figure 122**). The surfaces must be smooth with no sign of abrasion.

5. Measure the bearing inside diameters in the crankcase and oil pan. Maximum allowable camshaft bearing bore diameters is 16.136 mm (0.6352 in.).

6. Inspect the compression release mechanism. The mechanism should move freely without binding. Replace any worn components.

7. Refer to *Engine Reassembly* in this chapter for the procedure to install the camshaft into the engine.

NOTE
If the camshaft is being replaced, the valve tappets also should be replaced.

GOVERNOR

The engine is equipped with a flyball assembly mounted on the end of the camshaft. Movement of the governor flyballs through centrifugal force forces the outer plate thrust washer against the governor fork (B, **Figure 122**) in the oil pan. The governor fork shaft extends through the oil pan to operate the external governor linkage.

9

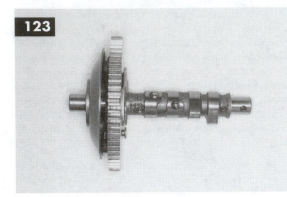

Removal/Installation

1. Refer to *Engine Disassembly* in this chapter to remove the oil pan for access to the internal governor components.

> *NOTE*
> *The internal engine components do not need to be removed to service the governor assembly unless the camshaft requires replacement.*

2. Remove the thrust washer on the camshaft.

> *NOTE*
> *The flyballs will be loose after removing the outer plate.*

3. Remove the outer snap ring (A, **Figure 125**), slider thrust washer (B) and outer plate (C).

4. Remove the inner snap ring (A, **Figure 126**), flyball holder (B) and flyballs (C).

5. Remove the inner plate (**Figure 127**).

6. Inspect the governor components for excessive wear and damage.

7. Remove the governor shaft and fork (B, **Figure 122**) for access to the shaft seal (**Figure 128**).

8. To install a new shaft seal, proceed as follows:

   a. Install the governor shaft into the oil pan.

   b. Note that one side of the new seal is marked.

   c. Install the new seal over the shaft and into the oil pan so the marked side is toward the outside of the oil pan.

   d. The outer face of the governor shaft seal should be flush to 1.0 mm (.040 in.) below the edge of the seal bore.

9. Reverse the removal steps to install the governor. After assembly, be sure the slider thrust washer moves smoothly.

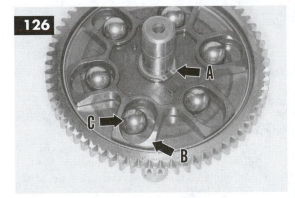

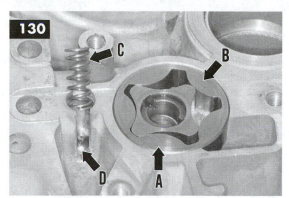

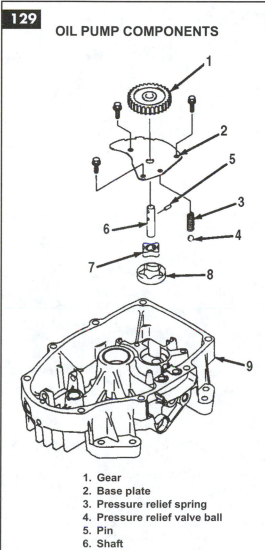

OIL PUMP COMPONENTS

1. Gear
2. Base plate
3. Pressure relief spring
4. Pressure relief valve ball
5. Pin
6. Shaft
7. Inner rotor
8. Outer rotor
9. Oil pan

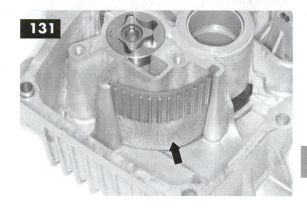

9

OIL PUMP

Removal

The rotor-type oil pump is located in the oil pan (**Figure 129**). The crankshaft gear drives the oil pump gear.

1. Remove the oil pan for access to the oil pump.

2. Remove the oil pump gear (1, **Figure 129**), retaining screws and cover (2). The outer rotor (A, **Figure 130**), inner rotor (B), relief valve spring (C) and ball (D) are now accessible.

3. Remove the pick-up screen (**Figure 131**).

4. Thoroughly clean and inspect all pump components.

Inspection

1. Make certain the oil passages are clear.

2. Inspect the pump housing in the oil pan for damage.

3. Measure the clearance between the inner rotor and outer rotor (**Figure 132**). Maximum allowable inner-to-outer rotor clearance is 0.2 mm (0.008 in.).

4. Measure the outside diameter of the outer rotor (**Figure 133**). Minimum allowable outside diameter of outer rotor is 40.470 mm (1.5933 in.).

5. Measure the thickness of the outer rotor. Minimum allowable thickness of the outer rotor is 9.830 mm (0.3870 in.).

6. If the rotors do not meet Step 3-5 specifications, re-place the rotors as a set.

7. Measure the inside diameter of the oil pump bore in the oil pan (**Figure 134**). Maximum allowable inside diameter in oil pan is 40.801 mm (1.6063 in.).

8. Measure the oil pump bore depth in the oil pan. Maximum allowable depth in the oil pan is 10.230 mm (0.4028 in.).

9. Measure the diameter of the oil pump shaft (**Figure 135**). Minimum allowable oil pump shaft diameter is 10.923 mm (0.4300 in.).

10. Measure the oil pump shaft bore in the oil pan. The maximum allowable oil pump shaft bore is 11.072 mm (0.4359 in.).

11. Measure the length of the pressure relief spring (**Figure 130**). Minimum pressure relief spring free length is 19.50 mm (0.768 in.).

Installation

Install the oil pump by reversing the removal steps while noting the following:

1. Fill the oil pump cavity with clean engine oil.

2. Position the oil pump cover so the 6 mm hole is centered over the relief valve spring (**Figure 136**).

3. Tighten the oil pump cover retaining screws to 5.9 N•m (52 in.-lb.).

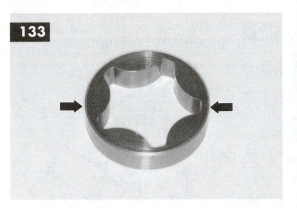

ENGINE REASSEMBLY

Refer to the appropriate previous sections when assembling the internal engine components and installing the external engine components as applicable. Refer to **Figure 89** for internal engine component identification.

Before assembling the engine, be sure all components are clean. Any residue or debris left in the engine will cause rapid wear and/or major damage when the engine runs.

> *NOTE*
> *Thoroughly lubricate all internal component contact/wear surfaces with fresh engine oil immediately prior to assembly.*

Lightly coat all fastener threads, except the cylinder head bolts and the connecting rod bolts, with Loctite 242 or equivalent immediately prior to assembly. Do not use threadlock compound on the head or rod bolts.

During final installation, ensure that new gaskets are installed and the correct torque sequences and values are strictly followed. Torque values are listed in **Table 7**.

The following components should be already assembled before proceeding:

1. Pistons, piston rings and connecting rods.

2. Oil pump assembly.

3. Camshaft and flyball governor.

4. Governor lever and governor shaft.

Use the following procedure to assemble internal engine components:

1. Lubricate the flywheel-side main crankshaft bearing with engine oil.

2. Insert the crankshaft into the crankcase.

3. Proceed as follows to install the piston/connecting rod assembly for the No. 1 cylinder (nearer the flywheel):

    a. Lubricate the piston, piston pin and piston rings with engine oil.

    b. Position the piston ring end gaps as specified in the previous *Pistons, Reassembly* section.

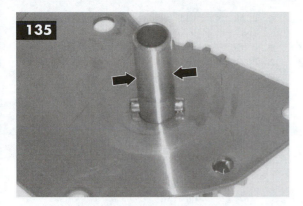

f. Insert the connecting rod and piston through the top of the engine so the piston ring compressor rests against the engine.

g. Liberally lubricate the connecting rod bearing and the crankshaft crankpin with engine oil.

h. Push the piston into the cylinder bore while guiding the connecting rod onto the crankshaft crankpin.

CAUTION
Do not use excessive force when installing the piston and rod. If binding occurs, remove the piston and rod and try again. Excessive force can damage or break the piston rings, piston ring lands, connecting rod or crankshaft.

i. Mate the connecting rod with the crankshaft crankpin, then rotate the crankshaft so the cap can be installed.

j. Install the rod cap. Apply oil to the connecting rod bolts before installation. Tighten the rod bolts to 5.9 N•m (52 in.-lb.) on Models FH451V and FH500V. Tighten the rod bolts to 21 N•m (186 in.-lb.) on Model FH641V.

4. Repeat Step 3 for the No. 2 cylinder.

5. Lubricate the valve lifters with engine oil and install them into the crankcase.

6. Lubricate the camshaft and camshaft bearings with engine oil.

7. Install the camshaft. Align the timing marks (**Figure 92**) on the crankshaft and camshaft gears.

8. Install the thrust washer onto the end of the camshaft (16, **Figure 89**).

9. Be sure the locating sleeves are installed in the appropriate crankcase holes.

10. Install the crankcase gasket.

11. Lubricate the crankshaft main bearing and camshaft bearing in the oil pan.

12. Install the oil pan. Rotate the crankshaft to help engage the oil pump gear.

NOTE
Do not force the oil pan onto the crankcase. If binding occurs, remove the oil pan, then determine and correct the cause.

13. Install the oil pan bolts. Tighten the oil pan bolts in 5.0 N•m (45 in.-lb.) increments in the sequence shown in **Figure 90** or **Figure 91**. Tighten the screws to a final torque of 25 N•m (221 in.-lb.).

14. Install the oil seals. Follow the steps in the *OIL SEAL* section.

15. Install the PTO shaft keys, pulley and clutch. The assembled engine block can now be installed onto the mower, if desired, for installation of the external components.

c. Using a full-band ring compressor (**Figure 137**), compress the piston rings. Ensure that the top and bottom edges of the snugged compressor band are not misaligned. The projections on the compressor band must be toward the piston skirt and the oil ring must be at least 6 mm (1/4 inch) above the bottom edge of the compressor.

d. Install the piston and rod assembly in the cylinder so the arrow stamped on the piston crown (**Figure 103**) points toward the flywheel side of the engine.

e. Lubricate the cylinder bore with Lubriplate White Grease or fresh engine oil.

16. Paying close attention to the location and orientation marks made during disassembly, install the external components.

    a. Crankcase breather.
    b. Push rods.
    c. Cylinder heads.
    d. Rocker arm assemblies.
    e. Valve covers.
    f. Spark plugs.
    g. Electric starter motor, if used.
    h. Blower shroud base plate.
    i. External governor components.
    j. Blower housing base plate.
    k. Alternator stator.
    l. Flywheel.
    m. Ignition modules.
    n. Intake manifold, carburetor, and air filter assembly.
    o. Blower housing, cooling shrouds and baffles.
    p. Fuel pump.
    q. Exhaust system and muffler.
    r. Oil filter. Fill the oil filter and crankcase with the correct type and amount of oil.

17. Static-adjust the governor.

CAUTION
Prior to starting the engine, the governor linkage must have the static adjustment performed or serious engine overspeed damage could result. Once the engine is started, the governor must be adjusted for high speed. Refer to the Governor, External Service section for the adjustments.

Table 1 GENERAL ENGINE SPECIFICATIONS

Model	No. Cyls.	Bore	Stroke	Displacement	Power Rating
FH451V	2	68 mm (2.68 in.)	68 mm (2.68 in.)	494 cc (30.1 cu. in.)	15 hp 11.2 kW
FH500V	2	68 mm (2.68 in.)	68 mm (2.68 in.)	494 cc (30.1 cu. in.)	17 hp 12.6 kW
FH641V	2	75.2 mm (2.96 in.)	76 mm (2.99 in.)	675 cc (41.19 cu. in.)	21 hp 15.6 kW

Table 2 MAINTENANCE AND LUBRICATION SCHEDULE

After 5-hour break-in period (new unit; new or overhauled engine)	Change the engine oil and the oil filter. Check the fasteners and the linkages.
Every 8 hours or daily	Check the engine oil with the unit sitting level. Do not overfill. Check and/or clean the air filter. Clean the cooling system.
Every 40-50 hours or weekly	Service the air cleaner pre-filter. On electric-start units, check the battery electrolyte level. Lubricate the throttle and choke cables.
Every 100 hours or semi-monthly	Replace the air filter and pre-filter. Change the engine oil and oil filter.
Every 300 hours or semi-annually	Adjust the valve clearance.
Every 500 hours or annually	Replace the fuel filter and fuel hoses. Remove and clean the cylinder heads. Check all of the fasteners for proper tightness.

Table 3 RECOMMENDED ENGINE FUEL AND LUBRICANTS

Fuel	Unleaded gasoline with Octane rating of 87 or higher
Capacity	5.0 U.S. gallons (18.7 liters or 4.0 Imperial gallons)
Engine oil	API service rating of SH or above
Viscosity	
Above 70° F (20° C)	SAE 40
Above 32° F (0° C)	SAE 30
Between 0° F and 95° F (-18° C and 35° C)	SAE 10W-30
Capacity	
FH451V, FH500V, and FH641V	
With filter	Approximately 3.6 pints (1.75 liters)
Without filter	Approximately 3.2 pints (1.5 liters)

NOTE: Do not use 10W-40 oil in the engine. Recommended engine oil viscosities are for petroleum-based oils. Comparable synthetic oils may be used. DO NOT MIX synthetic oil with petroleum oil.

Table 4 CARBURETOR SERVICE SPECIFICATIONS (FH451V and FH500V)

Item	Specification
Float level	Parallel to body
Idle mixture screw initial setting	2 1/4 turns out
Idle speed	See text
Main air jet	1.7
Main jet	
0-3000 ft.	#125
3000-6000 ft.	#122.5
6000 and higher	#120
Pilot air jet	1.2
Pilot jet	#48.8

9

Table 5 CARBURETOR SERVICE SPECIFICATIONS (FH641V)

Item	Specification
Float level	Parallel to body
Idle mixture screw initial setting	
Left	2 1/4 turns out
Right	1 1/4 turns out
Idle speed	See text
Main air jet	1.7
Main jet	
0-3000 ft.	
Left	#136
Right	#140
3000-6000 ft.	
Left	#133
Right	#139
6000 and higher	
Left	#130
Right	#134
Pilot air jet	1.1
Pilot jet	
Left	#46
Right	#44

Table 6 STARTER MOTOR SERVICE SPECIFICATIONS

Item	Specification
Brush length (min.)	6.4 mm (0.25 in.).
Commutator diameter (min.)	31.1 mm (1.225 in.)

Table 7 TORQUE SPECIFICATIONS

Item	N•m	ft.-lb.	in.-lb.
Air cleaner base retaining nut	6.9	–	61
Alternator stator retaining bolts	3.4	–	30
Breather cover	5.9	–	52
Cylinder head	25	–	221
Cylinder head cover	5.9	–	52
Exhaust manifold retaining nuts	15	–	133
Flywheel retaining nut	56	41	
Ignition module			
Stud nuts	7.8	–	69
Flanged bolts	5.9	–	52
Intake manifold	6.9	–	61
Oil pan	25	–	221
Oil pump cover	5.9	–	52
Starter motor retaining bolts	15	–	133

Table 8 ENGINE SERVICE SPECIFICATIONS

Item	Specification
Camshaft bearing bore (min.)	16.136 mm (0.6353 in.)
Camshaft bearing journal diameter (min.)	15.985 mm (0.6293 in.)
Camshaft lobe height—in. & ex. (min.)	
FH451V, FH500V	29.131 mm (1.1469 in.)
FH641V	29.621 mm (1.1662 in.)
Connecting rod big end diameter (max.)	
FH451V, FH500V	35.055 mm (1.3801 in.)
FH641V	38.055 mm (1.498 in.)
Connecting rod big end width (min.)	
FH451V, FH500V	18.80 mm (0.740 in.)
FH641V	19.90 mm (0.783 in.)
Connecting rod small end diameter (max.)	16.05 mm (0.632 in.)
Crankshaft main journal diameter (min.)	
FH451V, FH500V	
PTO end	34.90 mm (1.374 in.)
Flywheel end	34.93 mm (1.375 in.)
FH641V	
PTO end	39.896 mm (1.571 in.)
Flywheel end	39.896 mm (1.571 in.)
Crankshaft connecting rod journal	
Diameter (min.)	
FH451V, FH500V	34.94 mm (1.3756 in.)
FH641V	37.94 mm (1.494 in.)
Taper, out-of-round	0.006 mm (0.0002 in.)
Crankshaft runout	0.05 mm (0.002 in.)

(continued)

Table 8 ENGINE SERVICE SPECIFICATIONS (continued)

Item	Specification
Cylinder head warpage (max.)	0.05 mm (0.002 in.)
Cylinder bore diameter	
FH451V, FH500V	
Standard size	67.98-68.00 mm (2.676-2.677 in.)
Wear limit	68.10 mm (2.681 in.)
0.50 mm oversize	68.48-68.50 mm (2.696-2.697 in.)
Wear limit	68.60 mm (2.701 in.)
FH641V	
Standard size	75.18-75.20 mm (2.960-2.961 in.)
Wear limit	75.28 mm (2.964 in.)
0.50 mm oversize	75.68-75.70 mm (2.979-2.980 in.)
Wear limit	75.78 mm (2.983 in.)
Ignition module air gap	0.20-0.40 mm (0.008-0.016 in.)
Main bearing diameter (max.)	
Crankcase & oil pan	
FH451V, FH500V	35.15 mm (1.384 in.)
FH641V	40.15 mm (1.581 in.).
Oil pump bore (max.)	40.801 mm (1.6063 in.)
Oil pump bore depth (max.)	10.230 mm (0.4028 in.)
Oil pump inner-to-outer rotor clearance (max.)	0.2 mm (0.008 in.)
Oil pump outer rotor OD (min.)	40.470 mm (1.5933 in.)
Oil pump outer rotor width (min.)	9.830 mm (0.3870 in.)
Oil pump relief spring free length (min.)	19.50 mm (0.768 in.)
Oil pump shaft bore (max.)	11.072 mm (0.4359 in.)
Oil pump shaft diameter (min.)	10.923 mm (0.4300 in.)
Piston diameter (min.)	
FH451V, FH500V	67.79 mm (2.669 in.)
FH641V	74.99 mm (2.952 in.).
Piston pin bore (max.)	16.08 mm (0.633 in.)
Piston pin diameter (min.)	15.96 mm (0.628 in.)
Piston ring side clearance (max.)	
FH451V, FH500V	
Top compression ring	0.15 mm (0.006 in.)
Second compression ring	0.12 mm (0.005 in.)
FH641V	
Top compression ring	0.18 mm (0.007 in.)
Second compression ring	0.16 mm (0.006 in.)
Piston ring end gap (max.)	
FH451V, FH500V	
Top compression ring	0.70 mm (0.028 in.)
Second compression ring	0.78 mm (0.031 in.)
Oil control ring rails	1.05 mm (0.041 in.)
FH641V	
Top compression ring	0.65 mm (0.026 in.)
Second compression ring	0.78 mm (0.031 in.)
Oil control ring rails	1.05 mm (0.041 in.)
Valve clearance (in. & ex.)	0.075-0.125 mm (0.003-0.005 in.)
Valve spring length (min.)	26.7 mm (1.05 in.)
Valve stem diameter (min.)	
Intake	5.950 mm (0.2342 in.)
Exhaust	5.930 mm (0.2335 in.)
Valve stem runout (max.)	0.05 mm (0.020 in.)

(continued)

9

Table 9   VALVE SERVICE DIMENSIONS

Ref.	Description	Dimension
A	Seat Angle	45° from guide centerline
B	Insert Diameter (OD)	Not serviceable
C_1	Guide Depth	Not serviceable
C_2	Guide Protrusion	Not serviceable
D	Guide Diameter (ID)	
	Wear limit	6.08 mm (0.239 in.)
E	Valve Head Diameter	Not specified
F	Valve Face Angle	45° from stem centerline
G	Valve Margin (Minimum)	0.35 mm (0.014 in. or 1/64 in.)
H	Valve Stem Wear limit:	
	Intake	5.95 mm (0.2342 in.)
	Exhaust	5.93 mm (0.2335 in.)
J	Valve Seat Width	
	FH451, FH500 Intake & Exhaust	0.6-0.9 mm (0.024-0.035 in.)
	FH641	
	Intake	0.8-1.4 mm (0.030-0.050 in.)
	Exhaust	1.1-1.6 mm (0.040-0.060 in.)
K	Valve Spring Free Length	
	Minimum	26.7 mm (1.050 in.)

CHAPTER TEN

BRIGGS & STRATTON ENGINE

This section covers the Briggs & Stratton Model 303776, 303777 and 350776 Vanguard V-twin engines. These engines are air-cooled, four-stroke, vertical-crankshaft engines equipped with overhead valves. They are pressure lubricated and equipped with an oil filter.

The Tables at the end of this chapter list the engine specifications.

ENGINE IDENTIFICATION

Engine model, type and code numbers are located on a plate (**Figure 1**) mounted on the side of the blower housing, cylinder shroud or valve cover. All the numbers are required when ordering parts or a replacement engine and for using applicable service procedures.

1. The model number decodes as follows:
   a. The first two digits indicate the cubic inch displacement.
   b. The third digit tells the factory design series.
   c. The fourth digit tells that the engine is a vertical shaft model with a float-style carburetor and a mechanical governor.
   d. The fifth digit indicates the engine has plain bearings with filtered, full-pressure lubrication.
   e. The last digit indicates the engine has a 12-volt gear-drive electric starter with a recharging alternator.
2. The type number is a factory code used to identify the options of each engine.
3. The date of manufacture is the first six digits of the code number; the first two digits is the year, the third and

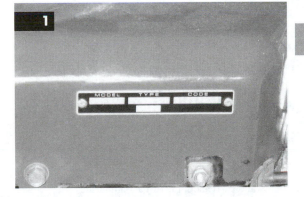

fourth digits are the month and the fifth and sixth digits are the day. The remaining digits are factory production codes.

The next two sections in this chapter provide information on removing and reinstalling the engine as a complete, assembled unit. Subsequent sections provide disassembly, inspection, adjustment, repair/overhaul and reassembly information for the engine components.

The engine must be removed from the equipment before undertaking repairs on the internal components. In the case of external components such as the carburetor or a cylinder head, engine removal may not be necessary, as the repair job may be performed with the engine mounted on the equipment.

Briggs & Stratton tools, or suitable equivalent tools, may be recommended for some procedures outlined herein. The tools are available from Briggs & Stratton dealers and service centers. Good quality tools are also available from small engine parts suppliers. Be careful when substituting a homemade tool for a recommended tool. Although an existing or fabricated tool may be made to work, consider the possibilities if the substitute tool damages the engine. The cost to repair the damage, and the lost time, may exceed the cost of the recommended tool.

NOTE
Some procedures may require that work be performed by a professional shop. Be sure to get an estimate, then compare it with the cost of a new rebuilt engine or shortblock (a basic engine sub-assembly).

NOTE
Metric fasteners are used throughout the engine except the threaded hole in the PTO end of the crankshaft, the flange mounting holes and the flywheel puller holes, which are inch-size threads.

CYLINDER IDENTIFICATION

The top cylinder (nearest the flywheel) is the number 1 cylinder (**Figure 2**). The cylinder number also appears on the cylinder head underneath the valve cover (**Figure 3**).

The No. 1 cylinder is always the cylinder closest to the flywheel. The cylinder numbers are marked on the cylinder sides facing the flywheel.

ENGINE REMOVAL

Drain the crankcase oil before removing the engine. Always drain the oil with the engine warm so the oil flows freely and carries out the dirt and impurities.

1. Be sure the engine is stopped and the ignition switch is in the OFF position. Allow the engine to cool to ambient temperature.

2. Engage the parking brake.

3. Disconnect the battery cables, negative terminal first, and remove the battery.

4. Close the fuel tank valve (**Figure 4**).

WARNING
Some gasoline will drain from the fuel hose during the next procedure. Wipe up any spilled gasoline immediately. Work in a well-ventilated area at least 50 feet away from any open flame, including pilot lights in gas appliances. Do not allow anyone to smoke in the area. Do not work near any grinding or any other source of sparks.

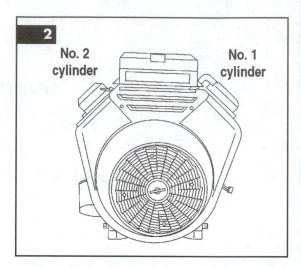

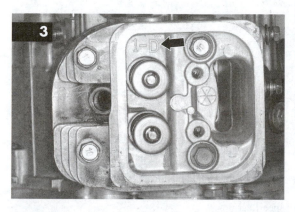

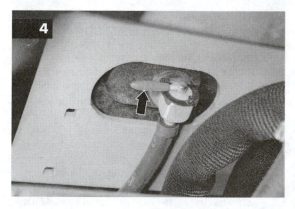

5. Detach the fuel hose clamp at the inlet connection to the fuel pump. Disconnect the fuel hose from the pump.

6. Disconnect the spark plug wires from the spark plugs. Ground the spark plug wires to the engine.

7. Identify and unplug the chassis wiring harness connectors and, on electric-start units, the starter motor cable.

8. Disconnect the throttle and choke control cables.

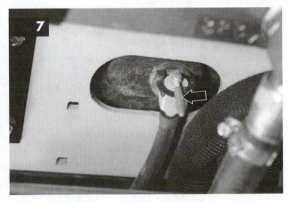

NOTE
Prior to removal, mark cable positions for proper reconnection during engine installation.

9. Remove the deck drive belt shield, then slacken the belt running from the engine:

   a. On fixed-idler drives (**Figure 5**), back off the idler adjusting nut to allow slack in the belt.

   b. On spring-loaded idler drives (**Figure 6**), move the idler pulley bracket away from the belt. Secure the bracket to allow slack in the belt, or work the belt off the idler.

10. Block the front wheels. Safely raise and support the rear of the mower to gain access to the underside of the engine.

11. Unplug the PTO clutch wire connector (**Figure 6**). Support the PTO clutch while removing the clutch bolt from the crankshaft. Slide the clutch off the shaft, then remove the belt from the clutch pulley.

12. Move the hydrostatic drive idler pulley away from the drive belt so the belt slackens. Work the belt off the engine pulley, then remove the belt.

13. Remove the engine mounting bolts.

14. Carefully lift the engine off the frame.

15. Note the position and orientation of the hydrostat pulley on the crankshaft. Remove the pulley.

16. Clean the engine mounting area on the frame.

ENGINE INSTALLATION

1. Ensure that the engine mounting areas on both the frame and the bottom of the engine are clean and dry.

2. Lightly coat the crankshaft, including keyway, with anti-seize compound.

3. Install the hydrostat pulley on the crankshaft in the same position and orientation as that noted during removal.

4. Set the engine in position on the frame.

5. Apply Loctite 271 or equivalent to the engine-mount fastener threads. Tighten the fasteners securely. On fasteners with lock washers, use new lock washers.

6. Install the hydrostat belt onto the pulleys, then allow the spring-loaded idler to exert tension on the belt.

7. Insert the PTO clutch belt into the clutch pulley groove. Align the clutch locator bracket, ensuring that the clutch wire is not pinched or kinked. Align the clutch key with the crankshaft keyway, then slide the clutch onto the crankshaft. Install the clutch bolt and tighten to the proper torque using the torque tables at the end of Chapter 1.

8. Remove the mower supports and lower the unit onto the floor. Make sure that the parking brake is still set, then remove the front wheel chocks.

9. Reapply tension to the deck drive belt. Refer to the adjustment procedure under *Drive Belts* in Chapter Three to properly tension the belt.

10. Install the deck drive belt shield.

11. Reconnect the throttle and choke cables using the marks noted during engine removal.

12. Reconnect the chassis wiring harness connectors to the appropriate engine plugs.

13. Connect the starter motor cable and the battery cables, negative cable last.

14. Reconnect the spark plug leads to the plugs.

15. Install the fuel hose between the fuel filter and the fuel pump.

16. Refill the crankcase with oil.

17. Open the fuel tank valve (**Figure 7**).

10

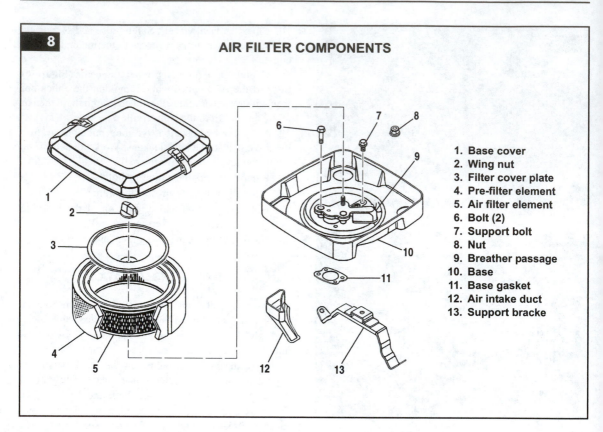

AIR FILTER COMPONENTS

1. Base cover
2. Wing nut
3. Filter cover plate
4. Pre-filter element
5. Air filter element
6. Bolt (2)
7. Support bolt
8. Nut
9. Breather passage
10. Base
11. Base gasket
12. Air intake duct
13. Support bracke

LUBRICATION

All models are equipped with a filtered pressure lubrication system. Refer to the *OIL PUMP* section for oil pump service information.

NOTE
It is recommended that the oil filter be filled with oil before installation to assure adequate componet lubrication during initial engine restart. Pour the oil into the filter through the center threaded hole only. Do not fill past the bottom of the threads.

Periodically check the oil level; do not overfill. To check the oil level:

1. Make sure that the mower is sitting on a level surface.

2. Clean the area around the dipstick cap to prevent dirt and debris from falling into the crankcase when the cap is removed.

3. Remove the dipstick and wipe the oil from the level indicator.

4. Reinsert the dipstick, screwing it back down into the tube.

5. Remove the dipstick and check the oil level. The oil level should be up to, but not over, the "FULL" line on the dipstick.

It is recommended that a new oil filter be installed at each oil change. Apply a light coating of clean engine oil to the filter gasket. Install the oil filter until the rubber gasket contacts the filter adapter plate, then tighten an additional 1/2-3/4 turn.

Crankcase oil capacity is approximately 3-1/2 pints (1.65 L) with oil filter.

Engine oil specifications are listed in **Table 1** at the end of this chapter.

In new or overhauled engines or short blocks, use SAE 30 oil for the first 5 hours of operation, then change oil according to ambient temperature requirements. The recommended oil change interval after the 5-hour break-in period is every 50 hours of operation. The oil should be drained while the engine is warm for the most effective crankcase sludge removal.

The engine may be equipped with a low-oil sensor. If the oil level is low, the sensor circuit will either stop the engine or trigger a warning device.

AIR FILTER

These engines are equipped with a paper-type air filter and a foam precleaner element (**Figure 8**).

Remove and clean the air filter at the interval indicated in **Table 2**. Replace the element at the specified interval or whenever it is damaged or starting to deteriorate. Ser-

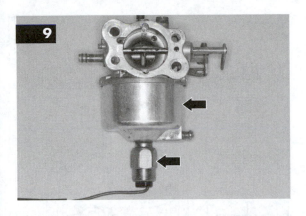

ning, fuel is drawn into the nozzle through the removable main jet. Fuel in the nozzle then exits into the carburetor bore through a discharge hole. Fuel is also drawn into the idle circuit to the idle fuel jet and then to the idle mixture adjustment screw. Air flow through the carburetor is controlled by throttle and choke plates.

If the engine does not perform well at high altitude, a high altitude main jet is available.

The carburetor is equipped with a fuel shut-off solenoid (**Figure 9**). The solenoid is controlled by the equipment electrical system. When 12 volts is directed to the solenoid, the solenoid rod retracts and allows fuel to flow into the main fuel circuit of the carburetor.

Adjustment

Idle speed and mixture adjustment

The idle speed is governed. Use the following procedure to adjust the idle speed. To comply with emissions requirements, the idle mixture screw may be equipped with a limiter cap. Use pliers to remove the limiter cap.

NOTE
Be sure the choke is wide open and the engine is at normal operating temperature when performing the adjustment procedure.

NOTE
The air cleaner is removed for clarity. The air cleaner must be installed when the engine is running. The idle speed and mixture screws are accessible through holes in the top grille.

1. If so equipped, remove the idle mixture screw limiter cap.
2. Turn the idle mixture screw (A, **Figure 10**) 1-1/4 turns out from a lightly seated position.
3. With the parking brake on, the blade PTO disengaged, the speed control in neutral, and the neutral locks locked, start the engine and run it for 5-10 minutes to reach normal operating temperature.

WARNING
Make sure ventilation is adequate if the engine will be run in a confined area. Exhaust fumes are toxic and deadly.

4. Place the remote speed control in the idle position.
5. Hold the carburetor throttle lever against the idle speed adjusting screw (B, **Figure 10**) and adjust the idle speed screw so the engine runs at 1400 rpm.
6. With the throttle lever against the idle speed adjusting screw, turn the idle mixture screw clockwise until the engine speed decreases. Mark the screw position.
7. Slowly back out the idle mixture screw until the engine speed decreases again. Mark the screw position.

vice more frequently if the engine is operated in severe conditions.

To service the filter assembly, refer to *Periodic Maintenance, Air Filter Service* in Chapter Three.

NOTE
Inspect the crankcase breather hose between the breather and the air filter base each time the air filter is serviced. If the hose is loose, cracked, or dry and brittle, replace it.

FUEL FILTER

Service the fuel filter at the interval indicated in **Table 2**. Service more frequently if the engine is operated in severe conditions.

To service the fuel filter, refer to *Periodic Maintenance, Fuel Filter Service* in Chapter Three.

CARBURETOR

Operation

The carburetor operates according to the principles outlined in Chapter Two. A float in the fuel bowl controls the amount of fuel in the bowl. When the engine is run-

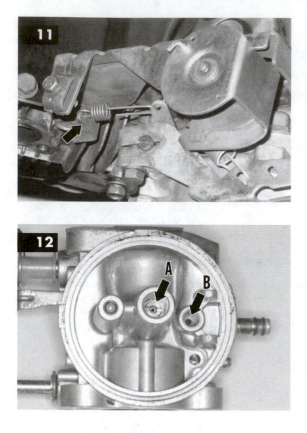

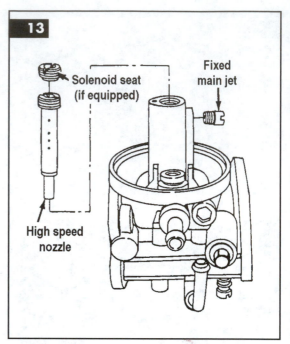

Solenoid seat
(if equipped)

Fixed
main jet

High speed
nozzle

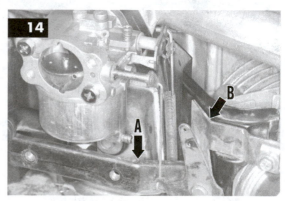

8. Rotate the idle mixture screw so it is halfway between the two marked positions. If so equipped, install a new limiter cap onto the idle mixture screw.

9. With the throttle lever against the idle speed screw, readjust the idle speed to 1200 rpm.

10. Release the throttle lever. With the remote control in governed idle position, bend the governed idle speed tab (**Figure 11**) so the engine idles at 1400 rpm.

High Speed Mixture Adjustment

A fixed main fuel jet inside the carburetor controls the high-speed fuel mixture. **Figure 12** (A) shows the main jet position inside the column on the Aisan carburetor. On the Mikuni carburetor, the jet screws into the side of the column (**Figure 13**). No external high-speed mixture adjustments can be made to this carburetor. For high-altitude operation, the main fuel jet may be removed and replaced with a jet having a smaller orifice size to alter the high speed fuel mixture.

Removal

WARNING
Some gasoline will drain from the fuel hose and/or the carburetor during this

procedure. Wipe up any spilled gasoline immediately. Work in a well-ventilated area at least 50 feet away from any open flame, including pilot lights in gas appliances. Do not allow anyone to smoke in the area. Do not work near any grinding or any other source of sparks.

1. Disconnect the negative battery lead from the battery and the solenoid wire from the carburetor.

2. Turn the fuel tank valve off (**Figure 4**).

3. Remove the air cleaner cover and elements (1-5, **Figure 8**).

4. Remove the lower air cleaner base retaining screw (7, **Figure 8**).

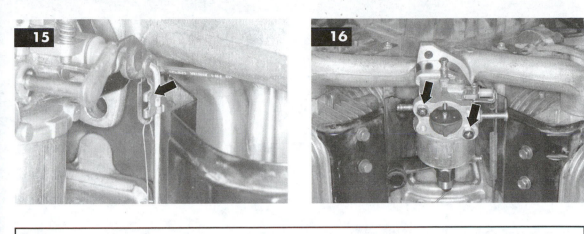

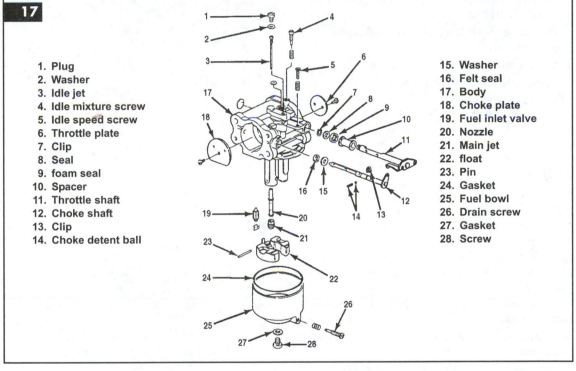

17

1. Plug
2. Washer
3. Idle jet
4. Idle mixture screw
5. Idle speed screw
6. Throttle plate
7. Clip
8. Seal
9. foam seal
10. Spacer
11. Throttle shaft
12. Choke shaft
13. Clip
14. Choke detent ball

15. Washer
16. Felt seal
17. Body
18. Choke plate
19. Fuel inlet valve
20. Nozzle
21. Main jet
22. float
23. Pin
24. Gasket
25. Fuel bowl
26. Drain screw
27. Gasket
28. Screw

10

5. Remove the upper air cleaner base and baffle retaining screws (6, **Figure 8**), then remove the air cleaner base (10). Remove and discard the base gasket (11).

6. Remove the air cleaner base bracket.

7. While disconnecting the choke control rod, remove the choke control bracket (B, **Figure 14**).

8. Remove the blower housing as described in this chapter. The blower housing must be removed for access to the fuel shutoff solenoid wire.

9. Detach the fuel hose from the carburetor.

10. Disconnect the spring and throttle control link from the throttle arm on the carburetor (**Figure 15**).

11. Remove the carburetor retaining bolts (**Figure 16**), then remove the carburetor.

12. Carefully clean all old gasket material from the carburetor and manifold flanges. Do not scratch, gouge or damage the gasket surfaces. Discard the old gasket.

Disassembly (AISAN Carburetor)

Refer to **Figure 17**.

1. Unscrew the fuel solenoid (A, **Figure 9**) and remove the fuel bowl (B) and gasket.

NOTE
The float pin is a drive fit. Exercise care when removing the pin.

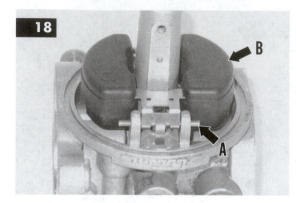

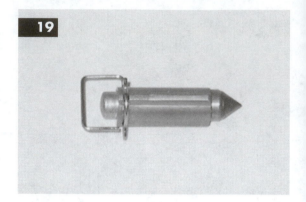

2. Remove the float pin (A, **Figure 18**) by carefully driving it out of the posts.

3. Remove the float (B, **Figure 18**) and fuel inlet valve (**Figure 19**).

4. Remove the main jet (**Figure 12** and A, **Figure 20**).

5. Remove the nozzle (B, **Figure 20**) from the carburetor column by carefully inserting a screwdriver into the carburetor throat and pushing the nozzle down and out.

6. Remove the idle mixture screw and spring (4, **Figure 17**).

7. Remove the idle jet plug (**Figure 21**) and idle jet (A, **Figure 22**).

8. Mark the throttle plate (**Figure 23**) so it may be reinstalled in its original position, then unscrew and remove the throttle plate.

9. Using a proper size pin punch, drive out the throttle shaft Welch plug (**Figure 24**) from the opposite side of the carburetor. Use care not to damage the throttle shaft bore.

10. Remove the snap ring (7, **Figure 17**) from the end of the throttle shaft.

11. Withdraw the throttle shaft and remove the shaft components.

12. Unscrew and remove the choke plate (A, **Figure 25**).

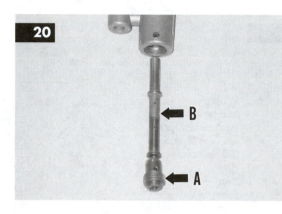

NOTE
The choke detent ball and spring will be free when the choke shaft is removed.

13. Remove the idle jet (**Figure 26**)..

14. Be prepared to remove the detent ball and spring (B, **Figure 27**) from the body, then remove the choke shaft assembly. When the shaft is pulled past the detent hole, the spring will push the ball into the choke shaft bore. Do not lose the ball or spring. Remove the felt seal, washer and E-ring from the choke shaft.

15. Pierce the Welch plug (B, **Figure 22**) on the top of the carburetor with a suitable tool, then pry out the plug.

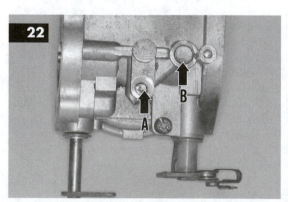

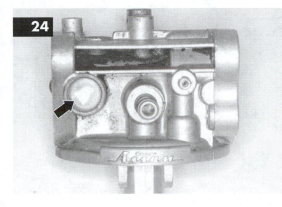

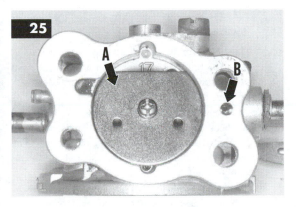

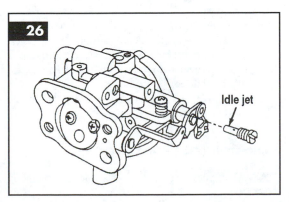

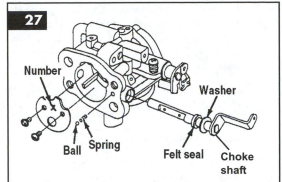

CAUTION
Do not damage the passage area behind the plug or the fuel-air mixture calibration will be altered.

Disassembly (MIKUNI Carburetor)

The differences between the Mikuni and the Aisan are:

Instead of a clip (7, **Figure 17**) on the end of the throttle shaft, Mikuni uses another shaft seal (8) and foam seal (9), with these two seals held in place by an exposed circular snap retainer.

The idle jet is screwed into the side of the carburetor (**Figure 26**) instead of being positioned on top of the carburetor.

The fixed main jet is screwed into the side of the column (**Figure 13**) instead of the center of the column. The Mikuni solenoid seat takes the place of the Aisan fixed main jet (**Figure 12** and **Figure 13**).

The Mikuni carburetor uses no Welch plugs.

To disassemble the carburetor:

1. Unscrew the fuel solenoid (A, **Figure 9**) and remove the fuel bowl (B) and gasket.

2. Remove the float pin by carefully pulling it out of the posts.

3. Remove the float and fuel inlet valve.

4. Unscrew and remove the solenoid seat (**Figure 12**).

5. Unscrew and remove the nozzle tube (B, **Figure 20**) from the carburetor column.

6. Remove the idle mixture screw and spring.

7. Note that the numbers on the throttle plate face out and down. Remove the throttle plate.

8. Remove the circular retainer from the end of the throttle shaft.

9. Withdraw the throttle shaft and remove the shaft components.

10. Unscrew and remove the choke plate (**Figure 27**).

NOTE
The choke detent ball and spring will be free when the choke shaft is removed.

11. Be prepared to remove the detent ball and spring (B, **Figure 25**) from the body, then remove the choke shaft assembly. When the shaft is pulled past the detent hole, the spring will push the ball into the choke shaft bore. Do not lose the ball or spring.

12. Remove the felt seal and washer from the choke shaft.

Cleaning and Inspection

> *CAUTION*
> *Do not dip any plastic or rubber carbure-tor parts into carburetor cleaner or other harsh solutions that can damage these parts.*

1. Inspect the carburetor and components.

> *CAUTION*
> *Do not use wire or drill bits to clean jets or passages. Even minor gouges in the jet can alter the fuel-flow rate and upset the air-fuel mixture.*

2. Inspect the tip of the idle mixture needle (**Figure 28**). Replace it if the tip is bent or grooved.

> *NOTE*
> *The tapered tip of the idle mixture adjust-ing needle is machined to precision di-mensions. If the needle is forced into its bottomed position, it will be damaged as shown in **Figure 29**. If this happens, the carburetor may need to be replaced, as the internal mixture passage is probably simi-larly damaged.*

3. Inspect the fuel inlet valve (**Figure 19**). Replace it if the tip is grooved.

4. Inspect the fuel valve seat (B, **Figure 12**):

   a. On an Aisan carburetor, the valve seat is not re-movable. Replace the carburetor body if the valve seat is worn or damaged.

   b. On a Mikuni carburetor, the seat is replaceable, but the seat retainer must be removed first.

5. To replace the Mikuni fuel valve seat:

   a. Take the Self-Threading Screw No. 93029 from the B&S Flywheel Puller Tool No. 19165.

   b. Thread the screw into the seat retainer approxi-mately four turns (**Figure 30**).

   c. Remove the screw from the retainer.

   d. Thread a 1/4-20 nut onto the screw followed by a flat washer.

   e. Position a 1/4-inch drive, 3/8-inch or 9 mm socket over the seat retainer so the socket hex is against

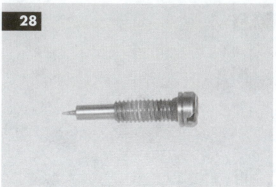

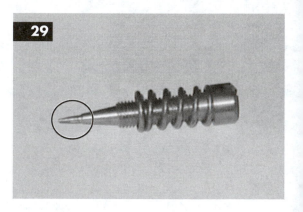

the retainer bore flange, straddling the retainer (**Figure 31**).

   f. Thread the screw into the retainer.

   h. Hold the bolt head stationary and thread the nut against the socket until the retainer pulls out.

   i. Remove the fuel valve seat.

6. Install the throttle and choke shafts in the carburetor body and check for excessive play between the shaft and body. Play must not exceed 0.25 mm (0.010 in.). The body must be replaced if there is excessive play as bush-ings are not available.

7. To test the fuel shutoff solenoid, proceed as follows:

   a. Connect one terminal of a 12-volt battery to the so-lenoid case.

   b. Momentarily connect and disconnect the other bat-tery terminal to the solenoid terminal a few times. The solenoid should audibly click and the plunger should extend and retract each time voltage is ap-plied and disconnected.

   c. If the solenoid does not operate, it is faulty and must be replaced.

Reassembly (AISAN Carburetor)

Always use new gaskets and seals when reassembling the carburetor.

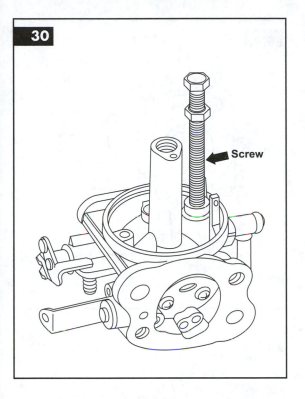

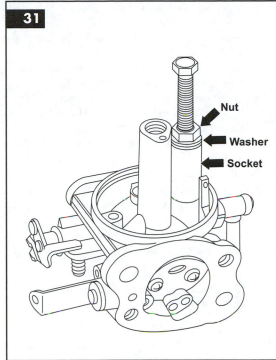

Refer to **Figure 17** when performing the following procedure:

1. Make sure that all fastener threads, threaded holes and Welch plug bores are clean and dry.

2. Install the idle mixture adjusting screw and spring (4). The initial setting of the idle mixture screw is 1 1/4 turns out from a *lightly bottomed* position.

> *NOTE*
> *If the idle mixture adjusting needle is forced into its bottomed position, it will be damaged (**Figure 29**). If this happens, the carburetor may need to be replaced, as the internal mixture passage is probably similarly damaged.*

3. If the idle mixture screw requires a limiter cap, do not install the cap until after the final adjustment has been made.

4. Install the choke shaft as follows:

a. Position the carburetor body (17) on the workbench with the manifold mounting flange down.

b. Install the E-ring (13) onto the groove of the shaft, followed by the washer and felt seal (15, 16).

c. Install the detent spring (14) into the detent hole, followed by the detent ball.

d. Use a small pin punch through the detent hole to press down on the ball while inserting the choke shaft (12) into the body. The flat choke-plate

mount area on the shaft must face out (away from the ball and spring) during shaft installation.

e. When the shaft contacts the punch, slowly remove the punch while continuing to feed the shaft through the body bore.

f. When the shaft is in position, rotate it to make sure the detent works properly.

5. Install the choke plate:

a. Lightly coat the choke plate screw threads with Loctite 222 or equivalent.

b. Install the choke plate (18) onto the shaft. The flat cutout must be at the top, and the alignment dimples must be in (**Figure 25**).

c. Install the screw finger-tight.

d. Close the choke to align the plate in the bore.

e. Tighten the choke plate screw.

f. Make sure that the choke shaft works freely. Realign, if necessary.

6. Install the throttle shaft seal (8) so the lip faces out.

7. Install the throttle shaft (11):

a. Lightly coat the throttle plate screw threads with Loctite 222 or equivalent.

b. Assemble the spacer (10) and foam seal (9) onto the shaft as shown.

c. Install the throttle shaft into the carburetor body.

d. If the idle speed screw and spring (5) were not removed for service, unscrew the idle speed screw exactly two turns so the throttle plate can be closed completely to align it with the bore.

10

e. Make sure that the beveled edges of the throttle plate (6) match the angle of the bore and that the disassembly marks align. Attach the plate to the shaft.

f. Work the shaft back and forth a few times to ensure free movement. Realign, if necessary.

g. Screw the idle speed screw to its original position to initially set the idle speed. The throttle plate should appear as in **Figure 23**.

h. Install the snap ring onto the end of the throttle shaft.

8. Install and measure the float:

a. Install the float valve (19) onto the float (22).

b. With the carburetor inverted, place the valve into the seat and position the float so the float hinge pin holes align with the body holes.

c. Install the hinge pin (23).

NOTE
The float pin is a drive fit. Exercise care when installing the pin.

d. Make sure that the float has freedom of movement.

e. Hold the carburetor hinge-pin up, float vertical (**Figure 32**), with the float arm just barely pressing the float valve against the seat. The bottom of the float should be parallel with the bowl gasket surface. If the float height is not correct, carefully bend the float tab (**Figure 33**) to adjust the float height.

9. Install the nozzle (B, **Figure 20**) into the carburetor column, followed by the main jet (A). Screw the main jet snugly against the nozzle (**Figure 12**) but do not overtighten.

10. Install the fuel bowl gasket and bowl (6). Position the bowl nut gasket (10) over the bowl. Tighten the screw (11) or solenoid (12) to 5.1-6.2 N·m (45-55 in.-lb.).

11. Install the idle jet (A, **Figure 22**) followed by the washer and plug (**Figure 21**).

12. Install the Welch plugs:

a. Using a flat-tipped pin punch with approximately the same diameter as the plug (**Figure 34**), carefully *flatten* the plug, but do not cave the plug in.

b. Apply a glyptol sealant or fingernail polish to the plug-to-carburetor seams. Permit the sealant to dry before proceeding.

Reassembly (MIKUNI Carburetor)

Always use new gaskets and seals when reassembling the carburetor.

Unless other figures are specified, refer to **Figure 17** when performing the following procedure. Instead of a clip (7) on the end of the throttle shaft, Mikuni uses another shaft seal (8) and foam seal (9), with these two seals

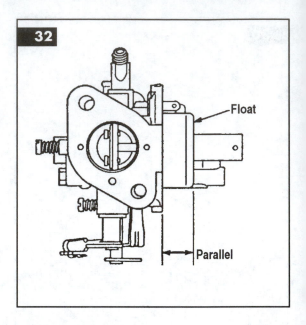

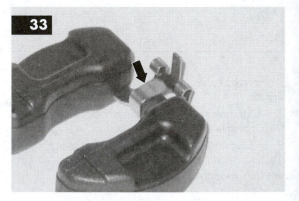

held in place by a circular retainer. The plug, washer and idle jet (1-3) are not used.

1. Make sure that all fastener threads and threaded holes are clean and dry.

2. If replacing the float valve seat:

a. Install the new seat with the inner recess out and the outer chamfer toward the carburetor body (**Figure 35**).

b. Use Tool No. 19135 to press the new seat retainer into the seat bore.

CAUTION
*If the idle mixture adjusting needle is forced into its bottomed position, it will be damaged (**Figure 29**). If this happens, the carburetor may need to be replaced, as the internal mixture passage is probably similarly damaged.*

3. Install the idle mixture adjusting screw and spring (4). The initial setting of the idle mixture screw is 1 1/4 turns

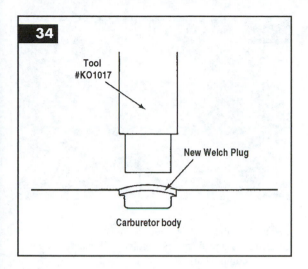

34

Tool
#KO1017

New Welch Plug

Carburetor body

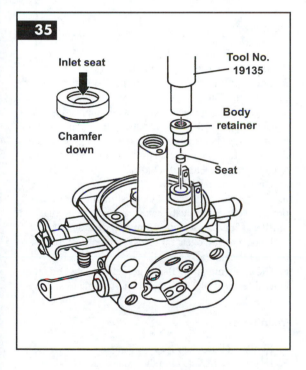

35

Inlet seat

Tool No.
19135

Chamfer
down

Body
retainer

Seat

out from a *lightly bottomed* position. If the idle mixture screw requires a limiter cap, do not install the cap until after the final adjustment has been made.

4. Install the choke shaft as follows:

   a. Position the carburetor body (17) on the workbench with the manifold mounting flange down.

   b. Install the washer and felt seal (15, 16) onto the choke shaft.

   c. Install the detent spring (14) into the detent hole, followed by the detent ball.

   d. Use a small pin punch through the detent hole to press down on the ball while inserting the choke

shaft (12) into the body. The flat choke-plate mount area on the shaft must face out (away from the ball and spring) while installing the shaft.

   e. When the shaft contacts the punch, slowly remove the punch while continuing to feed the shaft through the body bore.

   f. When the shaft is in position, rotate it to make sure the detent works properly.

5. Install the choke plate:

   a. Lightly coat the choke plate screw threads with Loctite 222 or equivalent.

   b. Install the choke plate (18) onto the shaft. The cutout must be at the top with the number facing out (**Figure 27**).

   c. Install the screws finger-tight.

   d. Close the choke to align the plate in the bore.

   e. Tighten the choke plate screws.

   f. Make sure that the choke shaft works freely. Realign, if necessary.

6. Install the throttle shaft seals (8) so the lips face out.

7. Install the throttle shaft (11):

   a. Lightly coat the throttle plate screw threads with Loctite 222 or equivalent.

   b. Assemble the spacer (10) and foam seal (9) onto the shaft as shown.

   c. Install the throttle shaft into the carburetor body.

   d. If the idle speed screw and spring (5) were not removed for service, unscrew the idle speed screw exactly two turns so the throttle plate can be closed completely to align it with the bore.

   e. Be sure that the beveled edges of the throttle plate (6) match the angle of the bore and that the numbers on the plate are down. Screw the plate to the shaft.

   f. Work the shaft back and forth a few times to ensure free movement. Realign, if necessary.

   g. Screw the idle speed screw to its original position to initially set the idle speed.

   h. Install the foam seal and circular retainer onto the end of the throttle shaft.

8. Install and measure the float:

   a. Install the float valve (19) onto the float (22).

   b. With the carburetor inverted, place the valve into the seat and position the float so the float hinge pin holes align with the body holes.

   c. Install the hinge pin (23).

NOTE
One end of the float pin is larger than the other. The larger end should be toward the choke side of the carburetor.

   d. Make sure that the float has freedom of movement.

   e. The float height is not adjustable. With the carburetor inverted and the float lightly resting on the float valve, the bottom of the float should be parallel or nearly parallel with the bowl gasket surface.

10

The float should not contact the carburetor body. If a major variation exists, check the float arm, float valve and seat. If the seat was replaced, make sure the position is correct. If necessary, replace the float.

10. Screw the nozzle tube (**Figure 13**) into the carburetor column, followed by the solenoid seat.

11. Screw the fixed main jet into the side of the column.

12. Install the fuel bowl gasket and bowl (6). Position the bowl nut gasket (10) over the bowl. Tighten the screw (11) or solenoid (12) to 5.1-6.2 N·m (45-55 in.-lb.).

13. Install the idle jet (A, **Figure 21**) followed by the washer and plug (**Figure 20**).

Installation

1. Lightly coat the carburetor mounting bolt threads with Loctite 242 or equivalent.

2. Install the bolts through the carburetor.

3. Position a new gasket onto the carburetor bolts.

4. Install the carburetor onto the manifold, then tighten the carburetor mounting screws to 7.0 N·m (62 in.-lb.).

5. Reconnect the throttle control link, clip and spring to the throttle lever (**Figure 15**). Check the linkage for freedom of movement.

6. Install a new fuel hose and clamps between the fuel pump and carburetor.

7. Reconnect the choke control rod and reinstall the choke control bracket (B, **Figure 14**).

8. Install the air filter base bracket (A, **Figure 14**).

9. Using a new gasket (11, **Figure 8**), mount the air filter base to the carburetor and bracket. Tighten the mount bolts to 7.0 N•m (65 in.-lb.).

10. Install the air filter elements and cover.

11. Reconnect and clamp the crankcase breather hose to the air filter base.

12. Turn the fuel tank valve ON and check for leaks.

13. Reconnect the negative battery lead to the battery.

14. Reset the static governor adjustment as described under *GOVERNOR, External Adjustment* in this chapter.

15. Start the engine and adjust the carburetor as described in the previous *Adjustment* section.

MUFFLER

The muffler is calibrated as part of the emission control system. It not only reduces exhaust noise to acceptable levels, but it also provides the proper amount of back pressure to allow the inlet and combustion components to produce rated horsepower as well as compliant emission levels.

For this reason, the exhaust system should be maintained in good repair. As the noise level increases, power decreases. Under no circumstances should the exhaust

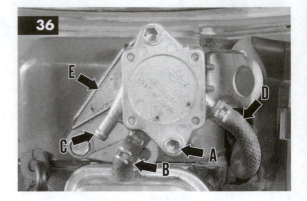

system be modified. Inspect the muffler, pipes, flanges, connections and fasteners regularly. Replace any questionable components.

Removal

1. Allow the unit to cool.

2. Remove the heat shield, if used.

3. Loosen all fasteners and clamps. Do not *remove* any fasteners until all of them have been loosened.

4. Begin removing the fasteners while supporting the exhaust system. Work from the outlet pipe inward. The nuts holding the exhaust pipe flange(s) to the engine should be the last fasteners removed, at which time the exhaust system can be removed and set aside.

5. Discard the gaskets.

6. Inspect the muffler and exhaust manifold for cracks, broken welds or indications of gas leakage. Replace the muffler if it is significantly damaged due to rust.

7. Inspect the brackets for cracks or breaks. Repair or replace as necessary.

8. Clean the mounting flange gasket surfaces and all fastener threads. Make sure the threads are clean and dry.

Installation

1. Replace all fastener lock washers.

2. Insert new gaskets onto the exhaust studs.

3. Align the exhaust system with all bracket and fastener holes, then install and hand-tighten the fasteners, beginning with the exhaust pipe flanges. Do not tighten any fasteners until all of them have been installed.

4. Beginning with the flanges, tighten all fasteners, working toward the outlet pipe.

5. Install the heat shield and spark arrestor, if used.

BLOWER HOUSING, SHROUDS AND BAFFLES

The fins on the cylinders and heads dissipate engine heat to the surrounding air. The flywheel fan creates a forced airflow to cool the engine. The blower housing on

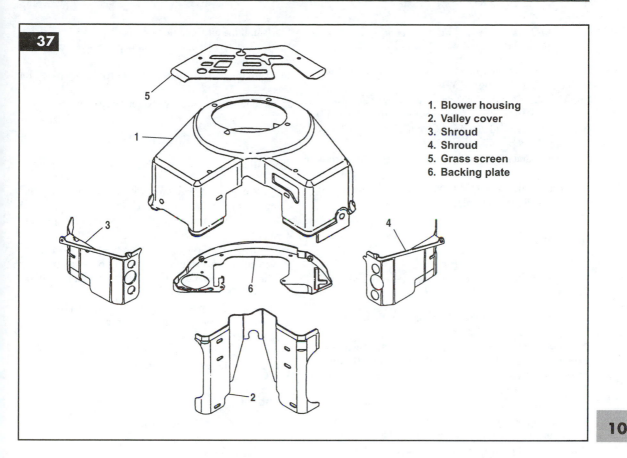

37

1. Blower housing
2. Valley cover
3. Shroud
4. Shroud
5. Grass screen
6. Backing plate

top of the engine and the shrouds around the cylinder heads direct the air over the cooling fins. Any time grass debris appears lodged where the blower housing or shrouds meet the engine, remove the housing and clean the cooling system.

Removal

CAUTION
*Remove the fuel pump before removing the blower housing. To prevent debris from entering the hoses or fittings, clean the hose fittings before disconnecting the hoses. When plugging hoses during service procedures, always use a straight-shank plug. **Never use a bolt to plug a hose.***

1. Refer to Steps 1-7 in the previous *Carburetor, Removal* section to remove the following:
   a. Air filter and base assembly.
   b. Air filter base mounting bracket.
   c. Choke control bracket.
2. Unplug and ground the spark plug leads.
3. If necessary, unclamp and disconnect the fuel tank-to-pump supply hose fitting (C, **Figure 36**).

WARNING
Some gasoline will drain from the fuel hose and/or the carburetor hose during this procedure. Wipe up any spilled gasoline immediately. Work in a well-ventilated area at least 50 feet from any open flame, including pilot lights in gas appliances. Do not allow anyone to smoke in the area. Do not work near grinding or other source of sparks.

4. Unbolt the fuel pump (A, **Figure 36**) from the blower housing bracket.
5. Unclamp and disconnect the breather pulse hose (B, **Figure 36**) from the No. 1 cylinder valve cover fitting. Carefully move the pump aside.
6. Remove the fuel pump mounting bracket (E, **Figure 36**) from the blower housing.
7. Remove the flywheel grass screen from the blower housing. Do not lose any of the four screen-to-fan spacers.
8. Unbolt and remove the blower housing (1, **Figure 37**).

NOTE
One of the blower housing bolts also holds the oil fill/dipstick tube to the engine. Be careful not to pull the tube from the crank-

case after removing the bolt, as oil spill-age could occur.

9. Unbolt and remove the shrouds for the No. 1 and No. 2 cylinders (3 and 4, **Figure 37**).

10. Unbolt and remove the valley cover (2, **Figure 37**).

11. If the blower housing backing plate (6, **Figure 37**) needs to be removed, the flywheel must be removed first. Refer to *Flywheel, Removal* in this chapter.

12. Clean and dry all fastener threads and mating threads.

13. Inspect all blower housing components for cracks and breaks. Repair or replace as necessary.

Installation

NOTE
Tighten all blower housing component fasteners to 7.0 N•m (65 in.-lb.).

1. If the blower housing backing plate (6, **Figure 37**) has been removed, install it first.

2. Follow the necessary steps in the subsequent *Flywheel, Installation* section and install the flywheel. Tighten the flywheel nut to 175 N•m (125 in.-lb.).

3. Install the valley cover (2, **Figure 37**).

   a. Position the valley cover between the cylinders.

   b. Reconnect the choke control rod and reinstall the choke control bracket (B, **Figure 14**).

   c. Install the air filter base bracket (A, **Figure 14**).

   d. Tighten all fasteners.

4. Install the No. 1 and No. 2 cylinder shrouds (3, 4, **Figure 37**).

5. Install the blower housing (1, **Figure 37**).

6. On engines without a rewind starter, install the flywheel grass screen (**Figure 37**). Make sure that the four spacers are properly positioned above the fan posts and inside the screen screw holes.

7. Install the fuel pump mounting bracket (E, **Figure 36**).

CAUTION
When reconnecting hoses to the pump, clean the hose fitting before reconnecting to prevent debris from entering the hoses or fittings. Always use new clamps.

8. Connect and clamp the breather pulse hose to the No. 1 cylinder valve cover fitting (B, **Figure 36**). Fasten the fuel pump (A, **Figure 36**) to the pump bracket. Tighten the pump-to-bracket screws.

9. Reconnect any disconnected fuel hoses to the pump. Refer to **Figure 36**:

   a. The hose from the tank connects to Fitting C.

   b. The carburetor feed hose connects to Fitting D.

10. Reconnect the spark plug leads.

11. Using a new air filter base gasket (11, **Figure 8**), mount the filter base to the carburetor and bracket.

12. Install the air filter elements and cover.

13. Reconnect and clamp the crankcase breather hose to the air filter base.

14. Turn the fuel tank valve on (**Figure 7**) and check for leaks.

15. Reconnect the negative battery lead to the battery.

FUEL PUMP

Operation

These engines are equipped with a diaphragm type fuel pump (A, **Figure 36**) mounted on the blower housing. A pulse hose (B) from the engine crankcase directs crankcase pulsations to the diaphragm in the fuel pump. Fuel enters the pump through the pump inlet (C). Diaphragm movement forces fuel through a pair of one-way valves to the fuel pump outlet, where the fuel is routed via the fuel hose (D) to the carburetor.

Specified fuel pump pressure is 1.5 psi (10.3 kPa). Connect a fuel pressure gauge to the fuel pump outlet hose to check fuel pressure.

Individual parts are not available for the fuel pump. Service the fuel pump as a unit assembly.

Removal

WARNING
Some gasoline will drain from the fuel hose and/or the carburetor hose during this procedure. Wipe up any spilled gasoline immediately. Work in a well-ventilated area at least 50 feet from any open flame, including pilot lights in gas appliances. Do not allow anyone to smoke in the area. Do not work near any grinding or other source of sparks.

CAUTION
*When disconnecting hoses from the pump, clean the hose fitting before disconnection to prevent debris from entering the hoses or fittings. When plugging hoses during service procedures, always use a straight-shank plug. **Never use a bolt to plug a hose.***

Refer to **Figure 36**.

1. Unplug and ground the spark plug leads.

2. Turn the fuel tank valve off (**Figure 4**).

2. Unclamp and disconnect the fuel tank-to-pump supply hose (Fitting C, hose removed).

3. Unclamp and disconnect the pump-to-carburetor hose (D).

4. Unbolt the fuel pump from the blower housing bracket.

5. Unclamp and disconnect the breather pulse hose (B) from the pump.

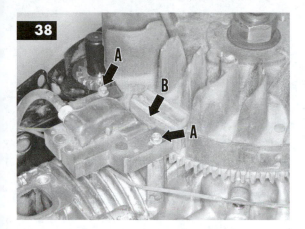

Installation

CAUTION
When reconnecting hoses to the pump,
clean the hose fitting before reconnection
to prevent debris from entering the hoses
or fittings.

1. Slide the pump pulse fitting into the pulse hose (B). Clamp the hose.
2. Bolt the pump to the blower housing bracket. Tighten the pump bolts to 7.0 N•m (65 in.-lb.).
3. Connect the carburetor feed hose to the pump (D).
4. Connect the fuel tank supply hose to the pump (C).
5. Turn the fuel tank valve on (**Figure 7**) and check for leaks.
6. Reconnect the spark plug leads.

IGNITION SYSTEM

The engine is equipped with a capacitor-discharge ignition system that uses two ignition modules. The ignition modules are located under the blower housing adjacent to the flywheel. The ignition switch grounds the modules to stop the engine. No periodic maintenance or adjustment is required for the ignition system other than setting the air gap for each module.

Spark Plugs

The recommended spark plug is Champion RC12YC, Autolite 3924 or equivalent. The recommended spark plug electrode gap is 0.75 mm (0.030 inch). Spark plug tightening torque is 20 N•m (180 in.-lb. or 15 ft.-lb.).

CAUTION
Do not use the abrasive-blast
(sand-blast) method to clean spark plugs.
This method causes abrasive grit to lodge
in the upper gap between the insulator

and the shell. During engine operation the plug heats and expands, and the grit then falls into the cylinder and combustion chamber area, causing rapid internal wear and damage.

Module-to-Flywheel Air Gap Adjustment

The air gap between the ignition module and the flywheel should be 0.20-0.31 mm (0.008-0.012 inch). If the ignition module has been removed or its position disturbed, use the following procedure to set the air gap between the ignition module and flywheel.
1. Remove the blower housing as outlined in Steps 1-8 in the previous *Blower Housing, Removal* section.
2. Disconnect the spark plug lead and turn the flywheel so that the magnets are not next to the ignition module.
3. Loosen the module retaining screws (A, **Figure 38**).
4. Extend the module to the limits allowed by the adjustment slots, then lightly tighten one screw to temporarily hold the module away from the flywheel.
5. Rotate the flywheel to center the magnets directly under the module legs.
6. Place a 0.25 mm (0.010 in.) plastic or brass flat feeler gauge between the flywheel and the ignition module armature legs.
7. Loosen the module screw, allowing the magnets to draw the module to the flywheel. While holding the module snugly against the flywheel, tighten the module screws to 3.0 N•m (25 in.-lb.).
8. Rotate the flywheel and remove the gauge.
9. Reconnect the spark plug lead.
10. Install the blower housing by following the applicable steps under *Blower Housing, Installation*.

Module Testing

1. To check spark, remove the spark plugs.
2. Connect each spark plug cable to a suitable ignition spark tester, such as Briggs & Stratton Tester No. 19051 or 19368. Be sure each tester is properly grounded. Follow the instructions included with the tester.
3. Operate the starter so the engine rotates at 350 rpm or more. On rewind-start engines, make sure the ignition switch is on. If sparks jump the tester gaps, the system is functioning properly.
4. If one or both testers produce little or no spark:
   a. Set the module air gap on the offending module by following the instructions in the preceding section.
   b. Disconnect the kill wire on the non-sparking module(s).
   c. Retest for spark.

10

5A. If Step 4 still produced no spark, the module is faulty and must be replaced.

5B. If Step 4 produced spark, the kill wire assembly is probably faulty.

Kill wire harness

The kill wire harness assembly contains two diodes, one in each kill wire (**Figure 39**), to prevent cross-firing between the two modules.

1. With the harness in the circuit and connected to both modules, kill wire harness faults will be displayed as one of the following:

    a. The engine will not start due to no spark from either module.

    b. The engine only runs on one cylinder.

    c. The engine kills one cylinder when the switch is turned off.

    d. The engine continues to run on both cylinders with the switch off.

2. If both modules test OK but the engine displays any of these symptoms, test the kill wire harness:

    a. Disconnect the harness terminals from the modules and the kill wire connector.

    b. Test one kill wire by attaching ohmmeter probes to the wire ends. Note the reading.

    c. Reverse the ohmmeter probes and again note the meter reading.

    d. The reading in one direction should read approximately 20 ohms; the other direction should read infinity.

3. Repeat Step 2 with the other kill wire.

4. If either wire fails its test, the harness is faulty and must be replaced.

> *NOTE*
> *Early models had individual module kill wires going to a ground terminal assembly (**Figure 40**) that was mounted on the outer shroud of the No. 1 cylinder, near the electric starter motor. The test procedure is the same, going from the stop switch wire terminal to one armature ground wire terminal at a time.*

Module Removal

1. Disconnect the applicable spark plug wire.

2. Remove the blower housing as described in the previous *Blower Housing, Removal* section.

3. Disconnect the ignition module kill wire.

4. Unscrew the module mounting screws (A, **Figure 38**), then remove the ignition module.

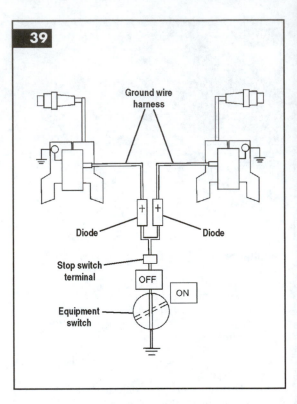

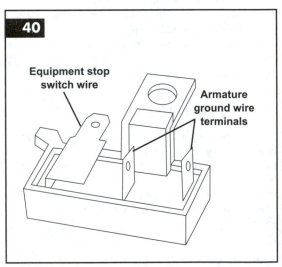

Module Installation

1. Rotate the flywheel so the magnet is away from the module mounting position.

2. Set the module in position on the cylinder posts.

3. Loosely install the module retaining screws (A, **Figure 38**).

4. Adjust the air gap between the module and the flywheel magnets as described in the *Module-to-Flywheel Air Gap Adjustment* section.

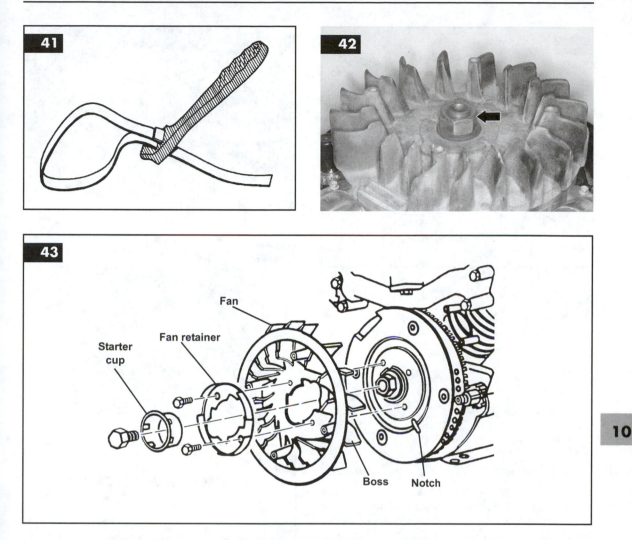

41

42

43

Fan

Fan retainer

Starter
cup

Boss   Notch

10

5. Reconnect the spark plug lead.

6. Install the blower housing by following the applicable steps under *Blower Housing, Installation*.

FLYWHEEL

Removal

The flywheel is secured to the crankshaft by a retaining nut. To remove the flywheel, proceed as follows:

1. Disconnect the spark plug wires from both spark plugs and properly ground the spark plug wire ends to the engine.

2. Remove the blower housing as described in this chapter.

3. Remove the ignition modules as described in this chapter.

4. On Series 303700, hold the flywheel using a strap wrench (**Figure 41**), then unscrew the flywheel retaining nut (**Figure 42**).

CAUTION
Do not use a bar or wedge in the fan blades or ring gear teeth to hold the flywheel. Doing so could damage the flywheel or engine block.

NOTE
*Not shown in **Figure 42** is the starter cup on engines equipped with a rewind starter. The typical starter cup is shown in the **Figure 43** exploded view. On Series 303700 engines, the flywheel nut secures the cup and the fan is not removable. On Series 350700 engines, the cup is held onto an elongated flywheel nut by the bolt shown in **Figure 43**.*

5. On Series 350700, hold the flywheel using B&S flywheel holder tool No. 19321 as shown in **Figure 44**, then unscrew the flywheel retaining nut.

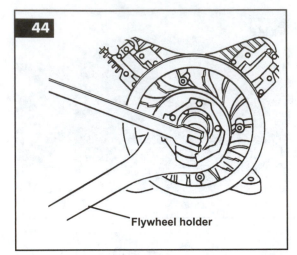

44

Flywheel holder

45

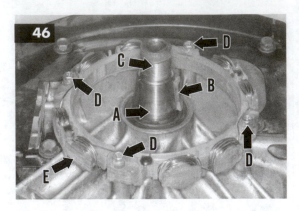

46

47

6. Install a flywheel puller as shown in **Figure 45** so the puller screws engage the two holes adjacent to the flywheel hub.

WARNING
Do not strike the flywheel. The flywheel must be replaced if the flywheel is cracked or any fins are damaged.

CAUTION
Do not use a "flywheel knocker" to break the flywheel loose from the crankshaft. The tool can damage the crankshaft and internal engine parts.

7. Rotate the puller screws evenly until the flywheel "pops" free. When the flywheel breaks loose from the crankshaft, *carefully* lift the flywheel straight up off the crankshaft so as not to damage the stator magnets under the flywheel.

8. Remove the flywheel key (B, **Figure 46**).

9. If additional engine work is planned, it is a good practice to wrap the crankshaft threads with tape to prevent damage to the threads.

48

STARTER DRIVE ASSEMBLY

1. **Bendix clutch**
2. **Retaining ring**
3. **Pinion retainer assembly**
4. **Pinion for aluminum or steel ring gear**
5. **Pinion for plastic composite ring gear**

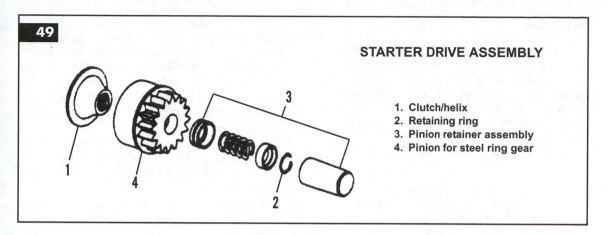

49

STARTER DRIVE ASSEMBLY

1. Clutch/helix
2. Retaining ring
3. Pinion retainer assembly
4. Pinion for steel ring gear

10. On Series 350700, remove the fan and retainer as shown in **Figure 43**.

Inspection

1. Thoroughly clean the flywheel, removing all dust and dirt from both the top and bottom of the flywheel, especially around the magnets.

2. Inspect the flywheel casting for cracks or damage. A cracked or damaged flywheel must be replaced.

3. Inspect the integrity of the inner ring of stator magnets and the outer ignition module magnet (**Figure 47**).

> *WARNING*
> *The magnets are not removable or serviceable. Do not attempt to reattach or tighten any loose magnet. If any magnet is loose or damaged, replace the flywheel.*

4. Inspect the starter ring gear. Remove any debris stuck between the teeth. Light nicks or scratches may be dressed. Damaged teeth will require replacement of the ring gear, if the ring gear is either plastic composite or aluminum alloy. Refer to the following section for ring gear replacement.

> *NOTE*
> *Steel ring gears are not replaceable. A damaged steel ring gear will require replacement of the flywheel assembly.*

5. Inspect the electric starter pinion gear. A steel flywheel ring gear requires a steel pinion; a plastic composite or aluminum alloy ring gear requires a plastic/fiber pinion. **Figure 48** shows a late model starter drive assembly for plastic composite, aluminum alloy or steel ring gears. Pinion A, made of plastic/fiber should be used with aluminum ring gears. Pinion A with a plastic/fiber hub helix and steel teeth should be used with steel ring gears. Pinion B should be used with plastic ring gears. **Figure 49**

shows the pinion and Bendix assembly on starters used exclusively with steel ring gears.

6. Inspect the tapers and keyways of both the crankshaft (A, **Figure 46**) and the flywheel (**Figure 47**). The tapered portion of the flywheel and crankshaft must be clean and smooth with no damage due to movement between the flywheel and crankshaft. A damaged flywheel keyway will require replacement of the flywheel. A damaged crankshaft keyway will require crankshaft replacement.

7. Inspect the flywheel key. Replace if questionable. Use only the correct Briggs & Stratton key. The key is made of aluminum to prevent or lessen the possibility of crankshaft or flywheel damage if the crankshaft is abruptly stopped. *Do not use* a steel key.

Ring Gear Replacement

Steel ring gears are not replaceable. A damaged steel ring gear will require replacement of the flywheel assembly.

The replacement ring gear for either a plastic or aluminum gear will be aluminum. Replace this gear as follows:

1. Mark the center of each rivet head in the ring gear (**Figure 47**) with a center punch.

2. Use a 6 mm (1/4-inch) drill bit to drill out the rivet heads. Remove *only* the heads.

3. Drive the rivets out of the flywheel with a long-shank 4.7 mm (3/16-in.) pin punch.

4. Remove the old ring gear.

5. Clean all rust and dirt from the ring gear mounting surface of the flywheel.

6. Using an 82° countersink bit, countersink the recessed replacement ring gear holes to a head diameter of 9.5 mm (3/8 inch).

7. Position the new ring gear onto the flywheel, aligning the screw holes.

8. Lightly coat the ring gear screw threads with Loctite 242 or equivalent.

9. Using the lock nuts provided with the replacement ring gear, install and tighten the screws and nuts.

10

Installation

1. Make sure that the matching tapers on the crankshaft (**Figure 46**) and inside the flywheel (**Figure 47**), as well as the crankshaft and bolt threads, are *clean and dry*. Ensure no metallic debris has stuck to any of the magnets.
2. Carefully lower the flywheel straight down onto the crankshaft, aligning the crankshaft keyway with the flywheel keyway.
3. Install the flywheel key.

> *NOTE*
> *Use only the correct Briggs & Stratton key. The key is made of aluminum to prevent or lessen the possibility of crankshaft or flywheel damage if the crankshaft is abruptly stopped. Do not use a steel key.*

4. On rewind-start units, position the starter cup over the flywheel.
5. With the flat washer in position on the crankshaft thread, install the nut onto the crankshaft.
6. On Series 303700, hold the flywheel using a strap wrench (**Figure 41**), then tighten the flywheel retaining nut (**Figure 42**) to 175 N•m (125 ft.-lb.).

> *CAUTION*
> *Do not use a bar or wedge in the fan blades or ring gear teeth to hold the flywheel. Doing so could damage the flywheel or engine block.*

7. On Series 350700:
   a. Install the fan and fan retainer (**Figure 43**). Make sure the fan boss is aligned with the flywheel notch. Tighten the retainer bolts to 17 N•m (150 in.-lb.).
   b. Hold the flywheel using the B&S Flywheel Holder Tool No. 19321 as shown in **Figure 44**, then tighten the flywheel retaining nut to 175 N•m (125 ft.-lb.).
8. Install the ignition modules as described in the previous *Module Installation* section.
9. Install the blower housing as outlined in the previous *Blower Housing, Installation* section.
10. Reconnect both spark plug leads.

ALTERNATOR/CHARGING SYSTEM

Figure 46 shows the alternator stator, which mounts under the flywheel. The stator connects to the rectifier-regulator, which mounts onto the side of the blower housing.

Operation

If the alternator is functioning correctly, current is produced whenever the flywheel rotates. The stator produces AC and the rectifier-regulator changes the AC to DC while controlling the amount of DC based on the battery state-of-charge and/or the demands of the chassis electrical system. There are no adjustments possible to the system.

For the system to perform properly and to avoid damage to the charging system, observe the following precautions:

1. Prevent possible grounding of the AC lead(s).
2. The negative post of the battery must be connected to the engine ground and correct battery polarity must be observed at all times.
3. The rectifier-regulator must be connected in common ground with the engine and with the battery on electric-start units.
4. Disconnect the leads at the rectifier-regulator and the battery if electric welding is to be done on equipment in common ground with the engine.
5. Remove the battery or disconnect the battery cables when recharging the battery with an external battery charger.
6. Do not operate the engine with the battery disconnected.

Stator Testing (Rewind-start units)

> *CAUTION*
> *The mower blades will be engaged during this test. Use all necessary precautions to prevent injury.*

1. Disconnect the green connector from the regulator/rectifier lead.
2. Connect one lead of an AC voltmeter to the stator lead; connect the other voltmeter lead to engine ground.
3. Start the engine and run it at 3600 rpm. The voltmeter should indicate 40V AC.
4. Replace the alternator stator if the voltage is less than the specified voltage.

Regulator Testing (Rewind-start units)

> *CAUTION*
> *The mower blades will be engaged during this test. Use all necessary precautions to prevent injury.*

1. Make sure the stator is producing the correct output.
2. Unplug the red regulator output connector from the chassis harness.
3. Connect the positive lead of a minimum 10-Amp DC test meter to the red regulator output terminal.
4. Connect the negative ammeter test lead to the chassis harness terminal.

CAUTION
Make sure the ammeter test leads cannot touch ground.

5. Start the engine, and allow it to reach normal operating temperature.

6. Engage the PTO switch, then bring the engine up to full throttle (3600 rpm).

7. Note the meter reading. The meter should show 3-9 Amps.

8. If the meter read less than 3 Amps or if the blades did not engage when the PTO switch was activated:

   a. Disengage the PTO switch, stop the engine and disconnect the test equipment.

   b. Test the chassis wiring for continuity between the regulator and the PTO switch and between the PTO switch and the blade clutch.

   c. Refer to Chapter 14 and test the blade clutch and the PTO switch for continuity.

   d. If substeps 8b and 8c met specification, the regulator is faulty and must be replaced.

Stator testing (Electric-start units)

1. Disconnect the yellow connector from the regulator/rectifier lead.

2. Connect the leads of an AC voltmeter to the two black-wire terminals inside the yellow connector.

3. Run the engine at 3600 rpm. The voltmeter should indicate 30V AC.

4. Replace the alternator stator if the voltage is less than the specified voltage.

Regulator Testing (Electric-start units)

1. Make sure the stator is producing the correct output.

2. Unplug the red regulator output connector from the chassis harness.

3. Connect the positive lead of a minimum 10-Amp DC test meter to the red regulator output terminal.

4. Connect the negative ammeter test lead to the chassis harness terminal.

CAUTION
Make sure the ammeter test leads cannot touch ground.

5. Start the engine and allow it to warm up briefly. Run the engine at 3600 rpm.

6. Note the meter reading. The meter should show 3-16 Amps. The output will depend on the state-of-charge of the battery. The battery *must* have a minimum charge of 5 volts to energize the regulator.

7. Slow the engine and engage the PTO switch, then bring the engine up to full speed again.

8. Note the meter reading. The meter should again show 3-16 Amps, with more output than Step 6 due to the blade clutch requirements.

9. If preceding test Steps 6 and 8 failed to meet specification, the regulator is faulty and must be replaced.

10. Disengage the PTO switch, stop the engine and disconnect the test equipment.

Stator Removal

1. Remove the blower housing as outlined previously in this chapter.

2. Remove the flywheel as described previously in this chapter.

3. Disconnect the alternator stator wire from the regulator. Note the orientation and position of the wire.

4. On electric-start units, remove the starter motor.

5. Remove the alternator stator retaining screws (**Figure 46**), then remove the stator.

Stator Installation

1. Noting the orientation and position of the stator harness wire from the disassembly procedure, position the stator onto the mounting posts.

2. Lightly coat the stator mounting screw threads with Loctite 222 or equivalent. Install the screws (**Figure 46**). Tighten the screws to 2.0 N•m (20 in.-lb.).

3. Install the flywheel as outlined in the preceding *Flywheel, Installation* section.

4. Install the blower housing as instructed in the previous *Blower Housing, Installation* section.

5. On electric-start units, install the starter motor.

   a. Use care not to pinch or kink the stator wires that run behind the starter.

   b. Due to the starter location, bolt installation is made easier by using a 13 mm, 12-point, 1/4-inch drive swivel socket. This socket is available from B&S as Tool No. 19353.

   c. Tighten the starter bolts to 16.0 N•m (140 in.-lb.).

ELECTRIC STARTER MOTOR AND SOLENOID

In this section, "starter" refers to the electric starter motor assembly. Unless otherwise noted, starter component descriptions will refer to **Figure 50** for starters used with plastic composite, aluminum alloy or steel flywheel ring gears and **Figure 51** for starters used only with steel ring gears.

Starter Operation

1. When voltage is applied to the starter through the brushes and ground, the armature rotates.

10

50 **ELECTRIC STARTER MOTOR**

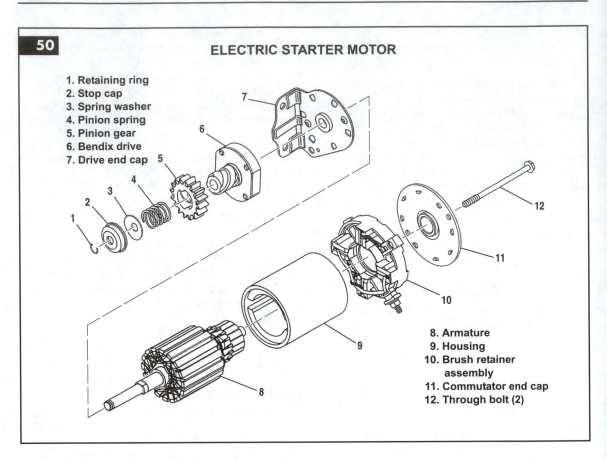

1. Retaining ring
2. Stop cap
3. Spring washer
4. Pinion spring
5. Pinion gear
6. Bendix drive
7. Drive end cap

8. Armature
9. Housing
10. Brush retainer assembly
11. Commutator end cap
12. Through bolt (2)

2. As the armature spins, centrifugal force causes the drive pinion to travel up the helical splines, meshing with the flywheel ring gear teeth.

3. When the drive pinion reaches the end of the armature shaft splines, it turns the flywheel and cranks the engine.

4. When the engine starts, the increased flywheel speed turns the drive pinion faster than the starter is spinning, causing the pinion to travel back down the armature shaft splines.

5. When 12 volts is cut off from the starter, the armature stops and the anti-drift spring holds the pinion away from the ring gear until power is again applied to the starter.

Starter Precautions

1. Do not operate the starter continuously for more than 10 seconds. If the engine does not start, allow at least a 60-second cooling period between each 10-second operational period. Failure to allow sufficient cool-down time will burn out the starter.

2. Do not activate the starter while the engine is already turning. Engaging the starter into a rotating flywheel will damage the starter and the flywheel.

3. If the engine does not crank when the starter is engaged and the pinion contacts the ring gear, disengage the

starter immediately. Correct the engine problem prior to attempting a restart. Do not attempt to overcome the problem by jump-starting with a larger battery. Serious starter damage will result.

4. To avoid damage to the permanent magnets inside the starter frame housing, do not:
   a. Drop the starter.
   b. Strike the starter frame.
   c. Clamp the starter frame in a vise.

Starter Troubleshooting

Starter fails to energize

Check the following:

1. Battery. Check the voltage and the specific gravity of the electrolyte. Recharge or replace the battery as necessary.

2. Wiring.
   a. Check for corroded or loose battery or solenoid connections. Clean or tighten as necessary. Soaking the corroded terminal in a baking soda and water solution is the best cleaning method. Do not allow any solution to get into any of the cells, as it will neutralize the electrolyte. Coat the clean con-

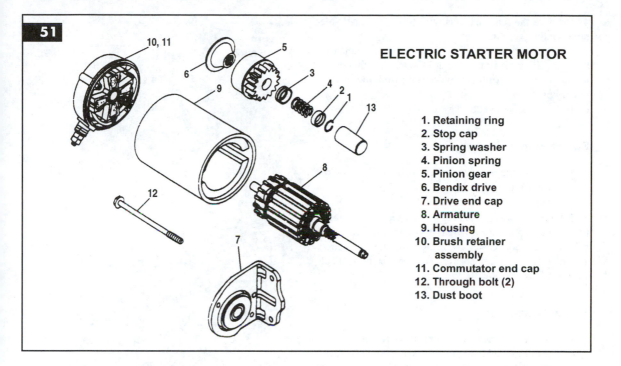

51

ELECTRIC STARTER MOTOR

1. Retaining ring
2. Stop cap
3. Spring washer
4. Pinion spring
5. Pinion gear
6. Bendix drive
7. Drive end cap
8. Armature
9. Housing
10. Brush retainer
    assembly
11. Commutator end cap
12. Through bolt (2)
13. Dust boot

nections with NoCo NCP-2 or equivalent to prevent further corrosion.

b. Replace any frayed wires or wires with disintegrated terminals.

c. Check for corroded or rusted ground connections on the equipment chassis. Remove the rust and treat the connection with NoCo or equivalent.

3. Solenoid. Use a jumper cable across the two large solenoid terminals to momentarily bypass the solenoid. If the starter energizes, the fault is in either the solenoid or the wiring to the solenoid. The *Solenoid Testing* section follows this *Starter Troubleshooting* section.

4. Starter components.

a. Check the brushes. Dirty or worn brushes and/or commutator will slow a starter.

b. Check the armature commutator. The commutator is an integral part of the armature. Cracked, chipped, broken, or badly grooved commutator sections are not repairable. In these cases, the armature will need replacement. Dirty or rough commutators should be cleaned with a suitable solvent, then lightly sanded with ScotchBrite or crocus cloth.

c. Check the armature shaft and bearings. A worn shaft or bearings will allow the armature laminations to rub against the frame magnets, causing drag. Replace faulty components.

Starter energizes but turns slowly

Check the following:

1. Battery. Check the voltage and the specific gravity of the electrolyte. Recharge or replace the battery as necessary.

2. Parasitic load on the engine. Attempting to start an engine that is connected to a hydrostatic drive system places an additional load on the starter motor, especially in cooler temperatures. If possible, disconnect the load from the engine and retry the starter. If the starter now turns the engine properly, check the hydrostatic system to find the reason for the excessive load.

3. Internal load on the engine.

a. Dirty, thick crankcase oil past its change schedule will cause slow turnover.

b. Scored or galled internal engine components such as bearing journals, pistons and cylinders will overload the starter.

4. Starter components. (Same checks as Step 4 in the preceding *Starter fails to energize* section.)

Solenoid Testing

The solenoid is not serviceable and must be replaced if faulty. Troubleshooting a solenoid can usually be done quickly with the solenoid on the starter.

To troubleshoot the solenoid:

1. Remove the ignition key from the switch so the engine does not start.

2. Ensure that the unit is in neutral and that the parking brake is set.

3. Place the throttle control in the SLOW position.

10

4. Remove the main harness wire from the small solenoid winding terminal.

5. Using a short jumper wire, connect one end of the wire to the small terminal; momentarily touch the other end to the large terminal of the cable coming from the positive battery post.

6. If the starter activates, the solenoid is OK.

Starter Removal

1. Disconnect the negative battery cable and secure the cable away from the battery.

2. Disconnect the starter cable.

3. Remove the bolts holding the starter to the engine, then remove the starter. Due to the starter location, bolt removal is made easier by using a 13 mm, 12-point, 1/4-inch drive swivel socket. This socket is available from B&S as Tool No. 19353.

Starter Disassembly

Starter component descriptions listed in this section will refer to **Figure 50** for starters used with plastic composite, aluminum alloy or steel flywheel ring gears and **Figure 51** for starters used only with steel ring gears. The spiral helix for the pinion gear in **Figure 50** is on the Bendix drive; on the **Figure 51** starter, it is part of the armature shaft (**Figure 53**). Depending on the problem, the starter motor can be either partially or completely disassembled. It is not necessary to remove the drive assembly if the brushes require service.

To disassemble the starter:

1. To disassemble the drive assembly:

   a. Depress the cap (2) for access to the C-clip (1). Briggs & Stratton provides a tool (#19436) to ease clip removal. On **Figure 51** starters, pry the dust boot off (13) prior to depressing the cap.

   b. Remove the C-clip at the end of the armature shaft and remove the drive assembly components.

   c. If the starter drive has a roll pin instead of a C-clip (**Figure 54**), support the end of the armature shaft while using a pin punch to drive out the pin.

2. Before disassembling the motor, make marks on the drive plate, housing and end cap so they can be reassembled in their original positions.

3. To service the brushes and check the condition of the commutator, unscrew the tswo through bolts (12) and remove the end cap (11) and brush retainer (10). Before removing the brushes, note the position of the brushes and wires.

4. To remove the armature:

   a. Remove the drive assembly (1-6, 13).

   b. Remove the two through bolts (12).

   c. Set the starter on the workbench with the commutator end cap (11) down.

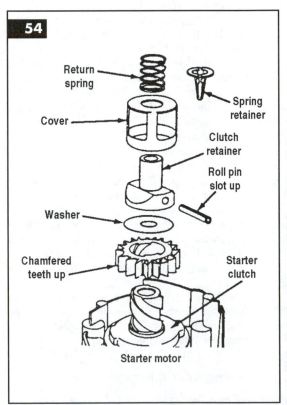

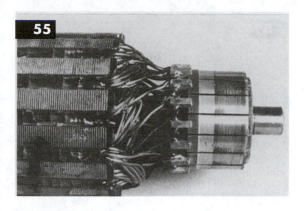

55

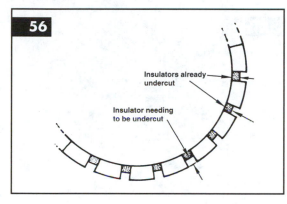

56

Insulators already undercut

Insulator needing to be undercut

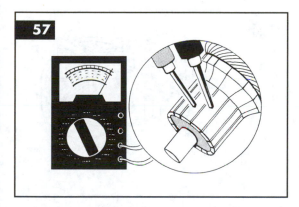

57

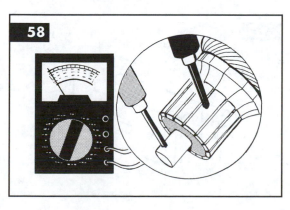

58

d. While pushing down on the drive end of the armature (8), lift the drive end cap (7) off the starter.

e. Push firmly down on the drive end of the armature, holding the end cap against the bench, then lift the housing (9) up off the armature.

5. Note the position and orientation of any spacers and/or washers on the armature shaft.

Starter Inspection

1. Clean the starter components but do not use cleaning solvents that will damage the armature.

2. Measure the length of each brush:

a. On **Figure 50** starters, the minimum allowable brush length is 1/8 inch (3.2 mm) measured from the commutator curve of the brush to the wire.

b. On **Figure 51** starters, the minimum allowable brush length is 1/4 inch (6.4 mm) measured from the brush face to the brush bottom.

3. Check the strength of the brush springs. The spring must force the brush against the commutator with sufficient pressure to ensure good contact. Be sure the brushes do not bind in the holders.

4. Inspect the condition of the commutator (**Figure 55**, typical). The mica between the commutator bars should be slightly undercut as shown in **Figure 56**. Undercut the mica or clean the slots between the commutator bars using a piece of hacksaw blade. After undercutting, remove burrs by sanding the commutator lightly with crocus cloth. Remove all crocus cloth grit before proceeding. Inspect the commutator bars for discoloration. If a pair of bars are discolored, grounded armature coils are indicated. Replace the armature.

5. Measure the diameter of the commutator on the **Figure 50** starter. The minimum allowable commutator diameter is 1.23 inches (31.24 mm).

6. Use an ohmmeter and check for continuity between the commutator bars (**Figure 57**); there should be continuity between pairs of bars. If there is no continuity between pairs of bars, the armature is open. Replace the armature.

7. Connect an ohmmeter between any commutator bar and the armature shaft (**Figure 58**); there should be no continuity. If there is continuity, the armature is grounded. Replace the armature.

8. Inspect the bushings in the drive plate and end cap (**Figure 59** and **Figure 60**). If the bushings are damaged or excessively worn, then the drive plate and/or end cap must be replaced; individual bushings are not available. If the bushings are worn, also check the corresponding armature journal.

10

Starter Reassembly

Starter component descriptions listed in this section will refer to **Figure 50** for starters with plastic composite, aluminum alloy or steel flywheel ring gears and **Figure 51** for starters with only steel ring gears.

To reassemble the starter:

1. Reinstall any armature shaft washers and/or spacers removed during disassembly.

2. Assemble the brushes into the end cap (10):

   a. On starters with radial-style brushes (**Figure 50**), insert homemade U-shaped wire pins or equivalent into the slots in the end cap to hold in the brushes (**Figure 61**). The pin legs should be approximately 1/2 inch (13 mm) long with 3/4 inch (19 mm) between the legs.

   b. On starters with axial-style brushes (**Figure 51**), fabricate a sheet-metal tool as shown in **Figure 62**. Compress the brushes against the brush springs while sliding the tool over each brush as its spring is compressed. When assembled, the end cap will appear as in **Figure 63**.

   NOTE
   To ensure proper brush polarity when replacing brushes, always follow the instructions included with the new brushes.

3. Apply a drop of SAE 20 oil into each end cap bushing (Figures 59 and 60).

4. Lightly coat the threads of the two through bolt with Loctite 242 or equivalent.

5. To assemble the brush retainer (10), end cap (11), armature (8) and housing (9) on **Figure 50** starters:

   a. Carefully assemble the armature into the housing. Do not damage the housing magnets. The housing magnets go toward the drive end of the armature.

   b. Align the brush retainer with the housing. Push the brush retainer over the armature commutator and against the housing.

   c. Remove any brush holder pins that did not fall out in the previous step. Make sure that the brushes are making firm contact with the commutator.

   d. Install the end cap onto the brush end of the armature shaft, against the brush retainer. Align the through-bolt holes.

   e. Install the drive end cap (7) onto the armature shaft and housing, aligning the marks made during disassembly.

   f. Install and tighten the two through-bolts (12).

6. To assemble the brush retainer/end cap (10), armature (8) and housing (9) on **Figure 51** starters:

   a. Carefully assemble the armature into the housing. Do not damage the housing magnets. The housing magnets go toward the drive end of the armature.

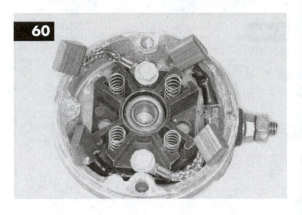

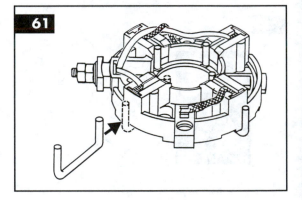

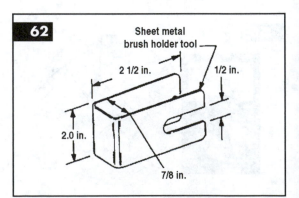

Sheet metal brush holder tool

2 1/2 in.

1/2 in.

2.0 in.

7/8 in.

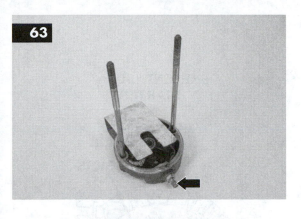

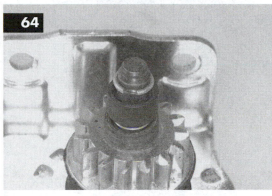

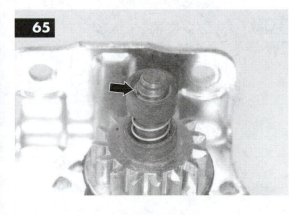

b. Install the drive end cap (7) onto the armature shaft and housing, aligning the marks made during disassembly.

c. Align the brush cap with the housing. Push the brush cap onto the armature shaft end.

d. While lightly holding the brush cap against the armature, slide the brush holder tool off the brushes.

e. Continue to hold the brush cap against the armature while installing the through-bolts (12). Tighten the bolts.

7. After assembling the starter, rotate the armature. The armature should rotate without binding, although magnetic force will inhibit rotation. If the armature is difficult to turn, recheck the assembly procedure.

8. Assemble the Bendix drive assembly onto the **Figure 50** starter as follows:

a. Lightly coat the ramps of the Bendix drive (6) with Lubriplate White Grease or equivalent.

b. Assemble the Bendix drive, pinion, spring, washer and stop cap (items 6-2) as shown. The Bendix drive has a D-hole in the base that must fit over the cutouts on the armature shaft. Style A pinion has beveled-edge teeth on one side of the gear: The beveled edges must face the ring gear. Style B pinion has straight-cut teeth with rounded edges on the gaps between the teeth: The round-edge gaps must face the ring gear. The concave part of the washer (3) must face the stop cap (2).

c. While compressing the spring with the stop cap, install the retaining ring into its armature shaft groove. B&S C-ring Tool No. 19435 makes this installation easy.

d. If the starter drive has a roll pin instead of a C-clip (**Figure 54**), support the end of the armature shaft while carefully driving the pin into the shaft. Make sure the pin does not protrude past the sides of the clutch retainer.

9. Assemble the Bendix drive assembly onto the **Figure 51** starter as follows:

a. Lightly lubricate the helix on both the armature shaft and pinion drive with an all-temperature grease.

b. Assemble the Bendix drive, pinion, spring, washer and stop cap (items 6-2) as shown. Make sure that the recess in the spring washer (3) faces the spring (4).

c. While compressing the spring with the stop cap, install the retaining ring into its armature shaft groove (**Figure 64**).

d. Release the stop cap. Ensure the stop cap cavity fits over the retaining ring (**Figure 65**).

e. Install the dust boot onto the groove of the spring washer (**Figure 66**).

10

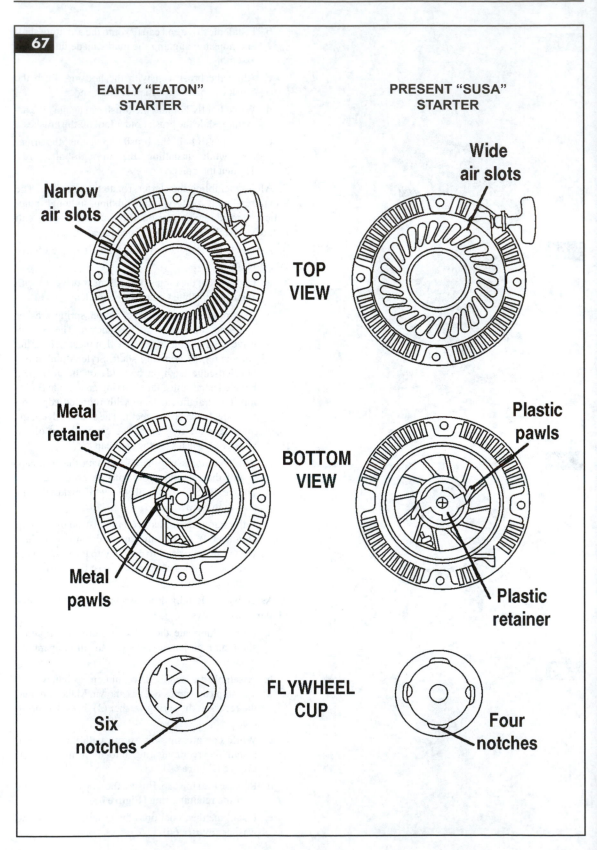

67

EARLY "EATON"
STARTER

PRESENT "SUSA"
STARTER

Narrow
air slots

Wide
air slots

TOP
VIEW

Metal
retainer

Plastic
pawls

BOTTOM
VIEW

Metal
pawls

Plastic
retainer

FLYWHEEL
CUP

Six
notches

Four
notches

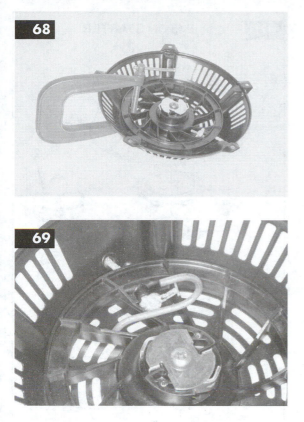

Starter Installation

1. Position the starter on its mount on the side of the crankcase.

2. Lightly coat the mount bolt threads with Loctite 242 or equivalent.

3. Install the bolts. Due to the starter location, bolt installation is made easier by using a 13 mm, 12-point, 1/4-inch drive swivel socket. This socket is available from B&S as Tool No. 19353.

4. Torque the bolts to 16.0 N•m (140 in.-lb.).

5. Install the starter cable. Do not overtighten the nut.

6. Reconnect the negative battery cable.

REWIND STARTER

The rewind starter is a pawl-type starter. When the rope is pulled, two pawls extend outward to engage notches in the starter cup that is attached to the flywheel.

Two starter designs have been used on these engines. The differences are shown in **Figure 67**.

In this section, "starter" refers to the rewind starter assembly.

Removal

To remove the starter:

1. Mark the direction of pull of the handle.

2. Remove the four hex flange screws holding the starter to the blower housing.

   3 To remove the starter drive cup after removing the starter:

   a. Remove the blower housing by following the necessary steps in the previous *BLOWER HOUSING, Removal* section.

   b. Use the strap wrench to hold the flywheel.

   c. Using the proper 6-point socket and ratchet or breaker bar, loosen the nut or bolt assembly holding the flywheel to the crankshaft. Remove the fastener.

CAUTION
If using an impact wrench to remove the flywheel fastener, be sure the wrench is set to turn counterclockwise, viewing the fastener. Accidentally applying additional tightening force to the fastener will damage the flywheel and crankshaft. **Do not use an impact wrench to tighten the fastener.**

   d. Remove the drive cup.

Replace an Unbroken Starter Rope

1. Pull the rope out about 12 inches (30 cm). Tie a slip knot in the rope at the housing to prevent the rope from rewinding.

2. Remove the rope retainer and handle.

3. Remove the slip knot and pull the rope all the way out. This will cause the pulley to rotate counterclockwise when viewed from inside the starter housing.

4. After performing Step 3, the spring will be almost completely tensioned, but the pulley must be held in this position to replace the rope. Three acceptable methods are:

   a. Have an assistant hold the pulley and housing to prevent the pulley from rotating;

   b. Use a C-clamp around the edge of the housing (**Figure 68**). *Do not* clamp the pulley to the housing. Place the foot of the clamp screw *between* the pulley ribs; or

   c. When the rope is all the way out and the rope hole in the pulley is aligned with the rope hole in the housing, rotate the pulley one more rib counterclockwise. Place a small S-hook through one of the small-diameter slots in the housing, then allow spring tension to lock the rib against the S-hook (**Figure 69**). The pulley and housing holes should then be nearly aligned.

5. Pull the old rope out of the starter from the inside, through the pulley hole.

6. Obtain a new No. 5½ rope (4.5 mm [11/64 inch] diameter) 178 cm (70 inches) long for the early Eaton starter or

10

200 cm (80 inches) long for the late SUSA starter. Burn both ends to prevent fraying. Tie a single knot at one end.

7. Feed the free end of the rope through the pulley hole, then through the housing hole. Pull the rope all the way out to where the knot meets the pulley.

8. Feed the rope through the handle grip, then through the rope retainer.

9. Tie a single knot at the end of the rope. Slide the knot into the retainer. Fit the retainer into the handle.

10. Unlock the pulley, allowing the spring to slowly draw the rope back into the starter. The rope should draw in completely and the handle should stop against the housing hole.

11. Check starter operation.

Replace a Broken Starter Rope

1. Invert the starter and remove what remains of the rope from the pulley groove.

2. Obtain a new No. 5 1/2 rope (4.5 mm [11/64 in.] diameter) 178 cm (70 in.) long for the early Eaton starter or 200 cm (80 inches) long for the late SUSA starter. Burn both ends to prevent fraying. Tie a single knot at one end.

3. Allow the pulley to unwind on the spring, then while holding the housing stationary, rotate the pulley counterclockwise (viewed from inside the starter housing):

    a. On the early Eaton starter, rotate the pulley until the spring is tight. This will require approximately six full turns of the pulley. *Do not force* the pulley once the spring is tight.

    b. On the late SUSA starter, rotate the pulley exactly six complete turns.

4. Rotate the pulley clockwise only until the pulley rope hole aligns with the housing rope hole. Hold the pulley in this position. Three acceptable methods of holding the pulley are:

    a. Have an assistant hold the pulley and housing to prevent the pulley from rotating;

    b. Use a C-clamp around the edge of the housing (**Figure 68**). *Do not* clamp the pulley to the housing. Place the foot of the clamp screw *between* the pulley ribs; or

    c. When the rope is all the way out and the rope hole in the pulley is aligned with the rope hole in the housing, rotate the pulley one more rib counterclockwise. Place a small S-hook through one of the small-diameter slots in the housing, then allow spring tension to lock the rib against the S-hook (**Figure 69**). The pulley and housing holes should then be nearly aligned.

5. Feed the free end of the rope through the pulley hole, then through the housing hole. Pull the rope all the way out until the knot seats against the pulley.

6. Feed the rope through the handle grip, then through the rope retainer.

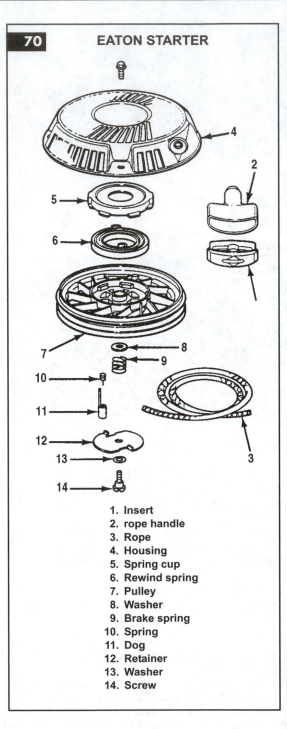

70   **EATON STARTER**

1. Insert
2. rope handle
3. Rope
4. Housing
5. Spring cup
6. Rewind spring
7. Pulley
8. Washer
9. Brake spring
10. Spring
11. Dog
12. Retainer
13. Washer
14. Screw

7. Tie a single knot at the end of the rope. Slide the knot into the retainer. Fit the retainer into the handle.

8. Unlock the pulley, allowing the spring to slowly draw the rope back into the starter. The rope should draw in completely and the handle should stop against the housing hole.

9. Check starter operation.

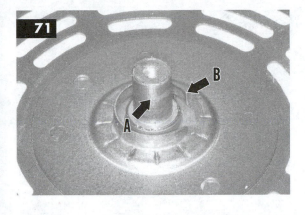

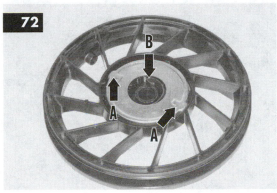

Repair, Eaton Starter

CAUTION
The rewind spring is under tension. Always wear eye protection when servicing rewind starters. Follow repair instructions accurately.

NOTE
If the rope is broken, proceed to Step 4.

Refer to **Figure 70**.
1. Pull the rope out about 12 inches (30 cm). Tie a slip knot in the rope at the housing to prevent the rope from rewinding.

2. Remove the rope retainer and handle (1, 2).

3. Remove the slip knot. Allow the rope to *slowly* wind back into the starter.

4. Remove the retaining screw and washer (14, 13) from the center of the starter.

5. Remove the pawl retainer (12), brake spring and washer (9, 8), pawls and pawl springs (11, 10). Note the position and orientation of the pawls and pawl springs.

6. Rotate the pulley (7) *two turns clockwise* to make sure the spring tension is relieved and the spring is disengaged from the housing.

7. While holding the pulley in the housing, invert the starter, aiming the pulley away from yourself or others.

8. Carefully remove the pulley by rotating it back and forth a few degrees. The containerized spring (5, 6) should remain in the pulley when the pulley is removed.

NOTE
If the pulley cannot be easily removed from the housing, there may still be tension on the spring or the spring could still be connected to the housing. Repeat Steps 6-8 and again try to remove the pulley.

9. Note the orientation of the spring cup assembly inside the pulley. Carefully remove the spring and cup as an assembly.

CAUTION
The spring and spring cup are serviced as an assembly. Do not attempt to remove the spring from the cup.

10. Clean and dry all parts, including the center screw and housing center post threads. Carefully inspect all components for wear or damage. Repair or replace as necessary.

11. Lightly lubricate the spring and the housing shaft (A, **Figure 71**) with all-temperature bearing grease.

12. Install the spring cup assembly into the pulley with the exposed spring face against the pulley and the cup tabs in the pulley slots (A, **Figure 72**). Note that the keeper tabs are offset, allowing the keeper to fit into the pulley one way only.

13. Install the pulley and spring assembly into the starter housing with the spring cup against the housing. Rotate the pulley assembly counterclockwise as necessary to make sure the spring end hook (B, **Figure 72**) catches on the housing tab (B, **Figure 71**).

14. Install the pawl springs into the pawl slots in the pulley (**Figure 73**). Pull the spring arms aside and insert the pawls.

15. Position the brake washer onto the center shaft, inside the pulley recess (**Figure 74**).

10

16. *Lightly* grease the brake spring ends. Set the spring onto the brake washer, making sure no grease gets into the center post threads (**Figure 75**).

17. Position the pawl retainer onto the pulley as shown in **Figure 76**.

    a. Lightly coat the center screw threads with Loctite 271 or equivalent.

    b. Place the washer onto the screw shoulder.

    c. Install the screw and tighten to 7.4-8.5 N•m (65-75 in.-lb.).

18. Install the rope and tension the spring by following Steps 1-9 under *Starter Rope Replacement* in this chapter.

Repair, SUSA Starter

Figure 77 shows an exploded view of the late-style starter manufactured by SUSA. Component reference numbers in this section are for **Figure 77** unless otherwise noted.

> *CAUTION*
> *The rewind spring is under tension. Always wear eye protection when servicing rewind starters. Follow repair instructions accurately.*

> *NOTE*
> *If the rope is broken, proceed to Step 4.*

1. Pull the rope out about 12 inches (30 cm). Tie a slip knot in the rope at the housing to prevent the rope from rewinding.

2. Remove the rope retainer and handle (1, 2).

3. Remove the slip knot. Allow the rope to *slowly* wind back into the starter.

4. Remove the retaining screw (11) from the center of the starter.

5. Remove the pawl friction plate (9), brake spring (4) and pawls (8). The ring (10) should remain attached to the plate.

> *CAUTION*
> *Wear appropriate safety eyewear and gloves before disengaging the pulley from the starter as the spring may uncoil uncontrolled.*

6. Rotate the pulley clockwise so the inner spring end disengages from the inner spring anchor.

7. Place rags around the pulley and lift the pulley out of the housing; the rewind spring should remain with the pulley.

8. If necessary, remove the rewind spring from the pulley.

9. Clean and dry all parts, including the center screw and housing center post threads. Inspect all components for wear or damage. Repair or replace as necessary.

10. Lightly lubricate the spring and the housing shaft (A, **Figure 71**, typical) with all-temperature bearing grease.

11. If the rewind spring was removed, install the spring into the pulley. The spring outer hook must seat properly into the pulley slot. The correct spring rotation is shown in **Figure 77**.

12. Install the pulley and spring assembly into the starter housing. Rotate the pulley assembly counterclockwise as necessary to ensure the inner spring-end hook catches on the housing anchor adjacent to the center post.

13. Install the pawl springs and pawls onto the posts in the pulley.

77

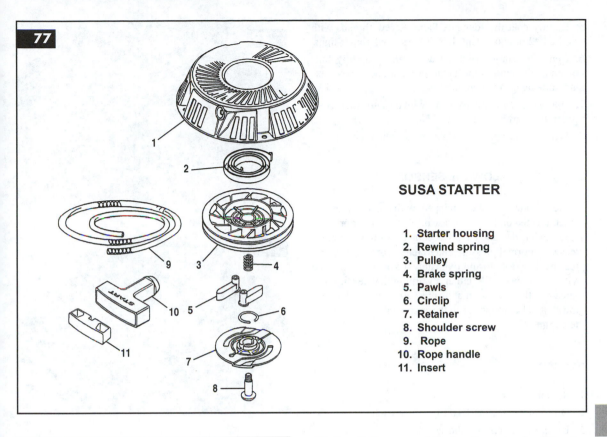

SUSA STARTER

1. **Starter housing**
2. **Rewind spring**
3. **Pulley**
4. **Brake spring**
5. **Pawls**
6. **Circlip**
7. **Retainer**
8. **Shoulder screw**
9. **Rope**
10. **Rope handle**
11. **Insert**

10

78

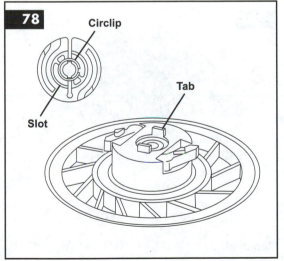

14. Be sure the friction plate ring fits in the groove in the retainer (**Figure 78**).

15. Position the friction plate onto the pulley. The slots on the underside of the plate engage the tabs on the pulley (**Figure 78**).

16. Lightly coat the center screw threads with Loctite 271 or equivalent. Install the screw and tighten to 8.0 N•m (70 in.-lb.).

17. Install the rope and tension the spring by following Steps 1-9 under the preceding *Starter Rope Replacement* section.

Installation

1. Install the starter cup onto the flywheel if it was removed.
   a. On Series 303700 engines, the cup fits over the crankshaft threads.
   b. On Series 350700 engines, the cup fits against the extended flywheel nut.

2. Using the strap wrench shown in **Figure 41**, hold the flywheel in position while tightening the cup fastener:
   a. On Series 303700 engines, install the flat washer and nut onto the crankshaft. Tighten the nut to 175 N•m (125 ft.-lb.).
   b. On Series 350700 engines, lightly coat the cup bolt threads with Loctite 242 or equivalent, then install the bolt through the cup and into the extended flywheel nut. Tighten the bolt to 135 N•m (100 ft.-lb.).

3. Reinstall the blower housing as instructed in the previous *Blower Housing, Installation* section.

4. Position the starter onto the blower housing. Be sure the handle is oriented in the proper direction.

5. Lightly coat the four hex flange screw threads with Loctite 242 or equivalent. Install the screws finger-tight.

6. Center the starter pawls inside the cup by lightly pulling out on the starter rope handle grip until both pawls extend and engage the cup notches.

7. While the pawls are in contact with the cup, alternately tighten the starter fasteners to 7 N•m (62 in.-lb.).

8. When the fasteners are tight, release the rope grip.

LOW OIL SENSOR

The engine may be equipped with an oil pressure switch located on the crankcase oil filter adapter bracket. The switch is designed to break contact as oil pressure increases to normal pressure and to make contact when oil pressure decreases to approximately 0.3 bar (4.5 psi). The switch is connected to either a warning device (light) to indicate to the operator that oil pressure is low and the engine should be stopped or to the engine kill circuit to stop the engine.

Removal

1. Stop the engine and let it cool.

2. Disconnect the wire lead from the switch.

3. Unscrew and remove the switch.

Testing

To check the sensor switch, a regulated supply of compressed air and a continuity tester are required.

1. Remove the oil pressure sensor switch as described in the previous section.

2. Connect the tester probes to the body of the switch and to the switch terminal.

3. The tester should indicate continuity between the switch terminal and the switch body.

4. Gradually apply air pressure to the switch oil passage.

5. As pressure increases past approximately 0.3 bar (4.5 psi), the switch should open and the tester should indicate no continuity.

6. If the switch fails the test, install a new switch.

Installation

1. Before installing the switch, apply Loctite 592 or equivalent pipe sealant with Teflon to the switch threads.

2. Install the switch. Tighten the switch to 4.5 N•m (40 in.-lb.).

3. Reconnect the wire lead.

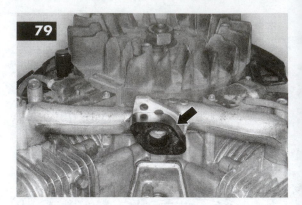

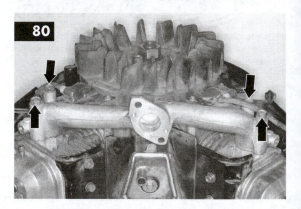

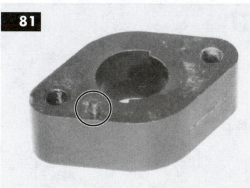

INTAKE MANIFOLD

Removal

1. Remove the blower housing as described in this chapter.

2. Remove the carburetor as described in this chapter. Remove the carburetor insulator from the manifold (**Figure 79**).

3. Remove the intake manifold mounting bolts (**Figure 80**) and remove the intake manifold. Discard all old gaskets.

82

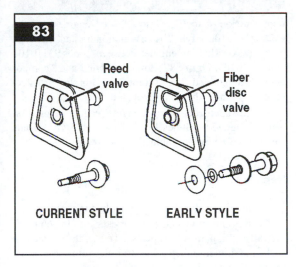

83

Reed valve

Fiber disc valve

CURRENT STYLE   **EARLY STYLE**

4. Inspect the manifold and insulator for cracks and other damage. Ensure that the insulator locator tab (**Figure 81**) is not broken off. Clean the manifold using a suitable solvent or parts cleaner. Carefully remove any gasket material on the manifold or cylinder heads. Do not scratch or gouge the gasket surfaces.

5. Clean and dry the mounting bolt threads and matching cylinder head threads.

Installation

1. Position new manifold gaskets onto the cylinder head openings.

2. Set the manifold onto the heads.

3. Lightly coat the manifold bolt threads with Loctite 242 or equivalent.

4. Install the manifold bolts (**Figure 80**). Tighten the bolts to 16 N·m (142 in.-lb.).

5. Using new gaskets, install the carburetor as detailed in the previous *Carburetor, Installation* section in this chapter. Use new gaskets.

NOTE
*The insulator locator pin (**Figure 81**) fits into the hole in the intake manifold (**Figure 82**).*

6. Install the blower housing as outlined in the previous *Blower Housing, Installation* section in this chapter.

CRANKCASE BREATHER

Figure 83 shows the two types of crankcase breathers used on these engines. The early style was used on engines before Code 90111500; the late style has been used since Code 90111400.

The valve in the breather maintains a vacuum in the crankcase by venting crankcase pressure through the breather hose into the air filter. A faulty breather will result in excessive oil consumption. A missing internal crankcase baffle will also cause excessive oil consumption. Refer to the *Engine Reassembly* section to check the baffle.

The breather assembly is located in the valley between the cylinders, below the carburetor. The breather is visible in **Figure 80**, just below the carburetor opening in the intake manifold.

Removal

1. Remove the air filter assembly as described in this chapter. Remove the breather hose from the air filter base plate.

2. If necessary, remove the carburetor as described in this chapter. If the carburetor must be removed, first remove the blower housing as outlined in the previous section of this chapter.

3. Remove the breather mounting bolt.

4. Remove the breather. It may be necessary to carefully pry the breather off the block. Do not bend the breather mounting surface.

5. Carefully clean all old gasket material from the block and breather surfaces. Do not scratch or gouge the surfaces. Discard old gaskets and sealing washers.

6. Clean and dry the breather bolt and matching block threads.

Inspection

1. Inspect the breather for cracks, breaks or damaged valve.

2. On the early breather, there should be a 1.0-1.15 mm (0.040-0.045 inch) gap between the fiber disc and the body opening. Check this dimension with a bent wire gauge. Do not force the gauge. Replace the breather if the gap is insufficient or excessive.

3. On late-style breathers, check to make sure the reed seats correctly against the body opening. *Do not press*

10

against the reed. Replace the breather if damage is evident.

4. Inspect the breather hose. Replace the hose if it is dry, cracked or brittle.

Installation

1. Place a new breather gasket onto the crankcase and a new sealing washer onto the breather bolt.
2. Lightly coat the breather bolt threads with Loctite 242 or equivalent.
3. Bolt the breather to the block. Tighten the bolt to 3.0 N•m (30 in.-lb.). Fit the breather hose to the breather fitting.
4. If the anti-afterfire solenoid was removed from the carburetor bowl, reinstall it. Torque the solenoid to 5.0 N•m (45 in.-lb.). Reconnect the solenoid wire.
5. Turn the fuel tank valve on (**Figure 7**).
6. If the carburetor was removed, reinstall it and the air filter assembly as described in the previous *Carburetor, Installation* section. Connect the breather hose to the air filter base plate.
7. Reinstall the blower housing as outlined in the previous *Blower Housing, Installation* section.

VALVE COVERS

Removal

1. Remove the valve cover retaining nuts (A, **Figure 84**).
2. Remove and discard the valve cover sealing washers (B, **Figure 84**).
3. On the No. 1 cylinder, unclamp the fuel pump pulse hose from the valve cover fitting (**Figure 36**).
4. Remove the valve covers. On the No. 1 cylinder, pull the cover away from the head slightly, then twist the cover back and forth gently to remove the fuel pump hose.
5. Remove the gaskets and clean the mating surfaces on the covers and cylinder heads. Discard the old gaskets.

Installation

1. Install a new gasket into each valve cover.
2. On the No. 1 cylinder, work the valve cover fitting into the fuel pump pulse hose, then install the cover onto the studs. Clamp the hose.
3. Install the No. 2 valve cover.
4. Install new sealing washers. Install the retaining nuts and tighten evenly to 3.0 N•m (27 in.-lb.).

ROCKER ARMS AND PUSH RODS

Three styles of rocker arms have been used (**Figure 85**). Style 1 is stamped steel (A, **Figure 86**) and was used

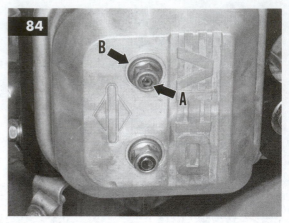

with a rocker shaft (B, **Figure 86**) on engines prior to Code 93110100. Style 2 is cast aluminum and was used with a rocker shaft on engines between Codes 93110100 and 96040100. **Figure 87** shows the Style 1 and 2 components disassembled. The current Style 3 is stamped steel mounted on an individual pivot stud.

Style 2 supercedes Style 1. Style 3 cannot be used on heads designed for Styles 1 or 2. However, Style 3 heads can be used on earlier engines.

Removal

1. Remove the valve cover as described in this chapter.
2. Depress the valve end of the rocker arm to compress the valve spring, move the push rod out of the rocker arm socket, and release the rocker arm. Perform this step on the remaining rocker arm.
3. Mark the rocker arms so they may be reinstalled in their original positions.
4. Unscrew the rocker shaft studs.
5. If so equipped, remove the rocker shaft assembly.

> *NOTE*
> *The push rod for the exhaust valve is aluminum; the push rod for the intake valve is steel.*

6. If necessary, remove the push rods. Mark the push rods so they may be reinstalled in their original positions and direction.
7. Inspect the rocker arm components for excessive wear or damage.
8. Check the push rods for straightness.
9. Clean and dry all fastener threads.

Installation

1. On Styles 1 and 2:
   a. Loosen the rocker arm adjusting nuts and back the adjusting screws out about one turn.

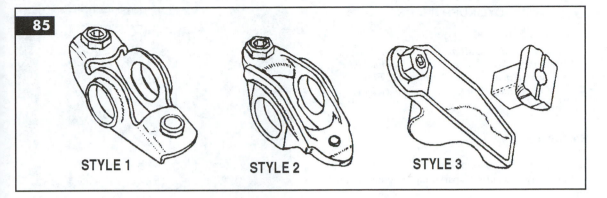

STYLE 1   STYLE 2   STYLE 3

86

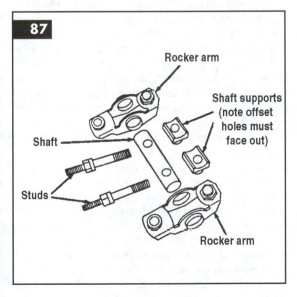

87

Rocker arm

Shaft supports
(note offset
holes must
face out)

Shaft

Studs

Rocker arm

e. Fit the shaft supports up onto the studs in between the sides of the arms.

NOTE
Make sure the offset support holes face out as shown in Figure 87.

f. Position the shaft assembly onto the cylinder head, threading the studs in finger-tight. Ensure that the adjusting screws are positioned over the push rod area.

g. Tighten the studs to 16.0 N•m (140 in.-lb.).

h. When finished, the rocker shaft assembly will appear as in **Figure 86**.

2. On Style 3:

a. Lubricate the rocker arm and support pivot areas with fresh engine oil.

b. Assemble the long shank of the rocker arm stud into the support.

c. Place the support into the arm, then screw the studs into the head. Ensure that the adjusting screws are positioned over the push rod area.

d. Torque the studs to 11.0 N•m (100 in.-lb.).

3. If necessary, install the push rods according to the marks made during disassembly.

NOTE
The push rod for the exhaust valve is aluminum; the push rod for the intake valve is steel.

4. Make sure that the lifter end of the push rod is seated properly in the lifter socket. Using thumb pressure, depress the valve end of the rocker arm to compress the valve spring, move the push rod into the rocker arm socket, and release the rocker arm. Perform this step on the remaining rocker arm.

5. Adjust the valve clearance as outlined under *Valve Adjustment* in this chapter.

6. Install the valve covers as described in the preceding section.

b. Lubricate the rocker arms and shaft with fresh engine oil.

c. Fit the rocker arms onto the shaft so the gap in each arm straddles a shaft hole and the adjusting nuts are up.

d. Install the long shanks of the studs through the shaft holes.

10

CYLINDER HEADS

NOTE
*The cylinder heads are not identical. Each cylinder head has an identifying number located near the valve springs (A, **Figure 88**) on the flywheel side of the cylinder head.*

Removal

1. Disconnect the spark plug wire from each spark plug and properly ground the spark plug wire end to the engine.
2. Remove the exhaust manifold and muffler as described in this chapter.
3. Remove the intake manifold as detailed in this chapter.
4. Remove any air shrouds or heat shields attached to the cylinder heads as described under *Blower Housing*.
5. Remove the valve covers as instructed in the previous section.
6. Remove the rocker arms as described in the preceding section.
7. In a crossing pattern, remove the cylinder head bolts (B, **Figure 88**). Note the sealing washers (C) under the inner bolts.

NOTE
Sealing washers are not used under the inner cylinder head bolts on engines after Code 94043000.

8. Loosen the cylinder head by tapping around the perimeter with a rubber or soft-faced mallet. Do not use a metal hammer.
9. Remove the cylinder head and gasket. Discard the gasket.

Disassembly

NOTE
Prior to or during disassembly, mark all components so they can be reinstalled in the same positions if they are to be reused.

Refer to **Figure 89**.
1. Remove the spark plug, if not already removed.
2. Place the head (3) on the workbench, combustion chamber down, with a folded shop rag or short section of fuel hose between the valve heads and the bench. This will hold the valves closed against spring pressure while disassembling the head.
3. Using B&S Valve Spring Compressor Tool No. 19347, compress the valve springs and remove the split keepers (8). Follow the instructions included with the tool.
4. Remove the valve spring caps (7) and springs (5, 6).
5. Remove the valves (1, 2).

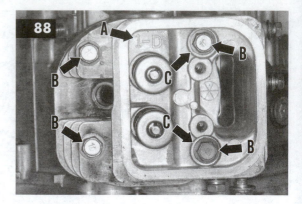

NOTE
*If the valves are difficult to remove, check the keeper groove at the base of the stem (**Figure 90**). Using a fine file, carefully remove any burrs or flaring on the stem at the bottom end of the groove. Attempting to remove the valves with stem burrs will damage the valve guides.*

6. Remove and discard the intake valve stem seal (4).

Inspection

1. Carefully remove all traces of gasket material from the cylinder head and valve cover mating surfaces. Do not gouge or damage the mating surfaces.
2. Carefully remove all traces of gasket material from the cylinder head and cylinder block mating surfaces. Do not gouge or damage the mating surfaces.
3. Remove all carbon deposits from the valves, combustion chamber area and valve ports with a rotary wire brush. A blunt screwdriver or chisel may be used if care is taken not to damage the head, valves and spark plug threads.
4. Examine the spark plug threads in the cylinder head for damage. If damage is minor or if the threads are dirty or clogged with carbon, use a spark plug thread tap (**Figure 91**) to clean the threads. If thread damage is severe, repair can sometimes be made by the installation of a Heli-Coil or equivalent replacement thread.
5. Inspect the threads in all threaded cylinder head and crankcase holes for damage. If damage is slight, dress the threads with an appropriate size metric tap if necessary. If thread damage is severe, a Heli-Coil or equivalent replacement thread may be installed.
6. After the carbon is removed from the combustion chamber and the valve intake and exhaust ports, clean the entire head in cleaning solvent. Blow dry with compressed air.
7. Carefully clean all carbon from the piston crown. Do not score the crown.

89

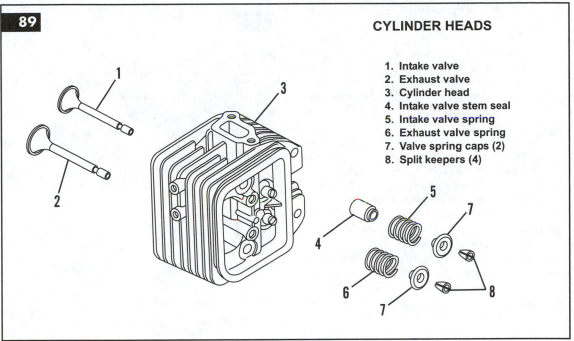

CYLINDER HEADS

1. Intake valve
2. Exhaust valve
3. Cylinder head
4. Intake valve stem seal
5. Intake valve spring
6. Exhaust valve spring
7. Valve spring caps (2)
8. Split keepers (4)

90

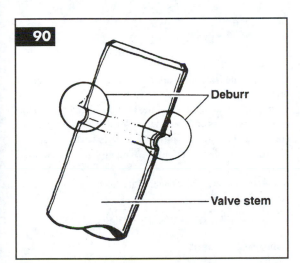

Deburr

Valve stem

91

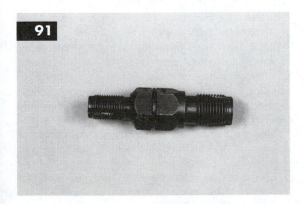

8. Check for cracks or other damage to the head, especially in the combustion chamber and exhaust port. Replace the cylinder head if it is cracked or damaged, or if any cooling fins are broken off.

9. After the head has been thoroughly cleaned, place the cylinder head gasket surface on a surface plate. Measure the warpage by inserting a flat feeler gauge between the plate and the cylinder head at various locations. Replace the cylinder head if warpage exceeds 0.1 mm (0.004 in.). Machining or grinding the cylinder head surface to remove warpage is not recommended.

10. Valve, valve guide and valve seat service will be covered in the following *Valves And Valve Components* section.

Reassembly

Refer to **Figure 89**.

1. Make sure all threads are clean and dry.

2. Lightly lubricate the intake valve stem, guide and stem seal wiping lip with fresh engine oil. Always use a new stem seal (4). Install the intake valve stem seal and valve (1). Install the stem seal first, pushing it down until it bottoms against the guide. Rotate the valve while passing it through the seal to prevent damaging the seal. Push the valve all the way in until it bottoms against the seat. **Figure 92** shows the intake stem seal in place with the valve installed.

3. Lightly lubricate the exhaust valve stem with Led-Plate or equivalent. Lightly lubricate the exhaust

10

valve guide with fresh engine oil. Install the exhaust valve (2).

4. Place the head (3) on the workbench, combustion chamber down, with a folded shop rag or short section of fuel hose between the valve head and the bench. This will hold the valve closed against spring pressure while assembling the valve spring, spring cap and split keepers.

5. If the valve springs are being replaced, obtain the correct springs:

    a. On engine Series 303700, the intake and exhaust springs are not interchangeable, and the springs are different before and after Code 94011700.

    b. On engine Series 350700, the springs are interchangeable and are the same for all codes.

6. Position the intake valve spring (5) over the valve stem. Install the spring cap (7). Use a valve spring compressor tool to compress the valve springs.

7. Apply a small amount of grease to the valve keeper groove on the valve stem prior to installing the split keepers (8) to help hold the keepers in place on the valve stem. Make sure the keepers fit snugly into the groove in the valve stem. When the keepers are installed on both valves, they will appear as shown in **Figure 93**.

8. Position the exhaust valve spring (6) onto the valve. Install the spring cap (7). Compress the spring and install the split keepers (8).

9. Repeat Steps 1-8 for the other cylinder head.

Installation

Refer to **Figure 89**.

1. If removed, install the cylinder head locating dowels (21, **Figure 94**).

> *NOTE*
> *Do not apply sealer to the cylinder head gasket.*

2. Install a new head gasket.

> *NOTE*
> *Engines prior to Code 96040100 use a metal head gasket. Engines after Code 96033100 use a carbon-graphite head gasket. Use the correct gasket.*

3. Install the cylinder head onto the cylinder.

4. Lightly coat the head bolt threads with Led-Plate, B&S Lubricant No. 93963 or equivalent.

5. Install the cylinder head bolts. On engines before Code 94050100, be sure to install the washers (**Figure 95**) on the inner bolts.

6. Tighten the cylinder head bolts in 5.0 N•m (45 in.-lb.) increments using the sequence shown in **Figure 96**. The specified final torque reading is 19.0 N•m (165 in.-lb.).

7. Install the rocker arms and push rods as instructed in the preceding section.

8. Install the valve covers as specified in the previous section.

9. Install any air shrouds or heat shields that attach to the cylinder heads as outlined in the *Blower Housing* section.

10. Install the intake manifold as detailed in this chapter.

11. Install the exhaust manifold and muffler as described in this chapter.

12. Reconnect the spark plug wire to each spark plug.

VALVES AND VALVE COMPONENTS

Valve Adjustment

The engine must be cold for valve adjustment.

1. Remove the valve covers as previously described.

2. Remove the spark plugs.

3. Rotate the flywheel so the piston for the cylinder being adjusted is at top dead center on the compression stroke. Be sure both valves are closed.

4. Using a suitable measuring device inserted through the spark plug hole, rotate the flywheel *clockwise* so the piston is 6.35 mm (0.250 in.) *below* TDC.

5. Measure the clearance gap between the valve stem and rocker arm. Valve clearance should be 0.10-0.16 mm (0.004-0.006 in.) for both valves.

6. Loosen the locknut (C, **Figure 86**) and turn the adjustment screw (D) to obtain the specified clearance.

94

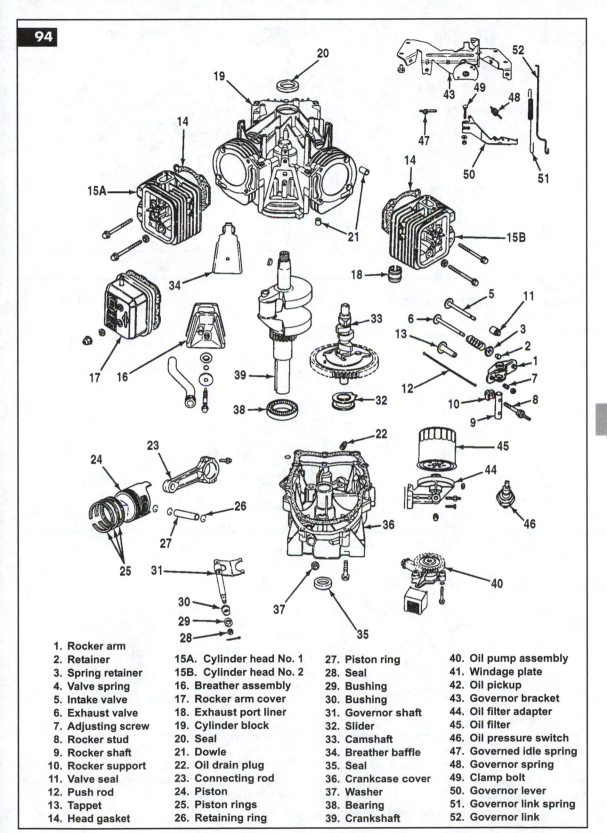

1. Rocker arm
2. Retainer
3. Spring retainer
4. Valve spring
5. Intake valve
6. Exhaust valve
7. Adjusting screw
8. Rocker stud
9. Rocker shaft
10. Rocker support
11. Valve seal
12. Push rod
13. Tappet
14. Head gasket

15A. Cylinder head No. 1
15B. Cylinder head No. 2
16. Breather assembly
17. Rocker arm cover
18. Exhaust port liner
19. Cylinder block
20. Seal
21. Dowle
22. Oil drain plug
23. Connecting rod
24. Piston
25. Piston rings
26. Retaining ring

27. Piston ring
28. Seal
29. Bushing
30. Bushing
31. Governor shaft
32. Slider
33. Camshaft
34. Breather baffle
35. Seal
36. Crankcase cover
37. Washer
38. Bearing
39. Crankshaft

40. Oil pump assembly
41. Windage plate
42. Oil pickup
43. Governor bracket
44. Oil filter adapter
45. Oil filter
46. Oil pressure switch
47. Governed idle spring
48. Governor spring
49. Clamp bolt
50. Governor lever
51. Governor link spring
52. Governor link

10

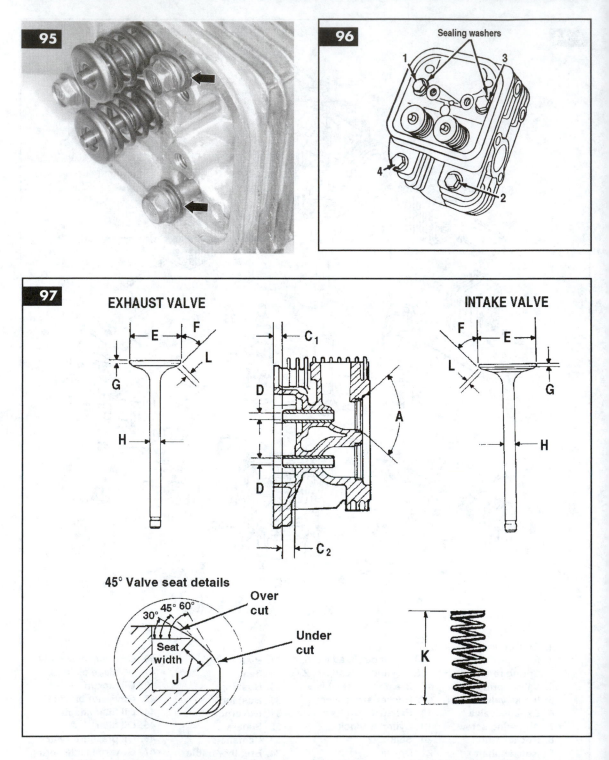

95

96

Sealing washers

1   3

4

2

97

EXHAUST VALVE

E   F

L

G

H

C₁

D

A

D

C₂

INTAKE VALVE

F   E

L

G

H

45° Valve seat details

30°   45° 60°

Over cut

Under cut

Seat width

J

K

8. While holding the locknut, tighten the adjustment screw to 7.0 N•m (60 in.-lb.). Recheck the valve clearance gap.

9. Reinstall the spark plugs. Tighten the plugs to 23 N•m (16.5 ft.-lb. or 200 in.-lb.).

10. Using new gaskets and sealing washers, reinstall the valve covers as specified in the previous *Valve Covers, Installation* section.

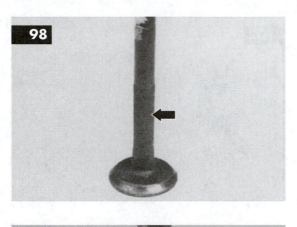
98

99

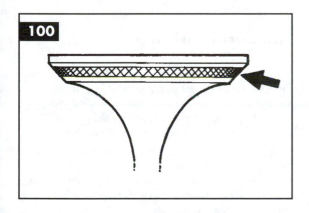
100

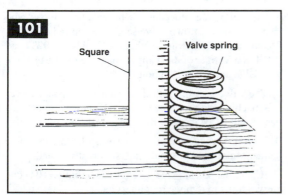
101

Square

Valve spring

Valve Removal

To remove the valves, follow the steps outlined in the preceding *Cylinder Head, Disassembly* section.

Valve Inspection

For valve system dimensions, refer to **Table 6** at the end of this chapter and **Figure 97**.

1. Inspect the valve for damage and excessive wear. Inspect the valve before cleaning. Gummy deposits on the intake valve (**Figure 98**) may indicate that the engine has run on gasoline that was stored for an extended period. Hard deposits on the intake valve are due to burnt oil, while hard deposits on the exhaust valve (**Figure 99**) are due to combustion byproducts and burnt oil. Moisture in the engine during storage can cause corroded or pitted valves, which should be replaced.

2. Check the valve face and seat for an irregular contact pattern. The seating ring around the valve face should be centered on the face, concentric with the valve head and equal in thickness all around the valve (**Figure 100**). If the seating pattern is irregular, then the valve may be bent or the valve face or seat is damaged.

3. Remove deposits either with a wire brush or soak the valve in parts cleaner.

4. Using a micrometer, measure the valve stem diameter in multiple locations where the valve rides in the guide. Replace the valve if the stem is worn.

5. The valve stem must be perpendicular to the valve head. To check for a bent valve, carefully install the valve stem in a drill chuck and rotate the drill. Be sure the valve stem is centered in the drill chuck. If the stem or head wobbles, replace the valve.

6. Measure the valve head margin (**Figure 97**). Replace the valve if the margin is less than specified.

7. If the valve and valve seat are worn, but serviceable, they can be restored by machining. Use the specifications in **Figure 97**.

8. The valves ride in renewable valve guides. Refer to *Valve Guide Reconditioning* in this chapter.

9. If valve machining is not necessary, the valve should be lapped against the valve seat to restore the seating surfaces. Refer to *Valve Lapping* in this chapter.

10. Check the valve springs:
    a. The spring should be straight and square as shown in **Figure 101**. Check multiple locations around the spring circumference.
    b. Use a micrometer to measure the spring free length (**Figure 102**). Replace the valve spring if the free length is less than 41.0 mm (1.614 in.).

Valve Lapping

Valve lapping is a simple operation that can restore the valve seal without machining if the amount of wear or

10

distortion is not excessive. Lapping requires the use of lapping compound and a lapping tool (**Figure 103**). Lapping compound is available in either coarse or fine grade, water- or oil-mixed. Fine grade water-mixed compound is recommended. To lap a valve, proceed as follows:

1. Make sure that the valve head is smooth. Wire brush or lightly sand the head, if necessary.

2. Apply a light, even coat of lapping compound to the valve face. Too much compound can fall into the valve guide and cause damage.

3. Insert the valve into the valve guide.

4. Moisten the end of the lapping tool suction cup and place it on the valve head.

5. Rotate the lapping tool back and forth between your hands several times.

> *NOTE*
> *For the most accurate lapping, slowly hand-rotate the lapping tool back and forth between 1/4 and 3/8 of a turn (90°-135°). Do not spin the tool rapidly through a revolution or two, then reverse direction. Do not use a drill to rotate the lapping tool.*

6. Lap the valve so that the sealing ring of the valve face is in the center of the face (**Figure 100**). Make the first lap pass *very light* to check the sealing ring position. If, after initial lapping, the sealing ring is too high or too low on the valve face:

    a. If necessary, recut the seat as described under *Valve Seat Reconditioning* in this chapter.

    b. Relap the valve.

7. If the initial lap indicates the sealing ring is centered on the valve face, proceed with a full lapping.

8. Clean the compound from the valve and seat frequently to check the progress of the lapping. Lap only enough to achieve a precise seating ring around the valve head. The pattern on the valve face should be an even width as shown in **Figure 100**.

9. Closely examine the valve seat in the cylinder head. It should be smooth and even with a smooth burnished seating ring.

10. After lapping has been completed, thoroughly clean the valve face and valve seat areas using dampened cloths to remove all grinding compound. Any lapping compound residue left in the engine will cause rapid wear.

11. After the valve assemblies have been installed into the engine, test each valve seal by pouring solvent into the intake and exhaust ports. There should be no leakage past the seat. If fluid leaks past any of the seats, remove the valve and repeat the lapping procedure until there is no leakage.

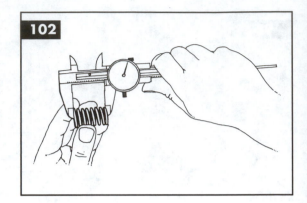

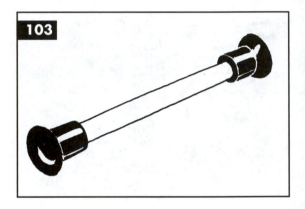

Valve Seat Reconditioning

These cylinder heads use hardened alloy steel intake and exhaust valve seat inserts pressed into the head. The inserts are not replaceable. If the inserts are loose, cracked or seriously warped, replace the head. If the inserts are in good condition, they can be reworked.

Special valve cutter tools and the proper expertise are required to recondition the valve seats in the cylinder heads properly. If the necessary tools are not available, take the cylinder heads to a shop that is equipped to recondition the valve components.

The following procedure is provided for those who choose to do their own valve service. Required tools are: Valve seat cutters (Briggs & Stratton Tool Nos. 19237 and 19343), a Vernier or dial caliper, machinist's dye or Prussian Blue and a valve lapping stick.

The valve seat for both the intake and exhaust valves are machined to the same angles. The valve contact surface is cut to a 45° angle from center (90° total angle).

1. Carefully rotate and insert the solid pilot into the valve guide. Make sure the solid pilot is correctly seated.

2. Using the 45° cutter, rotate the tool (**Figure 104**) one or two turns to remove roughness and clean the seat.

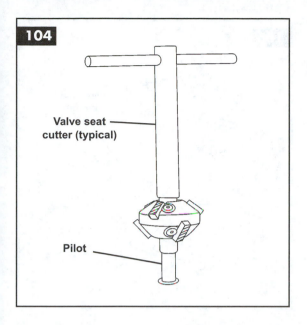

104

Valve seat cutter (typical)

Pilot

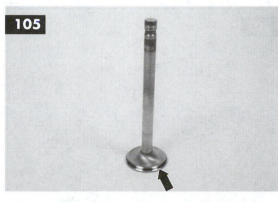

105

CAUTION
Measure the valve seat contact area in the cylinder head after each cut to make sure the contact area is correct and to prevent removing too much material. If too much material is removed, the cylinder head must be replaced.

3. If the seat is still pitted or burned, turn the 45° cutter additional turns until the surface is clean. Avoid removing too much material from the cylinder head.

4. Remove the valve cutter.

5. Inspect the valve seat-to-valve face impression as follows:

   a. Spread a thin layer of Prussian Blue or machinist's dye evenly on the valve face.

   b. Moisten the suction cup tool (**Figure 103**) and attach it to the valve. Insert the valve into the guide.

   c. Using the suction cup tool, tap the valve up and down in the cylinder head. Do *not* rotate the valve or a false indication will result.

   d. Remove the valve and examine the impression left by the Prussian Blue or machinist's dye.

6. Note the impression the dye left on the valve face (**Figure 105**).

   a. If the contact area is too *low* on the valve (too close to the stem), use the 60° cutter and remove a portion of the lower area of the valve seat material. This will raise the contact area. If this narrows the seat width, use the 45° cutter again to bring the seat width back into specification.

   b. If the contact area is too *high* on the valve, use the 30° cutter and remove a portion of the top area of the valve seat material. This will lower the contact area. If this narrows the seat width, use the 45° cutter again to bring the seat width back into specification.

7. Once the contact area is properly positioned on the valve face, adjust the valve seat width:

   a. If the width is too narrow, use the 45° cutter to widen the seat.

   b. If the width is too wide, use the 30° and 60° cutters equally to remove material from both above and below the seat contact area. When the seat width is correct, repeat Step 5 to ensure the correct seat-to-face position.

8. After the desired valve seat position and width is obtained, use the 45° cutter and very lightly clean off any burrs that may have been caused by the previous cuts.

9. Check that the finish has a smooth surface. It should not be rough or show chatter marks.

10. Repeat Steps 1-9 for the remaining valve seat.

11. Lap the valves as detailed in the preceding *Valve Lapping* section.

12. Thoroughly clean the cylinder head and all valve components in solvent or detergent and hot water to remove all cutting and lapping debris.

10

Valve Guide Reconditioning

Check for valve guide inside diameter for wear by inserting Briggs and Stratton Rejection Gauge No. 19382 into the valve guide. If the gauge can be inserted more than 6.0 mm (1/4 inch) into the guide, the valve guide is excessively worn and should be replaced.

When valve guides are worn so that there is excessive valve stem-to-guide clearance or valve tipping, the guides must be replaced. Special tools are required to correctly perform this job. If the valve guide is replaced, also replace the matching valve.

1. Position the cylinder head on the workbench so the combustion chamber side is facing down.

2. Support the cylinder head on wooden blocks so the guide can be pressed down and out.

3. From the rocker arm side of the cylinder head, drive or press out the old valve guide (**Figure 106**) using Briggs &

Stratton Valve Guide Remover Tool No. 19367. Remove the special tool when the guide clears the head.

4. Inspect the valve guide bore in the cylinder head for damage.

5. Apply penetrating oil to the new valve guide and the valve guide bore in the cylinder head.

6. From the top side (valve spring side) of the cylinder head, use Briggs & Stratton Valve Guide Installer Tool No. 19416 and press or drive in the new valve guide (**Figure 107**). Push the guide in until the installation tool bottoms on the cylinder head boss.

7. After installation, ream the new valve guide as follows:

   a. Use Briggs & Stratton Reamer No. 19444 and Pilot Guide No. 19345.

   b. Apply cutting oil to both the new valve guide bore and the valve guide reamer.

CAUTION
Always rotate the valve guide reamer clockwise to prevent damaging the new guide.

   c. Rotate the reamer *clockwise*. Continue to rotate the reamer and work it down through the entire length of the new valve guide. Apply additional cutting oil repeatedly during this procedure.

   d. Rotate the reamer *clockwise* until the reamer has traveled all the way through the new guide.

   e. While continuing to rotate the reamer *clockwise*, completely withdraw the reamer from the valve guide.

8. If necessary, repeat Steps 1-8 for the other valve guide.

9. Thoroughly clean the cylinder head and valve guides with solvent to wash out all metal particles. Dry with compressed air. Apply a light coat of engine oil to all bare metal surfaces to prevent any rust formation.

10. Reface the valve seats as described in the preceding section.

Valve Installation

To install the valves, follow the steps outlined under *Cylinder Head, Reassembly* in this chapter.

GOVERNOR (External Service)

Static Adjustment

1. Remove the air cleaner assembly for access to the governor linkage.

2. Loosen the governor lever clamp nut (A, **Figure 108**).

3. Rotate the governor lever (B, **Figure 108**) counterclockwise so the carburetor throttle plate is wide open. Hold the lever in that position.

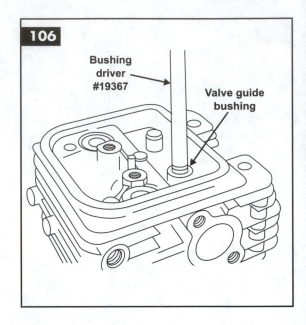

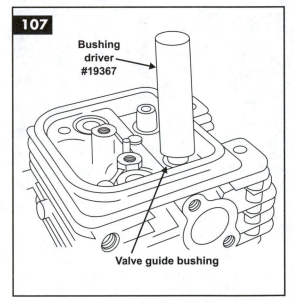

4. Turn the governor shaft (C, **Figure 108**) counterclockwise as far as possible, then tighten nut (A) to 8.0 N•m (71 in.-lb.).

Dynamic Adjustment

These engines use a governed idle system. The idle rpm must be adjusted prior to adjusting top no-load rpm. Follow the adjustment instructions precisely.

To make this adjustment properly, the following tools will be needed: An accurate tachometer such as B&S

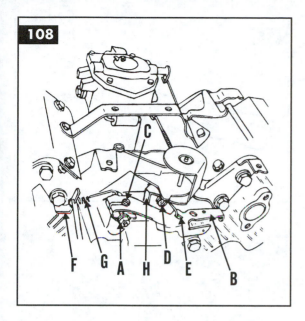

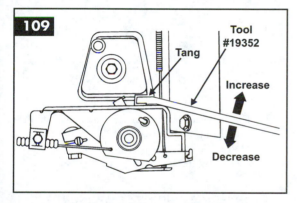

a. If the governed-idle spring (G) is red, rpm should be 1750.

b. If the governed-idle spring is white, rpm should be 1100.

5. With the speed control in the Idle position and the engine operating at the governed-idle rpm, bend the throttle-restrictor tang (H) so that it just touches the governor lever (B).

6. Move the remote speed control to the Fast position. Note the engine rpm. Top no-load rpm should be 3600. To adjust, bend the tang shown in **Figure 109** as necessary.

OIL SEALS
(SERVICE WITH CRANKSHAFT INSTALLED)

Oil seals at the flywheel end of the crankshaft and at the PTO end prevent the oil in the engine from leaking out. Wear or damage can reduce their effectiveness and oil leakage can become a problem, particularly if excessive amounts of oil are lost.

In some instances, it is possible to remove and install an oil seal without removing the crankshaft. Depending on the location of the engine and which oil seal is leaking, it may be necessary to remove the engine from the equipment.

If the oil seal at the flywheel end of the crankshaft is leaking, the flywheel must be removed (see the *Flywheel, Removal* section). If the oil seal at the output end of the crankshaft is leaking, any parts attached to the crankshaft that deny access to the oil seal must be removed. Refer to the previous *Engine Removal* section if the engine must be removed from the mower.

NOTE
Drain the engine oil if replacing the lower crankshaft oil seal.

Removal

Before removing an oil seal, note the position of the seal in the crankcase or oil pan. Install the new seal so it is located at the same depth as the original seal.

CAUTION
Exercise care when extracting the seal so the metal in the seal bore or the crankshaft seal surface is not scratched or damaged.

1. Special oil seal removal tools are available from small engine tool suppliers (**Figure 110**), or inexpensive oil seal removal tool can be made by modifying a linoleum knife as shown in **Figure 111**. Carefully grind the blade to the contour shown in the figure, then round all the blade edges so the blade will not damage the crankshaft or seal cavity.

2. Using a small pin punch, carefully tap the seal in a couple of places around its outer edge so as to break it

Tool No. 19389 Tiny-Tach, and B&S Tang Bending Tool No. 19352 or equivalent.

To make this adjustment, refer to **Figure 108** and proceed as follows:

NOTE
*The air cleaner is removed for clarity. The air cleaner **must be installed when the engine is running.***

1. Make sure that the end of the governor spring (D) is installed in lever hole No. 1 (E).

2. With the parking brake on, the blade PTO disengaged, the speed control in neutral, and the neutral locks locked, start the engine and run it for 5-10 minutes to reach normal operating temperature.

3. Place the remote speed control in the Idle or Slow position.

4. Bend the governed-idle tang (F) to obtain the specified idle rpm:

10

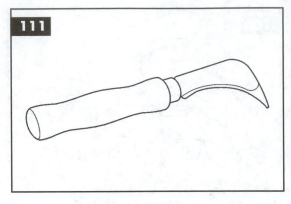

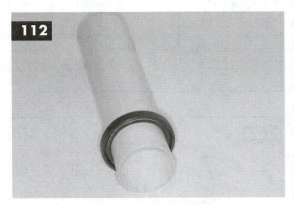

loose from the crankcase cavity. Only tap it enough to break it loose. Do not drive it deeper into the cavity.

3. Carefully insert the tool blade under the oil seal lip and against the inside periphery of the seal, next to the crankshaft (**Figure 110**). Pry out the seal. It may be necessary to work around the seal in more than one spot before the seal will break loose.

4. Clean and dry the seal seating area so the new seal will seat properly.

5. Check the oil seal bore in the engine and dress out any burrs created during removal. Only remove metal that is raised and will interfere with the installation of the new seal. If a deep gouge is present, carefully clean and dry the area around the gouge, then fill the depression with a suitable epoxy so it is level with the surrounding metal.

6. Check the crankshaft seal area. Scoring, grooves, or sharp edges on the crankshaft will require that the crankshaft be replaced.

Installation

1. Apply Loctite 598 or an equivalent oil resistant non-hardening sealer to the periphery of the oil seal prior to installation.

2. Coat the lips of the seal with light grease.

3. Cover keyways and threads on the crankshaft with the proper size seal protector sleeve from B&S Sleeve Kit No. 19334 or 19356, or thin tape so the oil seal lip will not be cut when passing the oil seal down the crankshaft. **Figure 112** shows the seal installed onto a protector sleeve.

4. Position the seal so the seal lip is slanted toward the inside of the engine. Most seals are spring-loaded. The spring must be toward the engine when installing the seal.

5. Use a suitable tool with the same outside diameter as the oil seal to drive the oil seal into the engine. Suitable sizes of tubing or pipe may be used (**Figure 113**).

a. The flywheel-end crankcase seal should be flush with the face of the seal bore.

b. The oil pan seal should be 1.5 mm (1/16 in.) below the edge of the seal bore.

INTERNAL ENGINE COMPONENTS

Although some internal components can be serviced without a complete disassembly, damage to one internal engine component often affects some or all of the other parts inside the engine. Failing to inspect all of the components may result in a future repair that could have been avoided.

Refer to **Figure 94** when performing internal component procedures.

ENGINE DISASSEMBLY

Use the following procedure to disassemble the engine, referring to previous sections where necessary to remove the external components. If the components are to be reused, mark them as necessary to identify them for proper placement upon reassembly.

WARNING
Some gasoline may drain from the fuel pump and/or the carburetor during this

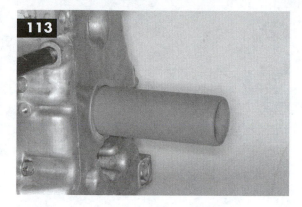

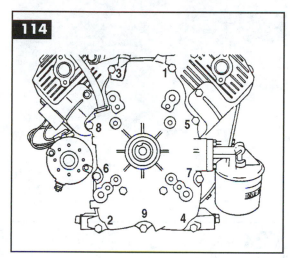

procedure. Wipe up any spilled gasoline immediately. Work in a well-ventilated area at least 50 feet from any open flame, including pilot lights in gas appliances. Do not allow anyone to smoke in the area. Do not work near any grinding or other source of sparks.

1. On electric-start units, disconnect the battery, negative cable first.

2. Turn the fuel tank valve off (Figure 4).

3. Drain the engine oil and remove the engine from the equipment. Remove the oil filter.

4. Remove the following components:
   a. Muffler and exhaust system.
   b. Fuel pump, blower housing, cooling shrouds and baffles.
   c. Air filter assembly, carburetor and intake manifold.
   d. Ignition modules.
   e. Flywheel.
   f. Alternator stator.
   g. External governor controls.
   h. Blower shroud base plate.

   i. Electric starter motor, if used.
   j. PTO clutch, pulley and key(s).
   k. Spark plugs, valve covers, rocker arm assemblies and cylinder heads.

   NOTE
   The push rod for the exhaust valve is aluminum; the push rod for the intake valve is steel.

   l. Push rods.
   m. Crankcase breather.

5. Remove the carbon ridge at the top of the cylinder bore. Run a fingernail over the top portion of the cylinder to determine if a wear ridge exists. Use a ridge reamer to remove the ridge at the top of the cylinder. Remove any shavings or grit from the ridge removal process.

6. Remove any rust or burrs from the crankshaft extensions. This will prevent damage to the main bearings. A strip of emery cloth can be used to remove rust. Burrs may be found adjacent to the keyways. It may be necessary to file down the end of the crankshaft to the original crankshaft diameter.

7. Unscrew the oil pan retaining screws (**Figure 114**).

8. Remove the oil pan by tapping with a soft-faced mallet. Do not pry between the mating surfaces. Do not use excessive force against the oil pan. Applying excessive force may damage the main bearing or oil pan. If binding occurs, determine if an obstruction on the crankshaft, such as a burr, is causing the binding. If no obstruction is present, then the crankshaft may be bent. If the crankshaft is bent, then a replacement short block should be considered, depending on the condition of the other internal engine components.

WARNING
When a crankshaft becomes bent, stress points are introduced into the crankshaft. When a bent crankshaft is straightened, additional stresses are introduced, further weakening the shaft. For this reason, straightening a bent crankshaft is not recommended.

9. Position the engine so the tappets will not fall out.

10. Rotate the crankshaft so the timing marks on the crankshaft gear and camshaft gear are aligned (**Figure 115**).

11. Remove the camshaft.

12. Mark the tappets prior to removing them so they can be reinstalled in their original positions.

13. Unscrew the connecting rod cap retaining screws and remove the rod cap on the No. 2 cylinder connecting rod (nearer the crankshaft PTO end).

NOTE
Care must be exercised not to damage the bearing surface of the crankshaft, connecting rod and rod cap.

10

14. Push the connecting rod and piston in the No. 2 cylinder out the top of the engine.

15. Repeat steps 13 and 14 for the No. 1 cylinder.

16. Remove the crankshaft.

17. If necessary, remove the oil pump and governor shaft assemblies from the oil pan as described in subsequent sections.

The major components of the engine should now be removed from the engine crankcase. Refer to the following sections for further disassembly and inspection of major components.

PISTONS, PISTON RINGS AND PISTON PINS

The aluminum-alloy pistons are each fitted with two compression rings and one oil control ring. Pistons and rings are available in standard size as well as 0.010 in., 0.020 in. and 0.030 in. (0.25 mm, 0.51 mm and 0.76 mm) oversize.

To remove the pistons, follow Steps 1-17 in the preceding *Engine Disassembly* section.

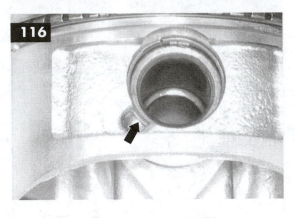

Disassembly

Use the following procedure to separate the piston from the connecting rod:

1. Using a small pry tool inserted into the piston pin retainer cutout (**Figure 116**), extract the piston pin retaining clips.

2. Push or tap out the piston pin. If the piston or connecting rod might be reused, take care not to damage the pin bores.

> *NOTE*
> *If the piston pin is stuck in the piston, a puller tool like that shown in **Figure 117** can be fabricated to extract the pin.*

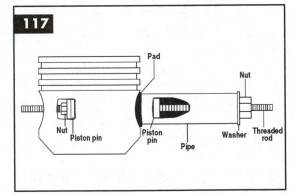

3. Separate the piston from the connecting rod.

> *NOTE*
> *A suitable piston ring expander tool (**Figure 118**) should be used to remove or install the compression rings. Although the rings can be removed or installed by hand, there is less chance of piston ring breakage or gouging the piston ring grooves when the ring expander tool is used.*

4. Remove the piston rings while noting the following:
   a. Remove the top compression ring (closest to the piston crown) first.
   b. Remove the No. 2 compression ring second.
   c. Remove the oil control ring last.
   d. Move the rings toward the piston crown for removal. Use care not to gouge the ring lands. Due to

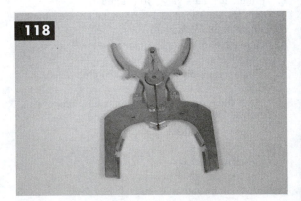

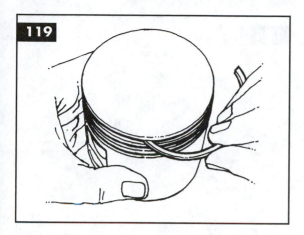

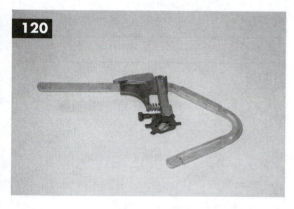

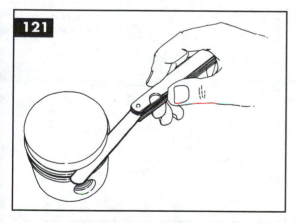

Inspection

1. Clean the top of the piston using a soft wire brush. Soaking the piston in carburetor cleaner can help loosen hard deposits.

2. Inspect the piston for damage. Replace the piston if it is cracked, scored, scuffed or scratched. Be sure to inspect the underside of the piston around the piston pin bosses for cracks, as well as the piston ring grooves. The piston crown must be smooth except for machining or casting marks. The piston should fit snugly in the cylinder bore, provided the cylinder bore is within specification.

3. Piston diameter sizes are not specified by Briggs & Stratton. Measure the cylinder bore as described in the *CYLINDER* section. If a cylinder overbore is required, then piston inspection is unnecessary.

> *NOTE*
> *Pistons and rings are available in standard size as well as 0.010 in., 0.020 in. and 0.030 in. (0.25 mm, 0.51 mm and 0.76 mm) oversize. Be sure the proper size is available before machining the cylinder or purchasing components.*

4. Place a new piston ring in the clean top piston ring groove and measure the side (ring land) clearance using a feeler gauge as shown in **Figure 121**. Replace the piston if a new top or second piston ring has a side clearance of 0.10 mm (0.004 in.).

5. Inspect the piston pin and the piston pin bores in the piston for scoring and other damage. The piston pin is only available in the standard size; replace the piston and pin if wear exceeds specification.

    a. Measure the piston pin diameter at several points to determine if the piston pin is out-of-round. The piston pin should be replaced if it is out-of-round by 0.01 mm (0.0005 in.) or more.

    b. Replace the piston pin if it is worn at any point to 17.064 mm (0.6718 in.) or less.

    c. Replace the piston if the piston pin bore diameter is equal to or greater than 17.12 mm (0.674 in.).

6. Measure the end gap of each piston ring. Place the piston ring in the cylinder bore, then push the piston ring down into the bore with the piston so the ring is square in the bore. Position the piston ring 1.0 inch (25 mm) down in the bore from the top of the cylinder and measure the piston ring end gap as shown in **Figure 122**. Reject size for the piston ring end gap is 0.76 mm (0.030 in.).

Reassembly

1. Use a suitable piston ring expander tool (**Figure 118**) to install the piston rings. Although the rings can be removed or installed by hand, there is less chance of piston ring breakage or gouging the piston ring grooves when the ring expander tool is used.

the flexibility of the oil control ring rails, carefully twist them out of the groove rather than use the expander tool. Discard the piston rings. Reusing worn rings is not recommended.

5. Clean the piston ring grooves. One method for cleaning piston ring grooves is to pull the end of a broken piston ring through the groove as shown in **Figure 119**. Use care not to gouge or otherwise damage the groove. Professional piston ring groove cleaning tools are also available (**Figure 120**).

10

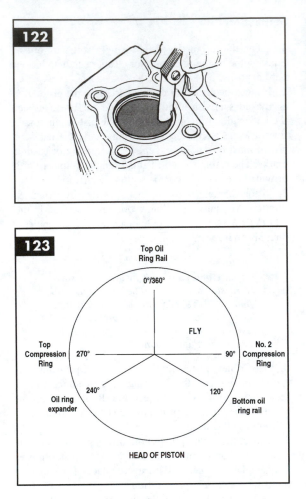

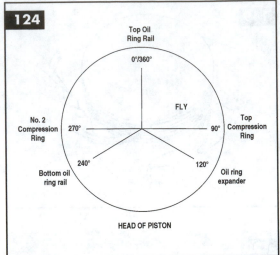

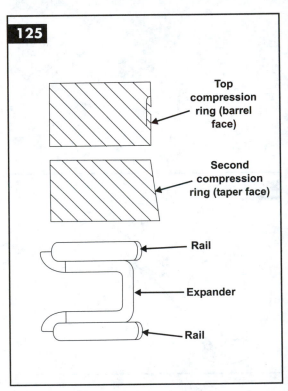

2. For maximum engine power and longevity, as well as precise emission control, the ring end gaps should be spaced around the piston circumference in the approximate intervals shown in **Figure 123** and **Figure 124**. **Figure 123** is the gap spacing recommendation for the No. 1 piston; **Figure 124** is for No. 2 piston.

    a. The arrow or notch mark on the piston head will indicate the 0°/360° position. Degree readings will advance counterclockwise for the No. 1 piston and clockwise for No. 2 piston.

    b. Refer to **Figure 125** for a cross-sectional view of the rings.

    c. The top (No. 1) compression ring has a barrel-shaped face. It should have its gap at the 90° position.

    d. The No. 2 compression ring (center groove) has a tapered face that is larger at the bottom of the piston. It should have its gap at the 270° position.

    e. The seam or gap of the oil control ring expander should be in the 120° position.

    f. The top oil control ring rail should have its gap at the 0°/360° position.

    g. The bottom oil control ring rail should have its gap at the 240° position.

3. Lubricate the rings and ring grooves in the piston prior to assembly.

4. Install the oil control ring (**Figure 126**) first using the following procedure:

    a. Install the ring expander in the ring groove. The expander ring ends must abut, not overlap (**Figure 127**).

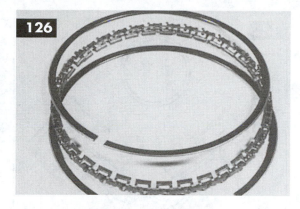

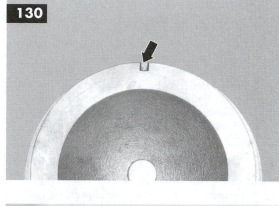

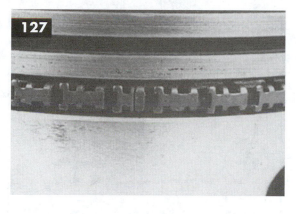

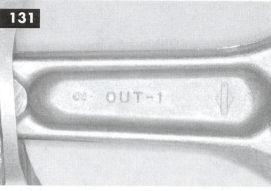

10

b. Twist one of the rails in a spiral and work it into the top piston ring groove (**Figure 128**), then into the center groove, and finally into the oil ring groove, placing the first rail against the bottom of the expander ring.

c. Install the second rail using the same procedure so it fits above the expander and the end gap is properly positioned. The installed oil control ring should appear as shown in **Figure 129**. The oil control ring assembly must rotate without binding in the piston ring groove.

5. Install the center compression ring, then the top compression ring. Note that the top side of each compression ring (toward the piston crown) is marked with a T.

6. Assemble the piston and connecting rod so the arrow or notch on the piston crown (**Figure 130**) is toward the flywheel and opposite the respective cylinder number on the side of the connecting rod (**Figure 131**).

NOTE
*One connecting rod part number services both cylinders. The rod has a "1" on one side and a "2" on the other side (**Figure 132**). The rods must be installed with their corresponding cylinder numbers facing outward, toward the PTO end of the crankshaft.*

7. Lubricate the piston pin bores and pin.
8. Install one of the piston pin clips in its piston pin bore groove.

> *CAUTION*
> *Make sure that the gap of the clip is at either the top or bottom of the piston. Installing the clips with the gap towards the sides could cause the clips to work loose during engine operation, resulting in serious engine damage.*

9. Insert the piston pin.
10. Install the remaining piston pin retaining clip.
11. Be sure the piston pin retaining clips are securely positioned in the piston grooves.

CONNECTING ROD

Disassembly

The piston and connecting rod are removed from the engine as an assembly, then separated, as outlined in the preceding section.

Inspection

1. Connecting rod specifications are listed in **Table 5** at the end of this chapter.
2. The connecting rod rides directly on the crankshaft crankpin. Inspect the bearing surfaces for signs of scuffing and scoring. If any damage is observed, also inspect the surface of the mating crankpin or piston pin.

> *NOTE*
> *If either rod bearing surface is worn due to abrasive particles (the surface texture is dull and rough), the connecting rod should be replaced even if it is not worn beyond the specified wear limit. Grit may be embedded in the aluminum, which will continue to cause wear on the mating surfaces.*

3. Inspect the connecting rod for cracks, twisting and other damage.
4. Measure the inner diameter of the connecting rod big end (A, **Figure 133**) after installing the rod cap. Be sure the match marks (B) on the rod and cap are aligned. Tighten the connecting rod screws to 13 N·m (115 in.-lb.).
5. Replace the connecting rod if the big end diameter is equal to or greater than 37.122 mm (1.4615 in.).

> *NOTE*
> *Connecting rods that are 0.020 in. (0.51 mm) undersize are available to fit a reground crankshaft crankpin. If the crankpin is reground, both rods must be*

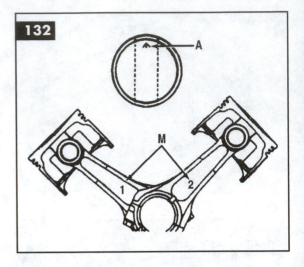

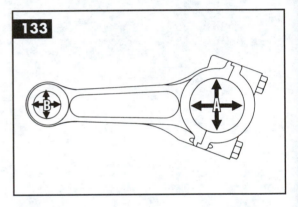

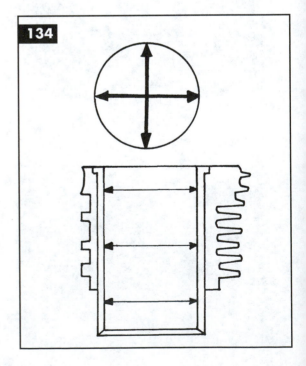

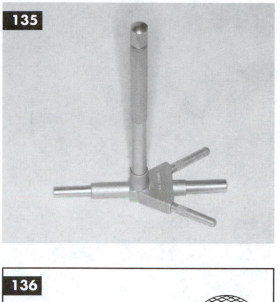

135

136

45°-50°

Inspection and Reconditioning

1. Remove all gasket and sealant material from the sealing surfaces. Sealing surfaces must be free from nicks, gouges or deep scratches.

2. Inspect the fastener holes for damaged threads or broken fasteners. Restore damaged threads with an appropriate size metric tap or install a replacement thread such as a Heli-Coil if necessary.

3. Check for broken cooling fins. A small broken edge or corner may not affect performance. A large piece of broken-off fin will cause the cylinder to overheat. Replace the cylinder block if major fin damage is evident.

4. Check for debris packed in between the fins. Carefully and completely remove any heat-caked debris.

5. Check the bores for scoring or other damage.

6. If the cylinder has been previously rebored, the piston will be marked .010, .020 or .030 to show its oversize. A block whose cylinder will not clean up at .030 inch oversize or one that has already been rebored to .030 inch oversize and then worn beyond limits will need to be replaced.

7. Measure the cylinder bore parallel with the crankshaft and at right angles to the crankshaft at the top, center and bottom of ring travel (**Figure 134**). A B&S Telescoping Bore Gauge No. 19404 (**Figure 135**) or an inside micrometer can be used to precisely measure cylinder bores. Compare the measurements to the dimensions listed in **Table 5**.

8. If the cylinder bore is within wear specifications, the bore will need to be honed so new rings will seat properly. The crosshatch angle of the bore surface after finish honing should be 45°-50° as shown in **Figure 136**. Too large an angle will cause high oil consumption; too small an angle will make the rings skip and wear rapidly. If the honing is being done in-shop, follow the hone manufacturer's instructions.

9. If the cylinder is being rebored oversize, rebore to the specified original-plus-oversize dimension. Always follow the bore machine manufacturer's instructions. The final step of a rebore should always be a finish honing. The crosshatch angle of the cylinder bore surface after finish honing should be 45°-50° as shown in **Figure 136**.

10. After honing, thoroughly wash the cylinder with plenty of soap and hot water, then rinse in clean warm water. Blow dry with compressed air. This will remove grinding particles from the surface of the cylinder bore. A grease-cutting dishwashing detergent is good cleanser. Do not use petroleum solvents (mineral spirits, kerosene, etc.) as they will not remove embedded grinding dust.

11. After drying the cylinder:

    a. Spray the bore with a moisture-displacing lubricant such as WD-40 or equivalent.

10

replaced. Instructions are included with the new rod.

6. Measure the inside diameter of the small end of the connecting rod (C, **Figure 133**). Replace the connecting rod if the piston pin bore in the connecting rod is equal to or greater than 17.12 mm (0.674 in.).

Reassembly

Refer to the preceding *Piston, Rings And Pin* section for the procedure to assemble the connecting rod and piston.

CYLINDERS/CYLINDER BLOCK/CRANKCASE

The cylinders are cast-iron alloy sleeves integrally cast into the aluminum alloy crankcase and block assembly.

To access the cylinders, follow the steps outlined in the previous *Engine Disassembly* section.

Pistons and ring sets are available in standard size as well as 0.010 in., 0.020 in. and 0.030 in. (0.25 mm, 0.51 mm and 0.76 mm) oversize to fit rebored cylinder bores.

b. Use a clean lint-free cloth to wipe the lubricant from the bore. If gray residue shows up on the wiping cloth, the cylinder is not clean. Repeat Step 11.

c. Apply a light coat of engine oil to the bore to prevent rust.

> *CAUTION*
> *Failure to properly clean a cylinder after honing will cause rapid cylinder and piston wear and severe engine damage.*

CRANKSHAFT AND MAIN BEARINGS

These engines use a replaceable sleeve-style upper main bearing (A, **Figure 137**) on the flywheel side.

The lower main bearing is an integral part of the oil pan, machined into the oil pan casting (A, **Figure 138**).

The crankshaft is pictured in **Figure 139**.

> *NOTE*
> *When replacing a crankshaft, short block, or engine, ensure that the threads on the PTO bolt that was removed from the old crankshaft are compatible with the threads in the new crankshaft.*

The crankshaft and main bearing specifications are listed in **Table 5**.

Removal

To remove the crankshaft, follow the steps in the previous *ENGINE DISASSEMBLY* section.

Inspection and Reconditioning

1. If considerable effort was required to remove the oil pan from the crankshaft, then the crankshaft is probably bent and must be discarded. If some effort was required during removal, then the crankshaft should be checked for straightness. If the oil pan was easy to remove, and the bearings are within specifications, then the crankshaft is probably straight.

2. Inspect all bearing surfaces on the crankshaft for indications of scoring, scuffing or other damage. This includes the main and thrust bearing faces. Make sure that the oil galleries (**Figure 140**) are clean and clear.

3. Check the fastener threads, such as the flywheel and PTO threads (**Figure 139**), for damage.

4. Inspect the keyways (**Figure 139**) and carefully remove any burrs. The keyways must be straight and unworn. The PTO extension must also be straight and unworn.

5. The crankshaft gear is removable.

a. Check the crankshaft gear (A, **Figure 141**) for broken or pitted teeth. If the gear teeth are question-

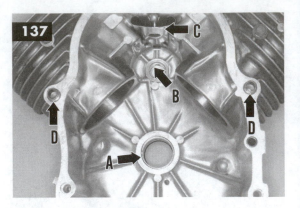

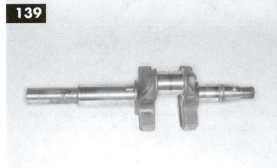

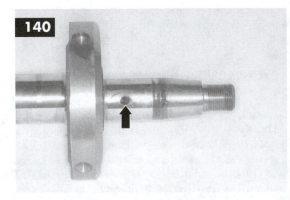

141

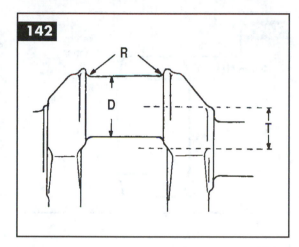

142

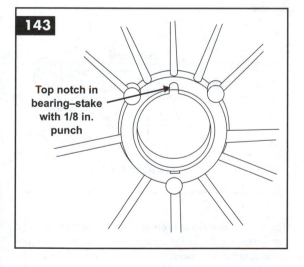

143

Top notch in
bearing–stake
with 1/8 in.
punch

able, also inspect the camshaft and oil pump gear
teeth.

b. Check the crankshaft gear key. The key should remain tightly fitted in the keyway.

6. Measure the connecting rod (crankpin) journal (**Figure 139**).

a. Regrind the crankshaft if the crankpin diameter is
36.96 mm (1.455 in.) or less. Connecting rods that
are 0.020 inch (0.51 mm) undersize are available
to fit a reground crankshaft crankpin.

b. If the crankpin is reground, both rods must be replaced, as one crankpin serves both rods.

c. If the crankpin is reground, refer to **Figure 142** and
the crankpin regrind chart for finish dimensions.

7. Measure the main bearing journals (**Figure 139**). Note
the engine code number for the flywheel journal dimension. Replace the crankshaft if:

a. The PTO journal diameter is equal to or less than
34.92 mm (1.375 in.).

b. The flywheel journal diameter is 29.95 mm (1.179
in.) before Code 97050100.

c. The flywheel journal diameter is 34.95 mm (1.376
in.) after Code 97043000.

8A. Crankcase main bearing before Code 97050100 –
Inspect the main bearing (bushing) surface in the crankcase (A, **Figure 137**). The surface must be smooth with
no sign of abrasion. The reject size for the bushing diameter is 30.08 mm (1.1845 in.). Use the following procedure
to replace the bushing in the crankcase:

a. If the oil seal is still in place, remove it.

b. Measure the depth of the bushing in the crankcase
so the new bushing can be installed in the same position.

c. Use Briggs and Stratton Driver No. 19450 or other
suitable tool to press out the old bushing. Be sure
to adequately support the crankcase bore area to
prevent cracking the crankcase.

d. Note the position of the oil holes in the bushing and
the crankcase bore. They must align after bushing
installation.

e. Using Briggs and Stratton Driver No. 19450 or
other suitable tool, press in the new bushing to the
previously measured depth. Be sure to adequately
support the crankcase bore area to prevent cracking the crankcase. Be sure the oil holes in the bushing and crankcase are aligned.

f. Use a 1/8-inch punch to stake the edge of the bushing into the notch in the crankcase (**Figure 143**).

g. Install a new oil seal so it is flush with the crankcase.

8B. Crankcase main bearing after Code 97043000 – Inspect the main bearing (bushing) surface in the crankcase
(A, **Figure 137**). The surface must be smooth with no
sign of abrasion. The reject size for the bushing diameter
is 35.12 mm (1.383 in.). Use the following procedure to
replace the bushing in the crankcase:

a. If still in place, remove the oil seal.

b. Measure the depth of the bushing in the crankcase
so the new bushing can be installed in the same position.

10

c. The bushing is held in place by a roll pin. Using a suitable punch, drive the roll pin into the oil passage in the crankcase (**Figure 144**).

d. Use Briggs and Stratton Driver No. 19349 or other suitable tool to press out the old bushing. Be sure to adequately support the crankcase bore area to prevent cracking the crankcase.

e. The replacement roll pin is tapered at both ends. Grind off the tapered portion of one end of the pin (**Figure 145**). Quench the pin in water as needed during grinding to prevent loss of temper. Deburr the ground end, then clean the pin.

f. Note the position of the oil holes in the bushing and the crankcase bore. They must align after bushing installation.

g. Use Briggs and Stratton Driver No. 19349 or other suitable tool to press in the new bushing to the previously measured depth. Be sure to adequately support the crankcase bore area to prevent cracking the crankcase. Be sure the oil holes in the bushing and crankcase are aligned.

h. Install the roll pin, tapered end first. Use Briggs and Stratton Driver No. 19344 to drive the pin into the bushing and crankcase (**Figure 146**). Drive in the pin until the tool bottoms.

i. Install a new oil seal so it is flush with the crankcase.

10. Measure the inside bearing (bushing) diameter in the oil pan (**Figure 138**). Replace the oil pan if the bushing diameter is equal to or more than 35.07 mm (1.381 in.).

Installation

To install the crankshaft, follow the necessary steps in the subsequent *Engine Reassembly* section.

> *CAUTION*
> *When reinstalling the gear onto the crankshaft, ensure that the timing mark on the gear faces out (**Figure 142**).*

CAMSHAFT, LIFTERS AND COMPRESSION RELEASE

The camshaft (**Figure 147**) rides directly in bores machined into the aluminum of the crankcase and oil pan (B, Figures 137 and 138).

To remove the camshaft from the engine, follow the necessary steps in the previous *Engine Disassembly* section.

The camshaft is equipped with a compression release mechanism to aid starting. The sliding weight mechanism on the camshaft gear (**Figure 148**) and inside the camshaft moves balls inside the exhaust cam lobes. At rest or during starting, the spring (A, **Figure 148**) holds the actuator cam weight (B) inward against the actuator rod (C).

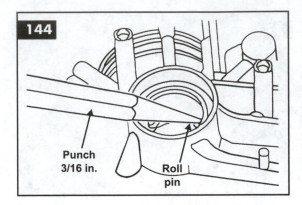

144

Punch 3/16 in.   Roll pin

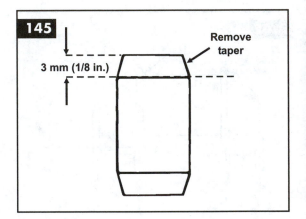

145

3 mm (1/8 in.)   Remove taper

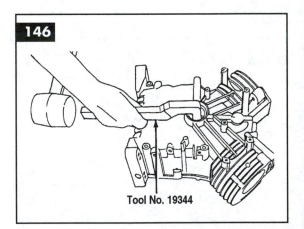

146

Tool No. 19344

This causes the balls to protrude beyond the bottom of the cam lobes and forces the exhaust valves to stay open longer during the compression stroke, thereby reducing compression. At running speed, centrifugal force causes the weight to pivot outward against the spring, freeing the actuator rod mechanism. This moves the balls below the surface of the cam lobes, allowing the engine to develop full power.

On the side of the camshaft gear opposite the lobes, the camshaft also contains the flyweight governor assembly.

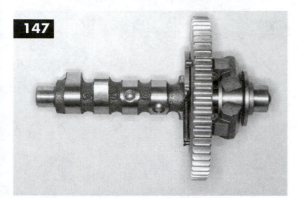

147

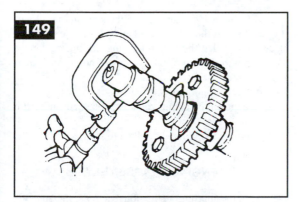

148

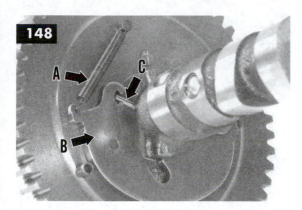

149

150

Inspection

Camshaft specifications are listed in **Table 5**.

1. Inspect the camshaft and gear for wear on the journals, cam lobes and gear teeth.

2. Measure the diameter of the flywheel-end bearing journal. The reject diameter is 15.933 mm (0.6273 in.).

3. Measure the diameter of the PTO-end bearing journal. The reject diameter is 19.926 mm (0.7845 in.).

4. Measure the height of the intake and exhaust lobes (**Figure 149**). Replace the camshaft if the lobe height is 30.25 mm (1.191 in.) or less.

5. Inspect the camshaft bearing surfaces in the crankcase (B, **Figure 137**) and oil pan (B, **Figure 138**). The surface must be smooth with no sign of abrasion.

    a. Measure the inside bearing diameter in the crankcase. Replace the crankcase if the diameter is 16.08 mm (0.633 in.) or greater.

    b. Measure the inside bearing diameter in the oil pan. Replace the oil pan if the diameter is 20.04 mm (0.788 in.) or greater.

6. Inspect the compression release mechanism. The mechanism should move freely without binding. No individual components are available.

7. Inspect the tappets for excessive wear on the camshaft contact surfaces. Check for excessive side play with the tappet installed in the crankcase bore.

10

GOVERNOR (Internal Service)

The governor weight assembly is attached to the camshaft. A spool (A, **Figure 150**) fits into the flyweight fingers (B) and moves in and out according to the flyweight position. The governor shaft located in the oil pan transmits motion from the thrust face on the camshaft spool to the governor linkage. The shaft rides in two bushings in the oil pan (**Figure 151**).

> *NOTE*
> *The spool is the only replaceable camshaft/governor component. If any other components are worn or damaged, the camshaft must be replaced.*

1. Inspect the flyweight assembly on the camshaft (B, **Figure 150**) for broken or excessively worn components.

2. Inspect the bushings in the oil pan (**Figure 151**). The lower flange bushing is replaceable. The pressed-in upper oil pan bushing is not replaceable.

3. Replace the seal in the oil pan (**Figure 151**). The seal lip should be in toward the pan. The seal outer face should be *slightly* below flush with the pan bore.

4. Inspect the governor shaft assembly (**Figure 151**).

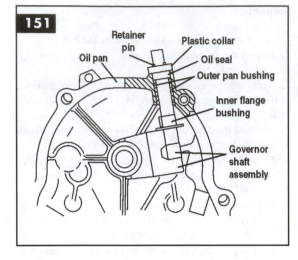

Retainer pin — Plastic collar
Oil pan — Oil seal
— Outer pan bushing
— Inner flange bushing
— Governor shaft assembly

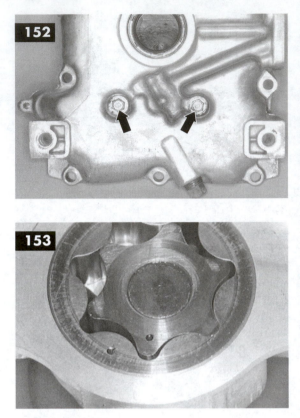

5. Assemble the governor shaft assembly as shown in **Figure 151**.

6. Assemble the governor flyweight and spool as shown in **Figure 150**. Be sure the slot in the spool fits around the pin (C).

OIL PUMP

The rotor-type oil pump is located in the oil pan. The crankshaft gear drives the oil pump gear. The oil pump is serviced as an assembly; individual components are not available.

Removal

1. To access the oil pump assembly inside the engine, remove the oil pan by following the necessary steps in the previous *Engine Disassembly* section.

2. Remove the oil pump bolts from the outside of the pan (**Figure 152**). Remove the oil pump rotors (**Figure 153**).

3. Remove the pick-up screen (**Figure 154**).

4. Clean the pan and all the pump components.

Inspection

1. Inspect the oil pump housing and gears (**Figure 153**). If the pump components are excessively worn, badly scored or damaged, replace the pump.

2. Inspect the oil pan surface (**Figure 153**). If damaged, replace the pan.

3. Inspect the pick-up screen. Replace the screen if damaged.

Installation

1. If removed, install the rotors so the dimples on the rotors are visible (**Figure 153**).

2. Install the pick-up screen into the slots in the oil pan (**Figure 154**). A flange on the oil pump holds the screen in place. Ensure that the screen housing fits slightly below the pan pump surface or the pump will not torque down and operate properly.

3. Install the oil pump to the pan:
   a. Be sure the sealing rings are installed under the bolt heads.
   b. Tighten the bolts to 7.0 N•m (62 in.-lb.).

ENGINE REASSEMBLY

Refer to the appropriate previous sections when installing the external engine components as applicable. Refer to **Figure 94** for internal engine component identification.

Before assembling the engine, be sure all components are clean. Any residue or debris left in the engine will cause rapid wear and/or major damage when the engine runs.

NOTE
Lubricate all internal component contact surfaces with fresh engine oil immediately prior to assembly.

1. Make certain that the crankcase breather baffle is positioned above the tappet bore castings (C, **Figure 137**).

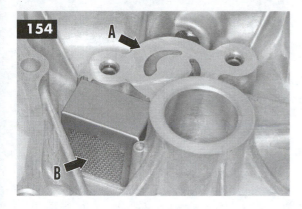

2. Install the crankshaft into the crankcase. If the flywheel-side oil seal has already been installed, use the proper size seal protector sleeve from B&S Sleeve Kit No. 19334 or 19356 or a rolled-up microfiche card or other thin plastic to prevent the crankshaft from damaging the seal. Coat the lip of the seal with light grease. Insert the sleeve into the seal before installing the crankshaft.

3. Install the piston and connecting rod assemblies into the engine:

a. Rotate the crankshaft so the connecting rod journal is at BDC on the No. 1 cylinder.

b. Double-check the ring end-gap alignment for the No. 1 piston assembly as specified in the *Pistons, Reassembly* section. Use a ring compressor (**Figure 155**) to compress the piston rings. Make sure that the top and bottom edges of the compressor band are not misaligned, the projections on the compressor band are toward the piston skirt and the oil ring is at least 6 mm (1/4 in.) above the bottom edge of the compressor.

c. Lightly coat the cylinder bore surface with Lubriplate White Grease or fresh engine oil.

d. With the rod cap removed, install the piston and rod assembly into the cylinder so the ring compressor rests on the cylinder head gasket surface. The casting notch or arrow stamped on the piston

crown should point toward the flywheel side of the engine (**Figure 132**). The No. 1 cylinder number on the connecting rod beam will then be facing out, toward the PTO end of the crankshaft.

e. Use the grip end of a hammer to carefully push the piston into the cylinder while guiding the end of the connecting rod so it does not scratch the cylinder.

CAUTION
Do not use excessive force when installing the piston and rod. If binding occurs, remove the piston and rod and try again. Excessive force can damage or break the piston rings, piston ring lands, connecting rod or crankshaft.

f. When the piston clears the ring compressor, stop pushing and set the compressor aside.

g. Continue pushing the piston into the cylinder by hand until the rod journal bearing is completely into the crankcase area.

h. Rotate the crankshaft and carefully guide the connecting rod onto the crankshaft journal. Do not allow the end of the rod to scratch the crankshaft.

i. Install the cap onto the rod, making sure the match marks align (**Figure 156**). Install and torque the rod bolts to 13.0 N•m (115 in.-lb.).

j. Repeat Steps a-i for the No. 2 cylinder. All step references to No. 1 cylinder will be for No. 2 cylinder. Ensure that the No. 2 rod and cap match marks align (**Figure 157**).

4. Rotate the crankshaft to check for freedom of movement of the pistons and rods. Stop the crankshaft with the camshaft timing mark pointing toward the camshaft location (**Figure 141**).

5. Position the engine so the tappets will not fall out, then install the tappets in their original positions.

6. Install the camshaft so the timing marks on the gears are aligned (**Figure 115**).

10

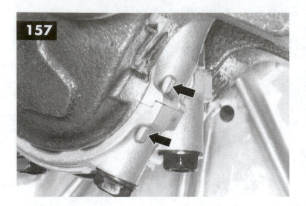

7. Be sure the governor spool is installed on the camshaft. The spool must engage the flyweights. The spool flange must index on the pin shown in **Figure 150**.

8. Be sure the locating sleeves are installed in the crankcase (A, **Figure 158**, 1 of 2 shown).

9. Install the O-ring (B, **Figure 158**) into the recess in the crankcase oil passage.

10. Install the crankcase gasket with a nonhardening sealer. At least one 0.015-inch thick crankcase gasket must be installed.

11. Rotate the governor shaft so the arm contacts the oil pan (**Figure 159**).

12. If the oil pan seal has already been installed, use the proper size seal protector sleeve from B&S Sleeve Kit No. 19334 or 19356 or a rolled-up microfiche card or other thin plastic to prevent the crankshaft from damaging the seal. Coat the lips of the seal with light grease. Insert the sleeve into the seal before installing the oil pan.

13. Install the oil pan, being careful to mesh the oil pump gear with the crankshaft gear. Remove the seal protector.

NOTE
Do not force the oil pan onto the crankcase. If binding occurs, remove the oil pan and determine the cause.

14. Install the oil pan bolts. Tighten the bolts in 4.5 N•m (40 in.-lb.) increments to 17 N•m (150 in.-lb.) in the sequence shown in **Figure 160**.

15. Measure the crankshaft end play. Recommended end play is 0.08-0.40 mm (0.003-0.015 in.). If end play does not meet specification, remove the oil pan and adjust the end play with the different thicknesses of thrust washers available in B&S Thrust Washer Kit No. 807625. Fit the washer between the crankshaft gear and the oil pan. The kit includes one washer each of the following thicknesses: 1.0 mm (0.039 in.), 1.25 mm (0.049 in.) and 1.5 mm (0.059 in.).

16. Repeat Steps 12-14. Recheck end play.

17. Install the PTO shaft keys, pulley and clutch. The assembled engine block can now be installed onto the

mower, if desired, for installation of the external components.

18. Paying close attention to the location and orientation marks made during disassembly, install the following components:

   a. Crankcase breather.

   b. Cylinder heads.

   c. Push rods.

NOTE
The push rod for the exhaust valve is aluminum; the push rod for the intake valve is steel.

   d. Rocker arm assemblies.

   e. Valve covers.

   f. Spark plugs.

   g. Electric starter motor, if used.

   h. Blower shroud base plate.

   i. External governor components.

   j. Alternator stator.

   k. Flywheel.

   l. Ignition modules.

   m. Intake manifold, carburetor, and air filter assembly.

   n. Blower housing, cooling shrouds and baffles.

   o. Fuel pump.

   p. Exhaust system and muffler.

19. During final installation, tighten all fasteners to the correct torques and in the correct sequence. Torque values are listed in **Table 4**.

20. Static adjust the governor.

CAUTION
Prior to starting the engine, the governor linkage must have the static adjustment performed or serious overspeed damage could result. Once the engine is started, the governor must be dynamically adjusted. Refer to the Governor, External Service section for the adjustments.

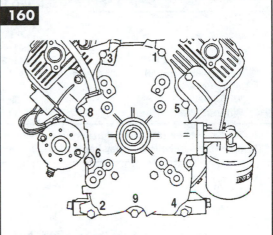

Table 1   GENERAL ENGINE SPECIFICATIONS

Model	No. Cyls.	Bore	Stroke	Displacement	Power Rating
303700	2	68 mm (2.68 in.)	66 mm (2.60 in.)	480 cc (29.3 cu. In.)	16 hp 11.9 kW
350700	2	72 mm (2.83 in.)	70 mm (2.75 in.)	570 cc (34.75 cu. In.)	18 hp 13.5 kW

Table 2   MAINTENANCE AND LUBRICATION SCHEDULE

After 5-hour break-in period (new or overhauled engine)	Change the engine oil and the oil filter.
	Check all the fasteners and the linkages for security.
Every 8 hours or daily	Check the engine oil with the unit sitting level.
	Check and/or clean the air filter.
	Clean the cooling system.
Every 40-50 hours or weekly	Service the air cleaner pre-filter.
	On electric-start units, check the battery electrolyte level.
	Lubricate the throttle and choke cables.
Every 100 hours or semi-monthly	Replace the air filter and pre-filter.
	Change the engine oil and oil filter.
Every 500 hours or annually	Replace the fuel filter.
	Remove cylinder heads and clean the combustion chamber.
	Check all fasteners and tighten as necessary.

Table 3 RECOMMENDED ENGINE FUEL AND LUBRICANTS

Fuel	Unleaded gasoline with pump octane rating of 87 or higher
Capacity	5.0 U.S. gallons (18.7 liters or 4.0 Imperial gallons)
Engine oil	API service rating of SH or above
Above 40° F (4° C)	SAE 30
Between 0° F and 40° F (-18° C and +4° C)	SAE 10W-30
Capacity	
With filter	3.5 pints (1.7 liters)
Without filter	3.0 pints (1.42 liters)

NOTE: Do not use 10W-40 oil in the engine. Recommended engine oil viscosities are for petroleum-based oils. Comparable synthetic oils may be used. Do not mix synthetic oil with petroleum oil.

Table 4 FASTENER TIGHTENING TORQUES

Item	N.m	ft.-lb.	in.-lb.
Spark plug	23	16.5	200
Alternator stator	2.0	–	20
Air filter base to carburetor	7.0	–	65
Blower housing mount plate	7.0	–	65
Blower housing	7.0	–	65
Breather cover	3.0	–	30
Carburetor mounting screws	7.0	–	65
Connecting rod	13	–	115
Cylinder head bolts	19	–	165
Cylinder head cover nuts	3.0	–	27
Cylinder shields	7.0	–	65
Electric starter mount bolts	16	–	140
Electric starter through-bolts	6.0	–	50
Exhaust manifold	17	–	150
Fan retainer	17	–	150
Flywheel nut	175	125	–
Governor control bracket	16	–	140
Governor lever nut	8.0	–	70
Ignition module	3.0	–	25
Intake manifold	16	–	142
Oil pan	17	–	150
Oil pump	7.0	–	65
Rewind starter mount bolts.	7.0	–	60
Rocker arm lock nut	7.0	–	60
Rocker arm studs (current)	11	–	100
Rocker shaft studs (early)	16	–	142

Table 5 ENGINE CLEARANCES AND SPECIFICATIONS

Angle of Operation, Maximum	
Continuous operation	15°
Intermittent operation (one minute)	30°
Compression Ratio	8.5:1
Oil pressure	
Normal engine at 3000 rpm	Up to 50 psi
Hot engine at idle	Down to 10 psi
	(continued)

Table 5 ENGINE CLEARANCES AND SPECIFICATIONS (continued)

Camshaft		
End bearing journal diameters		
Cylinder block end		
Standard	15.95-15.97 mm	(0.6280-0.6287 inch)
Wear limit	15.93 mm	(0.6273 inch)
Oil pan end		
Standard	19.94-19.96 mm	(0.7855-0.7860 inch)
Wear limit	19.92 mm	(0.7845 inch)
Bearing bore diameters		
Cylinder block end		
Standard	16.00-16.03 mm	(0.630-0.631 inch)
Wear limit	16.08 mm	(0.633 inch)
Oil pan end		
Standard	Not specified	
Wear limit	20.04 mm	(0.789 inch)
Lobe height dimension		
Intake	30.25 mm	(1.191 inches)
Exhaust	30.25 mm	(1.191 inches)
Connecting rod		
Crankpin, standard	37.06-37.08 mm	(1.459-1.460 inches)
Crankpin wear limit	37.12 mm	(1.4615 inches)
Crankpin side play	Not specified	
Wrist pin bore inside diameter		
Standard	17.09-17.10 mm	(0.6728-0.6735 inch)
Wear limit	17.12 mm	(0.6740 inch)
Crankshaft		
End play	0.08-0.40 mm	(.003-.015 inch)
Main bearing journal, flywheel end		
Before Code 97050100		
Standard diameter	29.98-30.00 mm	(1.180-1.181 inches)
Wear limit	29.95 mm	(1.179 inches)
After Code 97043000		
Standard diameter	34.99-35.01 mm	(1.3776-1.3784 inches)
Wear limit	34.95 mm	(1.376 inches)
Main bearing journal, PTO end		
Standard diameter	34.96-34.97 mm	(1.3765-1.3770 inches)
Wear limit	34.92 mm	(1.375 inches)
Crankpin		
Standard diameter	37.00-37.02 mm	(1.4565-1.4575 inch)
Wear limit	36.95 mm	(1.4550 inch)
Top main bearing		
Inside diameter, standard		
Before Code 97050100	30.03-30.06 mm	(1.1825-1.1835 inches)
After Code 97043000	35.02-35.06 mm	(1.3790-1.3805 inches)
Maximum wear limit		
Before Code 97050100	30.08 mm	(1.1845 inches)
After Code 97043000	35.12 mm	(1.3830 inches)
Oil pan bearing		
Inside diameter, standard	Not specified	
Maximum wear limit	35.07 mm	(1.3810 inches)
Cylinder bore		
Model 303700		
Standard diameter	68.000-68.030 mm	(2.677-2.678 inches)
Wear limit	68.100 mm	(2.681 inches)
Model 350700		
Standard diameter	72.000-72.030 mm	(2.835-2.836 inches)
Wear limit	72.160 mm	(2.839 inches)
Out of round	0.04 mm	(.0015 inch)
Cylinder head warpage, maximum	0.10 mm	(.004 inch)

(continued)

10

Table 5 ENGINE CLEARANCES AND SPECIFICATIONS (continued)

Ignition		
Module to flywheel magnet air gap	0.20-0.30 mm	(0.008-0.012 inch)
Spark plug gap	0.76 mm	(0.030 inch)
Oil seal		
Distance of outer face below crankcase surface		
PTO seal	2.0 mm	(0.079 inch)
Flywheel seal	Flush	
Governor shaft seal	Flush-to-1.0 mm	(0.040 inch)
Piston rings		
End gap (all except oil ring expander)		
Standard	0.20-0.40 mm	(0.008-0.016 inch)
Wear limit	0.76 mm	(0.030 inch)
Ring land clearance		
Top and middle compression rings		
Standard	0.045-0.076 mm	(0.0018-0.0030 inch)
Wear limit	0.010 mm	(0.004 inch)
Oil-control ring		
Standard	0.11-0.15 mm	(0.0045-0.0060 inch)
Wear limit	0.20 mm	(0.008 inch)
Piston pin		
Diameter		
Standard	17.07-17.08 mm	(0.6722-0.6725 inch)
Wear limit	17.06 mm	(0.6718 inch)
Out-of-round	0.01 mm	(0.0005 inch)
Bore inside diameter (piston)		
Standard	17.09-17.10 mm	(0.6728-0.6735 inch)
Wear limit	17.12 mm	(0.6740 inch)
Out-of-round	0.01 mm	(0.0005 inch)
Valves		
Valve clearance at rocker arm		
Intake and Exhaust (cold)	0.10-0.15 mm	(0.004-0.006 inch)

Table 6 VALVE SYSTEM DIMENSIONS

Ref.	Description	Dimension
A	Seat Angle	45° from guide centerlixne
B	Insert Diameter (OD)	Not serviceable
C_1	Guide Depth	Not specified; see C_2
C_2	Guide Protrusion	7.0 mm (0.276 in.)*
D	Guide Diameter (ID)	Wear limit: 6.057 mm (0.2385 in.)
E	Valve Head Diameter	Not specified
F	Valve Face Angle	45° from stem centerline
G	Valve Margin (Minimum)	0.75 mm (0.031 in. or 1/32 in.)
H	Valve Stem Diameter	Wear limit: 5.92 mm (0.233 in.)
J	Valve Seat Width	1.2-1.6 mm (0.046-0.062 in. or 3/64-1/16 in.)
K	Valve Spring Free Length	Minimum 41.0 mm (1.614 in.)
L	Valve Face Width	Not specified

*Protrusion should be measured only when using Guide Driver No. 19274 or No. 19367. Guide Driver No. 19416 automatically sets the protrusion dimension.

CONTROL LINKAGES

This chapter covers the linkages necessary to operate the mower propulsion system. Engine linkages (throttle, choke, and governor) are covered in each appropriate engine chapter. The brake linkage is covered in Chapter Fifteen.

CONTROL LINKAGE ADJUSTMENTS

Three functions on Scag SWZ(U) mowers are controlled by adjustments made to various linkages: neutral, steering, and tracking.

> *NOTE*
> *It is recommended that the adjustments be performed in the order listed.*

In order for the linkages to be properly adjusted, there must not be excessive play in the linkage pivot points. Common sense should be used in determining whether linkage pivot wear is beyond reasonable limits.

The following sections detail the correct procedures for performing these adjustments.

Neutral Adjustment

Scag SWZ(U) mowers use two types of neutral adjustment, the knob style (**Figure 1**) and the handle-and-wingnut style (**Figure 2**).

Knob-style neutral adjustment

To properly locate neutral on the knob-style adjustment:

1. Locate the tracking adjustment knobs just inboard of each drive wheel. Each wheel has its own respective adjustment knob.

2. Block the front wheels so the unit cannot move.

3. Carefully lift the rear of the unit off the floor enough so the drive wheels are not touching the floor. Support the unit in this position, taking care to not allow the supports to interfere with the operation of any linkages.

4. Engage the parking brake.

5. Place the speed control lever in neutral (**Figure 3**).

6. Make sure that the steering control levers are in the neutral lock position (**Figure 4**, right side shown). In neu-

2

NEUTRAL ADJUSTMENT HANDLE

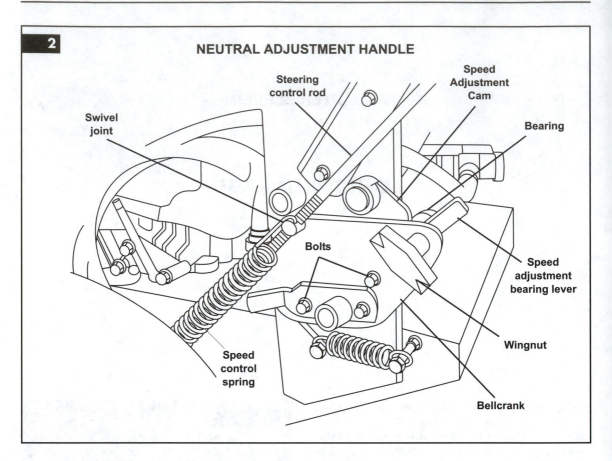

Steering control rod

Speed Adjustment Cam

Swivel joint

Bearing

Bolts

Speed adjustment bearing lever

Speed control spring

Wingnut

Bellcrank

tral lock, the bend at the end of the control rod will be all the way forward in the horizontal slot of the latch.

7. Start the engine.

WARNING
Make sure ventilation is adequate if the engine is to be run in a confined area. Exhaust fumes are toxic and deadly.

8. Release the parking brake. If the drive wheels rotate, note which direction they rotate:

   a. If a wheel rotates forward, turn the tracking adjustment knob clockwise until the wheel stops;

   b. If a wheel rotates backward, turn the tracking adjustment knob counterclockwise until the wheel stops.

9. Working with one wheel at a time, begin by turning the adjustment knob counterclockwise until the wheel *just* begins to rotate forward. Note or mark the knob position.

10. Turn the adjustment knob clockwise until the wheel *just* begins to rotate in reverse. Note or mark the knob position.

11. Neutral is midway between the two noted positions. Turn the knob to that position.

12. Repeat Steps 9-11 with the other side drive wheel.

13. Stop the engine, engage the parking brake, lower the unit down onto the floor and remove the front wheel chocks.

Handle-and-wingnut style neutral adjustment

To properly locate neutral on the handle-and-wingnut style adjustment:

1. Block the front wheels so the unit cannot move.

2. Carefully lift the rear of the unit off the floor far enough so the drive wheels are not touching the floor. Support the unit in this position, taking care to not allow the supports to interfere with the operation of any linkages.

3. Disengage the parking brake, and place the speed control handle in neutral.

4. Disconnect the speed control spring from its lower anchor.

5. Remove the control rod swivel joint from the bellcrank. This will allow the control to move into the neutral position.

6. Loosen the wingnut on the speed adjustment bearing lever. This will allow the bearing to move away from the speed adjustment cam.

7. Start the engine.

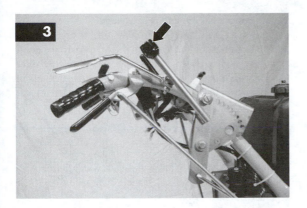

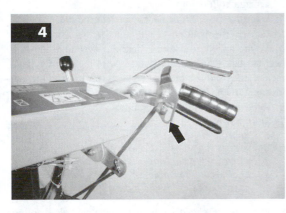

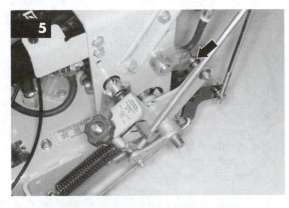

8. If either side drive wheel rotates with the engine running, continue with the adjustment procedure. Each side has its own adjustment. Perform one adjustment at a time. If neither drive wheel rotates, proceed with Step 14.

9. Loosen the two neutral adjustment handle bolts. Slowly move the handle down or up to stop the wheel.

10. Slowly move the handle to just start the wheel rotating *forward*, then reverse the handle until the wheel just stops rotating.

11. Hold the bellcrank to keep from losing the adjustment, then tighten the handle bolts.

12. Use the handle to move the bellcrank into forward and reverse, then release the handle. The system should return to neutral, confirming proper adjustment.

13. Repeat Steps 9-12, if necessary, until neutral self-locates after performing the forward-reverse test.

14. Stop the engine.

15. Reinstall the control rod swivel joint into the bellcrank.

16. Reconnect the speed control spring to its lower anchor.

17. Make sure that the speed control handle is still in neutral. Position each speed-adjustment bearing lever so that the speed control cam lightly contacts the bearing, then tighten the wingnut.

Steering Control Rod Adjustment

Scag SWZ(U) mowers use two steering control rod adjustment designs, the knob style (**Figure 1**) and the handle-and-wingnut style (**Figure 2**). The method of adjustment is the same for both types.

NOTE
The purpose of this adjustment is to prevent engaging reverse when moving the steering control levers out of the neutral latches.

To properly adjust the steering control on the knob-style adjustment:

1. Place the speed control lever in neutral.

2. Make sure that the steering control levers are in the neutral latch position (**Figure 4**).

3. Locate the bellcrank just inboard of each drive wheel (**Figure 5**, left side shown with outer plate removed for clarity).

4. Make sure that the speed control bearing barely contacts the speed control cam (**Figure 5**), and that the bellcrank ball bearing (**Figure 6**) is in the center of the neutral cam groove curve.

11

5. Remove the clevis pin and speed control spring from the steering control rod swivel pin end.

6. Hold the steering control rod swivel pin in the bellcrank slot. If it does not ride in the center of the slot, remove it from the slot and thread it up or down the control rod until it rides in the center of the slot.

7. Reinstall the spring and clevis pin onto the swivel pin end.

8. Repeat Steps 4-7 for the opposite side.

Tracking Adjustment

If the unit pulls to one side while attempting to mow in a straight line, the tracking needs adjusting.

Scag SWZ(U) mowers use two types of tracking adjustment, the knob style (**Figure 1**) and the handle-and-wingnut style (**Figure 2**).

> *NOTE*
> *Before performing the tracking adjustment, ensure that the neutral adjustment has been performed, the steering control rod adjustments have been performed, and the tire pressures are set at 25 psi (165 kPa) front and 15 psi (100 kPa) rear.*

Knob-style tracking adjustment

To adjust the tracking:

1. Note which side the mower pulls toward. During this adjustment, this will be called the slower side.

2. Place the mower on a level, flat surface.

3. Engage both neutral lock latches.

4. Start the engine.

> *WARNING*
> *Make sure ventilation is adequate if the engine is to be run in a confined area. Exhaust fumes are toxic and deadly.*

5. Position the speed adjustment lever into the driving speed which will be used most regularly.

6. Release the neutral latches by depressing the steering control levers, then allow the mower to move forward by slowly releasing the steering control levers.

7. Slowly rotate the tracking adjustment knob counterclockwise on the slower side until the mower tracks straight.

8. Return the steering control levers to the neutral lock position.

9. If the mower creeps forward in neutral on the adjusted side, the adjustment is out of the neutral range. Rotate the tracking adjustment knob clockwise until the creeping stops.

10. Repeat Steps 5 and 6. If the mower again pulls to one side, repeat Steps 7-10.

11. If proper tracking and neutral cannot be obtained by the previous adjustments, inspect all linkages, pivot points, bushings and bearings for wear. Repair as necessary and readjust. If hydrostatic trouble is suspected, refer to the *Troubleshooting* and *Hydrostatic Drive* chapters in this manual.

Handle-and-wingnut style tracking adjustment

To adjust the tracking:

1. Note which side the mower pulls toward. During this adjustment, this will be called the slower side.

2. Place the mower on a level, flat surface.

3. Engage both neutral lock latches.

4. Place the speed adjustment lever in the neutral position.

5. Loosen the bellcrank wingnut on the slower side. Move the speed adjustment bearing lever to where the bearing just lightly makes contact with the speed adjustment cam. Hold the bearing to keep from losing the adjustment, then tighten the wingnut.

6. Repeat Step 5 on the other side.

7. Start the engine.

> *WARNING*
> *Make sure ventilation is adequate if the engine is to be run in a confined area. Exhaust fumes are toxic and deadly.*

8. Position the speed adjustment lever into the driving speed which will be used most regularly.

9. Release the neutral latches by depressing the steering control levers, then allow the mower to move forward by slowly releasing the steering control levers.

10. If the mower still pulls to one side:

   a. Return the speed adjustment lever to the neutral position;

   b. Note the slower side; and

   c. Stop the engine.

11. On the slower side:

   a. Loosen the bellcrank wingnut;

   b. Move the speed adjustment bearing 1/16 inch (1.5 mm) away from the speed adjustment cam;

   c. Tighten the wingnut.

12. Repeat Steps 7-11.

13. If proper tracking and neutral cannot be obtained by the previous adjustments, inspect all linkages, pivot points, bushings and bearings for wear. Repair as necessary and readjust. If hydrostatic trouble is suspected, refer to the *Troubleshooting* and *Hydrostatic Drive* chapters in this manual.

System Test

After making all adjustments, the drive system should operate as follows:

1. Engage the parking brake.

2. Place the speed control lever in neutral (**Figure 3**).

3. Make sure that the steering control levers are in the neutral lock position (**Figure 4**, right side shown).

4. Start the engine and allow it to warm up to operating temperature.

WARNING
Make sure ventilation is adequate if the engine is to be run in a confined area. Exhaust fumes are toxic and deadly.

5. Release the parking brake.

6. Move the speed adjustment lever to the desired speed.

7. While squeezing both steering brake levers, release the neutral latches.

8. After releasing both steering brake levers, the mower should travel straight.
   a. To turn right, squeeze the right-hand lever.
   b. To turn left, squeeze the left-hand lever.

9. To stop:
   a. Squeeze both levers,
   b. Lock the neutral latches, and
   c. Move the speed adjustment lever to neutral.

10. To back up, squeeze up on both steering control levers. To turn in reverse, follow substeps 8a and 8b.

11

CHAPTER TWELVE

HYDROSTATIC DRIVE

DRIVE SYSTEM FUNDAMENTALS

Scag SWZ(U) units use a 2-pump, 2-motor hydrostatic drive system to propel the mower. **Figure 1** shows a flow diagram of the drive circuit. The tank (reservoir) and filter are the only components shared by the system. The right-side components (pump and motor) propel only the right drive wheel; the left-side components propel only the left drive wheel.

> *WARNING*
> *Hydrostatic systems operate under high pressure and uncomfortable heat. Wear appropriate protective apparel when servicing hydrostatic components. Never service a hydrostatic system with the machine running, unless specific instructions state otherwise. Always allow the engine and hydrostatic system to cool prior to servicing.*

> *NOTE*
> *Cleanliness is of paramount importance on a hydrostatic system. Make sure that the external areas of the hydrostatic components are kept clean, as dirt buildup causes the pumps and motors to run hot.*

Refer to **Figure 1**.

The 2-pump, 2-motor hydrostatic system functions as follows:

1. The hydrostatic reservoir (A) is the tank which holds most of the oil for the system. The reservoir serves three functions.

   a. It contains the oil for the system.

   b. It cools the oil. As oil is pumped through the system to perform work, it becomes hot. Oil returning to the reservoir transfers some of this heat to the tank walls, where it is dispersed into the surrounding air. This is also why tanks are thin and long, as a long, thin tank has more surface area than a square-shaped tank, thus providing better cooling capacity.

   c. It allows small air bubbles in the system to break up.

2. The oil is drawn from the reservoir, through the oil filter (B).

3. Filtered oil then splits into two lines, one line feeding the charge pump (C) on each main pump (D). The charge pump is a preliminary pump which keeps the main pump filled with oil.

4. In the main pump, the oil is pressurized and fed to the wheel motors (E).

5. After doing its work in the wheel motors, the oil returns to the main pumps where it is either sent back to the reservoir or slightly cooled and pumped back to the wheel motor.

The arrows in **Figure 1** show the direction of oil flow to propel the wheel motors forward. For reverse, the arrows between the main pumps and the wheel motors would point the opposite direction.

Figure 2 shows the hydrostatic pumps (A) and the wheel motors (B) as they are mounted on the mower. The pumps mount on the top of the engine deck directly behind the engine. The wheel motors mount on either side of

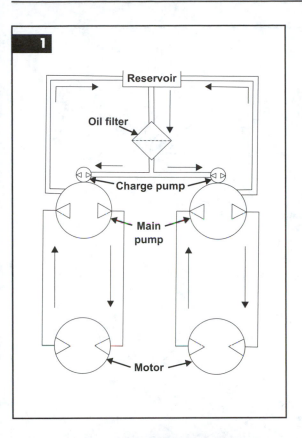

the engine deck, with the drive wheel/tire assemblies mounted directly to the wheel motor shaft hubs. **Figure 3** shows the left-side wheel motor mounted to the frame, with the wheel and brake assemblies removed for clarity.

Hydrostatic Pumps

Scag SWZ(U) units use Hydro-Gear Model BDP-10L pumps to create the pressure necessary to drive the wheel motors. The BDP-10L is a variable-displacement pump with a maximum displacement of 0.61 cubic inch (10 cc) per revolution. **Figure 4** shows an exploded view of the BDP-10L components. **Figure 5** and **Figure 6** show two cutaway views of the BDP-10L. **Figure 6** is rotated 90° away from **Figure 5**.

The BDL-10L pumps use spherical-nosed pistons arranged axially around the input shaft. The pistons are spring-loaded in order to be held tightly against a thrust bearing race. The thrust bearing rides inside a cradle-style swashplate. The swashplate uses an externally-operated lever to give direct-proportional displacement control, depending on the lever position. Reversing the direction of the swashplate angle, or tilt, reverses the flow of oil from the pump. This reverses the direction of rotation of the output shaft of the motor being powered by the pump. A fixed-displacement gerotor-style charge pump feeds a constant supply of oil from the reservoir and filter to the axial pistons.

Figure 7 is a flow chart showing the internal oil paths. Line A and Line B are the output pressure lines to the wheel motors.

The pumps are belt-driven from a pulley on the engine crankshaft, above the blade clutch (**Figure 8**, hydrostatic filter removed for clarity). A spring-loaded idler pulley keeps the belt in constant tension, except when the tension is manually released during cold-weather starts. **Figure 9** shows the tension-releasing chain in the tensioned normal-run position; **Figure 10** shows the chain in the slack-belt position. In cold weather, the chain is pulled out and locked as shown in **Figure 10** to reduce the starting load on the engine. If the chain is not in the tensioned position while mowing, the belt will slip and the traction drive will not propel the mower correctly, if at all.

Bypass valve

At times, it may be necessary to move the mower without the engine running. To do this, each pump is equipped with a bypass valve, sometimes referred to as a dump valve. Activating the bypass valve allows oil to be internally routed directly from the inlet side of the pump through the wheel-motor circuit to the pump's outlet side.

Figure 11 shows the location of the valve on the pump. It is a screw-type bypass valve and is fully open when unscrewed two (2) turns maximum. The left-side valve is al-

12

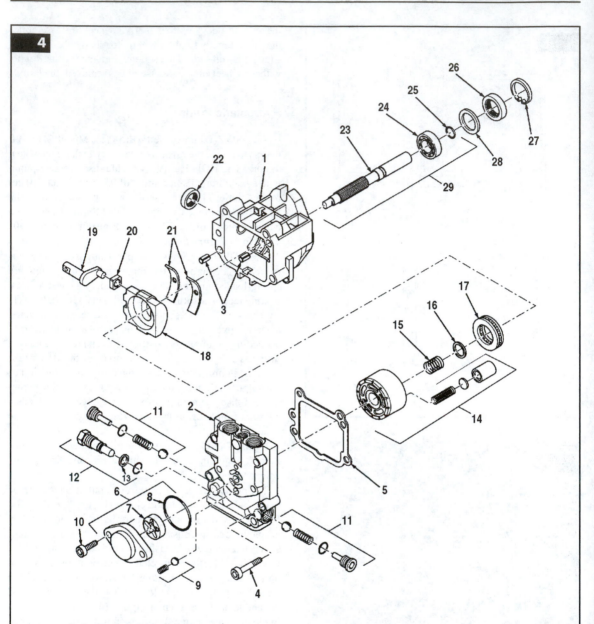

1. Pump housing assembly
2. End cap housing
3. Locator pins
4. End cap socket head screw
5. End cap gasket
6. Charge pump, gerotor, and O-ring assembly
7. Gerotor pump
8. Charge pump O-ring
9. Charge pump relief valve assembly
10. Charge pump cap socket head screw
11. Check valve assembly
12. Bypass valve assembly
13. Bypass valve backup ring
14. Cylinder block assembly, including five
each pistons, piston springs, and spring seats

15. Cylinder block spring
16. Block thrust washer
17. Thrust bearing assembly
18. Swashplate
19. Trunnion arm control lever
20. Guide block
21. Swashplate cradle bearings
22. Control lever seal
23. Pump input shaft
24. Input shaft ball bearing
25. Bearing inner retaining ring
26. Input shaft seal
27. Bearing outer retaining ring
28. Bearing-to-seal spacer
29. Input shaft kit

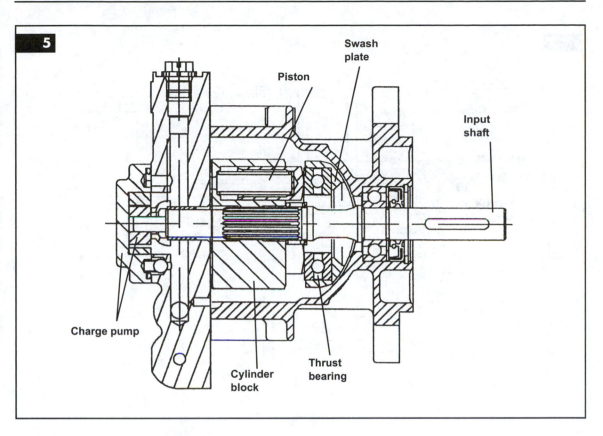

5

Piston

Swash plate

Input shaft

Charge pump

Cylinder block

Thrust bearing

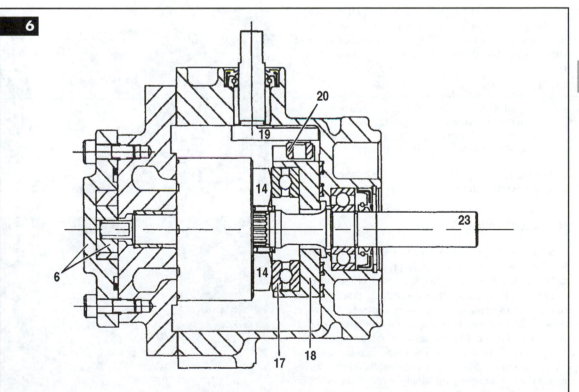

6

20

19

14

23

14

6

17   18

12

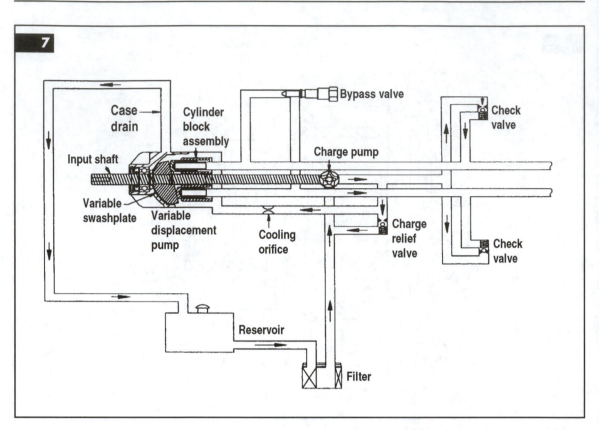

7

Case drain — Cylinder block assembly — Bypass valve — Check valve — Input shaft — Charge pump — Variable swashplate — Variable displacement pump — Cooling orifice — Charge relief valve — Check valve — Reservoir — Filter

ways accessed from the rear of the mower. Depending on the model, the right-side valve can be accessed from either the rear or the front of the right-side pump. **Figure 12** shows the right-side bypass valve as accessed from the front.

> *WARNING*
> *Opening the bypass valve(s) will cause a loss of hydrostatic braking. Exercise extreme care when opening the bypass valves, especially on sloping ground.*

Always remember to fully close the bypass valve(s) prior to operating the mower.

Hydrostatic Wheel Motors

Scag SWZ(U) units use a pair of Ross Model MB or MF Torqmotor wheel motors to propel the mowers. A cutaway view of these motors is shown in **Figure 13**.

Pressurized oil from the hydrostatic pumps is fed through the system's high-pressure hoses to the wheel motors. This oil travels through the motor's internal passages (A, **Figure 13**) where it is forced against the roller-style rotor vanes (B). The vanes, in turn, cause the vane housing (C, **Figure 13**) to rotate. Reversing the direction of the incoming oil supply reverses the direction of the vanes and vane housing, thereby reversing the mo-

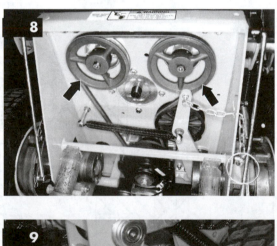

8

9

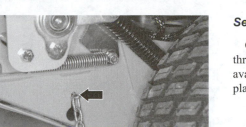

tor. The vane housing is splined to the output shaft (D, **Figure 13**), and the output shaft is splined to the wheel hub shaft (E). The wheel hub shaft is held in position inside the flanged motor mount housing (F) radially by a pair of needle-style roller bearings (G) and axially by a pair of needle-style thrust bearings (H). Contaminants are prevented from entering the motor by the outer dirt-and-water seal (I) and the inner high-pressure seal (J). The flanged motor mount housing fastens directly to the mower frame, holding the wheels in alignment (**Figure 3**).

Service and parts

Only complete wheel motor assemblies are available through Scag. Individual Ross wheel motor parts are not available from Scag. A faulty wheel motor will require replacement of the entire motor.

DRIVE SYSTEM TROUBLESHOOTING

No Drive Forward Or Reverse

1. Pump bypass valves open.
2. Hydrostatic drive belt broken or slipping.
3. Control linkage not operating.
4. Low hydrostatic fluid level.

No Drive At Normal Maximum Speed

1. Engine RPM not set correctly.
2. Control linkage binding or damaged.
3. Bypass valves partially open.
4. Charge check valve stuck open (problem one direction only).
5. Internal component wear or leakage.

Drive Jerky Or Erratic

1. Plugged filter.
2. Inlet air leak.

Drive OK On Level, No-load; Sluggish Under Load

1. Hydrostatic drive belt slipping.
2. Low hydrostatic fluid level.
3. Water in hydrostatic fluid.
4. Internal component wear or leakage.

Unit Does Not Track Straight

1. Improperly inflated tire(s).
2. Control linkage misadjusted or damaged.
3. One bypass valve partially open or loose.
4. Inlet air leak.
5. Internal component wear or leakage.
6. Incorrectly-adjusted brake.

Drive Runs Noisy

1. Low or contaminated oil.
2. Excessive RPM.
3. Air in hydrostatic fluid.
4. Bypass valve loose.
5. Pump belt drive faulty.

12

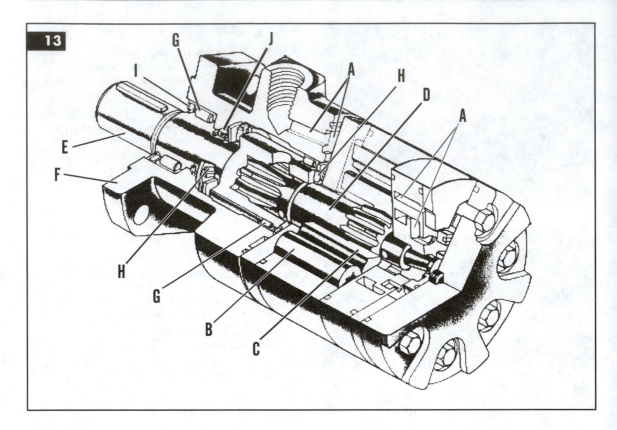

6. Damaged or blocked line or filter.

Drive Components Overheating

1. Debris buildup.
2. Oil contaminated or low.
3. Air in system or air leak.
4. Overloaded.

Leaking

1. Loose connections or fasteners.
2. Faulty gaskets or worn seals.
3. Air trapped in oil.
4. Hydrostatic reservoir overfilled.

DRIVE SYSTEM MAINTENANCE

Lubrication

NOTE
The reservoir is full when the oil level is one inch below the bottom of the filler neck.

Clean oil is the lifeblood of a hydrostatic drive system. Scag recommends draining the hydraulic system and in-

stalling fresh oil and a new oil filter every 500 hours or annually.

Factory-installed lubricant is SAE 20W-50 petroleum-base oil with an API classification of SH or above. Acceptable substitutes are Mobil Super HP, Amoco Ultimate, Viscosity Oil, Shell Gemini, Aero Shell, or Helix Ultra in SAE 5W-40, SAE 10W-40, or SAE 15W-50 grades.

If synthetic oil is preferred after a complete system flush, Mobil 1 SAE 15W-50 is recommended; 5W-30 or 10W-30 are acceptable substitutes.

If troubleshooting indicates an oil problem, siphon a sample of oil from the reservoir. Siphon part of the sample from the bottom of the tank and part from the top. The sample should be clean and clear.

If the oil is bubbly or cloudy, it indicates a suction-side air leak. The suction side includes the reservoir, filter, and all hoses and fittings between the reservoir and the main pumps. Air in the system will also cause the unit drive to be jerky and/or noisy. To solve the problem, check and secure all hoses, connections, and fittings. After the air leak has been corrected, the system will need to be purged of any remaining air. The amount of time needed for purging will depend on the amount of air previously drawn in. Purging the system will be covered in the next section.

Oil with a milky appearance indicates water in the oil. The two most likely sources of water contamination are

high-pressure washing of the unit and leaving the unit out in rainy weather. Water-contaminated oil must be flushed and replaced. Hydrostatic oil changing will be covered after the *Purging* section.

If the oil has a burnt, foul odor, the system has been overheated. Locate and correct the cause, then flush and replace the oil.

Periodically check all hoses for chafing or cracking. Replace any questionable hose(s). Replacing a hose will require flushing and replacing the oil.

Purging the system

> *NOTE*
> *Cleanliness is of paramount importance when working on a hydraulic system. Make sure that no dirt or debris is allowed to come into contact with any internal hydrostatic component. Also make sure that the external areas of the hydrostatic components are kept clean, as dirt buildup causes the pumps and motors to run hot.*

To purge the system:

1. Jack up the rear of the mower so the drive wheels do not touch the floor. Safely support the mower in this position.

2. With the parking brake on, the cutter blades disengaged, the speed adjustment lever in the neutral position, and the neutral latches in the neutral lock position, start the engine and run the engine at idle speed.

3. Release the parking brake.

4. Operate one of the wheel drive systems, going slowly from neutral to full forward, back to neutral, then into reverse and back into neutral again. Continue this process until the drive wheel operates smoothly and quietly, usually about 6-10 cycles. Check the reservoir oil level; add oil as needed. Remember that the reservoir is full when the oil level is one inch below the bottom of the filler neck.

5. Repeat Step 4 with the other side drive wheel.

6. Stop the engine and reset the parking brake.

7. Set the mower back down onto the floor.

8. Test-run the mower to ensure that all air has been purged from the system. Repeat the purging, if necessary.

Flushing and replacing the oil

1. Jack up the rear of the mower so the drive wheels do not touch the floor. Safely support the mower in this position.

2. Locate the supply hose which runs from the reservoir outlet fitting to the inlet side of the oil filter base (**Figure 14**).

3. Pinch the hose just above the filter base fitting, then loosen the hose clamp and remove the hose from the base fitting.

4. Drain the reservoir oil into an approved container.

5. Loosen the two main pump return hoses from the side reservoir fittings (**Figure 15**). Direct these hose ends into a container.

6. Replace the hydrostat oil filter. Using the same new oil which the system will be refilled with, fill the new filter prior to installation.

7. Using a separate flush/supply tank with the same new oil the system will be refilled with, connect the tank to the filter base inlet fitting.

8. With the parking brake on, the cutter blades disengaged, the speed adjustment lever in the neutral position, and the neutral latches in the neutral lock position, start the engine and run the engine at idle speed.

> *WARNING*
> *Make sure ventilation is adequate if the engine is to be run in a confined area. Exhaust fumes are toxic and deadly.*

9. Release the parking brake.

10. While carefully monitoring the oil supply in the flush tank, operate one of the wheel drive systems, going slowly from neutral to full forward, back to neutral, then into reverse and back into neutral again. Continue this process until the oil coming from the return hose is clean and clear.

12

11. Repeat Step 10 with the other side drive wheel.

12. Stop the engine and reset the parking brake.

13. Disconnect the flush tank.

14. Carefully clean the fitting barbs on the fittings. Install the hoses and snugly secure all hose clamps.

15. Refill the reservoir with the proper oil to within one inch of the bottom of the filler neck.

16. Repeat Steps 8-12 to purge any remaining air from the system. Note that the tank being monitored in Step 10 is now the mower reservoir, and the oil will be returning to the reservoir. Continue to monitor the reservoir oil level while final-purging.

17. Stop the engine and set the mower back down onto the floor.

Controls

If maintaining neutral or straight tracking is difficult or impossible, check the linkage. All linkage adjustments are covered in Chapter Eleven. Also check tire pressure. Uneven tire pressures will affect tracking. Tire pressure should be 25 psi (165 kPa) on the front caster wheels and 15 psi (100 kPa) on the rear drive wheels. Check tires, as well. Never mix old and new tires; always replace old tires in pairs. Tires with worn tread will have different diameters than new-tread tires. Tire service is covered in Chapter Three.

Pump Drive

If drive performance seems poor, check the drive belt for wear and/or slippage. **Figure 8** shows a drive system with a spring-loaded idler. Some units have a fixed idler drive. Check and adjust as follows.

> *NOTE*
> *If a hydrostatic drive belt needs replacing,*
> *the deck drive belt will need to be removed*
> *first. Refer to Clutch Removal and Clutch*
> *Replacement in Chapter Fourteen.*

1. On the spring-loaded idler system, the spring pulling the idler pulley bracket is engineered to apply the correct amount of tension to the belt. When checking the spring-loaded system:

  a. Make sure that the spring ends and the spring-end mating areas are not broken or worn, and that the spring coils are not rubbing against other components, causing drag.

  b. Make sure that the idler bracket pivot bearings/bushings allow the bracket to swing freely through the required horizontal arc of travel. Remove the belt from the idler, making sure the bracket continues to arc on its pivot, not binding or jamming at or near the point of normal belt tension. Make sure that the bracket pivot is not worn to the

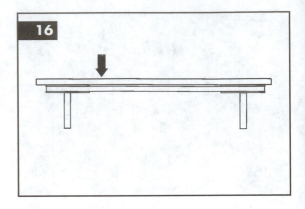

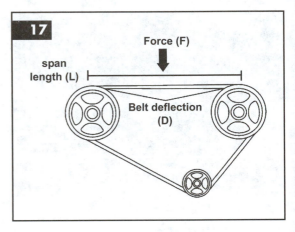

point of allowing the idler to droop vertically, causing idler and belt misalignment.

  c. Inspect the integrity of the belt and the idler pulley, including the idler bearing(s). If questionable, replace the belt or pulley.

  d. Make sure that the driven pulleys have not slipped on their shafts. Inspect pulley alignment as well as key and setscrew placement. To check the alignment of pulleys, place a straightedge across the faces of the pulleys as shown in **Figure 16**. If the inner and outer edges of both pulleys contact the straightedge, the pulleys are aligned.

2. To adjust belt tension on the fixed-idler drive system:

  a. Apply penetrating oil to the J-bolt threads on both sides of the idler adjusting nut.

  b. Inspect the integrity of the belt, the driven pulleys on the pumps, the drive pulley on the crankshaft and the idler pulley, including the idler bearing(s). To check the alignment of pulleys, place a straightedge across the faces of the pulleys as shown in **Figure 16**. If the inner and outer edges of both pulleys contact the straightedge, the pulleys are aligned. If questionable, replace the belt or pulley(s). Loosen the adjusting nut enough to work the belt off the idler, then install the new component(s).

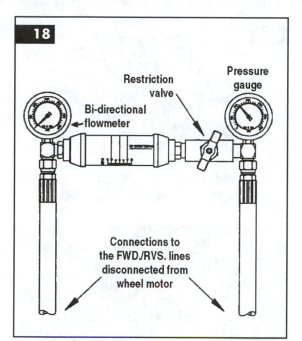

Bi-directional flowmeter

Restriction valve

Pressure gauge

Connections to the FWD./RVS. lines disconnected from wheel motor

Tester Nos. 70661 or 70511 supercede Tester No. BB-76810. Tester 70661 has 22-inch (56 cm) long hoses. Tester 70511 has 18 in. (46 cm) long hoses. The following instructions apply to either tester.

NOTE
Cleanliness is of paramount importance when working on a hydraulic system. Ensure that no dirt or debris is allowed to come into contact with any internal hydrostatic component. Also ensure that the external areas of the hydrostatic components are kept clean, as dirt buildup causes the pumps and motors to run hot.

To test a pump:

1. Disconnect the pressure hoses from either the pump or wheel motor, whichever is most convenient.

NOTE
Pump-to-motor oil flow is directional. Mark the hoses so they are reinstalled in the same positions. Failure to do so could result in a reverse-rotating wheel motor.

2. Connect the tester. The flow gauge on Testers 70511 and 70661 is bi-directional, so connection polarity is unimportant. The flow gauge on Tester BB-76810 is one-way; carefully follow the connection instructions with this tester.

3. Chock the front wheels to prevent the unit from moving.

4. Jack up the rear of the mower so the drive wheels do not touch the floor. Safely support the mower in this position.

5. Open (unscrew) the tester restriction valve completely.

6. With the parking brake on, the cutter blades disengaged, the speed adjustment lever in the neutral position, and the neutral latches in the neutral lock position, start the engine and allow it to reach operating temperature. Once warm, increase the engine speed to 3600 rpm.

WARNING
Make sure ventilation is adequate if the engine is to be run in a confined area. Exhaust fumes are toxic and deadly.

7. Release the parking brake.

8. Move the speed adjustment lever to the top speed position (**Figure 19**). Run the unit in this speed for 1-2 minutes to allow the system oil to reach operating temperature for accurate test results.

9. Close the restriction valve until the pressure gauge reads 300 psi (21 bar).

10. Record the gallon-per-minute (gpm) gauge reading on the flowmeter.

11. Close the restriction valve further until the pressure gauge reads 1100 psi (76 bar).

12. Record the gpm gauge reading on the flowmeter.

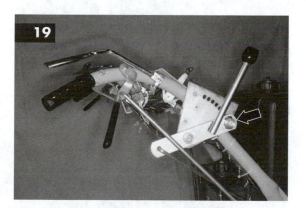

c. When the new components are in place, refer to **Figure 17**, and calculate the amount of deflection needed as follows: Divide the longest span lentth (L) by 64. The result is the amount of deflection (D) required for proper tension. For example, if the span length were 32 inches, 32 divided by 64 equals 1/2. The belt should deflect 1/2 inch when a force (F) of 8-10 pounds is applied at the center of the belt span..

d. Apply the 8-10 pounds of force while measuring belt deflection. Tighten the adjusting nut as necessary to achieve proper deflection.

System Test

The Hydro-Gear BDP Flow Test Kit (**Figure 18**) isolates the pump from the wheel motor to determine where a fault lies by simulating a wheel-motor load. Current

12

13. Subtract the Step 12 reading from the Step 10 reading. The maximum allowable difference is 1.5 gpm (5.6 liters per minute).

    a. A difference within this specification indicates a satisfactory pump.

    b. A difference beyond this specification indicates a faulty pump.

HYDRO-GEAR BDP-10L PUMP SERVICE

Removal

1. Drain the system as outlined in Steps 1-4 under *Flushing and Replacing the Oil* in this chapter.

2. Disconnect the pump-to-wheel-motor (pressure) hose fittings and the pump-to-filter-base (supply) hose fitting at the pump. **Figure 2** shows the hoses mounted to a typical right-side pump. The pump hose fittings pictured in **Figure 14** are the connections for a left-side pump. **Figure 20** shows both pump-supply hose connections at the filter base.

> *NOTE*
> *Pump-to-motor oil flow is directional. Mark the hoses so they are reinstalled in the same positions. Failure to do so could result in a reverse-rotating wheel motor.*

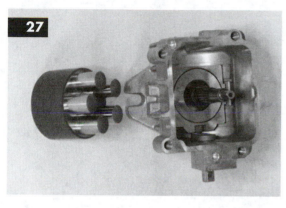

3. Mark the linkage orientation at the pump. Disconnect the linkage.

4. Remove the pump drive belt by following the necessary steps in the preceding *Pump Drive* section.

5. Mark the position and orientation of the pulley on the pump shaft. Loosen the setscrew and remove the pulley.

6. Loosen and remove the two bolts holding the pump to the chassis. Remove the pump.

Disassembly

NOTE
Cleanliness is of paramount importance when working on a hydraulic system. Make sure that no dirt or debris is allowed to come into contact with any internal hydrostatic component.

1. Mark the position of the charge pump cover on the end cap housing (**Figure 21**). Incorrect reassembly of the charge pump will prevent the main pump from developing correct pressure.

2. Carefully remove the charge pump cover. This will expose the pump rotors and relief valve (**Figure 22**).

3. Remove the charge pump rotors. Remove the relief valve spring and spool or ball. **Figure 23** shows the charge pump components removed.

CAUTION
If the check valve has a ball instead of a spool, do not permit the ball to drop into the end-cap passages.

4. Slowly and alternately remove the four end-cap screws from the pump. As the screws are loosened, the pump piston springs will push the end cap away from the pump housing (**Figure 24**). When the screws are removed and the end cap is free, the cylinder block may stick to the end cap. Carefully move the end cap sideways slightly to break contact.

5. Remove and discard the end cap gasket. Be careful not to damage the gasket sealing surfaces.

6. Remove the bypass valve (A, **Figure 25**) and check valve (B) assembly from the end cap.

7. Remove the locator pins from the housing (**Figure 26**).

8. Remove the cylinder block assembly from the shaft and housing (**Figure 27**).

9. Disassemble the cylinder block assembly (**Figure 28**).

10. Remove the cylinder block spring and thrust washer from the pump shaft (**Figure 29**).

11. Remove the thrust bearing assembly from the swashplate (**Figure 30**).

12. Remove the swashplate. Remove the swashplate cradle bearings from the locator posts in the base of the housing (**Figure 31**). The guide block can be removed from the control lever pin at this time.

12

13. Turn the pump housing over and remove the seal snap ring (**Figure 32**).

14. Carefully and lightly tap on the end-plate end of the pump shaft with a brass, plastic or lead mallet to push the seal and the bearing spacer out of the housing (**Figure 33**).

15. Push the shaft and bearing assembly from the housing (**Figure 34**).

16. With the shaft removed, the control lever can be removed from inside the housing (**Figure 35**). If the lever guide block was not removed in Step 12, remove it with the lever. Take care not to allow it to fall out and become lost.

17. Remove the control lever seal.

18. Discard all old seals and O-rings.

Inspection

1. Clean all parts thoroughly.

2. Inspect the seal areas on the pump shaft and control lever for corrosion or wear. Polish, if necessary.

3. Inspect the bypass valve, check valve and mating seats for wear, damage or debris. Clean as necessary.

4. Inspect the charge pump components for wear or debris. Clean or replace as necessary.

5. Inspect all main pump components for discoloration and excessive or unusual wear. Replace as necessary.

6. Inspect the seal bores.

7. Inspect the pump shaft bushing in the end cap. The bushing is not replaceable.

8. The mating surfaces of the cylinder block and end cap must be flat and scratch-free. If more than 0.0004 inch (0.01 mm) polishing is required to obtain a flat, scratch-free surface, replace the component(s).

9. Inspect the cylinder block, pistons, springs and spring seats. Compare spring lengths: All springs should be the same length. Inspect the pistons and bores for scratches. If any components are faulty, the cylinder block assembly must be replaced as a unit.

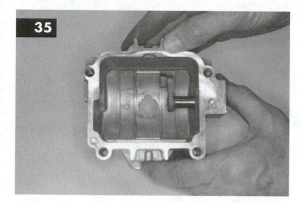

35

36

37

38

Reassembly

NOTE
Cleanliness is of paramount importance when working on a hydraulic system. Make sure that no dirt or debris is allowed to come into contact with any internal hydrostatic component.

NOTE
Lubricate all internal pump components with fresh oil prior to assembly.

1. Install the control shaft into the pump housing from the inside (**Figure 35**). If installing the guide block at this time, make sure the block does not fall out during subsequent assembly.

2. If previously disassembled, assemble the input shaft bearing onto the shaft. Use care not to deform the retaining ring.

3. Install the shaft and bearing assembly into the housing from the outside (**Figure 34**). Be sure the bearing seats completely in its bore.

4. Place the bearing spacer into the bearing bore.
   a. Use a seal protector tube or wrap the keyed end of the input shaft with thin plastic to protect the seal.
   b. Lubricate the inner seal lip with a light grease.
   c. Using a proper-sized driver, press the seal into the housing far enough to allow the retaining ring to be installed.
   d. Install the seal retaining ring (**Figure 32**).

5. Position the swashplate cradle bearings onto the locator posts in the housing (**Figure 31**).

6. Make sure the control lever guide block is properly positioned on the lever pin. Install the swashplate into the housing (**Figure 30**).

7. Hold the swashplate in the neutral position (plate face perpendicular to the input shaft). Using a depth gauge or dial indicator, measure the control lever end play. End play should be 0.020-0.060 inch (0.5-1.5 mm). If excessive, use a proper-sized sleeve to press the control shaft bushing into the housing as needed.

8. Assemble and install the thrust bearing into the swashplate bore (**Figure 29**).

9. Install the cylinder block thrust washer and spring onto the input shaft (**Figure 38**).

10. Lubricate and assemble the cylinder block (**Figure 36**):
    a. Install the spring seats into the piston cavities.
    b. Install the springs into the pistons.
    c. Hold the cylinder upside-down and install the pistons into the cylinder.

NOTE
Install the pistons carefully to prevent scratching either the pistons or the bores.

12

11. Carefully install the cylinder block assembly (**Figure 27**) over the shaft and into the housing. It helps to hold the housing assembly in a near-horizontal position (control lever up or down), with the end-plate end of the housing slightly higher than the flange-mount end.

12. With the cylinder block installed, position the pump on the workbench with the flange-mount end down (**Figure 26**).

13. Make sure the housing and end-plate gasket surfaces are clean and dry. Install the two locator pins into the housing, followed by a new end-plate gasket.

14. Make sure that the cylinder and end cap mating surfaces are lubricated. Position the end cap onto the cylinder, aligned with the locator pins. If everything is properly assembled, the internal springs will keep the end cap approximately 3/8-inch (9.5 mm) from the housing (**Figure 24**).

15. Lightly coat the four end-cap screw threads with Loctite 242 or equivalent.

   a. Set the screws into position in the end cap holes.

   b. Press the end cap down onto the housing, making sure everything is properly aligned. Do not force the end cap.

   c. Finger-tighten the four end cap screws.

   d. Rotate the input shaft to verify proper assembly. Minimum force should be required.

   e. Torque the screws to 120-180 in.-lb. (10-15 ft.-lb. or 13.5-20 N•m).

   f. Again rotate the input shaft to verify proper assembly.

16. Install the control-shaft seal:

   a. Use a seal protector tube or wrap the exposed end of the input shaft with thin plastic to protect the seal.

   b. Lubricate the inner seal lip with a light grease.

   c. Using a proper-sized driver, press the seal into the housing.

17. Install the bypass valve and check valve assemblies into the proper end-cap holes (**Figure 25**). Torque the bypass valve to 85-120 in.-lb. (9.6-13.5 N•m). Torque the check valve to 180-240 in.-lb. (20-27 N•m).

18. Assemble the charge pump rotors and relief valve ball and spring into the end cap (**Figure 22**).

19. Install a new O-ring into the end-cap groove. Noting the position of the end cap and charge pump cover marks (**Figure 21**), install the cover onto the end cap. The relief valve spring must fit into the recess in the cover. Torque the screws to 85-120 in.-lb. (9.6-13.5 N•m).

20. Fill the pump by pouring fresh oil directly into the pump inlet and high-pressure ports prior to installation and start-up.

Installation

> *NOTE*
> *Cleanliness is of paramount importance when working on a hydraulic system. Make sure that no dirt or debris is allowed to come into contact with any internal hydrostatic component.*

1. Position the pump flange slots over the mounting holes in the chassis. Install and tighten the pump-mount bolts.

2. Lightly coat the pump shaft with Led-Plate anti-seize or equivalent. Install the key into the keyway. Fit the pulley onto the shaft, orienting it hub-up and aligning it in the same position as noted during removal. If the removal position has been lost, align it with the other pump pulley or the engine pulley by placing a straightedge across the faces of the pulleys as shown in **Figure 16**. If the inner and outer edges of both pulleys contact the straightedge, the pulleys are aligned. Tighten the setscrew.

3. Install the drive belt by following the steps in the previous *Pump Drive* section.

4. Reconnect the linkage. Refer to the necessary steps in Chapter Eleven and adjust the linkage after the system is refilled with oil.

5. Noting the directional hose markings made during disassembly, reconnect the pump hoses. Torque the fittings to 180-240 in.-lb. (20-27 N•m)

6. Fill the reservoir with oil. Factory-installed lubricant is SAE 20W-50 petroleum-base oil with an API classification of SH or above. Acceptable substitutes are Mobil Super HP, Amoco Ultimate, Viscosity Oil, Shell Gemini, Aero Shell, or Helix Ultra in SAE 5W-40, SAE 10W-40, or SAE 15W-50 grades.

   If synthetic oil is preferred after a complete system flush, Mobil 1 SAE 15W-50 is recommended; 5W-30 or 10W-30 are acceptable substitutes.

> *NOTE*
> *The reservoir is full when the oil level is one inch below the bottom of the filler neck.*

7. Purge the air from the system by following Steps 2-8 under *Purging the system* in this chapter.

ROSS WHEEL MOTOR SERVICE

Only complete wheel motor assemblies are available through Scag. Individual Ross wheel motor parts are not available from Scag. A faulty wheel motor will require replacement of the entire motor.

Removal

NOTE
Cleanliness is of paramount importance when working on a hydraulic system. Thoroughly and carefully clean the outside of the motor, especially around the hose connections. Ensure that no dirt or debris is allowed to come into contact with any internal hydrostatic component.

1. Chock the front wheels to prevent the unit from moving.

2. Raise the rear of the mower so the drive wheels do not touch the floor. Safely support the mower in this position.

3. Remove the lug nuts, wheel and tire assembly, brake drum and band from the side requiring service (**Figure 37**).

4. Bend the lock tab back away from the hub nut (**Figure 38**). Remove the nut, then remove the lock plate. Turn the nut around and rethread it onto the motor shaft so the nut face is flush with the end of the shaft.

5. Apply penetrating oil to the tapered shaft-to-hub mating area.

CAUTION
Either a 2-jaw or 3-jaw puller can be used. Whichever one is used, align one of the jaws with the hub keyway for easiest hub removal.

6. Install a puller onto the hub (**Figure 39**). Break the hub free, then remove the hub (**Figure 40**).

7. Remove the two pump-to-motor pressure hoses (**Figure 40**). Wipe up any spilled fluid.

NOTE
Pump-to-motor oil flow is directional. Mark the hoses so they are reinstalled in the same positions. Failure to do so could result in a reverse-rotating wheel motor.

8. Remove the four bolts securing the motor to the chassis.

9. Slide the motor toward the inside of the frame to remove it.

10. Clean the motor mounting face on the frame bracket.

Installation

NOTE
Cleanliness is of paramount importance when working on a hydraulic system. Thoroughly and carefully clean the outside of the motor, especially around the hose connections. Make sure that no dirt or debris is allowed to come into contact with any internal hydrostatic component.

1. Make sure that the motor mounting face on the frame bracket is clean and dry, as well as the motor mount bolt and housing threads.

2. Fill the motor by pouring fresh oil directly into the high-pressure ports prior to reinstallation and start-up.

3. Fit the motor into the frame cutout and against the mount bracket with the feed holes up.

4. Lightly coat the four mount bolts with Loctite 262 or equivalent. Insert the bolts into the motor. Torque the bolts incrementally and alternately to 28-35 ft.-lb. (38.0-47.5 N•m).

5. Noting the proper hose orientation as marked during disassembly, connect the two pump-to-motor pressure hoses. Torque the fittings to 180-240 in.-lb. (20-27 N•m).

CAUTION
Make sure all hose connections are secure due to the high system pressures.

6. Make sure that the matching tapers on the pump shaft and inside the hub are clean and dry. Install the shaft key, making sure that the flat of the key is parallel to the taper of the hub.

7. Align the wheel hub keyway with the motor shaft key. Fit the hub all the way onto the motor shaft.

8. Inspect the lock plate. If the inside-diameter locator tab is damaged in any way, replace the plate. Install the lock plate onto the shaft, aligning the locator tab with the shaft thread keyway. While holding the lock plate against the hub, thread the nut onto the shaft, notches out. Tighten the nut securely. Do not overtighten. With the nut tight,

12

locate whichever lock plate tab is aligned with a flat side of the nut, then bend the tab down onto the flat.

9. Reinstall the brake components and wheel and tire assembly.

10. Fill the reservoir with oil. Factory-installed lubricant is SAE 20W-50 petroleum-base oil with an API classification of SH or above. Acceptable substitutes are Mobil Super HP, Amoco Ultimate, Viscosity Oil, Shell Gemini, Aero Shell, or Helix Ultra in SAE 5W-40, SAE 10W-40, or SAE 15W-50 grades.

If synthetic oil is preferred after a complete system flush, Mobil 1 SAE 15W-50 is recommended; 5W-30 or 10W-30 are acceptable substitutes.

NOTE
The reservoir is full when the oil level is one inch below the bottom of the filler neck.

11. Purge the air from the system by following Steps 2-8 under *Purging the System* in this chapter.

Table 1   TORQUE VALUES

Item	in.-lbs.	ft.-lbs.	N•m
Case drain fitting, 9/16-18 with O-ring	180-240 in.-lb.	15-20 ft.-lb.	20-27 N•m
System ports, 3/4-16 with O-ring	180-240 in.-lb.	15-20 ft.-lb.	20-27 N•m
Inlet fitting/plug, 7/16-20 with O-ring	95-120 in.-lb.	8-10 ft.-lb.	10.7-13.5 N•m
Check valve plugs, 9/16-18 with O-ring	180-240 in.-lb.	15-20 ft.-lb.	20-27 N•m
Bypass valve	85-120 in.-lb.	7-10 ft.-lb.	9.6-13.5 N•m
Charge pump cover	85-120 in.-lb.	7-10 ft.-lb.	9.6-13.5 N•m
End-cap-to-housing screws	120-180 in.-lb.	10-15 ft.-lb.	13.5-20 N•m

CHAPTER THIRTEEN

MOWER DECK

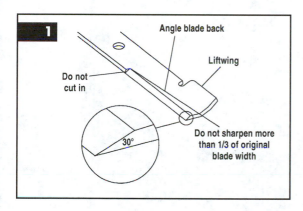

Angle blade back

Liftwing

Do not cut in

30°

Do not sharpen more than 1/3 of original blade width

This chapter covers the blades, spindles and deck housing. Chapter Fourteen covers the deck drive system including the PTO clutch, belts, pulleys, idlers and belt idler adjustments.

BLADES

Many problems associated with poor cutting are the result of dull blades. Dull or improperly sharpened blades not only cut unsatisfactorily, they can also overheat the engine by making it work harder to cut the grass, as well as overheating the deck belt(s), pulleys, and spindles due to the additional drag. **Figure 1** shows the proper method of sharpening a blade.

Figure 1 shows the correct cutting-edge angle as well as the maximum amount of sharpening a blade can accept before the cutter end becomes weak and dangerous. The

30° angle is recommended for normal cutting in average soils. Decrease the angle to 20°-25° for sandy soils. Increase the angle to 35°-40° for clay or heavy soils. "Original blade width" is the narrowest part of the blade – in this case, from the cutting edge to the inside edge of the clearance notch between the blade center and the liftwing.

WARNING
Never mount a blade upside-down. Never straighten a bent blade. Never heat, bend or weld a damaged blade. Reworking a bent or damaged blade does not remove the stresses introduced by the damage. It merely creates more stresses, further weakening the blade and increasing the potential for blade breakage at speed under load.

NOTE
*The cutting edge of the blade (**Figure 1**) should always be at the bottom of the blade, closest to the grass. When sharpening a blade, always remove cutting-edge metal from the top of the blade, never from the bottom. A very light deburring pass is all that should be done to the bottom of the cutting edge after the top is sharpened.*

When sharpening with a grinding wheel, always keep the wheel dressed. *Never* allow the blade cutting edge to become hot enough to turn blue. This will remove the temper from the edge, thereby softening and weakening the cutting edge. Keep the cutting edge quenched while sharpening. If quenching produces bubbling steam, the

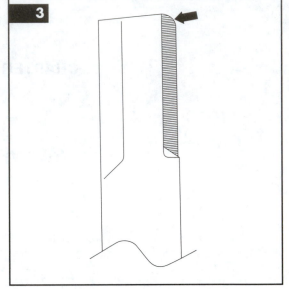

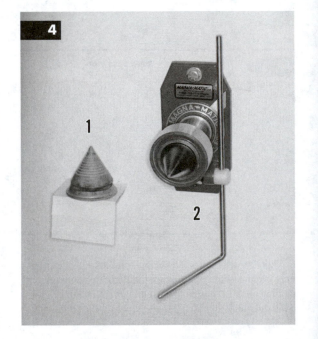

cutting edge is too hot, and the metal will crystallize, further weakening the cutting edge. A quality quenching solution can be purchased from any machine-tool supply house.

Figure 2 shows the clearance angle which must be maintained on the blade ends. This prevents the end of the blade from hacking or chopping what the tip of the cutting edge may have not cut due to the traveling speed of the mower. **Figure 3** shows an unacceptable rounded cutting edge tip. This will tear the grass, giving an unsatisfactory cut. Always sharpen the blade tip as shown in **Figure 1** and **Figure 2**.

Whenever a blade is sharpened, it must also be balanced. Prior to balancing, always clean all the grass debris from the blade – top, bottom, and edges. The vibration caused by out-of-balance blades is not only uncomfortable for the operator but also destructive to the mower. Vibration from out-of-balance blades causes problems in three major areas:

1. It loosens fasteners, causing parts to fall off the mower.

2. It creates stress cracks on the frame, especially around the spindle mounting areas. This weakens the frame.

3. It causes spindle bearing failure.

Figure 4 shows two types of blade balancers. The first balancer (1) is an inexpensive balancer which, if used correctly, will satisfactorily balance the blade. The second balancer (2) is a more precise balancer which can also check the blade for straightness. Always follow the balancer manufacturer's instructions.

Figure 5 shows blade erosion where the flat part of the blade bends up to form the liftwing. Erosion is usually caused by cutting heavy wet grass or cutting in sandy or abrasive conditions. Blades with eroded liftwing edges

should always be replaced to prevent the liftwings from breaking off and becoming missile hazards.

NOTE
Use the Blade Buddy Tool (Scag part No. 9212) to prevent the blades from rotating while loosening the blade bolt nut and removing the blade. When balancing a blade, remove metal from the cutting edge only. When reinstalling sharpened and balanced blades, torque the blade bolt nut to 75 ft.-lb. (102 N•m).

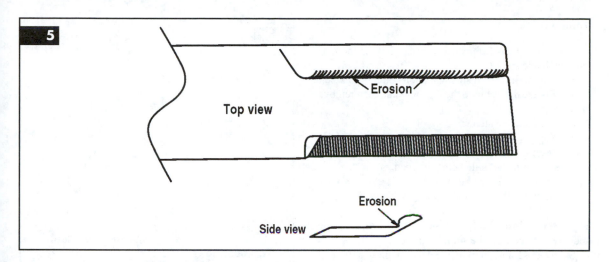

5

Top view

Erosion

Erosion

Side view

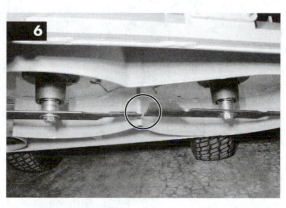

6

Checking Blade Straightness

To check the blades, spindle bolts or spindle shafts for straightness, refer to **Figure 6** and perform the following test:

1. Remove the blade drive-belt shield from the top of the deck.

2A. On units with spring-loaded belt idlers, carefully rotate the belt off the idler pulley.

2B. On units with fixed idlers, loosen the locknut on the J-bolt to create enough slack in the belt so the belt can be rotated off the idler pulley. This will give the spindles and blades the freedom to rotate individually.

3. Set the parking brake.

4. Raise the front of the mower to access the blades. Ensure that the mower is safely supported.

5. Using heavy gloves to guard against injury from sharp blades, rotate the left and right blades (left and center blades on 3-blade decks) so that the tips of the cutting edges align. Note the alignment.

6. While holding the left blade in position, rotate the right (center) blade 180° so that the opposite tip lines up with the stationary blade tip. Note the alignment.

7. Hold the right (center) blade in position, then rotate the left blade 180° to align the blade tips. Note the alignment.

8. On 3-blade decks, repeat Steps 4-6 with the center and right blades.

9. There should not be more than 1/16 inch misalignment between any of the tip match-ups. Any serious misalignment indicates either bent blades, bent blade bolts, bent spindle shafts, or faulty spindle bearings.

   a. If the cause of misalignment is not readily apparent, begin by rocking the spindle to check for loose bearings.

   b. If the bearings appear loose, service the spindle as described in this chapter.

   c. If the bearings are good, continue by replacing one suspect blade and blade bolt at a time.

   d. If, after replacing a pair of blades, there is still misalignment, the suspect spindle shaft is probably bent and must be replaced. Again, refer to the spindle service procedures.

   e. The deck could also be bent in the area where the spindle housing mounts. Although straightening the deck is possible, it must be attempted with the utmost caution. Replacing the deck is the recommended solution.

10. Carefully reinstall the belts onto the idler pulleys. On fixed-idler systems, refer to *Drive Belts, Fixed-idler system* in this chapter for proper belt tension adjustment.

BLADE SPINDLES

WARNING
When working on the cutter deck, maintain a safe working environment and practice safe working procedures.

13

Removal

Refer to **Figure 7** for an exploded view of the cutter-deck blade spindle.

1. Loosen the front and side wing bolts on the deck belt guard (**Figure 8**). Remove the top wing nut, then remove the belt guard.

2. On fixed-idler systems:

   a. Apply penetrating oil to the J-bolt threads (**Figure 8**) on both sides of the adjusting nut for the idler serving the spindle being serviced.

   b. Loosen the adjusting nut enough to be able to work the belt off the spindle pulley *without damaging the belt*.

3. On spring-loaded idlers, push the idler bracket aside and work the belt off the spindle pulley.

4. Safely raise and support the deck to allow sufficient working room underneath.

5. Remove the blade bolt and blade. Use the Blade Buddy (Scag part No. 9212) to prevent the blades from rotating while loosening the blade bolt nut.

6. Note the distance the spindle shaft protrudes from the hub of the belt pulley. This dimension must be maintained during reassembly.

7. Remove the two hub-to-pulley bolts (**Figure 9**).

8. Remove any dirt or debris from the threaded holes in the hub flange. Lightly run a bottoming tap into the holes to ensure complete cleanliness.

9. Insert the two hub-to-pulley bolts into the hub flange threads until they contact the pulley hub flange.

10. Tighten the bolts incrementally and progressively 1/4 turn at a time until the pulley is loose from the hub. At this point, the hub and pulley can be removed from the shaft.

11. Remove the square key from the shaft keyway.

12. Remove the four bolts and nuts holding the spindle to the bottom of the cutter deck. Remove the spindle.

13. Clean the spindle-mount area of the deck and the spindle flange.

Disassembly

The following tools will be needed for proper spindle repair:

1. Half-inch drive ratchet wrench.
2. Half-inch drive torque wrench.
3. Six-point 11/2-inch socket.
4. Seal-removal tool.
5. Drive punch.
6. Ball-peen hammer.
7. Bench vise.
8. 5/32-inch Allen wrench.
9. Scag spindle repair kit No. 47003 (**Figure 10**) which includes:

   a. 43322 Spindle Tool
   b. 43320 Shaft Holder
   c. 04063-08 Key

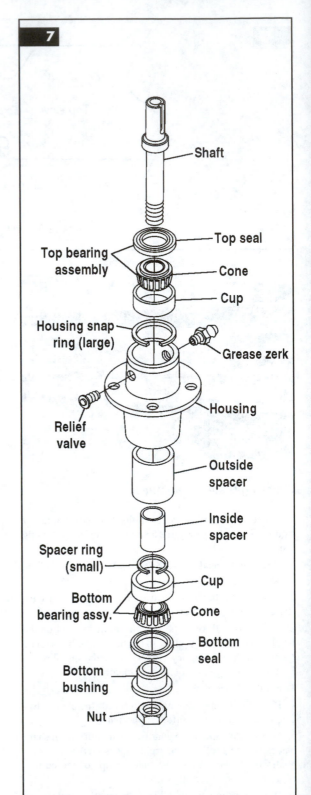

7

Shaft

Top bearing assembly

Top seal

Cone

Cup

Housing snap ring (large)

Grease zerk

Housing

Relief valve

Outside spacer

Inside spacer

Spacer ring (small)

Cup

Bottom bearing assy.

Cone

Bottom seal

Bottom bushing

Nut

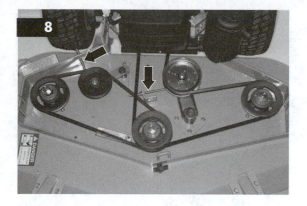

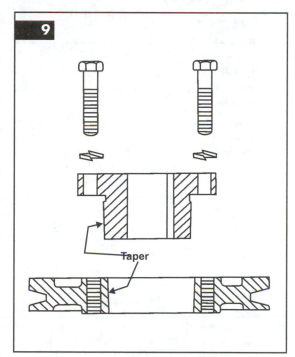

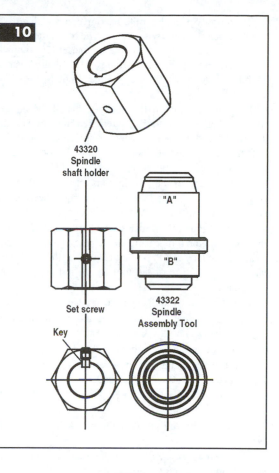

43320
Spindle
shaft holder

"A"

"B"

43322
Spindle
Assembly Tool

Set screw

Key

NOTE
Unless the large snap ring is damaged, it can be left in the housing and reused.

8. Thoroughly clean and inspect the housing, all housing components and the shaft. Remove all grease from inside the housing, as it may contain small metal particles. Discard any damaged or questionable items. Always discard the seals.

13

NOTE
If a tapered roller bearing cone assembly is being replaced, always replace the outer race cup.

Reassembly

1. If the large snap ring was removed, install a new one.
2. Slide the large outside spacer into the housing from the bottom. Slide it all the way up to the snap ring.
3. Fit the bottom bearing race cup into the housing. Use the spindle tool No. 43322 "A" end to press the cup up to the spacer.
4. Again using the 43322 "A" end, press the top bearing race cup into the housing against the snap ring.

Taper

d. 04012-04 Set Screw
e. Instruction Sheet

To disassemble the spindle

1. Clamp the shaft holder in the vise facing up.
2. Install the key into the spindle keyway.
3. Turn the spindle upside-down and install the keyed end of the shaft into the shaft holder.
4. Secure the shaft with the allen-head set screw.
5. Use the socket to remove the bottom spindle nut and bushing.
6. Mark the spindle housing "Top" and "Bottom." Remove the spindle housing from the shaft.
7. Remove all components from the housing. Remove the shaft from the holder.

5. Thoroughly pack the roller bearing cones with grease. Coat the bearing cups with grease. The recommended lubricant is US Lithium MP White Grease 2125. Compatible lubricants are Exxon's Ronex MP, Shell Alvania, Mobil's Mobilux #2, Conoco's Super Lube M EP #2, or Lidok EP #2.

6. From the bottom of the housing, install the bottom roller bearing cone into the bottom bearing cup. Use the 43322 "B" end to install the bottom seal. Press the seal in with the lip side toward the bearing until the tool flange is flush with the housing face.

7. From the top of the housing, install the small spacer ring into the housing, all the way to the roller bearing. Install the small spacer to meet the spacer ring.

8. From the top of the housing, install the top roller bearing cone into the top bearing cup. Use the 43322 "B" end to install the top seal. Press the seal in with the lip side toward the bearing until the tool flange is flush with the housing face.

9. Install the key into the spindle keyway.

10. Turn the spindle upside-down and install the keyed end of the shaft into the shaft holder.

11. Secure the shaft with the allen-head set screw.

12. Turn the housing upside-down and install the housing assembly onto the spindle shaft.

13. Fit the bottom spindle bushing over the shaft into the seal.

14. Install and torque the spindle nut to 150 ft.-lb (203 N•m).

15. Using the grease zerk fitting, lubricate the spindle assembly until grease overflows from the relief valve.

16. Rotate the housing a few turns to check for smooth operation.

17. Regrease until lubricant again comes from the relief valve.

18. Remove the spindle assembly from the vise holder. The spindle assembly is ready for installation onto the mower.

Installation

1. Make sure that the spindle housing flange and under-deck mount surfaces are clean.

2. Position the spindle assembly under the deck and align the housing and deck bolt holes so the grease fitting faces toward the inside of the mower deck.

3. Install and tighten the four housing-to-deck bolts.

4. Remove the hub-to-pulley bolts from the hub-removal holes and loosely install them through the hub and into the threaded pulley holes (**Figure 9**).

5. Fit the pulley and hub onto the shaft in the same position as noted during disassembly. If the pre-disassembly position is not known, the pulley will have to be realigned:

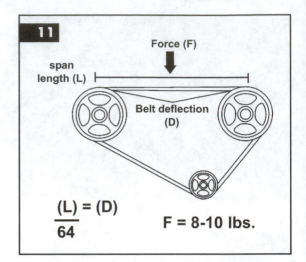

a. Lightly and incrementally tighten the bolts until the hub becomes difficult to slide up and down the shaft by hand.

b. Place a straightedge across the faces of the pulleys.

c. When the inner and outer edges of both pulleys contact the straightedge, the pulleys are aligned. On pulleys with different wall thicknesses, the difference between the thick and the thin wall must be compensated for along the straightedge.

6. Tighten the bolts incrementally and progressively 1/4 turn at a time until the hub is tight inside the pulley. Torque the bolts to the appropriate specifications, according to the tables in Chapter One.

CAUTION
Two-piece taper-hub pulleys must always be assembled clean and dry. Do not use any lubricants on the tapered surfaces, the screw and pulley threads, or the shaft surfaces. If penetrating oil is used to aid in removal of the pulley and hub, remove all traces of the penetrating oil prior to reassembly.

7. Install the blade bolt, flat washer, blade and spacer(s) onto the spindle. Install and torque the blade bolt nut to 75 ft.-lb. (102 N•m).

8. Safely remove the deck supports and lower the deck onto the floor.

9. Install the drive belt onto the pulleys. If the drive is a fixed-idler system, adjust the belt tension as follows:

a. A quality belt-tensioning tool is the best way to check belt tension. Always follow the instructions which come with the tool. The second-best way of checking belt tension is with an accurate fishing scale. Tension should be checked in the center of the longest belt span between two pulleys (**Figure 11**). Use a straight-edge ruler to measure the span.

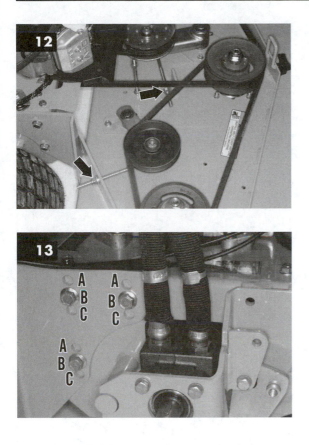

The straight-edge can also be used to help gauge the amount of deflection.

b. Using the formula in **Figure 11**, determine the longest belt span, then calculate the amount of deflection needed.

c. Apply the 8-10 pounds of force while measuring belt deflection. Turn the adjusting nut (**Figure 12**) as necessary to achieve proper deflection.

10. Reinstall the deck belt guard and tighten the wing nuts and bolt.

CUTTER DECK ADJUSTMENTS

SWZ Models

Two types of cutting adjustments can be made to these mowers, height and pitch.

1. Height is the distance from the cutting edge of the blade to the ground. It is measured with the blades in a side-to-side direction.

2. Pitch is measured with the blades in a front-to-rear direction. It is the difference between the front cutting-edge height and the rear cutting-edge height. The recommended ideal pitch is a downward pitch, with the front cutting edge 1/4-inch (6 mm) lower than the rear cutting edge.

Cutting adjustments can be accomplished using a combination of any of three methods built into these mowers.

The chart in **Table 2** shows how combining the three areas of adjustability produces the desired cut. The highlighted specifications are the recommended cutting positions. Cutting heights are computed for a 61-inch deck. Other size decks may produce slightly different dimensions.

NOTE
All adjustments must be made with the mower sitting on a smooth, flat, level floor.

Cutter Deck Mounting

The cutter deck is mounted to the engine deck using brackets with three sets of bolt holes (**Figure 13**). For adjustment purposes, these holes are identified as A, B, and C, top-to-bottom.

NOTE
Always use the same hole positions on both the left and right side brackets.

The cutter deck mounting adjustment is performed upon initial mower set-up and should never need to be changed under normal circumstances.

To reposition the cutter-deck mounting:

1. Shut off the engine. Disconnect the spark plug lead.

2. Engage the parking brake.

3. Safely support both the front and rear of the engine deck, as well as the rear of the cutter deck.

4. Remove tension from the engine-to-cutter deck drive belt. Refer to Steps 1-3 under *Blade Spindles, Removal* in this chapter.

5. Loosen and remove the mounting bolts.

5. Adjust the deck supports to move the mounting brackets to the desired holes.

6. Lightly coat the mount bolt threads with Loctite 262 or equivalent. Install and tighten the bolts.

7. Install and tension the cutter-deck drive belt. Follow Steps 9 and 10 under *Blade Spindles, Installation* in this chapter

8. Remove the mower floor supports and reconnect the spark plug lead.

Caster Wheel Spacers

The caster wheel yoke pivot (**Figure 14**) has four spacers which can be mounted in varying quantities below the caster support to either raise or lower the front of the mower deck. Pitch is adjusted by varying the caster wheel spacers in conjunction with the cutter deck mounting hole position.

NOTE
Always use the same number of spacers between the caster yoke and caster support on both sides of the mower.

13

To move the caster wheel spacers:

1. Shut off the engine. Disconnect the spark plug lead.

2. Engage the parking brake.

3. Safely lift and support the front of the cutter deck high enough so the caster pivot shaft can be removed from the caster support.

4. Support the caster wheel and remove the caster pin and any upper spacers.

5. Remove the caster.

6. Install or remove spacers as necessary.

7. Reinstall the caster into the support, followed by any remaining spacers and the caster pin.

8. Repeat with the other caster.

9. Remove the cutter deck floor support(s) and lower the mower onto the floor.

10. Reconnect the spark plug lead.

Cutter Blade Spacers

The blade bolt is long enough for five 1/4-inch (6 mm) spacers (**Figure 15**). A minimum of three spacers is recommended between the spindle and blade for the best cut and maximum clipping discharge.

To change the spacers:

1. Shut off the engine. Disconnect the spark plug lead.

2. Engage the parking brake.

3. Loosen the front and side wing bolts on the deck belt guard (A, Figure 6). Remove the top wing nut, then remove the belt guard.

4. Safely lift and support the front of the cutter deck high enough so the blade bolt can be removed.

5. Remove the blade bolt nut and any upper spacer(s) from the top of the spindle. Remove the blade bolt, flat washer, blade and any blade spacer(s) from the spindle bottom.

6. Adjust the spacer positions as required.

NOTE
All blades should be spaced equally.

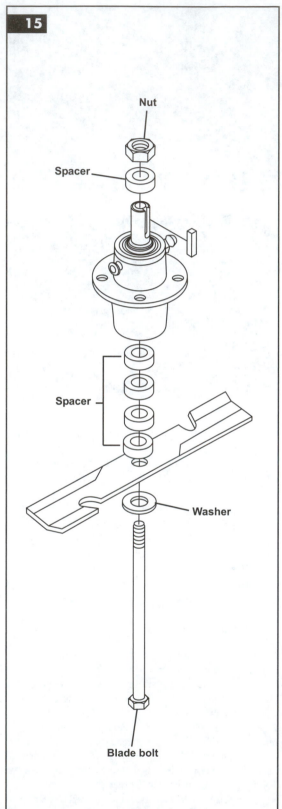

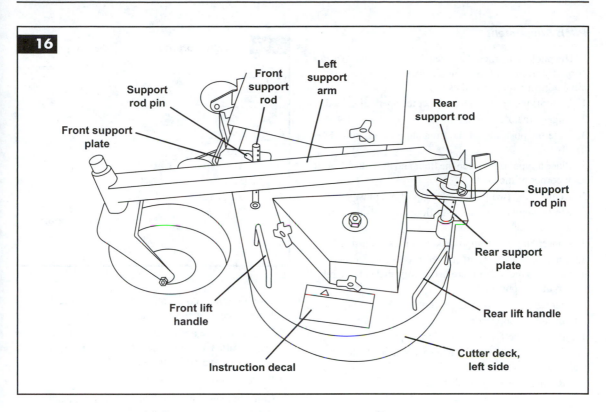

16

Support rod pin

Front support rod

Left support arm

Rear support rod

Support rod plate

Front support plate

Support rod pin

Rear support plate

Front lift handle

Rear lift handle

Instruction decal

Cutter deck, left side

7. Install the blade bolt, flat washer, blade and required spacer(s) onto the bottom of the spindle.

8. Install the remaining spacer(s) onto the top of the spindle.

9. Install the blade bolt nut onto the bolt. Torque the nut to 75 ft.-lb. (102 N•m).

10. Repeat Steps 5-9 for the other blade(s).

11. Remove the cutter deck support(s) and lower the mower onto the floor.

12. Reconnect the spark plug lead.

13. Reinstall the deck belt guard and tighten the wing nuts and bolt.

CUTTER DECK ADJUSTMENTS

SWZU Models

Two types of cutting adjustments can be made to these mowers, height and pitch.

1. Height is the distance from the cutting edge of the blade to the ground. It is measured with the blades in a side-to-side direction.

2. Pitch is measured with the blades in a front-to-rear direction. It is the difference between the front cutting-edge height and the rear cutting-edge height. The recommended ideal pitch is a downward pitch, with the front cutting edge 1/4-inch (6 mm) lower than the rear cutting edge.

Cutting adjustments can be accomplished on these models by moving the deck support rod pins, adjusting the support rods when necessary, and repositioning the cutter deck.

NOTE
All adjustments must be made with the mower sitting on a smooth, flat, level floor.

Height Adjustment

Eight height adjustment positions are available from 1.0 inch to 4.5 inch (2.5 cm to 11.5 cm).

1. Shut off the engine. Disconnect the spark plug lead.

2. Engage the parking brake.

3. Note the positions of the support rod pins (**Figure 16**).

4. Hold up on the front deck lift handle of one side of the deck. Remove the front support rod pin. Release the handle or place a wooden block support under the edge of the deck.

5. Hold up on the rear deck lift handle and remove the rear support rod pin. Lift or lower the deck as required and reinstall the pin into the desired hole.

6. Repeat Step 5 with the front support rod and pin.

7. Repeat Steps 3-6 with the other side of the deck.

8. Double-check the height measurement. Readjust as necessary.

9. Reconnect the spark plug lead.

13

Pitch Adjustment

The pitch adjustment has been factory-set and does not normally need readjustment. If deck service requires a pitch adjustment, proceed as follows:

1. Shut off the engine. Disconnect the spark plug lead.

2. Engage the parking brake.

3. Note the positions of the front support rod pins (**Figure 16**).

4. Place a support between the floor and the cutter deck at each corner of the deck.

5. Remove the two front deck support rod pins.

6. Move the two front deck-to-floor supports to achieve the correct pitch dimension.

7. Loosen the front support rod jam nuts (**Figure 17**).

8. Turn the deck support rods to raise or lower them as necessary so the rod pins are in their original holes in relation to the support plates.

9. Tighten the support rod jam nuts.

10. Install the support rod pins.

11. Remove the four deck-to-floor supports.

12. Double-check the pitch measurement. Readjust as necessary.

13. Reconnect the spark plug lead.

DECK HOUSING

The Scag cutter deck housing is robotically cut, formed and welded in precision jigs. There are no adjustments other than the ones previously listed in this chapter. If, after performing necessary adjustments, the blade dimen-

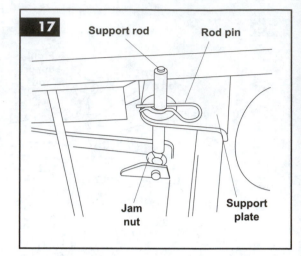

sions or alignment do not meet specification, the deck has probably been warped or twisted.

Clean under the deck and remove packed grass debris daily or as often as is necessary to maintain a proper cut. Grass debris underneath the deck will:

1. Prevent proper clipping discharge.

2. Contribute to rust, corrosion and scaling, leading to a weakening of the deck structure.

3. Wear down the liftwings on the blades.

Periodically check the integrity of the welds on the deck, deck supports and caster wheel attachments. Repair or replace as necessary. For service on the caster wheels, tires or bearings, refer to Chapter Three.

Table 1 CUTTING HEIGHT SPECIFICATIONS FOR SWZ WALK BEHIND MOWERS

		DECK MOUNTED IN TOP HOLE					A
		Number of Spacers Above Blades					
		0	1	2	3	4	5
Number of Spacers Above Blades	0	2 1/4	2	1 3/4	1 1/2	1 1/4	1
	1	2 1/2	2 1/4	2	1 3/4	1 1/2	1 1/4
	2	2 7/8	2 5/8	2 3/8	2 1/8	1 7/8	1 5/8
	3	3 1/4	3	2 3/4	2 1/2	2 1/4	2
	4	3 1/2	3 1/4	3	2 3/4	2 1/2	2 1/4

Table 1 CUTTING HEIGHT SPECIFICATIONS FOR SWZ WALK BEHIND MOWERS (continued)

		DECK MOUNTED IN TOP HOLE					B
		Number of Spacers Above Blades					
		0	1	2	3	4	5
Number of Spacers Above Blades	0	2 1/2	2 1/4	2	1 3/4	1 1/2	1 1/4
	1	2 3/4	2 1/2	2 1/4	2	1 3/4	1 1/2
	2	3 1/8	2 7/8	2 5/8	2 3/8	2 1/8	1 7/8
	3	3 1/2	3 1/4	3	2 3/4	2 1/2	2 1/4
	4	4	3 3/4	3 1/2	3 1/4	3	2 3/4

		DECK MOUNTED IN TOP HOLE					C
		Number of Spacers Above Blades					
		0	1	2	3	4	5
Number of Spacers Above Blades	0	3	2 3/4	2 1/2	2 1/4	2	1 3/4
	1	3 1/4	3	2 3/4	2 1/2	2 1/4	2
	2	3 1/2	3 1/4	3	2 3/4	2 1/2	2 1/4
	3	4	3 3/4	3 1/2	3 1/4	3	2 3/4
	4	4 1/4	4	3 3/4	3 1/2	3 1/4	3

13

CHAPTER FOURTEEN

CLUTCH AND DRIVE BELTS

This chapter will cover the electric PTO clutch, belts, pulleys and idlers necessary for transmitting engine power to the blades.

PTO CLUTCH

The PTO clutch is mounted on the bottom of the engine crankshaft (**Figure 1**, hydrostatic filter removed for clarity). It is keyed to the crankshaft and is secured to the shaft with a bolt, lock washer and flat washer.

> *NOTE*
> *When the PTO switch is activated and deactivated, engaging and disengaging the clutch, a squealing sound may be momentarily heard under the engine. This sound is normal. It is caused by the clutch plate coming up to speed upon activation and the brake slowing the blade pulley upon deactivation. For long PTO clutch life, do not engage or disengage the clutch under full throttle, but only between 1/2 and 3/4 throttle. After the clutch is engaged, immediately bring the engine to full throttle.*

Prior to testing the circuit, the PTO clutch windings must be checked for shorts and opens and the airgap must be set to 0.015 inch. To access the clutch for testing and gapping:

1. Block the front wheels so the unit cannot move.

2. Carefully lift the rear of the unit off the floor high enough to access the clutch (**Figure 1**). Support the unit in this position, taking care not to allow the lift or supports to interfere with the clutch removal.

> *WARNING*
> *The clutch must be serviced from the bottom of the mower. When working under the mower, maintain a safe working environment and practice safe working procedures.*

Testing For Shorts And Opens

Shorted windings will feed DC current into the engine crankshaft. To return to ground, the current arcs through

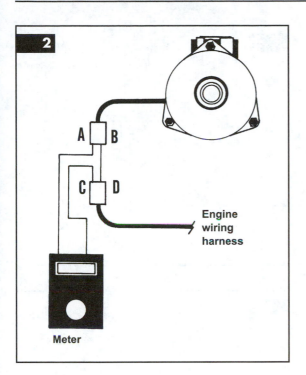

2

A B

C D

Engine
wiring
harness

Meter

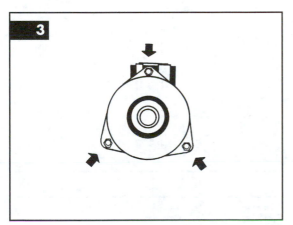

3

the oil film at the main bearing surfaces, eroding and pitting the bearings and causing major engine damage. Perform the following tests with the engine off to check for shorted windings.

1. Disconnect the main harness connector from the clutch connector (**Figure 1**).

NOTE

Resistance specifications in Step 2 are for an ambient temperature of 70° F (21° C) and may vary depending on the winding temperature and the test-equipment accuracy. If the mower has just been used, allow the engine and clutch to cool prior to testing.

2. Zero an ohmmeter on the Rx1 scale, then measure resistance between the two clutch-lead terminals. Resistance should read 2.4-2.9 Ohms on the Warner Electric Model CVX clutch and 2.8-3.2 Ohms on the Ogura Model MA-GT-EXM3X clutch. If resistance meets specification, proceed to Step 4.

3. If the clutch failed to read specified resistance in Step 2, the clutch has open windings. Inspect the clutch connector and lead for breaks or corrosion. Clean as necessary; repair if possible. If the connector and lead are good, the clutch must be replaced.

4. Measure resistance between each clutch-lead terminal and a clean ground spot on the clutch housing. Resistance should read infinity/no-continuity at both terminal-to-ground tests.

5. Connect a 14 gauge or larger jumper wire from the positive terminal of a fully charged battery to one of the clutch-lead terminals. Touch an equal-sized jumper wire from the negative battery terminal to the engine crankshaft. Listen and watch for the clutch to engage.

6. Repeat Step 5 with the other clutch-lead terminal.

7. Reverse the battery jumper connections and repeat Steps 5 and 6.

8. If the clutch engaged during any of test Steps 5-7, the clutch has shorted windings and must be replaced.

9. A current-draw test should also be used to check for shorted windings. This test is also performed with the engine off and the main-harness-to-clutch connectors disconnected. Refer to **Figure 2** and perform the following:

   a. Set the test meter to the 10 amp scale.

   b. Connect one ammeter lead to one terminal in the clutch-wire connector plug (A).

   c. Connect the second ammeter lead to the main harness terminal which feeds the meter-connected terminal in the clutch plug (C).

   d. Connect a jumper between the remaining clutch and main harness terminals (B and D).

   e. Turn the ignition switch on, but *do not start the engine*.

   f. Activate the PTO switch. The ammeter should show a draw of approximately 4.0 amps. If the reading is significantly higher or lower than 4.0 amps, the clutch winding may be shorted or the PTO switch may be faulty. PTO switch testing will be covered under*Component Testing* in this chapter.

   g. Turn the ignition switch off and deactivate the PTO switch.

Setting The PTO Clutch Airgap

To check and adjust the airgap:

1. Access the three adjustment nuts on the bottom of the clutch (**Figure 3**).

14

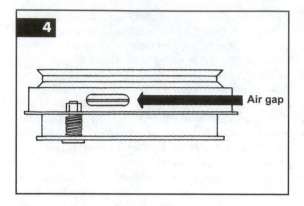

Air gap

2. Locate the airgap inspection windows on the side of the clutch housing (**Figure 4**). There is one window next to each adjusting nut.

3. Using a .015 inch feeler gauge, measure the gap between the armature and the rotor. If necessary, loosen or tighten the adjusting nut to set the airgap to specification. Do this at all three windows.

4. Repeat Step 3 two more times to make sure that the airgap did not change on one side of the clutch when the gap was adjusted on the opposite side.

5. Carefully rotate the clutch rotor pulley by hand to ensure smooth operation.

Testing The PTO Switch

Two styles of PTO switches are used—the toggle type (**Figure 5**) and the push-pull type. The push-pull type has two variations—the 5-terminal switch (**Figure 6**) and the 8-terminal switch (**Figure 7**).

Refer to the switch-terminal diagrams in **Figures 5-7** and the PTO Switch Terminal Continuity Chart in **Figure 8** to test the PTO switch. Connect the ohmmeter test leads to the applicable PTO swtich terminals, indicated in the chart (**Figure 8**). Note the continuity/no-continuity readings with the PTO switch OFF, then ON.

Replace the PTO swtich if it fails any of the continuity/no-continuity tests.

Clutch Removal

WARNING
The clutch must be removed from the bottom of the mower. When working under the mower, maintain a safe working environment and practice safe working procedures.

1. Block the front wheels so the unit cannot move.

2. Carefully lift the rear of the unit off the floor high enough to access the clutch (**Figure 1**). Support the unit in this position, taking care not to allow the lift or supports to interfere with the clutch removal.

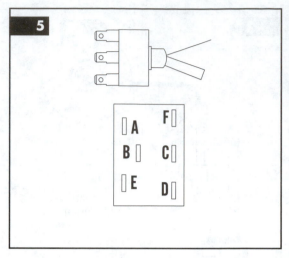

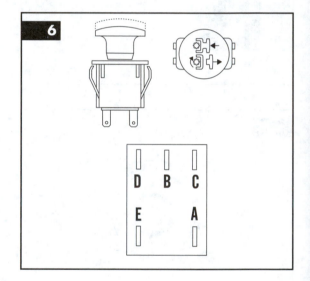

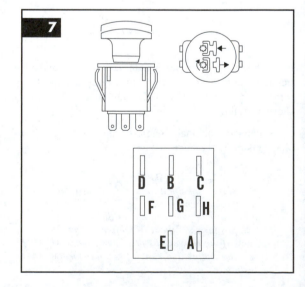

8

PTO SWITCH TERMINAL CONTINUITY CHART

SWITCH	Toggle		5-Terminal Push-Pull		8-Terminal Push-Pull	
POSITION	**OFF**	**ON**	**OFF**	**ON**	**OFF**	**ON**
Continuity terminal pairs	B-E C-D	A-B C-F	A-E C-D	B-C	C-D F-H	A-E B-C G-H
No continuity terminal pairs	A-B C-F	B-E C-D	B-C	A-E C-D	A-E B-C G-H	C-D F-H

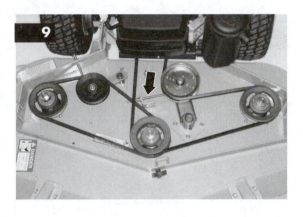

9

3. Access the blade drive belt. Loosen the front and side wing bolts on the deck belt guard. Remove the top wing nut(s), then remove the belt guard.

4. On fixed-idler drives, loosen the belt idler adjusting nut (**Figure 9**) enough to remove the belt from the idler pulley *without damaging the belt*.

5. On spring-loaded idler drives, push against the idler pulley arm enough to be able to work the belt off the pulley.

6. Feed the blade belt backwards, removing it from the clutch pulley, then feed it forward again to get it out of the way.

7. Repeat Step 4 or 5 as applicable to remove the hydrostatic drive belt (**Figure 1**). On spring-loaded idler systems, the idler spring can be removed for less interference.

8. Unplug the clutch harness connector (**Figure 1**).

9. Using a strap wrench, hold the engine-mounted hydrostatic drive pulley while loosening the clutch bolt.

10. Support the clutch. Remove the clutch bolt. Note the location of the clutch locator bracket. Remove the clutch.

11. Clean the engine crankshaft and clutch bore as necessary. Clean the clutch bolt and matching crankshaft threads.

12. Inspect the condition of the crankshaft keyway and key, the clutch keyway and the clutch bearing. The bearing should turn smoothly.

Clutch Installation

1. Ensure that the clutch key is in its proper position in the crankshaft keyway.

2. Lightly coat the crankshaft and clutch bore with Led-Plate or an equivalent anti-seize compound.

3. Note the position of the crankshaft key in relation to the clutch locator bracket (**Figure 1**). Align the clutch keyway and locator bracket to match the crankshaft key and frame bracket.

4. Lightly coat the clutch bolt threads with Loctite 262 or equivalent.

5. Slide the clutch into position on the crankshaft. Ensure that the key and locator bracket are properly aligned. Ensure that the clutch leads are not pinched or kinked. Install the clutch bolt, lock washer and flat washer.

6. While holding the crankshaft-mounted hydrostatic drive pulley with a strap wrench, torque the clutch bolt to 75-80 ft.-lb. (102-108 N•m).

7. Install and tension the hydrostatic drive belt. On spring-loaded idler systems, align the belt in all the pulley V-grooves, then pull the idler arm aside and work the back side of the belt onto the idler. On fixed-idler systems:

    a. Align the belt in all the pulley V-grooves.

    b. Work the back side of the belt onto the idler.

    c. Check belt tension in the center of the longest belt span between two pulleys (**Figure 10**). The following formula can be used to calculate the proper belt deflection when a force of 8-10 pounds. (3.6-4.5 kg) is applied to the center of the belt. Belt span length (L) divided by 64 equals the amount of deflection (D). For example, if the span length (L) were 24 inches (61 cm), 24 divided by 64 equals

14

0.375 or 3/8. Applying 8-10 pounds (3.6-4.5 kg) of force should produce a deflection of 3/8 inch (13 mm).

    d. Tighten the idler adjusting nut as necessary to achieve the proper deflection.

8. Reconnect the clutch harness connector (**Figure 1**).

9. Install the blade drive belt guard. Tighten the side wing bolts and the top wing nut(s).

10. Carefully lower the mower back down onto the floor and unchock the front wheels.

DRIVE BELTS

Misalignment

    Belts operate best when the pulleys are properly aligned. A, **Figure 11** illustrates a belt running between two properly-aligned pulleys.

    Tests have shown that just over six percent of belt life is lost for every degree of misalignment. B, **Figure 11** illustrates two pulleys with plane misalignment. C, **Figure 11** illustrates two pulleys with compound misalignment — plane misalignment plus shaft misalignment. The situation illustrated by C, **Figure 11** is almost always caused by shaft bearing problems, especially with spring-loaded idler pulleys, as belt tension tends to pull the two pulleys together.

    To check the alignment of pulleys, place a straightedge across the faces of the pulleys as shown in **Figure 12**. If the inner and outer edges of both pulleys contact the straightedge, the pulleys are aligned. On pulleys with different wall thicknesses, the difference between the thick and the thin wall must be compensated for along the straightedge. If misalignment is evident, locate and correct the cause.

Belt cross-section

    Figure 13 shows a deep cross-section belt in a leading-groove pulley. This is an "engineered-misalignment" pulley, and the deep cross-section belt not only resists twisting in this application, but also has a large contact surface area on both sides of the belt to provide the maximum amount of grip. The more the grip, the less the slip, provided the belt is tensioned properly.

    Figure 14 shows the same pulley as **Figure 13**, but with a shallow cross-section belt such as those fractional horsepower belts offered by some aftermarket suppliers. In some cases, the depth of the belt is less than the top width. Even in perfect alignment situations, these belts provide unsatisfactory results in two areas. They do not have sufficient gripping capacity, and so may slip or overheat, especially under heavy loads. They also are more prone to twisting and rolling-over due to the momentary slack created during periods of engagement and disengagement.

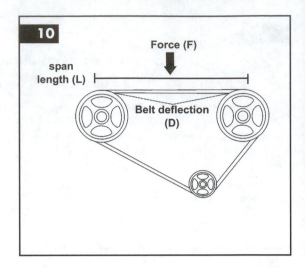

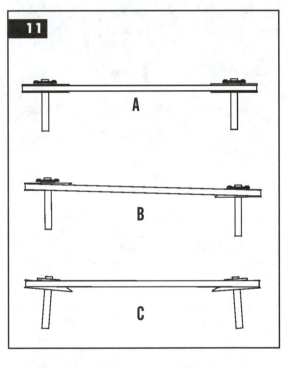

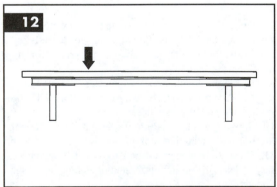

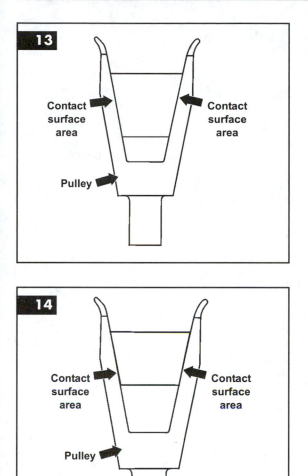

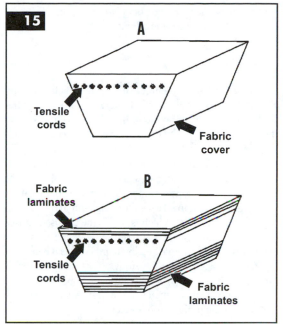

Figure 15 shows cross-sectional views of the two types of belt construction.

A, **Figure 15** illustrates the wrapped belt. This belt receives its name from the fact that each belt is individually manufactured, then wrapped with a rubberized fabric material covering all of the belt's internal structure. The wrap surface is not seriously affected by a slight amount of slippage, and it increases belt life by helping the belt retain its shape. This type of belt construction works well in situations where good clutching characteristics and smooth engagements are required.

B, **Figure 15** illustrates the raw edge or raw-sided belt. These belts are cut from a continuous band composed of the layers which make up the belt's internal structure. This is especially helpful when a matched set of belts is needed, as all the belts cut from the band are identical in length. The raw sides, being exposed, provide superior gripping qualities over the wrapped belt. They normally have higher strength, thereby being able to handle more

horsepower, than wrapped belts. Because of their grip, they have limited clutch-slip ability, and are usually slightly noisier when engaged. Instead of being wrapped in rubberized fabric, these belts have laminated layers of fabric at the bottom and the top of the belt.

Although all of a belt's components are important, the component which contributes most to the strength of the belt is the layer of tensile cords which runs lengthwise inside the belt. Two types of material are usually used — polyester and Kevlar. Polyester is used most often, but, during the life of the belt, it will stretch, requiring adjustments. Kevlar is the strongest belt cord material and has negligible stretch, requiring minimal maintenance.

Figure 15 illustrations show the tensile cords mounted toward the wide top of the belt. On some belts which flex both directions — forward around the drive pulleys, then backward around the "flat" idler pulleys — the layer of tensile cords is placed closer to the center of the belt to equalize flexing.

Improper Tension

Correct tension is critical toward proper belt operation and life expectancy, mainly because of heat. Testing has shown that belt life is reduced by half for every 25° F increase in belt temperature above the temperature at which the belt was designed to operate.

Over tensioning and under tensioning both create additional heat: over tensioning due to the excess heat of friction from the belt being too tight, and under tensioning by slippage and the slapping of the belt against the pulley groove. Over tensioning also overheats the pulleys, shafts

14

and bearings due to the belt being too tight, thereby transferring additional heat to the belt.

Heat

As mentioned in the preceding section, belt life is reduced by 50% for every 25° F increase in belt temperature. Improper misalignment, like that shown in **Figure 11**, is one source of excess belt heat. Incorrect tension is another.

A third source of excess heat is the pulleys, themselves. A pulley running hot due to a faulty bearing will pass the heat to the belt. Grass debris buildup in the bottom of the pulley groove (**Figure 16**) reduces the normal belt-to-pulley side contact areas which is where the belt is supposed to get its traction. Debris buildup requires the load to be taken from the bottom of the belt and creates a belt rocking motion inside the pulley groove. This causes slippage, further increasing belt temperature. It also causes rapid wear on the inside diameter of the belt. Always keep the bottoms of the pulley grooves clean.

On units which operate in humid environments, especially a mower which may have been out of service for some time, check the pulley grooves for rust and corrosion. These cause additional friction between the belt and pulley grooves, producing higher belt temperatures. The roughness of the rust and corrosion also cause more rapid wear on the sides of the belt.

Other Problem Sources

Load shock

A belt which seems to be in otherwise good condition but has a break area where it appears to have been pulled apart or snapped in two is a victim of load shock. When the mower is mowing, and one blade is stopped suddenly by a tree root, large rock, or other unseen solid object, the shock can be transferred to the belt. This sometimes snaps the belt in two. If this happens, also inspect the blades, blade bolts, shafts and pulleys for straightness and alignment, as the belt is the secondary recipient of the load shock, with the primary damage being done elsewhere.

Twigs

Even with the best of guards and shields, twigs, wire, hay twine and other debris can make its way into belt drive systems. Debris can:
1. Jam the drive, preventing it from turning.
2. Cause the belt to jump off the pulley, sometimes damaging the belt.
3. Jam against a part of the frame while rubbing against the belt or pulley, overheating one or both. A large enough

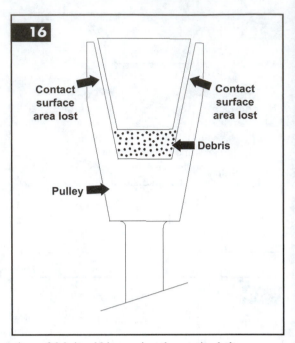

piece of debris rubbing against the rotating belt can cause the belt to smoke.

Vibration

If some part of a drive system is stopped momentarily – jammed, for instance – and the engine continues to run, the part of the belt which rubs against the pulley on the stopped component will burn and harden. In the future, whenever this burned spot passes around a pulley, it will cause vibration. If the mower has a vibration problem and all other apparent sources have been checked unsuccessfully, inspect the belts.

Dimensioning

Some belt problems can be traced to having the wrong-sized belt, especially if the belt was recently replaced. In addition to the cross-sectional differences between belts, there can also be variations in length. These differences can lead to improper tensioning and insufficient or too much idler adjustment, resulting in interference between drive components and adjoining chassis members. Always make sure that replacement belts exactly match the original equipment specifications.

Pulley groove damage

Pulleys should be checked for groove damage.

A pinched groove, for example, will cause binding and momentary belt tightening every time the pulley rotates to the pinched spot.

Cast pulleys, when struck, may sometimes break off a piece of groove which may not be noticed immediately, especially if the break is on the hidden side of the pulley. The edge of the break will then scrape the belt every time the belt passes the break.

Pulley-to-shaft integrity

Pulleys should always be securely mounted to their shafts, with keys and setscrews tight.

Some of the pulleys on these mowers use a separate tapered hub which locks onto the shaft by being tightened into a matching taper in the pulley. If the bolts holding the hub to the pulley should loosen, the pulley will slip on the shaft. Servicing these tapered hub pulleys will be covered later on in this chapter.

Drive Belt Systems

Fixed-idler system

To adjust belt tension on fixed-idler drives, refer to **Figure 9** and perform the following:

1. Loosen the front and side wing bolts on the deck belt guard. Remove the top wing nut, then remove the belt guard.

2. Apply penetrating oil to the J-bolt threads on both sides of the adjusting nut.

3. Inspect the integrity of the belt(s), the fixed pulleys, and the idler pulley(s), including the idler bearing(s). If questionable, replace the belt(s) or pulley(s). Pulley replacement will be covered in the *Deck and Drive* chapter.

4. Refer to **Figure 10**. Determine the longest belt span. Use the following formula to calculate the proper belt deflection when a force of 8-10 pounds. (3.6-4.5 kg) is applied to the center of the belt. Belt span length (L) divided by 64 equals the amount of deflection (D). For example, if the span length (L) were 24 inches (61 cm), 24 divided by 64 equals 0.375 or 3/8. Applying 8-10 pounds 3.6-4.5 kg) of force should produce a deflection of 3/8 inch (13mm).

5. Turn the adjusting nut as necessary to achieve proper deflection.

Spring-loaded idler system

Refer to **Figure 1**.

The spring pulling the idler pulley bracket is engineered to apply the correct amount of tension to the belt. When checking the spring-loaded system:

1. Make sure that the spring ends and the spring-end mating areas are not broken or worn, and that the spring coils are not rubbing against other components, causing drag.

2. Make sure that the idler bracket pivot bearings/bushings allow the bracket to swing freely through the required horizontal arc of travel. Remove the belt from the idler, making sure the bracket continues to arc on its

pivot, not binding or jamming at or near the point of normal belt tension. Make sure that the bracket pivot is not worn to the point of allowing the idler to droop vertically, causing idler and belt misalignment.

3. Inspect the integrity of the belt and the idler pulley, including the idler bearing(s). If questionable, replace the belt or pulley.

4. Make sure that the driven pulleys have not slipped on their shafts. Inspect pulley alignment as well as key and setscrew placement. On two-piece pulleys with tapered hubs, refer to the next section for proper service.

BELT-DRIVE PULLEYS

To check the alignment of pulleys, place a straightedge across the faces of the pulleys as shown in **Figure 12**. If the inner and outer edges of both pulleys contact the straightedge, the pulleys are aligned. On pulleys with different wall thicknesses, the difference between the thick and the thin wall must be compensated for along the straightedge. If misalignment is evident, locate and correct the cause.

Two-Piece Taper-Hub Pulleys

Some of the pulleys on these mowers use a separate tapered hub which locks onto the shaft by being tightened into a matching taper in the pulley (**Figure 17**). The correct procedure for servicing these pulleys is as follows:

Removal

> *CAUTION*
> *Two-piece taper-hub pulleys must always be assembled clean and dry. Do not use any lubricants on the tapered surfaces, the screw and pulley threads, or the shaft surfaces. If penetrating oil is used to aid in removal of the pulley and hub, remove all traces of the penetrating oil prior to reassembly.*

1. Remove the hub-to-pulley bolts.

2. Remove any dirt or debris from the threaded holes in the hub flange. Lightly run a bottoming tap into the holes to ensure complete cleanliness.

3. Insert the hub-to-pulley bolts into the hub flange threads until they contact the pulley hub flange.

4. Beginning with the bolt farthest from the split in the hub, tighten the bolts incrementally and progressively 1/4 turn at a time until the pulley is loose from the hub. At this point, the hub can be removed from the shaft.

5. If necessary, remove the square key from the shaft keyway at this time.

14

Installation

> *CAUTION*
> *Two-piece taper-hub pulleys must always be assembled clean and dry. Do not use any lubricants on the tapered surfaces, the screw and pulley threads, or the shaft surfaces. If penetrating oil is used to aid in removal of the pulley and hub, remove all traces of the penetrating oil prior to reassembly.*

1. Properly position the square key into the shaft keyway.
2. Set the pulley onto the shaft with the large diameter of the taper facing up.
3. With the hub flange up, slide the hub onto the shaft so the keyway slides over the key.
4. Lightly slide the pulley up onto the hub, aligning the threaded pulley holes with the unthreaded hub flange holes.
5. Loosely insert the bolts through the unthreaded hub flange holes, into the threaded pulley holes.
6. Lightly and incrementally tighten the bolts until the hub becomes difficult to slide up and down the shaft by hand.
7. Align the pulley position with a straightedge (**Figure 12**), then incrementally and alternately torque the bolts to the specifications in **Table 1**.

> *CAUTION*
> *When tightening the hub bolts on a taper-hub pulley, the applied torque is multiplied considerably by the wedging action of the hub and pulley tapers. Over-torquing the bolts or applying lubricants to any part of the shaft, pulley, hub or bolts will create bursting pressures in the pulley hub flange, cracking the pulley. Torque the bolts incrementally and alternately. Do not over-torque.*

8. Double-check the alignment of the pulley. Readjust as necessary.

Fixed-hub Pulleys

Removal

The pulley on the engine crankshaft which drives the blade belt is a one-piece fixed-hub pulley. To remove this pulley:
1. Remove the electric PTO clutch by following Steps 1-12 under *PTO Clutch Removal* in this chapter.
2. Mark the position and orientation of the pulley on the crankshaft.
3. Loosen the setscrew in the pulley hub.
4. Slide the pulley off the crankshaft. It may be necessary to apply penetrating oil to the crankshaft/pulley hub area

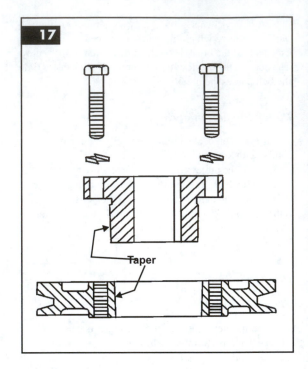

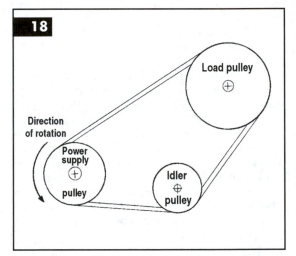

to aid in removal. *Light* tapping on the pulley hub with a small ball-peen hammer may also help.

Installation

1. Lightly coat the crankshaft and pulley hub bore with Led-Plate or an equivalent anti-seize compound.
2. Make sure that the crankshaft key is properly positioned.
3. Orient the pulley as noted during removal. Slide the pulley into the position noted during removal.
4. Tighten the pulley hub setscrew.
5. Install the electric PTO clutch by following Steps 1-10 under *PTO Clutch Installation* in this chapter.

Idler Pulleys

Idler pulleys provide a path for the belt to follow in order to clear obstructions or to apply more grip on the pulley, and apply tension on the belt to prevent slippage.

Figure 1 shows a typical Scag hydrostatic-drive system. This system uses a spring-loaded idler pulley to automatically provide tension against the belt. The direction of rotation of the drive belt in **Figure 1** is counterclockwise.

Figure 9 shows a typical Scag blade-drive system for a 3-blade cutter deck. The primary idler pulley (I, **Figure 9**) and the secondary idler pulley (J) keep the blade drive belts properly tensioned while allowing adjustment when needed. This system uses a manually-adjusted fixed-idler system to keep correct tension on the drive belts. To adjust belt tension, refer to the previous *Fixed-idler system* section in this chapter. The direction of rotation of the drive belts in **Figure 9** is clockwise.

On a multi-belt system such as the one in **Figure 9**, the belt coming from the power source, the engine, is referred to as the primary belt, with the idler pulley being the primary idler. This is the right-side belt and idler in the figure. The left-side drive, being driven by a pulley which is already driven by the engine belt, contains the secondary belt and idler.

Note that on both **Figure 1** and **Figure 9** belt-drive systems, the primary idler is always on the slack, or return, side of the belt. This is so the side of the belt being pulled by the rotation of the engine is always tight, thereby exerting the maximum amount of grip on the belt (**Figure 18**). This is especially critical on spring-loaded idlers.

Table 1 Torque Values For 2-Piece Taper-Hub Pulleys

Bolt	Thread	Torque Value
1/4	Inch	108 In.-lb. (12 N•m)
5/16	inch	180 In.-lb. (20 N•m)
3/8	inch	360 In.-lb. (40.5 N•m)

14

CHAPTER FIFTEEN

BRAKE

Since the Scag SWZ(U) units are hydrostatic drive, moving the drive control to the neutral position stops the mower, making driving brakes unnecessary. The brakes on these units are used as parking brakes only. **Figure 1** shows a disassembled view of the wheel brake components. With the wheel and tire removed, **Figure 2** shows the left-side brake engaged. **Figure 3** shows the brake linkage.

WARNING
Opening the bypass valve(s) on the hydro-static pumps will cause a loss of hydro-static braking. Exercise extreme care when opening the bypass valves, especially on sloping ground.

NOTE
For operator comfort, the handlebars can be mounted in any one of three positions, depending on the height of the operator. Anytime the handlebar position is changed, the brakes and the steering control linkage rods must be readjusted. The steering adjustment procedure can be found in the Linkage Adjustment section in either Chapter Three or Chapter Eleven.

BRAKE ADJUSTMENT

The brakes are external band-style brakes and are located on the rear drive wheels, just inside each wheel (**Figure 2**). To check and adjust the brakes:

1. Block the front wheels so the unit cannot move.

2. Carefully lift the rear of the unit off the floor slightly so the drive wheels are not touching the floor. Support the unit in this position, taking care to not allow the lift or supports to interfere with the operation of any linkages.

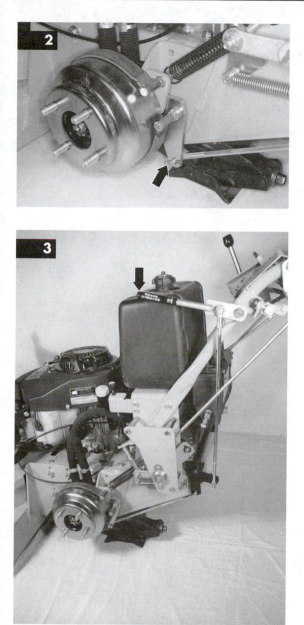

3. Open both hydrostatic pump bypass valves completely. They are screw-type valves and are fully open when unscrewed two turns maximum. **Figure 4** shows the location of the valve on the pump. The left-side valve is always accessed from the rear of the pump. Depending on the model, the right-side valve can be accessed from either the rear or the front of the pump.

4. With the parking brake handle in the down position (**Figure 3**; wheel removed for clarity) and the brakes released, the brake actuators (**Figure 5**; left side shown with hub, drum, band and wheel assembly removed for clarity) should rest against the wheel motor bracket stops on the frame. Both drive wheels should then rotate without brake drag when turned by hand. If drag is noticed due to the actuator not contacting the frame stop, adjust the brake actuator rod (**Figure 2**) incrementally on the dragging wheel until the actuator contacts the frame and the wheel turns freely. To adjust the rod:

   a. Remove the clevis pin from the rod swivel (**Figure 2**).
   b. Remove the rod swivel from the hole in the brake actuator.
   c. Unscrew the swivel to allow more brake slack.
   d. Reinsert the swivel into the actuator hole and reinstall the clevis pin. Note that the swivel fits inside the actuator with the clevis pin on the outside.

5. Pull the parking brake handle up into the engaged position (**Figure 6**). It should rest against the interlock-switch button on the handle bar and should only require light to moderate hand force to activate.

6. At this point, the drive wheels should not be able to be turned by hand.

7. Lower the machine back down onto the floor, then remove the chocks.

8. Attempt to push and pull the mower. The brakes should prevent any movement.

9. If the wheels moved in either Steps 6 or 8, adjust the brake actuator rod (**Figure 2**) on the non-braking wheel until the wheel stops properly. It will be necessary to disengage the brake to perform the adjustment(s). If, after adjusting the brakes to prevent mower movement, the actuator does not contact the frame (Step 4), do not readjust the actuator. Proper brake function is more important than actuator-to-frame contact.

10. Close both hydrostatic pump bypass valves completely.

BRAKE DRUM AND LINING

1. Block the front wheels so the unit cannot move.

2. Loosen the four wheel-mount nuts on each wheel (**Figure 1**) just enough to break torque. Do not remove the nuts at this time.

3. Carefully lift the rear of the unit off the floor slightly so the drive wheels are not touching the floor. Support the

15

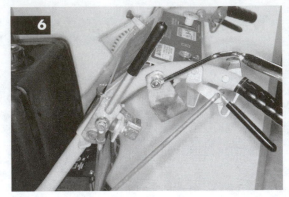

unit in this position, taking care to not allow the supports to interfere with the operation of any linkages.

4. Open both hydrostatic pump bypass valves completely. **Figure 4** shows the location of the valve on the pump. They are screw-type valves and are fully open when unscrewed two turns maximum. The left-side valve is always accessed from the rear of the pump. Depending on the model, the right-side valve can be accessed from either the rear or the front of the pump.

5. Remove the wheel-mount nuts, then remove the wheels.

6. Check the brake bands (**Figure 2**):

   a. Lining thickness should be a minimum of 1/16 inch (1.5 mm).

   b. There should be no cracks or broken welds on the bands.

   c. If substep 6a or 6b shows faults, replace the band(s).

7. Check the drums (**Figure 2**):

   a. There should be no scoring on the lining area of the drums.

   b. There should be no cracks anywhere on the drums, including the lining area and the 4-hole mounting area.

   c. If Steps 7a or 7b show faults, replace the drum(s).

8. Check the actuator mounting bolts (**Figure 5**) and the band mounting bolts (**Figure 2**). Replace any bent bolts.

CHAPTER SIXTEEN

ELECTRICAL SYSTEM

The electrical systems on these units consist of five main circuits:

1. Operator presence circuit.
2. Engine cranking circuit.
3. Engine ignition circuit.
4. Engine charging circuit.
5. Cutter deck PTO clutch circuit.

This chapter will cover most of the chassis electrical system components on these mowers (circuits 1 and 2), including ignition switches, safety-interlock switches and the battery and solenoid on electric-start units. The electrical systems for the engines are covered in each appropriate engine chapter. The electric PTO clutch blade-drive system is covered in Chapter Fourteen. *Electrical System Fundamentals* are located in Chapter Two.

ELECTRICAL SYSTEM TROUBLESHOOTING

CAUTION
Never perform a resistance test on a "hot" circuit, one which is powered by the mower's battery or by a running engine. Serious meter damage will result; personal injury may also occur.

NOTE
Resistance specifications are for an ambient temperature of 70° F (21° C) and may

vary depending on the winding temperature and the test-equipment accuracy.

Operator Presence Circuit

The operator presence circuit, sometimes referred to as the safety-interlock circuit, uses the safety-interlock switches and wiring to prevent the engine from starting or continuing to run if certain operating procedures are not followed.

The engine will not start unless:

1. The neutral latches are in the neutral lock position.
2. The speed adjustment lever is pulled back into the neutral position.
3. The parking brake is locked.
4. The cutter blade PTO switch is in the OFF position.

Once started, the operator presence levers (**Figure 1**) must be held down anytime the PTO switch is activated. If the PTO switch is on and the operator presence controls are released, the engine will stop.

Troubleshooting

To troubleshoot the operator presence circuit, refer to Chapter Two. Prior to testing the circuit:

1. Make sure that the fuses are good;

16

2. Engage the parking brake. **Figure 2** shows the brake switch activated with the brake handle up, in the ON position.

3. Place the motion drive lever in neutral (**Figure 3**). **Figure 4** shows the neutral switch in the OFF position, located between the right-side frame upright and the right-side hydrostatic pump.

4. Place the PTO switch in the OFF (down) position (the PTO safety interlock switch is built into the PTO switch as shown in **Figure 5**).

5. Start the test with the ignition switch off.

The test can be performed using either a test light or a voltmeter. Connect the positive tester lead to the positive battery terminal; connect the other tester lead to the white wire at the engine harness connector. If using a voltmeter, the meter should read battery voltage anytime a test step calls for the light to illuminate; the meter should read no voltage when a test step calls for the test light off.

Engine Cranking Circuit

The engine cranking circuit covers the wiring and components necessary to start the engine.

To troubleshoot the engine cranking circuit, refer to Chapter Two. Prior to testing the circuit:

1. Test the battery.

    a. The battery should have a minimum of 12.0 volts. If not, hydrometer-test and load-test the battery. Recharge and/or replace the battery as necessary. Refer to *Battery Service* in this chapter.

    b. With the ignition key turned to the START position, the battery should have a minimum of 9.0 volts. Also test the starter motor and cables.

2. Make sure that the fuses are OK.

3. Engage the parking brake. **Figure 2** shows the brake switch activated with the brake handle up, in the ON position.

4. Place the motion drive lever in neutral (**Figure 3**). **Figure 4** shows the neutral switch in the OFF position, located between the right-side frame upright and the right-side hydrostatic pump);

5. Place the PTO switch in the OFF (down) position (the PTO safety interlock switch is built into the PTO switch as shown in **Figure 5**).

6. Turn the ignition switch ON.

7. Depress and hold either operator presence lever (**Figure 1**).

The test can be performed using either a voltmeter or a test light. Connect the negative tester lead to the negative battery terminal. If using a test light, the light should illuminate whenever a test step calls for voltage to be present.

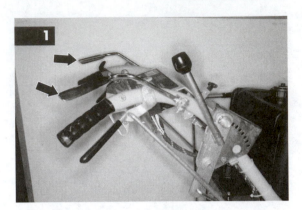

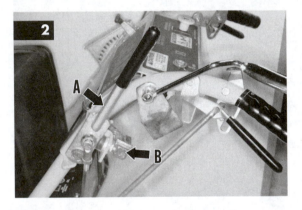

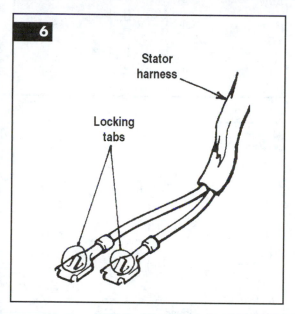

Stator harness

Locking tabs

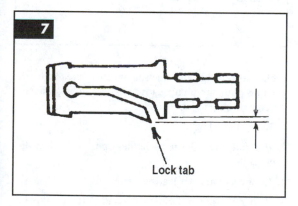

Lock tab

Component Testing

Switches and other individual components may be removed and bench-tested, but for system accuracy, they should be tested in-place to ensure that the linkages which operate them are working properly. Otherwise, a switch

may be thought to be at fault when the real problem is a linkage adjustment or malfunction.

Continuity (resistance) testing should be performed with an ohmmeter.

> *CAUTION*
> *Never perform a resistance test on a "hot" circuit, one which is powered by the mower's battery or by a running engine. Serious meter damage will result; personal injury may also occur.*

Wires, connectors and harnesses

Prior to testing individual components when electrical troubles develop, perform a thorough inspection of the wiring of the faulty system. Many electrical components are replaced only to discover that corrosion or a broken wire was the cause.

Inspect the harness in question to make sure it is not pinched or chafed. Reroute and clamp as necessary.

To check an individual wire:

1. Unplug both wire-end connectors from the system components.

2. Inspect the integrity of the connectors and component terminals. Are the connectors melted? Are the terminals rusted or corroded?

3. Use an ohmmeter and connect one probe to each end of the questionable wire. Wires are color-coded. Ensure that the probes are connected to both ends of the same-color wire.

4. Continuity indicates a good wire.

5. If no continuity is noted, remove the wiring terminals from the connectors.

    a. **Figure 6** shows the female harness terminals removed from the connector. To remove the terminals, use a tiny eyeglass repair style flat screwdriver to carefully flatten and unlock the terminal locking tabs from the locking slots in the harness connector. The blade tip must be inserted into the open end of the connector. Remove the terminals from the connector.

    b. The male harness terminal (**Figure 7**) typically fits into a connector. To remove this terminal, carefully pry sideways on the lock tab until the tab clears the terminal slot. Remove the terminal.

6. Bypass the terminal and retest the wire. If the wire tests good, replace the faulty terminal(s). New terminals must be soldered to the wire for proper contact and future corrosion prevention.

7. If the wire still does not test continuity, replace the wire.

8. Using the same eyeglass-repair screwdriver which was used in Step 5, carefully bend the terminal locking tabs back to the lock positions shown in **Figure 6**.

    a. Do not raise the tabs more than 3/32 inch (2.3 mm) on the female harness terminal.

16

b. Do not spread the tab more than 1/16 inch (1.6 mm) on the male harness terminal.

9. Align the terminal lock tabs with the connector slots. Insert the terminals into the connector completely. Ensure that the terminals are locked into the connector by lightly tugging on the wire after insertion. If the terminal pulls out, check the connector for obstructions, clear or replace as necessary, then reinsert and lock the terminal.

Single-pole switch

Scag single-pole switches (**Figure 8**) normally have one pair of terminals and are used in the operator presence circuit as neutral interlock switches. They are classified as normally-closed (NC) switches since, in the switch's normal position, with the spring-loaded activation plunger out, the internal contacts are closed, allowing current to pass across the two exposed terminals. To test these switches:

1. Unplug the harness connector from the switch terminals.
2. Connect the ohmmeter probes to the switch terminals.
3. The ohmmeter should read continuity between terminals A and B with the plunger out and infinity/no-continuity with the plunger in.

Double-pole switch

Scag double-pole switches (**Figure 9**) normally have two pair of terminals and are used as neutral-lever interlock switches. Only one pair of side-by-side terminals will pass current at a time, depending upon the plunger position. The switch activation plunger is spring-loaded to a normally-out position. To test these switches:

1. Unplug the harness connector(s) from the switch terminals.
2. Connect the ohmmeter probes to one pair of switch terminals at a time.
3. The ohmmeter should read continuity between the A terminals and infinity/no-continuity between the B terminals with the plunger in the out, relaxed position.
4. The ohmmeter should read continuity between the B terminals and infinity/no-continuity between the A terminals with the plunger pushed in.

Relays

On some Scag units with electric-start Kawasaki engines, a start relay is used in the wiring harness instead of the usual solenoid mounted on or near the starter. **Figure 10** shows the relay terminal arrangement as well as the internal schematic of the relay.

Terminals B and D are connected to the internal relay winding. Terminals A and C are normally not connected, as the internal plunger is spring-loaded to keep the A-C contact strip away from the terminals. When voltage is

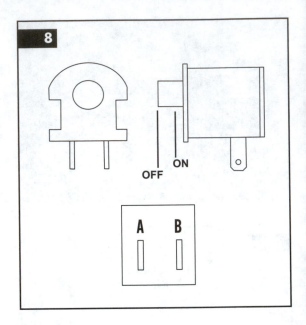

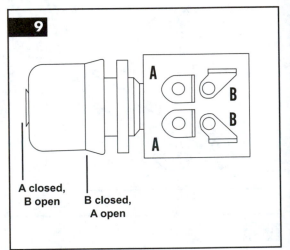

applied to B and D, the electromagnetism created by the winding pulls the plunger toward the winding, causing the contact strip to join A and C.

To test the relay:

1. Carefully note the relay harness positions, then disconnect the wires.

2. Connect ohmmeter leads to terminals A and C.

3. Apply 12 volts to terminals B and D (polarity is not important).

4. Note the ohmmeter reading.

If the relay is functioning properly, there will be no continuity between A and C until power is applied to B and D, at which time A and C should read continuity. Any other test results indicate a faulty relay.

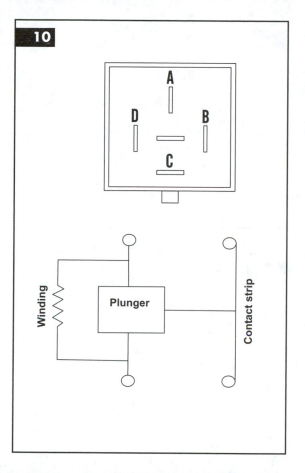

10

A

D   B

C

Winding   Plunger   Contact strip

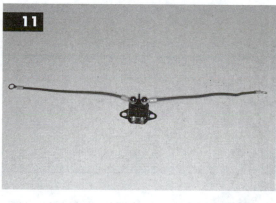

11

Solenoids

Solenoids are of two basic types: internally grounded or externally grounded. The grounding refers to the primary, low-current circuit. They can be identified by the number of terminals on the solenoid case.

All solenoids used in the starting circuits of the engines on these units have two large secondary-circuit terminals. These terminals use either 1/4 inch or 5/16 inch terminal studs, and are for the battery-to-starter cables.

Externally-grounded solenoids (**Figure 11**) have two smaller primary-circuit terminals. Internally-grounded solenoids only have one small terminal.

Troubleshooting a solenoid can usually be done quickly with the solenoid in the system.

To troubleshoot an internally-grounded solenoid:

1. Remove the ignition key from the switch so the engine does not start.
2. Make sure that the unit is in neutral and that the parking brake is set.
3. Place the throttle control in the SLOW position.
4. Remove the main harness wire from the small solenoid terminal.
5. Using a short jumper wire, connect one end of the wire to the small terminal; momentarily touch the other end to the large terminal of the cable coming from the positive battery post.
6. If the starter activates, the solenoid is good.

To troubleshoot an externally-grounded solenoid:

1. Remove the ignition key from the switch so the engine does not start.
2. Ensure that the unit is in neutral and that the parking brake is set.
3. Place the throttle control in the Slow position.
4. Remove the main harness wires from the small solenoid terminals.
5. Taking a pair of jumper wires, use one wire to connect one small solenoid terminal to the positive battery post. Connect one end of the other jumper to the other small solenoid terminal. Momentarily touch the other end of the second jumper wire to the negative battery post.

CAUTION
Do not allow the two jumper wires to contact each other.

6. If the starter activates, the solenoid is good.

Ignition switches

Two styles of ignition switches may be used: one for recoil-start engines (**Figure 12**) and one for electric-start engines (**Figure 13**). The alphabetical legend for these switches is as follows:

A = Accessories L = Lights
B = Battery M = Magneto
G = Ground S = Start

16

To test the recoil-start switch, connect the ohmmeter leads to the two terminals, M and G. With the key off, there should be continuity between M and G. With the key in the RUN position, there should be no continuity between M and G.

To test the electric-start switch, connect the ohmmeter leads to the terminals noted in the following list:

1. With the key in the OFF position, there should be continuity between terminals A-M-G.

2. With the key in the RUN position, there should be continuity between terminals A-B-L.

3. With the key in the START position, there should be continuity between terminals B-L-S.

Battery Service

On electric-start units, the battery is an important component in the electrical system. Many electrical system troubles can be traced to battery neglect. Clean and inspect the battery at periodic intervals.

Original equipment batteries have cell caps which can be removed to check the electrolyte level and specific gravity. Some battery manufacturers offer a maintenance-free battery as a replacement. This is a sealed battery, so the electrolyte level and specific gravity cannot be checked.

On all models covered in this manual, the negative side is grounded. When removing the battery, disconnect the negative cable first, then disconnect the positive cable. This minimizes the chance of a tool shorting to ground if the positive battery cable is disconnected first.

Battery service specifications are given in this chapter for a normal room temperature of 68° F (20° C). When taking hydrometer readings, add .004 to the reading for every 10° F increase above 68° F; subtract .004 from the reading for every 10° F decrease below 68° F. Refer to **Table 1** for the battery state of charge as determined by the specific gravity reading.

Ambient temperature affects battery charging and discharging. A cold battery will charge slower than a warm battery, but, by the same token, it will also discharge slower. For this reason, when the mower is not in use for an extended period, it is more beneficial to the battery to be stored in a cool location, provided the battery is fully-charged at the start of storage. A fully-charged battery will not freeze, even in below-zero temperatures, because the electrolyte acts as an anti-freeze. A half-charged or discharged battery will, on the other hand, freeze more readily, since the weaker electrolyte more closely resembles regular water.

> *WARNING*
> *Battery fluid splashed into the eyes is extremely harmful. Safety glasses must always be worn while working with a battery.*

> *CAUTION*
> *Battery electrolyte is very corrosive. Avoid spilling or splashing electrolyte on skin or clothing, as it will cause burns.*

Battery removal/installation

1. Turn the ignition switch OFF.
2. Remove the insulated battery shield (3, **Figure 14**).

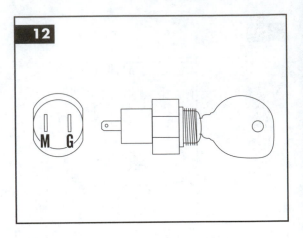

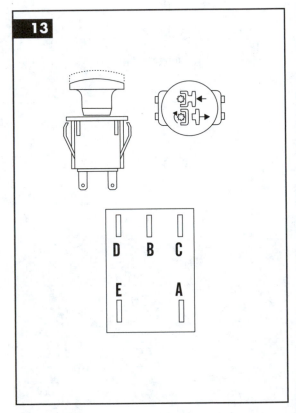

3. Disconnect the negative battery cable from the negative battery terminal.

4. Move the negative cable out of the way so it will not accidentally contact the negative battery terminal.

5. Remove the protective terminal boot from the positive battery terminal. Disconnect the positive battery cable from the positive battery terminal.

6. Remove the two carriage bolt battery holders and wingnuts (9 and 10, **Figure 14**), then remove the battery from the mower.

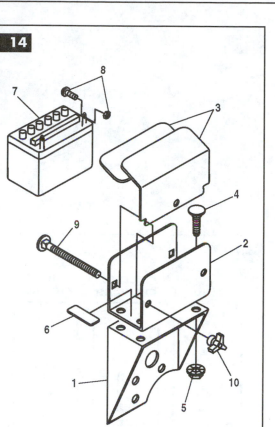

14

1. **Support mount**
2. **Tray**
3. **Shield with insulator pad**
4. **Tray bolts (4)**
5. **Tray nuts (4)**
6. **Rubber pad (2)**
7. **Battery**
8. **Terminal bolt assembly (2)**
9. **Holder bolt (2)**
10. **Holder wingnut (2)**

NOTE
When purchasing a replacement battery, always obtain one with the terminals in the same positions as the original battery. This will prevent cable mix-up as well as allowing the cables to reach their proper battery terminals.

7. To install the battery, set the battery into the battery box.

CAUTION
Be sure the battery is positioned so the cables will connect to their proper terminals.

On units with color-coded cables, the red battery cable must connect from the positive battery terminal to the starter solenoid post; the black battery cable must connect from the negative battery terminal to the mower chassis ground. On units with same-color cables, the ground cable is the cable with one end fastened to the mower chassis; the opposite end of this cable *must* be connected to the negative battery terminal. Connecting the battery backwards will reverse the polarity and damage the electrical system.

8. Install and tighten the positive battery cable.
9. Install and tighten the negative battery cable.
10. Coat the battery connections with No-Co NCP-2 or dielectric grease to retard corrosion. Reinstall the protective terminal boot over the positive battery terminal.

Inspection, cleaning and testing

Battery service specifications are given in this chapter for a normal room temperature of 68° F (20° C). When taking hydrometer readings, add .004 to the reading for every 10° F increase above 68° F; subtract .004 from the reading for every 10° F decrease below 68° F. Refer to **Table 1** for the battery state of charge as determined by the specific gravity readings. To clean and inspect the battery:

1. Remove the battery as described in this chapter. Do not clean the battery while it is mounted in the frame.
2. Inspect the battery box, holddown bolts and top shield for corrosion or damage. Clean the box and components with a baking soda and water solution, then rinse thoroughly and dry.
3. Set the battery on a stack of newspapers or cardboard to protect the workbench surface. Setting the battery on a concrete floor is not recommended.
4. Check the entire battery case for cracks or other damage. If the battery case is warped or has a raised top, the battery has overheated from overcharging.
5. Check the battery terminals and bolts for corrosion or damage. Clean parts thoroughly with a baking soda and water solution, then rinse and dry. Replace severely corroded bolts.
6. If corroded, clean the top, sides and bottom of the battery with a stiff bristle brush using a strong baking soda and water solution. Do *not* allow the soda solution to seep past the cell caps into the cells. Doing so will neutralize the cells' electrolyte and ruin the battery. When clean, rinse the battery case with clean water, then wipe dry.
7. Check the battery cable terminals for corrosion and damage. If corrosion is minor, clean the terminals by soaking them in a container of baking soda and water. Replace severely worn or damaged cables.
8. Connect a voltmeter across the negative and positive battery terminals. Note the following:
   a. If the battery voltage is 12.0-12.8 volts at 68° F (20° C), the battery is fully charged.

16

b. If the battery voltage is below 12.0 volts at 68° F (20° C), the battery is undercharged.

9. If the battery has removable cell caps, use a hydrometer (**Figure 15**) to test the specific gravity of the electrolyte. **Table 1** shows the percent of battery charge at 68° F (20° C) based on the hydrometer float reading. When hydrometer testing the electrolyte (**Figure 16**), ensure that there is sufficient fluid in the tube to buoy the float and do not let the float contact the sides of the glass tube. A battery with cells below 85% is considered not fully charged.

10. If either Step 8 or 9 shows the battery to be discharged, recharge it as described in this chapter. Once the battery is fully charged, reinstall the battery, then test the charging system as described in the appropriate engine chapter.

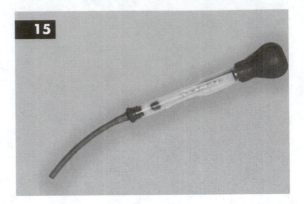

Charging

Refer to *Battery Initialization* in this chapter if the battery is new.

If recharging is required on a maintenance-free battery, a digital voltmeter and a charger with either an adjustable amperage output or a tapering output are required. Excessive voltage and amperage from an unregulated charger can damage the battery and shorten service life.

The battery should only self-discharge approximately one percent each day. If a battery not in use loses its charge within a week after charging, with no loads connected, the battery is defective.

If the mower is not used for long periods of time, an automatic battery charger with variable voltage and amperage outputs is recommended for optimum battery service life. Once the battery is fully charged, an automatic trickle charger should suffice.

Ambient temperature affects battery charging and discharging. Battery service specifications are given in this chapter for a normal room temperature of 68° F (20° C). When taking hydrometer readings, add .004 to the reading for every 10° F increase above 68° F; subtract .004 from the reading for every 10° F decrease below 68° F.

A cold battery will charge slower than a warm battery, but, by the same token, it will also discharge slower. For this reason, if the mower is not in use for an extended period, it is more beneficial to the battery to be stored in a cool location, provided the battery is fully-charged at the start of storage. A fully-charged battery will not freeze, even in below-zero temperatures, because the electrolyte acts as an anti-freeze. A half-charged or discharged battery will, on the other hand, freeze more readily, since the weaker electrolyte more closely resembles regular water.

> *WARNING*
> *During charging, highly-explosive hydrogen gas is released from the battery. Only charge the battery in a well-ventilated area away from open flames (including pi-*

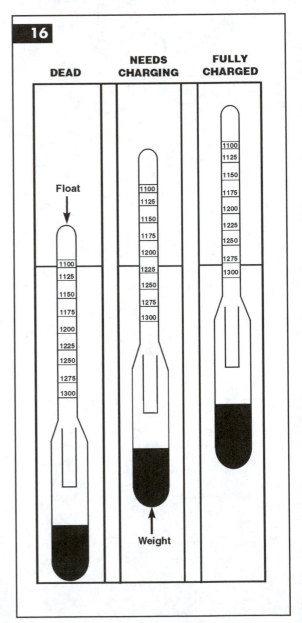

lot lights on gas home appliances) and sparks of any kind. Do not allow any smoking in the area. Do not do any grinding in the area. Never check the charge of the battery by arcing across the terminals; the resulting spark can ignite the hydrogen gas and cause a serious explosion. Never charge a battery in an area where sensitive equipment is stored, since the corrosive vapors can damage the equipment.

CAUTION
Always disconnect the battery cables from the battery, and disconnect the ground cable first. If the cables are left connected during the charging procedure, the charger may destroy the diodes in the voltage regulator/rectifier.

1. Remove the battery from the mower as described in this chapter.
2. Set the battery on a stack of newspapers or cardboard to protect the workbench surface. Setting the battery on a concrete floor is not recommended.
3. Always follow the charger manufacturer's instructions.
4. Make sure the battery charger is turned to the OFF position prior to attaching the charger leads to the battery.
5. Connect the positive charger lead to the positive battery terminal and the negative charger lead to the negative battery terminal.
6. Set the charger to 12 volts.
7. If the amperage output of the charger is variable, select the low setting. Normally, a battery should be charged at 1/10th its given capacity. A 40-ampere-hour battery should be charged at a maximum of 4 amps.

CAUTION
Never set the battery charger to more than 5 amps. A charge of more than 5 amps can overheat and warp the cell plates, ruining the battery, as well as creating a danger of explosion.

8. The charging time depends on the discharged condition of the battery. Again, refer to the charger manufacturer's instructions concerning charging times. As a general rule, the battery state-of-charge should be checked every half-hour while the battery is on charge, unless the charger is equipped with an automatic regulator.
9. Turn the charger to the ON position.
10. After the battery has been charged for the pre-determined time, turn the charger to the OFF position and disconnect the leads. Wait 30 minutes, measure the battery voltage and test the specific gravity of the electrolyte. Refer to the following:

a. If the battery voltage is 12.0-12.8 volts with all cells reading at least 1.260 specific gravity at 68° F (20° C), the battery is fully charged;
b. If the battery voltage is below 12.0 volts with all cells reading below 1.260 specific gravity, the battery is undercharged and requires additional charging time.
c. If most of the cells read at least 1.260 specific gravity after an ample charge time, with one or two cells reading significantly below 1.260, the low cells are weak and the battery is faulty.

11. If the battery remains stable for one hour, the battery is charged.
12. Install the battery into the mower as described in this chapter.

Battery initialization

A new battery must be *fully* charged to a specific gravity of 1.260-1.280 before installation. To bring the battery to a full charge, give it an initial charge. Using a new battery without an initial charge will cause permanent battery damage by preventing the battery from ever being able to hold more than an 80% charge. Charging a new battery *after* it has been used will not bring its charge to 100%. To initialize a new, dry battery:

1. Remove the cell covers.
2. Fill each cell to the bottom of the cell opening. There is usually a split ring at the bottom of each cell-fill tube to note the full position. On clear-case batteries, Low and Full level marks or lines are normally printed on the outside of the case, with the electrolyte level visible through the case.

It may be necessary to fill each cell initially, then refill after a few minutes when the first fill settles into the plates. Top off each cell as needed. Do not overfill.
3. Allow the electrolyte to stabilize for 30 minutes.
4. Make sure the battery charger is turned to the OFF position prior to attaching the charger leads to the battery.
5. Connect the positive charger lead to the positive battery terminal and the negative charger lead to the negative battery terminal.
6. Set the charger to 12 volts.
7. Slow-charge the battery at 3-5 amps for two hours.
8. After the battery has been charged for the pre-determined time, turn the charger to the OFF position and disconnect the leads. Wait 30 minutes, measure the battery voltage and test the specific gravity of the electrolyte. Refer to the following:

a. If the battery voltage is 12.0-12.8 volts with all cells reading at least 1.260 specific gravity at 68° F (20° C), the battery is fully charged;
b. If the battery voltage is below 12.0 volts with all cells reading below 1.260 specific gravity, the battery is undercharged and requires additional charging time.

16

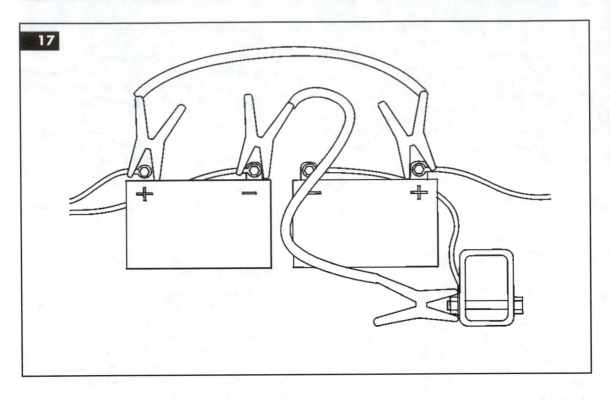

17

9. If the battery remains stable for one hour, the battery is charged.

> *NOTE*
> *Recycle the old battery. When a new battery is purchased, turn in the old one for recycling. Most battery sales outlets will accept the old battery in trade when purchasing a new one. Never place an old battery in the household trash since it is illegal, in most states, to place any acid or lead (heavy metal) contents in landfills.*

Jump-starting

If it becomes necessary to temporarily jump-start the mower, it is important to use the correct procedure not only for personal safety but also to safeguard the mower's electrical system. To jump-start:

1. Use color-coded red and black jumper cables.

2. Connect one end of the red cable to the positive terminal of the dead battery. Connect the other end to the positive terminal of the good battery (**Figure 17**).

3. Connect one end of the black cable to the negative terminal of the dead battery.

4. Connect the loose end of the black cable to a good, clean ground on the engine block or chassis of the unit

with the good battery. This will prevent possible sparks from occurring near the cell caps.

5. When the machine with the dead battery starts, always disconnect the black chassis-ground connection first, followed by the black dead-battery connection. Finish by unclamping both red cable connections.

Wiring Diagrams

Engine wiring diagrams are located in each particular engine chapter.

Mower wiring diagrams are divided into three groups: engine deck harness, handle harness, and relay harness. These diagrams follow this chapter.

Refer to **Table 1** at the end of this chapter for a sequential listing of unit serial numbers showing all possible wiring harnesses used in that series, depending on equipment options. Refer to **Table 2** at the end of this chapter for a sequential listing of wiring harnesses by part number and description.

As an example, the 320001 to 3349999 series show both the 487074 and the 481073 engine deck harnesses being used, with both of these harnesses able to be used with Briggs & Stratton engines. In cases where similar harness numbers are listed for one series, carefully inspect the harnes and compare it to the diagram prior to troubheshooting in order to enxure proper testing is performed.

Table 1 WIRING HARNESS – SERIAL NO. CROSS-REFERENCE

SERIAL NO. RANGE	MOWER MODEL	WIRING HARNESS DIAGRAMS USED			
xxx70001 – xxx79999	SWZ	481014	481051	481073	481074
		481075	481266	481267	481275
3230001 – 3239999	SWZ36-14KA,				
3240001 – 3249999	SWZ36-14KH,				
3250001 – 3259999	SWZ48-14KA,				
3260001 – 3269999	SWZ48-14KH,				
3270001 – 3279999	SWZ48-14KAE,				
3280001 – 3289999	SWZ48-16BV,				
3300001 – 3309999	SWZ-14KA,				
3310001 – 3319999	SWZ-16BV,				
3320001 – 3329999	SWZ-16BVE,				
3330001 – 3339999	SWZ-18BV,				
3340001 – 3349999	SWZ-20CVE	481014	481051	481073	481074
		481075	481275	481406	481407
4040001 – 4049999	SWZ36-14KA,				
4050001 – 4059999	SWZ36-15KH,				
4060001 – 4069999	SWZ48-14KA,				
4070001 – 4079999	SWZ48-15KH,				
4080001 – 4089999	SWZ48-17KA,				
4100001 – 4109999	SWZ-17KA	481073	481074	481075	
		481275	481680	481681	
780001 – 4789999	SWZU36-15KH,				
4790001 – 4799999	SWZU48-17KA	481073	481865	482008	482026
5120001 – 5129999	SWZ36-14KA,				
5130001 – 5139999	SWZ36-15KH,				
5140001 – 5149999	SWZ48-14KA,				
5150001 – 5159999	SWZ48-15KH,				
5160001 – 5169999	SWZ48-17KA,				
5170001 – 5179999	SWZ48A-17KA,				
5180001 – 5189999	SWZ52-17KA,				
5190001 – 5199999	SWZ52A-17KA,				
5210001 – 5219999	SWZ-21KAE	481073	481074	481075	
		481275	481680	481681	
5260001 – 5269999	SWZU36-15KA,				
5270001 – 5279999	SWZU48-17KA,				
5280001 – 5289999	SWZU52-17KA	481073	481865	482008	482026
5970001 – 5979999	SWZ52-17KAE	481073	481074	481075	
		481275	481680	481681	
6230001 – 6239999	SWZ36A-14KA,				
6260001 – 6269999	SWZ48A-17KA,				
6280001 – 6289999	SWZ52A-17KA,				
6290001 – 6299999	SWZ-17KA				
6300001 – 6309999	SWZ-21KAE	481073	481074	481075	481275
		481680	481681	482008	482026
6340001 – 6349999	SWZU,				
6350001 – 6359999	SWZU,				
6360001 – 6369999	SWZU,				
6370001 – 6379999	SWZU,				
6380001 – 6389999	SWZU,				
6390001 – 6399999	SWZU	481073	481865	482008	482026
7190001 – 7199999	SWZ36A-15KA	481073	481074	481075	481275
		481680	481681	482008	482026

16

(continued)

Table 1 WIRING HARNESS – SERIAL NO. CROSS-REFERENCE (continued)

SERIAL NO. RANGE	MOWER MODEL	WIRING HARNESS DIAGRAMS USED		
7370001 – 7379999	SWZ36A-15KA,			
7380001 – 7389999	SWZ48-17KA,			
7390001 – 7399999	SWZ52A-17KA	481073	481074	481865
		482008	482026	
7400001 – 7409999	SWZU36A-15KA,			
7410001 – 7419999	SWZU48A-17KA,			
7420001 – 7429999	SWZU52A-17KA			
7430001 – 7439999	SWZ-17KA,			
7440001 – 7449999	SWZ-21KAE,			
7450001 – 7459999	SWZ,			
7460001 – 7469999	SWZ	481073	481074	481865
		482008	482026	
7470001 – 7479999	SWZU-21KAE			

Table 2 WIRING HARNESS IDENTIFICATION

481014	Engine deck wiring harness used with 16hp Briggs & Stratton engines.
481051	Engine deck wiring harness used with Kawasaki electric-start engines.
481073	Engine deck wiring harness used with 1-cylinder Kohler Model CV engines, 15hp and 17hp Kawasaki engines, and Briggs & Stratton engines.
481074	Engine deck wiring harness used with Kawasaki engines.
481075	Engine deck wiring harness used with 2-cylinder Kohler Model CV engines.
481266	Handle wiring harness used with recoil-start engines.
481267	Handle wiring harness used with electric-start engines.
481275	Relay wiring harness used with some electric-start engines.
481406	Handle wiring harness used with recoil-start engines.
481407	Handle wiring harness used with electric-start engines.
481680	Handle wiring harness used with recoil-start engines.
481681	Handle wiring harness used with electric-start engines.
481865	Handle wiring harness used with recoil-start engines.
482008	Engine deck wiring harness used with Kawasaki electric-start engines.
482026	Handle wiring harness used with Kawasaki electric-start engines.

INDEX

17

F

G

H

I

17

17

Part Number 481014

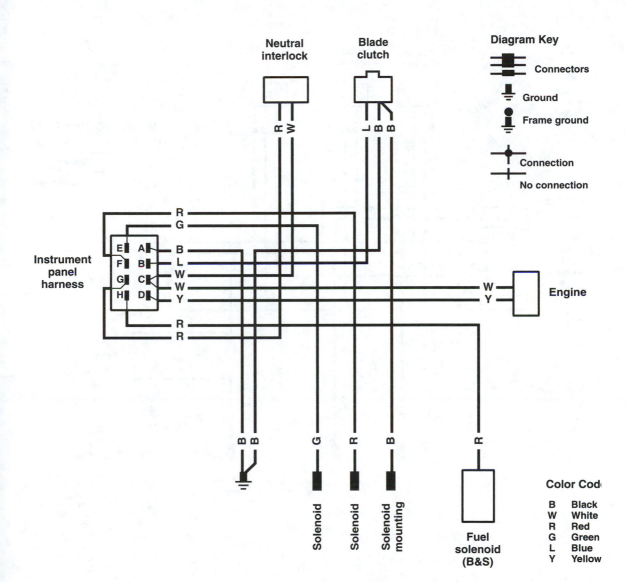

Part Number 481051

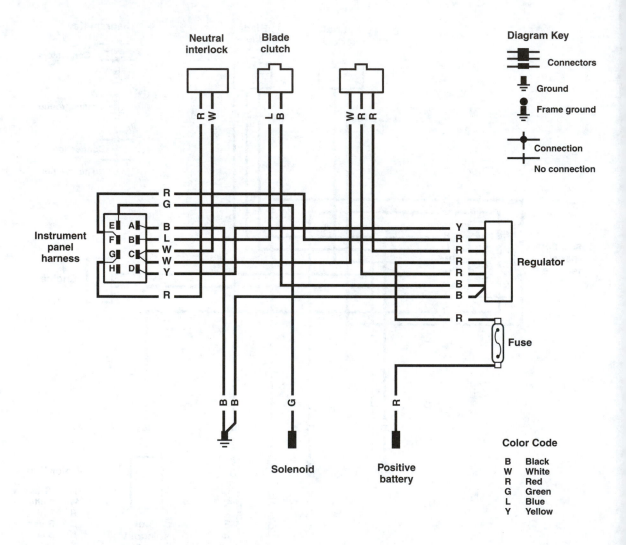

Part Number 481073

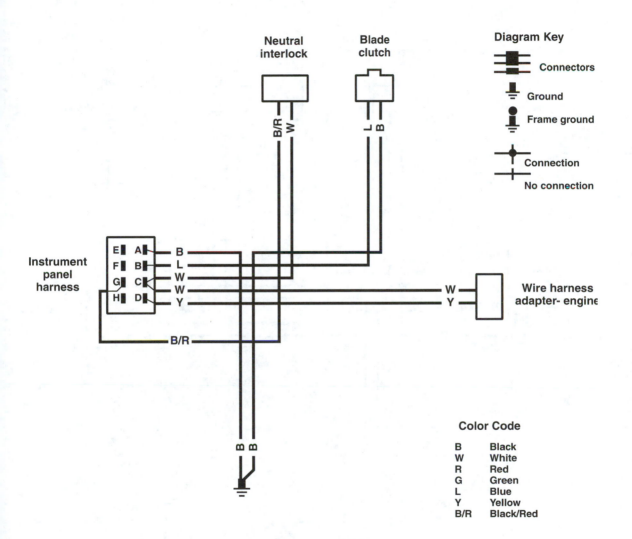

Part Number 481074

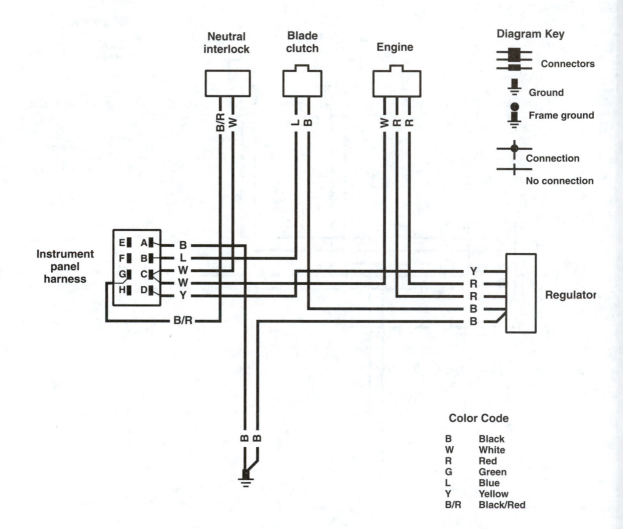

Part Number 481075

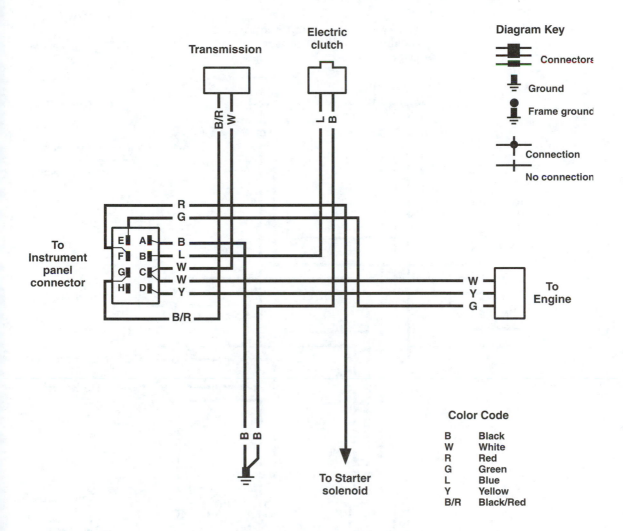

Transmission

Electric clutch

Diagram Key

Connectors

Ground

Frame ground

Connection

No connection

To Instrument panel connector

To Engine

To Starter solenoid

Color Code

B	Black
W	White
R	Red
G	Green
L	Blue
Y	Yellow
B/R	Black/Red

18

Part Number 481266

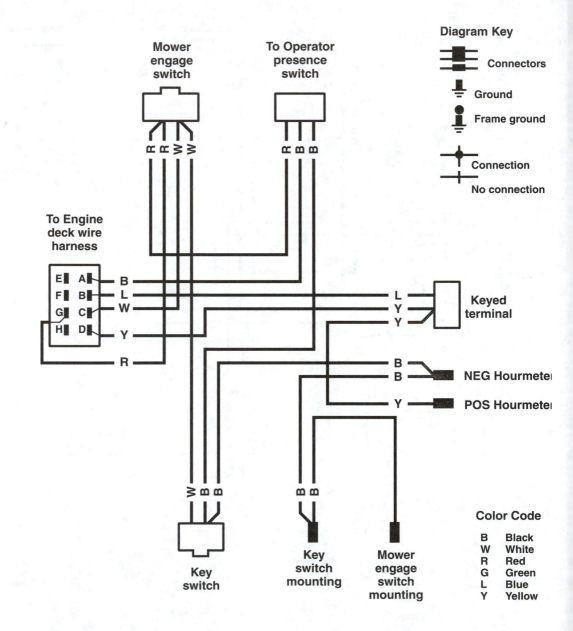

Part Number 481267

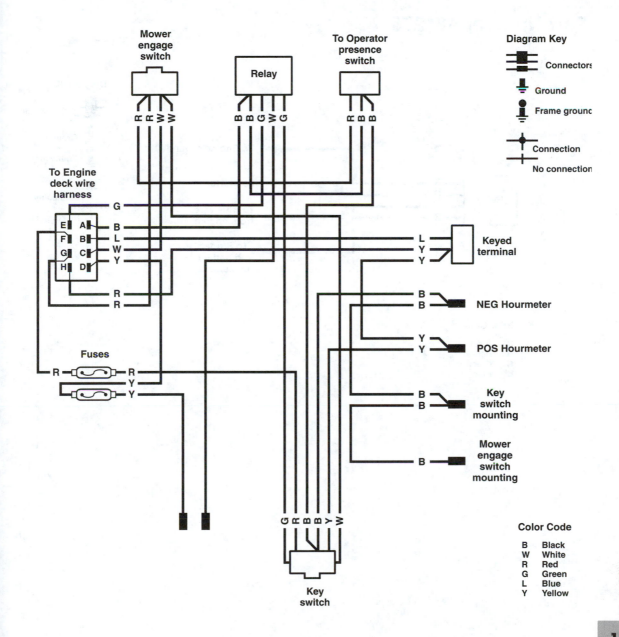

Part Number 481275

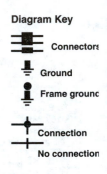

Diagram Key

Connectors

Ground

Frame ground

Connection

No connection

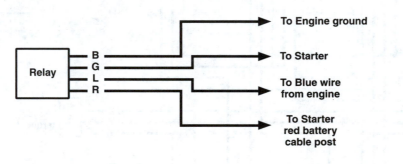

Relay

B — To Engine ground
G — To Starter
L — To Blue wire from engine
R — To Starter red battery cable post

Color Code

B   Black
R   Red
G   Green
L   Blue

Part Number 481406

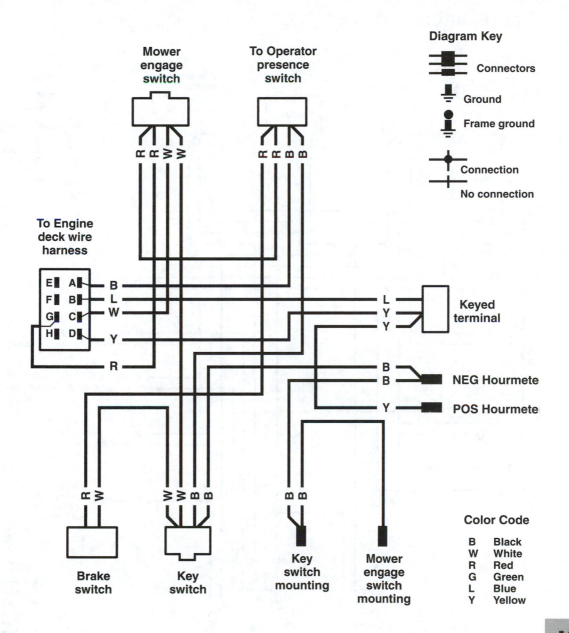

Diagram Key

Connectors

Ground

Frame ground

Connection

No connection

Color Code

B   Black
W   White
R   Red
G   Green
L   Blue
Y   Yellow

Part Number 481407

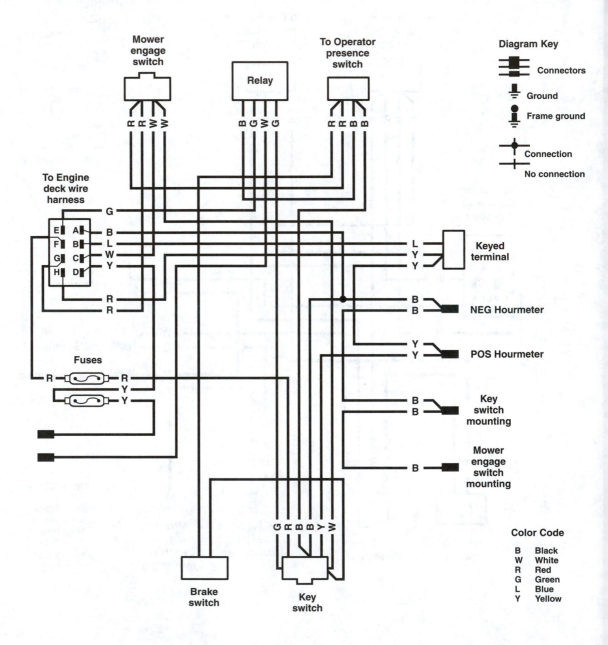

Part Number 481680

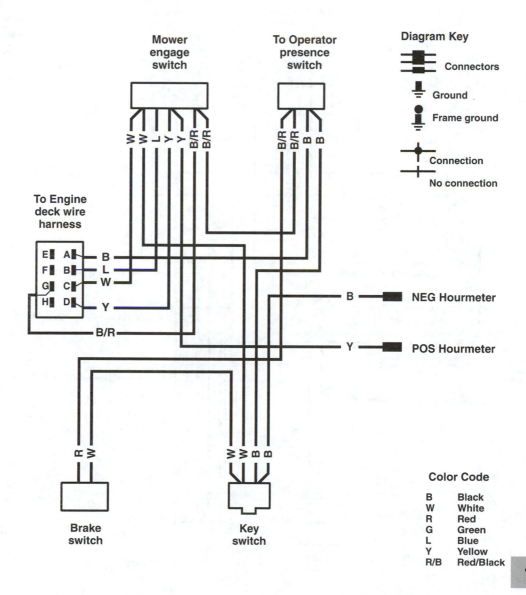

Mower engage switch

To Operator presence switch

Diagram Key

Connectors

Ground

Frame ground

Connection

No connection

To Engine deck wire harness

E A — B
F B — L
G C — W
H D — Y

B/R

B — NEG Hourmeter

Y — POS Hourmeter

Brake switch

Key switch

Color Code

B   Black
W   White
R   Red
G   Green
L   Blue
Y   Yellow
R/B   Red/Black

18

Part Number 481681

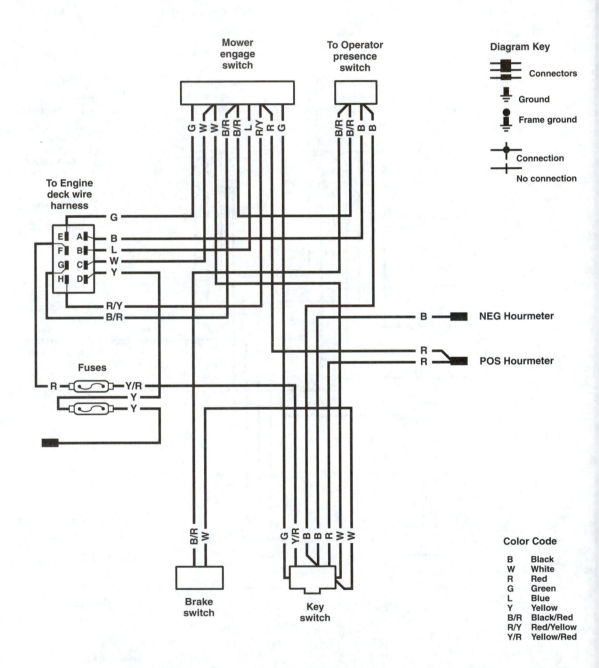

Part Number 481865

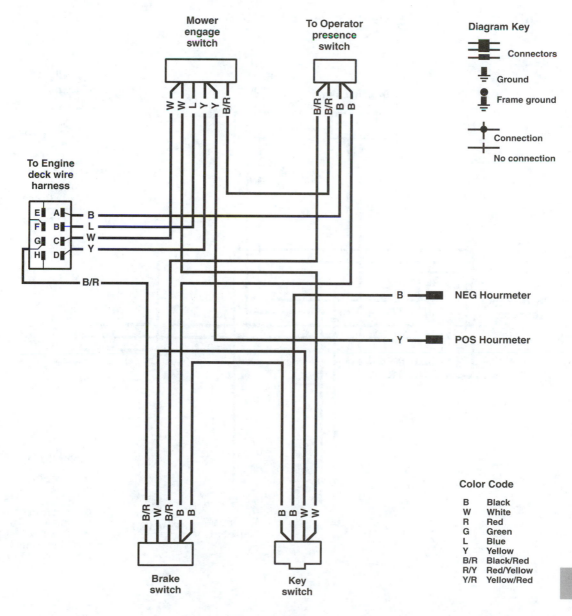

Part Number 482008

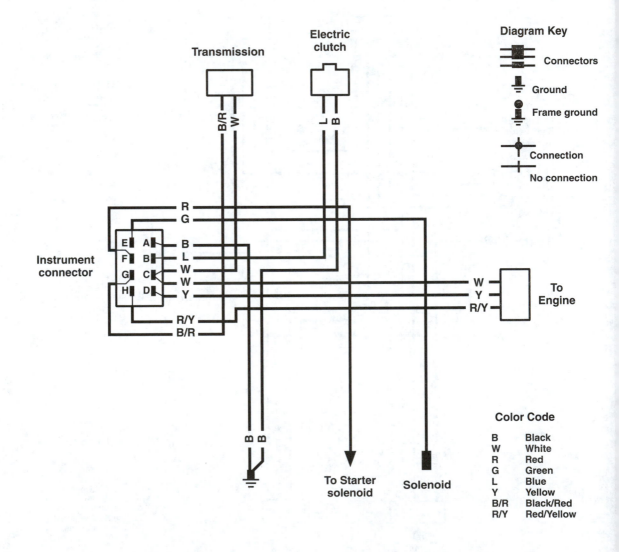

Part Number 482026

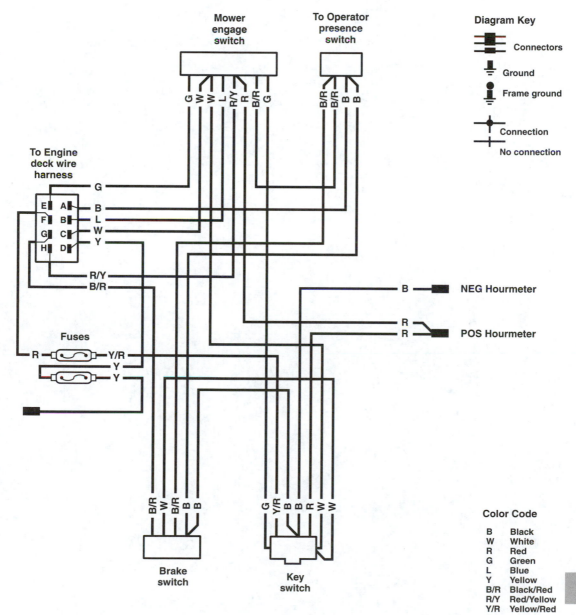

Mower engage switch

To Operator presence switch

Diagram Key

Connectors

Ground

Frame ground

Connection

No connection

To Engine deck wire harness

NEG Hourmeter

POS Hourmeter

Fuses

Brake switch

Key switch

Color Code

B	Black
W	White
R	Red
G	Green
L	Blue
Y	Yellow
B/R	Black/Red
R/Y	Red/Yellow
Y/R	Yellow/Red

18

NOTES

NOTES

NOTES

MAINTENANCE LOG

Date	Hours	Type of Service